Culture and Psychology

FOURTH EDITION

David Matsumoto
San Francisco State University
Linda Juang
San Francisco State University

THOMSON
␜␜␜␜␜
WADSWORTH

Australia • Brazil • Canada • Mexico • Singapore • Spain
United Kingdom • United States

THOMSON

★ ™

WADSWORTH

Culture and Psychology, **Fourth Edition**
David Matsumoto and Linda Juang

Publisher: Michele Sordi
Assistant Editor: Magnolia Molcan
Editorial Assistant: Erin Miskelly
Marketing Manager: Kim Russell
Marketing Assistant: Melanie Cregger
Marketing Communications Manager: Linda Yip
Project Manager, Editorial Production: Marti Paul
Creative Director: Rob Hugel
Senior Art Director: Vernon Boes
Print Buyer: Linda Hsu

Permissions Editor: Mardell Glinski Schultz
Production Service: Samirendra Ghosh
Photo Researcher: Kelly Carter, Writer's Research Group
Copy Editor: Debbie Stone
Illustrator: ICC Macmillan Inc.
Cover Designer: Paula Goldstein
Cover Image: Day And Night Face ©Images.com/Corbis
Compositor: ICC Macmillan Inc.
Text and Cover Printer: Thomson West

Printed in the United States of America
1 2 3 4 5 6 7 11 10 09 08 07

Library of Congress Control Number: 2007924876

ISBN-13: 978-0-495-09787-7
ISBN-10: 0-495-09787-X

Thomson Higher Education
10 Davis Drive
Belmont, CA 94002-3098
USA

For more information about our products, contact us at:
Thomson Learning Academic Resource Center
1-800-423-0563
For permission to use material from this text or product, submit a request online at
http://www.thomsonrights.com.
Any additional questions about permissions can be submitted by e-mail to
thomsonrights@thomson.com.

About the Authors

David Matsumoto is Professor of Psychology and Director of the Culture and Emotion Research Laboratory at San Francisco State University. He has studied culture, emotion, social interaction, and communication for 20 years, and has written more than 250 works in these areas. His books include well-known titles such as *The Handbook of Culture and Psychology* (Oxford University Press, translated into Russian), and *The New Japan* (Intercultural Press). He is the recipient of many awards and honors, including being named a G. Stanley Hall lecturer by the American Psychological Association. He also holds a sixth-degree black belt in judo, a Class A Coaching Certificate from USA Judo, and a Class A International Referee License from the International Judo Federation. He is the recipient of the 1999 U.S. Olympic Committee's Developmental Coach of the Year Award in Judo, the 2001 U.S. Judo Federation's Senior and Junior Female Coach of the Year Award, and an acclamation from the City and County of Honolulu in 1977. In addition to his works in psychology, he is the author of *The History and Philosophy of Kodokan Judo* (Hon no Tomosha) and *Judo: A Sport and a Way of Life* (International Judo Federation).

Linda Juang is an Associate Professor of Psychology at San Francisco State University. She earned her B.A. in Child Development from the University of Minnesota and her M.A. and Ph.D. in Developmental Psychology from Michigan State University, and she was also a postdoctoral fellow at the University of Jena in Germany for three years. Her research focuses on adolescent development in various family and cultural contexts. She has published and presented studies concerning issues of ethnic identity, autonomy, acculturation, and adjustment of culturally diverse adolescents in the United States and Germany.

Brief Table of Contents

Table of Contents

CHAPTER 11   Culture and Abnormal Psychology 282

Preface

First of all, we would like to thank you sincerely for using our book. This fourth edition brings together some excellent suggestions by reviewers and users of the previous edition with contemporary new and exciting work in cross-cultural psychology. Foremost among these evolutions in the field concerns our understanding of exactly what culture is in the first place. Our perspective is that there is much to be gained by first understanding why it is that all humans have culture and how human culture is different from nonhuman cultures. We believe this provides another, perhaps deeper and definitely more complex, understanding of culture and its relationship to psychological processes. Understanding human culture within this larger perspective will help us better understand differences among human cultures.

Concretely, we bring this new understanding of what culture is to the first chapter of the book. We include work on animal as well as human culture to highlight how important it is for all humans to have a culture. This provides us with a framework to understand how the many psychological processes are universal among humans, and why they are meaningful to all.

We then use the framework we introduced in Chapter 1 to build the material in each chapter, which covers topics surveying the field of psychology. In each, we begin with a discussion of how and why that psychological process is universal to all humans. Afterward, we engage in a discussion of how various human cultures are different.

Adopting this approach can provide a consistent framework that can be used as a unifying theme for all the topics in the book. And it provides a better, more sophisticated, more nuanced, understanding of culture and its relationship to psychological processes. As you can see below, we have also made some structural changes to the book, such as splitting the material in the previous social behavior chapter into two chapters and rearranging the order of some of the material. In doing so, we believe the book has now come to represent mainstream approaches to the teaching of psychology topically. We have also eliminated many superfluous studies that were in the previous edition, and now spend more time discussing more recent and influential studies in each area. We have improved the pedagogy of the book by including chapter outlines, adding more tables and figures highlighting the illustrative research we discuss, and expanding the glossary to include relevant terms.

Here is a brief synopsis of the changes made in each chapter:

Chapter 1: An Introduction to Culture and Psychology
- Included new material concerning the origins of culture, the contrast between human and animal cultures, and a new definition of culture
- Included new material on the psychological contents of culture
- Reorganized the entire chapter
- Pedagogical improvements: outline, figures, tables, pictures, and new glossary

Chapter 2: Cross-Cultural Research Methods
- Reorganized the chapter around four major research methods:
  - Cross-cultural comparisons
  - Ecological-level studies
  - Cultural studies
  - Linkage studies
- Described the evolution of cross-cultural research methods across time
- Added information about response bias and cultural attribution fallacies

Chapter 3: Enculturation
- Added new material on
  - Cultural learning
  - Whiting and Whiting's Children of Six Cultures Study
  - Parental ethnotheories
  - Review of cross-cultural studies on authoritative and authoritarian parenting
  - Perception of parental warmth among Chinese American adolescents
  - Review of cross-cultural studies using the OME: Observation and Measurement of the Environment Inventory
  - Sibling relationships
  - Siblings and gender role attitudes
  - National Institute on Child Health and Human Development study of early child care
- Updated research throughout

Chapter 4: Culture and Developmental Processes
- Added new material on
  - Description of Ainsworth's attachment styles
  - Comparison of U.S. and Japanese maternal attachment behaviors
- Updated research throughout

Chapter 5: Culture and Cognition
- Reorganized the material to focus exclusively on cognition
- Added new sections on
  - Culture as cognition
  - Dialectical thinking
  - Counterfactual thinking
- Added exciting new research by Nisbett and colleagues in cognition section
- Added more information on Hofstede's Long- versus Short-Term Orientation with country scores in culture and time section

Chapter 6: Culture and Gender
- Reorganized the material to weave a better story
- Substantially improved the chapter by adding new material on
  - Gender differences in division of labor in the home from Georgas et al.'s 30-country study
  - Research on aggression
  - Differences in gender roles
  - Research on sex and sexuality
  - Research on mate selection, mate poaching, and jealousy
  - Research on personality
  - Changing gender roles because of changing and clashing cultures

Chapter 7: Culture and Health
- Added new material on
  - Racism and stress
  - Increasing social isolation in the United States
  - Overweight and obesity
- Updated research throughout

Chapter 8: Culture and Emotion
- Added a new section on the evolution of human emotions, tying the chapter into the message of Chapter 1
- Reorganized the material into two major sections, one dealing with universal processes and the other dealing with cultural differences
- Used the framework of Basic Emotions Theory to guide the entire discussion

Chapter 9: Culture, Language, and Communication
- Added new section on the dual evolution of language and culture, tying the chapter into the message of Chapter 1

- Added a new section on culture and nonverbal behaviors
- Reorganized the chapter for better flow
- Updated the research throughout, including new studies on bilingualism and code frame switching

Chapter 10: Culture and Personality
- Totally new organization
- Added new material on
  - Five-Factor Model
  - Accuracy of national character stereotypes
  - Five-Factor Theory
  - Control
  - Autonomy
  - Chinese and Filipino Traits
  - Dominance

Chapter 11: Culture and Abnormal Psychology
- Added new material on
  - Attention-deficit/hyperactivity disorder
  - Ethnic disparities in the diagnosis of serious mental illnesses
  - Large national study on prevalence of psychiatric disorders and service use among various African American, Latino, Asian American, and Native American groups
  - Immigrant paradox
  - Mental health of Chinese, Vietnamese, and Laotian refugees in Canada
- Updated the research throughout

Chapter 12: Culture and the Treatment of Abnormal Behavior
- Added new material on
  - Strategies for higher service-utilization rates among ethnic minorities
  - The increasing importance of training cross-culturally competent psychologists
  - Reiki, Qigong, and pranic healing
- Updated the research throughout

Chapter 13: Culture and Social Behavior, I: Self and Identity
- Totally new organization
  - Moved the material on self and attributions to this chapter
- Added new material on
  - Culture and identity
  - Self-esteem and self-enhancement
- Updated the research throughout

Chapter 14: Culture and Social Behavior, II: Interpersonal and Intergroup Relations
- Totally new organization
- Added new material on
  - Mate poaching
  - Sex
  - Acculturation
  - Volunteerism
  - Cooperative behaviors
  - Explicit and implicit prejudice
  - Collective threat
  - Model minority
  - Cultures of honor
- Updated the research throughout

Chapter 15: Culture and Organizations
- Added new material on
  - Long- versus Short-Term Orientation
  - Climate and leadership
  - Fairness, including distributive and procedural justice
  - Sexual harassment
- Updated the research throughout

We are excited about the changes that were made, and we hope you will share in our excitement! To assist you in your course preparation, an Instructor's Manual with Test Bank is available online, containing lecture slides, activities, suggested newspaper articles on culture, and a test bank containing at least 50 questions per chapter. If you have any comments or suggestions on how we can continue to improve on this text, please don't hesitate to let us know. You can email us at dm@sfsu.edu or ljuang@sfsu.edu.

We would also like to thank our reviewers, whose generous critique guided the progress of this text: Ganie DeHart, State University of New York, Geneseo; Becky Munoz, University of Houston; Mar Rodriguez, University of Central Florida; Joy Stratton, California State University, Northridge; and Nan Sussman, College of Staten Island.

David Matsumoto and Linda Juang
San Francisco, CA

An Introduction to Culture and Psychology

CHAPTER CONTENTS

What a difference a hundred years makes. Think about this: in 1904,

- The average life expectancy in the United States was 47 years.
- Only 14 percent of the homes in the U.S. had a bathtub.
- Only 8 percent of the homes had a telephone.
- A 3-minute call from Denver to New York City cost 11 dollars.
- There were only 8,000 cars in the United States, and only 144 miles of paved roads.
- The maximum speed limit in most cities was 10 mph.
- Alabama, Mississippi, Iowa, and Tennessee were each more heavily populated than California. With a mere 1.4 million residents, California was only the 21st most-populous state in the union.
- The average wage in the United States was 22 cents an hour; the average U.S. worker made between $200 and $400 per year.
- More than 95 percent of all births in the United States took place at home.
- Ninety percent of all U.S. physicians had no college education; instead, they attended medical schools, many of which were condemned in the press and by the government as "substandard."
- Sugar cost 4 cents a pound; eggs were 14 cents a dozen; coffee cost 15 cents a pound.
- Most women washed their hair only once a month, and used borax or egg yolks for shampoo.
- The five leading causes of death in the United States were pneumonia and influenza, tuberculosis, diarrhea, heart disease, and stroke.
- The population of Las Vegas was 30.
- Crossword puzzles, canned beer, and iced tea had not yet been invented.
- There was no Mother's Day or Father's Day.
- One in 10 U.S. adults could not read or write.
- Only 6 percent of Americans had graduated high school.
- Marijuana, heroin, and morphine were all available over the counter at corner drugstores. According to one pharmacist, "Heroin clears the complexion, gives buoyancy to the mind, regulates the stomach and the bowels, and is, in fact, a perfect guardian of health."
- Eighteen percent of households in the United States had at least one full-time servant or domestic.
- There were only about 230 reported murders in the entire United States.
- And I got this from someone else whom I have never met, without typing it myself, on the Internet, which did not exist, on a computer, which did not exist.

The world is changing at an amazingly rapid pace, and one of the most important ways in which it is changing is in terms of cultural diversity. Here in the United States, and everywhere else in the world, people live, work, and play with an increasing number of people from all cultures, countries, and walks of life. This increasingly diversifying world has created a wonderful environment for personal challenge and growth, but it also brings with it an increased potential for misunderstandings, confusion, and conflict.

Cultural diversity is one of our biggest challenges. At the same time, however, the challenges that face us in the name of cultural diversity and intercultural relations also represent our biggest opportunities. If we can meet those challenges and turn them to our favor, we can actualize a potential in diversity and intercultural relations that will result in far more than the sum of the individual components that comprise that diverse universe. This sum will result in tremendous personal growth for many individuals, as well as in positive social evolution.

It is with this belief that this book was written—to meet the challenge of diversity and turn that challenge into opportunity. Doing so is not easy. It requires each of us to take an honest look at our own cultural background and heritage, and at their merits and limitations. Fear, rigidity, and sometimes stubborn pride come with any type of honest assessment. Yet without that assessment, we cannot meet the challenge of diversity and improve intercultural relations.

In academia, that assessment brings with it fundamental questions about what is taught in our colleges and universities today. To ask how cultural diversity colors the nature of the truths and principles of human behavior delivered in the halls of science is to question the pillars of much of our knowledge about the world and about human behavior. From time to time, we need to shake those pillars to see just how sturdy they are. This is especially true in the social sciences and particularly in psychology—the science specifically concerned with the mental processes and behavioral characteristics of people.

THE STUDY OF CULTURE IN PSYCHOLOGY

The Goals of Psychology

No field is better equipped to meet the challenge of cultural diversity than psychology. And in fact, psychology has met, and continues to meet, the challenge of culture through a subfield known as cross-cultural psychology. In order to get a better handle on what cross-cultural psychology is all about, it is important first to have a good grasp of the goals of psychology.

Psychology essentially has two main goals. The first is to build a body of knowledge about people. Psychologists seek to understand behavior when it happens, explain why it happens, and even predict it before it happens. Psychologists achieve this by conducting research and creating theories of behavior.

The second goal of psychology involves taking that body of knowledge and applying it to intervene in people's lives, to make those lives better. Psychologists achieve this in many ways: as therapists, counselors, trainers, and consultants. Psychologists work on the front lines, dealing directly with people to affect their lives in a positive fashion.

The two goals of psychology—creating a body of knowledge and applying that knowledge—are closely related. Psychologists who are on the front lines take what psychology as a field has collectively learned about human behavior and use that knowledge as a basis for their applications and interventions. This learning initially comes in the form of academic training in universities. But it continues well after formal education has ended, through continuing education programs and individual scholarship—reviewing the literature, attending conferences, and joining and participating in professional organizations. Applied psychologists engage in a lifelong learning process that helps them intervene in people's lives more effectively.

Likewise, researchers are cognizant of the practical and applied implications of their work, and many are well aware that the value of psychological theory and research is often judged by its practical usefulness in society (see, for example, Gergen, Gulerce, Lock, & Misra, 1996). Theories are often tested for their validity not only in the halls of science but also on the streets, and they often have to be revised because of what happens on those streets.

Cross-Cultural Research and Psychology

In the past, most research on human behavior conducted in the United States involved American university students as study participants. Thus, most theories in psychology are based on studies with students. There is nothing wrong with such research, and the findings obtained from American samples are definitely true for those samples. These findings may be replicated across multiple samples using different methods, and many findings may weather tests for scientific rigor that would normally render them acceptable as a truth or principle about human behavior. However, a basic question still remains: Is what we know about human behavior true for all people, regardless of gender, race, ethnicity, culture, class, or lifestyle?

Cross-cultural psychology asks these questions by testing them in people of differing cultural backgrounds. Cross-cultural psychology is a research method that tests the cultural parameters of psychological knowledge. Cross-cultural research does this by including participants of more than one cultural background and then comparing data obtained across those cultures. This method allows psychologists to examine how knowledge about people and their behaviors from one culture may or may not hold for people from other cultures.

Cross-cultural psychology, therefore, is a matter of *scientific philosophy*— that is, the logic underlying the methods used to conduct research and generate knowledge in psychology. This idea is based on a few premises. First, the results of psychological research are bound by our methods, and the very standards of care we use when we evaluate the scientific rigor and quality of research are also bound by the cultural frameworks within which our science occurs (Pe-Pua, 1989). Theories depend on research to confirm or disconfirm them; research involves methods designed to collect data to test theories (or more precisely, hypotheses based on theories). Methods involve many parameters, one of which includes decisions about the nature of the participants in the study. Cross-cultural research involves the inclusion of people of different cultural backgrounds—a specific type of change in one of the parameters of research methods.

The contribution that cross-cultural psychology makes to psychology as a whole, however, goes far beyond simple methodological changes in the studies. It is a way of understanding principles about human behaviors within a global perspective. Cross-cultural research not only tests whether people of different cultures are similar or different; it also tests possible limitations in our knowledge, by examining whether psychological theories and principles are **universal** (true for all people of all cultures) or **culture-specific** (true for some people of some cultures).

Because cross-cultural psychology is a method, it is not topic-specific. Cross-cultural researchers are interested in a broad range of phenomena related to human behavior—from perception to language, child rearing to psychopathology. What distinguishes cross-cultural psychology from a mainstream approach, therefore, is not the phenomenon of interest but the testing of limitations to knowledge by examining whether that knowledge is applicable to people of different cultural backgrounds. The approach, not the topic, is what is important in cross-cultural psychology.

The Growth of Cross-Cultural Psychology

Although cross-cultural research has been conducted for over a century, cross-cultural psychology has truly made a substantial impact in psychology not only in the United States but also worldwide in the past decade or two. Much of this popularity is due to the increased awareness of the importance of culture as an influencing factor on behavior in research, and, unfortunately, to increased awareness of the frequency of intercultural conflicts within and between countries, which have also led to much interest in cross-cultural psychology. The flagship journal of the International Association of Cross-Cultural Psychology, the *Journal of Cross-Cultural Psychology,* has now passed its 35th year of publishing top-level cross-cultural research. Other specialty journals also exist, such as *Cross-Cultural Research* and *Culture and Psychology.* The number of research articles incorporating people of different cultures has increased tremendously in all top-tier mainstream journals as well, such as the *Journal of Personality and Social Psychology, Developmental Psychology,* and *Psychological Science* (see Figure 1.1). Theoretical models are increasingly incorporating culture, and the number of books involving culture has also increased.

In a broad perspective, an increased interest in cross-cultural psychology is a normal and healthy development in psychology. As psychology has matured, many scientists have come to recognize that much, but not all, of the research and theories once thought to be universal for all people is indeed culture-bound. The increasing importance and recognition of cross-cultural psychology are reactions to this realization.

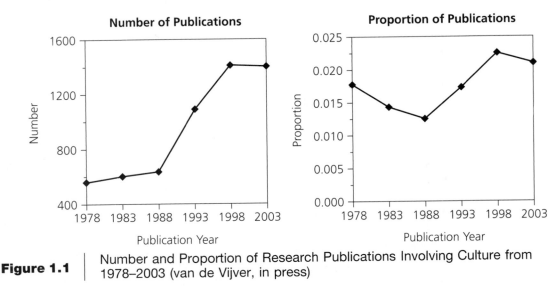

Figure 1.1 | Number and Proportion of Research Publications Involving Culture from 1978–2003 (van de Vijver, in press)

van de Vijver, F.J.R. Culture and psychology: A swot analysis of cross-cultural psychology from *Progress in Psychological Science Around the World. Volume 2.* London: Psychology Press.

DEFINING CULTURE

Unfortunately, many psychologists and laypersons use the words *culture, race, nationality,* and *ethnicity* interchangeably, as if they were all terms denoting the same concepts. They are not, and as we begin our study of culture and psychology, it is important to define exactly what we mean by the term *culture*.

Clearly, we use the word **culture** in many different ways in everyday language and discourse. Kroeber and Kluckholn (1952/1963) and later Berry, Poortinga, Segall, and Dasen (1992) described six general categories in which culture is discussed:

- *Descriptive* uses highlight the different types of activities or behaviors associated with a culture.
- *Historical* definitions refer to the heritage and tradition associated with a group of people.
- *Normative* uses describe the rules and norms that are associated with a culture.
- *Psychological* descriptions emphasize learning, problem solving, and other behavioral approaches associated with culture.
- *Structural* definitions emphasize the societal or organizational elements of a culture.
- *Genetic* descriptions refer to the origins of a culture.

In an early work, Murdock, Ford, and Hudson (1971) described 79 different aspects of life with which culture had something to do. Barry (1980) rearranged this list into eight broad categories, which were also reported by Berry et al. (1992):

- General characteristics
- Food and clothing

- Housing and technology
- Economy and transportation
- Individual and family activities
- Community and government
- Welfare, religion, and science
- Sex and the life cycle

Thus, we use the concept of culture to describe and explain a broad range of activities, behaviors, events, and structures in our lives. It is used in many different ways because it touches on so many aspects of life. Culture, in its truest and broadest sense, cannot simply be swallowed in a single gulp (Malpass, 1993)—not in this book, not in a university course, not in any training program. Although we will attempt to bring you closer to a better understanding of what culture is and how it influences our lives, we must begin by recognizing and admitting the breadth, scope, and enormity of culture.

And, the concept of culture may have different meanings in other cultures. If you refer to culture in Japan, for instance, a Japanese person may think first of flower arranging or a tea ceremony rather than the aspects of culture Americans normally associate with the word. In Paris, culture might refer to art, history, or food. Because we use *culture* to refer to so many different things about life, it is no wonder that it generates so much confusion and ambiguity.

Where Does Culture Come From?

In order to understand and define culture, it is necessary to start with some assumptions about human nature. One view that can be used to ground an understanding of culture is that of evolutionary psychology, which suggests that people have evolved a set of motives and strivings that are ultimately related to reproductive success (Boyer, 2000; Buss, 2001). Reproductive success and other functions such as eating and sleeping are biological imperatives if people are to survive. Survival is related to the degree to which people can adapt to their environments and to the contexts in which they live. Over history people must have solved a host of distinct social problems in order to adapt and thus achieve reproductive success. These social problems include negotiating complex status hierarchies, forming successful work and social groups, attracting mates, fighting off potential rivals for food and sexual partners, giving birth and raising children, and battling nature (Buss, 1988, 1991, 2001). In fact we need to do these things in our everyday lives today as well.

Thus, biological imperatives are associated with social motives. All individuals and groups have a universal problem of how to adapt to their environments in order to address these needs and motives, and must create solutions to these universal problems. These solutions can be very specific to each group because the contexts in which each group lives—the physical environment, social factors, and types and sizes of their families and communities—are different. These solutions are culture (Figure 1.2). Culture is the product of the interaction between universal biological needs and functions,

Human Nature and Culture

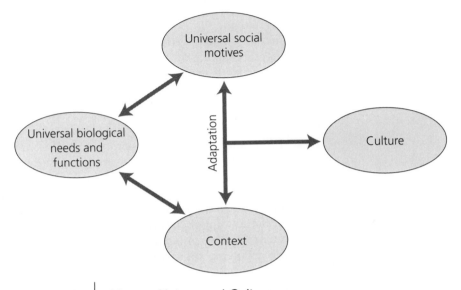

Figure 1.2 | Human Nature and Culture

universal social problems created to address those needs, and the context in which people live. Culture is a solution to the problem of individuals' adaptations to their contexts to address their social motives and biological needs.

What kinds of needs produce cultural responses? There are many possible ways to conceptualize basic human needs. For example, Malinowski suggested that all individuals had universal basic needs related to metabolism, reproduction, bodily comforts, safety, movement, growth, and health (Malinowski, 1927/1961, 1944/1960). According to Malinowski all cultures must create ways to deal with each of these social motives, producing a cultural "response" that corresponds ultimately to the universal biological functions (Table 1.1).

Is Culture a Uniquely Human Product?

If we understand culture as a response or solution to the problem of adapting to our contexts in order to meet basic biological and social needs, then one question that arises is whether humans are the only beings that have culture. After all, *all* living beings need to adapt to their life contexts in order to meet basic needs and survive. In fact, there are many characteristics of human cultural life that are shared with other animals. For example, consider:

- Many animals are social; that is, they work and live in groups. Fish swim in schools, wolves hunt in packs, and lions roam in prides.
- In animal societies, there are clear social networks and hierarchies. The staring game played by us humans as children is used by animals to create

Table 1.1 | Malinowski's Conceptualization of Basic Needs and Cultural Responses

Basic Needs	Cultural Response
Metabolism	Commissariat
Reproduction	Kinship
Bodily comforts	Shelter
Safety	Protection
Movement	Activities
Growth	Training
Health	Hygiene

dominance hierarchies. And like the human game, the animal that smiles or averts its gaze loses and becomes the subordinate.

- Many animals invent and use tools (Whiten, Horner, & De Waal, 2005). Perhaps the most famous initial example of this were the monkeys who used twigs to get insects to eat. Japanese monkeys at Koshima Island washed sweet potatoes and bathed in the sea (Matsuzawa, 2001).
- Many animals communicate with each other. Bees communicate via a complex dance concerning the source of flowers. Ants leave trails to communicate their paths to themselves and others. And relatives of monkeys who wash sweet potatoes at Koshima Island themselves began to wash sweet potatoes.

And the list goes on and on. Thus, it is clear that animals have culture, or at least a rudimentary form of culture consisting of social customs (McGrew, 2004), as we defined it above (responses and solutions to the problem of adapting to context in order to meet basic needs for survival) (Boesch, 2003). So the answer to the question—Is culture a uniquely human product?—appears to be *no*.

What Is Unique about Human Culture?

Yet, human cultures are different from animal cultures, and understanding how we are different serves as an important basis to understanding how all humans are universally similar in important ways. Addressing the uniqueness of human culture begs the question of what unique skills humans have that other animals don't.

Of course humans can do many things that other animals cannot (and vice versa). Of the many differences, there are two that stand out in terms of their contribution to unique, human cultures: language and complex social cognition.

Language Humans, unlike other animals, have the unique ability to symbolize their physical and metaphysical world (Premack, 2004), to create sounds representing those symbols (morphemes), to create rules connecting those symbols to meaning (syntax and grammar), and to put this all together in sentences (see Figure 1.3). Moreover, since the use of papyrus to develop paper, humans developed writing systems, so we can reduce those oral expressions to words on paper. This book, in fact, is a uniquely human product.

Complex Social Cognition One of the most important thinking abilities that humans have that other animals apparently do not have is the ability to believe that other people are intentional agents—that is, that they have wishes, desires, and intentions to act and behave. We know that we have our own intentions. But we also know that other people have their own intentions. And we know that they know that we have intentions. Being in the "public eye," therefore, takes on special meaning for humans, because we know that others can make judgments about us. Thus, we have causal beliefs (which form the basis for the study of *attributions,* which we will discuss later in Chapter 13). *Morality,* a uniquely human product, is probably rooted in this unique human cognitive ability (and we will discuss this more in Chapter 4). This ability apparently turns on in humans around 9 months of age (Tomasello, 1999), which is a critical time of development of many cognitive abilities (we will discuss these more in Chapter 4). That is probably why we don't just take off our clothes in the middle of the street, have sex in the middle of the park in broad daylight, or just bop on the nose those with whom we disagree. Other animals, however, seem to not care as much.

Another important ability that humans have that animals do not is the ability to continually build upon improvements. When humans create something that is good, it usually evolves to a next generation, in which it is even better. This is true for computers, cars, audio music players, and unfortunately,

Faculties	Human	Chimpanzee	Monkey
Voluntary control of the voice, face, hands	+	Hands	Hands
Imitation, level 2	+	Only with human training	–
Teaching	+	–	–
Theory of mind recursive/nonrecursive	Recursive	Nonrecursive	–
Capacity to acquire recursive and/or nonrecursive grammar	Both	Nonrecursive	Nonrecursive

Figure 1.3 | Faculties That Underlie the Evolution of Language

Premack, D. (2004). Is Language the Key to Intelligence? *Science,* 303 (16), 319. (http://www.sciencemag.org)

weapons. Tomasello, Kruger, and Ratner (1993) call this the **ratchet effect.** Like a ratchet, an improvement never goes backward; it only goes forward and continues to improve on itself. The ratchet effect does not occur in other animals. Monkeys may use twigs to catch insects, but they never improve on that tool.

Thus, there are three characteristics of human social and cultural life that differentiates it from those of animals: *complexity, differentiation,* and *institutionalization.* For example, not only do humans make tools. We make tools to make tools. We automate the process of making tools and mass distribute tools around the world for mass consumption. Because humans have complex social cognition, language, and ratcheting, human social and cultural life is much more complex than that of other animals. We are members of multiple groups, each having its own purpose, hierarchy, and networking system.

In short, humans have evolved to have human cultures, and human cultures ensure a great diversity in life. Increased diversity, in fact, greatly aids in survival, and humans appear to be doing a good job at surviving (Figure 1.4).

A Definition of Culture

Over the years many scholars have attempted to define culture. Well over 100 years ago, for example, Tylor (1865) defined culture as all capabilities and habits learned as members of a society. Linton (1936) referred to culture as

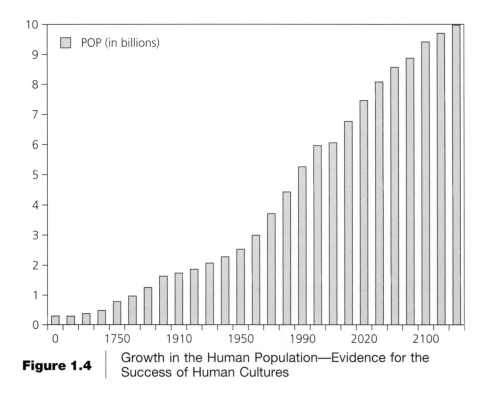

Figure 1.4 | Growth in the Human Population—Evidence for the Success of Human Cultures

social heredity. Kroeber and Kluckholn (1952/1963) defined culture as patterns of and for behavior acquired and transmitted by symbols, constituting the distinct achievements of human groups, including their embodiments in artifacts. Rohner (1984) defined culture as the totality of equivalent and complementary learned meanings maintained by a human population, or by identifiable segments of a population, and transmitted from one generation to the next. Jahoda (1984) argued that culture is a descriptive term that captures not only rules and meanings but also behaviors. Pelto and Pelto (1975) defined culture in terms of personality, whereas Geertz (1975) defined it as shared symbol systems transcending individuals. Berry et al. (1992) defined culture simply as the shared way of life of a group of people, and Baumeister (2005) defined culture as an information-based system that allows people to live together and satisfy their needs.

To be sure, there is no one accepted definition of culture in either psychology or anthropology. What is important, however, is that we have a working definition of culture for our own use. In this book, therefore, we define human culture as *a unique meaning and information system, shared by a group and transmitted across generations, that allows the group to meet basic needs of survival, pursue happiness and well-being, and derive meaning from life.*

Of course, human cultures exist first to enable us to meet basic needs of survival. Human cultures help us to meet others, to procreate and produce offspring, to put food on the table, to provide shelter from the elements, and to care for our daily biological essential needs.

But human culture is so much more than that. It allows for complex social networks and relationships. It allows us to enhance the meaning of normal, daily activities. It allows us to pursue happiness. It allows us to be creative in music, art, and drama. It allows us to seek recreation and to engage in sports and organize competition, whether in the local community Little League or the Olympic Games. It allows us to search the sea and space. It allows us to create mathematics, an achievement no other species can claim, as well as an educational system. It allows us to go to the moon, to create a research laboratory on Antarctica, and send probes to Mars and Jupiter. Unfortunately, it also allows us to have wars, create weapons of mass destruction, and create terrorists.

Human culture does all this by creating and maintaining complex social systems, institutionalizing and improving cultural practices, creating beliefs about the world, and communicating the meaning system to other humans and subsequent generations. It is the product of the evolution of the human mind, increased brain size, and complex cognitive abilities.

The Difference Between "Society" and "Culture"

The analysis presented here suggests a very large distinction between the concepts "society" and "culture." We define society as "a system of inter-relationships among people." *Society* refers to the fact that relationships among individuals exist, and in human societies, individuals have multiple relationships with multiple groups, and the groups themselves have interrelationships with other groups. Thus, human societies are complex. Nonhuman animals are also social and have societies.

Culture, however, is different. *Culture* refers to the meanings and information that are associated with social networks. "Family," for example, is a social group that exists in both the human and nonhuman animal world. But human cultures give the concept of family its own unique meaning, and individuals draw specific information from these meanings. Moreover, different human cultures assign different meanings to this social group. Thus, although nonhuman animals have social groups, like humans, they do not have human cultures associated with those social groups.

FACTORS THAT INFLUENCE CULTURE

Because cultures are adaptational responses to the environment, it follows that factors in the environment can influence culture. Given the necessity to survive, cultures help to select behaviors, attitudes, values, and opinions that may optimize the tapping of resources to meet survival needs. Thus, as suggested by Poortinga (1990), out of all the myriad behaviors possible in the human repertoire, cultures help to focus people's behaviors and attention on a few limited alternatives in order to maximize their effectiveness, given their resources and their environment.

Ecological Factors

Geography, climate, and amount of natural resources all affect culture. For example, a land void of natural resources may encourage teamwork and community spirit among its members and interrelationships with other groups that have abundant resources in order to survive. These needs and relationships will foster certain psychological characteristics and attributes that complement teamwork, community spirit, and interdependence. In a land with abundant resources, however, a society would have less need for such values and attitudes, and these attributes would be less important in its culture.

Climate also affects culture, and global changes in climate across history may have even affected the evolution of humans (Behrensmeyer, 2006). Groups that live near the equator, in hot, humid, tropical areas, will exhibit a lifestyle that is very different from that of groups living in temperate or arctic zones, with seasonal changes and extremely cold weather. Differences in climate will affect the clothes people wear, the types of foods they eat, storage and container systems for food supplies, health (infectious and parasitic diseases tend to be more frequent in hotter climates), and many other facets of living. People in hotter climates tend to organize their daily activities more around shelter, shade, and temperature changes that occur during the day. Part of Spanish culture is to shut down shops and offices in the midafternoon, during the hottest time of the day, and reopen later, pushing back the working hours. There, it is not uncommon for people to be having dinner outside at 11:00 P.M.

or even midnight. People who live nearer the poles may organize their lives around available sunlight. All these factors are likely to influence people's attitudes, beliefs, and behaviors, and hence their culture.

Social Factors

There are several social factors that affect culture, including population density, affluence, technology, type of government, institutions, media, sociocultural history, and religion. For instance, societies with higher population densities may require greater social order in order to function effectively. These societies may encourage hierarchy and groupism, with related psychological attributes, more than societies with relatively less population density. Affluence has been shown to be related not only to a cultural dimension known as individualism (Hofstede, 1980, 1983) but also to national characteristics in emotionality (Wallbott & Scherer, 1988). As societies become more affluent, they are more able to obtain resources with less reliance on others, fostering these types of psychological characteristics. Communication technology (such as cellular phones and electronic mail), for instance, brings with it its own brand of communication culture, in which rules regarding interactions and interpersonal engagement change rather rapidly. The widespread use of computers has brought with it the ability to work independently, loosening the reliance on others to get work accomplished and the need to interact with coworkers. These types of changes have the potential to bring about changes in psychological functioning and behavior, which, in turn, lead to changes in culture.

Biological Factors

A final factor that may influence culture is the aggregate temperament and personality of the members of a culture. As we will learn in Chapter 10, many cultures of the world are associated with differences in mean levels of several personality traits. Although it is possible that cultures shaped the average personalities of its members, it is also possible that groups of individuals with certain kinds of personalities and temperaments banded together in certain geographic regions and thus influenced culture. For example, cultures high on the dimension known as Uncertainty Avoidance (see below) happen to be associated with higher means on the personality trait known as Neuroticism. It could be that Uncertainty Avoidant cultures produce more neurotic individuals; but it is also possible that more neurotic individuals exist in these areas in the first place, and they help to create cultural systems that are more Uncertainty Avoidant.

GROUPS THAT HAVE CULTURES

Given our definition of culture and what influences it, the next question that arises is, Which human groups have culture? Certainly there are many groups of individuals that have culture, and here we discuss only a few.

Culture and Nationality

Nationality refers to a person's country of origin, and countries have their own cultures. This is because countries are associated with each of the factors that influence culture. For example, countries are defined by specific boundaries that describe their ecology—geography, climate, and natural resources. Countries also have their own unique sociocultural history, government, and economic base, all of which affect culture. Countries also have differences in mean levels of aggregate personality traits, which can affect culture.

Of course, this is a generalization, and although countries can certainly have a dominant culture, they can also have many subcultures. For example, even within countries like France or Japan, subcultures differ depending on region. This is surely true within the United States as well, with the differences between the East and West Coasts, the South, the Midwest, Alaska, and Hawaii. Thus, we need to engage in a study of culture and psychology by first acknowledging the multicultural reality that exists around the world.

Culture and Ethnicity

The word *ethnicity* is derived from the Greek *ethnos,* meaning people of a nation or tribe, and is usually used to denote one's racial, national, or cultural origins. In the United States, for example, ethnic groups include African Americans, Asians and Pacific Islanders, Hispanics and Latinos, and Native Americans. Thus, ethnicity is generally used in reference to groups characterized by a common nationality, geographic origin, culture, or language (Betancourt & Lopez, 1993).

Understanding the relationship between ethnicity and culture can be tricky. To the extent that ethnicity refers to national origins, it may denote aspects of culture. But psychologists and laypersons often equate ethnicity with race, and as we will discuss below, this is problematic. Moreover, ethnicity as a label has no explanatory value; although information about ethnic differences on a broad range of psychological phenomena can be useful, such information by itself does not explain the nature of the relationship between ethnicity and psychology. Exactly what variables related to ethnicity account for psychological differences among groups of individuals? The use of ethnicity (or race, for that matter) as a categorical descriptor does little to address this important concern. Put simply, just knowing the ethnicity (or race) of a person does little to explain psychological outcomes in cognition, emotion, motivation, or health (Phinney, 1996). Given these limitations, psychologists need to go beyond the use of ethnic labels to explain individual and group differences in psychology. Phinney (1996) has outlined three key aspects of ethnicity that deserve further attention: cultural norms and values; the strength, salience, and meaning of ethnic identity; and attitudes associated with minority status. We agree with the emphasis on culture as an underlying determinant of psychological functioning. Culture makes ethnic group differences meaningful, and psychologists should focus on it, as well as the other two aspects outlined by Phinney (1996), in understanding and describing ethnicity.

Culture and Gender

Sex refers to the biological differences between men and women, the most obvious being the anatomical differences in their reproductive systems. Accordingly, the term *sex roles* is used to describe the behaviors and patterns of activities men and women may engage in that are directly related to their biological differences and the process of reproduction (such as breast-feeding). In contrast, *gender* refers to the behaviors or patterns of activities that a society or culture deems appropriate for men and women. These behavior patterns may or may not be related to sex and sex roles, although they oftentimes are. *Gender role* refers to the degree to which a person adopts the gender-specific and appropriate behaviors ascribed by his or her culture.

Describing and understanding psychological gender differences requires us to go beyond the biological differences between men and women. Gender differences arise because of differences in the psychological cultures transmitted to men and women. Gender differences are thus cultural differences, and men and women can be said to belong to different cultures. Of course, they may also belong to a larger culture (such as a national culture), and their gender cultures may coexist within the larger culture. This is yet another example of how culture can be understood on multiple levels of analysis, as the definition of culture presented earlier in the chapter suggests.

Culture and Disability

Persons with disabilities differ from those without disabilities in that they share some type of physical impairment in their senses, limbs, or other parts of their bodies. Although the lay public has generally viewed the main distinction of persons with disabilities as the physical impairments they have, a growing body of work in psychology has found important sociopsychological characteristics of disability as well (for example, Clymer, 1995; Hughes & Paterson, 1997; Marks, 1997). Persons with disabilities share the same feelings, ways of thinking, and motivations as everyone else. Beyond that, however, they also share some unique ways of thinking and feeling that may be specific to the fact of their impairment. To the extent that they share certain unique psychological attitudes, opinions, beliefs, behaviors, norms, and values, they share a unique culture.

In recent years, a number of authors have begun to describe the culture of disability (for example, Rose, 1995; Slee & Cook, 1994). These works highlight the unique psychological and sociocultural characteristics of this group of people, refocusing our attention on a broader picture of the person in understanding the psychological characteristics of persons with disabilities. Seen in this light, psychological studies involving participants with disabilities can be viewed as yet another example of cross-cultural studies, as they involve comparisons not only of the presence or absence of impairment, but of more important conditions of culture.

Culture and Sexual Orientation

People form different sexual relationships with others, and the persons with whom they form such relationships constitute a major aspect of their sexual orientation. We often view these relationships as the sole or major defining characteristic of a person's sexual orientation. Yet one of the most important aspects of any sexual orientation—whether straight or gay, mono or bi—is the particular psychological outlook and characteristics that are shared by and unique to each orientation.

These distinctive psychological characteristics may indeed be cultural. Understanding shared psychological attributes among people sharing the same sexual orientation as cultural (for example, gay culture) has become not only fashionable in recent years but well accepted in psychology (Abramson & Pinkerton, 1995; Suggs & Miracle, 1993).

The common thread in this section is that people are often grouped on the basis of shared characteristics that are oftentimes visible or otherwise easily identifiable (race, ethnicity, nationality, sex, disability, or sexual orientation). Although there may or may not be objective bases underlying these classifications or groupings, we cannot forget that they are important social constructs and categories. We use these groupings as mental categories, as Hirschfield (1996) has suggested with race. Problems occur, however, when we consider these mental categories as endpoints in and of themselves, instead of as gate-keepers to important sociopsychological—that is, cultural—differences (and similarities) among the categories. Thus, it is crucial to recognize that one of the most important features of each of these social categories is its underlying culture—that unique set of shared attributes that influences its members' psychologies.

Is culture the only important underlying feature of these social groupings? Of course not. There may be a host of other factors, personal and social, psychological and biological, innate and environmental, that affect the psychologies and behaviors of these, and all, individuals. But culture is probably a very important factor in understanding individuals.

CONTRASTING CULTURE, RACE, PERSONALITY, AND POPULAR CULTURE

Culture and Race

Race is not culture, although many people use the terms interchangeably. The problem with race is that there is considerable controversy surrounding what it is (Anderson & Nickerson, 2005). Many contemporary scholars suggest that there are three major races—Caucasoid, Mongoloid, and Negroid—but past studies of the origins of race have proposed as many as 37 different races (Yee, Fairchild, Weizmann, & Wyatt, 1993). Although laypersons typically use skin color, hair, and other physical characteristics to define race, most physical anthropologists use population gene frequencies. Regardless of which biological or physical characteristics one uses to define race, the very concept of race is much less clear-cut than previously believed (Lewontin, Rose, & Kamin, 1984). Some authors have suggested that the distinctions among races are arbitrary and dubious at best (Zuckerman, 1990). Even studies of genetic systems, including blood groups, serum proteins, and enzymes, have shown considerably more within-group than between-group variation, suggesting that racially defined groups are actually more similar than different.

There is also controversy about the origins of race. Prevalent theories posit a common ancestor originating in Africa 200,000 years ago, whose descendants then migrated to other parts of the world. Evidence for these theories comes from physical anthropology and archaeology. Other theories and apparently conflicting sets of evidence, however, suggest that humans may have existed in multiple regions of the world as far back as 2 million years ago and that intermixing among regions occurred (Wolpoff & Caspari, 1997).

Many psychologists today agree that race is more of a social construction than a biological essential. Hirschfield (1996) suggests that people have a natural propensity to create categories, especially those dealing with human characteristics. Because easily identifiable physical characteristics are often used in this category-formation process, "race" becomes central to these folk theories and thus gains cognitive and social meaning and importance. And of course, although race as a biological construct may be questionable, race as a social construct is real (Smedley & Smedley, 2005).

But race as a social construction does have problems. Category boundaries among the socially constructed races are ambiguous and vary with social context (Davis, 1991; Eberhardt & Randall, 1997; Omi & Winant, 1994). And people of different cultures differ in their definitions of race. In some cultures, race is a continuum along a dimensional scale, not a categorical or nominal entity (Davis, 1991). Many Brazilians believe that race is not heritable and varies according to economic or geographic mobility (Degler, 1971, reported in Eberhardt & Randall, 1997). In some countries, socioeconomic mobility is associated with changes in perceptions of physical properties such as skin color and hair texture (Eberhardt & Randall, 1997).

Thus, our view is that "racial" differences are of little scientific or practical use without a clear understanding of the underlying causes of the similarities and differences observed (Betancourt & Lopez, 1993; Helms, Jernigan, & Mascher, 2005; Zuckerman, 1990). These causes will necessarily involve culture, as defined in this book, because culture as a functional psychological phenomenon determines what is psychologically meaningful and important for different races. Culture is what gives race its meaning, and it is culture with which psychologists should be concerned.

Culture and Personality

Culture is a macro, social, group-level construct. *Personality* refers to the individual differences that exist among individuals within groups. *Culture* is the social psychological frame within which individuals reside, much like the structure of our houses and homes. *Personality* refers to the unique constellation of traits, attributes, qualities, and characteristics of individuals within those frames.

Now it is true that individuals can have their own, special mental representations of culture, and these representations may differ across people. And this may be an aspect of their personality. But individual-level mental representations of culture on the macro-social level is not culture on the macro-social level. Besides, culture as we have defined it involves a meaning and information system that is shared among individuals and transmitted across generations. Personality and individual differences are not shared. Culture is relatively stable across individuals, whereas personality is vastly different.

Culture versus Popular Culture

From time to time, it is fashionable to refer to fads that come and go as "culture." This is also referred to as "popular culture" by the mass media and in everyday conversation. *Popular culture* generally refers to trends in music, art, and other expressions that become popular among a group of people.

Certainly popular culture and culture as we have defined it share some similarities—perhaps most important, the sharing of an expression and its value by a group of people. But there are also important differences. For one, popular culture does not necessarily involve sharing a wide range of psychological attributes across various psychological domains. Culture as defined in this chapter involves a system of rules that cuts across attitudes, values, opinions, beliefs, norms, and behaviors. Popular culture may involve sharing in the value of a certain type of expression, but does not necessarily involve a way of life.

A second important difference concerns cultural transmission across generations. Popular culture refers to values or expressions that come and go as fads or trends within a few years. Culture is relatively stable over time and even across generations (despite its dynamic quality and potential for change).

Thus, although culture and popular culture have some similarities, there are important differences as well. The cross-cultural literature in psychology and the culture described in this book is the culture defined in this chapter, not popular culture (although the psychology of popular culture is a topic well deserving of consideration).

THE PSYCHOLOGICAL CONTENTS OF CULTURE

Culture involves both objective, explicit elements that are physical (e.g., architecture, clothes, foods, art) as well as subjective, implicit elements that are psychological (Kroeber & Kluckholn, 1952/1963; Triandis, 1972). Although both are important, of course, psychologists have been typically interested in the psychological contents of culture. Research over the past several decades has begun to identify exactly what those psychological contents are, and we review three major lines of this research here.

Hofstede's Cultural Dimensions

Hofstede studied work-related values around the world, and to date has reported data from 72 countries involving the responses of more than 117,000 employees of a multinational business organization, spanning over 20 different languages and seven occupational levels to his 63 work-related values items (Hofstede, 2001). In his original work Hofstede (Hofstede, 1980) generated four dimensions that he suggested could differentiate cultures, as discussed below.

Individualism versus Collectivism   This dimension refers to the degree to which cultures will encourage on one hand the tendency for people to look after themselves and their immediate family only, or on the other hand for people to belong to ingroups that are supposed to look after its members in exchange for loyalty.

Power Distance   This dimension refers to the degree to which cultures will encourage less powerful members of groups to accept that power is distributed unequally.

Uncertainty Avoidance   This dimension refers to the degree to which people feel threatened by the unknown or ambiguous situations, and have developed beliefs, institutions, or rituals to avoid them.

Masculinity versus Femininity   This dimension is characterized on one pole by success, money, and things, and on the other pole by caring for others and quality of life. It refers to the distribution of emotional roles between males and females.

Recently Hofstede incorporated a fifth dimension called **Long- versus Short-Term Orientation** (Hofstede, 2001). This dimension refers to the degree to which cultures encourage delayed gratification of material, social, and emotional needs among its members.

Schwartz's Values

Schwartz's work focuses on values, which are desirable goals that serve as guiding principles in people's lives (Rokeach, 1973; Schwartz, 1992, 1994). Schwartz has measured values in many countries using a 56-item instrument, and has identified seven values that are universal (all descriptions taken from Schwartz & Ros, 1995, pp. 96–97).

Embeddedness   The degree to which cultures will emphasize the maintenance of the status quo, propriety, and restraint of actions or inclinations that might disrupt the solidarity of the group or the traditional order. It fosters social order, respect for tradition, family security, and self-discipline.

Hierarchy   The degree to which cultures emphasize the legitimacy of hierarchical allocation of fixed roles and resources such as social power, authority, humility, or wealth.

Mastery   The degree to which cultures emphasize getting ahead through active self-assertion or by changing and mastering the natural and social environment. It fosters ambition, success, daring, and competence.

Intellectual Autonomy   The degree to which cultures emphasize promoting and protecting the independent ideas and rights of the individual to pursue his/her own intellectual directions. It fosters curiosity, broadmindedness, and creativity.

Affective Autonomy   The degree to which cultures emphasize the promotion and protection of people's independent pursuit of positive experiences. It fosters pleasure and an exciting or varied life.

Egalitarianism   The degree to which cultures emphasize transcending selfish interests in favor of the voluntary promotion of the welfare of others. It fosters equality, social justice, freedom, responsibility, and honesty.

Harmony   The degree to which cultures emphasize fitting in with the environment. It fosters unity with nature, protecting the environment, and a world of beauty.

Leung and Bond's Social Axioms

Social axioms are general beliefs and premises about oneself, the social and physical environment, and the spiritual world. They are assertions about the relationship between two or more entities or concepts; people endorse and use them to guide their behavior in daily living, such as "belief in a religion helps one understand the meaning of life." Leung et al. (2002) demonstrated the universal existence of five types of social axioms on the individual level in 41 cultural groups. Bond et al. (2004) then conducted cultural-level analyses on these data, and demonstrated that two social axiom dimensions existed on the cultural level, as discussed below.

Dynamic Externality   This dimension represents an outward-oriented, simplistic grappling with external forces that are construed to include fate and a supreme being. It is the culture-level reflection of the belief structures that form part of a psychological constellation that aids citizens to mobilize psychologically to confront environmental difficulties. Cultures high on this dimension tend to be more collectivistic, conservative, hierarchical; have high unemployment levels, less freedom, and fewer human-rights activities; and have aspirations for security, material resources, and a longer life. There is a strong sense of spirituality in this dimension.

Societal Cynicism   This dimension represents a predominantly cognitive apprehension or pessimism of the world confronting people. Cultures high on this dimension believe that the world produces malignant outcomes, that they are surrounded by inevitable negative outcomes, and that individuals are suppressed by powerful others and subjected to the depredations of willful and selfish individuals, groups, and institutions.

Hofstede's, Schwartz's, and Leung and Bond's perspectives of culture are not mutually exclusive. Individualism, for instance, refers to a constellation of qualities that involve values related to autonomy and individuality. Power Distance involves values related to the primacy of ingroups, the maintenance of hierarchies, situational beliefs, and long-term time perspectives. Masculinity involves values related to Mastery, and Uncertainty Avoidance refers to values and beliefs related to risk versus caution. These links have been supported by country-level correlational findings; Hofstede's Individualism is positively correlated with Schwartz's Affective and Intellectual Autonomy and Egalitarianism (Schwartz, 2004). Power Distance is positively correlated with Long-Term Orientation, Embeddedness, Hierarchy, and Dynamic Externality (Bond et al., 2004; Schwartz, 2004). And Individualism, Affective and Intellectual Autonomy, and Egalitarianism tend to be negatively correlated with Power Distance, Long-Term Orientation, Embeddedness, Hierarchy, and Dynamic Externality.

At the same time, there are important differences among the dimensions. Individualism, for instance, refers more to the relationships between individuals and ingroups, whereas Power Distance refers more to the differentiation of power and status within groups. The same distinction can be made concerning Hierarchy and Embeddedness. Thus, although these dimensions are conceptually and empirically related to each other, they reflect different conceptualizations about the psychological contents of culture.

Behaviors and Worldviews

Culture affects different types of psychological processes, and we draw a distinction here between behaviors and cultural worldviews. Of course, culture affects actual overt, observable behaviors; how we express our emotions in social situations (Chapter 8), how we seek help when we are sick (Chapter 12), how we greet each other (Chapter 9), and how we interact with strangers (Chapter 14). But cultures also differ importantly in **cultural worldviews**. These are culturally specific belief systems about the world; they contain attitudes, beliefs, opinions, and values about the world. They are assumptions people have about their physical and social realities (Koltko-Rivera, 2004). People have worldviews because of evolved, complex cognition; thus, having a worldview is a universal psychological process. The specific content of worldviews, however, is specific and different to each culture, and we will discuss these more in Chapter 13.

More importantly, sometimes behaviors and cultural worldviews are not related to each other. For example, people of different cultures may have a belief about something that may not correspond with what their actual behaviors are

(Matsumoto, 2006); what people say is not always what they do. This distinction also needs to be taken into account when understanding the relationship between culture and psychology: cultural differences in worldviews may or may not be associated with cultural differences in behaviors.

HOW DOES CULTURE INFLUENCE HUMAN BEHAVIORS AND MENTAL PROCESSES?

How can we understand the influence of culture on human behaviors and mental processes? Clearly, with the distinctions we have drawn here, cultures are learned phenomena. Newborns have no culture (although they may very well have biological and temperamental dispositions to learning certain cultural tendencies; see Chapters 3 and 4). As children grow older, they learn specific behaviors and patterns of activities appropriate and inappropriate for their culture, and they either adopt or reject those cultural values and mores.

We believe that culture influences psychological processes—behaviors and mental processes—through the process outlined in Figure 1.5. First, as we described above, culture is an adaptational response to three factors—Ecology, Social Factors, and Biological Factors. These three factors combine to produce cultures on a macro-social level. Individuals are first welcomed into their worlds at birth and begin a process of learning about their culture through a process known as **enculturation,** which we will discuss in Chapter 3. The enculturation process gradually shapes and molds individuals' psychological characteristics, including how individuals perceive their worlds, think about the reasons underlying their and other people's action, have and express emotions, and interact with others.

Although Figure 1.5 summarizes how culture influences psychological processes, there are several important points to remember. First, the system described in Figure 1.5 is not static or unidirectional. The entire system is dynamic and interrelated; it feeds back on and reinforces itself. Cultures themselves change over time as the psychology of its members change. These

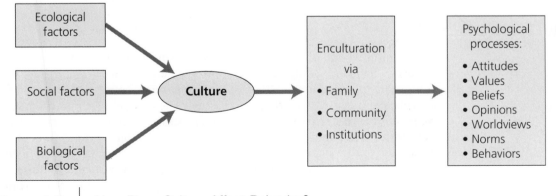

Figure 1.5 | How Does Culture Affect Behavior?

changes also affect the factors that influence culture in the first place, just as how our lifestyles today affect our ecologies and environment.

Also, although culture is an important factor influencing behavior, it is important to realize that it is one of many factors. Other factors include personality and context, and the influence of these factors in understanding behavior cannot be underestimated. Depending on context, cultural influences may be magnified or minimized.

Understanding Culture in Perspective: Universals and Culture-Specifics

The evolution of human culture the way we described it earlier suggests that there are many psychological processes in which all humans engage. For example, because humans have the unique ability to recognize that others are intentional agents, we can draw inferences about the reasons underlying other people's behavior. These are called **attributions,** and the process of making attributions may be something that is universal to all humans (we'll discuss this more in Chapter 11).

But because all human cultures exist in their own specific, unique environment, there are differences among them. Thus, while making attributions may be something universal to all humans, people of different cultures may differ in the *way* they make them. That is, there are probably cultural differences in attributional styles among different human cultures.

This approach provides us with a relatively nuanced way of understanding the relationship between culture and psychology, and of the discipline of cross-cultural psychology. With this approach we can understand how, at one level comparing human cultures with nonhuman animal cultures, the same psychological process may be universal to all humans. At another level, comparing human cultures among themselves, the same psychological process may be done differently. This is true for attributions, emotions, cognition, and motivation, and one of the goals of this book is to highlight the universal *and* culture-specific aspects of these psychological processes. (See Lonner, 1980; Norenzayan & Heine, 2005, for more discussion on universal psychological processes.)

Etics and Emics

Cross-cultural psychologists have a vocabulary for talking about universal and culture-specific psychological processes. **Etics** refer to those processes that are consistent across different cultures; that is, etics refer to universal psychological processes. **Emics** refer to those processes that are different across cultures; emics, therefore, refer to culture-specific processes. These terms originated in the study of language (Pike, 1954), with *phonetics* referring to aspects of language and verbal behaviors that are common across cultures, and *phonemes* referring to aspects of language that are specific to a particular culture and language. Berry (1969) was one of the first to use these linguistic concepts to describe universal versus culturally relative aspects of behavior.

THE CONTRIBUTION OF THE STUDY OF CULTURE

The impact of the growth in cross-cultural research on mainstream psychology has been enormous, and is related to both goals described earlier: the creation of knowledge, and the application of that knowledge.

On Psychological Truths: The Cultural Revolution in Psychology

Despite the wealth of knowledge that has already been gathered in mainstream psychology, it is vitally important to incorporate a cross-cultural approach into our knowledge and learning base. We need to examine whether the information we have learned, or will learn in the future, is applicable to all people of all cultures or only to some people of some cultures. Scientific philosophy suggests that we have a duty and an obligation to ask these questions about the scientific process and about the nature of the truths we have learned, or will learn, about human behavior.

Why is it important to ask and answer these questions? The knowledge that is created in psychology should be accurate and descriptive of all people, not only of people of a certain culture (or race, ethnicity, nationality, gender, or sexual orientation). For too many years, students and faculty alike in psychology have been handed information garnered from research that they have questioned as being truly applicable to themselves. Certainly psychology instructors can learn and understand a theory and the research that supports it and then teach it; likewise, students can learn and memorize these theories and facts. But the mere fact that people can teach and learn something does not mean that it accurately reflects all people, and students and faculty members alike have lamented this issue for years.

The field of psychology has an obligation—to its teachers, students, practitioners, and especially all the people whose lives are touched by its knowledge—to produce accurate knowledge that reflects and applies to them. Cross-cultural research plays an important role in helping psychologists produce that accurate knowledge for all because it tests whether what is true for some is also true for others.

This is not an easy challenge for the field to embrace. In almost any contemporary resource in psychology, cultural diversity in findings and cultural differences in research are widespread and commonplace in all areas. These differences are forcing psychologists to take a good, hard look at their theories and, in many cases, to call for revisions, sometimes major, in the way we have conceptualized many aspects of behavior. As a result, many psychologists see an evolution in psychology, with culture incorporated as a necessary and important ingredient in mainstream psychology. Some authors have even argued that the move toward a cultural psychology should really be a move toward a multicultural psychology—one that incorporates the unique psychologies of the multitude of cultures around the world that may not be assimilable into a single psychology (Gergen et al., 1996). Whether or not that position is accepted, current mainstream psychology clearly needs to move in this direction, finding ways to educate and be educated by other psychological approaches in other cultures. This move involves basic changes in the way psychologists understand many aspects of human behavior. We are in the midst of this evolution in knowledge right now, making it a very exciting time for psychology.

In Our Own Lives

Psychological theories are only as good as their applicability to people in their real lives (Amir & Sharon, 1988; Gergen et al., 1996), and one of the main contributions of cross-cultural psychology to applied psychology is the process it fosters in asking questions. Practicing cross-cultural psychology is an exercise in critical thinking. Is what we know true for all people regardless of their cultural backgrounds? If not, under what conditions do differences occur, and why? What is it about culture that produces such differences? What factors other than culture, such as socioeconomic class, heredity, or environment, may contribute to these differences? The generation of these questions, the harboring of skepticism, and the inquisitive nature of the cross-cultural approach together define its process. And this process is even more important than the content; it can be applied to all areas of our lives, especially in this multicultural world.

THE GOAL OF THIS BOOK

After all is said and done, what do we intend that you gain from this book? In challenging the traditional, we do not mean to disregard its importance or the importance of the work that produced that knowledge. Instead, we seek to raise questions about the traditional, mainstream knowledge of human behavior. We want to know whether what we know of organizations, development, personality, emotion, communication, and many other aspects of human behavior is applicable to people of all cultural backgrounds. We want to challenge the traditional by seeking out answers to these questions in the cross-cultural literature. And if the research suggests that people are different from what is typically believed, we want to find better ways to understand those differences than are available today. We want to impart the flavor of the evolution in science and knowledge that is now occurring.

We offer this book to you as a way to understand, appreciate, respect, and feel cultural diversity and its influence on human behavior. In this book, there should be no right and wrong, no good and bad. In learning about others—in meeting the challenge of cultural diversity—our biggest challenge is within ourselves.

GLOSSARY

attributions Beliefs about the underlying causes of behavior.

cross-cultural psychology A research methodology that tests the cultural parameters of psychological knowledge. Traditionally, it involves research on human behavior that compares psychological processes between two or more cultures. In this book, we also incorporate knowledge contrasting human cultures versus nonhuman animal cultures. This approach is primarily concerned with testing the possible limitations of knowledge gleaned from one culture by studying people of different cultures.

cultural worldviews Culturally specific belief systems about the world. They contain attitudes, beliefs, opinions, and values about the world. People have worldviews because of evolved, complex cognition; thus, having a worldview is a universal psychological process. The specific content of worldviews, however, is specific to and different for each culture.

culture A unique meaning and information system, shared by a group and transmitted across generations, that allows the group to meet basic needs of survival, pursue happiness and well-being, and derive meaning from life.

culture-specific A psychological process that is considered to be true for some people of some cultures but not for others.

enculturation The process of learning about and being indoctrinated into a culture.

emics Aspects of life that appear to differ across cultures; truths or principles that are culture-specific.

etics Aspects of life that appear to be consistent across different cultures; universal or pancultural truths or principles.

ratchet effect The concept that humans continually improve on improvements, that they do not go backward or revert to a previous state. Progress occurs because improvements move themselves upward, much like a ratchet.

social axioms General beliefs and premises about oneself, the social and physical environment, and the spiritual world. They are assertions about the relationship between two or more entities or concepts; people endorse and use them to guide their behavior in daily living, such as "belief in a religion helps one understand the meaning of life."

universal A psychological process that is found to be true or applicable for all people of all cultures.

2 CHAPTER | # Cross-Cultural Research Methods

CHAPTER CONTENTS

One of the points we tried to make in Chapter 1 was that most findings in psychology are limited to the parameters of the research that generated them, and cross-cultural psychology examines the boundaries of that knowledge by altering *one* of those methodological parameters—the cultural background of the participants in the studies. Yet, cross-cultural research is conducted within its own set of parameters. Thus, not only is it important to be able to read cross-cultural research and understand its contributions to knowledge; you also need to be able to evaluate it on its own merits. As active consumers of research in your everyday and academic lives, you need to review cross-cultural research with a critical but fair and open mind, accessing the literature directly and evaluating it with established criteria for quality.

This chapter describes some of the most important issues that determine the quality of cross-cultural research. We organize our discussion of those methodological issues around four major types of studies: cross-cultural comparisons, ecological-level studies, cultural studies, and linkage studies.

CROSS-CULTURAL COMPARISONS

Cross-cultural comparisons are studies that compare cultures on some psychological variable of interest. Cross-cultural comparisons serve as the backbone of cross-cultural research, and are the most prevalent type of cross-cultural study. Several writers have referred to the different phases through which cross-cultural research has evolved over the years (Bond, 2004; Matsumoto & Yoo, 2006). Different types of cross-cultural studies are prominent at different times, each with its own set of methodological issues that have an impact on its quality. Cross-cultural comparisons served as the primary type of study in Phase I of cross-cultural psychology, which began about 100 years ago and continued prominently until the early 1980s. In fact, cross-cultural comparisons are still very prevalent today as well, and serve as the bases for Phase III and IV studies, which we discuss further below.

Equivalence

By far the most important methodological concern that is associated with all types of cross-cultural comparisons, in all phases of cross-cultural research, is **equivalence,** which can be defined as a state or condition of similarity in conceptual meaning and empirical method between cultures that allows comparisons to be meaningful. In its strictest sense, equivalence means that if any aspect of a cross-cultural study is not entirely equal in meaning or method across the cultures being compared, then the comparison loses its meaning. Lack of equivalence in a cross-cultural study creates the proverbial situation of comparing apples and oranges. Only if the theoretical framework and hypotheses have equivalent meaning in the cultures being compared—and if the methods of data collection, management, and analysis have equivalent meaning—will the results from that comparison be meaningful. Apples in one culture can be compared only to apples in another. Lack of equivalence is also known as *bias*.

Linguistic Equivalence   Researchers need to be concerned about equivalence in all aspects of their research, and one arena in which equivalence quickly becomes apparent is in language. Cross-cultural research is unique because it often involves collecting data in multiple languages, and researchers need to establish the **linguistic equivalence** of the research protocols. *Linguistic equivalence* refers to whether the research protocols—items on questionnaires, instructions, etc.— used in a cross-cultural study are semantically equivalent across the various languages included in the study.

There are generally two procedures used to establish linguistic equivalence. One is known as back translation (Brislin, 1970). **Back translation** involves taking the research protocol in one language, translating it to the other language(s), and having someone else translate it back to the original. If the back-translated version is the same as the original, they are generally considered equivalent. If it is not, the procedure is repeated until the back-translated version is the same as the original. The concept underlying this procedure is that the end product must be a semantic equivalent to the original language. The original language is **decentered** through this process (Brislin, 1970, 1993), with any culture-specific concepts of the original language eliminated or translated equivalently into the target language. That is, culture-specific meanings and connotations are gradually eliminated from the research protocols so that what remains is something that is the closest semantic equivalent in each language. Because they are linguistic equivalents, successfully back-translated protocols are comparable in cross-cultural hypothesis-testing research.

A second approach to establishing language equivalence is the committee approach, in which several bilingual informants collectively translate a research protocol into a target language. They debate the various forms, words, and phrases that can be used in the target language, comparing them with their understanding of the language of the original protocol. The product of this process reflects a translation that is the shared consensus of a linguistically equivalent protocol across languages and cultures.

Researchers may combine the two approaches. Here, a protocol may be initially translated and back-translated. Then, the translation and back-translation can be used as an initial platform from which a translation committee works on the protocol, modifying the translation in ways they deem most appropriate, using the back-translation as a guideline.

Measurement Equivalence   Perhaps the most important arena with regard to equivalence may concern the issue of measurement. **Measurement equivalence** refers to the degree to which measures used to collect data in different cultures are equally valid and reliable. **Validity** refers to whether a measure accurately measures what it is supposed to measure; **reliability** refers to how consistently a measure measures what it is supposed to measure.

To be sure, one of the most important lessons to learn about cross-cultural research methods is that linguistic equivalence alone does not guarantee measurement equivalence. This is because even if the words being used in the two languages are the same, there is no guarantee that those words have exactly the same meanings, with the same nuances, in the two cultures. A successful translation gives the researcher protocols that are the closest linguistic equivalents in two or more languages. However, they still may not be exactly the same. In translating the English word *anger,* for example, we might indeed find an equivalent word in Cantonese or Spanish. But would it have the same connotations, strength, and interpretation in those languages as it does in English? It is very difficult to find exact translation equivalents of most words. Thus, cross-cultural researchers need to be concerned with measurement equivalence in addition to linguistic equivalence.

One way to think about measurement equivalence is on the conceptual level. Different cultures may conceptually define a construct differently and/or measure it differently. Just because something has the same name in two or more cultures does not mean that it has the same meaning (Wittgenstein, 1953/1968, cited in Poortinga, 1989) or that it can be measured in the same way. If a concept means different things to people of different cultures, or if it is measured in different ways in different cultures, then comparisons are meaningless. Cross-cultural researchers need to be keenly aware of the issue of equivalence with regard to their conceptual definitions and empirical **operationalization** of the variables (the way researchers conceptually define a variable and measure it) in their study.

In the past, debates concerning cross-cultural studies of intelligence highlight issues concerning conceptual equivalence. Intelligence typically is thought to consist of verbal and analytical critical-thinking skills, and tests such as the Wechsler Adult Intelligence Scale (WAIS) have been widely used to assess IQ. Different cultures, however, may have a different conception of what constitutes intelligence. For example, a culture may consider nobility of character and sincerity to be markers of intelligence. Another culture may consider the ability to have smooth, conflict-free interpersonal relationships a marker for intelligence. Yet another culture may consider creativity and artistic abilities to be indices of intelligence. Comparisons of WAIS data from all of these cultures may not be a meaningful cross-cultural comparison of intelligence.

Another way to think about measurement equivalence is on the statistical level—that is, in terms of **psychometric equivalence.** Psychometric equivalence can be ascertained in several different ways. One of the most important ways, especially when using questionnaires to collect data (which is used in many cross-cultural studies), is to determine whether the questionnaires in the different languages have the same structure. For example, researchers often use a technique called **factor analysis** to examine the structure of a questionnaire. Factor analysis creates groups of the items on a questionnaire based on how the responses to them are related to each other. The groups, called factors, are thought to represent different mental constructs in the minds of the participants responding to the items. Scores are then computed to represent each of these mental constructs.

When using questionnaires across cultures, one concern that arises is whether the same groups of items, or factors, would emerge in the different cultures. If so, then the measure is said to have **structural equivalence.** If not, however, the measure is structurally nonequivalent, which suggests that people of different cultural groups have different mental constructs operating when responding to the same questionnaire. Thus, their responses may not be comparable to each other.

Another way in which psychometric equivalence can be ascertained is by examining the **internal reliability** of the measures across cultures. Internal reliability can be assessed by examining whether the items on a questionnaire are all related to each other. If they are supposed to be measuring the same mental construct, then items should be related to each other; that is, they should have high internal reliability. If the items are working in the same way across cultures, then they should have high internal reliability in each of the cultures being tested.

Cross-Cultural Validation Studies   Because cross-cultural researchers are concerned with measurement equivalence, and because they know that just translating a measure does *not* ensure measurement equivalence, there is a need to conduct studies to test the reliability and validity of measures in different cultures in order to be sure they can be used in the various cultures, thereby ensuring the cross-cultural measurement equivalence of the measure used. **Cross-cultural validation studies** do so. They examine whether a measure of a psychological construct that was originally generated in a single culture is applicable, meaningful, and most importantly psychometrically equivalent (that is, equally reliable and valid) in another culture. These studies do not test a specific hypothesis about cultural differences; rather, they test the equivalence of psychological measures and tests for use in other cross-cultural comparative research.

Sampling Equivalence   There are two issues with regard to **sampling equivalence,** which refers to whether cross-cultural samples can be compared. One concerns whether the samples are appropriate representatives of their culture. Most cross-cultural studies are, in fact, not just cross-cultural; they are cross-city, and more specifically cross-university studies. A "cross-cultural comparison" between Americans and Mexicans may, for instance, involve data collected in Seattle and Mexico City. Are the participants in Seattle representative of American culture? Would they provide the same responses as participants from Beverly Hills, the Bronx, or Wichita? Would the participants in Mexico City provide the same results as those in San Luis Portosi, Guadalajara, or the Yucatan Peninsula? Of course the answer is "we don't know," and it is important for cross-cultural researchers, and consumers of that research (you) to recognize that sound cross-cultural comparisons would entail the collection of data from multiple sites within the same cultural group, either in the same study or across studies, to demonstrate the replicability of a finding across different samples within the same culture.

A second question concerning sampling equivalence concerns whether the samples are equivalent on noncultural demographic variables, such as age, sex, religion, socioeconomic status, work, and other characteristics. For example, imagine comparing data from a sample of 50 Americans from Los Angeles with 50 individuals from Bombay, India. Clearly, the Americans and the Indians come from entirely different backgrounds—different socioeconomic classes, different educational levels, different social experiences, different forms of technology, different religious backgrounds, and so on.

To deal with this issue, researchers need to find ways of controlling these noncultural demographic factors when comparing data across cultures. They do this in one of two ways: experimentally controlling them by holding them constant in the selection of participants (e.g., conducting studies in which only females of a certain age can participate in the study in all cultures) or statistically controlling them when analyzing data.

The conceptual problem that arises in cross-cultural research is that some noncultural demographic characteristics are inextricably intertwined with culture, such that researchers cannot hold them constant across samples in a comparison. For example, there are differences in the meaning and practice of religions across cultures that make them oftentimes inextricably bound to culture. Holding religion constant across cultures does not address the issue, because being Catholic in the United States does not mean the same thing as being Catholic in Japan or Malaysia. Randomly sampling without regard to religion will result in samples that differ not only on culture but also on religion (to the extent that one can separate the influences of the two). Thus, presumed cultural differences often reflect religious differences across samples as well. The same is often true for socioeconomic status (SES), as there are vast differences in SES across cultural samples from around the world.

Procedural Equivalence   The issue of equivalence also applies to the procedures used to collect data in different cultures. For instance, in many universities across the United States, students enrolled in introductory psychology classes are strongly encouraged to participate as research subjects in partial fulfillment of class requirements. American students generally expect to participate in research as part of their academic experience, and many American students are "research-wise."

Customs differ in other countries. In some countries, professors simply collect data from their students or require them to participate at a research laboratory. In some countries, students may consider it a privilege rather than a chore or course requirement to participate in an international study. Thus, expectations about and experience with research participation may differ.

All the decisions researchers make in any other type of study are made in cross-cultural studies as well. But those decisions can mean different things in different countries. Laboratory or field, day or night, questionnaire or observation—all these decisions may have different meanings in different cultures. Cross-cultural researchers need to confront these differences in their work and establish procedures, environments, and settings that are equivalent across the cultures being compared. By the same token, consumers need to be aware of these possible differences when evaluating cross-cultural research.

Theoretical Equivalence   Aside from the methodological issues described above, a major concern of cross-cultural research is the equivalence in meaning of the overall theoretical framework being tested and the specific hypotheses being addressed in the first place. If these are not equivalent across the cultures participating in the study, then the data obtained from them are not comparable, because they mean different things. If, however, the theoretical framework and hypotheses are equivalent across the participating cultures, the study may be meaningful and relevant.

For example, people trained to do research in the United States or Europe may be bound by a sense of "logical determinism" and "rationality" that is characteristic of such formal and systematic educational systems. In addition, because we are so used to drawing two-dimensional theories of behavior on paper, that medium affects the way we think about people and psychology. People of other cultures who have not been exposed to such an educational system or who are not used to reducing their thoughts about the world onto a two-dimensional space may not think in the same way. If this is the case, then a real question arises as to whether a theory created within a Western European or American cultural framework is meaningful in the same way to people who do not share that culture. If the theory is not meaningful in the same way, then it is not equivalent.

Response Bias

In addition to the methodological issues concerning equivalence described above, cross-cultural researchers need to be aware of the fact that different cultures can promote different types of response biases. A **response bias** is a systematic tendency to respond in a certain way to items or scales. Obviously, if culturally-based response biases exist, then it is very difficult to compare data between cultures, because it is not clear whether differences refer to "true" differences in what is being measured or are merely differences in how people respond using scales.

There are, in fact, several different types of response biases. **Socially desirable responding,** for instance, is the tendency to give answers that make oneself look good (Paulhaus, 1984), and it may be that people of certain cultures have greater concerns that lead them to respond in socially desirable ways than people of other cultures. There are two facets of socially desirable responding, which include self-deceptive enhancement—seeing oneself in a positive light—and impression management. Lalwani, Shavitt, and Johnson (2006) demonstrated that European American university students score higher on self-deceptive enhancement than both Korean Americans and students from Singapore, but the latter score higher on impression management than do European Americans (Figure 2.1).

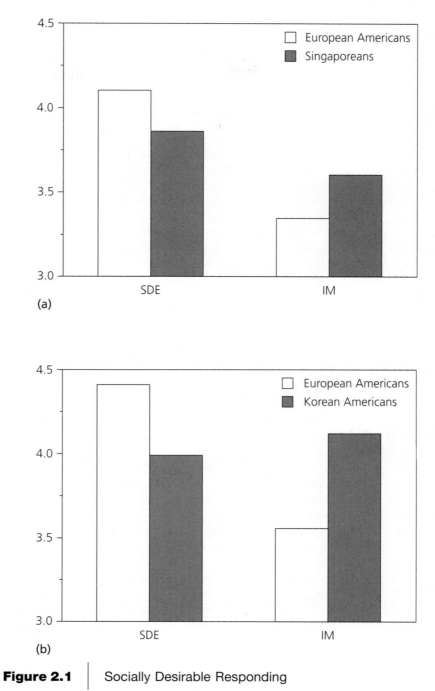

Figure 2.1 | Socially Desirable Responding

(a) Comparison of European Americans and Singaporeans. (b) Comparison of European Americans and Korean Americans. SDE = self-deceptive enhancement; IM = impression management. (Adapted from Lalwani et al., 2006.)

Lalwani et al. (2006) also demonstrated that individuals with more individualistic cultural orientations engaged in more self-deceptive enhancement, while individuals with more collectivistic orientations engaged in more impression management. In a related vein, Matsumoto (2006b) showed that differences between Americans and Japanese university students' individualistic versus collectivistic cultural orientations disappeared once socially desirable responding was statistically controlled.

Two other types of response bias are **acquiescence bias,** which is the tendency to agree rather than disagree with items on questionnaires, and **extreme response bias,** which is the tendency to use the ends of a scale regardless of item content. Van Herk, Poortinga, and Verhallen (2004) examined responses on marketing surveys regarding household behaviors (e.g., cooking, use of products, shaving, washing clothes) in six European countries. They reported that countries near the Mediterranean (Greece, Italy, and Spain) exhibited more of both acquiescence bias and extreme response bias than countries in northwestern Europe (France, Germany, and the United Kingdom). Interestingly, their degree of the two response biases were *not* correlated with national differences in actual behaviors with regard to the issues raised. (If there were differences in rates of actual behaviors, it could be argued that the response styles were not biases, but were reflective of actual differences in behaviors, but this was not the case.)

A final type of response bias we will cover is known as the **reference group effect** (Heine, Lehman, Peng, & Greenholz, 2002). This idea is based on the notion that people make implicit social comparisons with others when making ratings on scales, rather than relying on direct inferences about a private, personal value system (Peng, Nisbett, & Wong, 1997). That is, when completing rating scales, people will *implicitly* compare themselves to others in their group. For example, Japanese individuals may appear to be fairly individualistic on questionnaires, even more so than Americans. But Heine et al. (2002) argue that this may be because the Japanese implicitly compare themselves to their own groups, who are actually fairly collectivistic, when making such ratings, and thus inflate their ratings of individualism. Likewise, Americans may inflate their ratings of collectivism because they implicitly compare themselves to others, who are actually fairly individualistic. Peng et al. (1997) examined four different value survey methods: the traditional ranking, rating, and attitude scaling procedures, and a behavioral scenario rating method. The only method that yielded reasonable validity estimates was the behavioral scenario rating method, the most unorthodox of all the measures tested.

What aspects of culture account for response biases? Johnson, Kulesa, Cho, and Shavitt (2004) examined these biases in 19 countries around the world, and correlated indices of the biases with each country's score on Hofstede's cultural dimensions (see Chapter 1 for a review). (This study is an example of an ecological-level study, which is described more fully below.) On one hand, they found that extreme response bias occurs more in cultures that encourage masculinity, power, and status. They suggested that this response style achieves clarity, precision, and decisiveness in one's explicit verbal statements, characteristics that are valued in these cultures. On the other hand, they also found respondents from individualistic cultures to be less likely to engage in acquiescence bias, probably because maintaining harmony and conveying agreeableness and deference are less emphasized in these cultures.

Response biases can be viewed as methodological artifacts that need to be controlled in order to get to "true" responses, or as an important part of cultural influence on data. Regardless of how researchers choose to view this issue, we agree with Smith (2004) that their effects should be acknowledged and incorporated in data analysis in cross-cultural comparisons.

Interpreting and Analyzing Data from Cross-Cultural Comparisons

Effect Size Analysis   In testing cultural differences on target variables of interest, researchers often use inferential statistics such as chi-square or analysis of variance (ANOVA). These statistics compare the differences observed between the groups to the differences one would normally expect on the basis of chance alone and then compute the probability that the results would have been obtained solely by chance. If the probability of obtaining the findings they did is very low (less than 5 percent), then researchers infer that the findings did not occur because of chance—that is, that the findings reflect actual differences between the cultural groups from which their samples were drawn. This "proof by negation of the opposite" is at the heart of the logic underlying hypothesis testing and statistical inference.

Just because differences between group means are statistically significant, however, does not by itself give an indication of the degree of practical difference between the groups. Group means may be statistically different even though there is considerable overlap among the scores of individuals comprising the two groups.

One mistake that researchers and consumers of research alike make when interpreting group differences is that they assume that most people of those groups differ in ways corresponding to the mean values. Thus, if a statistically significant difference is found between Americans and Japanese, for instance, on emotional expressivity such that Americans had statistically significantly higher scores than the Japanese, people often conclude that all Americans are more expressive than all Japanese. This, of course, is a mistake in interpretation that is fueled by the field's fascination and single-minded concern with statistical significance and perhaps stereotypes.

Statistical procedures are available that help to determine the degree to which differences in mean values reflect meaningful differences among individuals. The general class of statistics that do this is called "effect size statistics"; when used in a cross-cultural setting, Matsumoto and his colleagues call them "cultural effect size statistics" (Matsumoto, Grissom, & Dinnel, 2001). Matsumoto et al. present four such statistics that they deem most relevant for cross-cultural analyses, with reanalyses from two previously published studies as examples. Whether cross-cultural researchers use these or other statistics, it is incumbent on them to include some kind of effect size analysis when comparing cultures so that informed readers can determine the degree to which the differences reported reflect meaningful differences among people. With these statistics, researchers and consumers can have an idea of the degree to which the between-group cultural differences actually reflect differences among the individuals tested, helping to break the hold of stereotypic interpretations based on group difference findings.

Cause–Effect versus Correlational Interpretation In hypothesis-testing cross-cultural studies, cultural groups are often treated as independent variables in research design and data analysis, making these studies a form of quasiexperiment. Data from such studies are basically correlational, and inferences drawn from them can only be correlational inferences. For example, if a researcher compared data from the United States and Japan on social judgments and found that Americans had significantly higher scores on a person-perception task, any interpretations of these data would be limited to the association between cultural membership (American or Japanese) and the scores. Cause–effect inferences (for example, being American causes one to have higher person-perception scores) are unwarranted. For such causal statements to be justified, the researcher would have had to: (1) create the conditions of the experiment (the cultural groups) and (2) randomly assign people to each of the conditions. These experimental conditions cannot apply in any study in which one of the main variables is cultural group. It makes no more sense to assume a causal relationship between cultural membership and a variable of interest than it does to assume such a relationship on the basis of sex, hair color, or height.

Cultural Attribution Fallacies A related type of mistaken interpretation is to suggest specific reasons why cultural differences occurred even though the specific reasons were never measured in the study. Matsumoto and Yoo (2006) call these **cultural attribution fallacies,** which occur when researchers claim that between-group differences are cultural when they really have no empirical justification to do so. For instance, a researcher might take the significant American–Japanese differences found in the previous example and suggest that these differences occurred because of differences between individualism and collectivism in the two cultures. Unless the researchers actually measured individualism and collectivism in their study, found that the two cultures differed on this dimension, and showed that it accounted for the cultural-group differences on social judgments, the interpretation that this construct (IC) is responsible for the group differences is unwarranted. Linkage studies (described more fully below) address this problem.

Researcher Bias Just as culture can bias formulation of the research questions in a cross-cultural study, it can also bias the ways researchers interpret their findings. Most researchers inevitably interpret the data they obtain through their own cultural filters, and these biases can affect their interpretations to varying degrees. For example, for years American–Japanese cultural differences in emotionality have been interpreted by researchers as indicative of Japanese suppression of emotion (Matsumoto & Ekman, 1989). Later studies, however, have provided evidence that it may not be so much that the Japanese suppress, but that the Americans exaggerate their emotional responses (Matsumoto, Kasri, & Kooken, 1999). Thus, our own interpretations of the data were biased in implicitly considering the American data as the "true" responses and non-American data as somehow different.

Dealing with Nonequivalent Data   Despite the best attempts to establish equivalence in theory, hypothesis, method, and data management, cross-cultural research is often inextricably, inherently, and inevitably nonequivalent. It is impossible to create any cross-cultural study that means exactly the same thing to all participating cultures, both conceptually and empirically. What cross-cultural researchers often end up with are best approximations of the closest equivalents in terms of theory and method in a study. Thus, researchers are often faced with the question of how to deal with nonequivalent data. Poortinga (1989) outlines four different ways in which the problem of nonequivalence of cross-cultural data can be handled:

1. *Preclude comparison.* The most conservative thing a researcher could do is not make the comparison in the first place, concluding that it would be meaningless.
2. *Reduce the nonequivalence in the data.* Many researchers take steps to identify equivalent and nonequivalent parts of their methods and then refocus their comparisons solely on the equivalent parts. For example, if a researcher used a 20-item scale to measure anxiety in two cultures and found evidence for nonequivalence on the scale, he or she might then examine each of the 20 items for equivalence and rescore the test using only the items that are shown to be equivalent. Comparisons would then be based on the rescored items.
3. *Interpret the nonequivalence.* A third strategy is for the researcher to interpret the nonequivalence as an important piece of information concerning cultural differences.
4. *Ignore the nonequivalence.* Unfortunately, what many cross-cultural researchers end up doing is simply ignoring the problem, clinging to beliefs concerning scale invariance across cultures despite a lack of evidence to support those beliefs.

How researchers handle the interpretation of their data given nonequivalence depends on their experience and biases and on the nature of the data and the findings. Because of the lack of equivalence in much cross-cultural research, researchers are often faced with many gray areas in interpreting their findings. Culture itself is a complex phenomenon, neither black nor white but replete with gray. It is the objective and experienced researcher who can deal with these gray areas, creating sound, valid, and reliable interpretations that are justified by the data. And it is the astute consumer of that research who can sit back and judge those interpretations relative to the data in their own minds and not be unduly swayed by the arguments of the researchers.

ECOLOGICAL-LEVEL STUDIES

Although most hypothesis-testing cross-cultural research uses individual participants as the unit of analysis, **ecological-level studies** use countries or cultures as the unit of analysis. Data may be obtained from individuals in different cultures, but they are often summarized or averaged for each culture, and those averages are used as data points for each culture. Table 2.1 gives an example of how data are set up in an individual-level study, which is the typical way psychology studies are conducted, compared with an ecological-level study.

Ecological-level studies comprised an important part of Phase II studies in cross-cultural psychology. Many cross-cultural researchers came to realize how limited the cross-cultural comparisons in Phase I were, because just showing a difference between two cultural groups does not demonstrate that the difference occurs because of any cultural difference between them. After all, differences

Table 2.1 A Comparison of the Data Used in an Individual-Level Study, Typical in Psychology, v. an Ecological-Level Study, Comparing the Relationship between Self-Esteem and Academic Performance

Individual-Level Study			Ecological-Level Study		
Level of Analysis	Self-Esteem	Academic Performance	Level of Analysis	Self-Esteem	Academic Performance
Participant 1	Participant 1's score on self-esteem	Participant 1's score on academic performance	Country 1	Country 1's mean on self-esteem	Country 1's mean on academic performance
Participant 2	Participant 2's score on self-esteem	Participant 2's score on academic performance	Country 2	Country 2's mean on self-esteem	Country 2's mean on academic performance
Participant 3	Participant 3's score on self-esteem	Participant 3's score on academic performance	Country 3	Country 3's mean on self-esteem	Country 3's mean on academic performance
Participant 4	Participant 4's score on self-esteem	Participant 4's score on academic performance	Country 4	Country 4's mean on self-esteem	Country 4's mean on academic performance
Participant 5	Participant 5's score on self-esteem	Participant 5's score on academic performance	Country 5	Country 5's mean on self-esteem	Country 5's mean on academic performance
Etc	Etc	Etc	Etc	Etc	Etc

between two cultural groups could occur because of many factors, including and not including culture. Thus, researchers became interested in identifying the kinds of psychological dimensions that underlie cultures in order to better understand cultures on a subjective level (as opposed to an objective level; see Triandis, 1972) and to explain differences better when observed in research.

The most-well-known ecological-level study of culture is Hofstede's seminal work. In his original work, Hofstede (1980) reported data from 40 countries, and soon thereafter from an additional 13 (Hofstede, 1984). Most recently, he has reported data from 72 countries involving the responses of more than 117,000 employees of a multinational business organization, spanning over 20 languages and seven occupational levels to his 63 work-related values items (Hofstede, 2001). Respondents completed a 160-item questionnaire; 63 were related to work values. Hofstede conducted ecological-level analyses on the country means of the 63 items and generated three dimensions that he suggested could describe the cultures of the countries sampled. Hofstede split one of the dimensions into two based on theoretical reasoning and the fact that controlling for country-level gross national product produced a different set of scores. This resulted in his well-known set of four dimensions, introduced in Chapter 1: Individualism versus Collectivism, Power Distance, Uncertainty Avoidance, and Masculinity versus Femininity. Most recently, Hofstede incorporated a fifth dimension called "Long- versus Short-Term Orientation" (Hofstede, 2001; Hofstede & Bond, 1984), which was derived from Bond's work on Asian values (Connection, 1987).

To give you a flavor of the nature of ecological-level data, we reproduce for you the scores of each of the countries and regions in Hofstede's (2001) data set in Appendix A. Other ecological sets of cultural data do exist, such as Schwartz's value orientations (Schwartz, 2004), and Leung and Bond and colleagues' (Bond, Leung, Au, Tong, Reimel de Carrasquel, Murakami, et al., 2004) social axioms, both of which were introduced in Chapter 1. Ecological-level data also have been published for many other psychological constructs, such as personality traits (McCrae, Terracciano, Khoury, Nansubuga, Knezevic, Djuric Jocic, et al., 2005; discussed more fully in Chapter 10) and emotional display rules (Matsumoto, Yoo, Anguas-Wong, Arriola, Ataca, Bond et al., 2005).

The identification of ecological-level dimensions of culture by Hofstede, Schwartz, and others has been extremely important to the field, for several reasons. First, they allowed researchers to use them as a theoretical framework to predict and explain cultural differences in their research (more below in the section on "Cultural Studies"). Also, they allowed other researchers to examine how they relate to other types of ecological-level data. For instance, Triandis, Bontempo, Villareal, Asai and Lucca (1988) showed that the incidence rates of heart attacks were correlated with Individualism versus Collectivism across cultures. Matsumoto and Fletcher (1996) demonstrated a relationship between Hofstede's cultural dimensions and incidence rates for six diseases. And Matsumoto (1989) demonstrated a relationship between Hofstede's cultural dimensions and judgments of emotion across 15 cultures.

CULTURAL STUDIES

After the identification of meaningful cultural dimensions of variability, as mentioned above, the field began to use these dimensions in creating elaborate and exciting theories about exactly what it was about culture that produced differences, and why. By far the most widely used cultural dimension to date has been that of Individualism versus Collectivism. Triandis (1994, 1995), in particular, championed the cause of this dimension, demonstrating how many cultural differences could be explained by this dimension. Also contributing greatly to this evolution in cross-cultural research was Markus and Kitayama's (1991) landmark work linking Individualism versus Collectivism on the cultural level with the concept of self on the individual level (more about this in Chapter 13).

These developments spurred on culturally based studies that comprise Phase III of the evolution of cross-cultural research. **Cultural studies** are characterized by rich descriptions of complex theoretical models of culture that predict and explain cultural differences. Mesquita (Mesquita, 2001; Mesquita & Karasawa, 2002), for instance, describes how cultural systems produce different concepts of the self, which in turn produce different types of specific concerns. According to her framework, individualistic cultures encourage the development of independent senses of self that encourage a focus on personal concerns and the view that the emotions signal internal, subjective feelings; collectivistic cultures, contrastingly, encourage the development of interdependent senses of self that encourage a focus on one's social worth and the worth of one's ingroup, and the notion that emotions reflect something about interpersonal relationships.

Similarly, a number of lines of research have incorporated complex views of culture to predict cultural differences in a number of psychological processes, including morality (Shweder, 1993), attributional style (Nisbett et al., 2001), eye movements when viewing scenes (Masuda & Nisbett, 2001), the nature of unspoken thoughts (Kim, 2002), the need for high self-esteem (Heine, Lehman, Markus, & Kitayama, 1999), and many others. We will, in fact, be discussing much of this research throughout the book.

LINKAGE STUDIES

As mentioned above, cultural studies were definitely a step in the right direction for the field of psychology because they highlighted the rich, complex, and comprehensive influence of culture on a wide array of psychological processes. Thus, they have been extremely important in the evolution of cross-cultural research methods. Still, however, they were limited, because in a strict sense, most cultural studies did not link the theoretical frameworks about culture with the psychological phenomena of interest in the study to demonstrate that those frameworks were actually empirically related to the psychological processes and influenced them in the manner hypothesized. Without this empirical linkage of the theorized contents of culture with the variables of interests, scientists in a strict sense are not empirically justified in claiming that those rich and complex aspects of culture were precisely those that influenced the variables of interest.

For instance Iwata and Higuchi (2000) compared Japanese and American students using the State–Trait Anxiety Inventory (STAI) (Spielberger & Sydeman, 1994), and reported that Japanese were less likely to report positive feelings, and more likely to report higher state and trait anxiety, than Americans. In interpreting these findings, they wrote:

> In traditional Japan, a typical collectivistic society, individual psychological well-being is subordinate to the well-being of the group; that is, maintenance of social harmony is one of the most important values.... The healthy collectivist self is characterized by compliance, nurturance, interdependence, and inhibited hedonism.... The inhibition of positive affect seems to represent a moral distinction and reflect socially desirable behavior in Japan.... For this reason, the Japanese are taught from childhood to understate their own virtues and avoid behaving assertively.... *Because of this socialization, the Japanese seem less likely to generate positive feelings and more likely to inhibit the expression of positive feelings.* (Iwata & Higuchi, 2000, p. 58) (emphasis added)

The problem with this interpretation is that *none* of the factors that are suggested to account for the country differences in anxiety were actually measured in the study and empirically linked to the observed differences. In order to make the causal statement above, the following would need to be established with data in the study: (1) Japan is a collectivistic society; (2) individual psychological well-being is subordinate to the well-being of the group; (3) maintenance of social harmony is one of the most important values; (4) Japanese selves are characterized by compliance, nurturance, interdependence, and inhibited hedonism; (5) the inhibition of positive affect represents a moral distinction and is socially desirable; (6) the Japanese underestimate their own virtues; and (7) the Japanese avoid behaving assertively. Moreover, these observed differences need to empirically mediate the country differences in the STAI data. None of this was done, essentially rendering the authors' claims as speculations.

Most recent researchers have come to recognize the importance of establishing such linkages between the contents of culture and the variables of interest in the study. This has led to the emergence of a class of studies we call **linkage studies** that attempt to do just that. This type of study comprises Phase IV of the evolution of cross-cultural research, a stage we are entering in the field today. There are two types of linkage studies conducted in the field today: unpackaging studies and experiments.

Unpackaging Studies

Unpackaging studies are extensions of basic cross-cultural compariso[...] include the measurement of a variable that assesses the contents of cu[...] are thought to produce the differences on the variable being com[...] cultures. The underlying thought to these studies is that cultures a[...]

for which layer after layer needs to be peeled off until nothing is left. Poortinga, Van de Vijver, Joe, and van de Koppel (1987) expressed the view this way:

> In our approach culture is a summary label, a catchword for all kinds of behavior differences between cultural groups, but within itself, of virtually no explanatory value. Ascribing intergroup differences in behavior, e.g., in test performance, to culture does not shed much light on the nature of these differences. It is one of the main tasks of cross-cultural psychology to peel off cross-cultural differences, i.e., to explain these differences in terms of specific antecedent variables, until in the end they have disappeared and with them the variable culture. In our approach culture is taken as a concept without a core. From a methodological point of view, culture can be considered as an immense set of often loosely interrelated independent variables. (p. 22; see also Segall, 1984; Strodtbeck, 1964)

In unpacking studies, culture as an unspecified variable is replaced by more specific variables in order to truly explain cultural differences. These variables are called **context variables,** and should be measured to examine the degree to which they can account for cultural differences. When measured, researchers then examine the degree to which they statistically account for the differences in the comparison. If the context variables do indeed statistically account for differences, then the researchers are empirically justified in claiming that that specific aspect of culture—that is, that context variable—was related to the differences observed. If they do not, then researchers know that that specific context variable did *not* produce the observed differences. In either case, researchers are empirically justified in making claims about aspects of culture being related to the variables of interest.

Individual-Level Measures of Culture   Over the past few years, one of the more common types of context variables used in research has been **individual-level measures of culture.** These are measures that assess psychological dimensions related to meaningful dimensions of cultural variability and that are completed by individuals. That is, these measures operationalize cultural dimensions on the individual level.

By far, the most common dimension of culture operationalized on the individual level is Individualism versus Collectivism. As mentioned earlier, Harry Triandis, a noted cross-cultural scientist, championed the cause for this dimension. Being heavily influenced by Hofstede's (1980) work, for years Triandis used the Individualism versus Collectivism framework to organize and explain many different types of cultural differences (Triandis, 1994, 1995). the Individualism versus Collectivism framework has been used by archers to explain cultural differences in topics such as ingroup group relationships (Triandis et al., 1988); expression, perception, edents of emotion (Gudykunst & Ting-Toomey, 1988; Matsumoto, 91; Wallbott & Scherer, 1988); self-monitoring and communication s in ingroup and outgroup relationships (Gudykunst et al., 1992); the ial effects of speech rate on perceptions of speaker credibility (Lee & 1992); family values (Georgas, 1989, 1991); teaching styles (Hamilton,

Blumenfeld, Akoh, and Miura, 1991); and conflict avoidance (Leung, 1988). Oyserman, Coon, and Kemmelmeier (2002) conducted a meta-analysis of 83 studies examining group differences on Individualism versus Collectivism (IC) and the possible contribution of IC to various psychological processes. They found that European Americans were more individualistic and less collectivistic than others in general. But they were not more individualistic than African Americans or Latinos, nor were they less collectivistic than Japanese or Koreans, contrary to common stereotypes. In addition, this review indicated that IC had moderate effects on self-concept and relationality, and large effects on attributions and cognitive styles across the studies examined.

Because of the large emphasis on IC as a grounding theoretical framework of culture, most attempts at developing individual-level measures of culture have tried to operationalize it. Triandis himself was a leader in this movement, producing many different types of individual-level measures of IC. Hui (1984, 1988), for example, developed the Individualism–Collectivism (INDCOL) scale to measure an individual's IC tendencies in relation to six collectivities (spouse, parents and children, kin, neighbors, friends, and coworkers and classmates). Later Triandis, Leung, Villareal, and Clack (1985) used items from the INDCOL and further broadened them by adding scenarios and other ratings. Triandis et al. (1986) used items from Hui (1984), Triandis et al. (1985), and items suggested by colleagues in other cultures to measure IC. Triandis et al. (1988) used items from the INDCOL and U.S.-originated items to measure IC. Triandis, McCusker, and Hui (1990) used a multiple-method approach to measuring IC that represented an evolution not only in method but also in thinking. These researchers viewed IC as a cultural syndrome that includes values, beliefs, attitudes, and behaviors (see also, Triandis, 1996); they treated the various psychological domains of subjective culture as an entire collective rather than as separate aspects of culture. Their multiple-method approach included ratings of the social content of the self, perceptions of homogeneity of ingroups and outgroups, attitude and value ratings, and perceptions of social behavior as a function of social distance. Participants were classified as either individualist or collectivist on the basis of their scores on each method. On the individual level, Triandis refers to individualism and collectivism as **idiocentrism** and **allocentrism,** respectively (Triandis et al., 1986).

Most recently, Triandis and his colleagues (Singelis, Triandis, Bhawuk, & Gelfand, 1995) have developed measures that include items assessing a revised concept of individualism and collectivism they call "horizontal and vertical individualism and collectivism," representing yet further advances in the conceptual understanding of IC. In horizontal collectivism, individuals see themselves as members of ingroups in which all members are equal. In vertical collectivism, individuals see themselves as members of ingroups that are characterized by hierarchical or status relationships. In horizontal individualism, individuals are autonomous and equal. In vertical individualism, individuals are autonomous but unequal.

Matsumoto, Weissman, Preston, Brown, and Kupperbusch (1997) also developed a measure of IC for use on the individual level that assesses context-specific

IC tendencies in interpersonal situations—the IC Interpersonal Assessment Inventory (ICIAI). Matsumoto, Consolacion, Yamada, Suzuki, Franklin, Paul, et al. (2002) used it in an unpackaging study examining American and Japanese cultural differences in judgments of emotion. They showed that Americans and Japanese differed in how strongly they perceived facial expressions of emotion. More importantly, however, they also demonstrated that these differences were linked with differences in individual-level measurement of IC (using the ICIAI), and that this linkage empirically accounted for the cultural differences in judgment of faces. Thus, they were empirically justified in claiming that IC accounted for this difference, exemplifying the utility of an unpackaging study.

Self-Construal Scales Spurred on by the IC framework, Markus and Kitayama (1991) proposed that individualistic and collectivistic cultures differed in the kinds of self-concepts they fostered, with individualistic cultures encouraging the development of independent self-construals, and collectivistic cultures encouraging the development of interdependent self-construals (we will discuss these more fully in Chapter 13). This theoretical advance led to the development of scales measuring independence and interdependence on the individual level, most notably the Self-Construal Scale (Singelis, 1994). Using this scale, Singelis, Bond, Sharkey, and Lai (1999) showed that cultural differences in self-esteem and embarassability were empirically linked to individual differences on these types of self-construals, again exemplifying the utility of unpackaging studies.

Personality Any variable that is thought to vary on the cultural level and that may be thought to affect psychological processes can be used as context variables. One such possibility is personality. There are differences in aggregate personality traits across cultures. The United States, Australia, and New Zealand, for example, are noted for their relatively high degrees of extraversion, while France, Italy, and the French Swiss are associated with high levels of neuroticism. Thus, cultural differences may be a product of different levels of personality traits in each culture.

For instance, Matsumoto (2006a) measured emotion regulation—the ability that individuals have to modify and channel their emotions—in the United States and Japan, and demonstrated the existence of cultural differences in emotion regulation. He also measured several personality traits, and demonstrated that the personality traits known as extraversion, neuroticism, and conscientiousness were linked to emotion regulation, and accounted for the cultural differences in it. Thus, what were apparent "cultural" differences on a variable could be explained by differences in aggregate levels of personality between the two cultures studied.

Cultural Practices Another important type of context variable that is important in linkage studies are those that assess cultural practices such as child-rearing, the nature of interpersonal relationships, or cultural worldviews. Heine and Renshaw (2002), for instance, showed that Americans and Japanese were different in their liking of others, and that differences in liking were linked to different cultural practices. Americans liked others they thought were similar to them or shared their own views. For Japanese, liking was related to familiarity and interdependence with others.

Experiments

Another major type of linkage study are experiments. **Experiments** are studies in which researchers create conditions to establish cause–effect relationships. Participants are generally assigned randomly to participate in the conditions, and researchers then compare results across conditions. These studies are fundamentally different from cross-cultural comparisons because in cross-cultural comparisons, researchers cannot create the cultural groups, nor can they randomly assign participants to those groups. (Cross-cultural comparisons are generally examples of what are known as quasiexperimental designs.) True experiments, however, differ because researchers create the conditions and assign participants to those conditions.

There are different types of experiments conducted in cross-cultural psychology today. Here we cover two types: priming studies and behavioral studies.

Priming Studies Priming studies are those that involve experimentally manipulating the mindsets of participants and measuring the resulting changes in behavior. These are interesting because researchers have attempted to manipulate mindsets supposedly related to culture in order to see if participants behave differently as a function of the primed mindset. If they do, researchers can infer that the primed cultural mindset caused the observed differences in behavior, thereby providing a link between a cultural product (the mindset) and a psychological process (the behavior).

One of the first studies that primed cultural contents of the mind was that by Trafimow, Triandis, and Goto (1991). In this study, American and Chinese participants were primed to think in either a private or collective, group-oriented way. Participants primed in the private way read instructions that stated:

> For the next two minutes, you will not need to write anything. Please think of what makes you different from your family and friends.

Participants primed in the collective, group-oriented way, however, were primed with these instructions:

> For the next two minutes, you will not need to write anything. Please think of what you have in common with your family and friends. What do they expect you to do?

Then all participants were asked to complete a self-attitude instrument that involved their completing a series of incomplete questions that started "I am. . . ." Their responses were then coded according to whether it was individually oriented or group-oriented.

The findings indicated that, as expected, Americans as a whole produced more individually oriented responses than the Chinese, while the Chinese

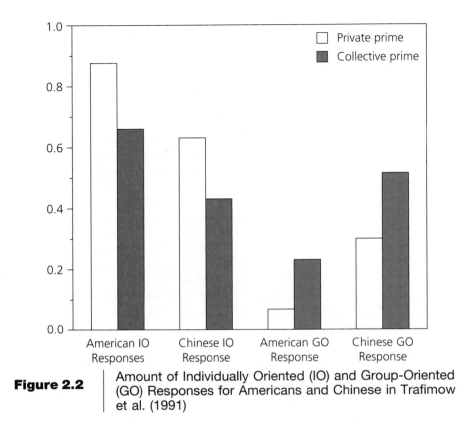

Figure 2.2 | Amount of Individually Oriented (IO) and Group-Oriented (GO) Responses for Americans and Chinese in Trafimow et al. (1991)

produced more group-oriented responses. But, the results also showed that the priming worked. Individuals who were primed privately—that is, to think about how they were *different* from others—produced more individually oriented responses, regardless of whether they were American or Chinese. Likewise, individuals who were primed collectively—that is, to think about how they were similar to others—produced more group-oriented responses, regardless of whether they were American or Chinese (Figure 2.2).

A number of other priming studies have appeared in the literature (Gardner, Gabriel, & Lee, 1999; Trafimow, Silverman, Fan, & Law, 1997), all of which provide evidence for linkage between mental processes and behaviors with the cultural contents of the mind.

Behavioral Studies   Perhaps the most stringent experiments involve manipulations of actual environments and the observation of changes in behaviors as a function of these environments. For example, it is commonly thought that members of collectivistic cultures cooperate more with each other, because cooperation is necessary for groups to function effectively and because of the group-oriented nature of collectivism. Two classic studies on cooperative behavior will elucidate the importance of experiments in identifying what about cultures produce such differences. In the first study, Yamagishi (1986) used a questionnaire to categorize Japanese participants who were high trusters and low trusters; all of the participants then participated in an experiment in which they could cooperate with others by giving money to them, either with a sanctioning system that provided for punishments or without such a system. The conditions, therefore, were the presence or absence of the sanctioning system. The results indicated that high trusters did indeed cooperate more than low trusters without the sanctioning system; when the sanctioning system was in effect, however, low trusters cooperated more than did the high trusters.

Yamagishi (1988) then replicated this study in the United States and compared American and Japanese responses. He found the same results for Americans as he did for the Japanese; when there was no sanctioning system, high-trusting Americans cooperated more than low-trusting Americans. When there was a sanctioning system, the findings reversed. Moreover, there were no differences between the Americans and the Japanese when the sanctioning system was in effect. This suggests, therefore, that the greater cooperation observed in Japanese culture exists because of the sanctioning system within which individuals exist; when Americans were placed in that same type of system, they behaved in the same ways.

SUMMARIZING ACROSS THE DIFFERENT METHODS OF CROSS-CULTURAL RESEARCH

Of course it is very difficult to summarize all of the information presented previously in this chapter in a concise way. In Table 2.2, however, we try to distill some of the major characteristics, and limitations, of the four major research methods that we have discussed until now. This table gives a flavor of how cross-cultural research methods have evolved across time (across the various phases); and it lists the basic methods involved in each approach, the units of analysis, what each type of research can demonstrate, and its limitations. Each type of research method is an answer to a limitation of a previous one.

THE IMPORTANCE OF UNDERSTANDING CROSS-CULTURAL RESEARCH METHODS

Today, cross-cultural research involves studies that involve *all* of the types of cross-cultural studies. Thus, it is important to realize that the methods associated with each of the phases of cross-cultural research are not mutually exclusive. It is more accurate to say that the relative emphasis on the different types of studies has increased across time.

To be sure, just as all research methods have their own limitations, there are limitations to the linkage studies discussed above and that characterizes Phase IV of cross-cultural research. The major limitation to them is that, even if researchers

Table 2.2 | Summary of the Major Characteristics of the Different Types of Cross-Cultural Research

	Cross-Cultural Comparison	Ecological-Level Studies	Cultural Studies	Linkage Studies
Basic research question being addressed	Are the cultures being compared different on the psychological variable of interest?	1. What are the dimensions of culture that exist on the ecological (e.g., country) level. Or, 2. How are cultural dimensions related to psychological variables on the ecological level?	What aspects of culture are probably related to psychological processes?	How are specific and measurable aspects of culture empirically related to psychological processes?
Corresponding phase of research in the history of cross-cultural research	Phase I	Phase II	Phase III	Phase IV (now)
Unit of analysis	Individuals	Cultures	Individuals	Individuals
Basic methodology	Participants in two or more cultures are measured on a psychological variable of interest, and their responses are compared to each other.	Data for cultures, either averages of responses from members of each culture, or data associated with each culture (e.g., average rainfall per year) are compared to each other.	Same as cross-cultural comparison, but within a theoretical framework that attempts to explain why differences may occur in the first place.	Specific aspects of culture that are thought to produce differences are either measured or manipulated, and then empirically related to the psychological variable of interest.
What does this type of research demonstrate?	That people of different cultural groups differ on the psychological variable of interest.	That cultural means on psychological variables are related to dimensions of cultural variability on the cultural level.	That people of different cultural groups differ on the psychological variable of interest.	That specific aspects of culture are empirically related and thus account for cultural differences on a psychological variable of interest.

Limitations to this approach	Cannot be sure of what aspect of culture, if any, produced the differences.	Cultural-level findings may not be applicable on the individual level.	Cannot be sure that the cultural processes associated with the theoretical framework is what really accounts for the differences.	Cannot be sure that other specific aspects of culture may be better explanations of the observed differences, or that the causal link is in the direction hypothesized. That is, the differences in the psychological variable may be what causes the differences in the specific aspects of culture to occur.

demonstrate linkage in their studies, one can never be sure that the specific aspects of culture they measured are the *best* explanatory factors of differences. It may be that others, and more precisely combinations of others, are better.

Another limitation to linkage studies concerns inferences about the types of causal links they allow. The philosophy underlying linkage studies is that the specific aspect of culture measured *causes* the observed differences in the psychological variable of interest. Yet as we discussed in Chapter 1, it may very well be that differences in people's mental processes, behaviors, temperaments, or personalities combined to create cultures, and thus culture-specific practices, in the first place.

A final limitation to linkage studies is that they tend to ignore the advantages of the previous types of studies. Ecological-level factors, such as cultural dimensions, climate, macro-economy, geopolitics, and the like, may contribute to cultural differences, as may culture-specific types of cultural practices. Thus, cross-cultural research in the future—perhaps Phase V of cross-cultural research—will need to incorporate ecological-level data, cultural theories, and linkage variables together, at different levels of analysis, to try to explain differences, and similarities, in mental processes and behaviors.

CONCLUSION

Research is the primary way in which scholars and scientists generate knowledge about the world. Cross-cultural research brings with it its own special set of issues. Many of these are extensions of general experimental research issues in the cross-cultural arena. Other issues, however, are specific to cross-cultural research. To be a critical reader and evaluator of cross-cultural research, you need to be alert to these issues.

Cross-cultural research is tough. As you read above, there are many threats to the validity of any cross-cultural study, including threats to linguistic equivalence, measurement equivalence, sampling equivalence, procedural equivalence, and theoretical equivalence. Threats to the validity of cross-cultural studies come from the existence of different types of response biases, and the proper interpretation of findings. Even when cultures are compared correctly, there is the additional problem of how we can link the differences to meaningful aspects of culture. Ecological-level studies, cultural studies, and linkage studies are all steps in that direction.

All in all, the issues discussed in this chapter are so daunting that you may well wonder whether any cross-cultural study can tell us anything. All studies have at least some imperfections, and every study has its limitations. But that does not necessarily mean we cannot learn something from those studies. The real question is whether the flaws of a study so outweigh its procedures as to severely compromise the trust you place in its data. If a study is so compromised that you don't trust the data, you shouldn't believe it, whether it is cross-cultural or not, even if you agree with its nebulous conclusions. But if a study's problems are less serious, you should be able to glean information from it about cultural differences. If you can do this over a number of studies in an area, they might cumulatively or collectively say something about that area, even though any single study might not.

Despite all the inherent difficulties, cross-cultural research offers a number of exciting and interesting opportunities not available with traditional research approaches. Through cross-cultural research, we can test the limits and boundaries of our knowledge in psychology and about human behavior. We can push the envelope of knowledge and understanding about people in ways that are impossible with traditional research approaches. The cross-cultural enterprise itself offers a process by which scientists and laypersons from disparate and divergent cultures can come together and work toward common goals, thereby improving human relations across what otherwise may seem a considerable chasm. The findings from cross-cultural research offer scientists, scholars, and the public ways to further our understanding of human diversity that can serve as the basis for renewed personal and professional interrelationships and can help to focus public and social policy. Methodologically, cross-cultural studies offer researchers a way to deal with empirical problems related to the conduct of research, such as confounding variables present in traditional research approaches.

This process of evaluating the merits of each study in terms of the trust you would place in the data and then accumulating bits and pieces of information across the studies you trust is integral to learning about a field. In this chapter, we have tried to provide a solid basis for developing and practicing these skills. The material presented in this chapter is just the tip of the iceberg. Many excellent resources, other than those cited throughout this chapter, explain cross-cultural research issues in greater detail for specialists in the field, including issues of method (for example, Van de Vijver & Leung, 1997a, 1997b; Van de Vijver & Matsumoto, 2007), interpretation (Leung, 1989), and data analysis (Leung & Bond, 1989; Matsumoto, Grissom, & Dinnel, 2001). It is this cumulative process that we went through in selecting studies and findings from the various fields of cross-cultural psychology to present to you in the remainder of this book. But do not take our word for it; you need to evaluate that research for yourself. It is a skill that takes practice in order to do well, but like many skills, it can be learned. As you read and evaluate the studies presented in this book and elsewhere, we hope you will find that while cross-cultural research has its own problems and limitations, it has advantages and potentialities that far outweigh the difficulties.

GLOSSARY

acquiescence bias The tendency to agree rather than disagree with items on questionnaires.

allocentrism Refers to collectivism on the individual-level. On the cultural level, collectivism refers to a how a culture functions. Allocentrism refers to how individuals may act in accordance with collectivistic cultural frameworks.

back translation A technique of translating research protocols that involves taking the protocol as it was developed in one language, translating it into the target language, and having someone else translate it back to the original. If the back-translated version is the same as the original, they are generally considered equivalent. If it is not, the procedure is repeated until the back-translated version is the same as the original.

context variables Variables that operationalize aspects of culture that researchers believe produce differences in psychological variables. These variables are actually measured in unpackaging studies.

cross-cultural comparisons A study that compares two or more cultures on some psychological variable of interest, often with the hypothesis that one culture will have significantly higher scores on the variable than the other(s).

cross-cultural validation study A study that examines whether a measure of a psychological construct that was originally generated in a single culture is applicable, meaningful, and thus equivalent in another culture.

cultural attribution fallacies A mistaken interpretation in cross-cultural comparison studies. Cultural attribution fallacies occur when researchers infer that something cultural produced the differences they observed in their study, despite the fact that they may not be empirically justified in doing so because they did not actually measure those cultural factors.

cultural studies Studies that use rich, complex, and in-depth descriptions of cultures and cultural differences to predict and test for differences in a psychological variable.

decenter The concept underlying the procedure of back translation that involves eliminating any culture-specific concepts of the original language or translating them equivalently into the target language.

ecological-level studies A study in which countries or cultures, not individuals, are the unit of analysis.

equivalence A state or condition of similarity in conceptual meaning and empirical method between cultures that allows comparisons to be meaningful.

experiments Studies in which researchers create conditions to establish cause–effect relationships. Participants are generally assigned randomly to participate in the conditions, and researchers then compare results across conditions.

extreme response bias The tendency to use the ends of a scale regardless of item content.

factor analysis A statistical technique that allows researchers to identify groups of items on a questionnaire. The grouped items are thought to represent mental constructs underlying the responses to the items.

idiocentrism Refers to individualism on the individual level. On the cultural level, individualism refers to a how a culture functions. Idiocentrism refers to how individuals may act in accordance with individualistic cultural frameworks.

individual-level measures of culture Measures that assess psychological dimensions related to meaningful dimensions of cultural variability and that are completed by individuals. They are often used to ensure that samples in different cultures actually harbor the cultural characteristics thought to differentiate them. They are often used as context variables.

internal reliability The degree to which different items in a questionnaire are related to each other, and give consistent responses.

linguistic equivalence The semantic equivalence between protocols (instruments, instructions, questionnaires, etc.) used in a cross-cultural comparison study.

linkage studies Studies that attempt to measure an aspect of culture theoretically hypothesized to produce cultural differences and then empirically link that measured aspect of culture with the dependent variable of interest.

measurement equivalence The degree to which measures used to collect data in different cultures are equally valid and reliable.

operationalization The ways researchers conceptually define a variable and measure it.

priming studies Studies that involve experimentally manipulating the mindsets of participants and measuring the resulting changes in behavior.

procedural equivalence The degree to which the procedures used to collect data in different cultures are equivalent to each other.

psychometric equivalence The degree to which different measures used in a cross-cultural comparison study are statistically equivalent in the cultures being compared—that is, whether the measures are equally valid and reliable in all cultures studied

reliability The degree to which a finding, measurement, or statistic is consistent.

response bias A systematic tendency to respond in certain ways to items or scales.

reference group effect The idea that people make implicit social comparisons with others when making ratings on scales. That is, people's ratings will be influenced by the implicit comparisons they make between themselves and others, and these influences may make comparing responses across cultures difficult.

sampling equivalence The degree to which different samples in different cultures are equivalent to each other.

socially desirable responding Tendencies to give answers on questionnaires that make oneself look good.

structural equivalence The degree to which a measure used in a cross-cultural study produces the same factor analysis results in the different countries being compared.

theoretical equivalence The degree to which a theory or set of hypotheses being compared across cultures are equivalent—that is, whether they have the same meaning and relevance in all the cultures being compared.

unpackaging studies Studies that unpackage the contents of the global, unspecific concept of culture into specific, measurable psychological constructs and examine their contribution to cultural differences.

validity The degree to which a finding, measurement, or statistic is accurate, or represents what it is supposed to.

APPENDIX A LISTING OF COUNTRIES AND REGIONS AND THEIR SCORES ON THE FIVE HOFSTEDE CULTURAL DIMENSIONS (FROM HOFSTEDE, 2001; REPRODUCED BY PERMISSION OF GEERT HOFSTEDE)

Exhibit A2.1 | Index Scores for Countries and Regions From the IBM Set

Country	Index				
	Power Distance	Uncertainty Avoidance	Individualism Collectivism	Masculinity/ Feminity	Long-/Short-Term Orientation
Argentina	49	86	46	56	
Australia	36	51	90	61	31
Austria	11	70	55	79	31
Belgium	65	94	75	54	38
Brazil	69	76	38	49	65
Canada	39	48	80	52	23
Chile	63	86	23	28	
Colombia	67	80	13	64	
Costa Rica	35	86	15	21	
Denmark	18	23	74	16	46
Ecuador	78	67	8	63	
Finland	33	59	63	26	41
France	68	86	71	43	39
Germany	35	65	67	66	31
Great Britain	35	35	89	66	25
Greece	60	112	35	57	
Guatemala	95	101	6	37	
Hong Kong	68	29	25	57	96
Indonesia	78	48	14	46	
India	77	40	48	56	61
Iran	58	59	41	43	
Ireland	28	35	70	68	43
Israel	13	81	54	47	
Italy	50	75	76	70	34
Jamaica	45	13	39	68	
Japan	54	92	46	95	80

Exhibit A2.1 | (*continued*)

Country	Power Distance	Uncertainty Avoidance	Individualism Collectivism	Masculinity/ Feminity	Long-/Short-Term Orientation
Korea(South)	60	85	18	39	75
Malaysia	104	36	26	50	
Mexico	81	82	30	69	
Netherland	38	53	80	14	44
Norway	31	50	69	8	44
New Zealand	22	49	79	58	30
Pakistan	55	70	14	50	0
Panama	95	86	11	44	
Peru	64	87	16	42	
Philippines	94	44	32	64	19
Portugal	63	104	27	31	30
South Africa	49	49	65	63	
Salvador	66	94	19	40	
Singapore	74	8	20	48	48
Spain	57	86	51	42	19
Sweden	31	29	71	5	33
Switzerland	34	58	68	70	40
Taiwan	58	69	17	45	87
Thailand	64	64	20	34	56
Turkey	66	85	37	45	
Uruguay	61	100	36	38	
United States	40	46	91	62	29
Venezuela	81	76	12	73	
Yugoslavia	76	88	27	21	
Regions:					
Arab countries	80	68	38	53	
East Africa	64	52	27	41	25
West Africa	77	54	20	46	16

3 CHAPTER | Enculturation

CHAPTER CONTENTS

When the study of culture and psychology uncovers cultural differences among people, some natural questions are: How did these differences arise in the first place? What happens during development that makes people of different cultures different? What are the relative influences of parents, families, extended families, schools, and other social institutions? Are people born with inherent, biological predispositions to behavioral and cultural differences, or are such differences due entirely to environment and upbringing? This chapter examines how the process of enculturation works. That is, how do people come to acquire their cultures? Research in this area has focused on parenting, peer groups, and institutions such as day care, the educational system, and religion, each of which will be discussed here. First, we'll discuss how humans are different from other animals in their ability to acquire culture. Then, we define and compare two important terms in this area of study: enculturation and socialization.

HUMANS ENGAGE IN CULTURAL LEARNING

In Chapter 1 we learned that one of the most important thinking abilities that humans have that other animals do not is the ability to understand that others have wishes, desires, and intentions to act and behave. In other words, humans can get into another person's mind and see things from that person's point of view. Being able to take the perspective of others has important consequences for learning and, more specifically, how we learn to become a member of our culture. Tomasello, Kruger, and Ratner (1993) argue that this unique ability of humans to engage in perspective-taking allows us to engage in "cultural learning"—that is, learning not only *from* others but *through* others. For instance, nonhuman animals, such as young chimpanzees, learn from adult chimpanzees, such as how to fish for termites. Yet, this learning is very different from how young humans learn. Young humans learn not only by mimicking adults, but also by internalizing the knowledge of another person through social cognition. We can do this because we have the ability to understand another person's perspectives, intentions, and goals; internalize them; and learn from them. Thus, Tomasello argues, culture is something that is uniquely learned by humans.

ENCULTURATION AND SOCIALIZATION

Childhood in any society is a dynamic period of life. One aspect of childhood that is probably constant across cultures is that people emerge from this period with a wish to become happy, productive adults. Cultures differ, however, in exactly what they mean by "happy" and "productive." Despite similarities in the overall goals of development, cultures exhibit a tremendous degree of variability in its content.

Each culture has some understanding of the adult competencies needed for adequate functioning (Kagitcibasi, 1996b; Ogbu, 1981), but these competencies differ by culture and environment. For example, children who need a formal education to succeed in their culture are likely to be exposed to these values early in childhood. These children are likely to receive books and instruction at a young age. Children in another culture may have to do spinning and weaving as part of their adult livelihood. These children are likely to receive early exposure to those crafts.

We are all truly integrated in our own societies and cultures. By the time we are adults, we have learned many cultural rules of behavior and have practiced those rules so much that they are second nature to us. Much of our behavior as adults is influenced by these learned patterns and rules, and we are so well practiced at them that we engage in these behaviors automatically and unconsciously.

Still, at some time in our lives, we must have learned those rules and patterns of behavior. Culture, in its truest and broadest sense, involves so many different aspects of life that it is impossible to simply sit somewhere and read a book and learn about, let alone thoroughly master, a culture. Culture must be learned through a prolonged process, over a considerable period of time, with much practice. This learning involves all aspects of the learning processes that psychologists have identified over the years, including classical conditioning, operant conditioning, and social learning. In learning about culture, we make mistakes along the way, but people or groups or institutions are always around to help us, and in some cases force us, to correct those mistakes.

Socialization is the process by which we learn and internalize the rules and patterns of the society in which we live. This process, which occurs over a long time, involves learning and mastering societal norms, attitudes, values, and belief systems. The process of socialization starts early, probably from the very first day of life.

Closely related to the process of socialization is the process called **enculturation**. This is the process by which youngsters learn and adopt the ways and manners of their culture. There is very little difference, in fact, between the two terms. *Socialization* generally refers more to the actual *process and mechanisms* by which people learn the rules of society—what is said to whom and in which contexts. *Enculturation* generally refers to the *products* of the socialization process—the subjective, underlying, psychological aspects of culture that become internalized through development. The similarities and differences between the terms *enculturation* and *socialization* are thus related to the similarities and differences between the terms *culture* and *society*.

Socialization (and enculturation) **agents** are the people, institutions, and organizations that exist to help ensure that socialization (or enculturation) occurs. The first and most important of these agents is parents, who help instill cultural mores and values in their children, reinforcing those mores and values when they are learned and practiced well and correcting mistakes in that learning.

Parents, however, are not the only socialization agents. Siblings, extended families, and peers are important socialization and enculturation agents for many people. Organizations such as school, church, and social groups such as Boy or Girl Scouts also become important agents of these processes. In fact, as you learn more about the socialization process, you will find that culture is enforced and reinforced by so many people and institutions that it is no wonder we all emerge from the process as masters of our own culture.

Super and Harkness (1986, 1994, 2002) suggest that enculturation occurs within a *developmental niche*. This niche forms the child's world within which the child comes to learn values and mores important to the culture. According to Super and Harkness, this niche includes three major components: the physical and social setting, the customs of child care and child rearing, and the psychology of the caregivers. The developing child is influenced by all three components, or more precisely by their interaction, all of which occurs within a larger environmental and human ecology. In their niche, developing children are influenced by the various socialization agents and institutions around them, ensuring their enculturation. At the same time, the child also brings his or her temperamental disposition to the interaction.

In recent years, researchers have examined the process of enculturation itself, looking at how people's interactions with the various socialization agents help to produce cultures. People are not passive recipients of cultural knowledge. Bronfenbrenner (1979) posits that human development is a dynamic, interactive process between individuals and their environments on several levels. These include the *microsystem* (the immediate surroundings, such as the family, school, peer group, with which children directly interact), the *mesosystem* (the linkages between microsystems, such as between school and family), the *exosystem* (the context that indirectly affects children, such as parent's workplace), the *macrosystem* (culture, religion, society), and the *chronosystem* (the influence of time on the other systems). We are not simply socialized by our families, peer groups, and educational and religious institutions; we also contribute to our own development by affecting the people and contexts around us. In other words, we are also active producers of our own development. In the following sections, we will review research that includes several important contexts of enculturation: the family, peer groups, day care, and educational and religious institutions.

PARENTING AND FAMILIES

Margaret Mead, the famous anthropologist, proposed that by observing parents we are observing the essence of a culture. Cultural rules are reinforced and passed on from generation to generation through the way that our parents interact with us (Mead, 1975). As such, a study of parenting gives us a good idea of what is important to that culture.

One of the most in-depth and well-known studies of children and culture was conducted by Beatrice and John Whiting in their Children of Six Cultures study (Whiting & Whiting, 1975). The Whitings were anthropologists who collected field data in Mexico, India, Kenya, the United States, Okinawa, and the Philippines. The major focus of their project was to understand child rearing and children's behavior in these varied cultural contexts. Their observations revealed that children's social behavior could be described along several dimensions ranging from nurturant-responsible (caring and sharing behaviors) to dependent-dominant (seeks help and asserts dominance) and sociable-intimate (acts sociably) to authoritarian-aggressive (acts aggressively). These social behaviors depended, in part, on characteristics of the culture such as household structure. For instance, in cultures with nuclear families, in which husbands and wives slept and ate together and husbands helped with the children, children scored high on sociability and low on aggression. In contrast, in cultures with patrilineal extended families, in which husbands and wives did not sleep and eat together and husbands were not allowed to be present at childbirth or expected to help care for infants, the children scored low on sociability and high on aggression. Women's work roles also contributed to children's social behavior. In cultures in which women contributed greatly to the subsistence base of the family, the children learned to share in family responsibilities and scored low on dependence. In contrast, in cultures in which women were not expected to contribute to the subsistence base of the family and who depended on the husbands for economic support, the children learned to be more dependent. The Six Cultures study demonstrated that variations in the cultural environment (economy, women's work roles) were linked to variations in child-rearing patterns and child development. The next sections delve into greater detail on child-rearing patterns in particular.

Parenting Goals and Beliefs

Clearly, our parents play an important, if not the most important, role in our development. Parenting has many dimensions: the goals and beliefs that parents hold for their children, the general style of parenting they exhibit, and the specific behaviors they use to realize their goals. The goals that parents have for their child's development are based on the caregiving context and the behaviors that each specific culture values (LeVine, 1977, 1997).

An example of how parenting goals may lead to variation in parenting behaviors across cultures is seen in the work of LeVine, LeVine, Dixon, Richman, Leiderman, and Keefer (1996). These researchers have contrasted the parenting goals of Gusii mothers in Kenya with those of American mothers living in a Boston suburb. The Gusii are an agricultural people. Children are expected to help their mothers in the household and fields at a young age. In this environment, one parenting goal Gusii mothers emphasize is protection of their infants. During infancy, soothing behaviors and keeping their infants in close proximity at all times are emphasized to attain this goal. For instance,

93 percent of the waking time and 100 percent of the nighttime is spent with mothers. In Boston, however, one parenting goal that mothers emphasize for their infants' development is active engagement and social exchange. During infancy, these mothers emphasize stimulation and conversation with their infants. Mothers use "baby talk" and adult speech with talking mostly in the form of questions. These mothers respond to 20 percent of any vocalization the baby makes (as compared with Gusii mothers who respond to only 5 percent). American parents believe they must stimulate and teach their children from the very beginning. Gusii mothers, in contrast, believe such stimulation leads to a self-centered adult. Perhaps both are correct. The goals and beliefs of parents are rooted in what is appropriate for that particular culture. As such, we cannot say that certain goals and beliefs are "right" or "wrong," only appropriate or inappropriate to a particular culture (Small, 1998).

Parents' beliefs concerning their roles as caregivers also influence their behaviors. Parents in Western countries (especially in the United States) believe that they play a very active, goal-directed role in the development of their children (Coll, 1990; Goodnow, 1988). In India, however, parents do not believe they "direct" their children's development, but rather focus on enjoying the parent–child relationship (Kakar, 1978). Similarly, Kagitcibasi (1996b) describes traditional Turkish mothers as believing that their children "grow up" rather than are "brought up." This range of parenting beliefs is reflected in the type and extent of involvement in children's upbringing, such as whether the mother transmits cultural knowledge by verbalization or by expecting her child to learn primarily by observation and imitation.

Current research has emphasized the importance of examining such **parental ethnotheories,** or parental cultural belief systems (Edwards, Knoche, Aukrust, Kimru, & Kim, 2006; Harkness & Super, 2006). Harkness and Super state that parental ethnotheories "are the nexus through which the elements of the larger culture are filtered and [are] an important source of parenting practices and the organization of daily life for children and families." Harkness and Super identify parental ethnotheories by conducting in-depth interviews with parents and asking them to keep a daily diary of what they do with their children. One study using these methods compared the parental ethnotheories of American and Dutch parents (Harkness & Super, 2006). The researchers found that American parents hold ethnotheories about the importance of spending *special time* with their children, whereas Dutch parents hold an ethnotheory of spending *family time* with their children. For instance, American parents talked extensively about creating time alone with their child in an activity (usually outside the home) that was focused primarily on attending to the needs of that particular child. Dutch parents, on the other hand, talked extensively about the importance of spending time together as a family, such as sitting down for dinner every night. They did not place as much importance on the belief that they must create a special time for each individual child. You can see how these different belief systems, or ethnotheories, motivate parents to socialize their children in culture-specific ways.

Parenting Styles

Parenting styles are another important dimension of caregiving. Baumrind (1971) has identified three major patterns of parenting. **Authoritarian parents** expect unquestioned obedience and view the child as needing to be controlled. They have also been described as being low on warmth and responsiveness toward their children. **Permissive parents** are warm and nurturing to their children; however, they allow their children to regulate their own lives and provide few firm guidelines. **Authoritative parents** are sensitive to the child's maturity and are firm, fair, and reasonable. They also express a high degree of warmth and affection to their children. This is the most common type of parenting.

Maccoby & Martin (1983) have identified a fourth type of parenting style, called uninvolved. **Uninvolved parents** are often too absorbed in their own lives to respond appropriately to their children and may seem indifferent to them. They do not seem committed to caregiving, beyond the minimum effort required to meet the physical needs of their child. An extreme form of this type of parenting is neglect.

Which of these parenting styles is optimal for a child's development? In general, research on American children indicates that children benefit from the authoritative parenting style. Compared to children of other parenting styles, children of authoritative parents demonstrate more positive mood, self-reliance, self-confidence, higher emotional and social skills, and secure attachment to caregivers (Baumrind, 1967, 1971; Denham, Renwick, & Holt, 1997; Karavasilis, Doyle, & Markiewicz, 2003). This style is seen as promoting psychologically healthy, competent, independent children who are cooperative and at ease in social situations. Children of authoritarian parents are found to be more anxious and withdrawn, lacking spontaneity and intellectual curiosity. Children of permissive parents tend to be immature; they have difficulty controlling their impulses and acting independently. Children of uninvolved parents fare the worst, being noncompliant and demanding.

The benefits of authoritative parenting also extend to the later years. Adolescents with authoritative parents tend to be creative, have high self-esteem, do well in school, and get along well with their peers (Baumrind, 1991; Collins & Laursen, 2004; Spera, 2005; Steinberg, Lamborn, Darling, Mounts, & Dornbusch, 1994). Why is authoritative parenting linked to such positive outcomes during adolescence? A study of college students found that the relation between authoritative parenting and student adjustment could be explained by the student's level of optimism. In other words, students who reported having authoritative parents were also more optimistic. Those who were more optimistic had lower depression, higher self-esteem, and a smoother adjustment to university life (Jackson, Pratt, Hunsberger, & Pancer, 2005). Thus, authoritative parenting may help young people develop positive characteristics, such as optimism, that in turn may encourage healthier development.

Because Baumrind's parenting styles were originally based on observations from a European American sample, Steinberg, Lamborn, Dornbusch, and Darling (1992) argued that the benefits of authoritative parenting may differ depending on the particular ethnic group. For example, when they compared several thousand U.S. adolescents from four ethnic groups (European American, African American, Asian American, and Hispanic American), they found that authoritative parenting significantly predicted higher school achievement for European American, African American, and Hispanic American adolescents, but not for Asian Americans. They also found that European American adolescents were the most likely, and Asian American adolescents the least likely, to report that their parents were authoritative.

Findings from the U.S. have expanded to include cross-cultural studies using the classifications of parenting derived from Baumrind's original research. For instance, a recent study of almost 3,000 Arab adolescents from eight Arab societies revealed that authoritative parenting was associated with greater family connectedness and better adolescent mental health (Dwairy, Achoui, Abouseire, & Farah, 2006). Another study of second-graders in China examined how children's school and social adjustment compared in authoritative versus authoritarian families (Chen, Dong, & Zhou, 1997). These researchers found that authoritarian parenting was related negatively, and authoritative parenting positively, to children's school and social adjustment. These findings are inconsistent with Steinberg et al.'s (1992) argument that the effects of authoritative parenting may be less pronounced for non-European American children. Still, further cross-cultural studies examining these parenting styles are needed before concluding that the authoritative style is optimal for all children.

Some researchers argue that the conceptualization of these parenting styles itself may not be appropriate for parents of other cultures. For instance, Chinese parents have been thought to be more authoritarian. However, the significance and meaning attached to this parenting style may originate from a set of cultural beliefs that may differ greatly from the European American cultural belief system (Chao, 1994, 2001; Gorman, 1998). Chao advocates that researchers identify parenting styles that are specific to the culture by first understanding the values of the culture. For example, based on Confucian philosophy, Chinese parenting may be distinguished by the concept of *chiao shun*, or "training," in child rearing. She argues that this training aspect, which is not considered in Baumrind's styles of parenting, may be more useful in predicting Chinese children's outcomes. Research in Pakistan has also found this notion of training to be an important component of parenting (Stewart, Bond, Zaman, McBride-Chang, Rao, Ho, & Fielding, et al., 1999).

Instigated in large part by Chao's work of Chinese-American parenting, researchers have hypothesized that authoritarian parenting may actually encourage positive outcomes in collectivistic cultures. Nonetheless, a recent review of studies applying Baumrind's parenting styles typology in cross-cultural studies concludes that, in general, authoritarian parenting is associated with psychological maladjustment in cultures as diverse as Egypt, China, India, and Turkey (Sorkhabi, 2005). In other words, there is evidence that when children and adolescents of collectivistic as well as individualistic cultures perceive parents as lacking warmth and exerting unilateral control (aspects of authoritarian parenting), this is seen as undesirable and hostile, not as positive, as some researchers have suggested. This negative perception of authoritarian parents also predicts less family harmony and more family conflict. Authoritative parenting, on the other hand, seems to be consistently associated with positive outcomes (e.g., getting good grades, positively regarded by peers, self-reliant) and has not been associated with negative outcomes across cultures such as Hong Kong, China, and Pakistan. Future studies are needed to examine how different cultures may express these parenting styles in different ways to determine which style is "optimal."

In addition to global parenting styles, the specific dimensions of parenting styles, such as warmth, may have different meanings or expressions in different cultures. For instance, Wu and Chao (2005) studied how perceptions of parental warmth changes as a process of **acculturation** (the process of adapting to, and in many cases adopting, a different culture from the one in which a person was enculturated) among Chinese American teenagers. Traditional Chinese notions of parenting are not based on open displays of affection, such as hugging and kissing. Chinese adolescents in the United States, however, are exposed to parenting in which open affection is encouraged. Thus, these adolescents may develop different ideals than what their parents exhibit. Indeed, Wu and Chao found that Chinese American teenagers were more likely than European American teenagers to believe that their parents were not as warm as they would like their parents to be (i.e., their "ideal" parent). These findings highlight the fact that perceptions of parenting are not static, but can be altered in a different social context.

Parenting Behaviors and Strategies

Over the past several decades, a considerable amount of cross-cultural research has examined differences in parenting behaviors across cultures and how these differences contribute to cultural differences on a variety of psychological constructs.

One of the most representative cultural difference in parenting behaviors concerns sleeping arrangements. One of the single greatest concerns of urban-dwelling Western parents, especially Americans, is getting their baby to sleep through the night, and to do so in a room separate from the parents'. Americans shun co-sleeping arrangements, with the underlying assumption that sleeping alone will help develop independence. Some assistance is offered to the child by way of "security objects," such as a special blanket or toy.

Most other cultures do not share this value. In rural areas of Europe, for example, infants sleep with their mothers for most, if not all, of their first year. This is true for many other cultures in the world, and comfort objects or bedtime rituals are not common in other cultures. In traditional Japanese families, the child sleeps with the mother, either with the father on the other side (symbolizing a river between two river beds) or the father in a separate room (Small, 1998). Swedish children often sleep with both their parents until the child is of school age (Welles-Nystrom, 2005). Mayan mothers allow their children to sleep with them for several years because of a commitment to forming a very close bond with their children. When a new baby comes along, older children move to a bed in the same room or share a bed with another member of the family (Morelli, Oppenheim, Rogoff, & Goldsmith, 1992). The Mayan mothers in this study expressed shock and concern that American mothers would leave their babies alone at night. Again, these practices foster behaviors and values that are consistent with the developmental goals of the culture.

Cultural differences in infant sleeping arrangements can also be seen *within* one culture, such as in the United States. For instance, in a study of Latinos in East Harlem, 21 percent of the children 6 months to 4 years of age slept with their parents, as compared with 6 percent of a matched sample of white middle-class children (Schachter, Fuches, Bijur, & Stone, 1989). In Appalachia or Eastern Kentucky, co-sleeping is the norm. The point is to create a very tightly knit family and keep children close. One mother says, "How can you expect to hold on to them in life if you begin by pushing them away?" (Sloane, 1978 as cited in Small, 1998). Independence is not the goal, but rather attachment to the family. These studies of sleeping arrangements across cultures illustrate how different parenting goals shape what we consider appropriate parenting practices.

Cross-cultural research has also shown differences in how parents structure the home environment for their children. One of the most widely used measures of the home environment is the Home Observation and Measurement of the Environment Inventory (HOME Inventory) created by U.S. researchers (Bradley, Caldwell, & Corwyn, 2003). To administer the HOME Inventory, a researcher visits a family in their home for about one hour. During this hour the researcher makes observations of parent–child interactions and also asks the parents a number of questions concerning how they interact with their child.

In a summary of cross-cultural studies that have used the HOME Inventory, Bradley and Corwyn (2005) describe three general areas in which cultures vary: warmth and responsiveness, discipline, and stimulation/teaching. For instance, warmth and responsiveness are conveyed differently in different cultures. In the United States, one way parents show responsiveness is through physical affection. The Yoruba of Nigeria, however, show responsiveness not by physical affection primarily, but through their tone of voice or praising their child. In many Western industrialized societies, responsiveness is also measured by how often the parent engages in spontaneous conversations with their child. In India, however, where children are expected to respect their elders, it is considered disrespectful to speak without permission. Thus, the type of home environment parents create will depend on the broader cultural belief systems.

Cross-cultural research has not only demonstrated cultural differences in parenting behaviors; it has documented numerous cultural similarities as well. Kelley and Tseng (1992), for example, found that both European American and Chinese American mothers place more emphasis on manners, school-related skills, and emotional adjustment when their children are 6 to 8 years of age than when they are 3 to 5. Solis-Camara and Fox (1995), using a 100-item rating scale—the Parent Behavior Checklist—found that Mexican and American mothers did not differ in their developmental expectations or in their parenting practices. Papps, Walker, Trimboli, and Trimboli (1995) found that mothers from Anglo-American, Greek, Lebanese, and Vietnamese ethnic groups all indicated that power assertion was their most frequently used disciplinary technique.

Thus, the available research evidence suggests both differences and similarities across cultures in parenting styles and child rearing. All of the studies have shown that parenting styles tend to be congruent with developmental goals dictated by culture; that is, cultural differences in specific values, beliefs, attitudes, and behaviors necessary for survival are associated with different developmental goals so that developing members of a society can carry on culture-relevant work related to survival. It seems that all people are similar in that their developmental processes are designed to meet cultural goals; people differ, however, in the specific nature of those goals.

Cultural differences in parenting reflect other social factors as well, such as the economic situation of the family, to which we now turn.

Diversity in Parenting as a Function of Economics

Parenting and child rearing often occur in very different economic conditions in different countries and cultures, and even within one culture, such as the United States. These diverse conditions produce socialization processes that vary widely from culture to culture. Applying one culture's standards to evaluate parenting in other countries and cultures can lead to harsh conclusions.

Consider the case of a slum-dwelling Brazilian mother who leaves her three children under the age of 5 locked in a bare, dark room for the day while she is out trying to meet their basic needs for food and clothing. Although this may seem cruel, we cannot judge the practices of others by the standards of the affluent and well-fed.

If a society has a high rate of infant mortality, parenting efforts may concentrate on meeting basic physical needs. Parents may have little choice but to disregard other developmental demands. Sometimes the response to harsh and stressful conditions is parenting behavior that we might consider positive. In the Sudan, for example, the mother traditionally spends the first 40 days after delivery entirely with her baby. She rests while her relatives tend to her, and she focuses all her energy on her baby (Cederblad, 1988). In other cultures the response to harsh and stressful conditions is parenting behavior that we might consider negative. For example, the anthropologist Scheper-Huges (1992) describes an impoverished community in northeast Brazil, where, if the infant is weak, mothers show little responsiveness and affection, and sometimes even neglect to the point of death, to the infant. Some of these mothers think of their infants as temporary "visitors" to their home. Scheper-Huges writes that in this community, "mother love grows slowly, tentatively, fearfully." These mothers are adapting to the harsh environment in which they must raise their children.

LeVine (1977) has theorized that the caregiving environment reflects a set of goals that are ordered in importance. First is physical health and survival. Next is the promotion of behaviors that will lead to self-sufficiency. Last are behaviors that promote other cultural values, such as morality and prestige. Many families in the United States are fortunate in that they can turn their attention to meeting the second two goals. In many countries, the primary goal of survival is all-important and often overrides the other goals in the amount of parental effort exerted. Indeed, this is true in many areas of the United States as well.

Siblings

The relationships we have with our siblings are likely to be the longest lasting. Siblings play an important role in the socialization of children (Dunn, 1988; Teti, 2002). However, research on family socialization has focused predominantly on parents and, for the most part, neglected the role of siblings (McHale, Crouter, & Whiteman, 2003). This is unfortunate, as siblings are an integral part of the social contexts of children's lives in almost every culture. For instance, in five of the cultures of Whiting and Whiting's Six Cultures Study (1975), other caretakers (which included mostly siblings) were observed to be present an equal or greater amount of time with the young child compared with the mother. In only one culture, the United States, were siblings less likely to be present with the young child than the mother.

The definition of who is considered a sibling may differ across cultures (Economic and Social Research Council, 2005). In many cultures siblings refer to family members who are biologically related. In other cultures, siblings may refer to people who are biologically and nonbiologically related. Changing family structures in many Western industrialized countries are also redefining who is a sibling. Because of the high rates of divorce, separation, remarriage, and creation of step-families, children can now have full siblings (sharing both biological parents), half siblings (sharing one parent) and stepsiblings (sharing no biological parent).

Siblings can fulfill many roles; they can be tutors, buddies, playmates, or caretakers (Parke, 2004). In many cultures, it is common practice for older siblings to act as caretakers for younger siblings (Weisner & Gallimore, 1977). An autobiographical account by Lijembe (1967), a Western Kenyan, describes his role as a caretaker for his younger sister:

> Because there was no older sister in the family, and my mother had to go off to work in the *shamba* [gardens] everyday, it wasn't long before I obliged, though still a very young child myself, to become the day-to-day "nurse" for my baby sister. For my mother to make me succeed in this function, she had to train me—to give me instructions and to see how well I carried them out. . . . As her *shamba* work increased so did my nursing duties . . . before moving off to the *shamba*, she would give me instructions: Do not leave the home unguarded, she would tell me. . . . (as quoted in Weisner & Gallimore, 1977, p. 171)

In his account Lijembe tells of the many important caretaking duties he was responsible for: he plays with his younger sister, bathes her, feeds her, and toilet-trains her. Clearly, studies of caretaking in different cultures would be incomplete if they focused solely on the mother and father and ignored the role of siblings.

Another example of siblings as highly involved caregivers can be seen among the Kwara'ae in the Solomon Islands. In this culture, the responsibilities involved in caregiving are viewed as a training ground for siblings to become mutually dependent on one another in adulthood. For example, one sibling may be designated to go to school while the others combine their resources to support that sibling. In turn, this sibling will support the family financially once he has finishing his schooling and found a job (Watson-Gegeo, 1992). Thus, many of the culture's values, such as family interdependence, are transferred through siblings (Zukow-Goldring, 1995).

Through our interactions with our siblings we learn important skills important to all cultures, such as perspective-taking, social understanding, and conflict negotiation (Parke, 2004; Whiting & Whiting, 1975). Our sibling relationships provide a context to learn prosocial and antisocial behaviors such as empathy and aggression (Ostrov, Crick, & Staffacher, 2006; Tucker, Updegraff, McHale, & Crouter, 1999). Importantly, what children learn with siblings (the good and bad) can transfer into relationships with other children (Parke, 2004; Stauffacher & DeHart, 2006; Teti, 2002).

One study of early adolescents examined how older siblings influenced younger siblings' perspectives on gender (McHale, Updegraff, Helms-Erikson, & Crouter, 2001). These researchers followed a group of sibling pairs over one year. They found that younger siblings tended to model their older siblings in terms of their gender-role attitudes, gendered personality traits, and gender-stereotyped leisure activities. Gender-role attitudes referred to how traditional their attitudes toward women were; gendered personality traits referred to stereotypical traits such as "kind" and "active"; and gender-stereotyped activities referred to activities such as sports and craftwork. Interestingly, the study showed that it was the older siblings', and not parents', gendered attitudes, personality, and activities that were a better predictor of younger siblings' attitudes, personality, and activities. These findings speak to the powerful socializing role that siblings play in our lives. More research is needed to explore the profound ways in which siblings contribute to children's development across cultures.

Extended Families

Extended families are a vital and important feature of child rearing, even when resources are not limited. Many cultures view extended-family child rearing as an integral and important part of their cultures. The extended family can provide a buffer to stresses of everyday living. It is also an important means of transmitting cultural heritage from generation to generation.

In many non–European American cultures, extended families are prevalent. In the United States in 2000, for example, 14 percent of African American and 15 percent of Asian and Pacific-Islander children lived in multigenerational families, compared with only 5 percent of European American children (U.S. Bureau of the Census, 2000). As such, ethnic minority families in the U.S. have been characterized as extended and generally more conservative than European American families. For example, Japanese American families have strict age and sex roles, and emphasize children's obedience to authority figures (Trankina, 1983; Yamamoto & Kubota, 1983). Arab American families are also characterized by an extended family system, in which loyalty, emotional support, and financial assistance are emphasized (Nydell, 1998). Of course, not all ethnic minority families are extended, and caregiving between nuclear and extended families may differ. For instance, African American extended families tend to emphasize cooperation and moral and religious values more than African American nuclear families do (Tolson & Wilson, 1990).

In an extended family situation, even though mothers are still seen as the primary caregiver, children experience frequent interaction with fathers, grandparents, godparents, siblings, and cousins. Hispanic and Filipino families see godparents as important models for children, and as sources of support for the parents. Sharing households with relatives, characteristic of extended families, is seen as a good way of maximizing the family's resources for successful child rearing.

One need not look outside the United States to recognize the importance of extended families. One major difference, however, is that participation in child rearing via extended families in the United States is often seen as a consequence of poor economics rather than a desirable state of affairs. Limited resources are a reality, with 16.3 percent of children in the United States living in poverty in 2001 (U.S. Census Bureau, 2002). Many are born to single mothers, and here the extended family plays an important role in the child-rearing process.

Grandmothers are more actively involved with their grandchildren when they live with their single adult daughters. These children experience a greater variety of principal caregivers and have different social interactions than children from middle-class, two-parent families. Compounding this picture is the reality that ethnicity also confounds social class.

Teenage parenting also forces us to think differently about traditional notions of parenting. The presence of the maternal grandmother in these families has been found to cancel out some of the negative results associated with teen mothering (Baydar & Brooks-Gunn, 1998; Garcia-Coll, 1990; Leadbeater & Way, 2001). The grandmother often serves as a valuable source of information about child development. She also tends to be more responsive and less punitive with the child than the teen mother is. The grandmother in these three-generation households plays a very important role as teacher and role model to her daughter and can provide favorable, positive social interaction for her grandchild.

Extended families differ in their composition from one culture to another but have in common a sharing of resources, emotional support, and caregiving. The experiences of a child growing up in these situations can be quite different from those of a child in a European American nuclear family. In addition, we need to be aware that the traditional two-parent household is changing for many European Americans as well. Future studies will undoubtedly change the way we view parenting in this culture as well.

CULTURE AND PEERS

One's peer group is another critical context for enculturation. How much do your peers influence your development? It may depend on how rapidly your culture is changing. Margaret Mead (1978) described three types of cultures with differing levels of peer influence on the socialization of its young people. In **postfigurative cultures,** in which cultural change is slow, socialization occurs primarily by elders transferring their knowledge to their children. In this case, elders hold the knowledge necessary for becoming a successful and competent adult. In **cofigurative cultures,** in which cultural change occurs more rapidly, adults continue to socialize their children, but peers play a greater role in socializing each other. Young people may have to turn to one another for advice and information. In **prefigurative cultures,** the culture is changing so rapidly that young people may be the ones to teach adults. The knowledge that adults hold may not be sufficient for the next generation, and adults may need to look to younger people for advice and information.

Exposure to Peer Groups

Researchers have studied how cultures vary in the exposure that children have to their peer groups. In industrialized countries, children spend a significant amount of time with same-aged peers. Fuligni and Stevenson's (1995) comparison of the number of hours that teenagers spend with one another outside of school reveals that American teenagers spend more hours (18 hours) with their peers compared with Japanese (12) and Taiwanese (8) teens. The nature and strength of peers as socializing agents in these highly industrialized cultures will differ from other cultures. For instance, children growing up in solitary farm settlements will have limited options to interact with a wide range of potential playmates. Or, children growing up in a hunting/gathering society may be socialized by their peers within the context of multiple-age groups instead of the same-age groups that are characteristic of countries such as the United States, where age-stratified schooling is the norm (Krappmann, 1996). Thus, depending on the specific culture, the extent to which children interact with their peers may be quite significant in terms of enculturation.

CULTURE AND DAY CARE

Variations in Day Care

The differences we see across cultures in day care are a window into different cultural attitudes about children, parenting roles, and social organization. Variations in cultural attitudes concerning how children should be socialized affect the quality and availability of day care around the world. For instance, in the United States, there is a controversy regarding whether child care should be a public responsibility or a private, individual concern (Lamb & Sternberg, 1992). Perhaps because of this tension, there is no national day-care policy, and day-care facilities and practices vary greatly. Unfortunately, the quality of many day-care facilities in the United States appears to be inadequate. Many caregivers do not receive specialized training for teaching young children, and a majority of private day-care homes are unlicensed and therefore not subject to close monitoring to ensure that children are receiving high-quality care (Howes, Whitebrook, & Phillips, 1992; Kontos, Howes, Shinn, & Galinsky, 1995). In contrast, parents in other countries, such as Israel, take for granted that all citizens should share the responsibility of rearing and educating young children. Rosenthal (1992) points out that most Israeli parents believe it is appropriate and important for young children to interact in a group setting with their peers and not be kept at home. Cultural attitudes such as this contribute to the quality and availability of day care.

Day Care and Child Development

Whether day care is beneficial or detrimental to a child's development has been a hotly debated topic. The answer is complex. It is important to examine several factors: the quantity, quality, and type of child care. Since the early 1990s in the United States, a large-scale study of over 1,000 children has been funded by the National Institute of Child Health and Human Development (NICHD) with the goal of understanding how early child care is related to child development. Concerning time spent in child care (quantity), one alarming finding was that 17 percent of children in child care for more than 30 hours a week received high scores on items such as "gets in lots of fights," "talks too much," and "argues a lot" in kindergarten (Belsky, 2002). Whereas only 6 percent of those in child care for less than 10 hours a week reported these problems. Nonetheless, it is important to note that other factors, such as parent–child interactions, was a better predictor of children's behavior than number of hours spent in child care.

What may be even more important to child development is not the quantity, but quality, of child care. Studies in the United States demonstrate that low-quality day care can be detrimental to a child's social and intellectual development (Haskins, 1989; Howes, 1990). Conversely, high-quality day care can enhance children's development, especially for those from underprivileged families of low socioeconomic status (Phillips, Voran, Kisker, Howes, & Whitebrook, 1994). For example, the NICHD study found that high-quality care is linked to greater social competence and fewer behavior problems in the first three years of life (NICHD, 2001). Further, high-quality care is linked to higher scores in math, reading, and memory for children in the third grade (NICHD, 2005). *High-quality care* is defined as a rich learning environment with toys, books, and other learning materials available, a low ratio of caregivers to children, high language stimulation, and individualized attention to children. Studies of young children in Sweden, where day care is of uniformly high quality, show that those in day care have slightly more advanced cognitive and social development compared with those cared for at home (Hwang & Broberg, 1992). Day care in all cultures can be a context in which children's development can be enriched, better preparing them to fill their expected roles in their societies (Lamb & Sternberg, 1992).

CULTURE AND EDUCATION

The single most important formalized mechanism of instruction in many societies and cultures today is the educational system. Most of us think of a country's educational system solely as an institution that teaches thinking skills and knowledge. But a society's educational system is probably the most important institution that teaches and reinforces its cultural values. Much of the cross-national and cross-cultural research in this area has focused on cross-national differences in math achievement.

Cross-National Differences in Math Achievement

Mathematics learning occupies a special place in our understanding of culture, socialization, and the educational system. Of course, learning math skills is crucial to the ultimate development of science in any society, which is probably why learning math has received so much research attention, as well as funding from government and private sources.

Still, math and culture have a very special relationship because, as Stigler and Baranes (1988) put it, math skills "are not logically constructed on the basis of abstract cognitive structures, but rather are forged out of a combination of previously acquired (or inherited) knowledge and skills, and new cultural input" (p. 258). Culture is not only a stimulator of math, but is itself represented in math, and how a society teaches and learns it.

Cross-national research on math learning in schools has traditionally compared the math abilities of students around the world. An early study conducted by the International Association for the Evaluation of Education Achievement (IEA) (Husen, 1967), for example, measured math achievement scores in 12 different countries at the 8th- and 12th-grade levels. The overall performance of the American 8th-graders was ranked 11th, and their mean scores were below the international mean in every area of math assessed. The performance of the American 12th-graders was even worse. A more recent IEA study comparing 45 countries found that American students scored above the international average in math. However, compared to the industrialized countries, 8th-grade American students scored among the lowest (National Center for Education Statistics, 2003). Asian countries such as Singapore, Korea, and Hong Kong top the list (see Chapter 5 for a detailed list).

These findings have been corroborated by other research involving primary-school children (for example, Chen, Lee, & Stevenson, 1996). Even in first grade, the superiority of the Japanese and Chinese in math performance is already striking, reaching "dynamic" proportions by fifth grade (Stevenson, Lee, & Stigler, 1986; Stigler & Baranes, 1988, p. 291). The relatively poor performance of American children has also been documented in comparisons with Korean children (Song & Ginsburg, 1987). Moreover, the differences were observed not only in computational tests but in all math tests produced and administered by the researchers. Finally, more recent research with very young children shows cross-cultural differences in counting performance already emerging at the age of 3 (see Figure 3.1).

Of course, such findings have been alarming to educators at all levels in the United States for many years. The relatively poor performance of American youth in these skills is not only an important social concern; it is also of major concern for the future health of the U.S. economy, as more and more potentially unskilled or underskilled employees enter the workforce (Geary, 1996). Math abilities—and, more importantly, the logical reasoning skills underlying math and the mental discipline associated with math—are essential in many walks of life.

In searching for the possible causes of these differences, Geary (1996) has suggested a distinction between primary and secondary math abilities. *Primary math abilities* refer to natural abilities that are shaped by evolutionary processes that all people presumably share (for example, language, counting). *Secondary abilities* refer to unnatural abilities that are based in large part on primary systems. Whereas the motivation to acquire primary abilities is likely to be inherent, the motivation to acquire secondary abilities may be more strongly influenced by culture.

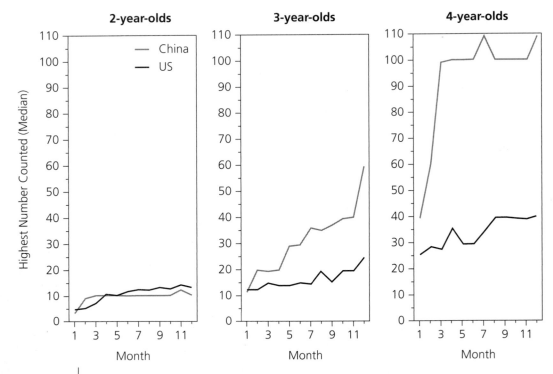

Figure 3.1 | Preschooler's Mathematical Development in China and the United States

Source: Miller, K. M., Kelly, M., & Zhou, X. (2005). Learning mathematics in China and the United States: Cross-cultural insights into the nature and course of preschool mathematical development. In J. Campbell (Ed.), *Handbook of mathematical cognition* (pp. 163–177). New York: Psychology Press. Reprinted with permission.

Are differences in math abilities biologically caused? If biological factors were responsible for cross-national differences in math ability, then cross-national differences in primary math abilities should exist. But, although the research is not definitive, indirect evidence indicates no cross-national differences in primary math abilities. Those cross-national differences that have been found appear to be related to secondary, not primary, math achievements (Geary, 1996). Some people may suggest that research presented in Chapter 5 on possible racial differences in IQ or head (brain) size may also be related to differences in math achievement and thus imply biological causes for those differences. Those IQ differences, however, tend to be small, and not robust enough to account for the rather large differences in math abilities. Moreover, comparisons of mean IQ scores of American, Japanese, and Chinese children (for example, Stevenson et al., 1985) have found no differences; thus, IQ cannot possibly account for cross-national differences among these children. As noted throughout this book, moreover, interpretation of biological differences based on classifications of race are always problematic.

Social and Cultural Factors That Influence Math Achievement

That cross-national differences in math achievement are related to secondary rather than primary math abilities implies that social and cultural factors play a major role in producing those differences. A number of possible contributing factors have been examined in the literature, including differences in language, school systems, parental and familial values, teaching styles and teacher–student relationships, and attitudes and appraisals of students. Work in each of these areas supports the contribution of each factor to cross-national differences in math achievement, and collectively constitutes a wealth of evidence concerning the relationship between culture and education.

Language   Research by Stigler, Lee, and Stevenson (1986) has shown that cross-national differences among Chinese, Japanese, and American children in counting and memory exercises may be largely a function of differences in the Chinese, Japanese, and English languages related to counting and numbers. The Japanese language, for example, has unique verbal labels only for the numbers 1 through 10. Number 11 is then "ten-one," 12 is "ten-two," 20 is "two-ten," 21 is "two-ten-one," and so forth. English, however, has unique labels for numbers 1 through 19 as well as all the decade numbers (20, 30, 40, and so forth). Research has shown that East-Asian students make fewer errors than Americans in counting, and understand some basic math concepts related to counting and numbers better (Miller, Kelly, & Zhou, 2005; Miura, Okamoto, Vladovic-Stetic, Kim, & Han, 1999). These differences may account for some, but not all, of the cross-national differences in math abilities (Paik & Mix, 2003).

School Systems   Research has shown that the educational system in which children take part plays an important role in producing cross-national differences in math abilities, while at the same time imparting cultural values. First of all, the content of what is taught in the schools reflects a priori choices by that culture or society regarding what it believes is important to learn. Different cultures believe different topics to be important for later success in that society. By teaching a certain type of content, the educational system reinforces a particular view of cognition and intelligence.

Another important factor to consider is the environmental setting in which education occurs. Many industrialized societies have a formal educational system, with identifiable areas and structures (schools) and identifiable education agents (teachers) to "do" education. In other cultures, formalized education may take place in small groups led by elders of the community. In yet other cultures, formalized education may be a family task (for example, the mother tutoring her own children in cognitive and other skills necessary for members of their community). Regardless of the environmental setting, the vehicle by which education occurs reinforces certain types of cultural values in its recipients.

The organization, planning, and implementation of lesson plans are other important cultural socializers. Some cultures encourage a didactic model of teaching, in which an expert teacher simply gives information to students, who are expected to listen and learn. Other cultures view teachers as leaders through a lesson plan, providing the overall structure and framework by which students discover principles and concepts. Some cultures view the imparting of praise as an important process. Other cultures focus on mistakes made by students in the learning process. Some cultures have special classes and mechanisms to deal with many different types of students—for example, students with learning disabilities, physical handicaps, and special gifts or talents. Other cultures tend to downplay such differences among their students, treating them all as equals.

Once in school, children spend the majority of their waking hours away from their parents. The socialization process that began in the primary relationship with the parents continues with peers in play situations and in school. School institutionalizes cultural values and attitudes and is a significant contributor not only to the intellectual development of the child but, just as important, to the child's social and emotional development.

To highlight the role of the educational system as an enculturation agent, one need only recognize that not all cultures of the world rely solely on an institutionalized school setting to teach math. For example, important math skills are taught to Micronesian islanders in the Puluwat culture through navigation, to coastal Ghanaians by marketing fish, and even to bookies in Brazil (Acioly & Schliemann, 1986; Gladwin, 1970; Gladwin & Gladwin, 1971). Important math skills are imparted through nonschool activities not only in more "exotic" cultures, but also through activities such as dieting and athletic training in the United States (Stigler & Baranes, 1988).

Regardless of the way education occurs, the choices a society and culture make concerning its structure, organization, planning, and implementation all encourage and reinforce a certain view of culture. We are not always cognizant of our own cultural view because we are in the middle of it. To see our own biases and choices, we need to observe education in other cultures and compare what is done elsewhere to what we do. Through such comparisons, the differences and the similarities often become quite clear.

Parental and Familial Values   Cultural differences in parenting beliefs about education have an impact on children's educational experiences (Chao, 2000). For example, Japanese and Chinese parents are more likely to consider all children as equal, with no differences between them. American parents are more likely to recognize differences and find reasons to treat their children as special.

American parents are also more likely to consider innate ability more important than effort; for the Japanese and Chinese, however, effort is far more important than ability (Stevenson & Zusho, 2002). These cultural differences among the three countries have enormous implications for education.

American parents tend to be more easily satisfied at lower levels of competence than either the Japanese or the Chinese. Also, when problems arise, Americans are more likely to attribute the cause of the problem to something they cannot do anything about (such as ability). These cultural differences in attribution of causality are directly related to cultural differences in self-construals, discussed in Chapter 13.

Believing that ability is more important than effort has yet another side to it—a belief that each child is limited in his or her abilities. Once this belief becomes a cultural institution, it dictates how the educational system should respond. The resulting emphasis in the case of the American system is to seek unique, innate differences among the students, to generate separate special classes for these unique groups of students, and generally to individualize the process of education. As a result, more time is spent on individualized instruction and less on whole-group instruction.

Research has documented other interesting effects of parental and familial values related to achievement and academic success. Sy and Schulenberg (2005), for example, found that European American parents were more involved with in-school activities such as attending a school event or volunteering in their children's classroom compared with Asian American parents. However, Asian American parents were more involved in outside-school activities such as going to the zoo, library, or museum with their children. Furthermore, Asian American parents emphasized the importance of learning early academic skills (counting to 20 and knowing the alphabet by the time a child enters kindergarten), held higher educational expectations for their children (expecting their children to continue onto graduate school), and set more rules regarding watching TV. Chao's (1996) study found that Chinese mothers of preschoolers conveyed a high value on education, the high investment and sacrifice they themselves need to make in order for their children to succeed, their desire for direct intervention approaches to their children's schooling, and a belief that they play a major role in their children's success. American mothers of preschoolers in her study, however, conveyed a negation of the importance of academic skills, a desire for a less-directive approach in instruction, and concern for building their children's self-esteem. These findings suggest the importance of parental cultural values in understanding cultural differences in academic achievement.

Attitudes and Appraisals of Students   A number of studies have examined cultural differences between Asian or Asian American children and European Americans. Pang (1991), for example, studied the relationships among test anxiety, self-concept, and student perceptions of parental support in Asian American and European American middle-school students. This study found that Asian American students exhibited a stronger desire to please parents, greater parental pressure, but also higher levels of parental support, than did the European American students. Yan and Gaier (1994) looked at causal attributions for college success and failure in Asian and American college undergraduate and graduate students; they found that American students attributed academic achievement more often to ability than did Asian subjects. American students also believed that effort was more important for success than lack of effort was for failure, whereas Asian students considered effort equally important for success or failure. These results are consonant with similar tendencies in parental attitudes described earlier, and with attributional biases discussed elsewhere in this book.

Cross-national differences have been found in other samples as well. Little, Oettingen, Stetsenko, and Baltes (1995), for example, compared American, German, and Russian beliefs about school performance. They found that American children had the highest levels of personal agency and control expectancy, but the lowest belief–performance correlations. That is, Americans believed they had the most control over their academic outcomes, but this degree of perceived control was unrelated to their actual performance.

Together, these findings suggest that students around the world approach their academic work with quite different worldviews, attitudes, and attributional styles; that these differences are related to parental differences found in other research; that they may account for cross-national differences in academic achievement; and that they are intimately related to culture.

Teaching Styles and Teacher–Student Relationships   Stigler and his colleagues have examined classrooms to find possible roots of the cross-national differences in math achievement reported earlier (for example, Stigler & Perry, 1988). Several major differences in the use of classroom time appear to underlie math performance differences. The Japanese and Chinese spend more days per year in school, more hours per day in school, a greater proportion of time in school devoted to purely academic subjects, and a greater proportion of time devoted to math (Takahashi & Takeuchi, 2006). In addition, Japanese and Chinese teachers spend a greater proportion of time working with the whole class than do American teachers. This difference is even more dramatic because average class size is smaller in the United States than in Japan or China. As a result, American students spend less time working under the supervision and guidance of a teacher.

During class, it was observed, American teachers tend to use praise to reward correct responses. Teachers in Japan, however, tend to focus on incorrect answers, using them as examples to lead into discussion of the computational process and math concepts. Teachers in Taiwan tend to use a process more congruent with the Japanese approach. These teaching differences speak to the cultural emphasis in the United States on rewarding uniqueness and individualism and the emphasis in Japan and China on finding ways to engage in group process and sharing responsibility for mistakes with members of the group. Praise, while nice, often precludes such discussion.

Taken together, these studies highlight important differences that are present every day in the classroom in terms of teaching style, expectations, and actual behaviors that may account for cross-national differences in academic achievement.

Summary

We know that cross-national differences in academic achievement are not necessarily accounted for by biological differences between people of different cultures. And although differences in languages, especially related to counting systems, may be a factor, they cannot account for the size of the differences. Instead, research indicates that cross-national differences in academic achievement are the result of many social and cultural factors, some of which are institutionalized in educational systems, others found in parents and parental values, others in children's cognitive and attributional styles, and yet others in specific classroom practices. No research suggests that any single factor can fully account for cross-national differences in achievement; instead, it is a combination of these and other factors that leads to differences.

Nor are cross-national differences in academic performance, and the other cross-cultural differences that underlie them, solely products of culture. The performance of students of any culture, in any subject area, is the result of a complex interplay of economics, geography, resources, cultural values and beliefs, abilities, experiences, language, and family dynamics.

Research on differences in academic performance also highlights the role of the educational system as an important enculturation agent in any society. That is, not only do all of the differences discussed here contribute to cross-national differences in academic achievement; they also contribute to differences in culture itself. Parents' and children's attitudes, educational practices and curricula, teacher behaviors, and all other associated factors are important transmitters of culture. They impart important cultural knowledge to the students as members of a culture or society, and thus play a major role in the socialization and enculturation of the child members of many societies of the world. Differences in these institutions not only reflect but reinforce cultural differences in values, beliefs, attitudes, norms, and behaviors and help transmit this important cultural information from one generation to the next. The school-age period of life is indeed a critical time in any culture, when culture is strongly reinforced in children by society as a whole. This process is pervasive.

RELIGION

Religious institutions are another important vehicle of enculturation. In the United States, for most of the 20th century, psychologists neglected the role of religion in the development of individuals (Pargament & Maton, 2000). Religion, however, is an "ever present and extremely important aspect of the historical, cultural, social and psychological realities that humans confront in their daily lives" (Hood, Spilka, Hunsberger, & Gorsuch, 1996, p. 2). Religious institutions socialize children by setting rules for behavior, by preparing children for the roles they will play as men and women, and by helping individuals to create an identity (Arnett, 2001; Pargament & Maton, 2000). Furthermore, the religious community offers support to the developing child, a sense of belonging, and an affirmation of worthiness (Garcia-Coll, Meyer, & Brillon, 1995). Whether it is Islam, Christianity, Judaism, Buddhism, or another religious system, religion is a part of the human experience that can provide individuals with guidance, structure, and appropriate ways of behaving and thinking in many aspects of life.

The importance and pervasiveness of religion, however, vary across cultures. Goossens (1994) reports that only 30 percent of Belgian adolescents believe in God, and only 10 percent regularly attend religious services. In contrast, 95 percent of American adolescents believe in God, and 32 percent attend weekly religious services (Gallup & Bezilla, 1992; Wallace & Williams, 1997). In Poland, 92 percent of youth are members of the Catholic Church, and about 71 percent attend church regularly (Wlodarek, 1994). And in Korea, more than half of the adolescents report participating in some religion, ranging from Christianity to Buddhism to Catholicism (Choe, 1994).

Developmentally, religious ceremonies are an important part of child care and rites of passage in many cultures around the world. For instance, infants in India undergo a hair-shaving ceremony when they are born, and undergo a prayer and holy water ritual when they are named (Dosanjh & Ghuman, 1996). Some religious ceremonies mark the passage from childhood to adulthood, such as in Jewish culture, with the Bar (Bas) Mitzvah. In Islam, the beginning of adolescence is marked by participation in fasting during the holy month of Ramadan.

Dosanjh and Ghuman's (1997) study of Punjabi families living in England illustrates how parents use religion and religious practices in their daily lives to transmit the values and language of their culture to their children. A majority of the sample (87.5 percent) reported that religious education was "important" or "very important." They also reported discussing religion with their children, and actively encouraged them to attend religious services and engage in prayers at home. The authors note that for a majority of Punjabi families, religion plays a critical role in the development and maintenance of their personal identities.

Religious beliefs have been linked to the study of cognitive development in Jewish, Catholic, and Protestant children (Elkind, 1978); moral development in Africa (Okonkwo, 1997); attitudes toward sexuality in older adolescents in the United States (Fehring, Cheever, German, & Philpot, 1998); and attitudes toward suicide for Hindus and Muslims living in England (Kamal & Lowenthal, 2002). However, much still needs to be done to identify exactly what aspects of religion relate to what aspects of human development.

A major challenge for future cross-cultural researchers is to better understand the complex interplay between culture and religion and how they influence family beliefs and values, child-rearing goals and practices, and ultimately, the developing individual. In a world where religion is increasingly becoming a visible target of cross-cultural conflicts and misunderstandings, it is of utmost importance for us to continue exploring how religion defines and shapes an individual's personal experiences, belief systems, and identity.

CONCLUSION

The information presented so far speaks to just a few of the many ways in which enculturation occurs around the world. Differences in parenting styles and child rearing provide learning platforms for children that allow them to achieve developmental goals fostered by their particular cultures. Each culture's way of raising children—through parenting, sleeping arrangements, and other concrete mechanisms—represents that culture's way of ensuring that its values and norms are transmitted to those children. In all cultures, these practices are ritualized so that this transmission of information can occur generation after generation. Learning cultural values is as much a part of the process of socialization as it is an outcome of socialization.

What does contemporary cross-cultural research say about how all this occurs? According to Bornstein (1989), some early cross-cultural work in development (for example, Caudill & Frost, 1974; Caudill & Weinstein, 1969) focused primarily on the role of culture in "driving" parenting behaviors that resulted in changes in the infant and young child. This model suggests that culture unidirectionally provides the structure and environment for parents, particularly mothers, to affect their children in culturally appropriate ways: culture → mother → infant.

Others (for example, Shand & Kosawa, 1985) have focused on biology, proposing a developmental model that starts with the effects of genes, biology, and heredity on infant temperament, which then affects the mother's behaviors, which in turn produce cultural differences: genes → infant → mother → culture.

The available cross-cultural research provides support for both models of understanding. The work on parenting styles, for instance, supports the first model, while the work on temperament and attachment supports the second. More recent work in this area (for example, Super & Harkness, 2002) suggests a rapprochement between the two, conceptualizing both parents and children as interactive partners in the joint creation of cultural meanings. This view suggests that children's active processing of information results in the reproduction of culture and the production of new elements of culture. The interaction of language between parent and child provides the platform on which divergent points of view construct new realities. These recent theories also attempt to discover cultural meanings held in common between parents and children, rather than assuming a common understanding "imposed" by an outside culture.

In addition, the assumption in most of the literature on child rearing that the effect of caregiving flows from the caregiver to the child has been challenged (for example, Bell, 1968, Scarr, 1993). Is it really the case that authoritative parents produce more competent children? Or is it that children who are easygoing, cooperative, and obedient elicit authoritative parenting? Characteristics of the child, such as temperament (discussed in detail in Chapter 4), play an important role in the parenting the child receives. For instance, Ge, Conger, Cadoret, Neiderhiser, Yates, Throughton, and Stewart (1996) examined how an adolescent characterized by a difficult temperamental style might elicit negative parenting behaviors, leading to parent–adolescent conflict and subsequently to adolescent problem behavior. Ge et al. argue that the characteristics of both the adolescent and the parent must be considered in order to more fully understand how children and adolescents contribute to their own development. Current theories on parenting emphasize this dynamic interaction between the child and his or her parent (Collins, Maccoby, Steinberg, Hetherington, & Bornstein, 2000). Whoever the caregiver may be—whether mother, father, sibling, or grandparent—there is a mutual exchange between the child and the caretaker(s) that drives a child's development (Tronick, 1989).

Future research on the enculturation process will hopefully bridge the gaps among all of these various components, assessing the interplay of temperament, attachment, parenting styles, institutions, and psychological culture in the milieu. Ideally, longitudinal studies will enable researchers to examine the interactions among these various components of the enculturation process in the same individuals across time.

GLOSSARY

acculturation The process of adapting to, and in many cases adopting, a different culture from the one in which a person was enculturated.

authoritarian parent A style of parenting in which the parent expects unquestioned obedience and views the child as needing to be controlled.

authoritative parent A style of parenting that is viewed as firm, fair, and reasonable. This style is seen as promoting psychologically healthy, competent, independent children who are cooperative and at ease in social situations.

cofigurative culture A culture in which change occurs rapidly. Both adults and peers socialize young people. Young people may have to turn to one another for advice and information in this type of culture.

enculturation The process by which individuals learn and adopt the ways and manners of their culture.

parental ethnotheories Parental cultural belief systems.

permissive parents A style of parenting in which parents allow children to regulate their own lives and provide few firm guidelines.

postfigurative culture A culture in which change is slow and socialization occurs primarily by elders transferring their knowledge to their children. Elders hold the knowledge necessary for becoming a successful and competent adult.

prefigurative culture A culture that is changing so rapidly that young people may be the ones to teach adults cultural knowledge.

socialization The process by which we learn and internalize the rules and patterns of behavior that are affected by culture. This process, which occurs over a long time, involves learning and mastering societal and cultural norms, attitudes, values, and belief systems.

socialization agents The people, institutions, and organizations that exist to help ensure that socialization occurs.

uninvolved parents A style of parenting in which parents are often too absorbed in their own lives to respond appropriately to their children and may seem indifferent to them.

Culture and Developmental Processes

CHAPTER CONTENTS

Are people born with inherent, biological predispositions to behavioral and cultural differences, or are such differences due entirely to environment and upbringing? What psychological differences are there in childhood and development when people are raised in different cultures? This chapter examines the main question of what kind of psychological differences appear to exist across cultures during infancy and childhood, and throughout development. A considerable amount of cross-cultural research has been conducted on topics such as temperament, attachment, and cognitive and moral development; in this chapter, we review that literature, comparing and contrasting what that literature says in relation to mainstream knowledge. The information presented complements that in the previous chapter (Chapter 3); together they provide a comprehensive view of the influence of culture on developmental processes.

CULTURE AND TEMPERAMENT

As discussed in Chapter 3, the process of socialization starts early, probably from the very first day of life. Some people believe that the biological temperament and predispositions we bring with us into the world at birth are actually part of the socialization process. In other words, the characteristics we are born with determine, to some extent, how our caregivers react and interact with us, initiating the lifelong process of socialization. We begin this review by examining the possibility that children of different cultures are born with different biological predispositions to learn certain cultural practices—that is, the issue of **temperament.**

Traditional Knowledge

Any parent can tell you that no two babies are alike. It is not simply that they look different but that they differ from the very beginning in temperament. Each baby has its own way of being in the world—easygoing or fussy, active or quiet. These qualities of responsiveness to the environment exist from birth and evoke different reactions from people in the baby's world. Temperament is a biologically based style of interacting with the world that exists from birth.

Thomas and Chess (1977) have described three major categories of temperament: easy, difficult, and slow-to-warm-up. **Easy temperament** is defined by a very regular, adaptable, mildly intense style of behavior that is positive and responsive. **Difficult temperament** is an intense, irregular, withdrawing style generally marked by negative moods. **Slow-to-warm-up** infants need time to make transitions in activity and experiences. Though they may withdraw initially or respond negatively, given time and support they will adapt and react positively.

The interaction of a child's temperament with that of the parents, known as **goodness of fit,** seems to be a key to the development of personality. Parental reactions to a child's temperament can promote stability or instability in the child's temperamental responses to the environment. The parents' responses to the child's temperament may also affect subsequent attachment.

Cross-Cultural Studies on Temperament

Several studies have examined whether children of non-American cultures have general styles of temperament that differ from those described for American infants. The implications of differences in temperament, if they exist, are large. If children of other cultures have different temperaments at birth, they will respond to the environment differently. Moreover, they will evoke responses from the environment and caregivers that are different from what Americans would expect. These two fundamental differences—in temperament and environmental response—should produce a fundamental difference in the learning and social experiences of those children, and consequently in their worldview and culture as they grow older. Indeed, Freedman (1974) found that Chinese American babies were calmer and more placid than European American babies or African American babies. When a cloth was placed on their faces covering their noses, the Chinese American babies lay quietly and breathed through their mouths. The other babies turned their heads or tried to pull the cloth off with their hands. Another study supports similar cultural differences in temperament between Chinese and Anglo infants. It was found that Chinese infants were significantly less active, less irritable, and less vocal than American and Irish infants (Kagan, Snidman, Arcus, & Reznick, 1994).

Caudill (1988) found that Japanese infants cried less, vocalized less, and were less active than Anglo infants. Freedman (1974) also found similar differences with Japanese American and Navajo babies when compared with European Americans. Likewise, Chisholm (1983) extensively studied Navajo infants and found that they were much calmer than European American infants. Chisholm argues that there is a well-established connection between the condition of the mother during pregnancy (especially high blood-pressure levels) and the irritability of the infant. This connection between maternal blood pressure and infant irritability has been found in Malaysian, Chinese, and Aboriginal and white Australian infants, as well as in Navajo infants (Garcia Coll, 1990). Garcia Coll, Sepkoski, and Lester (1981) found that differences in the health of Puerto Rican mothers during pregnancy were related to differences in their infants' temperaments when compared with European American or African American infants. The Puerto Rican babies were alert and did not cry easily. The African American babies scored higher on motor abilities—behaviors involving muscle movement and coordination.

Cross-Cultural Studies Using the Neonatal Behavior Assessment Scale Much cross-cultural research has been conducted using T. Berry Brazelton's Neonatal Behavior Assessment Scale (NBAS) (Brazelton & Nugent, 1995). This instrument, used to assess newborns' behaviors in the first 30 days of life, is thought to give an indication of temperamental characteristics of newborns. Studies all over the world have been conducted with the NBAS. For instance, Saco-Pollit (1989) investigated how altitude may relate to newborn behaviors. She compared Peruvian infants who were raised in high-altitude (in the Andes) and low-altitude (Lima) environments. She reported that in comparison with low-altitude infants, those raised in the Andes were less attentive, less responsive, and less active, and had a more difficult time quieting themselves. The harsh environment of living in the high Andes may have contributed to the newborns' differences. A study of Nepalese infants, who by Western standards were undernourished, found that they were actually more alert and had better motor performance compared with a sample of U.S. infants (Walsh Escarce, 1989). The author hypothesizes that these results may reflect an adaptation on the part of the infant to years of poverty. She also noted that the cultural practice of daily massaging the infant, along with special rituals surrounding the baby, may have contributed to their higher performance on the NBAS.

Research conducted in the United States on Hmong infants in the Midwest, also using the NBAS, found that they were quieter and less irritable than Anglo infants (Muret-Wagstaff & Moore, 1989). These infant behaviors were also correlated with greater maternal sensitivity. The researchers raise an interesting question of how this culture in transition would be reflected in later infant–parent interactions. These studies with the NBAS illuminate how differences in temperament across cultures must be considered in relation to the cultural practices of infant caregiving, cultural goals for appropriate infant behaviors, and cultural ideas on the capabilities of infants. These studies also suggest that temperamental differences across cultures are indeed evident, even in infants only a few days after birth.

Temperament and Learning Culture The interaction between parents' responses and infant temperament is certainly one of the keys to understanding the development of culture and socialization processes. The quiet temperament and placidity that are notable in infants from Asian and Native American backgrounds are probably further stabilized in later infancy and childhood by the response of the mothers. Navajo and Hopi babies spend long periods of time tightly wrapped in cradle boards; Chinese parents value the harmony that is maintained through emotional restraint (Bond & Wang, 1983). Thus, differences in infant temperament may make it easier for parents of different cultures to engage in parenting styles and behaviors that teach and reinforce their particular cultural practices. Temperament, therefore, may serve as a baseline biological predisposition of the infant that allows this type of learning to occur.

The cultural differences that we find concerning temperament, evident very early in life, may give us a clue to what kinds of personalities and behaviors are valued in a culture as an adult. For instance, in Japan, nonreactivity (which is related to not expressing emotionality) is more valued than in Western cultures, where higher levels of reactivity (expression of emotionality) are more acceptable. Thus, the differences in temperament we see in the first few days of life may be a reflection of what each culture values concerning appropriate ways of acting and being (Lewis, 1989). As stated earlier, a child's temperament and the environmental response to his or her temperamental style will most likely result in differences in the learning and social experiences of those children, and consequently in their behaviors, personalities, and worldviews as they become adults.

The Goodness of Fit between Temperament and Culture   Research on Masai infants in Kenya has corroborated the importance of the goodness of fit between an infant's temperament and his or her environment. In other words, the adaptiveness of an infant's temperamental style to his or her development may be specific to the immediate environment. Based on Thomas and Chess's (1977) temperament classifications, deVries (1987, 1989) identified difficult and easy Masai infants and followed them for several years. What was considered a "difficult" temperament by Western standards became a protective factor against malnutrition during a time of drought. Those infants who were classified as difficult had a greater chance of survival compared with their easy counterparts. DeVries explains this surprising finding by suggesting that the difficult infants, who were very active and fussy, demanded and consequently received more feeding and caring from their mothers. In sum, a particular type of temperament may be adaptive in one culture and maladaptive in another. His findings highlight the need to consider the cultural context in analyzing the role of a child's characteristics in his or her development.

These findings also caution us about how we label the different temperamental styles. For instance, infants in the United States who have a "difficult" temperament have been found to be at risk for later behavior problems (Caspi, Henry, McGee, Moffitt, & Silva, 1995; Wachs & Bates, 2001). However, having a "difficult" temperament in an extreme situation (as in the context of a life-threatening drought) may be protective, rather than a risk factor, improving the infant's chances of survival. The way we interpret an infant's dispositions and behaviors must be considered in relation to the specific culture; the same dispositions and behaviors may have different meanings when placed in a different cultural context.

Sources behind Temperamental Differences   Why does temperament differ across cultures? It is possible that differences in temperament reflect differences in genetics and in reproductive histories. Thus, environmental and cultural pressures over generations may have helped to produce minor biological differences in infants through a functionally adaptive process. In addition, the cultural experiences of the mother during pregnancy, including diet and other culture-related practices, may contribute to a prenatal environment that modifies an infant's biological composition to correspond to those cultural practices. The fetal environment is one context in which significant stimulation occurs; however, the nature and consequences of this stimulation are largely unknown (Emory & Toomey, 1991).

Whatever the causal mechanism, temperamental differences that are evident from birth contribute to the personality differences we observe in adults of different cultures. Therefore, it is important to understand the magnitude of their contributions as building blocks in the development of adult members of the cultures of the world. Future research in this area should focus on the cultural practices and actual behaviors of people of different cultural groups, and examine the relationship between those and infant temperament.

In sum, cross-cultural research suggests that there are group differences across cultures in infants' and children's temperaments. These differences may be due to multiple factors—what temperamental styles are valued in each culture, specific environmental demands (such as living in poverty or in a high-altitude environment), or physiological aspects of the mother (for example, higher blood pressure). Examining the interaction between the child's temperament and the caregiving environment into which he or she is born can help us understand the process of how we eventually learn to internalize the values, attitudes, and behaviors appropriate to our culture.

CULTURE AND ATTACHMENT

Attachment refers to the special bond that develops between the infant and his or her primary caregiver. Many psychologists believe that the quality of attachment has lifelong effects on our relationships with loved ones. Attachment provides the child with emotional security. Once attached, babies are distressed by separation from their mothers (separation distress or anxiety). The studies on attachment in rhesus monkeys by the Harlows (Harlow & Harlow, 1969) highlighted the importance of contact and physical comfort in the development of attachment.

Bowlby's Theory of Attachment

Bowlby's (1969) evolutionary theory of attachment states that infants must have a preprogrammed, biological basis for becoming attached to their caregivers. This innate behavioral repertoire includes smiling and cooing to elicit physical attachment behaviors on the part of the mother. He argues that the attachment relationship between caregiver and child functioned as a survival strategy: Infants had a greater chance of survival if they remained close to the mother for comfort and protection.

Attachment as a survival strategy is illustrated in a study in Nigeria of Hausa infants and their caregivers (Marvin, VanDevender, Iwanaga, LeVine, & LeVine, 1977). The researchers report that the attachment relationship protected infants from the dangers of their environment, which included open fires and tools and utensils that were easily accessible. Infants explored their environment, but only when they were in close proximity to an attachment figure. True (1994) also found that secure attachment functioned as a protective factor against infant malnutrition among the Dogon of Mali.

Ainsworth's Classification System of Attachment

Based on Bowlby's attachment theory, Mary Ainsworth's (1967, 1977) famous study in Uganda led to the tripartite classification system of attachment relationships between infants and their mothers. Based on her careful observations of 28 mother–infant pairs over a span of one year, she described three attachment styles: **secure, ambivalent,** and **avoidant.** The latter two attachment styles she labeled as "insecurely attached." Infants who are securely attached will become distressed when their mother leaves them but are easily comforted by her when she returns. Infants who are ambivalent will also experience some distress when their mother leaves them but when she returns they send mixed signals—they want to be comforted by her yet, at the same time, appear to have a difficult time letting her soothe them. Infants who are avoidant do not seem to be distressed when their mother leaves and when she returns these infants will actively avoid reuniting with their mother and instead focus their attention elsewhere. Ainsworth later replicated her results in a sample of Baltimore mothers and their infants. In her samples, she found that approximately 57 percent of mothers and infants were classified as securely attached, 25 percent as ambivalent, and 18 percent as avoidant.

Some studies from other cultures have found a similar distribution of attachment classifications; others have found considerable differences. Some attachment styles are not reported in certain cultures; for example, no avoidant infants were found in a sample of Dogon of Mali (True, 1994). In other countries (such as Israel), higher percentages of certain attachment styles (ambivalent) have been found (Sagi et al., 1994, 1997).

Cross-Cultural Studies on Attachment

Since Ainsworth's early studies, hundreds of studies of attachment have been conducted in cultures all over the world. Van IJzendoorn and Sagi (1999) outline some important cross-cultural issues that Ainsworth's Uganda study raised, including whether maternal sensitivity is a necessary antecedent of attachment. For instance, mothers of securely attached infants are described as sensitive, warm, and more positive in their emotional expression. Mothers of avoidant children are suspected of being intrusive and overstimulating. Mothers of ambivalent children have been characterized as being insensitive and uninvolved. Thus, according to Ainsworth, a major determinant of attachment security is having a caregiver who is sensitive and responsive to the child's needs. In a review of 65 studies of attachment, caregiver sensitivity was related to security of attachment; however, this association was rather modest (DeWolff & van IJzendoorn, 1997). Studies with other cultures found an even weaker connection between parent sensitivity and security of attachment (van IJzendoorn & Sagi, 1999). More recently, researchers have highlighted how cultures may differ in what is considered sensitive parenting. For instance, Rothbaum, Weisz, Pott, Miyake, and Morelli (2000) contrast U.S. caregivers' with Japanese caregivers' sensitive responsiveness. In the United States, parents tend to wait for their child to communicate a need and then respond to that need. In other words, sensitive parenting in the United States allows the child to express his or her individual needs to the parent so that the parent can appropriately address those needs. In Japan, on the other hand, parents tend to prefer to anticipate their child's needs instead of waiting for their child to communicate a need. This can be done, for instance, by being aware of situations that may cause distress to a child and anticipating ways to minimize the stress. Rothbaum and colleagues argue that we need to pay more attention to how different cultures conceptualize sensitive parenting to better understand what type of parenting leads to secure attachment.

Cross-Cultural Validity of Assessing Attachment

The cross-cultural validity of the methods of assessing attachment and the meaning of the attachment classifications themselves have been questioned. The meaning of the Strange Situation, a widely used measure of attachment, has been challenged. In the Strange Situation, infants are separated from their mothers for a brief period of time. The quality of attachment is derived partly from an assessment of the infant's reaction to the separation and subsequent reunion with the mother. However, the meaning of the separation may differ across cultures (Takahashi, 1990). As noted earlier, Japanese infants are rarely separated from their mothers, and the separation during the Strange Situation may represent a highly unusual situation that may mean something different for Japanese infants and their mothers than for U.S. infants and their mothers.

Other researchers studying Chinese infants and their mothers question the validity of the avoidant category as an indication of insecure attachment (Hu & Meng, 1996, cited in van IJzendoorn & Sagi, 1999). The researchers state that Chinese mothers emphasize early independence in their infants and, at the same time, stress their reliance on nonparental (usually the grandparent) caregivers. These factors, rather than an insecure relationship between the mother and her infant, may be responsible for findings of avoidant attachment. It may also be the case that subtle attachment behaviors (for instance, those that characterize avoidant relationships) are difficult even for well-trained coders to observe in infants from different cultures (Crittenden, 2000; van IJzendoorn & Sagi, 1999).

Is Secure Attachment a Universal Ideal?

In the United States, secure attachment is assumed to be the ideal. The very term that Ainsworth and colleagues chose to describe this type of attachment, and the negative terms used to describe others, reflects this underlying bias. Some research suggests that cultures may differ, however, in their notion of "ideal" attachment. For example, north German mothers value and promote early independence and see the "securely" attached child as "spoiled" (Grossmann, Grossmann, Spangler, Suess, & Unzner, 1985). Of Israeli children who are raised on a kibbutz (collective farm), half display anxious ambivalent attachments, and only a third appear to be securely attached (Sagi et al., 1985). Children raised in traditional Japanese families are also characterized by a high rate of anxious ambivalent attachment, with practically no avoidant types (Miyake, Chen, & Campos, 1985). These traditional mothers seldom leave their children (such as with babysitters) and foster a strong sense of dependence in their children (which in itself is curious, because studies of U.S. culture have shown that ambivalent infants are generally associated with mothers who are less involved). This dependence supports the traditional cultural ideal of family loyalty. In nontraditional Japanese families, in which the mother may have a career, attachment patterns are similar to those in the United States (Durrett, Otaki, & Richards, 1984). Crittenden (2000) suggests that we should stop using value-laden terms such as "secure" and "insecure" in describing the attachment relationship. Instead, she proposes that it may be more useful to describe the attachment relationship as "adaptive" or "maladaptive" to the specific context, which would take into consideration how cultures differ in the particular attachment strategy that may be most appropriate for that culture.

Nonetheless, other studies suggest that securely attached infants may indeed be the ideal across cultures. For instance, Posada and his colleagues (1995) asked attachment experts to rate the characteristics of a securely attached child and mothers to rate the characteristics of the ideal child. Attachment experts and mothers from China, Colombia, Germany, Israel, Japan, and the United States were included in this study. The researchers report that in each of the countries, the characteristics of the securely attached child were closely associated with the characteristics of the ideal child. Thus, even cultures that vary on the dimension of individualism and collectivism may have similar views on the importance of having a secure attachment.

A review of 14 studies on attachment from Africa, China, Israel, and Japan reports that in each of these samples the majority of infants and their mothers were classified as being securely attached (van IJzendoorn & Sagi, 1999). Furthermore, there is evidence that 7- to 9-month-old infants in every culture studied show distress when they are separated from their primary caregiver (Grossman & Grossman, 1990). Thus, attachment between infants and their mothers is considered a universal phenomenon. What may differ across cultures, however, is the specific attachment behaviors exhibited by the infant that indicate secure or insecure attachment (van IJzendoorn & Sagi, 1999).

In sum, the vast literature concerning attachment in different cultures suggests that attachment between infants and their caregivers is a universal phenomenon. There is also some evidence that the "secure" attachment relationship may be preferred in many different cultures. However, this is an ongoing debate. As stated earlier, researchers such as Crittenden (2000) argue that viewing attachment through the lens of being "adaptive" and "maladaptive" may be more useful than using the evaluative terms *secure* and *insecure*. She defines adaptive attachments as relationships that promote the maximum level of safety for the child within a specific cultural context. This would then allow us to define an "optimal" relationship between infant and caregiver as one that may be achieved in different ways, under different circumstances, in different cultures.

Attachment and Child Development

Why is there such a keen interest in the development of a secure attachment to a parent? One reason is that attachment styles may predict child competence. Takahashi (1990) found that at 2 years old, securely attached Japanese infants, compared to resistantly attached infants, complied more with their mother's directions and demands, showed more curiosity about a new object, and demonstrated more social competence in how they related to unfamiliar peers. Security of attachment, however, did not predict infant competence in the third year of life. The long-term effects of the attachment relationship have been questioned. More longitudinal research that considers the stability of the caregiving environment (which is usually not measured), as well as the attachment relationship, is needed (van IJzendoorn, 1996).

Interestingly, the attachment relationship that an infant has with different caregivers may have implications for different areas of development. For instance, Gusii infants in Kenya who were securely attached to their non-maternal caregivers scored higher on the Bayley Scales of Infant Development, which include an assessment of cognitive development, than their insecurely attached counterparts. In this sample, an infant's security of attachment to his or her mother did not predict cognitive development. What the infant–mother attachment relationship did predict was the nutritional or health status of the infants: Infants who were securely attached to their mothers scored higher on nutritional status than insecurely attached infants. Thus, the various attachment relationships that infants experience may affect their development in different ways (Kermoian & Leiderman, 1986).

Studies involving an African tribe of forest-dwelling foragers known as the Efe show a very different pattern from the one psychologists have come to accept as necessary to healthy attachment (Tronick, Morelli, & Ivey, 1992). Efe infants are cared for by a variety of people in addition to their mothers; the time spent with caregivers other than their mothers increases from 39 percent at 3 weeks to 60 percent by 18 weeks. They are always within earshot and sight of about 10 people. They have close emotional ties to many people other than their mothers and spend very little time with their fathers. However, when infants are 1 year old, they clearly show a preference for being cared for by their mothers and become upset when left by their mothers. At this age, then, mothers once again become the primary caretakers. Thus, there is evidence that attachment to a primary caregiver is still formed and that children are emotionally healthy despite having multiple caregivers. The Efe have large extended families, and these families are permanent parts of the growing Efe children's lives.

Studies by Miyake and his colleagues (Miyake, 1993; Miyake et al., 1985) on infant attachment patterns in Japan summarize and highlight many of these points. In numerous studies on this topic, Miyake has reported finding no avoidantly attached children. In contrast to the United States, where most attachments are characterized as secure, attachments in Japan are overwhelmingly characterized as ambivalent, indicating a strong desire to prevent separation (and thus to foster dependence between mother and infant). Some of their other studies, moreover, have demonstrated a close relationship between temperament and attachment. These researchers measured irritability in response to interruption of sucking—a common measure of temperament—during the second and fifth days of life. They then classified the neonate's cries

Efe infants are cared for by multiple caretakers.
Source: Small (1998). Photographer: Michael Nichols, *National Geograhic*. Reprinted with permission.

as either smooth (fast rise time, brief duration, quick quieting) or effortful (prone to interruption, raucous in quality, and with facial and vocal expressions disorganized). They found that the nature of these cries in the second and fifth days of life predicted attachment 1 year later, with smooth criers being associated with secure attachments and effortful criers associated with ambivalent attachment (the Japanese mode). Other studies, however, do not find a relationship between temperament and attachment style (for example, Bates, Maslin, & Frankel, 1985; Vaughn, Lefever, Seifer, & Barglow, 1989). Thus, more work needs to be done before offering conclusive statements concerning the link between temperament and attachment.

TEMPERAMENT AND ATTACHMENT: A SUMMARY

Much still needs to be done to understand the attachment patterns in other cultures and the relationship among cultural milieu, infant temperament, and attachment style. Notions about the quality of attachment and the processes by which it occurs are qualitative judgments made from the perspective of each culture. What is considered an optimal style of attachment in one culture may not necessarily be optimal across all cultures. Furthermore, because nonparental caretaking is a frequent form in most cultures (Weisner & Gallimore, 1977), examining the attachment "network" instead of focusing solely on dyads, as has traditionally been done, is of crucial importance (van IJzendoorn & Sagi, 1999).

The information presented so far concerning temperament and attachment relationships speaks to just a few of the many ways in which enculturation occurs around the world. Children may be born with differences in biological predispositions or temperament that may make it easier for them to engage in the cultural learning that occurs throughout socialization and enculturation. Differences in attachment provide learning platforms for children that allow them to achieve developmental goals fostered by their particular cultures. Thus, the temperamental characteristics with which you were born, your caregiver's responses to your temperamental style, and the resultant attachment relationship you develop with your caregiver together play important roles in how you come to acquire the aspects of your specific culture.

We turn now to examine cultural similarities and differences in two major developmental processes: cognitive and moral development. These topics are of great interest to developmental psychologists, both mainstream and cross-cultural, and speak to the pervasive influence of culture on develop.

COGNITIVE DEVELOPMENT

Piaget's Theory

Cognitive development is a specialty in psychology that studies how thinking skills develop over time. Theories of cognitive development have traditionally focused on the period from infancy to adulthood. The theory that has dominated this field for the past half-century is Piaget's stage theory of cognitive development.

Piaget based his theories on observations of Swiss children. He found that these children tended to solve problems quite differently at different ages. To explain these differences, Piaget (1952) proposed that children progress through four stages as they grow from infancy into adolescence.

1. **Sensorimotor stage.** This stage typically lasts from birth to about 2 years of age. In this stage, children understand the world through their sensory perceptions and motor behaviors. In other words, children understand by perceiving and doing. The most important achievement of this stage is the capability to use mental symbols to represent objects and events. The acquisition of object permanence—that is, knowing that objects exist even when they cannot be seen—illustrates this achievement. Early in this stage, children appear to assume that when a toy or other object is hidden (for example, when a ball rolls under a sofa), it ceases to exist. Later in this stage, children will search under the sofa for the lost ball, demonstrating that they have come to understand that objects exist continuously.

Other cognitive developments that also depend on the development of mental representation typical of this stage include deferred imitation and language acquisition. These developments have important implications for later cognitive development and enculturation. Imitation is an important cognitive component of observational learning, and language skills are necessary to ensure proper communication of verbal socialization processes.

2. **Preoperational stage.** This stage lasts from about 2 to 6 or 7 years of age. Piaget described children's thinking at this stage in terms of five characteristics: conservation, centration, irreversibility, egocentrism, and animism. **Conservation** is the awareness (or in this stage, the lack of awareness) that physical quantities remain the same even when they change shape or appearance. **Centration** is the tendency to focus on a single aspect of a problem. **Irreversibility** is the inability to imagine "undoing" a process. **Egocentrism** is the inability to step into another's shoes and understand the other person's point of view. **Animism** is the belief that all things, including inanimate objects, are alive. For example, children in the preoperational stage may regard a book lying on its side as "tired" or "needing a rest," or they may think that the moon is following them. Children at this stage do not yet think in a logical and systematic manner.

3. **Concrete operations stage.** This stage lasts from about 6 or 7 years until about 11 years of age. During this stage, children acquire new thinking skills to work with actual objects and events. They are able to imagine undoing an action, and they can focus on more than one feature of a problem. Children also begin to understand that there are points of view different from their own. This new awareness helps children master the principle of conservation. A child in the concrete operations stage will understand that six apples are always six apples, regardless of how they are grouped or spaced and that the amount of clay does not change as a lump is molded into different shapes. This ability is not present in the preoperational stage. However, instead of thinking a problem through, children in this stage tend to rely on trial-and-error strategies.

4. **Formal operations stage.** This stage extends from around 11 years of age through adulthood. During this stage, individuals develop the ability to think logically about abstract concepts, such as peace, freedom, and justice. Individuals also become more systematic and thoughtful in their approach to problem solving.

The transition from one stage to another is often gradual, as children develop new abilities alongside earlier ways of thinking. Thus, the behavior of some children may represent a "blend" of two stages when they are in a period of transition from one to the other.

Piaget hypothesized that two primary mechanisms are responsible for movement from one stage to the next: assimilation and accommodation. **Assimilation** is the process of fitting new ideas into a preexisting understanding of the world. **Accommodation** refers to the process of changing one's understanding of the world to accommodate ideas that conflict with existing concepts.

Piaget believed that the stages were universal, and that progression through these stages was invariant in order. According to Piaget, knowledge is constructed through the interactions between the biological maturation of the child and his or her actions and experiences with the physical and social environment. Because there are similarities across cultures in how individuals mature physically and in how they act on the physical world (for example, in every culture individuals ask questions, exchange information, and work together), the stages are thought to be universal. The richness of Piaget's theory has prompted a multitude of studies of cognitive development in cultures all over the world. It is difficult to think of another theorist who has sparked so much comparative cross-cultural research.

Piaget's Theory in Cross-Cultural Perspective

Cross-cultural research on Piaget's theory has focused on four central questions. The findings to date show an interesting blend of cultural similarities and differences in various aspects of cognitive development that parallel Piaget's stages.

- Do Piaget's stages occur in the same order in different cultures? Studies that have addressed this question have convincingly demonstrated that Piaget's stages occur in the same fixed order in other cultures. For instance, a large cross-cultural survey that tested children in Great Britain, Australia, Greece, and Pakistan (Shayer, Demetriou, & Perez, 1988) found that schoolchildren in these different societies performed Piagetian tasks within the same stage of concrete operations. We do not find cultures in which 4-year-olds typically lack an awareness of object permanency or 5-year-olds understand the principle of conservation. Thus, we know that children from very different cultures do indeed learn groups of Piagetian tasks in a similar order.

- Are the ages that Piaget associated with each stage of development the same in all cultures? Studies have found surprising cultural variations in the ages at which children in different societies typically reach the third and fourth Piagetian stages. In some cases, the difference may be as much as 5 or 6 years. However, it has often been overlooked that children may have the potential to solve tasks sooner than their answers would indicate. For example, a child in the concrete operations stage will typically give the first answer that comes to mind during a test. If the child comes from a culture in which he or she has had practice performing the task in question, this answer is likely to be correct. However, a child who has never thought about the concept before may well utter the wrong answer and only later realize the mistake. When researchers checked for this possibility by repeating tests a second time at the end of testing sessions, they found that many children corrected their previous answers on the second attempt

(Dasen, 1982; Dasen, Lavallee, & Retschitzki, 1979; Dasen, Ngini, & Lavallee, 1979). Thus, it is important to remember that performance on a task may not reveal actual cognitive competence or ability.

- Are there cultural variations within, rather than between, Piaget's stages? There is considerable cultural variation in the order in which children acquire specific skills within Piaget's stages. In a comparative study of tribal children (the Inuit of Canada, the Baoul of Africa, and the Aranda of Australia), half of all Inuit children tested solved a spatial task at the age of 7 years, half of the Aranda solved it at 9 years, and the Baoul did not reach the halfway point until the age of 12 (Dasen, 1975). On a test of the conservation of liquids, however, the order changed dramatically: half of the Baoul children solved the problem when they were 8 years old, the Inuit at 9 years, and the Aranda at 12 years. Why did the ages at which these children could perform the same task vary so much? The Inuit and Aranda children live in nomadic societies, in which children need to learn spatial skills early because their families are constantly moving. The Baoul children live in a settled society, where they seldom travel but often fetch water and store grain. The skills these children used in their everyday lives seem to have affected the order in which they were able to solve Piagetian tasks within the concrete operations stage.

- Do non-Western cultures regard scientific reasoning as the ultimate developmental end point? Piaget's theory assumes that the scientific reasoning associated with formal operations is the universal end point of cognitive development—that the thinking most valued in Swiss and other Western societies (formal operations) is the yardstick by which all cultures should be judged. Because Piaget considered scientific reasoning to be the ultimate human achievement, his stage theory is designed to trace the steps by which people arrive at scientific thinking. This perspective has been widely accepted within North American psychology, and generally by the North American public, at least until very recently.

Cross-cultural research indicates that this perspective is by no means universally shared. Different societies value and reward different skills and behaviors. For example, until recently, the most respected scholars in traditional Islamic societies were religious leaders and poets. Although the Islamic educational system included science and mathematics, its primary goal was not to train people in the scientific method but to transmit faith, general knowledge, and a deep appreciation for poetry and literature. People from such cultures could be expected to be at a disadvantage when confronted with advanced Piagetian tasks, which are drawn almost exclusively from Western physics, chemistry, and mathematics.

Many cultures around the world do not share the conviction that abstract, hypothetical thought processes are the ultimate or desired end point in the cognitive development process. Many cultures, for example, consider cognitive development to be more relational—involving the thinking skills and processes needed to engage successfully in interpersonal contexts. What North Americans refer to as "common sense," rather than cognitive development per se, is considered a much more desired outcome in many cultures. This value structure is especially apparent in more collectivistic and group-oriented cultures, in which high-level, individualistic, abstract thinking is often frowned upon.

Piaget's Theory: Summary and Discussion

Cross-cultural studies of Piaget's stage of formal operations have found that in some cultures, very few people are able to complete fourth-stage Piagetian tasks. Does this mean that entire cultures are suspended at a lower stage of cognitive development? To answer this question, we must first ask whether Piagetian tasks are a culturally appropriate way of measuring an advanced stage of cognitive development. In fact, those tasks may not be meaningful in other cultures. Besides the issue of cultural appropriateness, there is also the issue of what is being tested. Tests of formal operations may tell us whether people can solve a narrow range of scientific problems, but they do not tell us whether people in different cultures develop advanced cognitive skills in areas other than those selected by Piaget.

We can say with certainty, however, that people who have not attended high school or college in a Westernized school system perform very poorly on tests of formal operations (Cole, 2006). These findings again raise the question of the degree to which Piagetian tasks depend on previous knowledge and cultural values rather than on cognitive skills. It is also important to remember the wide range of differences in cognitive development within a given culture. These within-culture differences make it extremely difficult to draw valid conclusions or inferences about differences in cognitive development between cultures. For example, not only do members of non-Western cultures have difficulty with tests of formal operations, but many adults in North American society also have such difficulties. Scientific reasoning does not appear to be as common in Western societies as Piaget thought, and it is frequently limited to special activities. Individuals who apply scientific logic to a problem on the job may reason quite differently in other situations.

Because large numbers of people are unable to complete Piagetian tasks of formal operations, it has not been possible to demonstrate the universality of the fourth stage of Piaget's theory of cognitive development. It is possible that most adults do possess the ability to complete Piagetian tasks but lack either motivation or knowledge of how to demonstrate such ability. To demonstrate success on a task purporting to measure some aspect of cognitive ability or intelligence, it is crucial that the test-taker and the test-maker agree on what is being assessed. Cultural differences in the desired endpoint of cognitive development, as well as in definitions of intelligence (see Chapter 5), contribute to this dilemma.

Other Theories of Cognitive Development

Although Piaget's theory is the most influential theory in the United States, it is only one of many stage theories that have been proposed by Western social scientists. The 18th-century German philosopher Hegel, for example, ranked all societies on an evolutionary scale based on a classification of religious beliefs, with Christianity at the top. Stage theories multiplied in the 19th century after Darwin's theory of evolution became well known. Several writers (for example, Morgan, 1877; Spencer, 1876; Tylor, 1865) proposed that humanity had progressed from savagery to civilization in a series of stages.

One of the most influential stage theories of the early 20th century was proposed by the French philosopher Levy-Bruhl (1910, 1922, 1949). In common with earlier scholars, Levy-Bruhl drew most of his conclusions from material related to the mystical and religious beliefs of non-Western peoples. Levy-Bruhl put forth the **great divide theory**, separating the thought of Westerners from that of people who lived in primitive societies. He described non-Western peoples as having a distinct way of thinking, which he attributed to the effects of culture. According to Levy-Bruhl, non-Westerners were not bothered by logical contradictions, and they lacked a clear sense of individual identity. More recently, some scientists (Goody, 1968, 1977; Hippler, 1980; Luria, 1976) have put forward new great divide theories. Although these researchers have various names for the two groups, their division of humanity breaks down along similar lines. In all these theories, the cultural development or thought of non-Westerners is usually judged as deficient or inferior to that of Europeans.

Several points need to be made about these theories. First, it is probably more than coincidence that stage theories produced by Westerners judge people from other cultures (and minorities within their own countries) in terms of how closely they resemble Westerners, thereby placing themselves at a relatively superior level of development. The popularity of stage theories in the 19th century, for example, coincided with the colonial imperialism of the period. Stage theories provided justification for imposing European rule around the world, based on the demonstrated superiority of European civilization.

Other problems also existed. Stage theorists persisted in evaluating the rationality of non-Westerners in terms of their magical and religious beliefs, while the rationality of Western beliefs was usually not questioned. Levy-Bruhl's theory has been fiercely attacked over the years by field anthropologists who have objected to both his methods and his conclusions. Levy-Bruhl based his work on stories told by missionaries and travelers, many of whom could barely speak native languages.

But Westerners are not the only ones who have ethnocentric assumptions. Cross-cultural studies have shown that people from many cultures prefer their own groups and rate them more positively than they rate outsiders. For example, a study that compared what people in 30 different East-African societies thought of themselves and others demonstrated that members of each society rated themselves highly and judged outsiders to be "advanced" when they were culturally similar to their own group (Brewer & Campbell, 1976).

This brings us back to Piaget's theory, which has several strong points. Piaget's theory is considerably more sophisticated than earlier theories. By devising tasks to measure concepts in an experimental setting, Piaget established a new standard by which to gauge cognitive development, one that appears to be less vulnerable to ethnocentric bias. Piaget's tests can be, and have been, administered cross-culturally, with clear-cut results that do not rest on the subjective beliefs of the researcher (although the choice of research instruments and the interpretation of data are still subject to researcher bias). Still, cognitive development is complicated, and it is unlikely that such tasks can capture all of its complexity.

MORAL REASONING

Another area of development crucial to our becoming functional adults in society and culture concerns moral judgments and reasoning. As they grow, children develop increasingly complex ways of understanding their world. These cognitive changes also bring about changes in their understanding of moral judgments. Why something is good or bad changes from the young child's interpretation of reward and punishment conditions to principles of right and wrong.

Morality and culture share a very close relationship. Moral principles and ethics provide guidelines for people's behaviors with regard to what is appropriate and what is not. These guidelines are products of a specific culture and society, handed down from one generation to the next. Morality is thus heavily influenced by the underlying, subjective, and implicit culture in which it is embedded. Morality also serves as the basis of laws, which are formalized guidelines for appropriate and inappropriate behavior. In this way, culture also affects the laws of a society. For these and other reasons, morality occupies a special place in our understanding of culture and cultural differences.

Our knowledge of the development of moral reasoning skills, at least in the United States, has been heavily influenced by the work of a psychologist named Lawrence Kohlberg. His model of moral reasoning and judgment is based in large part on Piaget's model of cognitive development.

Kohlberg's Theory of Morality

Kohlberg's theory of moral development (1976, 1984) proposes three general stages of development of moral reasoning skills. (Kohlberg further divided each of these three general stages into two stages, for a total of six substages of moral development.)

1. **Preconventional morality** involves compliance with rules to avoid punishment and gain rewards. A person operating at this level of morality would condemn stealing as bad because the thief might get caught and be thrown in jail or otherwise punished. The focus of the justification is on the punishment (or reward) associated with the action.
2. **Conventional morality** involves conformity to rules that are defined by others' approval or society's rules. A person operating at this level of morality would judge stealing as wrong because it is against the law and others in society generally disapprove of it.

3. **Postconventional morality** involves moral reasoning on the basis of individual principles and conscience. A person operating at this level of morality would judge stealing within the context either of societal or community needs or of his or her own personal moral beliefs and values, which supersede perceived societal and community needs.

Gilligan (1982) has challenged Kohlberg's theory by suggesting that its stages are biased toward the particular way in which males as opposed to females view relationships. She argues that male moral reasoning is based on abstract justice, whereas female moral reasoning is based on obligations and responsibilities. These two types of moral reasoning have been called "morality of justice" versus "morality of caring." Despite the fervor of the debate, however, reviews of the research seem to indicate few gender differences in moral reasoning (Walker, 1984, 1991). It appears that variations between males and females in moral reasoning can be explained by other variables, such as education, occupation, or types of issues under consideration. Cross-cultural research may shed more light on this issue.

Cross-Cultural Studies of Moral Reasoning

The universality or cultural specificity of moral principles and reasoning has been an area of interest for anthropologists and psychologists alike. A number of anthropological ethnographies have examined the moral principles and domains of different cultures (see review by Shweder, Mahapatra, & Miller, 1987). Many of these works have complemented and challenged traditional American views of morality, and for good reason. Culture, morality, ethics, and law share a close relationship.

The findings from a number of cross-cultural studies suggest that many aspects of Kohlberg's theory of morality are universal. Snarey (1985), for example, reviewed 45 studies involving participants in 27 countries and concluded that Kohlberg's first two stages could be regarded as universal. Others have reached similar conclusions, including Ma (1988), in a study involving Hong Kong and mainland Chinese as well as British participants; Ma and Cheung (1996), in a study involving Hong Kong, mainland Chinese, British, and Americans; and Hau and Lew (1989), in a study of Hong Kong Chinese participants.

However, a number of cross-cultural studies on moral reasoning raise questions about the universal generalizability of Kohlberg's higher stages. One of the underlying assumptions of Kohlberg's theory is that moral reasoning on the basis of individual principles and conscience, regardless of societal laws or cultural customs, represents the highest level of moral reasoning. This assumption is grounded in the cultural milieu in which Kohlberg developed his theory, which had its roots in studies involving American males in the Midwestern United States in the 1950s and 1960s. Although democratic notions of individualism and unique, personal conscience may have been appropriate to describe his samples at that time and place, it is not clear whether those same notions represent universal moral principles applicable to all people of all cultures.

In fact, some researchers have criticized Kohlberg's theory for harboring such cultural biases (Bronstein & Paludi, 1988). Miller and Bersoff (1992) compared the responses to a moral judgment task by respondents in India and the United States. The Indian subjects, both children and adults, considered not helping someone a moral transgression more than did the American subjects, regardless of the life-threatening nature of the situation or whether the person in need was related. These researchers interpreted the cultural differences as having to do with values of affiliation and justice, suggesting that Indians are taught a broader sense of social responsibility—individual responsibility to help a needy person.

One study suggests that Chinese and Icelandic children differ in a way similar to the differences between Indians and Americans concerning moral judgments (Keller, Edelstein, Schmid, Fang, & Fang, 1998). More specifically, Chinese children emphasized altruism and relationships when reasoning about moral dilemmas, whereas Icelandic children emphasized contractual and self-interest considerations. The issue of interpersonal responsiveness that Miller and Bersoff (1992) and Keller et al. (1998) raised is related to Gilligan's (1982) claims of gender bias in U.S. studies. It is entirely possible that Gilligan's findings were influenced by cultural as well as gender differences.

Snarey's (1985) review mentioned earlier also concluded that moral reasoning at the higher stages is much more culture-specific than Kohlberg originally suggested. Other reviews of the cross-cultural literature by Bergling (1981) and Edwards (1981) reached similar conclusions. Kohlberg's theory, as well as the methods for scoring moral stages according to verbal reasoning, may not recognize higher levels of morality as defined in other cultures. Should different cultures define those higher levels of morality along totally different dimensions, those differences would imply profound differences in people's judgments of moral and ethical appropriateness. Fundamental differences in the bases underlying morality and ethics across cultures are not at all impossible, given that they feed and are fed by subjective culture. Above all, those fundamental differences in morality as a function of culture form the basis for the possibility of major intercultural conflicts.

In order to better understand cultural differences in morality, researchers have highlighted the importance of the particular social structure and environment. For instance, Miller (2001) has argued that "the understanding of social structure entailed in Stage [substage] 4 and higher on the Kohlbergian scheme has relevance primarily in contexts that are closely tied to state or national governments, a finding that may explain, at least in part, the association observed cross-culturally between higher levels of Kohlbergian moral stage development and processes of modernization" (p. 159).

Miller (2001) also points out the need to consider other perspectives on morality that are overlooked in traditional theories of morality. She describes "moralities of community" that emphasize interpersonal relationships and community. For instance, in China, the concept of *jen,* which connotes love and filial piety, contributes to the way Chinese individuals view morality (Ma, 1997). In response to Kohlberg's moral dilemmas, Chinese individuals tend to emphasize the importance of filial piety—respecting and honoring parents and fulfilling their wishes—when judging what is right or wrong. Concerning Hindu Indians, Miller observes that "whereas European Americans tend to approach morality as freely given commitments or matters or personal choice . . . Hindu Indians tend to view interpersonal responsibilities as matters of moral duty that extend across a broader range of need and role situations" (p. 162). Miller also describes "moralities of divinity," in which religious beliefs and spirituality are central to moral development. For instance, Algerians' responses to Kohlberg's moral dilemmas are based on the belief that God is the creator and supreme authority of the universe (Bouhmama, 1984). In another example, fundamental Baptists in the United States consider divorce morally wrong based on their beliefs concerning the relationship between God, the church, and human relationships (Jensen, 1997).

One study exemplifies how the examination of morality at different levels of abstraction—from internalized ideals to actual behaviors—may be important to understanding cultural similarities and differences in moral judgment. In this study (Carlo, Koller, Eisenberg, DaSilva, & Frohlich, 1996), researchers examined prosocial moral reasoning in Brazilian and American adolescents. In addition, they assessed actual prosocial behaviors through peer ratings. In both cultures, age and gender differences in prosocial moral reasoning were the same, as was the relationship between prosocial moral reasoning and prosocial behaviors. There were, however, cultural differences in internalized moral reasoning, with American adolescents scoring higher than Brazilian adolescents. These findings suggest that cultural similarities and differences in moral reasoning and behavior may be explained by taking into account different levels of morality than are being examined. Future cross-cultural studies will need to incorporate such a multilevel view of morality to investigate similarities and differences in the same groups of participants across a broad range of morality-related psychological phenomena.

OTHER DEVELOPMENTAL PROCESSES

Cross-cultural research on psychological processes in development continues to be one of the most popular and thoroughly studied areas of the field, for good reason. This research offers important insights into the question of just how the differences observed in adults in many other studies over the years have come to be. In seeking to explain how and why cultural differences occur among adults, psychologists, mainstream and otherwise, have turned to developmental research to explicate the causes and contexts of the ontogenesis of cultural differences.

The past decade has witnessed a renewed interest in cross-cultural developmental research, no doubt due in large part to the increased interest in culture in all areas of psychology. This research has spanned many processes related to development, including future-oriented goals and commitments (Nurmi, Liiceanu, & Liberska, 1999; Nurmi, Poole, & Seginer, 1995), social expectations (Rotheram-Borus & Petrie, 1996), affective and romantic relationships in adolescence (Coates, 1999; Takahashi, 1990; Takahashi & Majima, 1994), political formation in adolescence (ter Bogt, Meeus, Raaijmakers, & Vollebergh, 2001), task persistence (Blinco, 1992), preschoolers' responses to conflict and distress (Zahn-Waxler, Friedman, Cole, Mizuta, & Hiruma, 1996), children's social pretend play and social competence (Farver, Kim, & Lee-Shin, 2000; LaFreniere et al., 2002), and children's understanding of mental states (Tardif, Wellman, Fung, Liu, & Fang, 2005). Other studies examining other developmental topics no doubt exist as well. Collectively, these studies highlight both similarities and differences in development across cultures, and pave the way for exciting new research in these areas in the future.

CONCLUSION

In this chapter, we have seen how culture produces similarities as well as differences in various areas of development, such as cognition and moral reasoning. The developmental research presented here provides a comprehensive view of how culture influences a number of developmental psychological processes. Still, much work remains to be done. In particular, cross-cultural developmental work has focused largely on infants and children, but mainstream psychology has come to recognize the importance of developmental processes throughout the life span, including adolescence; young, middle, and older adulthood; and old age.

The developmental differences discussed in this chapter all speak to how a sense of culture develops in each of us. As cultures exert their influence in their own special and unique ways, they produce specific tendencies, trends, and differences in their members when compared to others. When we are in the middle of a culture, as we all are, we cannot see those differences or how culture itself develops in us. Only when we look outside ourselves and examine the developmental and socialization processes of other cultures are we able to see what we are ourselves. Only then can we come to appreciate that those differences and similarities are our culture, or at least manifestations of our culture. Thus, while cultures produce differences in development that we observe in our research, these differences simultaneously contribute to the development of culture.

GLOSSARY

accommodation The process of changing one's understanding of the world to accommodate ideas that conflict with existing concepts.

ambivalent attachment A style of attachment in which children are uncertain in their response to their mothers,

going back and forth between seeking and shunning her attention. These mothers have been characterized as insensitive and less involved.

animism The belief that all things, including inanimate objects, are alive.

assimilation The process of fitting new ideas into a preexisting understanding of the world.

attachment The special bond that develops between the infant and his or her primary caregiver. The quality of attachment has lifelong effects on our relationships with loved ones.

avoidant attachment A style of attachment in which children shun their mothers, who are suspected of being intrusive and overstimulating.

centration The tendency to focus on a single aspect of a problem.

cognitive development A specialty in psychology that studies how thinking skills develop over time. The major theory of cognitive development is that of Piaget.

conservation An awareness that physical quantities remain the same even when they change shape or appearance.

conventional morality The second stage of Kohlberg's theory of moral development, emphasizing conformity to rules that are defined by others' approval or society's rules.

difficult temperament A type of temperament that is characterized by an intense, irregular, withdrawing style that is generally marked by negative moods.

easy temperament A type of temperament that is defined by a very regular, adaptable, mildly intense style of behavior that is positive and responsive.

egocentrism The inability to step into another's shoes and understand the other person's point of view.

goodness of fit The interaction of a child's temperament with that of the parents, considered a key to the development of personality.

great divide theory Theory of cognitive development that suggest that the thought of Westerners is superior to that of people who live in primitive societies.

irreversibility The inability to imagine "undoing" a process.

postconventional morality The third stage of Kohlberg's theory of moral development, emphasizing moral reasoning on the basis of individual principles and conscience.

preconventional morality The first stage of Kohlberg's theory of moral development, emphasizing compliance with rules to avoid punishment and gain rewards.

secure attachment A style of attachment in which infants are described as warm and responsive to their caregiver.

slow-to-warm-up A type of temperament in which infants need time to make transitions in activity and experiences. Though they may withdraw initially or respond negatively, given time and support they will adapt and react positively.

temperament Qualities of responsiveness to the environment that exist from birth and evoke different reactions from people in the baby's world. Temperament is generally considered to be a biologically based style of interacting with the world.

5

CHAPTER

Culture
and Cognition

CHAPTER CONTENTS

Just as atoms and molecules serve as the building blocks of matter, some psychological processes serve as the building blocks of other psychological constructs. In this chapter, we begin our exploration of cultural similarities and differences in psychology by examining the nature of those psychological building blocks under the name of cognition.

Psychologists use the term **cognition** to denote all the mental processes we use to transform sensory input into knowledge. The first cognitive processes to occur when people process stimuli are **sensation** and **perception**. Psychologists generally make a distinction between them, with sensation referring to the feelings that result from excitation of the sensory receptors (touch, taste, smell, sight, hearing), and perception referring to our initial interpretations of the sensations. Afterward, individuals engage in what are known as higher-order mental processes, including thinking and reasoning, language, memory, problem solving, decision making, and others.

In this chapter, therefore, we review cross-cultural research across a broad spectrum of cognitive processes, beginning with perception and attention, and then moving to higher-order processes such as categorization, memory, math, and thinking styles. Later we discuss the important topic of intelligence and what recent cross-cultural research has to say about this highly charged topic.

CULTURE AS COGNITION

The first issue we need to deal with regarding the relationship between culture and cognition is the fact that most scholars view culture itself *as* cognition. That is, in psychology, culture is generally viewed as a set of mental representations about the world. Hofstede (Hofstede, 1980), in fact, called culture "mental programming." He likened culture to computer software; just as different software exists to do different things even with the same computer equipment, different cultural "programs" exist that enable individuals to engage in different behaviors, even given the same hardware.

The view of culture as cognition has a long history in the social sciences and psychology. Many previous definitions of culture, for instance, defined culture as the norms, opinions, beliefs, values, and worldviews shared by a group of individuals and transmitted across generations (Berry Poortinga, Segall, & Dasen, 1992) (see also review in Chapter 1). Norms, opinions, beliefs, values, and worldviews are all cognitive products, and as such, one can view the contents of culture as being essentially cognitive.

More contemporary definitions of culture, like that adopted in this book, are also cognitive. In Chapter 1, we defined human culture as *a unique meaning and information system, shared by a group and transmitted across generations, that allows the group to meet basic needs of survival, pursue happiness and well-being, and derive meaning from life.* This definition of culture also essentially views culture as a knowledge system—one from which individuals create and derive knowledge about how to live. This knowledge system is shared, imperfectly, by a group of individuals, and this knowledge is manifested in concrete objects, behaviors, and other physical elements of culture. This knowledge system—culture—was created by groups to solve complex problems of living and social life, enabling them to survive more functionally and effectively.

Human culture is also essentially cognitive because of certain cognitive skills that humans have that other animals do not, and these skills allow humans to have the kinds of cultures that we do. As we discussed in Chapter 1, the two major cognitive advances that occurred in humans is the evolution of language, and the ability to know that others can make judgments about oneself as an intentional agent—that is, as a person who has motives, desires, and intentions. This ability begins in humans at around 9 months of age (Tomasello, 1999). One of the leading researchers in this area of study is Tomasello. In one of his most recent studies, for example, 18-month-old infants were presented with 10 situations in which an adult experimenter was having trouble achieving a goal (Warneken & Tomasello, 2006). For instance, one of these situations was when the experimenter accidentally dropped a marker and unsuccessfully tried to reach for it. More times than not, the infants were likely to help the adult experimenter, even though the experimenter neither asked for help nor made eye contact with the infant. The fact that human infants will help others achieve their goals even though there is no direct benefit to the infant suggests that they have an understanding of other people's goals, and an intrinsic motivation to help. These skills were *not* demonstrated in chimpanzees in the same study.

Thus, special cognitive abilities of humans allow for human cultures to be created in the first place, and cultures themselves are cognitive. That is, they are knowledge representations that include specific meanings and informations, translated into norms, opinions, attitudes, values, and beliefs. These in turn are manifested in overt behaviors and the physical elements of culture.

CULTURE AND PERCEPTION

Perception and Physical Reality

Before considering how culture affects our perceptions, we must first realize that regardless of culture, our perceptions of the world do not necessarily match the physical realities of the world, or of our senses. For instance, all humans have a **blind spot** in each eye—a spot with no sensory receptors, where the optic nerve goes through the layer of receptor cells on its way back toward the brain. But if you close one eye, you probably won't experience a hole in the world. There is no blind spot in our conscious perception, even though we have no receptors receiving light from one area of the eye. Our brains fill it in so it looks as if we see everything. It is only when something comes at us out of this spot that we get some idea that something is wrong with our vision in this particular location.

Or, fill three bowls with water—one with hot water, one with ice water, and one with lukewarm water. If you put your hand in the hot water for a few seconds and then in the lukewarm water, the lukewarm water will feel cold. If you wait a few minutes, then put your hand in the ice water and then the lukewarm water, the lukewarm water will feel warm. The lukewarm water will not have changed its temperature; rather, it is our perception of the water that has changed (compare Segall, 1979).

Once we begin to question our own senses, we want to know their limits. Do our experiences and beliefs about the world influence what we perceive? Do other people perceive things the same as we do? If others do not see things as we do, what aspects of their experiences and backgrounds might explain those differences? How does culture influence this process? These questions were addressed initially by research on the cultural influences on perception.

Cultural Influences on Visual Perception

Optical Illusions   Most of what we know about cultural influences on perception comes from cross-cultural research on visual perception. Much of this excellent work began with studies on optical illusions by Segall, Campbell, and Hersokovits (1963, 1966). **Optical illusions** are perceptions that involve an apparent discrepancy between how an object looks and what it actually is. They are often based on inappropriate assumptions about the stimulus characteristics of the object being perceived.

One of the best-known optical illusions is the Mueller–Lyer illusion (see Figure 5.1). Research has shown that subjects viewing these two figures typically judge the line with the arrowheads pointing in as longer than the other line—even though the lines are actually the same length. Another well-known illusion is the horizontal–vertical illusion (see Figure 5.2). When subjects are asked to judge which line is longer, they typically respond that the vertical line is longer—when, again, they are the same length. A third well-known example is the Ponzo illusion (see Figure 5.3). When subjects view this image, they typically report that the horizontal line closer to the origin of the diagonals is longer than the one away from the origin. Of course, they are the same length.

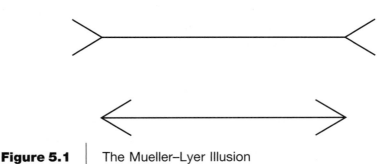

Figure 5.1 | The Mueller–Lyer Illusion

Which line is longer? To most people, the top line appears longer than the bottom line. The lines are actually identical in length.

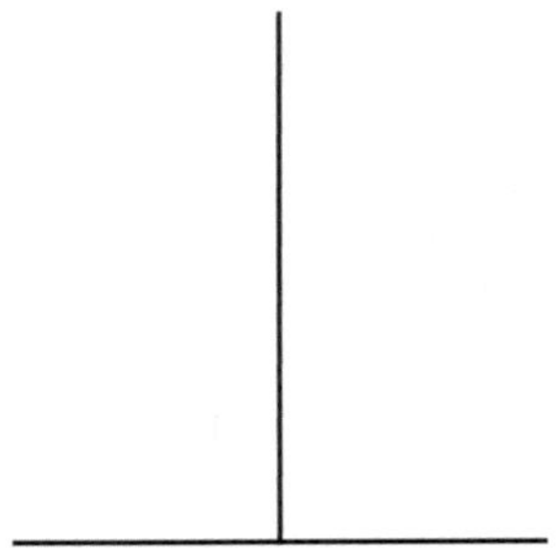

Figure 5.2 | The Horizontal–Vertical Illusion

Which line is longer? To most people, the vertical line appears longer than the horizontal line, although both lines are the same length.

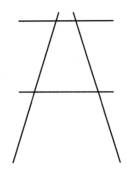

Figure 5.3 | The Ponzo Illusion

Which horizontal line is longer? To most people, the upper line appears longer, although both lines are the same length.

Several important theories have been developed to explain why optical illusions occur. One of these is the **carpentered world theory,** which suggests that people (at least most Americans) are used to seeing things that are rectangular in shape and unconsciously come to expect things to have squared corners. If we see a house from an angle and the light reflected off it does not form a right angle on the eye, we still perceive it as a house with square corners. In the Mueller–Lyer illusion, we tend to see the figures as having square corners that project toward or away from us. We know that things that look the same size to our eyes but are at different distances are actually different in size.

The **front-horizontal foreshortening theory** suggests that we interpret vertical lines as horizontal lines extending into the distance. In the horizontal–vertical illusion, we interpret the vertical line as extending away from us, and we know that a line of set length that is farther away from us must be longer.

These two theories share some common characteristics. Both assume that the way we see the world is developed over time through our experiences. What we see is a combination of the way the object reflects light to our eyes and our learning about how to see things in general. Although learning helps us see well most of the time, it is the very thing that causes us to misjudge optical illusions. The second idea these theories share is that we live in a three-dimensional world that is projected onto our eyes in two dimensions. Our eyes are nearly flat, and light striking the eye in two places right next to each other may be coming from very different distances. Thus, we need to interpret distance and depth from cues other than where the light falls on the eye.

A number of cross-cultural studies challenge our traditional notions about optical illusions, as would be expected if experience contributes to our perceptions. As early as 1905, W. H. R. Rivers compared the responses to the Mueller–Lyer and horizontal–vertical illusions using groups in England, rural India, and New Guinea. He found that the English people saw the lines in the Mueller–Lyer illusion as being more different in length than did the two other groups. He also found that the Indians and New Guineans were more fooled by the horizontal–vertical illusion than were the English. These results surprised Rivers and many other people from Europe and the United States. They believed that the people of India and New Guinea were more primitive and would therefore be more readily fooled by the illusions than the more educated and "civilized" people of England. The results showed that the effect of the illusion differed by culture, but that something other than education was involved. The researchers concluded that culture must have some effect on the way the world is "seen." How this difference in perception comes about has been a source of curiosity ever since.

Both the carpentered world theory and the front-horizontal foreshortening theory can be used to explain Rivers's results. Whereas the English people in Rivers's study were used to seeing rectangular shapes, people in India and New Guinea were more accustomed to rounded and irregular environments. In the Mueller–Lyer illusion, therefore, English people would tend to see the figures as squared corners projecting toward or away from them, but Indians and New Guineans would have less tendency to make the same perceptual mistake. The front-horizontal foreshortening theory can also account for the cultural differences obtained in Rivers's study. With fewer buildings to block long-distance vistas in India or New Guinea, the Indians and New Guineans had learned to rely more on depth cues than did the English. As a result, they were more likely to see the horizontal–vertical figure as three-dimensional, and therefore to misjudge the line lengths.

A third theory has been offered to explain cultural differences in visual perception. The **symbolizing three dimensions in two** theory suggests that people in Western cultures focus more on representations on paper than do people in other cultures—and in particular, spend more time learning to interpret pictures. Thus, people in New Guinea and India are less likely to be fooled by the Mueller–Lyer illusion because it is more "foreign" to them. They are more fooled by the horizontal–vertical illusion, however, because it is more representative of their lifestyle (although in this example it is unclear whether the differentiation between the cultures is Western versus non-Western or industrialized versus nonindustrialized).

To ensure that Rivers's findings held for cultures in general, Segall and colleagues (1963, 1966) compared people from three industrialized groups to people from 14 nonindustrialized groups on the Mueller–Lyer and the horizontal–vertical illusions. They found that the effect of the Mueller–Lyer illusion was stronger for the industrialized groups, whereas the effect of the vertical–horizontal illusion was stronger for the nonindustrialized groups. Rivers's findings were supported.

Segall and colleagues (1963, 1966), however, also found some evidence that did not fit with any of the three theories—namely, that the effects of the illusions declined and nearly disappeared with older subjects. Based on the theories, we might expect the effects of the illusions to increase with age because older people have had more time to learn about their environments than younger people.

Wagner (1977) examined this problem using different versions of the Ponzo illusion and comparing the performance of people in both rural and urban environments, some of whom had continued their education and some of whom had not. One version of the Ponzo illusion looked like Figure 5.3; another showed the same configuration of lines embedded in a complete picture. Wagner found that with the simple line drawing, the effect of the illusion declined with age for all groups. With the illusion embedded in a picture, however, he found that the effect of the illusion increased with age, but only for urban people and people who continued their schooling. This study provides more direct evidence of the effects of urban environments and schooling on the Ponzo illusion. There is also a physical theory that must be considered. Pollack and Silvar (1967) showed that the effects of the Mueller–Lyer illusion are related to the ability to detect contours, and this ability declines with age. They also noted that as people age and are more exposed to sunlight, less light enters the eye, and this may affect people's ability to perceive the lines in the illusion. In addition, they showed that retinal pigmentation is related to contour-detecting ability. Non-European people have more retinal pigmentation, and so are less able to detect contours. Thus, Pollack and Silvar (1967) suggested that the cultural differences could be explained by racial differences in retinal pigmentation (although how the researchers conceptually defined and actually measured race in their study may be problematic, given the ambiguity of that concept).

To test whether the racial or the environmental learning theory was more correct, Stewart (1973) noted that both race and environment need to be compared without being mixed together, as was done in the study by Segall and his colleagues. Stewart first tested the effects of the Mueller–Lyer illusion on both black and white children living in one American town (Evanston, Illinois). She found no differences between the two racial groups. She then compared groups of elementary school children in Zambia in environments that ranged from very urban and carpentered to very rural and uncarpentered. She found that the effects of the illusion depended on the degree to which the children lived in a carpentered environment. She also found that the effect declined with age, suggesting that both learning and physiology played roles in the observed cultural differences.

Hudson (1960) also conducted an interesting study that highlighted cultural differences in perception. He had an artist draw pictures, similar to those in the Thematic Apperception Test (TAT), that psychologists thought would evoke deep emotions in Bantu tribe members. They were surprised to find that the Bantu often saw the pictures in a very different way than anticipated; in particular, they often did not use relative size as a cue to depth. In Figure 5.4, for example, most Americans would see the hunter preparing to throw his spear at the gazelle in the foreground, while an elephant stands on a hill in the background. Many of the Bantu, however, thought the hunter in a similar picture was preparing to stab the baby elephant. In another picture, an orator, who we would see as waving his arms dramatically with a factory in the background, was seen as warming his hands over the tiny chimneys of the factory. Hudson (1960) found that these differences in depth perception were related to both education and exposure to European cultures. Bantu people who had been educated in European schools, or who had more experience with European culture, saw things as Europeans did. Bantu people who had no education and little exposure to Western culture saw the pictures differently.

Later work by McGurk and Jahoda (1975) found that children of different cultures, ranging in age from 4 to 10 years old, also saw things differently. For example, they found that Scottish children were more accurate than Ghanaian children in depicting spatial relationships in pictures in which a woman and child stood in different positions relative to one another.

One might suppose that the cultural differences found in fundamental psychological processes of perception would have considerable implications for conflicts that may arise in intercultural interactions. If people from different cultures have learned different ways of perceiving and interpreting the world, what happens when they interact across cultures? Those learned patterns that each culture takes for granted may no longer be valid.

At the same time, however, one has to question the generalizability of these findings beyond the sorts of the tasks used in the studies. For example, in most

Figure 5.4 | Hudson's (1960) Picture of Depth Perception

What is the hunter's target? Americans and Europeans would say it is the gazelle in the foreground. The Bantu in Hudson's research, however, said it was the elephant.

research on visual perception and optical illusions, the stimuli are presented in two dimensions—either on a piece of paper or projected on a screen. Cultural differences in depth perception may certainly exist using these types of stimuli (as shown in the studies described here, as well as in drawing and other artwork). But to what extent do such effects actually exist in the three-dimensional world? Would Bantu tribespeople see the hunter ready to stab the elephant, and not the gazelle, if the same scene were portrayed out in the open space of their actual environment?

Motivation may be a factor as well. That is, people of different cultures may be differently motivated to perceive certain types of objects, or to perceive them in certain ways. In one study that demonstrated this effect (Broota & Ganguli, 1975), Hindu, Muslim, and American children in India perceived faces associated with either a reward or a punishment in a pretraining session. In the testing session, the participants viewed these and other faces, and judged their characteristics. Significant differences were found between the groups: The Hindu and Muslim children perceived more of the faces associated with punishment than reward, whereas the American children perceived more faces associated with reward rather than punishment.

Attention   In recent years a very interesting line of research has emerged from the University of Michigan Culture and Cognition program. Much of this research focuses on the influence of culture on cognitive abilities and styles. Masuda and Nisbett (2001), for instance, asked American and Japanese university students to view an animated version of the scene in Figure 5.5 twice for

Figure 5.5 | Shot of Animated Swimming Fish Scene

Reprinted from Masuda and Nisbett (2001), with permission.

20 seconds each. Immediately after viewing the scene, they were asked to recall as many objects in the scene as possible. The researchers then categorized the responses of the respondents into whether the object recalled was a focal, main object of the picture, or a background object. They found that there were no differences in recalling the focal, main object of the scene between the Americans and Japanese; the Japanese did, however, remember more of the background objects.

In a second task, Masuda and Nisbett (2001) then showed respondents stimuli and asked them if they had seen them before in the original fish scene. The new stimuli were created so that some were objects that indeed were in the original and some were not. Also, the researchers varied the background, so that some stimuli included the old background, some the new, and some no background at all. They found that the Japanese were much more influenced by the changes in the background; when the Japanese saw new or no backgrounds, their rates of recognition were significantly worse than when they saw the original backgrounds. Background did not affect the Americans (Figure 5.6).

Nisbett and his colleagues have reckoned that these differences may occur because of differences in environment: Japanese environments may be more ambiguous and contain more elements than American scenes. To examine whether differences in this characteristic of the environments may have played

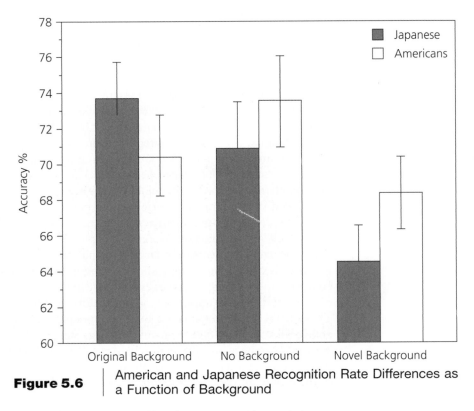

Figure 5.6 | American and Japanese Recognition Rate Differences as a Function of Background

Reprinted from Masuda and Nisbett (2001), with permission.

a part in the perceptual differences observed above, Miyamoto, Nisbett, and Masuda (2006) showed Americans pictures from a Japanese environment, and showed Japanese pictures from an American environment. After being shown these scenes, respondents were shown pairs of culturally neutral scenes in which they had to note the differences between them. The results indicated that both Americans and Japanese detected a larger number of contextual changes in the scenes after they saw pictures from a Japanese environment, suggesting that the environment affords the cultural differences in perception and attention.

CULTURE AND COGNITION

Culture and Categorization

One basic mental process is the manner in which people group things together into categories. People **categorize** on the basis of similarities and attach labels (words) to groups of objects perceived to have something in common. In so doing, people create categories of objects that share certain characteristics. People often decide whether something belongs in a certain group by comparing it to the most common or representative member of that category. For instance, a beanbag chair, a straight-backed dining room chair, and a seat in a theater differ in appearance from one another, but all belong to the basic category *chair*. All these things can be grouped together under the label *chair*, because all share a common function. When we say "That thing is a chair," we mean that the item can and should be used as something for people to sit on (Rosch, 1978).

The process of categorization is universal to all humans. Creating mental categories helps us sort out all the complex stimuli that we are exposed to every day. It helps us create rules and guidelines for behavior and to make decisions. Verbal language is based on categorization and concept formation; words are merely symbols for objects in our physical environment.

Some categories appear to be universal across cultures. Facial expressions that signal basic emotions—happiness, sadness, anger, fear, surprise, and disgust— are placed in the same categories across cultures (see Chapter 8). Likewise, there is widespread agreement across cultures about which colors are primary and which are secondary (more in Chapter 9). The way people select and remember colors appears to be largely independent of both culture and language. Regardless of whether people speak a language that has dozens of words for colors or one that distinguishes colors only in terms of whether they are bright or dark, individuals universally group colors around the same primary hues. They also remember primary colors with greater ease when asked to compare and recall colors in an experimental setting. Stereotypes are a type of category, and stereotyping is probably a universal psychological process (Chapter 14). And there is universality in how people across cultures categorize shapes in terms of the best examples of basic forms (perfect circles, equilateral triangles, and squares) rather than forming categories for irregular geometrical shapes.

These cross-cultural parallels suggest that physiological factors influence the way humans categorize certain basic stimuli. That is, humans seem to be predisposed to prefer certain shapes, colors, and facial expressions.

Although categorization itself is a universal psychological process, the way in which people categorize things may be culturally variable. For example, although all cultures may have a category for furniture, the prototype of a chair is likely to differ across cultures because the materials used to construct furniture differ across cultures.

One common way to study cultural differences in categorization involves the use of sorting tasks. When presented with pictures that could be grouped in terms of either function, shape, or color, young children in Western cultures tend to group by color. As they grow older, they group by shape, and then by function (Bruner, Oliver, & Greenfield, 1966). Western adults thus tend to put all the tools in one group and all the animals in another, rather than grouping all the red things or all the round things together. It had been assumed that this trend was a function of basic human maturation. But given similar sorting tasks, adult Africans showed a strong tendency to group objects by color rather than function (Greenfield, Reich, & Oliver, 1966; Suchman, 1966), suggesting that something other than simple maturation must be responsible for the category shifts.

East Asians may categorize differently altogether. In an early study by Chiu (1972), Chinese and American children were presented with sets of three objects and were asked to select two of the objects that should go together. The American children tended to group objects according to shared features, whereas the Chinese children tended to group objects according to shared contextual or functional relationships. For instance, when presented with a man, woman, and child, the Americans tended to group the man and woman together because they were both adults, while the Chinese tended to group the woman and child together because of their perceived relationship. More recently, Ji, Zhang, and Nisbett (2004) conducted similar tests with Americans and bilingual Chinese (mainland and Taiwan) participants and found similar results, suggesting that the cultural differences in categorization styles were not affected by language.

Culture and Memory

Many of us have heard the claim that individuals from nonliterate societies develop better memory skills because they do not have the ability to write things down to remember them (Bartlett, 1932). Is it true that our memories are not as good when we habitually use lists as aids in remembering? Ross and Millson (1970) suspected that reliance on an oral tradition might make people better at remembering. They compared the ability of American and Ghanaian college students to remember stories that were read aloud. They found that, in general, the Ghanaian students were better than the Americans at remembering the stories. But Cole, Gay, Glick, and Sharp (1971) found that nonliterate African subjects did not perform better when they were tested with lists of words instead of with stories. These findings suggest that cultural differences in memory as a function of oral tradition may be limited to *meaningful material*.

One of the best-known aspects of memory is the **serial position effect.** This effect suggests that we remember things better if they are either the first (primacy effect) or last (recency effect) item in a list of things to remember. Early cross-cultural comparisons challenge the universality of this effect. Cole and Scribner (1974), for instance, found no relation between serial position and the likelihood of being remembered in studying the memory of Kpelle tribes-people in Liberia. Wagner (1980) hypothesized that the primacy effect depends on rehearsal—the silent repetition of things you are trying to remember—and that this memory strategy is related to schooling. Wagner compared groups of Moroccan children who had and had not gone to school and found that the primacy effect was much stronger in the children who had been to school. This makes sense; in a classroom setting, children are expected to memorize letters, multiplication tables, and other basic facts. Participants who have been to school, therefore, have had more practice in memorizing than have unschooled individuals. They are also able to apply these skills in test situations that resemble their school experience. A study by Scribner (1974) with educated and uneducated Africans supported this idea. Educated Africans were able to recall lists of words to a degree similar to that of American subjects, whereas uneducated Africans remembered fewer words. It is not clear whether culture or schooling or both contribute to the observed differences.

There may be some constants about memory across cultures. For example, memory abilities tend to decrease as people get older (or at least people become more selective about what they remember!), and one study showed that such memory decreases with age were consistent across cultures (Crook, Youngjohn, Larrabee, & Salama, 1992).

Another aspect of memory that studies have found to be universal is in the effect known as **hindsight bias,** which refers to the process in which individuals adjust their memory for something after they find out the true outcome. For example, when someone is asked to guess the number of beads in a jar, they may say 350. When they find out later that the actual number is 647, people will often remember their original estimate to be 450, or some number *closer* to the true outcome. Choi and Nisbett (2000) found that Koreans exhibited more hindsight bias than Americans, but Heine and Lehman (1996) reported no differences between Japanese and Canadians. A more recent study involving participants from Asia, Australia, Europe, and North America also found no cultural differences in hindsight bias (Pohl, Bender, & Lachmann, 2002), providing evidence for its universality.

Culture and Math Abilities

One thing interesting about math is that it, like other symbolic languages, is unique to human cultures. Thus, the ability to do math is a universal human psychological process. Clearly, there are national differences in overall math abilities and achievements. For instance, the International Association for the

Evaluation of Educational Achievement conducts worldwide testing in mathematics and science. In its latest survey, conducted in 2003, they tested fourth and eight graders in 53 regions of the world. Their major findings were the following (http://www.iea.nl/timss2003.html) (see Table 5.1):

1. Asian countries outperformed the other participants. Singapore was the top-performing country at both the fourth- and eighth-grade levels in mathematics and science. Also Chinese Taipei, Hong Kong SAR, and Republic of Korea did very well.

2. At the eighth-grade level, countries that showed significant improvement in mathematics form 1995 to 2003 included the Republic of Korea, Hong Kong SAR, Latvia (Latvian-speaking schools), the United States, and Lithuania. At the fourth–grade level, they were Hong Kong SAR, Latvia (Latvian-speaking schools), England, Cyprus, New Zealand, and Slovenia. For science, improvement was registered in the Republic of Korea, Hong Kong SAR, the United States, Australia, Slovenia, Lithuania, and Latvia (Latvian-speaking schools) for grade eight, and Singapore, Hong Kong SAR, England, Hungary, Latvia (Latvian-speaking schools), New Zealand, Slovenia, Cyprus, and Iran for grade four.

3. Decreases in achievement were found in Japan, Belgium (Flemish), the Russian Federation, the Slovak Republic, Sweden, Bulgaria, Norway, Cyprus (mathematics, eighth grade), the Netherlands and Norway (mathematics, fourth grade), Sweden, the Slovak Republic, Belgium (Flemish), Norway, Bulgaria, Iran, and Cyprus (science, eighth grade), Japan, Scotland, and Norway (science, fourth grade).

4. Gender differences were negligible in many countries for mathematics, but in science at the eighth-grade level, boys had significantly higher achievement than girls in the majority of countries. Nevertheless, girls had greater improvement on average than boys, especially since 1999.

5. The home context (highly educated parents, speaking the language of the test at home, more books at home, and frequently using the computer) was important to fostering higher achievement.

6. Providing students the opportunity to learn the content assessed was fundamental. The content needed to be delivered in the classroom and in an effective way. Also, a positive school environment was related to higher achievement (positive climates for learning, fewer students from disadvantaged homes, and schools where teachers and students felt safe).

Differences across countries clearly exist in math and science abilities, however, it is not clear that these differences are cultural; they probably are more related to differences in the educational systems and practices across countries (see Chapter 3).

Studies of an area known as **everyday cognition** indicate that, even without formal educational systems, members of all cultures learn math skills (Schliemann & Carraher, 2001). Kpelle rice farmers, for instance, estimate amounts of rice as part of their work, and are better than Americans at volume estimation. Farmers in some areas of Brazil use a nonstandard system of

Table 5.1 | Average Math Scores for Eighth-Graders across All Countries in the 2003 Survey Conducted by the International Association for the Evaluation of Educational Achievement

Country	Average Score
International average	466
Singapore	605
Korea, Republic of	589
Hong Kong SAR	586
Chinese Taipei	585
Japan	570
Belgium-Flemish	537
Netherlands	536
Estonia	531
Hungary	529
Malaysia	508
Latvia	508
Russian Federation	508
Slovak Republic	508
Australia	505
(United States)	504
Lithuania	502
Sweden	499
Scotland	498
(Israel)	496
New Zealand	494
Slovenia	493
Italy	484
Armenia	478
Serbia	477
Bulgaria	476
Romania	475
Norway	461
Moldova, Republic of	460
Cyprus	459
(Macedonia, Republic of)	435

Table 5.1 | (continued)

Country	Average Score
Lebanon	433
Jordan	424
Iran, Islamic Republic of	411
Indonesia	411
Tunisia	410
Egypt	406
Bahrain	401
Palestinian National Authority	390
Chile	387
(Morocco)	387
Philippines	378
Botswana	366
Saudi Arabia	332
Ghana	276
South Africa	264

■ Average is higher than the U.S. average

☐ Average is not measurably different from the U.S. average

▨ Average is lower than the U.S. average

measures and formulas to calculate areas of land. Illiterate individuals in India can use the movements of sun, moon, and stars to tell time accurately. These examples abound all over the world, from Liberian tailors, to street vendors in South America, to carpenters in South Africa, to fisherman and cooks the world over. Knotted string devices known as khipu were used for bureaucratic counting devices in the Inke Empire in ancient Peru, and were used to keep census and tribe data (Urton & Brezine, 2005). Geometry, a topic we typically associate with middle- or high-school math classes, may in fact be a core intuition found in all humans. Even isolated indigenous groups of individuals living in the Amazon use geometric concepts to locate hidden objects (Dehaene, Izard, Pica, & Spelke, 2006). Findings from studies on everyday cognition provide fairly clear evidence that math abilities are universal to all humans.

Culture and Problem Solving

Problem solving refers to the process by which we attempt to discover ways of achieving goals that do not seem readily attainable. Psychologists have tried to isolate the process of problem solving by asking people from different cultures to solve unfamiliar problems in artificial settings. One such experiment (Cole et al., 1971) presented American and Liberian subjects with an apparatus containing various buttons, panels, and slots. After basic instruction in how to work the apparatus, subjects were to figure out how to open the device and obtain a prize. The solution involved combining two different procedures—first pressing the correct button to release a marble, and then inserting the marble into the appropriate slot to open a panel. American subjects under the age of 10 were generally unable to obtain the prize, but older American subjects combined the two steps with ease. However, Liberian subjects of all ages and educational backgrounds experienced great difficulty solving the problem; less than a third of the adults were successful.

This experiment, however, may have been biased in favor of the Americans. (Remember the first time you ever worked on a computer, or looked under the hood of a car?) Cole and his colleagues repeated their experiment with materials familiar to people in Liberia, using a locked box and keys instead of the mechanical contraption. In the new version of the two-step problem, the Liberian subjects had to remember which key opened the lock on the box and which matchbox container housed the correct key. Under these conditions, the great majority of Liberians solved the problem easily.

The success of the Liberians in solving a two-step problem with a familiar set of materials brings us back to the question of whether the experiment tested their ability to think logically or tested their previous knowledge and experience with locks and keys. In an attempt to clarify this issue, the researchers designed a third experiment, combining elements from both the first and second tests. Liberian and American subjects were again presented with a locked box, but the key that opened the box had to be obtained from the apparatus used in the first experiment. To the surprise of the researchers, the third test produced results similar to the first experiment. While Americans solved the problem with ease, most Liberians were not able to retrieve the key to open the box.

Cole and his colleagues concluded that the Liberians' ability to reason logically to solve problems depended on context. When presented with problems using materials and concepts already familiar to them, Liberians drew logical conclusions effortlessly. When the test situation was alien to them, however, they had difficulty knowing where to begin. In some cases, the problem went beyond confusion; uneducated Liberians appeared visibly frightened by the tests involving the strange apparatus and were reluctant to manipulate it. Although adult Americans did very well in these experiments in comparison to the Liberians, how might average Americans react if placed in a similar experimental situation that required the Americans to use wholly unfamiliar concepts and technology—for example, tracking animals by means of footprints and smells?

Another type of problem that has been studied cross-culturally involves syllogisms (for example: All children like candy. Mary is a child. Does Mary like candy?). In wide-ranging studies of tribal and nomadic peoples in East and Central Asia, Luria (1976) documented sharp differences in the way people approached these problems. As with other cultural differences in cognition and thought, the ability to provide the correct answer to verbal problems was found to be closely associated with school attendance. Individuals from traditional societies who were illiterate were generally unable to provide answers to syllogisms containing unfamiliar information. Individuals from the same culture and even from the same village who had received a single year of schooling could respond correctly.

Various explanations have been proposed to account for the inability of uneducated people to complete word problems. Luria (1976) concluded that illiterate people actually think differently from those who are educated. According to this hypothesis, logical reasoning is essentially artificial; it is a skill that must be learned in a Westernized school setting. Some studies lend support to this interpretation. Tulviste (1978) asked schoolchildren in Estonia ages 8 to 15 to solve verbal problems and explain their answers. Although the children were able to solve most of the problems correctly, they explained their answers by citing the logical premises of the problem only in areas in which they did not have firsthand knowledge. Elsewhere, their answers were justified with appeals to common sense or statements about their personal observations.

Scribner (1979) questioned whether illiterate subjects are truly incapable of thinking logically and looked more closely into the reasons uneducated people fail to give correct responses to verbal problems. When uneducated peasants were asked to explain illogical answers to syllogism problems, they consistently cited evidence that was known to them personally or stated that they did not know anything about the subject, ignoring the premises given to them. For example, in response to the word problem "All children like candy; Mary is a child; does Mary like candy?" subjects might shrug their shoulders and comment, "How would I know whether Mary likes candy? I don't even know the child!" or "Maybe she doesn't like candy; I've known children who didn't." These individuals appear to be unable or unwilling to apply concepts of scientific thinking to verbal problems. But this is not because they lack the capacity to reason logically; rather, they do not understand the hypothetical nature of verbal problems or view them with the same degree of importance. People who have been to school have had the experience of answering questions posed by an authority figure who already knows the correct answers. Uneducated people, however, have difficulty understanding the notion that questions need not be requests for information.

Culture and Creativity

Another aspect of cognition that has received attention in the literature is creativity. Creativity is an interesting area of study because it highlights a universal and unique human process. Creativity is what enables humans and only humans to create art and symphonies, explore space and the sea, and design machines to improve life. Unfortunately creativity also is what enables humans and only humans to create and improve on weapons of mass destruction and other terrible deeds.

Research on creativity in the United States suggests that it depends on divergent thinking, rather than on the convergent thinking that is typically assessed in measures of intelligence. Creative individuals have been shown to have a high capacity for hard work, a willingness to take risks, and a high tolerance for ambiguity and disorder (Sternberg & Lubart, 1995, 1999).

These same characteristics appear to be true of creative individuals in other cultures as well. For example, Khaleefa, Erdos, and Ashria (1996) highlighted these characteristics in their study of creativity in a conformist culture (Sudanese); Simonton (1996) documented them in his study of creative individuals in Japanese history; and Satoh (1996) described their implementation in kindergarten programs in Japan to foster the development of creativity in children in that culture. All of these examples are consistent with Sternberg and Lubart's (1995, 1999) studies of the processes that creative individuals go through, particularly in overcoming obstacles presented to them by conformist-centered organizations.

Some important differences have been noted, however, in the specific ways in which creativity can be fostered in different cultures. Shane, Venkataraman, and MacMillan (1995), for example, studied innovative strategies among a sample of 1,228 individuals from 30 countries who were employees of four different work organizations. The authors characterized the countries in terms of Hofstede's dimensions of individualism, power distance, and uncertainty avoidance (see Chapter 1 for a review). They found that countries high on uncertainty avoidance prefer creative individuals to work through organizational norms, rules, and procedures. Countries higher on power distance preferred creative individuals to gain support from those in authority before action is taken, or to build a broad base of support among members for new ideas. Collectivistic countries preferred creative people to seek cross-functional support for their efforts. Thus, although creative individuals may share some common core characteristics across cultures, they need to adapt their abilities to the specific cultural milieu within which they function, particularly in the implementation and adoption of their creative ideas (Csikszentmihalyi, 1999). Creativity requires people to "get outside of their own box" or framework; another area of cultural difference would be the degree to which this ability is fostered.

One area of creativity that has gained much attention in recent years is that of music. Music is universal to all human cultures. It helps to bring people together, and is a powerful way of expressing emotion. Music is thought to have evolved with language. The oldest known archaeological musical artifacts are flutes dated to be 32,000 years old (Balter, 2004), although music itself is widely considered to be as old as 150,000 years. Competing theories have emerged in recent years to try to account for music. The leading theory suggests that music plays an important role in social cohesion—maintaining and coordinating large networks of individuals—which would ultimately improve survival rates. Music may also have evolved to enable humans to show off their reproductive fitness. But convincing data confirming or disconfirming these theories still do not exist. Future studies, and their authors, will need to be creative to address these issues.

Culture and Dialectical Thinking

Dialectical thinking can be broadly defined as the tendency to accept what seem to be contradictions in thought or beliefs. This is in contrast to **positive logical determinism** that characterizes much of American and Western European thinking. Dialectical thinking tries to find the way in which both sides of an apparent contradiction are correct, tolerates the contradiction, and tries to find mutual middle ground. Logical deterministic thinking tends to see contradictions as mutually exclusive categories, as either–or, yes–no, one-or-the-other types of categories.

Cross-cultural research of the past decade has produced interesting cultural differences in dialectical thinking, demonstrating that East Asians tend to prefer dialectical thinking whereas Americans tend to prefer logical deterministic thinking. Peng and Nisbett (1999), for instance, conducted an interesting series of studies to demonstrate these differences. In one, American and Chinese graduate students at the University of Michigan were presented with the following two vignettes:

Mother–Daughter Conflict:
Mary, Phoebe, and Julie all have daughters. Each mother has held a set of values that has guided her efforts to raise her daughter. Now the daughters have grown up, and each of them is rejecting many of her mother's values. How did it happen, and what should they do?

School–Fun Conflict:
Kent, James, and Matt are college juniors. They are feeling very frustrated about their three years of routine tests, paper assignments, and grades. They complain that going through this process has taken its toll, undermining the fun of learning. How did it happen, and what should they do?

The participants were asked to write what they thought about both conflicts, including what they thought were the sources of the differences and what the persons in the vignettes should do. The researchers then categorized the participants' responses as either dialectical or not. A dialectical response was defined as one that "(a) addressed the issues from both sides and (b) attempted to reconcile the contradictions, for example, a response such as "both the mothers and the daughters have failed to understand each other" (p. 746). Nondialectical responses generally found exclusive fault with one side or the other, such as "mothers have to recognize daughters' rights to their own values" (p. 746). There were strong cultural differences in the responses (Figure 5.7), with the Americans responses being much more nondialectical, and the Chinese responses as more dialectical.

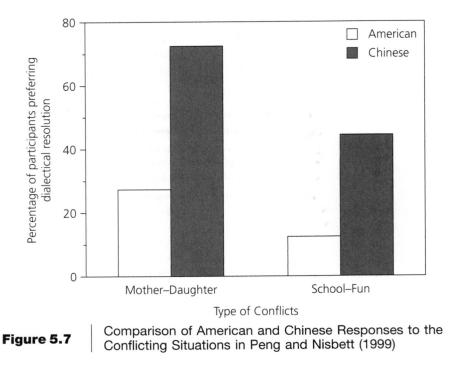

Figure 5.7 | Comparison of American and Chinese Responses to the Conflicting Situations in Peng and Nisbett (1999)

Reprinted with permission.

Culture, Regrets, and Counterfactual Thinking

Another interesting line of research that has blossomed in the past decade concerns counterfactual thinking and regret. **Counterfactual thinking** can be defined as hypothetical beliefs about the past that could have occurred in order to avoid or change a negative outcome. For example, if you got a bad grade on a test, an example of counterfactual thinking would be "If I had only studied harder." Previous research has demonstrated that these types of counterfactual thoughts often are related to feelings of regret (Gilovich, Medvec, & Kahneman, 1998).

Counterfactual thinking can be broadly classified into two types: actions and inactions. On one hand, "If I had only studied harder," "If I had only been a better parent," and "If I had only trained harder," are examples of counterfactual thinking related to inaction. On the other hand, "If I hadn't said what I said," "If I didn't eat that last piece of cake," and "If I weren't driving so fast," are examples of counterfactual thinking of actions.

Research in the United States has shown that regrets related to thoughts of inaction are more prevalent than regrets related to action (Gilovich & Medvec, 1995). But is this tendency culture-specific? Cultural differences in the concept of self as an active agent (described more fully in Chapter 13), would suggest so. Markus and Kitayama (1991) suggest that in individualistic cultures, people are active, autonomous agents in their world, and thus would regret *not* having done something more. In collectivistic cultures, however, these researchers claim that individuals' duty and responsibility are encouraged and take precedence over internal attributes. Thus, people in collectivistic cultures should experience more regret over action than inaction, if this framework were correct.

More recent research, however, has suggested otherwise. In a study of Americans, Chinese, Japanese, and Russians, all participants in all cultures experienced more regret over inaction than action (Gilovich, Wang, Regan, & Nishina, 2003). Moreover, the degree to which they experienced regret over inaction than over action was comparable across all cultures and to previous data involving just Americans. Thus, the emotion of regret, and the potential causes of it, appear to be universal.

Summary

Cross-cultural research on cognition highlights some interesting and important cultural similarities and differences in the ways people think. There appears to be universality in cognitive processes such as hindsight bias and regrets over inaction as opposed to action. At the same time, there are interesting cultural differences in perception and attention, categorization, some memory tasks, math abilities, problem solving, the factors that enhance creativity, and dialectical thinking.

The universal aspects of cognition point to important ways in which people are similar the world over. The differences, however, are also fascinating. Where do these differences come from? What is the *source* of these observed differences between countries?

Some researchers believe that the source of the differences observed in many cognitive processes so far is cultural. For example, Nisbett and his colleagues have suggested that the differences between Americans and East Asians in cognition are due to systemic cultural differences in individualism and collectivism (Nisbett, 2003; Nisbett, Peng, Choi, & Norenzayan, 2001). They suggest that these cultural differences are rooted in differences in ancient philosophies in Greece and China, the former promoting autonomy and independence, the latter promoting relations and interdependence. According to this framework, these ancient cultural systems produce differences in ways of perceiving and thinking about the world, with the Westerners characterized by analytic ways of thinking, whereas the East Asians are characterized by holistic thinking.

We believe that this theoretical framework is an interesting proposition. Still, it remains speculative, primarily because there are no studies conducted as of yet that link those specific cultural factors with the differences that have been observed. As we discussed in Chapter 2, the demonstration of differences in any psychological process between cultures cannot be used to make claims about any specific cultural factors *causing* those differences. It may very well be that ancient, systemic differences in culture produce those differences. But it may very well be that other cultural differences produced the observed differences.

And it may be that other, noncultural factors produced the differences observed to date. Future research will need to test these various sets of factors.

One important factor that we believe should be tested in producing cross-cultural differences in cognition is education. In the educational systems of Japan, China, and South Korea today, for example, there is much more emphasis on rote memorization and passive learning in a didactic environment. In a nutshell, the teachers lecture, and the students listen and memorize everything. This is in stark contrast to the typical European or American educational style, in which students are much more active learners, and discussion is promoted. It may very well be that, after 12 or 16 years of such educational practices, East Asian students, who are generally the participants in cross-cultural research, remember more things and think differently about things than do their American counterparts. Thus, the differences observed in research may be attributed to educational practices and not necessarily to cultural ideologies rooted in ancient philosophies.

The differences may be rooted in other sources as well, such as the amount and type of technology used in the countries today, or the type of animated video games played. Our position at this point is that future research will need to explore exactly what are the sources of the observed differences. Some of the sources may be cultural, others not.

CULTURE AND CONSCIOUSNESS

Culture and Dreams

There are considerable cultural differences in the manifest content of dreams. Punamaeki and Joustie (1998), for example, examined how culture, violence, and personal factors affected dream content among Palestinian children living in a violent environment (Gaza), Palestinian children living in a peaceful area, and Finnish children living in a peaceful area. Participants recorded the dreams they recalled every morning for 7 days, and researchers coded their manifest contents. The results indicated that the dreams of the Palestinian children from Gaza incorporated more external scenes of anxiety, whereas the Finnish children's dreams had more "inner" anxiety scenes. Cultural differences in manifest dream content were also reported by Levine (1991) in her study of Irish, Israeli, and Bedouin children, and by Kane (1994) in her study of Anglo American, Mexican American, and African American women.

The results of Punamaeki and Joustie's (1998) study, however, indicated that culture is not the only factor that influences dream content. That is, children living in the dangerous areas of Gaza had intensive and vivid dreams including themes related to persecution and aggression. These themes, of course, are present in these children's everyday lives, and affected the dreams considerably as well.

Some interesting research has also highlighted important differences in the role of dreams in different cultures. Tedlock (1992), for example, reported that dream sharing and interpretation was a common practice among Mayan Indians in Central America, regardless of the role or position of the person in the culture, and was important in the teaching of cultural folk wisdom. Thus, dreams were an important part of the cultural system, involving an organized, conventional set of signs. Likewise, Desjarlais (1991) examined dream usage among the Yolmo Sherpa of Nepal. Here, too, dreams constituted a local system of knowledge that helped in the assessment and communication of personal and social distress and conflict, and hence were an important vehicle for social understanding.

More recently, dream researchers have applied increasingly sophisticated technologies such as neuroimaging and electrophysiology to understanding dreams and their relationship to our psychology. Researchers such as Hobson (1999) have argued that Freud's (1900/1961) notion of dreams as reflecting unconscious motives (latent content) is outdated, with no empirical support. Hobson states that dreams, rather, may reveal emotionally salient concerns in an individual's life. Put another way, "In dreams we are often thinking about what we are already thinking about" (Flanagan, 2000, p. 190). Flanagan's work suggests that the content of our dreams is a reflection of our everyday experiences. Thus, it may not be the content of dreaming that is meaningful, but the emotions that it brings up, such as anxiety, which is "the leading emotion in all dreams and all dreamers" (Hobson, 1999, p. 170).

Dream content, the emotions associated with one's dreams, and dream usage may differ in important and interesting ways in different cultures. Because American culture does not place much emphasis on the importance of dreams as a symbol of individual and social concerns, American scientists have given relatively little consideration to the study of dreams as a way of understanding culture. Future studies will hopefully address this gap in our knowledge, and perhaps in our ways of understanding consciousness.

Culture and Time

People of different cultures experience time differently, even though time should be objectively the same for everyone. Differences in time orientation and perspective are often a source of confusion and irritation for visitors to a new culture. Many visitors from cultures in which time is respected and punctuality is cherished have difficulty adjusting to U.S. public transportation systems, which may not always be on time as scheduled. Visitors from other cultures, however, in which time is not so much of the essence and queuing is commonplace, seem less affected by such deviations from schedule, viewing them as trivial and to be expected.

Hall (1973) was one of the first to suggest that cultures differ in their time perspective and orientation. He analyzed differences among people of different cultures in their use of time, and how these differences manifested themselves in actual behavioral practices within such contexts as business. As you can imagine, cultural differences in the use and view of time can be especially agonizing in intercultural negotiation situations (see Chapter 15).

Today perhaps the largest-scale cross-cultural study on time perception is that of Hofstede (2001). As we discussed in Chapters 1 and 2, Hofstede suggested that Long- versus Short-Term Orientation was a cultural dimension that differentiates among cultures. People in Long-Term cultures delay gratification of material, social, and emotional needs, and think more about the future. Members of Short-Term cultures think and act more in the immediate present and the bottom line.

Hofstede surveyed Long- versus Short-Term Orientation across 36 countries of the world by asking their members to respond to a survey about their perceptions of time. He then characterized each of the countries in terms of their time orientations (Table 5.2).

Cultural differences in time orientations may be related to interesting and important aspects of our behaviors. Levine and his colleagues, for instance, have conducted an interesting set of studies on this topic (Levine & Bartlett, 1984; Levine, Lynch, Miyake, & Lucia, 1989; Levine & Norenzayan, 1999). In one of them (Levine & Norenzayan, 1999), experimenters measured how fast people walked a 60-foot distance in downtown areas of major cities, the speed of a transaction at the post office, and the accuracy of clocks in 31 countries. Pace of life was fastest in Switzerland, Ireland, Germany, Japan, and Italy, and slowest in Mexico, Indonesia, Brazil, El Salvador, and Syria. Pace of life was correlated with several ecological and cultural variables. Hotter cities were slower than cooler ones, cultures with vibrant and active economies were faster, and people in individualistic cultures were faster. Also, people in faster places tended to have worse health but greater happiness.

Table 5.2 | Results from Hofstede's (2001) Study on Time Orientation across Cultures

Short-Term Oriented	In the Middle	Long-Term Oriented
Ghana	Portugal	Norway
Nigeria	Australia	Denmark
Sierra Leone	Austria	Hungary
Philippines	Germany	Thailand
Spain	Poland	Czech Republic
Canada	Sweden	India
Botswana	Italy	Brazil
Malawi	Belgium	South Korea
Zambia	France	Japan
Zimbabwe	Switzerland	Taiwan
United States	Finland	Hong Kong
New Zealand	Netherlands	China

These types of cultural and individual differences in time orientation and perspective have important implications for real-life situations, such as in business (negotiation), working in groups in school or at work, or just in everyday life (riding the bus or train, getting help at a store). For instance, an orientation toward the future has been linked to lower rates of risky health behavior (Strathman, Gleicher, Boninger, & Edwards, 1994). Even though we may take such matters for granted within the cultural milieu in which we live, these differences can be a source of confusion, irritation, and conflict for many who travel across cultural boundaries. Although recent research in neuro-science has made advances in our understanding of how the brain represents and measures time (Buhusi & Meck, 2005), cultures clearly influence how it is perceived and used. Future research will need to explore more fully the nature of the relationship between culture and time, identifying what it is about culture that affects the perception of time. With such knowledge, we can better anticipate conflicts before they arise, and deal with them when they do occur.

Culture and the Perception of Pain

Cross-cultural psychologists and anthropologists alike have long been interested in the relationship between culture and pain, mainly because of anecdotal reports and observations of considerable differences in pain management and tolerance in different cultures. Almost 40 years ago, scientists began to formally recognize the influence of culture and attitudinal factors on the response to pain (Wolff & Langley, 1968). Today, we know that culture influences the experience and perception of pain in several ways, including: (1) the cultural construction of pain sensation, (2) the semiotics of pain expression, and (3) the structure of pain's causes and cures (Pugh, 1991). There is also a growing literature documenting the important implications and ramifications of cultural differences in the perception and management of pain, such as in doctor–patient interactions (Streltzer, 1997).

Although most cross-cultural research on pain has involved older children and adults, researchers are now recognizing that cultural differences in pain experiences, such as pain response, may occur quite early in life. For example, in a comparison of Chinese and non-Chinese Canadian 2-month-old infants, Chinese babies showed greater (more intense) response to pain as measured by facial expression and crying (Rosmus, Halifax, Johnston, Yip, & Yang, 2000).

One hypothesis concerning cultural differences in pain experience has to do with the effect of language on perception and cognition. The Sapir–Whorf hypothesis (discussed in Chapter 9) suggests that the structure of language, which is highly dependent on culture, affects our perceptions and cognitions of the world around us—including our pain experiences. Because the structure, content, and process of language differ across cultures, so does the experience of pain (Fabrega, 1989).

Another related topic is that of cultural display rules (discussed in Chapter 8). Just as people of different cultures may have different rules for the appropriate expression of emotion, they may have similar rules governing the expression, perception, and feeling of pain. And just as the strength of people's emotional expressions are correlated with the intensity of their emotional experiences, so the rules governing the expression of pain will ultimately affect people's subjective experiences of pain. For example, a recent study of Indian and American college students shows that Indians were less accepting of overt pain expression and also had a higher level of pain tolerance than Americans (Nayak, Shiflett, Eshun, & Levin, 2000). Furthermore, level of pain tolerance and acceptance of overt pain expression were linked: The less acceptable overt pain expression was, the greater was the tolerance of pain.

The tolerance of pain may also be rooted in cultural values. Sargent (1984), for example, interviewed females of reproductive age and 18 indigenous midwives in the Bariba culture of Benin, West Africa. In this culture, stoicism in the face of pain was idealized, and the "appropriate" response to pain was considered intrinsic to Bariban identity. Features such as the tolerance of pain through circumcision or clitoridectomy signaled courage and honor, and were considered crucial values within the culture. In a qualitative study of Finnish women and their experiences of childbirth, the participants described labor pain as something natural that they should accept. One mother said, "It is God's will for women to feel pain when giving birth" (as reported in Callister, Vehvilainen-Julkunen, & Lauri, 2001, p. 30). Thus, cultural values shape one's experience and tolerance of pain.

Although we know that there are considerable cross-cultural differences in the perception of pain, research has not yet examined systematically exactly what aspects of culture produce those differences, and why. For instance, concerning childbirth specifically, one aspect may be local attitudes toward childbirth—whether childbirth is a community celebration or requires purification of the woman giving birth (Newton & Newton, 1972). Future studies need to take up this important topic, which is of considerable practical importance to real-life events. Cultural differences in pain management affect how many professionals in the health services—physicians, nurses, dentists, psychotherapists, counselors, and others—interact with clients and patients. Even outside the clinical setting, these issues are becoming more real and more important for a growing number of people who deal with intercultural issues in their daily lives at home and at work. Future research needs to address these issues and their potential consequences.

CULTURE AND INTELLIGENCE

Traditional Definitions of Intelligence

The English word *intelligence* is derived from the Latin word *intelligentia*, coined 2,000 years ago by the Roman orator Cicero. In contemporary American psychology, intelligence has generally been considered a conglomeration of numerous intellectual abilities centering around verbal and analytic tasks. Piaget (described in Chapter 4) viewed intelligence as a reflection of cognitive development through a series of stages, with the highest stage corresponding to abstract reasoning and principles. Spearman (1927) and Thurstone (1938) developed factor theories of intelligence, viewing it as a general concept comprised of many subcomponents, or factors, including verbal or spatial comprehension, word fluency, perceptual speed, and others. Guilford (1985) built on factor theories to describe intelligence using three dimensions—operation, content, and product—each of which has separate components. Through various combinations of these three dimensions, Guilford suggested that intelligence is actually composed of more than 150 separate factors.

Spearman (1927) also proposed, along with the multiple factors of intelligence, a "general" intelligence representing overall mental ability. This factor, called g, is typically measured through a process of combining and summarizing the various component scores of a multiple-factor intelligence test. And aside from pure knowledge, the ability to reason logically and deductively about hypothetical and abstract issues and events is generally considered a part of intelligence. This definition of intelligence has dominated its measurement and, consequently, the research in this area.

Cross-Cultural and Multicultural Research on Intelligence

Numerous studies have documented cross-cultural differences in intelligence across a wide range of cultural groups, including Iranian children (Shahim, 1992), Bulgarians (Lynn, Paspalanova, Stetinsky, & Tzenova, 1998), Chinese and Germans (Willmann, Feldt, & Amelang, 1997), Filipinos (Church & Katigbak, 1988), Chinese and Australians (Keats & Fang, 1987), Indians and Nigerians (Nenty, 1986), New Zealanders (Petrie, Dibble, Long-Taylor, & Ruthe, 1986), Hindu Indians (Ajwani, 1982), Nigerian high-school students (Nenty & Dinero, 1981), Mexican Americans (Hays & Smith, 1980), Peruvians (Weiss, 1980), Costa Ricans (Fletcher, Todd, & Satz, 1975), Fijians (Chandra, 1975), Israelis (Miron, 1975), Irish (Hart, 1971), Metis and Eskimo schoolchildren (Rattan & MacArthur, 1968), Native Alaskans (Hanna, House, & Salisbury, 1968), Congolese (Claeys, 1967), Aborigines in central Australia (David & Bochner, 1967), secondary school pupils in Tanzania (Klingelhofer, 1967), and Guatemalan children (Johnson, Johnson, & Price-Williams, 1967).

Within the United States, cross-ethnic group differences in intelligence have been documented for years, and have been a source of academic and political controversy for decades. (Cross-ethnic group comparisons within the United States are called **multicultural studies.**) Modern intelligence tests were first developed in the early 1900s for the purpose of identifying cognitively challenged children. Intelligence tests provided a way to distinguish children in need of special education from those whose schoolwork suffered for other reasons. In the years that followed, intelligence tests came into widespread use in public schools and other government programs.

But not everyone benefited from the new tests of intelligence. Because such tests relied at least in part on verbal performance and cultural knowledge, immigrants who spoke English poorly and came from different cultural backgrounds were at a disadvantage. For example, when tests of intelligence were administered to immigrants at Ellis Island beginning in 1913, more than three-quarters of the Italian, Hungarian, and Jewish immigrants tested as mentally defective. Such low scores for certain immigrant groups provoked a storm of controversy. Some people defended the scientific nature of the new tests, charging that southern European immigrants were not fit to enter the country. Others responded that intelligence tests were biased and did not accurately measure the mental ability of people from different cultures.

There are ethnic group differences in measured intelligence (although the ethnic groups scoring low on standard tests change across time). The average scores of some minority groups in the United States are 12 to 15 percentage points lower than the average for European Americans. This does not mean that all the individuals in these groups test poorly—high-scoring individuals can also be found in all ethnic groups—it simply means that larger percentages of some ethnic groups score low. The question that has fueled great debates and controversy is this: What is the *source* of these differences? Is it biological or cultural?

Is IQ Biologically Predetermined?   The nature side of the debate argues that differences in IQ scores between different societies and ethnic groups are mainly heredity or innate. Arthur Jensen (1969, 1980, 1981) is one of the best-known proponents of this position. He conducted many different studies on this topic, mostly examining differences between African and European Americans (for example, Jensen, 1968, 1969, 1971, 1973, 1977, 1980, 1981, 1983, 1984), and found that African Americans typically scored lower on IQ tests than European Americans. Jensen takes the position that about 80 percent of a person's intelligence is inherited and suggests that the gap between the scores of European Americans and ethnic minorities in the United States is due to biological differences. Such a position has important ramifications for social policy; Jensen has argued that special educational programs for the under-privileged are a waste of money, time, and effort because inborn intellectual deficiencies of ethnic minorities are mostly responsible for their poorer per-formance on IQ tests. To support his claim, Jensen has also provided a sub-stantial database examining the effectiveness of educational and remedial programs to bolster the intellectual capacity and abilities of ethnic minorities. When extraneous factors are controlled, he concludes, those programs have had little or no effect on improving intelligence in ethnic minority groups.

Studies of twins provide some evidence for the nature hypothesis. The most important of these studies compared identical twins who grew up in separate homes to fraternal twins raised together (Bouchard & McGue, 1981). If test scores are determined by heredity, identical twins raised apart should have very similar scores. But if environment is primary, the scores of the fraternal twins raised together should be more similar. These twin studies revealed that the scores of identical twins raised in different environments were significantly more alike than those of fraternal twins raised together.

Jensen (1970) concluded that the correlation between twins on IQ was .824, which he interpreted as constituting an upper limit on the heritability of IQ.

Environmental factors, however, were normally distributed, and IQ was not correlated with those factors. Jensen concluded that environmental factors could not have been systematically related to the intelligence levels of twin pairs.

Today there is widespread agreement that at least 40 percent of intelligence can be attributed to heredity (Henderson, 1982; Jencks, Smith, Acland, Bane, Cohen, Gintis, Heyns, & Michaelson, 1972; Plomin, 1990). At the same time, one must keep in mind that heritability is a *population* statistic; it says nothing about IQ on an individual level. So, a heritability statistic of .40 for intelligence indicates that 40 percent of the variance in a population of IQ scores can be attributed to genetics, and the other 60 percent must be explained in some other way. It does not mean that 40 percent of an individual's IQ is determined by genetics.

Much of Jensen's research of the past two decades has involved studies that followed up his original thesis, in an attempt to uncover the biological bases underlying the ethnic and racial differences in IQ. For example, in some of his earlier research in this area, he documented differences in reaction and inspection times of different ethnic and racial groups of participants on a variety of cognitive tasks (for example, Jensen & Munro, 1979; Jensen & Reed, 1990; Jensen & Whang, 1993; Kranzler & Jensen, 1989). In subsequent research, he has examined the brain correlates of such reaction time measures and IQ, demonstrating a link between brain activity and processes on the one hand and reaction time and IQ on the other (for example, Reed & Jensen, 1992, 1993). Some of his latest research has also documented a relationship among brain size, reaction times, and IQ (for example, Jensen & Johnson, 1994; Reed & Jensen, 1993).

The considerable amount of research generated by Jensen, his colleagues, and others in this area provides a substantial base of data suggesting that at least a large portion of intellectual capacity, as measured by typical IQ tests, is associated with biological characteristics, many of which are genetically heritable. These biological characteristics appear to be related to brain size and function, which in turn appear to be related to racial or ethnic differences.

Is IQ Culturally Determined?   On the other hand, some scholars suggest that members of certain ethnic groups in the United States score lower because most subcultures in this country are economically deprived (Blau, 1981; Wolf, 1965). Advocates of this position have turned to studies showing that IQ scores are strongly related to social class. The average IQ score of poor whites, for instance, is 10 to 20 percentage points lower than the average score of members of the middle class. The effect of environment over race can be seen most clearly in studies showing that poor whites tested in Southern states scored lower than blacks who lived in Northern states. It is also possible that between-group differences in intelligence scores are the result of (1) different beliefs about what intelligence is or (2) culturally inappropriate measures of intelligence. What we do know is that intelligence tests are a good predictor of the verbal skills necessary for success in a culture associated with the formalized educational systems of modern industrial societies and increasingly adopted as a model throughout the world. However, such tests may not measure motivation, creativity, talent, or social skills, all of which are important factors in achievement.

A number of other authors and findings support this side of the debate. One recent theory that offers an alternative interpretation of the differences in IQ scores between African American and European American individuals is Claude Steele's work on **stereotype threat**—"the threat that others' judgments or their own actions will negatively stereotype them in the domain" (Steele, 1998, p. 613). In other words, he posits that societal stereotypes about a group—for instance, concerning academic or intellectual performance—can actually influence the performance of individuals from that group. In an interesting set of experiments with black and white college students at Stanford University, Steele and Aronson (1995) report that when black students were asked to record their race on a demographic questionnaire before taking a standardized test, they performed significantly worse as compared with black students who were not primed to think about their race before taking the test. Furthermore, they also found that when the exam was presented as a measure of intellectual ability, black students performed worse than white students. However, when the same test was presented as unrelated to intellectual ability, the detrimental effects of the stereotype threat disappeared.

Scarr and Weinberg (1976) also offer evidence for an environmental basis of intelligence. They showed that black and interracial children adopted by white families scored above the IQ and school achievement means for whites. Such a finding argues against biological predetermination and in favor of cultural and environmental factors. Greenfield (1997) has argued that intelligence tests can be understood in terms of symbolic culture, and therefore have little translatability (reliability or validity) when used with people of different cultural backgrounds—whether ethnic minorities within one country or across countries. Such arguments have been proffered for decades now, and have led to the development of a number of "culture-free" or "culture-fair" tests of intelligence, such as the Cattell Culture Fair Intelligence Test.

Collectively speaking, there appears to be an equally large and strong literature base suggesting that IQ is at least malleable to cultural and environmental factors, and that previous findings indicating racial or ethnic differences in IQ are equivocal because of problems of validity in the tests used to measure intelligence in different cultural groups.

Evaluating Both Positions   The debate on the origins of intelligence is a very involved one, and we have outlined only some of the issues. The topic of intelligence is one that is emotionally charged for many people, scientists and laypersons alike. It has important practical ramifications as well, including the development of appropriate and effective educational programs, and selection of individuals for employment or admission to organizations. These issues have been so emotionally and politically charged, in fact, that many people have suggested that doing research on intelligence is unethical. Such sentiments have undoubtedly persuaded many researchers and other psychologists to stay away from discussions of this topic, let alone conduct research on it.

We prefer to take an empirical approach to the issues, and to weigh evidence supporting or not supporting each of the positions. There are, in fact, problems on both sides of the issue. On the nature side, the use of race or ethnicity as a classifying variable is problematic because of the ambiguity of these concepts, which may not actually refer to anything meaningful about biology or psychology (Sternberg, Grigorenko, & Kidd, 2005). These concepts are basically a social construction—categories that we create in our minds to help us classify people in the world around us. In actuality, whether there are truly distinct races of people is still an unanswered question; if anything, the literature suggests that those distinctions really do not exist. Although observable differences in "traditionally" racial characteristics such as skin color, face morphology, and the like surely exist, evidence is not conclusive that they are correlated with distinctive biological differences among reliable racial categories.

Given the problems with the concept of race, therefore, we need to recast the findings provided by Jensen and his colleagues concerning the relationship between race or ethnicity and IQ. The findings may indeed exist (in general, data do not lie), and they may indeed be related to biological characteristics that have been examined until now, such as brain function, activity, and size. But should these findings be interpreted as indicative of an unchangeable biological condition? It is a fact that biology itself is influenced by cultural and environmental factors, not only over the long term through evolution, but also in the short term as a result of recent social history and even individual experience within a lifetime.

Some arguments on the nurture side of the controversy also have problems. If intelligence really is a cultural construct, then it would be impossible to construct a test that is indeed "culture-fair" or "culture-free," because any such test would, by definition, have to include specific items that are generated within a specific cultural milieu; that is, intelligence cannot be understood outside a cultural framework (Sternberg, 2004). Even culture-free tests and items would have the underlying bias of culture—a "culture of no culture." In fact, some studies have shown that such tests do suffer from the very biases they were designed to address. Nenty (1986), for example, administering the Cattell Culture Fair Intelligence Test to Americans, Indians, and Nigerians in order to test the validity of the scale, found that 27 of the 46 items administered were culturally biased, thus rendering scores for the three cultures incomparable to one another.

Proponents of the nurture view suggest that factors such as motivational levels of the participants, experience with similar tests, and difficulty of the items have affected previous ethnic-group differences in IQ testing. But, evidence does not support claims concerning such influences. For example, Herrnstein and Murray (1994) reviewed studies that examined whether the intelligence tests used in previous research had different external validities for different groups—that is, whether those tests predicted performance for African Americans in the real world (jobs, schooling) in the same way that they did for European Americans. Their review of hundreds of studies found no evidence of differential external validity, ruling out this potential cause of differences. They also reviewed studies that examined evidence of bias in internal validity by comparing the difficulty of specific items for different groups. They reported that differences between blacks and whites were actually found on culturally neutral items, not culturally biased items, thus ruling out this potential cause of the differences. They examined studies investigating differences in students' motivation to try to do well on the intelligence tests, and found that lack of motivation could not explain the differences in scores. They also examined whether blacks and whites differed in the amount of coaching they received on similar tests, the amount of experience and exposure to such tests, English language fluency, and the racial congruence of the test administrators. They found no effect for any of these variables on the differences between blacks and whites, and thus ruled these potential effects out as well. They examined the potential effect of socioeconomic status (SES), and found that this variable did account for some of the differences between blacks and whites, but not all; in fact, differences in intelligence between blacks and whites actually increased with higher SES. Comparisons were also made with studies involving black participants in Africa, the rationale being that these individuals would not have been subjected to the same social legacies as blacks in America. The results across studies, however, showed that the same differences occurred.

The debate continues. Herrnstein and Murray (1994) conclude the following on the basis of their literature review:

> We cannot think of a legitimate argument why any encounter between individual whites and blacks need be affected by the knowledge that an aggregate ethnic difference in measured intelligence is genetic instead of environmental. . . . In sum: If tomorrow you knew beyond a shadow of a doubt that all the cognitive differences between races were 100 percent genetic in origin, nothing of any significance should change. The knowledge would give you no reason to treat individuals differently than if ethnic differences were 100 percent environmental. By the same token, knowing that the differences are 100 percent environmental in origin would not suggest a single program or policy that is not being tried. It would justify no optimism about the time it will take to narrow the existing gaps. It would not even justify confidence that genetically based differences will not be upon us within a few generations. The impulse to think that environmental sources of differences are less threatening than genetic ones is natural but illusory. (pp. 313–315)

The Concept of Intelligence in Other Cultures

One of the positive outcomes from so much research on the relationship between culture and intelligence is an expanded view of what intelligence may be, and how it may be conceptually related to culture. This issue is intricately intertwined with cross-cultural research on intelligence because one of the possible confounding factors in previous studies that documented cultural differences has been cultural differences in the very concept and meaning of intelligence.

Researchers in this area have discovered that many languages have no word that corresponds to our idea of intelligence. The closest Mandarin equivalent, for instance, is a Chinese character that means "good brain and talented." Chinese people often associate this concept with traits such as imitation, effort, and social responsibility (Keats, 1982).

African cultures provide a number of examples. The Baganda of East Africa use the word *obugezi* to refer to a combination of mental and social skills that make a person steady, cautious, and friendly (Wober, 1974). The Djerma- Songhai in West Africa use the term *akkal,* which has an even broader meaning—a combination of intelligence, know-how, and social skills (Bissilat, Laya, Pierre, & Pidoux, 1967). Still another society, the Baoule, uses the term *n'glouele,* which describes children who are not only mentally alert but also willing to volunteer their services without being asked (Dasen et al., 1985).

Because of the enormous differences in the ways cultures define intelligence, it may be difficult to make valid comparisons from one society to another. That is, different cultures value different traits and have divergent views concerning which traits are useful in predicting future important behaviors (also culturally defined). People in different cultures not only disagree about what constitutes intelligence but also about the proper way to demonstrate those abilities. In mainstream North American society, individuals are typically rewarded for displaying knowledge and skills. This same behavior may be considered improper, arrogant, or rude in societies that stress personal relationships, cooperation, and modesty.

These differences are important to cross-cultural studies of intelligence because successful performance on a task of intelligence may require behavior that is considered immodest and arrogant in Culture A (and therefore only reluctantly displayed by members of Culture A) but desirable in Culture B (and therefore readily displayed by members of Culture B). Clearly, such different attitudes toward the same behavior could lead researchers to draw inaccurate conclusions about differences in intelligence between Culture A and Culture B.

Another reason it is difficult to compare intelligence cross-culturally is that tests of intelligence often rely on knowledge that is specific to a particular culture; investigators based in that culture may not even know what to test for in a different culture. For example, one U.S. intelligence test contains the following question: "How does a violin resemble a piano?" Clearly, this question assumes prior knowledge about violins and pianos—quite a reasonable expectation for middle-class Americans, but not for people from cultures that use different musical instruments.

Recent Developments in Theories about Intelligence in Contemporary Psychology

One of the most important contributions of cross-cultural psychology has been in expanding our theoretical understanding of intelligence in mainstream American psychology as well. Until very recently, for example, creativity was not considered a part of intelligence; now, however, psychologists are increasingly considering this important human ability as a type of intelligence. Other aspects of intelligence are also coming to the forefront. Gardner (1983) has suggested that there are really seven different types of intelligence: logical mathematical, linguistic, musical, spatial, bodily kinesthetic, interpersonal, and intrapersonal. According to this scheme, not only do the core components of each of these seven types of intelligence differ, but so do some sample end states (such as mathematician versus dancer). His theory of multiple intelligences has broadened our understanding of intelligence to include areas other than "book smarts."

Sternberg (1986) has proposed a theory of intelligence based on three separate "subtheories": contextual, experiential, and componential intelligence. Contextual intelligence refers to an individual's ability to adapt to the environment, solving problems in specific situations. Experiential intelligence refers to the ability to formulate new ideas and combine unrelated facts. Componential intelligence refers to the ability to think abstractly, process information, and determine what needs to be done. Sternberg's theory focuses more on the processes that underlie thought than on specific thought outcomes. Because this definition of intelligence focuses on process rather than outcome, it has the potential for application across cultures.

Perhaps the field is coming to realize that intelligence in its broadest sense may be more aptly defined as "the skills and abilities necessary to effectively accomplish cultural goals." If your culture's goals, for example, involve successfully pursuing a professional occupation with a good salary in order to support yourself and your family, that culture will foster a view of intelligence that incorporates cognitive and emotional skills and abilities that allow for pursuing such an occupation. Those skills and abilities may include deductive reasoning, logical thought, verbal and mathematical skills—the sorts of skills that are fostered in contemporary American culture. If your culture's goals, however, focus more on the development and maintenance of successful interpersonal relationships, working with nature, or hunting and gathering, intelligence will more aptly be viewed as the skills and abilities related to such activities. On one level, therefore, people of all cultures share a similar view of intelligence—a catchall concept that summarizes the skills and abilities necessary to live effectively in one's culture. At the same time, however, cultural differences naturally exist because of differences in how cultures define goals and the skills and abilities needed to achieve those goals. Future research will need to delve into these dual processes, searching for commonalities as well as differences across cultures and exploring what contextual variables affect intelligence-related behaviors, and why.

CONCLUSION

In this chapter, we have examined how culture influences the basic psychological processes of perception, cognition, consciousness, and intelligence. We have seen how there are many universals as well as culture-specific aspects of cognition. These findings have important implications for our understanding of the relationship between culture and psychological processes. I (the first author) remember fondly when I was first introduced to the material concerning cultural influences on visual perception and optical illusions. I had never thought that culture, and experience in general, could have the effect that it does on what I thought must be innate, basic properties. When I learned of cultural differences in optical illusions, it gave me a new perspective on the nature and pervasiveness of culture.

The issues discussed in this chapter serve as the basis for understanding findings from many cross-cultural studies to be discussed in subsequent chapters. Perception, cognition, and consciousness lie at the core of many psychological constructs, and cultural differences in these processes exemplify the various levels of psychology that culture influences. As consciousness reflects our subjective experience of the world, we take for granted that our consciousness is shared by others; research in this area, however, has shown that there may be large cultural, as well as individual, differences in consciousness.

These differences have important ramifications for intercultural interactions and applied settings. If people from different cultural backgrounds can view such things as optical illusions differently, it is no wonder they perceive so much of the rest of the world differently as well. When this information is coupled with information concerning other basic psychological processes such as attribution, emotion, and personality, the effect of culture on individual psychology is amazing.

Likewise, cultural differences and similarities in definitions and processes of intelligence have considerable relevance to various applied settings. Many current curriculum transformation movements in the United States, for example, are based on a particular view and definition of intelligence and cognitive development. It is not uncommon to hear allegations of cultural bias in these types of educational reforms. Indeed, if broad, sweeping educational changes are implemented in the United States without recognition and awareness of deeply embedded cultural differences in the nature and definition of intelligence, we may actually be broadening the gaps that already exist between groups and increasing, rather than decreasing, intergroup conflict in the name of "education."

Awareness of cultural differences in intelligence raises difficult questions concerning testing and the use of test scores. Should bias in testing be eliminated at the expense of the predictive validity of the test? Many educational institutions and business organizations today face this difficult question, which is compounded by legal ramifications and the constant threat of litigation. Perhaps we need to give consideration to yet another aspect of intelligence—that is, our attitudes regarding intelligence. A cross-cultural understanding of differences in the definitions and processes of intelligence should help to deepen our appreciation and respect for cultures different from our own, and help us to find similarities as well as differences among people.

GLOSSARY

blind spot A spot in our visual field where the optic nerve goes through the layer of receptor cells on its way back toward the brain, creating a lack of sensory receptors in the eye at that location.

carpentered world theory A theory of perception that suggests that people (at least most Americans) are used to seeing things that are rectangular in shape, and thus unconsciously expect things to have square corners.

categorize To classify objects on the basis of perceived similarities and attach labels (words) to those classifications.

cognition A term denoting all mental processes we use to transform sensory input into knowledge.

counterfactual thinking Hypothetical beliefs about the past that could have occurred in order to avoid or change a negative outcome.

dialectical thinking The tendency to accept what seem to be contradictions in thought or beliefs.

everyday cognition An area of study that examines cognitive skills and abilities that are used in everyday functioning that appear to develop without formal education, but from performing daily tasks of living and working.

front-horizontal foreshortening theory A theory of perception that suggests that we interpret vertical lines as horizontal lines extending into the distance. Because we interpret the vertical line in the horizontal–vertical illusion as extending away from us, we see it as longer.

hindsight bias The process in which individuals adjust their memory for something after they find out the true outcome.

multicultural studies Studies that examine cross-ethnic group differences within a country.

optical illusions Perceptions that involve an apparent discrepancy between how an object looks and what it actually is.

perception The process of gathering information about the world through our senses; our initial interpretations of sensations.

positive logical determinism A tendency to see contradictions as mutually exclusive categories, as either–or, yes–no, one-or-the-other types of categories.

problem solving The process by which we attempt to discover ways of achieving goals that do not seem readily attainable.

sensation The feelings that result from excitation of the sensory receptors such as touch, taste, smell, sight, or hearing.

serial position effect The finding that people tend to remember something better if it is either the first or the last item in a list.

stereotype threat The threat that others' judgments or one's own actions will negatively stereotype one in a domain (such as academic achievement).

symbolizing three dimensions in two A theory of perception that suggests that people in Western cultures focus more on representations on paper than do people in other cultures, and in particular spend more time learning to interpret pictures.

Culture and Gender

CHAPTER CONTENTS

As with so many other aspects of our lives, culture influences the behaviors associated with being male or female. In the past 30 to 40 years, we have witnessed many changes in the behaviors Americans consider appropriate for males and females. Certainly, American culture is one of the most dynamic in the exploration of sex and gender differences (or similarities). This dynamism has led to a great deal of confusion and conflict, but it has also produced excitement about the changing nature of human relations and culture itself.

Recent events around the world have brought international attention to gender issues. From the Taliban in Afghanistan to the World Conference on Women held in Beijing to global concern over female circumcision in Africa and Asia—gender roles, ideals, and expectations are heated topics widely discussed around the world. An example of a controversial cultural practice that is rooted in perceptions of gender and gender roles is female circumcision. It has been described as part of a female initiation ceremony and an important rite of passage marking the transition from childhood to adulthood (Lightfoot-Klein, 1989). Behind this practice lie many strongly held beliefs about women and the role of women. Those who defend the practice argue that it is a requirement for marriage and emphasize the importance of upholding tradition; those who condemn it emphasize the pain, suffering, and health risks involved. To understand this controversy, we need to first examine how our own cultural filters shape the way we view issues related to gender. If you find this practice abhorrent, why? How did you come to develop those beliefs? As will be discussed in Chapter 14, we perceive and make interpretations about others based on our cultural filters. When we encounter cultural practices that make us uncomfortable, we can engage in flexible ethnocentrism to attempt to understand the cultural viewpoint while not necessarily accepting or supporting it.

In this chapter, we will examine how culture influences behavior related to sex and gender. First, we will discuss some similarities between gender and culture concerns within psychology. Second, we will discuss some terminology and definitions concerning sex and gender that will help us understand what we are talking about and how to focus on cultural influences. Then, we will discuss cross-cultural research on gender stereotypes, gender roles, and self-concepts, all of which suggest the existence of a universality in stereotypes related to gender and gender roles around the world. Then we will discuss cross-cultural differences in gender-related psychological constructs, such as cognition, conformity and obedience, aggression, personality, and sex and sexuality. We will discuss some theoretical notions of how psychologists believe gender differences come to exist, and why cultures seem to differ in these differences. We will also discuss how changing cultures and clashes between cultures bring differences in gender roles to the forefront in the daily lives of many people today. Throughout this discussion, we will see that the issues surrounding gender and gender differences, both pancultural and culture-specific, are complex as well as interesting.

THE IMPACT OF GENDER AND CULTURE TO PSYCHOLOGY

Before turning to the cross-cultural literature on gender differences, it is interesting to note some parallels between the impact of gender and culture on psychology. Beginning 30 to 40 years ago, what is commonly known as the women's movement in the United States led American academic communities to evaluate the treatment and presentation of women in textbooks and research. They found that most research was conducted using men as subjects, and most information presented about "people" in academic textbooks and university courses was based on information gathered from men. This gender bias also affected what scholars considered important to study, the relative status of different studies and topics, and the probability and outlet for publication. Psychologists became increasingly aware of the possibility that men and women may differ psychologically, calling into question previous research findings and the theories based on them. Scholars, researchers, teachers, and students alike began to question whether knowledge based primarily on men was accurate for people in general.

One consequence of this growing awareness among researchers and scholars was a conscious effort to include women as research participants, to ensure that research findings would be applicable to women as well as men. At the same time, an increasing number of women became researchers and scholars, bringing different perspectives to the field, its theories, and its findings. Today, psychology enjoys more balanced contributions by both men and women, at least in the United States, and this combination of different perspectives and concerns makes for a dynamism that is rich, interesting, and important for the field.

As a result, we have come a long way toward improving our knowledge about both men and women in the social sciences. Although questioning the imbalance of research on men and women was difficult, many behavioral and social scientists have responded well to this inequity in our knowledge and practice. Today, studies of gender differences are commonplace in social science research, and textbooks routinely incorporate sex and gender differences when imparting knowledge about people (although the degree to which such material is presented and incorporated is still questioned and debated).

We have witnessed the same type of questioning with regard to cultural norms for women and men. Just as knowledge about women and women's concerns was missing from research and scholarship 30 years ago, so too was knowledge about cultural similarities and differences and cultural diversity. Much of this gap still exists today. Many of the same questions are still being raised concerning whether what we are learning in classes and in our laboratories is indeed true for people of all cultures and ethnicities. The answer so far has been "not necessarily." To address this gap, many researchers have made a conscious effort to study behaviors across cultures to learn what is similar across cultures and what is different. Academic institutions have also made a conscious effort to recruit and train people of diverse cultural backgrounds, so that they too can contribute to the research, teaching, and scholarship in psychology.

We interpret these changes as evidence of a continuing evolution in the field, similar to what has happened in relation to gender. That is, psychology is constantly changing and evolving, as the nature of the people it is supposed to be describing continues to change. As the United States and the entire world become increasingly diverse, the need for mainstream psychology to incorporate, explain, and describe that diversity increases. The field has become aware of this need only in the past decade or so (although cross-cultural psychology and cross-cultural research have a much longer history). Theories, research, and teaching are becoming more culturally sensitive, and this increasing awareness is bound to bring with it another evolution in the face and content of psychology. For this reason, it is an exciting time in both mainstream and cross-cultural psychology, as the gap between them narrows.

SEX AND GENDER ACROSS CULTURES

Definitions

Men and women coexist in all societies. They have to, in fact, if humans are to reproduce and survive. Psychologists generally differentiate between terms referring to the biological differences between men and women and other terms referring to psychological differences, the former referring to sex differences, the other referring to gender differences. In this chapter and throughout this book, we define the following terms as indicated:

Sex generally refers to the biological and physiological differences between men and women, the most obvious being the anatomical differences in their reproductive systems. Other biological differences between the sexes include physiological, hormonal, and biochemical differences. The term **sex roles** is used to describe the behaviors and patterns of activities men and women may engage in that are directly related to their biological differences and the process of reproduction. An example of a sex role for females is breast-feeding, a behavior in which only women can engage (Brislin, 1993). The term **sexual identity** is used to describe the degree of awareness and recognition of sex and sex roles an individual may have. Male sexual identity includes "his awareness that he has the potential to impregnate women and knows the necessary behaviors. Female sexual identity includes the woman's awareness of her reproductive potential and her knowledge about behaviors that lead to pregnancy" (p. 287).

In contrast, **gender** refers to the behaviors or patterns of activities that a society or culture deems appropriate for men and women. These behavior patterns may or may not be related to sex and sex roles, although they often are. For example, traditional gender roles that we all know about or have heard of suggest that males are aggressive and unemotional (with the exception of anger) and that the male should leave the home every day to make a living and be the principal wage earner. Traditional gender roles for females suggest that women are nurturant, caring, and highly emotional and that they should stay at home and take care of the home and children. **Gender role** refers to the degree to which a person adopts the gender-specific behaviors ascribed by his or her culture. **Gender identity** refers to the degree to which a person has awareness or recognition that he or she adopts a particular gender role. And **gender stereotypes** refer to the psychological or behavioral characteristics typically associated with men and women.

Not everyone can be pigeonholed into stereotypes according to sex or gender roles, as there are considerable individual differences from person to person with regard to these roles. In addition, gender-role stereotypes interact with other forms of group membership. African American women, for example, are generally not perceived in terms of the traditional gender roles just described (Binion, 1990), nor are women who are disabled or who have a different sexual orientation.

Separating the biological and physiological facts of sex from the behavioral aspects of gender is the first step in understanding differences between males and females. Indeed, it should become clear from this differentiation that we are mostly concerned with gender differences, not sex differences. Culture, as a macro construct, is likely to influence our perception of gender differences.

The Relationship between Sex and Gender across Cultures

While there are many similarities between men and women both physically and psychologically, there are differences as well. These sex differences include the fact that men are generally physically bigger and stronger than women, and that only women can carry a child, give birth, and breast-feed.

These types of real sex differences between men and women lead to some inevitable differences in sex roles. Men's larger size, on one hand, probably enabled them to take on the primary role of making and maintaining shelter, hunting for or producing food, and warding off enemies and rivals for food, mates, and other resources. Women, on the other hand, took on the primary role of caring for prenatal infants and newborns. Biological differences between men and women, therefore, are probably the platform by which decisions concerning a division of labor were made in our evolutionary history.

All societies, however, not only make decisions about what only men can do and what only women can do; they also come up with decisions about what men and women *should do*. And, these decisions are not necessarily what only men or women can do. For example, in many societies women take on the brunt of child care. Now, aside from a few things that only women can do, such as breast-feeding, both men and women can do many of the same tasks related to child care. But, despite this, the fact remains that women take on the primary job of caretaker within the family, handling most of the work within families and homes related to the care of children, cooking, cleaning, and other activities related to the maintenance of the home.

The study of families by Georgas, Berry, Van di Vijver, Kagitcibasi, and Poortinga (2006) highlights this issue. They assessed families in 30 countries around the world concerning a number of issues related to family functioning. One of the issues they assessed concerned division of labor related to household chores (housework). In all countries surveyed there was a very large gap between the amount of work men and women did. Needless to say, women took up the brunt of the housework in all societies surveyed (Figure 6.1). These differences were, in fact, some of the most robust and consistent findings in their study.

As we have discussed in Chapter 1 and throughout this book, however, different societies have different cultures. As we defined culture as a unique meaning and information system, that means that different cultures ascribe different and unique meanings to the sex differences and sex roles that exist within those cultures. These specific cultural meanings are gender. Thus, as you can see from Figure 6.1, while all cultures have large divisions of labor between men and women with regard to housework, some cultures have larger differences than others.

Or take for instance another piece of data from Georgas et al.'s (2006) study. They identified three types of roles mothers and fathers played in families: Expressive—focused on maintaining a pleasant environment and providing emotional support for one another; Financial—including contributing to and managing finances; and Childcare. In near all cultures surveyed, fathers were primarily concerned with Finances first, Expressive issues next, and

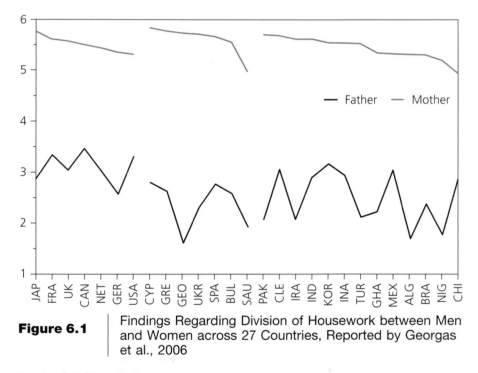

Figure 6.1 | Findings Regarding Division of Housework between Men and Women across 27 Countries, Reported by Georgas et al., 2006

Reprinted with permission.

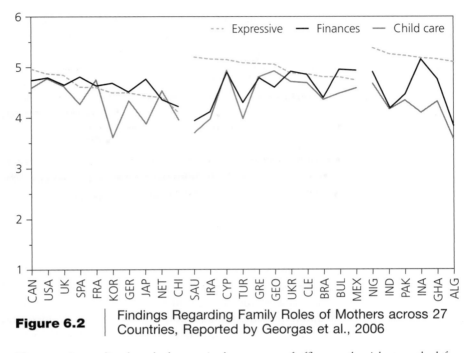

Figure 6.2 | Findings Regarding Family Roles of Mothers across 27 Countries, Reported by Georgas et al., 2006

The countries are listed on the bottom in three groups of affluence; the richest on the left, moderately affluent in the middle, and least affluent on the right.

Childcare last. The concerns of mothers, however, differed according to culture. Mothers were most concerned with Childcare, but only in less-affluent cultures. In more affluent cultures, mothers appeared to be equally concerned with all three family roles (Figure 6.2).

Thus, although differences in sex roles exist in all societies of the world, and are thus universal, cultures differ in the specific type and degree of differentiation they encourage between the sexes. Gender, gender roles, gender-role ideologies, and gender stereotypes, therefore, are culturally specific psychological constructs that differ across cultures.

CULTURE, GENDER ROLES, AND STEREOTYPES

The discussion above suggests that the existence of sex and gender roles is universal to all cultures. Does that mean that the *content* of those gender roles are also similar across cultures? The number of roles available to males and females is limitless. Some cultures foster one certain gender distinction, different cultures foster another. We are all familiar with traditional gender-role differentiations—the notion that males should be independent, self-reliant, strong, and emotionally detached, while women should be dependent, reliant, weak, nurturant, and emotional. To what degree is this an American or Western cultural phenomenon? Several programs of research have examined this interesting question over the years, and have shown that many gender-related stereotypes are, in fact, held universally across cultures.

Culture and Gender Stereotypes

The Williams and Best Studies   The best-known study of gender stereotypes across cultures is one conducted by Williams and Best (1982). These researchers sampled people in 30 countries, 52 to 120 respondents per country, for a total of almost 3,000 individuals. The study used a questionnaire known as the Adjective Check List (ACL). The ACL is a list of 300 adjectives. Respondents in each country were asked to decide whether each adjective was considered more descriptive of a male or of a female. Whether the subjects agreed with the assignment of an adjective to males or females was irrelevant; instead, they were asked merely to report the characteristics generally associated with males and females in their culture. The researchers tallied the data from all individuals. Looking at responses within each culture, Williams and Best established the criterion that if more than two-thirds of a sample from a country agreed on a particular term for either males or females, there was a consensus within that culture on that general characteristic. Then, looking at responses across the cultures, the researchers decided that if two-thirds of the cultures reached a consensus on the characteristic, there was a cross-cultural consensus on that characteristic as describing males or females. The results indicated a high degree of pancultural agreement across all the countries studied in the characteristics associated with men and women. Table 6.1 lists the 100 items of the pancultural adjective checklist reported by Williams and Best (1994).

The degree of consensus these adjectives received in describing males and females is amazing. In fact, Berry, Poortinga, Segall, and Dasen (1992) have suggested that "this degree of consensus is so large that it may be appropriate to suggest that the researchers have found a psychological universal when it comes to gender stereotypes" (p. 60), while at the same time cautioning against such sweeping generalizations. But the possibility of a universally accepted gender stereotype has interesting ramifications for possible evolutionary similarities across cultures in division of labor between males and females and the psychological characteristics that result from that universal division of labor.

Williams and Best (1982) conducted a second type of analysis on their data in order to summarize their major findings. They scored the adjectives in each country in terms of favorability, strength, and activity to examine how the adjectives were distributed according to affective or emotional meaning. They found surprising congruence in these analyses: The characteristics associated with men were stronger and more active than those associated with women across all countries. On favorability, however, cultural differences emerged: Some countries (such as Japan and South Africa) rated the male characteristics as more favorable than the female, whereas other countries (for example, Italy and Peru) rated female characteristics as more favorable.

Table 6.1 | The 100 Items of the Pancultural Adjective Checklist

Male-Associated		Female-Associated	
Active	Loud	Affected	Modest
Adventurous	Obnoxious	Affectionate	Nervous
Aggressive	Opinionated	Appreciative	Patient
Arrogant	Opportunistic	Cautious	Pleasant
Autocratic	Pleasure-seeking	Changeable	Prudish
Bossy	Precise	Charming	Self-pitying
Capable	Progressive	Complaining	Sensitive
Conceited	Rational	Confused	Sexy
Confident	Realistic	Curious	Shy
Courageous	Reckless	Dependent	Softhearted
Cruel	Resourceful	Dreamy	Sophisticated
Cynical	Rigid	Emotional	Submissive
Determined	Robust	Excitable	Suggestible
Disorderly	Serious	Fault-finding	Superstitious
Enterprising	Sharp-witted	Fearful	Talkative
Greedy	Show-off	Fickle	Timid
Hardheaded	Steady	Foolish	Touchy
Humorous	Stern	Forgiving	Unambitious
Indifferent	Stingy	Frivolous	Understanding
Individualistic	Stolid	Fussy	Unintelligent
Initiative	Tough	Gentle	Unstable
Interests wide	Unfriendly	Imaginative	Warm
Inventive	Unscrupulous	Kind	Weak
Lazy	Witty	Mild	Worrying

Source: Williams, J. E., & Best, D. L. (1994). Cross-cultural views of women and men. In W. J. Lonner & R. Malpass (Eds.), *Psychology and culture*, p. 193. Published by Allyn & Bacon, Boston, MA. Copyright © 1994 by Pearson Education. Reprinted by permission of the publisher.

How are we to interpret these results? It could be that a division of labor for males and females according to reproductive processes produced differences in behaviors that, in turn, produced differences in psychological characteristics. It may be that these psychological characteristics had some evolutionary and adaptive advantages for males and females to fulfill their roles as prescribed by the division of labor. It could be that men and women in all cultures became locked into these set ways, accounting for universal consensus on these descriptors. It could be that men and women become locked into a particular mindset about cultural differences because of perceived social inequality or social forces and indirect communication via mass media and the like. Or these findings could all be a function of the way the research was conducted, using university students as participants, which would tend to make the entire sample more homogeneous than if people from each culture were sampled randomly.

Although it is impossible to disentangle these factors, it is important to note that Williams and Best themselves collected and analyzed data concerning gender stereotypes from young children and found a considerable degree of agreement between the findings for children and those for university students (Williams & Best, 1990). These results argue against (but do not entirely eliminate) the notion that the original findings were due to homogeneity among university students.

Williams and his colleagues have since extended their earlier work on gender stereotypes in important ways. Williams, Satterwhite, and Best (1999), for example, took the ACL data from 25 countries in their previous work and rescored them in terms of five personality dimensions known as the Big Five, or Five-Factor Model of Personality. As you will see in Chapter 10, these terms refer to the five personality traits or dimensions that are considered universal or consistent around the world. They found that, overall, males were perceived to have significantly higher scores than females on all traits except agreeableness; females, however, were perceived to have significantly higher scores than males on this personality dimension.

In a subsequent follow-up study, Williams, Satterwhite and Best (2000) took their ACL data from 27 countries and rescored these data according to the Five-Factor Model of Personality. They then examined male–female differences on the personality traits separately in each country. They found that the results they had obtained earlier were generally supported in all the countries. In addition, they correlated the male–female differences with culture scores from two large value surveys (Hofstede, 1980; Schwartz, 1994), some demographic variables, and gender ideology scores from a previous study (Williams & Best, 1990). They found that gender-stereotype differentiation tended to be higher in countries that were conservative and hierarchical, with a lower level of socioeconomic development, a relatively low degree of Christian affiliation, and a relatively low proportion of women attending universities. Countries that valued harmony and egalitarianism, had less-traditional sex-role orientations, and viewed male stereotypes as less favorable than female stereotypes, were associated with less gender-stereotype differentiation on the five factors.

In summary, this set of studies informs us that gender stereotypes around the world are rather stable and are related to interesting and important psychological characteristics. Men are generally viewed as active, strong, critical, and adultlike, with psychological needs such as dominance, autonomy, aggression, exhibition, achievement, and endurance. Men are also associated more with the personality traits of conscientiousness, extroversion, and openness. Women are generally viewed as passive, weak, nurturing, and adaptive, with psychological needs such as abasement, deference, succorance, nurturance, affiliation, and heterosexuality. They are also associated with higher scores on the personality traits of agreeableness and neuroticism. As described earlier, the degree of stability of these findings across a wide range of countries and cultures provides a strong base of evidence for some pancultural universality in psychological attribution.

Other Studies   A number of other studies have also investigated gender- and sex-role stereotypes in different countries and cultures. Rao and Rao (1985), for example, examined sex role stereotypes in the United States and India; they found that Indians endorsed much more traditional stereotypes concerning mother, wife, and father roles than did the Americans. Trommsdorff and Iwawaki (1989) examined gender-role differences between German and Japanese adolescents. They found that Japanese mothers were seen as more controlling than fathers, but German mothers were viewed as less controlling. The Japanese also had more traditional gender-role orientations than did the Germans. In general, the results from these two studies support the overall findings of Williams and Best.

Perceiving gender differences in a stereotypical fashion is rather persistent. One reason for this persistence is that we tend to be more attuned to information that reinforces and supports our gender stereotypes. For instance, studies find that we tend to remember people and events better when they engage in gender-stereotyped rather than non–gender-stereotyped activities and behaviors (Furnham & Singh, 1986). Moreover, this tendency is greater for people who endorse stronger gender stereotypes.

Other studies have tried to shed light on how gender-role stereotypes develop. Albert and Porter (1986), for example, reported that gender stereotyping increase with age and that children are more likely to sex-type same-sex figures. Munroe, Shimmin, and Munroe (1984) found that children's understanding of gender- and sex-role preferences appear to be related to cognitive development. Other researchers have focused on the contribution of socializing agents, such as the media, to the development of gender-role stereotypes. Fejes (1992) argues that the way the media have historically portrayed women parallels the way media have historically portrayed people of color. An analysis of images of women in television reveals that overly simplified, blatantly stereotypical images of women dominated the earlier years of mass media. Current portrayals of men and women are somewhat more diverse. Nonetheless, some stereotypes persist; for example, women are less likely than men to be in leading roles or portrayed as having a high-status job, and more likely than men to be shown in the home (Fejes, 1992).

Many questions remain unanswered in this important area of psychology. How congruent are people's behaviors with their stereotypes, and does this congruence differ across cultures and countries? Are stereotypes related to important psychological constructs or behaviors that affect everyday lives? How do we come to develop such stereotypes—what are the factors that produce them, and their boundaries? These and other questions provide the basis for important future research.

Culture, Gender-Role Ideology, and Self-Concept

Another important topic that has been studied across cultures is **gender-role ideology**—judgments about what males and females ought to be like or ought to do. To examine gender-role ideologies, Williams and Best (1990) asked subjects in 14 countries to complete the ACL in relation to what they believe they are, and what they would like to be. The subjects also completed a sex-role ideology scale that generated scores between two polar opposites, labeled "traditional" and "egalitarian." The traditional scores tended to describe gender roles that were consistent with the traditional or universal norms found in their earlier research; egalitarian scores reflected a tendency toward less differentiation between males and females on the various psychological characteristics.

The most egalitarian scores were found in the Netherlands, Germany, and Finland; the most traditional ideologies were found in Nigeria, Pakistan, and India. Women tended to have more egalitarian views than men. Gender differences within each country were relatively small compared with cross-country differences, which were considerable. In particular, countries with relatively high socioeconomic development, a high proportion of Protestant Christians, a low proportion of Muslims, a high percentage of women employed outside the home, a high proportion of women enrolled in universities, and a greater degree of individualism were associated with more egalitarian scores. These findings make sense, as greater affluence and individualistic tendencies tend to produce a culture that allows women increased access to jobs and education, thus blending traditional gender roles.

In addition to studying gender stereotypes and ideologies, Williams and Best (1990) also examined gender differences in self-concept. The same students in the same 14 countries rated each of the 300 adjectives of the ACL according to whether it was descriptive of themselves or their ideal self. Responses were scored according to masculinity/femininity as well as in terms of favorability, strength, and activity. When scored according to masculinity/femininity, both self and ideal-self ratings for men were more masculine than they were for women. In contrast, both self and ideal-self ratings for women were more feminine than they were for men, across all countries. However, both men and women in all countries rated their ideal self as more masculine than their actual self. In effect, they were saying that they wanted to have more of the traits traditionally associated with males.

Gender-role ideologies have also been studied in younger populations by Gibbons and her colleagues (de Silva, Stiles, & Gibbons, 1992; Gibbons, Bradford, & Stiles, 1989; Gibbons, Stiles, Schnellman, & Morales-Hidalgo, 1990; Stiles, Gibbons, & Schnellman, 1990). These researchers have conducted several cross-cultural studies involving almost 700 adolescents ranging in age from 11 to 17 years from Spain, Guatemala, and Sri Lanka. In their surveys, adolescents were asked to draw and describe characteristics of the ideal man or woman. Interestingly, the most important quality in these countries for both boys and girls was being "kind and honest," a characteristic that was not gender-specific. Some gender differences emerged, however, with being good-looking more often mentioned as an ideal for women and being employed in a job as more of an ideal for men.

Gibbons conducted another study on adolescents' attitudes toward gender roles that involved 265 international students, ages 11 to 17, who attended school in the Netherlands. Students filled out an Attitude Towards Women Scale for Adolescents (Galambos, Peterson, Richards, & Gitelson, 1985) that included 12 statements such as "Boys are better than girls" and "Girls should have the same freedom as boys." Adolescents were asked to report their level of agreement with these statements. Results indicated that girls were less traditional than boys, and that adolescents from wealthier and more individualistic countries were less traditional than adolescents from poorer and more collectivist countries (Gibbons, Stiles, & Shkodriani, 1991).

Gibbons's study of Sri Lankan adolescents (de Silva et al., 1992) indicates that gender-role ideologies may be changing as societies undergo change. She found that more than half the girls in her study depicted the ideal woman as being employed outside the home, even though the traditional role of a Sri Lankan woman is that of homemaker. Mule and Barthel (1992) describe social change in Egypt, where there has been an increase in women's participation in the workforce and, to some extent, political life. Furthermore, globalization and exposure to Western culture have presented this traditionally Islamic country with alternative gender ideologies. Subsequently, gender-role ideologies may undergo modification or redefinition in these countries.

Nonetheless, maintaining, not modifying, traditional gender roles in the face of modernization is also likely. For instance, a study of Palestinian women and their families found that one's level of education, participation in political activities, and employment are not major factors predicting more egalitarian family roles (Huntington, Fronk, & Chadwick, 2001). The authors were surprised by this finding, and argue that cultural values, defined by Islamic beliefs and practices, are resisting the forces of modernity. In other words, Islamic teachings about women, the family, and relationships between men and women may be a powerful influence in maintaining traditional family functioning, and especially traditional ideas of women's roles in family and society. These findings highlight the important role of religion in understanding how gender-role ideologies are defined and preserved in different cultures.

Universality in gender-related stereotypes across cultures does not imply that all people of all cultures harbor those stereotypes to the same degree, or that they translate to exactly the same type of gender differences across cultures. Differences in the ecologies and environments in which people and cultures exist may lead to different ways in which the gender differences are manifested and expressed, a topic to which we turn next.

GENDER DIFFERENCES ACROSS CULTURES

Culture, biology, gender roles, and gender-role ideology all interact to produce differences between the genders on a variety of psychological and behavioral outcomes. That is, the division of labor and actual behaviors males and females engage in as a result of their biological and physiological differences help to produce a different psychology or mindset as well. These psychological differences between genders can be considered a product of the differences between males and females resulting at least partly because of the division of labor and behaviors surrounding reproduction.

Just as there will be psychological differences between males and females in any one culture, psychological differences can also be found across cultures. And the degree, direction, or exact nature of those gender differences may differ across cultures. That is, one culture may foster a certain type of gender difference, but another culture may not foster that difference to the same degree. A third culture may foster that difference even more than the first two cultures. Psychological gender differences across cultures are not simply products of biology and culture; they are also important reinforcers of culture, feeding back into the culture behaviors, gender roles, and gender-role ideologies. In this cyclical fashion, the psychological products of gender differentiation also become a crucial aspect of the culture–behavior–psychology linkage that exists among a people and their rituals, traditions, and behaviors.

Hofstede's Study

In Chapter 1, we discussed Hofstede's research on work-related attitudes across 50 countries. As you might remember, Hofstede (1980) conducted a large-scale survey of work-related values in a major multinational corporation. Based on the data obtained, he generated four dimensions of differentiation among the cultures in his sample. One of these dimensions was called "Masculinity versus Femininity." This dimension refers to the degree to which a culture will foster, encourage, or maintain differences between males and females. In Hofstede's research, Japan, Austria, Venezuela, and Italy had the highest masculinity scores, while Denmark, the Netherlands, Norway, and Sweden had the lowest scores.

Hofstede (2001) identified key differences between masculine and feminine cultures in terms of sexuality (Table 6.2). For instance, cultures high on masculinity tended to have moralistic attitudes about sex, had double standards about sex (i.e., women should be virgins at marriage but not men), and had norms encouraging passive roles of women. Cultures low on masculinity tend to have matter-of-fact attitudes about sex, a single standard concerning sex for men and women, and norms that encouraged an active role for women in society.

Masculine and feminine cultures also differed in their attitudes about religion. Masculine cultures tend to be more traditional, emphasize religion, and focus on God or gods. Feminine cultures tend to be less traditional, emphasize the importance of religion in life less, and focus on fellow humans.

Although Hofstede's study focused entirely on work-related values, his findings highlight a major point of this chapter—that cultures will vary in the ways they deal with differences between men and women. The behaviors men and women engage in produce different psychological outcomes that have

Table 6.2 | Key Differences between Low and High Masculine Societies Concerning Sexuality and Religion

Low Masculinity	High Masculinity
In Sexual Behavior	
Matter-of-fact attitudes about sex.	Moralistic attitudes about sex.
AIDS prevention campaigns very outspoken.	AIDS prevention campaigns restricted by taboos.
Single standard for women and men.	Double standard: Women should be chaste at marriage yet men needn't.
Norm of active role of woman.	Norm of passive role of woman.
Sexual attraction unrelated to career success.	Men become more attractive by career success, women less.
In uncertainty-accepting cultures, few teenage pregnancies.	In uncertainty-accepting cultures, frequent teenage pregnancies.
Young people more influenced by parents.	Young people more influenced by peers.
Other-oriented sex.	Ego-oriented sex.
Women enjoy first sex.	Women feel exploited by first sex.
Unwanted intimacies not major issue.	Sexual harassment major issue.
Homosexuality is a fact of life.	Homosexuality is a taboo and a threat.
Weak distinction between sex and love.	Sharp distinction between sex and love.
Sex and violence in media taboo.	Sex and violence in media frequent.
Lovers should be educated, social.	Lovers should be successful, attractive.
Happy lovers overbenefit from the other.	Happy lovers get equitable mutual deal.
Interaction with other sex more intimate.	Interaction with other sex less intimate.
Sex is a way of relating to someone.	Sex is a way of performing.
In Religion	
"Tender" religions and religious currents.	"Tough" religions and religious currents.
Secularization in Christian countries.	Maintenance of traditional Christianity.
Religion not so important in life.	Religion most important in life.
Religion focuses on fellow human beings.	Religion focuses on God or gods.
Children socialized toward responsibility and politeness.	Children socialized toward religious faith.
Exemplarism and mysticism.	Traditionalism, theism, and conversionism.
Dominant religions stress complementarity of the sexes.	Dominant religions stress male prerogative.
Men and women can be priests.	Only men can be priests.
Sex is for procreation and recreation.	Sex is primarily for procreation.
Positive or neutral attitude toward sexual pleasure.	Negative attitude toward sexual pleasure.
Sexuality as one area of human motivation.	Sexuality as primordial area of human motivation.

direct ramifications for actual life behaviors (such as work-related behaviors). Cultures vary in how they act on these gender differences, with some cultures fostering and encouraging great differences between the genders and other cultures minimizing those differences. It is precisely these cultural differences in gender roles that Hofstede's data on masculinity versus femininity address.

Perceptual/Spatial/Cognitive Differences

At least in American society, it is common folklore that males are better at mathematical and spatial reasoning tasks, whereas females are better at verbal comprehension tasks. An analysis of the scores for males and females on standardized tests in elementary school, college entrance examinations, and graduate-school entrance examinations shows some degree of support for these notions, although the difference between males and females seems to have narrowed in recent years. In their review of the literature, Maccoby and Jacklin (1974) also concluded that males tend to do better on spatial tasks and other tasks having a spatial component.

Years ago, however, Berry (1966) pointed out that such differences do not appear to exist among males and females of the Inuit culture in Canada. Berry suggested that the gender difference did not exist because "spatial abilities are highly adaptive for both males and females in Inuit society, and both boys and girls have ample training and experience that promote the acquisition of spatial ability" (Berry et al., 1992, p. 65).

Following up on the possibility of cultural differences on this gender difference, Berry (1976) conducted a study in which a block design task was given to males and females in 17 different cultures. A stimulus card depicting a geometric representation of a set of blocks was presented, and the task was to manipulate an actual set of blocks to emulate the design provided. The results were interesting and provocative. In a number of cultures, males indeed did better than females on the task; however, in other cultures, females did better than males. In interpreting these data, Berry et al. (1992) suggested that male superiority on the task tended to be found in cultures that were tight (that is, relatively homogeneous), sedentary, and agriculturally based, but that female superiority was found in cultures that were loose, nomadic, and based on hunting and gathering. In these latter cultures, the roles ascribed to males and females are relatively flexible, with more members performing a variety of tasks related to the survival of the group. Further research is needed to follow up these interpretations as hypotheses and investigate the exact nature of and reasons for the differences.

A similar finding was reported in a meta-analysis of the research literature by Born, Bleichrodt, and Van der Flier (1987). They reported that although no gender differences in overall intelligence were found, gender differences on various subtests of intelligence did occur. Although their findings leave open the question of the exact role of culture in creating or maintaining the gender difference, they do show that the differences in the cognitive test scores between males and females are variable across cultures. In another study (Pontius, 1997), the male advantage in spatial abilities was not found on two spatial tasks in eastern Ecuador, a culture that emphasizes women's traditional tasks, such as sewing and needlework, that require spatial representation.

Thus, some cultures foster male superiority in these types of tasks, but others foster female superiority, and still others foster no differences. Although some suggestions have been made as to the nature and causes of these various gender differences, research has yet to pinpoint exactly what factors influence which types of differences, and why. Future research will need to explore these and other issues regarding perceptual/spatial/analytic abilities. With the increasing pluralism of the world, this research will also need to be sensitive to the particular period during which the research is conducted, as differences may be decreasing in many societies and cultures today.

Conformity and Obedience

One of the most common gender-role stereotypes is that females are more conforming and obedient than males. This stereotype is no doubt related to the traditional gender roles females and males have occupied, with males traditionally being "head of the household," making primary decisions on big-ticket items that involve the family. In this traditional social arrangement, females were not to be concerned with authority and decision-making power; rather, the female role focused on caring for the children and managing the household affairs. In short, females were expected to conform to decisions imposed on them by males or by society in general.

The degree to which this difference is enacted varies considerably from culture to culture. In Berry's (1976) study, the researchers also obtained an index of the degree to which each person conformed in the 17 cultures included in the sample. Across the 17 cultures, clear variations emerged; as with gender differences in spatial reasoning, these variations appeared to be related to the cultural concept of tightness. Cultures that were tighter appeared to foster a greater gender difference on the issue of conformity, with females being more conformist than males; tight cultures may require a greater degree of conformity to traditional gender roles on the part of both males and females. In contrast, cultures that were looser fostered less gender difference on conformity, and in some of these cultures, males were found to be more conforming than females. Thus, traditional gender stereotypes of females as more conforming than males appear to have some validity, but considerable cross-cultural difference exists in the degree, and in some cases the direction, of this difference.

Future research needs to test these ideas further, examining the links between cultural variables such as tightness and psychological constructs such as conformity, and the degree to which gender differences on such constructs are fostered. Future research will also need to examine the degree to which gender differences on conformity are related to differences on perceptual, analytic, or spatial skills, or on other psychological traits and constructs such as aggressiveness.

Aggressiveness

Another common gender stereotype is that males are more aggressive than females. Indeed, there is support for this stereotype in all cultures for which documentation exists (Block, 1983; Brislin, 1993). Males account for a disproportionate amount of violent crime in both industrialized and non-industrialized societies. The focus in research on this topic has been adolescent males. Several researchers have searched for the biological correlates of aggression. In particular, some researchers have questioned whether increased levels of the hormone testosterone during male adolescence may account for or contribute to increased aggression in males. Increased testosterone levels have been associated with dominance hierarchies in some nonhuman primates, but the human analog is less clear. On the basis of the evidence available, it appears that hormones may contribute to aggressiveness to some degree, but culture and the environment can certainly act to encourage or discourage its emergence (Berry et al., 1992).

In fact, one study examining physical aggression between partners shed some light on this topic. In this study (Archer, 2006) male and female aggression toward their partners were examined in 52 countries. Both males and females committed acts of aggression toward their partners in developed, Westernized nations; but this did not generalize to all nations. The magnitude of the sex difference in physical aggression was related to levels of gender empowerment and individualism in each of the countries; cultures that were more individualistic and that empowered women more had less female victimization and more male victimization. Archer argued that these findings are best explained by social role theory (Eagley, 1987), which states that sex differences in social behavior result from the division of labor between women and men with regard to homemaker or worker outside the home. These roles, it is argued, produce expectancies that lead to different patterns of behavior in men and women, and these expectancies are transmitted across generations; that is, they are a part of culture. Expectancies associated with the male role include the use of direct aggression to resolve problems; expectancies associated with female roles include communal responses to resolve problems.

Studies of sex differences in development across cultures support these ideas. A study by Barry, Josephson, Lauer, and Marshall (1976), for instance, examined the degree to which cultures foster aggressive tendencies in the socialization of children. These researchers found a sex-related difference in the average amount of teaching about aggressiveness across 150 different cultures. Inspection of their data, however, reveals that this average difference was produced by a disproportionate number of high-scoring cultures in which teaching aggression actually occurs. In fact, a large majority of societies did not show a sex-related difference in teaching aggression.

Such interpretations have been bolstered by anthropological studies of some cultures known for their aggressive tendencies. Among these is the Yanomami culture of Venezuela and Brazil (see, for example, Sponsel, 1998), often referred to in anthropological circles as the "fierce people." Yet even with regard to these supposedly aggressive groups, more recent research and discussion have begun to call into question the potential bias in anthropological and comparative methods that may see only part of the culture (Sponsel, 1998). Such concerns affect cross-cultural research as well, bringing into question the specific definitions and measurements of aggressiveness and their degree of sensitivity to a variety of contexts.

Neither biology nor sex differences in teaching aggressive acts can account for gender differences in aggression observed across cultures. Some researchers (Berry et al., 1992; Segall, Dasen, Berry, & Poortinga, 1990) offer yet another possible explanation for gender differences in aggression across cultures. They suggest that male aggression may be a compensatory mechanism to offset the conflict produced by a young male's identification with a female care provider and his initiation into adulthood as a male. In this model, aggressiveness is viewed as "gender marking" behavior.

Regardless of the precise mechanisms that produce gender differences in aggression, it is clear that although the gender stereotype of aggressiveness may be generally true, considerable differences do exist across cultures. What is true for one culture may not be true for another. Future research needs to examine the exact mechanisms accounting for these differences, taking into account the complex interplay among biology, culture, and psychology. This research will need to be sensitive to the context specificity of aggressive acts, and the influence of the research method and data collection itself on the reporting or acting out of aggression.

Gender Roles

Although the studies by Williams and Best described above documented the universality of the existence and content of gender-related roles, stereotypes, and ideologies, they also showed how those constructs differed across cultures. Cultures that were more egalitarian, more affluent, individualistic, and Christian-based were more likely to have smaller degrees of differences between stereotypes concerning men and women.

Research within countries also point to important differences, especially among different ethnic groups. Some research, for instance, has suggested that the gender identities of African Americans are more androgynous than those of European Americans. **Androgyny** refers to a gender identity that involves endorsement of both male and female characteristics. Harris (1996), for example, administered the Bem Sex Role Inventory, a scale that is widely used to measure gender identity, to African American and European American males and females, and found that both African American males and females were more androgynous than European American males and females. In addition, he found that African American males and females have an equal propensity to endorse typically masculine traits, whereas European American males regard more masculine traits as self-descriptive than European American females do. Other studies conducted in the United States (Frome & Eccles, 1996), Israel (Orr & Ben-Eliahu, 1993), and Hong Kong (Lau, 1989) have found that adolescent girls who adopt an androgynous identity have higher levels of self-acceptance than either feminine or masculine girls. For boys, however, a masculine, not androgynous, identity is associated with the highest level of self-acceptance.

Many Asian American families have carried on traditional gender roles associated with males and females from their original culture. Asian American females are often expected to bear the brunt of domestic duties, to raise children, and to be "good" daughters-in-law. Asian American males are often raised to remain aloof, unemotional, and authoritative, especially concerning familial issues (D. Sue, 1998). Some studies, however, have suggested a loosening of these rigid, traditional gender roles for Asian American males and females. Although Asian American males may still appear as figurative head of the family in public, in reality much decision-making power within the family in private is held by the Asian American female head of the household (Huang & Ying, 1989).

As with Asian American gender roles, the traditional role of the Mexican American female was to provide for the children and take care of the home (Comas-Diaz, 1992). Likewise, Mexican American males were traditionally expected to fill the role of provider for the family. These differences are related to the concept of **machismo**, which incorporates many traditional expectations of the male gender role, such as being unemotional, strong, authoritative, aggressive, and masculine (see Table 6.1). However, more recent research has shown that these gender differences for Mexican American males and females are also on the decrease. Mexican American women are increasingly sharing in decision making in the family, as well as taking on a more direct role as provider by working outside the home (Espin, 1993). Although adolescent Mexican American males are generally still given more freedom outside the home than are females, gender differences may be decreasing in the contemporary Mexican American family. This is likely to continue, as increasing numbers of Latina women are employed and a Latina feminist movement has emerged (Espin, 1997). It is important to note, however, that this movement continues to place high value on the traditional emphasis of the role of wife and mother, yet offers a wider interpretation of roles acceptable for Latinas.

Gender-role differentiation for Native Americans seems to depend heavily on the patriarchal or matriarchal nature of the tribal culture of origin. In patriarchal tribes, women assume primary responsibility for the welfare of the children and extended family members. But males of the Mescalero Apache tribe often take responsibility for children when they are with their families (Glover, 2001). As with other ethnic groups, the passage of time, increased interaction with people of other cultures and with mainstream American culture, and the movement toward urban areas seems to have effected changes in these traditional values and expectations for Native American males and females.

Sex and Sexuality

It is really not surprising to find that there are major cultural differences in the degree of importance placed on values concerning chastity, especially for women. Many traditional, conservative cultures of the world view chastity as a virtue among unmarried women. Other cultures are more open and explicit about sex, approving and even encouraging multiple sexual partners before marriage. This is, in fact, one of the areas of contention between capitalistic societies found in the United States and western Europe with those of predominantly Muslim countries in North Africa and the Middle East, as changing values, attitudes, and behaviors concerning sex are often attributed as the "fault" of countries like the United States.

Not surprisingly, cultural differences in attitudes related to sex are also related to cultural differences in attitudes related to sexuality. Many traditional cultures view homosexuality as a curse or worse. These kinds of attitudes exist in many quarters of very egalitarian cultures, like the United States, as well. In some cultures, openly homosexual persons may be beaten, publicly humiliated and shamed, and even persecuted by the state. Attitudes concerning sex and sexuality are often linked with cultural values of honor, and transgressions— that is, premarital sex or homosexuality—can be seen as an injury to one's own or one's family's honor, and a disgrace, with sometimes deadly consequences.

Culture affects the practice of circumcision for males, and female genital mutilation (FGM) for females. The latter is a procedure that involves partial or complete removal of female genitalia or other injury to the female genital organs for nontherapeutic reasons (Organization, 1997). FGM is still practiced in some African, Middle Eastern, Asian, South American, and Pacific cultures. It can be carried out in settings as wide ranging as sterile, operating rooms in hospitals to homes with no anesthesia, antiseptics, antibiotics, or analgesics (Barstow, 1999). In many cultures in which FGM is practiced, it has traditional ties with attitudes concerning virtuousness, chastity, and honor for women. It is also considered a way to promote marital fidelity, control women's sex drives, and even to enhance fertility among women (Whitehorn, Ayonrinde, & Maingay, 2002). These kinds of attitudes were used in part to justify the enforcement of passive gender roles on women, much like the practice of foot binding in China.

The practice of FGM is associated with many complex issues. On the one hand, there appears to be no apparent health benefit to the practice, and in fact studies have demonstrated many health problems associated with it, including death, infertility, urinary-tract infection, and the like. As a result, many people in many affluent and more-egalitarian cultures view the practice as barbaric and outdated. On the other hand, the practice is tied with honor and virtue, and for many women in many cultures, not having FGM would prevent a woman from finding a husband, or to live life as a social outcast. For instance, a recent study of Egyptian female student nurses found that approximately 60 percent favored circumcising their own daughters and thought it beneficial (Dandash, Refaat, & Eyada, 2001). The clash of cultures brought about by immigration and improved communications technology has these issues at the forefront for many in the world today (more below).

Mate Selection, Mate Poaching, and Jealousy

In Chapter 14, we will discuss universal differences between men and women in their preferences for mates, and in the process of mate poaching—attempting to steal other's mates. These differences are typically explained using an evolutionary model that suggests that males look for younger, chaste mates to bear offspring, while females look for mates that can provide for offspring in the long term.

One important construct related to these concepts is fidelity of a mate. Research on sexual jealousy has demonstrated interesting gender differences in jealousy that appear to be universal (Buss & Schmitt, 1993; Fernandez, Sierra, Zubeidat, & Vera-Villarroel, 2006). This research has focused on two types of infidelity, sexual and emotional. Sexual infidelity occurs when a partner has sex or engages in sex-related behaviors with others. Emotional infidelity refers to the formation of an emotional bond with other people. Although both types of infidelity bring about feelings of jealousy in both men and women, studies have shown that males are relatively more jealous about sexual infidelity, while females are relatively more jealous of emotional infidelity. These findings have also been related to evolutionary theory. A woman sleeping with others threaten a man's ability to create offspring, or places him in the position of caring for someone else's offspring; men falling in love with other women threaten a woman's family and her offspring because the man may not be around to care for or provide for his offspring.

Personality

In Chapter 10, we will discuss how recent cross-cultural studies have documented the universal existence of a Five-Factor Model of Personality (McCrae & Costa, 1999). This theory suggests that five personality traits—Neuroticism, Extroversion, Agreeableness, Openness to Experience, and Conscientiousness—exist universally and can describe most human dispositions for behavior. In one study examining gender differences in personality traits around the world, Costa, Terracciano, and McCrae (2001) analyzed data obtained from 23,031 respondents in 26 cultures, and tested for gender differences on the five universal personality traits and their subfacets (each of the five personality traits are associated with six subfacets). They found that women universally reported higher scores on Neuroticism, Agreeableness, Warmth, and Openness to Feelings, while men scored higher on Assertiveness and Openness to Ideas. Interestingly, the differences between men and women were the largest in Europe and the United States, which typically promote more individualistic and egalitarian values. Studies have not yet followed up why this might be so.

Summary

There is little doubt that gender differences exist on a wide variety of psychological constructs, and that cultures differ in the exact degree and nature of those gender differences. Some research has examined how such culture and gender differences come to manifest themselves. Dasgupta (1998), for example, examined the relationship between ethnic identity and two scales related to women and dating among Asian Indian immigrants in the United States, and found a strong similarity between parents and children on many target attitudes. This finding provides evidence for the important role parents play as enculturation agents in maintaining traditional cultural values, including gender differences.

Another study (Glick, Lameiras, Fiske, Eckes, Masser, et al., 2004) also shed interesting light on this topic. In this study, 8,360 participants from 16 cultures responded to a questionnaire that assessed hostile and benevolent attitudes toward men. When people harbor both types of attitudes toward men at high degrees, they were labeled ambivalent. Ambivalent attitudes toward men were related to the degree of gender inequality in a country; that is, the more people in a country saw men as both hostile and benevolent, the greater the degree of gender inequality in the country. These findings suggested that gender inequality in a country may start with how the people view the role of men. (Women were rated more positively than men in all cultures.)

So how does culture influence gender? The process of learning gender roles begins very early in life. The importance of gender in organizing our expectations and thinking is illustrated in the first question that we ask when a baby is born: "Is it a boy or a girl?" In American culture, we tend to give boys and girls different types of toys to play with, and dress infants according to gender (although that may be changing). If you look back to your baby pictures, you may find that you were often dressed in either blue or pink. About 20 years ago, one U.S. study reported that 90 percent of the infants observed at a shopping mall were dressed in gendered colors and/or styles (Shakin, Shakin, & Sternglanz, 1985). By the age of 3, children begin to accurately label people by sex (Fagot, Leinbach, & Hagen, 1986). Gender-role socialization continues throughout life from various sources—expectations from parents, modeling of gender roles by peers, and images of males and females in the media, to name a few—that contribute to our ideas on what it means to be male or female.

In terms of the definitions presented earlier, a newborn has sex but no gender. Gender is a construct that develops in children as they are socialized in their environments. As children grow older, they learn specific behaviors and patterns of activities appropriate and inappropriate for their sex, and they either adopt or reject those gender roles. Sandra Bem (1981), a prominent theorist on gender, argues that gender is one of the fundamental ways we organize information and understand experiences about the world. For instance, we learn what behaviors, attitudes, objects, and conventions are associated with being "male" and what are associated with being "female," and apply these gender schemas to understand the people around us as well as ourselves.

Ensuring that reproduction occurs fulfills men's and women's sex roles. But what happens before and after that depends on a host of variables. One of these variables is culture. The biological fact and necessity of reproduction, along with other biological and physiological differences between men and women, lead to behavioral differences between men and women. In earlier days, these behavioral differences were no doubt reinforced by a necessary division of labor. Someone had to look after children while someone else had to find food for the family; no one person could have done it all. Thus, the existence of reproductive differences led to a division of labor advantageous to the family as a unit. These differences, in turn, produced differences in a variety of psychological traits and characteristics, such as aggressiveness, nurturance, and achievement.

As different societies live in different environments, survival requires that they balance a number of factors, including natural resources, affluence, and population density. These external factors help to frame and mold specific behaviors that may affect the division of labor between men and women originally necessitated by biological differences. These differential behaviors that occur because of differences in external, environmental factors lead to patterns of behaviors across time that are associated with men and women. This pattern of behaviors across time, of course, is culture. In turn, it feeds back reciprocally onto the pattern of behaviors, reinforcing behaviors, beliefs, attitudes, and values. Thus, as different cultures must deal with different external factors, it is only natural that gender differences vary by culture. One culture may foster considerable equality between women and men and relatively few differences in their cultural practices and psychological characteristics. Another culture may foster considerable differences between the sexes, their cultural practices related to reproduction, and psychological characteristics associated with sex roles. Some cultures may foster differences between the sexes in one direction (for example, males as primary decision makers, females compliant and obedient); another culture may foster differences in the opposite direction. This type of explanatory model may account for the range of differences obtained in previous cross-cultural research on psychological constructs.

Yet the evidence (see below) also suggests that stereotypes and attitudes concerning gender differences are relatively constant across cultures, despite actual differences in psychological behaviors brought about by real differences in demands placed on cultures and societies by their environment. Some researchers, in fact, go as far as to say that the persistence of gender stereotypes across culture cannot be attributed to sociocultural factors and can only be explained by sociobiological models (Lueptow, Garovich, & Lueptow, 1995).

Future research will need to tackle the important questions posed by this theoretical understanding of cultural and gender differences, elucidating on the mechanisms and factors that help produce and maintain those differences in individual cultures, and then across cultures. In addition, future research will need to explore the relationship between differences in actual behaviors and psychological constructs and gender-related stereotypes, investigating whether these are two different psychological systems of the mind or whether they are linked in ways that are not yet apparent. Indeed, research to date is rather silent on the mechanisms that produce gender and cultural differences, and the interrelationship among different psychological processes. The important point to remember is that different cultures may arrive at different outcomes through the same process. Men and women will have gender-specific roles in any society or culture. All cultures encourage particular behavioral differences between the genders and help to define the roles, duties, and responsibilities appropriate for males and females.

CHANGING CULTURES, CHANGING GENDER ROLES

Changing cultures, and the clash of cultures brought about by immigration, brings many of the issues discussed in this chapter to the forefront of many people's lives. In many cases they represent an interesting and complex interplay between culture, psychology, and law (Shweder, Minow, & Markus, 2002).

For instance, among the most pressing issues and concerns facing the United States today are gender differences across different ethnicities and the continuing struggle for gender equity across all cultural and ethnic groups. Just as people in different cultures in faraway lands may have different gender roles and expectations, people of different ethnic backgrounds in the United States can have different gender-role expectations as well. Many of these gender differences across ethnic lines are rooted in the cultures people of these ethnicities brought with them when they originally came to the United States. But gender differences in the United States today definitely reflect an "American" influence, making gender issues unique in American culture.

How is one to deal with the social isolation, physical beating, and even murder of young women that would be justified in another culture because of perceived dishonor brought about by premarital sex? What should be the response of communities and societies toward female genital mutilation, especially when condoned by the perpetrators and recipients? How can democracies deal with acts that they condemn in their laws while at the same time being open and embracing of cultural differences? These are tough questions that all of us have to face in today's pluralistic world.

Clearly, as we have mentioned throughout this book, culture is not a static entity; it is dynamic and ever changing. Cultural changes are brought about by many factors, especially economic. Witness the great cultural changes that have occurred in many countries of the world since the end of World War II. Japan, for instance, was decimated at the end of that war; yet, today it stands as one of the world's economic powers. Such changes bring with them a major change in the culture of the society, and we are witness to such changes in Japan today (Matsumoto, 2002).

Many of the cultural changes that are brought by economics give rise to tensions between tradition and progress, conservatism and liberalism. Images capture these tensions: watching young women in Japan dressed in traditional

Japanese *kimono* as they observe a centuries-old tradition of coming-of-age (*seijin-shiki*) while talking and sending instant messages on their cell phones as they ride the fastest trains in the world produce a stark contrast between tradition and progress, just as young adults in the Middle East may on one hand condemn the United States, yet on the other be willing to obtain a visa and immigrate to the United States.

Changing and clashing cultures bring about many confrontations between gender differences across culture. Changing culture in Japan and around the world, for example, that are associated with increased economic power, affluence, and individualism are associated with changing gender roles. More women work outside the home, are more economically independent, and have a greater say at home and at work. Yet there are social consequences of such cultural changes; in such cultures, divorce rates increase (Matsumoto, 2002; Yodanis, 2005); the amount and type of health-related problems for women increase, such as increased incidence of cardiovascular problems, alcoholism, and rates of smoking (Allamani, Voller, Kubicka, & Bloomfield, 2000). Changes in culture, therefore, have both positive and negative consequences, and full consideration should be given before weighing in on the pros and cons of such changes.

CONCLUSION

Sex refers to the biological and physiological differences between males and females. *Sex roles* are behaviors expected of males and females in relation to their biological differences and reproduction. *Gender* refers to the psychological and behavioral traits and characteristics cultures carve out using sex differences as a base. *Gender roles* refer to the degree to which a person adopts the gender-specific behaviors ascribed by his or her culture. Gender and its permutations—roles, identities, stereotypes, and the like—share an important link with culture.

Gender roles are different for males and females in all cultures. Some stereotypic notions about gender differences seem to be universal across cultures, such as aggressiveness, strength, and lack of emotionality for males, and weakness, submissiveness, and emotionality for females. Other research, however, has shown that the degree, and in some case the direction, of these differences varies across cultures. That is, not every culture will necessarily harbor the same gender differences in the same way as other cultures. Further research is needed to gain a better understanding of culture-constant and culture-specific aspects of gender differences.

Examining gender differences in the United States is especially challenging because of the cultural and ethnic diversity within this single country and the influence of interactions with mainstream American culture. Each ethnic group has its own cultural preferences for gender differentiation, but some blending of the old with the new, the traditional with the modern, appears to be taking place. Without evidence to the contrary, it is probably best to consider this blending as an addition of different cultural repertoires concerning gender differences rather than a subtraction from the old ways.

As we meet people from different cultural backgrounds, we may encounter gender roles that are different from our own. Often, we feel strongly and negatively about these differences. Yet despite our own personal outlook, we must exercise considerable care and caution in imposing our preferences on others. In most cases, people of other cultures feel just as strongly about their own way of living. Many people of many other cultures, particularly women, still harbor many of the traditional values of their ancestral culture, and we have seen conflicts arise because Americans—men and women alike—look down on these traditional ways, criticize them, and attempt to force change. Many women in many cultures want to marry early, stay home, and take care of the family; many men want to adopt the traditional male roles as well. These tendencies are alive in many different people within the most egalitarian cultures and societies, including the United States. We need to respect these differences, rather than attempt to change them because they are not consonant with our own individual or cultural preferences. Still, this is a delicate balancing act for all of us, because there is a fine line between cultural relativity (a desired state of comprehension) and the unacceptable justification of oppression.

GLOSSARY

androgyny A gender identity that involves endorsement of both male and female characteristics.

gender The behaviors or patterns of activities a society or culture deems appropriate for men and women. These behavioral patterns may or may not be related to sex and sex roles, although they often are.

gender identity The degree to which a person has awareness of or recognition that he or she has adopted a particular gender role.

gender role The degree to which a person adopts the gender-specific behaviors ascribed by his or her culture.

gender-role ideology Judgments about what gender roles in a particular culture ought to be.

gender stereotype The psychological or behavioral characteristics typically associated with men and women.

machismo A concept related to Mexican American gender role differentiation that is characterized by many traditional expectations of the male gender role, such as being unemotional, strong, authoritative, aggressive, and masculine.

sex The biological and physiological differences between men and women, the most obvious being the anatomical differences in their reproductive systems.

sex roles The behaviors and patterns of activities men and women may engage in that are directly related to their biological differences and the process of reproduction.

sexual identity The degree of awareness and recognition by an individual of his or her sex and sex roles.

7 CHAPTER | Culture and Health

CHAPTER CONTENTS

One major role of psychology is to improve the lives of the people we touch. Whether through research, service, or provision of primary or secondary health care, we look forward to the day when we can adequately diagnose and treat medical diseases, prevent abnormal behavior, and foster positive states of being in balance with others and the environment. This is not an easy task; a multitude of forces influences our health and our ability to prevent and treat illness.

As we strive to meet this challenge, the important role of culture in contributing to the etiology, maintenance, and treatment of disease has become increasingly clear. Although our goals of prevention and treatment of disease and maintenance of health may be the same across cultures, cultures vary in their definitions of what is considered "healthy" or "mature" (Tseng & McDermott, 1981). Cultural differences also exist in perceptions of problems and in preferred strategies for coping with them (Terrell, 1992). Our job is made more difficult because cultural beliefs and practices influence treatment, and they shape both the therapist's and the client's definitions and understandings of the problem (Berry, Poortinga, Segall, & Dasen, 1992). Traditional approaches to treatment of abnormal behavior may prove insensitive or inappropriate when applied across cultures.

This chapter explores how cultural factors influence physical health and disease processes, and our attempts to treat them. We begin with an examination of cultural differences in the definition of health, and then explore cultural differences in conceptions of the body. We then review the considerable amount of research concerning the relationship between culture and heart disease, other physical disease processes, eating disorders, and suicide. We will also explore the way cultural differences influence help seeking, treatment compliance, and issues of responsibility, trust, and self-control over personal health and disease processes. We will summarize the research in the form of a model, then use this information to consider ways of developing culturally relevant, sensitive, and effective treatment programs.

CULTURAL DIFFERENCES IN THE DEFINITION OF HEALTH

Before we look at how culture influences health and disease processes, we need to examine exactly what we mean by health. More than 50 years ago, the World Health Organization (WHO) developed a definition at the International Health Conference, at which 61 countries were represented. They defined health as "a state of complete physical, mental, and social well-being, and not merely the absence of disease or infirmity" (World Health Organization, 1948).

In the United States, our views of health have been heavily influenced by what many call the **biomedical model** of health and disease. This model views disease as resulting from a specific, identifiable cause originating inside the body. These causes, whether viral, bacterial, or other, are referred to as **pathogens** and are seen as the root of all physical and medical diseases. Cardiovascular disease, for example, has been linked to specific pathogens such as clotting from lipids and cholesterol. The biomedical model of disease has also influenced psychology's view of abnormal behavior and psychopathology. Traditional psychological approaches view the origin of abnormal behaviors as residing within the person. Such abnormalities may result from lack of gratification or over-gratification of basic, instinctual processes (as suggested by Freudian psychoanalytic theory) or from learned responses (as suggested by classical or operant conditioning).

The traditional biomedical model of health in both medicine and psychology has had a profound influence on treatment approaches. If specific medical or psychobehavioral pathogens exist within a person's body, those pathogens must be dealt with when treating disease. Medical treatment and traditional psychological approaches focus on making an intervention within a person. In the traditional biomedical model, health is characterized as the lack of disease. If a person remains free of disease, the person is considered healthy.

Views from other cultures suggest different definitions of health. People of China and ancient Greece, for example, viewed health not only as the absence of negative states but also as the presence of positive ones. Balance between self and nature and across the individual's various roles in life is viewed as an integral part of health in many Asian cultures. This balance can produce a positive state—a synergy of the forces of self, nature, and others—that many call health. Alternative views of health that incorporate the presence of positive as well as the absence of negative states are important in many cultures today.

In China, the concept of health, based on Chinese religion and philosophy, focuses on the principles of *yin* and *yang,* which represent negative and positive energies, respectively. The Chinese believe that our bodies are made up of elements of *yin* and *yang.* Balance between these two forces results in good health; an imbalance—too much *yin* or too much *yang*—leads to poor health. Many things can disturb this balance, such as eating too many foods from one of the elements; a change in social relationships, the weather, the seasons; or even supernatural forces. Maintaining a balance involves not only the mind and body, but also the spirit and the natural environment. From the Chinese perspective, the concept of health is not confined to the individual but encompasses the surrounding relationships and environment (Yip, 2005).

Incorporating balance as a positive aspect of health is not foreign in the United States today. In the past decade or two, we have seen a rising frustration with defining health solely as the absence of disease. Americans have become much more aware of how lifestyle factors can contribute not only to the absence of negative states but also to the presence of positive ones. In particular, the concept of **hardiness** has been used in recent years in contemporary psychology to denote not only a lack of disease but the presence of positive health states. Biobehavioral medicine and health psychology, nonexistent even a few years ago, represent responses by the health care and academic professions to a growing interest in definitions of health different from those afforded by the traditional biomedical model. We now know that many of the leading causes of death and disease are directly and indirectly attributable to lifestyle choices and unhealthy behaviors (Schneiderman, 2004), many of which will be explored in the remainder of this chapter. These findings contribute to our growing knowledge of the impact of behavior on health. And because behavior is heavily influenced by culture, an increased awareness of the links among health, lifestyle, and behavior can help us understand the sociocultural influences on health and disease.

Concepts of health may differ not only between cultures but also within a pluralistic culture such as the United States or Canada. Mulatu and Berry (2001) point out that health perspectives may differ between individuals from the dominant or mainstream culture and those of the nondominant social and ethnocultural group. They cite the example of Native Americans, who, based on their religion, have a holistic view of health and who consider good health to be living in harmony with oneself and one's environment. When one does not live in harmony and engages in negative behaviors such as "displeasing the holy people of the past or the present, disturbing animal and plant life, misuse of sacred religious ceremonies, strong and uncontrolled emotions, and breaking social rules and taboos" (p. 219), the result is ill health. This is in sharp contrast to the biomedical model, in which illnesses are thought to originate from viruses and bacteria.

Huff (1999) likewise argues that the concepts of health held by various ethnic and immigrant groups within the United States may differ from and even contradict the health concepts of the mainstream society. This may create problems in the identification and treatment of illnesses, as discussed later in the chapter. However, mainstream culture is also adapting and incorporating ideas of health that immigrants have brought with them, as seen in the rising popularity and interest in alternative health practices such as acupuncture, homeopathy, herbal medicines, and spiritual healing (Brodsky & Hui, 2006). Indeed, there is a growing field called Complementary and Alternative Medicine (CAM) that incorporates medical and health care systems and practices that are not considered conventional medicine to treat illness and promote health. Thus, our own views on health are changing as our culture becomes increasingly pluralistic.

CULTURE AND CONCEPTIONS OF THE BODY

Cultures differ in how they view the human body. These different conceptions of the human body influence how people of different cultures approach health and disease, treatment, and perhaps even the types of diseases that affect them.

MacLachlan (1997) has suggested that cultures have different metaphors for how they conceptualize the human body. The most widely held view, according to MacLachlan, involves the notion of balance and imbalance in the body: The various systems of the body produce harmony or health when in balance, illness and disease when in imbalance. A theory first developed by Hippocrates, which heavily influences views of the human body and disease in most industrialized countries and cultures today, suggests that the body is comprised of four humors: blood, phlegm, yellow bile, and black bile. Too much or too little of any of these throws the body out of balance, resulting in disease. Derivatives of these terms—such as sanguine, phlegmatic, and choleric—are widely used in health and medical circles today.

MacLachlan (1997) points out that common theories of disease in many Latin American cultures involve a balance between hot and cold. These terms do not refer to temperature, but to the intrinsic power of different substances in the body. Some illnesses or states are hot, others cold. A person who is in a hot condition is given cold foods to counteract the situation, and vice versa. The Chinese concept of *yin* and *yang* shows similarities to this concept.

Social and cultural factors play a major role in the perception of one's own and others' body shapes, and these perceptions influence the relationship between culture and health. For example, a number of studies have found an inverse relationship between social class and body weight in many American and European cultures; that is, individuals of higher social class generally have lower body weights than individuals of lower social class (reviewed in Furnham & Alibhai, 1983). The inverse, however, is true in many other cultures. And it has also been shown that the longer some immigrants have lived in traditionally Western cultures, the more their ideal body shape changes to one that is thinner. For instance, Furnham and Alibhai (1983) examined how Kenyan Asian, British, and Kenyan British females perceived female body shapes. In their study, participants were shown drawings of women ranging from extremely anorexic to extremely obese, and were asked to rate each on a series of bipolar adjectives. The results indicated that the Kenyan Asians rated larger figures more favorably and smaller figures less favorably than did the British, as predicted. The perceptions of the Kenyan British were similar to those of the British.

A later study by Furnham, Moutafi, and Baguma (2002) also confirmed the role of culture in the perception of body shape. In this study, British, Greek, and Ugandan students rated drawings of female figures. Again, the figures ranged from extremely anorexic to extremely obese. The results showed cultural differences on body shape preferences, with Ugandans rating the heavier figures as more attractive and the British and Greeks rating the thinner figures as more attractive. Other studies have documented cultural differences in body-shape preferences among ethnic groups in the United States. In one study African American male college students preferred heavier female body shapes while European American male college students preferred thinner female body shapes (Freedman, Carter, Sbrocco, & Gray, 2004). These findings point to the important role of culture and cultural stereotypes in the perception and evaluation of body shapes, which in turn has implications for health and disease processes. Future research will need to establish the links between these types of perceptions and actual health-related behaviors, in order to document the degree to which these perceptions influence health and disease processes.

SOCIOCULTURAL INFLUENCES ON PHYSICAL HEALTH AND MEDICAL DISEASE PROCESSES

Psychosocial Determinants of Health and Disease

In the past few years, psychology as a whole has becoming increasingly aware of the important role that culture may play in the maintenance of health and the production of disease processes. This awareness can be seen on many levels, from more journal articles published on these topics to the establishment of new journals devoted to this area of research. This increased awareness is related to a growing concern with psychosocial determinants of health and illness in general.

Scholars have long been interested in the close relationship between mental and physical health. Research linking Type A personality patterns and cardiovascular disease is a good example of this area of study. As most people are aware, research originally conducted three decades ago showed that individuals who were pressed for time; always in a rush, agitated, and irritable; and always on the go—characterized as Type A personality syndrome—appeared to be at greater risk for cardiovascular disease and heart attacks than non–Type A personalities. This linkage was important not only in informing us about the etiology and possible prevention of cardiovascular disease; it also opened the door to examining the close relationship between psychology and physiology—the field we now know as health psychology.

A number of important and interesting studies have documented the linkage between psychosocial factors and health/disease states. Steptoe and his colleagues (Steptoe, Sutcliffe, Allen, & Coombes, 1991; Steptoe & Wardle, 1994) have reviewed many of the previous studies, highlighting the links between unemployment and mortality, cardiovascular disease, and cancer; between goal frustration and negative life events and gastrointestinal disorders; between stress and myocardial ischemias and the common cold; between bereavement and lymphocyte functions; between pessimistic explanatory styles and physical illnesses; and between hardiness and physical illnesses, among others. Indeed, the field has come a long way beyond Type A personality patterns and cardiovascular disease in demonstrating the close relationship between psychosocial factors and health/disease outcomes.

Adler and her colleagues (1994) have reported that socioeconomic status (SES) is consistently associated with health outcomes, with people of higher SES enjoying better health than do people of lower SES, see Figure 7.1. This relationship has been found not only for mortality rates, but for almost every disease and condition studied. Adler and colleagues suggest that health-related behaviors such as smoking, physical activity, and alcohol use may explain the relation between SES and health, as these variables appear to be related to SES. In addition, psychological characteristics such as depression, hostility, stress, and social ordering—one's relative position in the SES hierarchy—may also explain the relationship between SES and health, because each of these variables appears to be related to SES. Interestingly, one's subjective *perception* of SES appears to better predict health and change in health rather than an objective assessment of SES (Singh-Manoux, Marmot, & Adler, 2006).

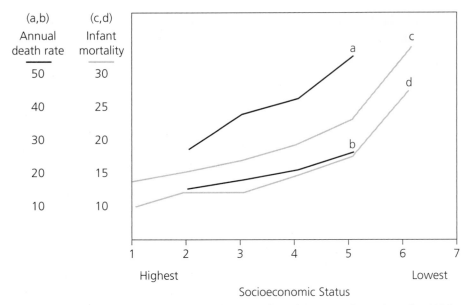

Note: (a) Annual death rate per 1,000 male (Feldman, Makuc, Kleinman, & Cornoni-Huntley, 1989), (b) Annual death rate per 1,000 female (Feldman et al., 1989), (c) Infant mortality per 1,000 live births male (Susser, Watson, & Hopper, 1985), (d) Infant mortality per 1,000 live births female (Susser et al., 1985).

Figure 7.1 | Mortality Rate by Socioeconomic Status Level

Adler, N. E., T. Boyce, M. A. Chesney, S. Cohen, S. Folkman, R. L. Kahn, and S. L. Syme. Socioeconomic Status and Health: The Challenge of the Gradient, *American Psychologist*, vol. 49, no. 1, pp. 15–24, 1994. Copyright © American Psychological Association. Adapted with author permission.

More recent studies have proposed that other psychosocial factors, such as perceived racism and discrimination contribute to negative health outcomes such as hypertension and cardiovascular disease (Brondolo, Rieppi, Kelly, & Gerin, 2003; Krieger, 1999). One study found that African American women were physiologically more stressed when encountering perceived racism than European American women (Lepore et al., 2005). In this study women were given three hypothetical scenarios to talk about: (a) being accused of shoplifting (racial stressor), (b) experiencing airport delays (nonracial stressor), and (c) giving a campus tour (control). The results showed that African American women had significantly greater mean diastolic blood pressure reactivity than European American women when talking about the racial stressor scenario. The authors concluded that perceived racism contributes to greater physiological stress for African American women, leading to poorer physical health.

Research of the past two decades has demonstrated convincingly that psychosocial factors play an important role in maintaining and promoting health, and in the etiology and treatment of disease. Still, many avenues remain open for future research, including establishing direct links between particular psychosocial factors and specific disease outcomes, and identifying the specific mechanisms that mediate those relationships. Hopefully, research of the next two decades will be as fruitful as that of the past two decades in providing much-needed knowledge about these processes.

Beyond looking at psychosocial factors, many scholars and health care practitioners alike have long been interested in the contribution of sociocultural factors to health. A number of important studies have shown how culture may play a major role in the development and treatment of illness. These studies, to be reviewed in this chapter, destroy the common notion that physical illness has nothing to do with sociocultural or psychological factors, and vice versa. Indeed, they contribute to our combined knowledge of psychological factors in physical disease processes. Changes in lifestyle (for example, in diet, smoking, exercise, and alcohol consumption) can be seen as our response to this increasing recognition of the complex interrelationship among culture, psychology, and medical processes.

Social Isolation and Mortality

Some of the earliest research on sociocultural factors in health and disease processes examined the relationship between social isolation or social support and death. Earlier research had highlighted the potential negative effects of social isolation and social disadvantage on health and disease (Feist & Brannon, 1988). One of the best-known studies in this area is the Alameda County study (Berkman & Syme, 1979), named after the county in California where the data were collected and the study conducted. Researchers interviewed almost 7,000 individuals to discover their degree of social contact; the final data set included approximately 4,725 people, as some people were dropped from the study. Following the initial assessment interview, deaths were monitored over a nine-year period. The results were clear for both men and women: Individuals with the fewest social ties suffered the highest mortality rate, and people with the most social ties had the lowest rate. These findings were valid even when other factors were statistically or methodologically controlled, including the level of physical health reported at the time of the initial questionnaire, the year of death, SES, and a number of health-related behaviors (such as smoking and alcohol consumption).

These findings become more poignant when one considers recent evidence that intimate social contact among individuals in the United States has declined in the past two decades (McPherson, Smith-Lovin, & Brashears, 2006). This nationally representative study reported the number of confidants that people turned to for discussion of important matters. In 1985, the most common response was having at least three confidants. In 2004, however, the most common response was having no one. The authors report that "The American population has lost discussion partners from both kin and outside the family. The largest losses, though, come from neighborhood and community ties" (p. 371). Thus, it appears that in the United States, social networks are shrinking and there is an increased risk of becoming socially isolated. As the study in Alameda County demonstrated, this has many negative implications for one's health and well-being.

The Alameda County study was one of the first to demonstrate clearly the enormous role that sociocultural factors may play in the maintenance of physical health and illness, and raised the awareness of scientists and theorists alike concerning the possible role of social factors in health/disease processes.

Individualism and Cardiovascular Disease

For many years now, researchers have examined how social and psychological factors influence the development and treatment of cardiovascular disease. Several factors have contributed to this focus. One is the previous work identifying a number of psychological and behavioral factors that appear to influence cardiovascular disease—notably, the Type A personality profile (see Friedman & Rosenman, 1974). This profile, found across various cultures (del Pino Perez, Meizoso, & Gonzalez, 1999), is characterized by competitiveness, time urgency, anger, and hostility. Another is the relatively high incidence of cardiovascular disease in the United States, making it a major health concern for many Americans.

Although there has not been a lot of research on the role of social and cultural (as opposed to personality) factors, some studies indicate that they also contribute to cardiovascular disease. Marmot and Syme (1976), for example, studied Japanese Americans, classifying 3,809 subjects into groups according to how "traditionally Japanese" they were (spoke Japanese at home, retained traditional Japanese values and behaviors, and the like). They found that those who were the "most" Japanese had the lowest incidence of coronary heart disease—comparable to the incidence in Japan. The group that was the "least" Japanese had a three to five times higher incidence. Moreover, the differences between the groups could not be accounted for by other coronary risk factors. These findings point to the contribution of social and cultural lifestyles to the development of heart disease.

Triandis, Bontempo, Villareal, Asai, and Lucca, N. (1988) took this finding one step further, using the individualism–collectivism cultural dimension and examining its relationship to heart disease across eight different cultural groups. European Americans, the most individualistic of the eight groups, had the highest rate of heart attacks; Trappist monks, who were the least individualistic, had the lowest rate. Of course, this study is not conclusive, as many other variables confound comparisons between Americans and Trappist monks (such as industrialization, class, and lifestyle). Nevertheless, these findings again highlight the potential contribution of sociocultural factors to the development of heart disease.

Triandis and his colleagues (1988) suggested that social support or isolation was the most important factor that explained this relationship, a position congruent with the earlier research on social isolation. That is, people who live in more collectivistic cultures have stronger and deeper social ties with others than do people in individualistic cultures. These social relationships, in turn, are considered a "buffer" against the stress and strain of living, reducing the risk of cardiovascular disease. People who live in individualistic cultures do not have the same types or degrees of social relationships; therefore, they have less of a buffer against stress and are more susceptible to heart disease.

Other Dimensions of Culture and Other Diseases

The study by Triandis and his colleagues (1988) was especially important because it was the first to examine the relationship between cultural differences and the incidence of a particular disease state (heart disease). Research has also been done on other disease states and health-related behaviors, such as cancer, smoking, stress, and pain (see Feist & Brannon, 1988). Collectively, these studies suggest the important role of sociocultural factors—most notably, social support—in contributing to health and disease.

Still, these studies are limited in that they have focused on only one aspect of culture—individualism versus collectivism—with its mediating variable of social support. As discussed in Chapter 1, however, culture encompasses many other important dimensions, including power distance, uncertainty avoidance, masculinity, tightness, and contextualization. Another limitation of the previous research is that it has looked almost exclusively at mortality rates or cardiovascular disease. Other dimensions of culture, however, may be associated with the incidence of other disease processes. If members of individualistic cultures are indeed at higher risk for heart disease, for example, perhaps they are at lower risk for other disease processes. Conversely, if collectivistic cultures are at lower risk for heart disease, they may be at higher risk for other diseases.

Matsumoto and Fletcher (1996) investigated this possibility by examining the relationship among multiple dimensions of culture and multiple disease processes, opening the door to this line of study. These researchers obtained the mortality rates for six different medical diseases: infections and parasitic diseases, malignant neoplasms (tumors), diseases of the circulatory system, heart diseases, cerebrovascular diseases, and respiratory system diseases. These epidemiological data, taken from the *World Health Statistics Quarterly* (World Health Organization, 1991), were compiled across 28 countries widely distributed around the globe, spanning five continents, and representing many different ethnic, cultural, and socioeconomic backgrounds. In addition, incidence rates for each of the diseases were available at five age points for each country: at birth and at ages 1, 15, 45, and 65 years. To get cultural data for each country, Matsumoto and Fletcher (1996) used cultural index scores previously obtained by Hofstede (1980, 1983), who analyzed questionnaire data about cultural values and practices from large samples in each of these countries and classified their responses according to four cultural tendencies: individualism versus collectivism (IC), power distance (PD), uncertainty avoidance (UA), and masculinity (MA).

Matsumoto and Fletcher then correlated these cultural index scores with the epidemiological data. The results were quite fascinating and pointed to the importance of culture in the development of these disease processes. See Table 7.1 for a summary of findings. The countries in this study differ economically as well as culturally, and it may well be that these economic differences—particularly with regard to the availability of treatment, diet, and sanitation—also contribute to disease. To deal with this possibility, Matsumoto and Fletcher (1996)

Table 7.1 | Summary of Findings on the Relationship between Four Cultural Dimensions and Incidence of Diseases

Cultural Dimension	Rates of Disease
Higher Power Distance	■ Higher rates of infections and parasitic diseases ■ Lower rates of malignant neoplasm, circulatory disease, and heart disease
Higher Individualism	■ Higher rates of malignant neoplasms and heart disease ■ Lower rates of infections and parasitic diseases, cerebrovascular disease
Higher Uncertainty Avoidance	■ Higher rates of heart disease ■ Lower rates of cerebrovascular disease and respiratory disease
Higher Masculinity	■ Higher rates of cerebrovascular disease

Source: Matsumoto & Fletcher, 1996.

recomputed their correlations, controlling for per capita gross domestic product (GDP) of each country. Even when the effects of per capita GDP were accounted for, the predictions for infections and parasitic diseases, circulatory diseases, and heart diseases all survived. The predictions for UA and cerebrovascular and respiratory diseases, and MA and cerebrovascular diseases, also survived. Thus, these cultural dimensions predicted disease above and beyond what is accounted for by economic differences among the countries. Only the prediction for malignant neoplasms was not supported, indicating that economic differences among the countries cannot be disentangled from cultural differences in predicting the incidence of neoplasms.

How and why does culture affect medical disease processes? Triandis and colleagues (1988) suggested that culture—specifically, social support—plays an important role in mediating stress, which affects health. The findings of Matsumoto and Fletcher (1996), however, suggest a much more complex picture. Although collectivistic cultures were associated with lower rates of cardiovascular diseases, replicating the previous findings, they were also associated with death from infectious and parasitic diseases and cerebrovascular diseases. Thus, although social support may be a buffer against life stress in the prevention of heart attacks, these data suggest that there is something else to collectivism that actually increases susceptibility to other disease processes. To be sure, these other factors may not be cultural per se. Collectivism, for example, is generally correlated with geographic location; countries nearer the equator tend to be more collectivistic. Countries nearer the equator also have hotter climates, which foster the spread of organisms responsible for infectious and parasitic diseases. The relationship between collectivism and death from these types of disease processes, therefore, may be related to geography rather than culture.

Still, these findings do suggest that individualism is not necessarily bad, and collectivism is not necessarily good, as earlier findings had suggested. The latest findings suggest, instead, that different societies and countries develop different cultural ways of dealing with the problem of living. Each way is associated with its own specific and different set of stressors, each of which may take its toll on the human body. Because different cultural ways of living take different tolls on the body, they are associated with different risk factors and rates for different disease processes. This view may be a more holistic account of how culture may influence health and disease processes.

Future research will need to investigate further the specific mechanisms that mediate these relationships. Some studies, for example, will need to examine more closely the relationship among culture, geography, and other noncultural factors in connection with disease incidence rates. Other studies will need to examine directly the relationship between culture and specific behavioral and psychological processes, to elucidate the possible mechanisms of health and disease. Matsumoto and Fletcher (1996), for example, suggested that culture influences human emotion and human physiology, particularly with respect to autonomic nervous system activity and the immune system. For example, the link between PD and circulatory and heart diseases may be explained by noting that cultures low on PD tend to minimize status differences among their members. As status and power differences diminish, people are freer to feel and express negative emotions, such as anger or hostility, to ingroup others. Containing negative emotions, as must be done in high-PD cultures, may have dramatic consequences for the cardiovascular system, resulting in a relatively higher incidence of circulatory and heart diseases in those cultures. A study by Ekman, Levenson, and Friesen (1983), documenting substantial increases in heart rate associated with angry expressions, lends further credence to this hypothesis. Hopefully, future research will be able to address these and other possibilities.

Cultural Discrepancies and Physical Health

Although the studies described so far suggest that culture influences physical health, later research suggests that culture per se is not the only culturally relevant variable. Indeed, the discrepancy between one's personal cultural values and those of society may play a large role in producing stress, which in turn leads to negative health outcomes. Matsumoto, Kouznetsova, Ray, Ratzlaff, Biehl, and Raroque (1999) tested this idea by asking university undergraduates to report what their personal cultural values were, as well as their perceptions of society's values and ideal values. Participants in this study also completed a scale assessing strategies for coping with stress; anxiety, depression, and other mood measures; and scales assessing physical health and psychological well-being. Discrepancy scores in cultural values were computed by taking the differences between self and society, and self and ideal, ratings. These discrepancy scores were then correlated with the scores on the eight coping strategies assessed. The results indicated that discrepancies between self and society's cultural values were significantly correlated with all eight coping strategies, indicating that greater cultural discrepancies were associated with greater needs for coping. These coping strategies were significantly correlated with depression and anxiety, which in turn were significantly correlated with scores on the physical health symptoms checklist scales. In particular, higher scores on anxiety were strongly correlated with greater health problems. The results of this study, therefore, suggest that greater discrepancy between self and societal cultural values may lead to greater psychological stress, which necessitates greater degrees of coping, which affects emotion and mood, which causes greater degrees of anxiety and depression, which then lead to more physical health problems.

Of course, this single study is not conclusive; future research will need to replicate these findings, and elaborate on them. They do suggest, however, the potential role of cultural discrepancies in mediating health outcomes, and open the door for new and exciting research in this area of psychology.

Culture and Eating Disorders

One health-related topic that has received considerable attention concerns eating disorders and obesity. As mentioned previously, a number of studies have reported a negative correlation between body weight and income in the United States: As people get wealthier, they tend to become thinner. In many other countries, the relationship is exactly the opposite: As people get wealthier, they tend to become larger; size is associated with wealth and abundance. A number of studies, in fact, have found considerable cultural differences in perceptions of and stereotypes about thinness and obesity. Cogan, Bhalla, Sefa-Dedeh, and Rothblum (1996), for example, asked university students in Ghana and the United States to complete questionnaires about their weight, frequency of dieting, social activities, perceptions of ideal bodies, disordered eating, and stereotypes of thin and heavy people. They found that the Ghanaians were more likely to rate larger body sizes as ideals in their society. Americans, especially females, were more likely to have dieted. American females also scored higher on dietary restraint, disordered eating behavior, and experiencing weight as a social interference.

Crandall and Martinez (1996) reported similar findings. These researchers compared attitudes about weight and being overweight in American and Mexican students, by asking students to complete an anti-overweight attitude scale and a scale on political ideologies and beliefs. The results indicated that Mexican students were less concerned about their own weight, and were more accepting of overweight people, than were the American students. In addition, anti-overweight attitudes in the United States appeared to be part of a social ideology that holds individuals responsible for their life outcomes. Attributions of controllability and responsibility were less important in predicting anti-overweight attitudes in Mexico, where antipathy toward overweight people did not appear to be related to any ideological framework.

Cultural differences in attitudes about being overweight and thinness appear to be related to cultural differences in attitudes toward eating behaviors. In Akan and Grilo's (1995) study, for instance, European Americans reported greater levels of disordered eating and dieting behaviors, and greater body dissatisfaction, than did Asian and African Americans. Low self-esteem and high public self-consciousness were associated with greater levels of problematic eating behaviors, attitudes, and body dissatisfaction. In Abrams, Allen, and Gray's (1993) study, white females demonstrated significantly greater disordered eating attitudes and behaviors than black females. Disordered eating behaviors, in turn, were related to depression, anxiety, and low self-esteem. In Hamilton, Brooks-Gunn, and Warren's (1985) study, none of the black dancers reported anorexia or bulimia, compared with 15 percent and 19 percent, respectively, of the white dancers. Self-reported anorectics had higher disordered eating attitudes, exhibited more psychopathology, and had poorer body images than nonanorectics. The bulimics valued their career less, dieted more, and exercised less frequently than nonbulimics.

More recent studies have focused on exposure to Western culture and acculturation in relation to eating attitudes and behaviors. For instance, a study of Pakistani females found that exposure to Western culture significantly predicted more disturbed eating attitudes (Suhail & Nisa, 2002). Along the same lines, a study of Mexican American females found that those who reported greater orientation to Anglo American culture also reported higher levels of eating disorders (Cachelin, Phinney, Schug, & Striegel-Moore, 2006).

Collectively, these studies demonstrate convincingly that attitudes toward body size and shape, and eating, are heavily influenced by culture. Cultural values, attitudes, beliefs, and opinions about wealth, abundance, beauty and attractiveness, power, and other such psychological characteristics likely play a major role in determining attitudes toward eating, thinness, and obesity. These latter attitudes, in turn, most likely directly affect health-related behaviors such as eating, diet, and exercise. The research also suggests that these tendencies may be especially prevalent in the United States, especially among European American females. However, such tendencies are not solely an American phenomenon. Cross-cultural research has pointed to similarities between Americans and members of other cultures—for example, the Japanese (Mukai & McCloskey, 1996)—in their attitudes toward eating and preoccupation with thinness.

Increasing attention has been paid to the growing rates of overweight and obesity in industrialized nations, especially among children and adolescents. This is a concern, as most overweight and obese children and adolescents become overweight and obese adults. For adults, the WHO's definition of overweight is body-mass index (BMI; calculated as the weight in kilograms divided by the square of the height in meters) at or above 25; for obesity, it is a BMI at or above 30. However, there is not a strong consensus on the definitions of overweight and

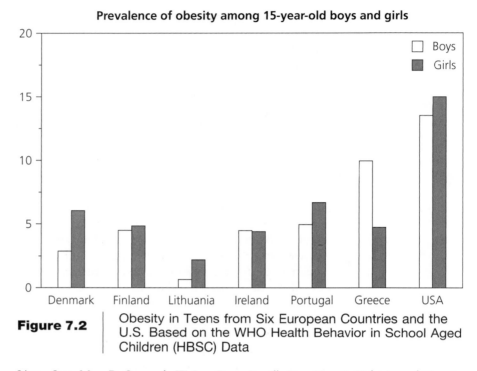

Prevalence of obesity among 15-year-old boys and girls

| | Figure 7.2 | Obesity in Teens from Six European Countries and the U.S. Based on the WHO Health Behavior in School Aged Children (HBSC) Data |

Lissau, Inge, Mary D. Overpeck, W. June Ruan, Pernille Due, Bjørn E. Holstein, and Mary L. Hediger. Body Mass Index and Overweight in Adolescents in 13 European Countries, Israel, and the United States, *Archives of Pediatrics & Adolescent Medicine*, vol. 159, no. 1, pp. 27–33, January 2004, published by American Medical Association. Reprinted with permission.

obesity for children and adolescents. To address this, The International Task Force on Childhood Obesity published a paper establishing appropriate cutoffs based on age and sex (Cole, Bellizzi, Flegal, & Dietz, 2000). The cutoffs are based on height and weight data from children in the United Kingdom, Brazil, the Netherlands, Hong Kong, Singapore, and the United States. Using this definition, the United States has by far the greatest percentage of young people who are obese compared with many European countries (see Figure 7.2).

In the United States, from 1974 to 2000, the obesity rate quadrupled for children (ages 6 to 11) and doubled for adolescents (ages 12 to 19) (Ogden et al., 2002). Some factors that may explain why the United States has such high rates compared with other countries are diet (consumption of fast food and soft drinks) and (lack of) exercise. For instance, a review of studies concluded that there is a clear link between the consumption of sugary soft drinks and obesity (Malik, Schulze, & Hu, 2006). These researchers suggest that the rising epidemic of obese American children and adolescents is partly due to increases in soft-drink consumption in the past several decades. In addition to unhealthy drinks, American children and adolescents tend to eat unhealthy foods. One study found that about one-third of American adolescents eat at least one fast-food meal a day (Bowman, Gortmaker, Ebbeling, Pereira, & Ludwig, et al.,

2003). Finally, American adolescents also tend to bike and walk less and rely on their cars more than adolescents from other industrialized countries (Arnett & Balle-Jensen, 1993). In sum, differences across cultures in food choice and behaviors play a role in contributing to differences in rates of overweight and obesity.

Future research will need to tackle the difficult question of exactly what it is about culture that influences attitudes about eating and stereotypes about thinness and obesity, and where cultures draw the line between healthy patterns and disordered eating behaviors that have direct, negative impacts on health. Future research will also need to tie specific eating behaviors to specific health and disease outcomes, and attempt to link culture with these relationships.

Culture and Suicide

No other behavior has health consequences as final as suicide—the taking of one's own life. Psychologists, sociologists, and anthropologists have long been fascinated by suicide, and have studied this behavior across many cultures. The research to date suggests many interesting cross-cultural differences in the nature of suicidal behavior, all of which point to the different ways in which people of different cultures view not only death, but life itself.

One of the most glorified and curious cultures with regard to suicidal behavior is that of Japan. Tales of Japanese pilots who deliberately crashed their planes into enemy targets during World War II stunned and mystified many people of other cultures. These individuals clearly placed the welfare, spirit, and honor of their country above the value of their own lives. To be sure, such acts of self-sacrifice were not limited to the Japanese, as men and women on both sides of war reach into themselves in ways many of us cannot understand to sacrifice their lives for the sake of others. But the Japanese case seems to highlight the mysterious and glorified nature of some acts of suicide in that culture.

Among the most glorified acts of suicide in Japan (called *seppuku* or *harakiri*—the slitting of one's belly) were those of the masterless samurai swordsmen who served as the basis for the story known as *Chuushingura*. In this factual story, a lord of one clan of samurai was humiliated and lost face because of the acts of another lord. In disgrace, the humiliated lord committed *seppuku* to save the honor of himself, his family, and his clan. His now masterless samurai—known as *ronin*—plotted to avenge their master's death by killing the lord who had humiliated him in the first place. Forty-seven of them plotted their revenge and carried out their plans by killing the lord. Afterward, they turned themselves into authorities, admitting to the plot of revenge and explaining the reasons for their actions. It was then decided that the only way to resolve the entire situation was to order the 47 *ronin* to commit *seppuku* themselves—which they did. In doing so, they laid down their lives, voluntarily and through this ritualistic method, to preserve the honor and dignity of their clan and families. Although these events occurred in the late 19th century, similar acts continue in Japan today. Some Japanese businessmen have committed suicide as a way of taking responsibility for the downturns in their companies resulting from the economic crisis in Japan and much of Asia.

Japan is by no means the only culture in which suicide has been examined psychologically and cross-culturally. Kazarian and Persad (2001) note that "suicide has been in evidence in every time period in recorded history and in almost every culture around the world. It is depicted, and reasons for its committal described, in tribal folklore, Greek tragedies, religious, philosophical, and historical writings, literature, modern soap operas, and rock music" (p. 275).

Many studies point to profound cultural changes as a determinant of suicidal behavior. Leenaars, Anawak, and Taparti (1998), for example, suggest this factor as an important influence on suicide rates among Canadian Inuits, primarily among younger individuals. Sociocultural change has long been identified as a predictor of suicide among Native Americans, whose suicide rates are higher than those of other Americans (Centers for Disease Control and Prevention, 2006). Stresses associated with social and cultural changes have also been implicated in the suicide rates of many other cultural groups, including Native Hawaiians (Takeuchi et al., 1987), Greeks (Beratis, 1986), English (Robertson & Cochrane, 1976), Eskimos (Parkin, 1974), and many other groups.

One factor that may be closely related to culture and suicide is religious beliefs. For instance, suicide is strictly forbidden in the Muslim and Jewish religions and was considered a mortal sin in the early history of Christianity (Kazarian & Persad, 2001). Kelleher, Chambers, Corcoran, Williamson, and Keeley (1998) examined data from suicide rates reported to the WHO and found that countries with religions that strongly condemned the act of suicide had lower reported rates of suicide than countries without religions that strongly condemned suicide. However, the researchers also suggested that the reports may have been biased. Those countries with religious sanctions against suicide may have been less willing to report and record suicides.

Cross-cultural research over the past few decades has given us important glimpses into this difficult yet fascinating topic. Still, many questions remain unanswered. What is it about culture that produces differences in suicidal behaviors, and why? Why are there still considerable individual differences in attitudes toward suicide even in cultures where it is relatively more acceptable? Despite the glorified stories concerning suicide in Japan, for instance, there is still a relatively strong stigma against it and intense prejudice toward the mental disorders related to it, resulting in reluctance to seek help (Takahashi, 1997). When may suicide be an acceptable behavior in any culture? Given recent and ongoing advances in medical technology, such questions that involve medicine, culture, and ethics are bound to increase in prominence. In the past decade, physician-assisted suicide, brought to national attention by Dr. Jack Kevorkian, has emerged as an issue in the United States. Future research within and between cultures may help to elucidate some of the important decision points as we approach these questions.

Summary

In this section, we have discussed a considerable amount of research concerning the influence of psychological, social, and cultural factors on health. We know that these factors can influence rates of mortality, heart disease, and several other disease processes. We also know that cultural discrepancies may be related to health, with greater discrepancies leading to greater stress and consequently more anxiety and greater health problems. We have seen how culture influences attitudes about body shape, eating, and eating disorders. And we have discussed how culture may play a role in suicidal behaviors. Future studies will begin to bridge the gap between culture as a macroconcept and specific medical disease processes in the body. Whatever the exact mechanisms, the contribution of culture to physical health and disease is clearer now than ever before. Future research will expand our understanding of how and why this relationship exists.

CULTURAL INFLUENCES ON ATTITUDES AND BELIEFS RELATED TO HEALTH AND DISEASE

Culture can influence health in many ways. Culture affects attitudes about health care and treatment, attributions about the causes of health and disease processes, the availability of health care and health care delivery systems, help-seeking behaviors, and many other aspects of disease and health care. We are only now becoming aware of the importance of sociocultural differences when developing treatment and intervention programs for medical and psychological problems.

In one study, Matsumoto and his colleagues (1995) recruited Japanese and Japanese American women over the age of 55 to participate in a study of attitudes and values related to osteoporosis and its treatment. Osteoporosis is a medical disorder in which a decrease in bone density leads to a gradual weakening of the bones. It can be a particularly devastating disease for older women of European or Asian descent. Among the most interesting results of this study were the cultural differences found in the attitude survey and the health care issues assessment. The entire sample of women was divided into two groups: those born and raised in the United States who spoke English as their primary language, and those born and raised in Japan who spoke Japanese as their primary language. When asked about the types of problems they would have if they were diagnosed with osteoporosis, more Japanese than American women reported problems with finances and with finding help. The major concern for American women was "other" problems, including mobility. This finding is especially interesting because mobility is such a central element of individualism, which is more characteristic of the United States than Japan.

If diagnosed with osteoporosis, Japanese women were more likely to attribute the cause of the illness to fate, chance, or luck; American women were more likely to attribute the illness to diet. Interestingly, there were no differences between the groups in degree of personal responsibility or control, nor in the number of women who specifically asked for osteoporosis examinations or in their feelings about estrogen therapy.

A final striking finding was that more Japanese women reported that they would comply with invasive treatment, even though fewer Japanese women had positive feelings about their physicians or reported that they trusted their physicians. This finding is related to the Japanese culture's emphasis on compliance with authority; it suggests that the relationship between interpersonal trust and compliance with authority figures in the Japanese culture is not the same as it is in the United States.

Many other studies also suggest the importance of culture in molding attitudes, beliefs, and values about illness and treatment. Jilek-Aall, Jilek, Kaaya, Mkombachepa, and Hillary (1997), for example, conducted a study on epilepsy in two isolated tribes in Africa; they reported significant differences in attitudes toward epilepsy, which influenced treatment approaches. Sun and Stewart (2000) found that internal locus of control was positively associated with psychological adjustment in a sample of Hong Kong patients with cancer, even though beliefs about supernatural forces are prevalent in this culture. Muela, Ribera, and Tanner (1998) reported on the influence of witchcraft on help-seeking behaviors of Tanzanians in regard to malaria. They found that such beliefs had consequences for noncompliance with treatment, and for delay in seeking diagnosis or treatment.

Other researchers have examined how perspectives on health may vary depending on level of acculturation. Quah and Bishop (1996) asked a group of Chinese Americans about their perceptions of health and also measured their level of acculturation by gathering information on generational status, language spoken, religious affiliation, and endorsement of traditional Chinese values. They found that those who rated themselves as being more Chinese believed that diseases were a result of imbalances in the body, such as excessive cold or excessive heat, in line with traditional Chinese views of illness. Those who rated themselves lower on being Chinese, in contrast, believed that diseases were a result of viruses, in line with the Western biomedical view of illness. The researchers also found that those who believed in the traditional Chinese views of health and disease were more likely to turn to a practitioner of traditional Chinese medicine when seeking medical help. Another study of acculturation and health involving Asian Canadians found that those with higher orientations toward Asian culture were more likely to endorse the traditional Chinese view of health than did those with higher orientations toward Western culture. Furthermore, those endorsing traditional Chinese medical beliefs also reported being less satisfied with Western medical care (Armstrong & Swartzmann, 1999).

Taken collectively, a growing literature in the field is showing an increased awareness of cultural influences on a host of psychological variables that ultimately have implications for health and disease. These findings suggest that health care providers need to deal not only with a patient's disease but also, and perhaps more importantly, with the psychological correlates of the disease.

These may include variables such as attributions and beliefs about the cause of disease; attitudes about health, illness, and treatment; preferences with regard to social support and networks; psychosocial needs with regard to autonomy versus reliance on others; and treatment compliance. Also, we cannot forget cultural differences in attitudes about body shapes and in definitions of health and disease, discussed earlier in this chapter. Contemporary health practitioners and the institutions in which they work—clinics, hospitals, laboratories—have become increasingly sensitized to these issues, and are now struggling with the best ways to understand and incorporate them for maximum effectiveness.

A MODEL OF CULTURAL INFLUENCES ON PHYSICAL HEALTH

So far in this chapter, we have reviewed a considerable amount of literature concerning the influence of culture on health and disease processes. This research has begun to affect the ways in which we deliver treatment and other services to people of varying cultural backgrounds, and the type of health care systems we create. It has also made scholars in the field more sensitive to the need to incorporate culture as a major variable in their studies and theories.

So, just how does culture influence physical health and disease processes? Figure 7.3 summarizes what we know so far. We know from other research, not reviewed in this chapter, that culture affects rates of alcohol consumption, tobacco use, and exercise and activity levels. Each of these variables, in turn, has implications for health and disease. The research concerning the relationship between cultural dimensions and the incidence of various diseases also implicates lifestyles and behaviors as possible mediators. In particular, research seems to suggest that stress and emotion, and the ways we cope with them, are important determinants of health and well-being.

We have also discussed the contribution to health and disease of other psychological factors, most notably attitudes and beliefs about disease processes, causations, treatment, and help seeking. Finally, although this chapter has focused on the role of sociocultural factors in health and disease, we cannot ignore the contributory roles of the environment and available health care systems in promoting health and well-being.

Figure 7.3 is meant to provide a general overview of the role that culture and other social factors may play in the area of physical health. All these factors will need to be fleshed out in greater detail, then tied together into a comprehensive and systematic whole to further our understanding of health and disease processes. Future research will also need to operationalize health according to dimensions other than mortality rates or incidence rates of various diseases. Incorporating cultural, environmental, social, and psychological factors in determining multiple definitions of health is an enormous job for the future, but it is one that we must work toward if we are to get a clearer and more complete picture of the relative contribution of all these factors.

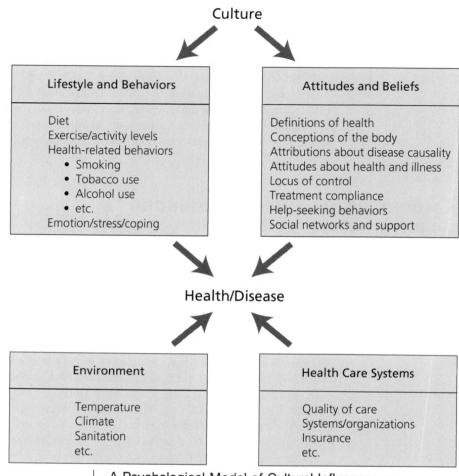

Figure 7.3 | A Psychological Model of Cultural Influences on Physical Health

CULTURAL DIFFERENCES IN DEALING WITH ILLNESS

In this final section of the chapter, we turn to the question of how health care professionals can provide appropriate and sensitive treatment and other health care services to a diverse population. We begin with a review of differences in health care and medical delivery systems around the world, and then look at some research on the development of culturally sensitive treatment approaches.

Differences in Health Care and Medical Delivery Systems

Different countries and cultures have developed their own unique ways of dealing with health care. A country's health care delivery system is a product of many factors, including social and economic development, technological advances and availability, and the influence of neighboring and collaborating countries. Also affecting health care delivery services are a number of social trends, including urbanization, industrialization, governmental structure, international trade laws and practices, demographic changes, demands for privatization, and public expenditures.

National health systems can be divided into four major types: entrepreneurial, welfare-oriented, comprehensive, and socialist (Roemer, 1991). Within each of these general categories, individual countries vary tremendously in terms of their economic level. For instance, the United States is an example of a country with a relatively high economic level that uses an entrepreneurial system of health care, characterized by a substantial private industry covering individuals as well as groups. The Philippines and Ghana also use an entrepreneurial system of health care, but have moderate and low economic levels, respectively. France, Brazil, and Burma are examples of high-, moderate-, and low-income countries with welfare-oriented health systems. Likewise, Sweden, Costa Rica, and Sri Lanka have comprehensive health care systems, and the former Soviet Union, Cuba, and China have socialist health systems.

A quick review of the countries listed here suggests that cultural differences are related to the type of national health system a country is likely to adopt. It makes sense that an entrepreneurial system is used in the United States, for example, because of the highly individualistic nature of American culture. Likewise, it makes sense that socialist systems of health care are used in China and Cuba, given their collectivistic, communal nature. However, cultural influences cannot be separated from the other factors that contribute to the existence of national health care systems. In the complex interactions among culture, economy, technology, and government, social aspects of culture are inseparable from social institutions.

The Development of Culturally Sensitive Treatment Approaches

In the past decade, a number of important studies have examined the issue of culturally sensitive treatment approaches for people of diverse cultural backgrounds. In the past, at least in the United States, health professionals and medical communities tended to approach health and the treatment of physical diseases in all people similarly, with the underlying assumption that people's bodies are all the same. As the American population has diversified, however, and as research continues to uncover more ways in which people of different cultural backgrounds differ from one another, health professions are slowly becoming aware of the need to develop culturally sensitive and appropriate treatment approaches.

The need for such approaches is borne out in the literature. Ponchillia (1993), for example, reports that cultural beliefs among Native Americans, Mexican Americans, and Pacific Islanders affect the success of health-related services to native peoples who are suffering vision loss as a result of diabetes. These cultural beliefs include the circle of life, identification with persons with disabilities, the value of silence, and even the healing power of blindness itself. Ponchillia also suggests that the increase in the incidence of diabetes among these cultural groups is due to their adoption of Western diets and lifestyles.

Other findings also suggest the influence of culture on treatment success. Wing, Crow, and Thompson (1995) examined barriers to seeking treatment for alcoholism among Muscogee Indians, and found that this group traditionally perceives alcoholism to be caused by a lack of spirituality. Admission of alcohol abuse thus causes embarrassment and shame, and the practice of humility in Western-oriented alcoholism programs hinders treatment. Talamantes, Lawler, and Espino (1995) examined issues related to caregiving and the use of hospice services by Hispanic American elderly persons, who are less likely to use such long-term care services. They found that factors affecting level of use included alienation; language barriers; availability of culture-sensitive services; beliefs regarding illness, suffering, coping, and death; socioeconomic and demographic factors; acculturation; and the availability of informal care, most notably via extended family and community support.

Studies of other cultural groups also highlight the importance of families and communities in the treatment of health-related problems. Nemoto and colleagues (1998), for example, examined cultural factors such as family support in the treatment and prevention of drug abuse in Filipino and Chinese individuals. More specifically, they examined factors that prevent drug abuse and the escalation of drug use in these groups, including family support, cultural competence, religious beliefs, and life satisfaction. One of the interesting findings of this study was that some drug users received financial support from family members who knew the recipients' drug habits. Family members tried not to talk about the problems in the family, yet continued to provide financial support to the user. The authors concluded that culturally sensitive and appropriate treatment needs to involve the immediate family and extended family members if the treatment is to be effective. These and other findings suggest that health problems arise as much from a collective system of individuals and social agents as from a single individual. This collective system, therefore, must be engaged if treatment is to be relevant and effective.

Armstrong and Swartzman (2001) also point out the need to understand how different cultures speak and communicate about illnesses. For instance, people from a collectivistic culture may not directly tell a doctor what is bothering them, but may be much more circumspect in describing their illness. If the doctor has an individualistic orientation and is much more direct in trying to find out what is ailing the patient by asking pointed, direct questions and expecting direct answers, this may cause distress for the patient and may hinder both the patient and the health care provider in dealing with the illness.

It is extremely difficult to grasp the complexity that culture brings to the development of successful and effective treatment approaches. Besides family issues, a host of variables may include religion and spirituality, social support networks, beliefs and attitudes about causes and treatments, socioeconomic factors, language barriers, shame, face, and many others. Although some culturally relevant programs have been shown to be successful (see, for example,

Damond, Breuer, & Pharr, 1993; Uziel-Miller, Lyons, Kissiel, & Love, 1998), others have not (see, for example, Rossiter, 1994). Thus, it is not clear what the exact ingredients for successful treatment interventions are, and whether these ingredients differ depending on the cultural group or on the individual who is seeking help. Basic educational programs about health and disease prevention that tap cultural groups in relevant ways may be a relatively easy way to access many individuals.

Clearly, the field is still struggling to discover what the most important culturally relevant variables are and whether these variables are similar or different across cultural groups. Our guess would be that there are some culture-constant needs that must be addressed, but that these needs are manifested in different ways in different attitudes, values, beliefs, social support, extended families, and the like. Future research has a large job in evaluating the host of potentially important variables to distill a set of guidelines that can be useful for health care professionals in their attempts to improve people's lives.

CONCLUSION

Many factors contribute to health and disease processes. Besides effects of the environment, diet, directly health-related behaviors (smoking, alcohol consumption), and health care availability, culture is also a major factor. Understanding the role that culture plays in the development of disease, whether medical or psychological, will take us a long way toward developing ways of preventing disease in the future. As research uncovers the possible negative consequences of cultural tendencies, we can also look to an understanding of cultural influences to help us treat people of different cultures better than we have in the past.

In this chapter, we have examined how cross-cultural research has attempted to explore the influence of culture on physical health. We have seen how different cultures have different definitions of health and disease, and different conceptions of the body. We have reviewed a considerable amount of research that shows how culture appears to be related to a number of different disease processes around the world. This literature complements the already large body of literature that highlights the importance of other psychosocial determinants of health and disease, such as personality and socioeconomic status. We have also seen how individual cultural discrepancies may be related to health, and how culture influences specific behaviors such as eating and suicide. We have explored the nature of culturally relevant and sensitive treatment approaches, including the importance of family and community in some cultural groups.

Still, much remains to be learned, and many questions remain unanswered. What is the relative contribution of cultural variables to the development of disease or the maintenance of health, in relation to other determinants such as psychological, social, demographic, economic, and environmental factors? What is it about culture that influences health and disease, and why? What are the basic ingredients of a culturally relevant and effective treatment approach, and to what degree are these ingredients constant across cultures and individuals?

Recognition of the role of culture in influencing the definition and expression of health suggests that we must modify our methods of assessing and treating disease. Developing adequate assessment strategies requires that culturally based definitions of health and disease be taken into account. Awareness of culture-specific systems of healing is also necessary to develop effective methods of both assessment and treatment. Culturally sensitive assessment and treatment methods are vital to improving our ability to meet the health needs of culturally diverse populations, both in the United States and globally.

GLOSSARY

biomedical model A model of health that views disease as resulting from a specific, identifiable cause originating inside the body.

hardiness A positive state of health that goes beyond the absence of disease.

pathogen In the biomedical model, a cause of disease, whether viral, bacterial, or other; the root of all physical and medical diseases.

Culture and Emotion

CHAPTER **8**

CHAPTER CONTENTS

THE EVOLUTION OF HUMAN EMOTION

It is impossible to imagine life without emotion. We treasure our feelings—the joy we feel at a ball game, the pleasure of the touch of a loved one, the fun we have with our friends on a night out, seeing a movie, or visiting a nightclub. Even our negative emotions are important: the sadness when we are apart from our loved ones, the death of a family member, the anger we feel when violated, the fear that overcomes us in a scary or unknown situation, and the guilt or shame we feel toward others when our sins are made public. Emotions color our life experiences. They inform us of who we are, what our relationships with others are like, and how to behave. Emotions give meaning to events. Without emotions, those events would be mere facts of our lives.

But what are emotions? In everyday discourse, laypersons generally do not distinguish between emotions and feelings. Yet, most emotion researchers consider feelings (subjective experience) to be a part of emotion, but not emotion itself. Emotion involves much more than feelings. We define emotions as a transient, neurophysiological response to a stimulus that excites a coordinated system of components; they inform us about our relationship to the stimulus, and prepare us to deal with it in some way. The system of components includes subjective experience (feelings); expressive behavior such as in the face, voice, or other nonverbal actions; physiological reactions such as increased heart rate, faster breathing, etc.; action tendencies such as moving toward or away from an object; and cognition—specific patterns of thinking.

There are many theoretical models of emotion today, and many differences among them. But there are many agreements across those models as well, and most would agree that a general model of emotion would look something like what is shown in Figure 8.1. Throughout this chapter we will be referring back to this model of emotion, and use it as a way of organizing the findings in the field.

Emotions are quick; they last only a few seconds or minutes. Thus, they are different from moods, which last longer—for hours or days. They are functional; when they occur, they tell us something important about our relationship to the emotion-eliciting stimulus, they help prepare our bodies for action, and have important social meanings (e.g., watch out when the boss is angry!). Thus, emotions help us solve complex social coordination problems that occur because human social life is complex.

All humans, regardless of culture, have emotions; thus, the existence of emotion is a universal aspect of human functioning. Like many other psychological processes we have been discussing throughout this book, human emotions evolved. Comparative research has demonstrated that nonhuman primates, for example, have some emotions, such as anger, fear, and disgust (de Waal, 2003). Thus, we share some emotions with our primate ancestors. Yet, human emotions are also different; they are more complex and differentiated. Our language ability, for instance, allows us to make many fine distinctions among emotions. Thus, we are not just angry; we are sometimes irritated, aggravated, agitated,

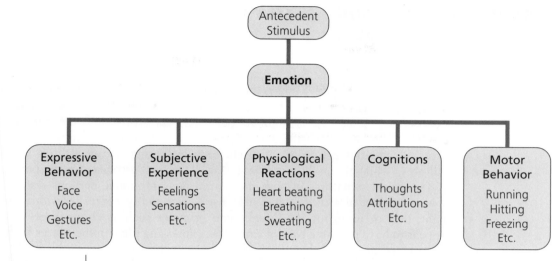

Figure 8.1   A General Model of Emotion Elicitation

annoyed, grouchy, grumpy, frustrated, hostile, exasperated, mad, enraged, or furious. Not only do humans have fear, as do animals, but humans also become anxious, nervous, tense, uneasy, worried, alarmed, shocked, frightened, horrified, terrorized, or mortified.

Also, because humans uniquely have cognitive representations of self and others as intentional agents, humans uniquely have emotions that are associated with self-reflective processes. These are called **self-conscious emotions**, and include emotions such as shame, guilt, pride, and embarrassment. Because humans uniquely have cognitive representations of self and others as intentional agents, humans uniquely have the construct of morality, in which moral emotions such as contempt and disgust play a particularly important role (Haidt, 2001; Rozin, Lowery, Imada, & Haidt, 1999). Disgust is especially interesting, because while nonhuman primates share with humans a biologically based version of disgust that helps them to avoid or expel nasty objects (e.g., through vomiting), probably only humans have the interpersonal version of disgust, in which we can be disgusted at others as people (i.e., a moral version of disgust). No wonder that contempt and disgust have been shown to be particularly explosive and devastating emotions when seen in marital interactions (Gottman, 1994; Gottman & Levenson, 2002). Humans also can feign emotion—lie about it by expressing it when they do not feel it, or expressing an emotion different from the one they are feeling.

Thus, human emotional life is varied and complex. Because emotions are neurophysiological realities, there are many pancultural aspects to them. These aspects are summarized in the perspective known as Basic Emotions Theory, which we describe below.

UNIVERSALITY IN EMOTION—THE BASIC EMOTIONS PERSPECTIVE

One of the great findings in psychology in the past half century of research is the fact that humans share a common base of emotion with their nonhuman primate relatives. Anger, disgust, fear, enjoyment, sadness, and surprise are known as **basic emotions** (Ekman, 1992, 1999). These are emotions that are expressed universally in all humans via facial expressions, regardless of race, culture, sex, ethnicity, or national origin. They are brought about by the same types of underlying psychological elicitors; loss brings about sadness in all cultures, while threat brings about fear. They are associated with unique physiological signatures in both the central and autonomic nervous systems, which are part of a coordinated response system that prepares individuals to fight, flee, or jump for joy. Nonhuman primates such as chimpanzees also appear to have the same base of emotions, expressing them in their faces in the same ways, and using them in the same manner to solve social problems.

The basic emotions perspective has its roots in evolutionary theory, and in studies that provided the first evidence for the universality of emotional expression, to which we now turn.

The Original Universality Studies

Although philosophers have argued and discussed the possible universal basis of facial expressions of emotion for centuries (see Russell, 1995, for a review), much of the impetus for contemporary cross-cultural research on facial expressions of emotion stems from the writing of Charles Darwin. Many people are familiar with Darwin's theory of evolution, outlined in his work *The Origin of Species* (1859). Darwin suggested that humans had evolved from other, more primitive animals, such as apes and chimpanzees, and that our behaviors exist today because they were selected through a process of evolutionary adaptation. In a subsequent volume, *The Expression of Emotion in Man and Animals* (1872; see also the new 1998 edition), Darwin suggested that facial expressions of emotion, like other behaviors, are biologically innate and evolutionarily adaptive. Humans, Darwin argued, express emotions in their faces in exactly the same ways around the world, regardless of race or culture. Moreover, those facial expressions can also be seen across species, such as in gorillas. According to Darwin, facial expressions of emotion have both communicative and adaptive value. They ensure the survival of the species by providing both intrapsychic information to the individual, about well-being and person–environment relationships, and social information for others in the community.

During the early to mid-1900s, several studies were conducted to test Darwin's ideas concerning the universality of emotional expressions (for example, Triandis & Lambert, 1958; Vinacke, 1949; Vinacke & Fong, 1955). Unfortunately, many of them had methodological problems that made drawing conclusions based on them difficult (see Ekman, Friesen, & Ellsworth, 1972, for a review). At the same time, prominent anthropologists such as Margaret

Mead and Ray Birdwhistell argued that facial expressions of emotion could not be universal; instead, they suggested that facial expressions of emotion had to be learned, much like a language (quoted in Ekman, Friesen, & Ellsworth, 1972). Just as different cultures had different languages, they also had different facial expressions of emotion.

It was not until the 1960s, when psychologists Paul Ekman and Wallace Friesen (Ekman, 1972) and, independently, Carroll Izard (1971) conducted the first set of methodologically sound studies that this debate was laid to rest. Spurred on by the work of Sylvan Tomkins (1962, 1963), these researchers conducted a series of studies now called the **universality studies.** Four different types of studies were originally included in the series. In the first of these, Ekman, Friesen, and Tomkins selected photographs of facial expressions of emotion they thought portrayed universally recognizable emotions (Ekman, 1972). The researchers showed these photographs to observers in five different countries (the United States, Argentina, Brazil, Chile, and Japan) and asked the observers to label each expression. If the expressions were universal, the researchers reasoned, judges in all cultures would agree on what emotion was being portrayed; if the expressions were culturally specific, the judges from different cultures should disagree. The data revealed a very high level of agreement across all observers in all five cultures in the interpretation of six emotions: anger, disgust, fear, happiness, sadness, and surprise. Izard (1971) conducted a similar study in other cultures and obtained similar results.

One problem with these studies was that all the cultures included in the research were literate, industrialized, and relatively modern. It was possible, therefore, that the observers in those cultures could have learned how to interpret the facial expressions in the photographs. The fact that these cultures shared mass media—television, movies, magazines, and so forth—reinforced this possibility. The research was criticized, therefore, on the basis of shared visual input across the cultures studied.

Ekman, Sorenson, and Friesen (1969) conducted similar studies in two preliterate tribes of New Guinea that address these concerns. Because of the nature of the participants in these studies, Ekman and his colleagues were forced to change the nature of the experiment, allowing participants to select a story that best described a facial expression instead of using emotion words. When these participants were asked to identify the emotions in the photographs, the data were amazingly similar to those obtained in literate, industrialized societies. Thus, judgments of posed expressions by preliterate cultures constituted a second source of evidence in support of universality.

Ekman and his colleagues took their research in New Guinea a step further, asking different tribe members to show on their faces what they would look like if they experienced the different emotions. Photographs of these expressions were brought back to the United States and shown to American observers, none of whom had ever seen the tribe members from New Guinea. When asked to label the emotions shown on the tribe members' faces, the data were again similar to those found in previous studies. Judgments of expressions posed by preliterate tribes thus constituted a third source of evidence for universality.

All the research conducted so far had involved judgments of facial expressions of emotion, and were based on the researchers' assumption that people of different cultures would agree on what emotion was being portrayed in a face if the expression were universal. Still, a question remained as to whether people actually spontaneously display those expressions on their faces when they experience emotion. To address this question, Ekman (1972) and Friesen (1972) conducted a study in the United States and Japan, asking American and Japanese subjects to view highly stressful stimuli as their facial reactions were videotaped without their awareness. Later analysis of the video records indicated that Americans and Japanese did indeed show exactly the same types of facial expressions at the same points in time, and these expressions corresponded to the same expressions that were considered universal in the judgment research. Data from spontaneous facial expressions of emotion, therefore, constituted the fourth line of evidence in the original set of universality studies. Collectively, these studies comprised what is commonly known in the field as the original universality studies that provided the initial evidence for the universality of anger, disgust, fear, happiness, sadness, and surprise.

Universality in Emotion Antecedents

The original universality research spurred a generation of research on emotion that continues today. Researchers in all areas of psychology study the various

Enjoyment

Sadness

Anger   Disgust

Examples of Emotional Expressions of Members of a Preliterate Culture

Example of American and Japanese Faces from Ekman (1972)
© Paul Ekman.

aspects of the emotion process described in Figure 8.1 and its response components. There has been considerable cross-cultural research in many of these, which inform us more about the universal basis for emotions.

Emotion antecedents are the events or situations that trigger or elicit an emotion. For example, losing a loved one may be an antecedent of sadness; getting an "A" in a class in which you wanted to do well may elicit happiness or joy. In the scientific literature, emotion antecedents are also known as emotion *elicitors*.

A considerable number of studies have supported the universality of emotion antecedents. Boucher and Brandt (1981), for example, asked participants in the United States and Malaysia to describe situations in which someone caused someone else to feel anger, disgust, fear, happiness, sadness, or surprise. Their selection of the emotions to study was guided by the previous universality research. A total of 96 antecedents to the various emotions were generated. A separate group of American participants then rated the antecedents, attempting to identify which emotion each elicited. The results indicated that the Americans correctly classified the antecedents equally well regardless of whether they were originally generated by Americans or by Malaysians; that is, culture of origin did not affect the classification. Subsequently, Brandt and Boucher (1985) replicated these findings using American, Korean, and Samoan participants.

The most prominent work to study emotion antecedents across a wide range of cultures has been that of Scherer and his colleagues, who have conducted a number of studies using questionnaires designed to assess the quality and nature of emotional experiences in many different cultures. Their largest study involved approximately 3,000 participants in 37 countries on five continents (Scherer, 1997a, 1997b; Scherer & Wallbott, 1994). They asked respondents about when they last felt anger, disgust, fear, joy, sadness, shame, and guilt. Respondents wrote about the situations that brought about each of these emotions. Trained coders then coded the situations described by participants into general categories such as good news and bad news, temporary and permanent separation, and success and failure in achievement situations. The findings indicated that no culture-specific antecedent category was necessary to code the data, indicating that all categories of events generally occurred in all cultures to produce each of the seven emotions studied. In addition, Scherer and his colleagues found many similarities across cultures in the relative frequency with which each of the antecedent events elicited emotions. For example, the most frequent elicitors of happiness across cultures were "relationships with friends," "temporary meetings with friends," and "achievement situations." The most frequent elicitors of anger were "relationships" and "injustice." The most frequent elicitors of sadness were "relationships" and "death." These findings supported the view that emotion antecedents are universal across cultures.

Universality in Emotion Appraisal Processes

When an antecedent occurs, most psychologists agree that it is appraised. **Emotion appraisal** can be loosely defined as the process by which people evaluate the events, situations, or occurrences that lead to their having emotions. The largest cross-cultural study on emotion appraisal processes is Scherer and colleagues', described above. In that study, respondents not only described the events that brought about their emotions (the antecedents described above); they were also asked about how they appraised or evaluated those events. For example, the respondents were asked to rate whether the antecedent helped them achieve their goals or blocked their goals; were expected or not; or were fair or unfair. The findings indicated that emotion appraisal processes were more similar than different across cultures.

Moreover, there was a very a high degree of cross-cultural similarity in emotion appraisal processes, and this cross-cultural agreement in appraisal has been replicated by other researchers as well (Mauro, Sato, & Tucker, 1992; Roseman, Dhawan, Rettek, Nadidu, & Thapa. 1995).These findings support the idea that the basic emotions appear to be appraised in the same way universally. Table 8.1 summarizes the universal latent content of emotion appraisals for each of the universal emotions.

Universality in Expressive Behavior

Once emotions are aroused, they trigger a series of events. One of these is expressive behavior. Since Ekman's (1972) study, there have been at least 25 other published studies in which individuals participated in emotionally

Table 8.1 | Underlying Psychological Themes That Elicit Emotions

Emotion	Universal Underlying Psychological Theme
Happiness	Accomplishing a goal
Anger	Being prevented from accomplishing a goal
Sadness	Being kept from something you desire or want
Disgust	Being sickened or repulsed by something
Fear	Sensing danger caused by unexpected, novel events and being completely helpless to do something about it
Surprise	Acknowledging something new or novel
Contempt	Feeling morally superior over someone else
Shame and guilt	Feeling a high level of responsibility for one's own behaviors, which conflict with one's own standards

arousing conditions and in which their facial expressions matched to the universal facial configurations of emotion originally found by Ekman (see review in Matsumoto, Keltner, O'Sullivan, & Frank, 2006). These studies demonstrate that the facial expressions postulated by Darwin and Tomkins are produced when emotion is aroused and there is no reason to modify the expression because of social circumstances. Moreover, the range of cultures across those studies is impressive. Matsumoto and Willingham's (2006) study, for instance, involved 84 athletes from 35 countries. Participants in other studies were Americans, Japanese, Germans, Canadians, and French. Collectively these studies demonstrate that the facial expressions reported originally by Ekman actually do occur when emotion is aroused in people of different cultures.

There is also evidence for universality in the developmental literature. The same facial musculature that exists in adult humans exists in newborn infants, and is fully functional at birth (Ekman & Oster, 1979). As such, infants have a rich and varied repertoire of facial expressions, including those that signal not only emotional states, but also interest and attention (Oster, 2005). There is widespread consensus that smiling; distaste, the infant precursor of adult disgust; and crying, the universal signal of sadness/distress, occur in neonates (Oster, 2005). Other than these, infants in the first year of life display relatively undifferentiated negative expressions, which ultimately transform into more differentiated, discrete expressions (Camras, Oster, Campos, & Bakeman, 2003; Oster, 2005). Discrete expressions of anger and sadness have been reported in the early part of the second year of life (Hyson & Izard, 1985; Shiller, Izard, Hembree, 1986). By the time they reach preschool age, children display discrete expressions of the other emotions as well (Casey, 1993).

One compelling line of evidence that suggests that facial expressions of emotion are genetically encoded and not socially learned are studies of congenitally blind individuals (Charlesworth & Kreutzer, 1973). Early observational studies concluded that congenitally blind children and adults showed the same facial expressions of emotion as sighted individuals, both spontaneously (Dumas, 1932; Eibl-Eibesfeldt, 1973; Freedman, 1964; Goodenough, 1932; Thompson, 1941) and posed (Fulcher, 1942). More recent studies have also shown that there are no differences in the spontaneous (Ortega, Iglesias, Fernandez, & Corraliza, 1983) or posed (Galati, Scherer, & Ricci-Bitti, 1997) expressions of emotion between blind and sighted individuals.

A final line of evidence for universality and the genetic encoding of facial expressions of emotion comes from studies of nonhuman primates. For years ethologists (Chevalier-Skolnikoff, 1973; Geen, 1992; Hauser, 1993; Snowdon, 2003; Van Hoof, 1972) have noted the morphological similarities between human expressions of emotion and nonhuman primate expressions displayed in similar contexts. Van Hoof (1972) described the evolution of the smile and laugh along two different evolutionary tracts across early mammals, monkeys, apes, chimpanzees, and humans. Redican (1982) suggested that among non-human primates, facial displays described as grimaces and open-mouth grimaces were akin to the human emotions of fear and surprise, that the tense-mouth display was similar to anger, that these two combined formed the often-identified threat display, and that nonhuman primates show a play face that is similar to the happy face of humans. He also suggested that the nonhuman pout served a function similar to that of the human sad face. Ueno, Ueno, and Tomonaga (2004) demonstrated that both infant rhesus macaques and infant chimpanzees showed different facial expressions in reaction to sweet and bitter tastes, but that the chimps' facial expressions were more similar to human facial expressions than to that of the macaques. However, even some of the smaller apes, such as siamangs (*Symphalangus syndactylus*), noted for their limited facial expression repertoire, have distinguishable facial expressions accompanying sexuality, agonistic behavior, grooming, and play (Liebal, Pika, & Tomasello, 2004). De Waal (2002) suggests that for some states a species less closely related to humans than chimpanzees, the bononos, may have more emotions in common with humans.

Thus, the available evidence to date clearly supports the notion that discrete facial expressions are universal, genetically encoded, and linked with those of our primate ancestors in evolution.

Universality in Physiological Responses to Emotion

Another part of the emotion response package is physiological reactions. For years there has been debate concerning whether different emotions are associated with a different, specific, and unique physiological profile of responding. Early research in this area was inconclusive. The first definitive evidence for this, however, came from a study that used the universal facial expressions as markers to signal when to examine physiological reactions. In this study, Ekman, Levenson, and Friesen (1983) demonstrated that each of the universal emotions, when signaled by the universal expressions, had a distinct and discrete physiological signature in the autonomic nervous system. Subsequent research has replicated these findings, and shown how there are specific patterns in central nervous system activity (the brain) as well (Davidson, 2003; Ekman, Davidson, & Friesen, 1990; Levenson, Carstensen, Friesen, & Ekman, 1991; Levenson & Ekman, 2002; Levenson, Ekman, & Friesen, 1990; Mauss, Levenson, McCarter, Wilhelm, & Gross, 2005).

Importantly for our discussion, these findings have been also replicated in cross-cultural samples. Tsai and Levenson (1997), for example, showed how the physiological responses of Chinese and European Americans were similar. Levenson, Ekman, Heider, and Friesen (1992) also showed that people from a very different culture—the Minangkabau of West Sumatra, Indonesia—also showed the same pattern of physiological response. These findings indicate that emotions help individuals to respond to emotional stimuli by preparing the body to engage in activity. Fear prepares us to flee, while anger prepares us to fight.

Universality in Subjective Emotional Experience

Another component of the emotion package is subjective experience. The most prominent study to examine subjective experiences across cultures is the work by Scherer and his colleagues, described earlier (Scherer & Wallbott, 1994). They asked respondents to rate their subjective feelings, physiological sensations, motor behaviors, and expressions when they felt anger, disgust, fear, joy, sadness, shame, and guilt. For all response domains, the seven emotions differed significantly and strongly among each other. Geographical and socio-cultural factors were much smaller than those for differences among the emotions. Thus, the researchers concluded that there are strong and consistent differences between the reaction patterns for the seven emotions, and that these are independent of the country studied. In other words, there were many more similarities in the responses across the cultures than there were differences, providing evidence for universal, psychobiological emotional patterning in subjective response.

Universality in the Coherence among Emotion Response Systems

Not only has the evidence shown that there is universality in the various responses of emotion—antecedent events, appraisals, expressive behavior, subjective experience, and physiology—but that there is also coherence among them. **Emotion response system coherence** refers to the idea that the various response components—face, voice, physiology, etc.—are related to each other in a meaningful way.

There are, in fact, many single-culture studies that demonstrate coherence among emotion response systems (reviewed in Matsumoto et al., 2006). The cross-cultural evidence, however, is just starting to emerge. Matsumoto et al. (2005), for example, reanalyzed the data from the Scherer studies described above, and examined the relationships among the self-reported expressive behaviors, emotional experiences, and physiological sensations. There were moderately sized correlations between these three systems of responses across the respondents in all 27 countries analyzed. There were also consistent correlations between verbal and nonverbal expressions, as well as between emotion intensity and physiological sensations, all of which suggest coherence in an underlying neurophysiological reality. Moreover, this coherence was true cross-culturally.

Universality in Emotion Recognition

One important aspect of basic emotions theory is the idea that not only are emotions universally expressed, but that they are universally recognized. Part of the original universality studies of emotion, in fact, were judgment studies, in which observers of different cultures viewed facial stimuli and judged the emotions portrayed in them. The earliest studies by Ekman and Izard demonstrated the existence of six universal expressions—anger, disgust, fear, happiness, sadness, and surprise—in literate and preliterate cultures (Ekman, 1972, 1973; Ekman & Friesen, 1971; Ekman, Sorenson, & Friesen, 1969; Izard, 1971).

Since the original studies by Ekman and Izard, 27 studies examining judgments of facial expressions have replicated the finding of universal recognition of basic emotion in the face (Matsumoto, 2001). In addition, a recent meta-analysis of 168 datasets examining judgments of emotion in the face and other nonverbal stimuli indicated universal emotion recognition well above chance levels (Elfenbein & Ambady, 2002). It would be very difficult to obtain such robust and consistent findings if expressions were not universally recognized. Even when low intensity expressions are judged across cultures (Ekman, Friesen, O'Sullivan, Chan, Diacoyanni-Tarlatzis, I., Heider, K., et al., 1987; Matsumoto, Consolacion, Yamada, Suzuki, Franklin, Paul, S., et al., 2002), there is strong agreement across cultures as to the emotion in the expression.

Research from the past two decades has also expanded the list of emotional expressions that are universally recognized. Ekman and his colleagues, for example, have reported data to support the universal recognition of contempt (Ekman & Friesen, 1986; Ekman & Heider, 1988; Matsumoto, 1992; Matsumoto & Ekman, 2004). There is also some evidence for the cross-cultural recognition of the self-conscious emotions of embarrassment and pride (Haidt & Keltner, 1999; Keltner, 1995; Tracy & Robins, 2004). Figure 8.2 shows examples of the seven emotions for which research has provided solid evidence for universal recognition.

Summary

In this section we have summarized the major cross-cultural findings to date concerning the basic emotions perspective (Ekman, 1999). This evidence suggests that emotions are a universal psychological phenomenon that is based in the evolution of the species. Humans appear to be born with a core set of basic emotions that are biologically innate and genetically encoded. They allow us to

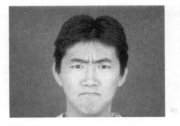

anger

disgust

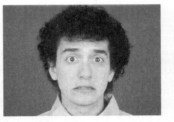

fear

happiness

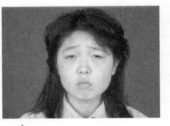

sadness

surprise

contempt

Figure 8.2 | The Seven Universal Expressions of Facial Emotion

appraise events and situations in reliable and predictable ways. When emotions are elicited, they trigger a host of responses, and these responses appear to be part of a universal emotion package. Humans can also universally recognize emotions in others, and this has important social meaning. Overall, these universal processes allow us to adapt, respond, and cope with problems that occur in our social lives and environments, aiding us to live, work, and function more effectively, regardless of the culture in which we are embedded.

CULTURAL DIFFERENCES IN EMOTION

Although humans may all universally start with the same base of emotions, cultures do influence a number of aspects of emotion in important ways. In this section we explore how that might occur, beginning with cultural influences on emotion antecedents.

Cultural Differences in Emotion Antecedents

As we discussed earlier, the same types of antecedents generally bring about the same kinds of emotions across cultures. But, cultural differences exist in the relative frequencies of the various antecedent events to bring about an emotion. For instance, in Scherer et al.'s data set, cultural events, the birth of a new family member, body-centered "basic pleasures," and achievement-related situations were more important antecedents of joy for Europeans and Americans than for the Japanese. Death of family members or close friends, physical separation from loved ones, and world news were more frequent triggers of sadness for Europeans and Americans than for the Japanese. Problems in relationships, however, produced more sadness for the Japanese than for Americans or Europeans. Strangers and achievement-related situations elicited more fear for Americans, whereas novel situations, traffic, and relationships were more frequent elicitors of fear for the Japanese. Finally, situations involving strangers were more frequent elicitors of anger for the Japanese than for the Americans or Europeans. Situations involving relationships brought about more anger for Americans than for Japanese.

Thus, emotions are elicited by the same underlying psychological theme described in Table 8.1. At the same time, cultures differ in the exact situations, events, or occurrences that are associated with the underlying content. That is, there is not always a one-to-one correspondence between latent and manifest content across cultures. Whereas death may produce sadness in one culture, for example, it may produce another emotion in another culture. In one culture, the manifest content of death may be associated with the latent content of loss of loved object, producing sadness; in another culture, the manifest content of death may be associated with a different latent content, such as achievement of a higher spiritual goal, producing a different emotion, happiness. Thus, the same manifest event may be associated with different underlying psychological themes, which give rise to different emotions. And an underlying theme may be associated with different manifest contents across cultures.

Cultural Differences in Emotion Appraisal

Despite the strong evidence for cross-cultural consistency in emotion appraisal processes, there are cultural differences as well. For example, one early study comparing American and Japanese responses (Matsumoto, Kudoh, Scherer, & Wallbott, 1988) showed that emotions had a more positive effect on self-esteem and self-confidence for Americans than they did for the Japanese.

Attributions of causality of emotions also varied by culture: Americans attribute the cause of sadness-producing events to others, whereas Japanese attribute the cause of sadness to themselves. Americans are also more likely to attribute the causes of joy, fear, and shame to other people, whereas the Japanese tend to attribute the causes of these emotions to chance or fate. Japanese believe more than Americans do that no action or behavior is necessary after an emotion is elicited. For emotions such as fear, more Americans than Japanese believe they can do something to influence the situation in a positive way. For anger and disgust, more Americans believe they are powerless and dominated by the event and its consequences. For shame and guilt, more Japanese than Americans pretended that nothing had happened and tried to think of something else. Cultural differences have been found by other researchers as well (Roseman et al., 1995; Mauro et al., 1992).

The largest cross-cultural study of emotion appraisal is Scherer's, reported above. In both of his studies, Scherer (1997a, b) reported cultural differences in emotion appraisal. In the first, Scherer (1997a) classified each of the 37 countries into one of six geopolitical regions: North/Central Europe, Mediterranean Basin, New World, Latin America, Asia, and Africa. Correlations among the appraisal dimensions across regions indicated great similarities across regions in appraisal processes, but Latin America and Africa seemed to differ slightly from the other regions. Scherer's further analyses (1997b) indicate that for all emotions except happiness, participants from African countries appraised the emotion-eliciting events as higher on unfairness, external causation, and immorality than did people from other regions. Respondents from Latin America had lower scores on perceptions of immorality than did people from other regions. Analyses involving climate, cultural values, and socioeconomic and demographic factors did not account for these differences. Still, Scherer suggested that a general factor of urbanism may account for both sets of findings (Africa and Latin America).

Collectively, these studies suggest that although many appraisal processes appear to be universal across humans, there is room for some cultural differences, especially in appraisal dimensions that require judgments relative to cultural or social norms such as fairness and morality. It would appear, therefore, that cultural differences may occur on these more "complex" appraisal dimensions, but not on more "primitive" dimensions, as suggested by Roseman and associates (1995). There appears to be something inherent to all humans that allows for the elicitation of a set of universal emotional experiences, but a role for culture in complex cognitive processes that allow for finer distinctions among emotions.

Cultural Differences in Expressive Behavior: Display Rules

The Original Display Rule Study   Despite the fact that facial expressions of emotion may be universal, many of us have experienced uncertainty about how to interpret the expressions of someone from a different cultural background. We may also wonder whether our own expressions are being interpreted in the way we intend. Although we see emotional expressions that are similar to ours in people from very diverse backgrounds, more often than not we see many differences as well.

Ekman and Friesen (1969) pondered this question many years ago and came up with the concept of **cultural display rules** to account for the discrepancy. They suggested that cultures differ in the rules governing how universal emotions can be expressed. These rules center on the appropriateness of displaying each of the emotions in particular social circumstances. These rules are learned early, and they dictate how the universal emotional expressions should be modified according to the social situation. By adulthood, these rules are automatic, having been very well practiced.

Ekman and Friesen (1969) suggested that there are multiple ways in which display rules can act to modify expressions. People can:

1. Express *less* than actually felt (Deamplification)
2. Express *more* than actually felt (Amplification)
3. Show nothing (Neutralization)
4. Show the emotion but with another emotion to comment on it (Qualification)
5. Mask or conceal feelings by showing something else (Masking)
6. Show an emotion when they really don't feel it (Simulation)

The existence of cultural display rules were supported by Ekman (1972) and Friesen's (1972) studies of spontaneous expressions of Americans and Japanese described above (one of the original universality studies). In the study described earlier, American and Japanese subjects were asked to view highly stressful films while their facial reactions were videotaped. That experiment actually had two conditions. In the first condition, subjects viewed the stimuli by themselves. In a second condition, an older, higher-status experimenter came into the room and asked the subjects to watch the films again, with the experimenter observing them. Their facial reactions were again videotaped. Analyses showed that the Americans in general continued to show negative feelings—disgust, fear, sadness, and anger. The Japanese, however, invariably smiled in these instances. These findings show how universal, biologically innate emotional expressions can interact with culturally defined rules of display to produce appropriate emotional expressions. In the first condition, when display rules did not operate, the Americans and the Japanese exhibited the same expressions. In the second condition, display rules were operative, forcing the Japanese to smile in order not to offend the experimenter, despite their obvious negative feelings. These findings are especially impressive because the subjects in the second condition that produced differences were the same individuals as in the first condition that produced similarities.

Recent Cross-Cultural Research on Display Rules   In recent years, a number of cross-cultural studies have extended our knowledge of the influence of culture on expression and display rules (e.g., Stephan, Stephan, and de Vargas, 1996; Pittam, Gallois, Iwawaki, & Kroonenberg, 1995; Pennebaker,

Rime, & Blankenship, 1996; McConatha, Lightner, & Deaner, 1994; Matsumoto, Takeuchi, Andayani, Koutnetsouva, & Krupp, 1998). To date, the largest cross-cultural study on display rules has been conducted by Matsumoto, Yoo, Anguas-Wong, Arriola, Ataca, Bond, et al. (2005). These researchers obtained data from approximately 5,000 respondents in 30 countries around the world for their Display Rule Assessment Inventory. This measure asks respondents to report what they would do if they felt each of seven emotions in 42 different situations. One of the major findings Matsumoto et al. reported concerned cultural differences in display rules as a function of emotion and interactant, using the concept of ingroups and outgroups (see Chapter 14).

In general, the familiarity and intimacy of self–ingroup relations in all cultures provide the safety and comfort to express emotions freely, along with tolerance for a broad spectrum of emotional behaviors. Part of emotional socialization involves learning who are ingroup and outgroup members and the appropriate behaviors associated with them. In Matsumoto et al.'s study, collectivistic cultures encouraged more positive and less negative emotions toward ingroups because ingroup harmony is more important to them. Positive emotions ensure maintenance of this harmony; negative emotions threaten it. Individualistic cultures, however, fostered more negative emotions and fewer positive emotions toward ingroups; because harmony and cohesion are less important to these cultures, it is considered appropriate to display emotions that may threaten group cohesion. Individualistic cultures foster more positive and less negative emotions toward outgroups, because it is less important in individualistic cultures to differentiate between ingroups and outgroups; thus, they allow expression of positive feelings and suppression of negative ones toward outgroup members. Collectivistic cultures, however, foster more negative expressions toward outgroups to distinguish more clearly between ingroups and outgroups and to strengthen ingroup relations (via the collective expression of negative feelings toward outgroups). These variations in the expressions of personal emotions are summarized in Table 8.2.

Table 8.2 | Expression of Personal Emotions in Self–Ingroup and Self–Outgroup Relationships in Individualistic and Collectivistic Cultures

	Type of Culture	
	Individualistic	Collectivistic
Self–Ingroup Relations	Okay to express negative feelings; less need to display positive feelings	Suppress expressions of negative feelings; more pressure to display positive feelings
Self–Outgroup Relations	Suppress negative feelings; okay to express positive feelings as would toward ingroups	Encouraged to express negative feelings; suppress display of positive feelings reserved for ingroups

Research has also documented the existence of cultural differences in emotional expression among ethnic groups in the United States. In one study (Matsumoto, 1993), Caucasian, black, Asian, and Latino American participants viewed the universal facial expressions of emotion and rated the appropriateness of displaying them in different social situations. The findings showed that Caucasians rated contempt as more appropriate than Asians, disgust as more appropriate than blacks and Latinos, fear as more appropriate than Latinos, and sadness as more appropriate than blacks and Asians. In addition, Caucasians rated the expression of emotions in public and with children as more appropriate than Latinos; with casual acquaintances as more appropriate than blacks, Asians, and Latinos; and with lower-status others as more appropriate than blacks or Latinos. Interestingly, however, blacks reported expressing anger more often than Caucasians, Asians, and Latinos.

Thus, although humans universally have the same base of emotional expressions, the research shows that culture exerts considerable influence over when and how to use them via culturally learned display rules. Facial expressions of emotion are under the dual influence of universal, biologically innate factors and culturally specific, learned display rules (see Figure 8.3). When an emotion is triggered, a message is sent to the facial affect program (Ekman, 1972), which stores the prototypic facial configuration information for each of the universal emotions. This prototypic configuration is what constitutes the universal aspect of emotional expression, and it is biologically innate. At the same time, however, a message is sent to the area of the brain storing learned cultural display rules. The resulting expression represents the joint influence of both factors. When display rules do not modify an expression, the universal facial expression of emotion will be displayed. Depending on social circumstances, however, display rules may act to neutralize, amplify, deamplify, qualify, or mask the universal expression. This mechanism explains how and why people can differ in their emotional expressions despite the fact that we all share the same expression base.

Cultural Differences in Judging Emotions in Others

Although the original universality research showed that subjects recognized emotions at well over chance rates, no study has ever reported perfect cross-cultural agreement (100 percent of the judges in any or all of the cultures agreeing on what emotion is portrayed in an expression). In fact, research has demonstrated the existence of reliable cross-cultural differences in recognition accuracy rates. Matsumoto's (1992) study, for instance, compared American and Japanese recognition of emotion, and showed that Americans were better at recognizing anger, disgust, fear, and sadness than were the Japanese, but accuracy rates did not differ for happiness or surprise.

Some findings suggest the cultural source of these differences. Matsumoto (1989) selected recognition data from 15 cultures reported in four studies and correlated these with Hofstede's (1980, 1983) four cultural dimensions— power distance (PD), uncertainty avoidance (UA), individualism (IN), and

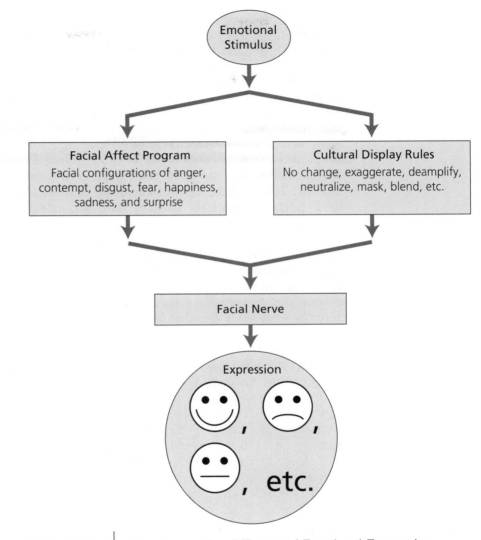

Figure 8.3 | The Neurocultural Theory of Emotional Expression

Adapted from P. Eckman, Universals and Cultural Differences in Facial Expressions of Emotion, in J. Cole (ed.), *Nebraska Symposium of Motivation*, 1971, vol. 19 (Lincoln: University of Nebraska Press, 1972).

masculinity (MA)—for each culture. (See Chapter 1 for a review of these dimensions.) He found that individualism was positively correlated with mean intensity ratings for anger and fear, supporting the claim that Americans (individualistic culture) are better at recognizing negative emotions than are Japanese (collectivistic culture). A meta-analysis by Schimmack (1996) also found differences in emotion perception as a function of culture. Individualism was a better predictor of recognition of happiness than ethnicity (operation-alized as Caucasian/non-Caucasian), supporting the notion that sociocultural dimensions account for differences in the perception of emotion. These data suggested that emotion recognition rates are influenced by culturally learned **decoding rules** about how to perceive expressions, especially given the fact that all posers were Caucasian. Like display rules, these are probably culturally dependent rules learned early in life that govern how emotional expressions are recognized.

An interesting development in the recent literature is the notion of an **ingroup advantage** in emotion recognition. This is defined as the ability of individuals from a certain culture to recognize the emotions of others of the same culture relatively better than of those from a different culture. Indeed several studies have provided some support for this claim (Elfenbein & Ambady, 2002, 2003a, 2003b; Elfenbein, Mandal, Ambady, & Harizuka, 2002; Elfenbein, Mandal, Ambady, Harizuka, & Kumar, 2004). But these studies have been challenged because of problems in the stimuli used, and when stimuli that are equivalent across the cultures—a methodological requirement in cross-cultural comparison (Chapter 2)—are judged, there is no evidence for the ingroup advantage effect (Matsumoto, 2002). Elfenbein & Ambady (2002) have suggested that the ingroup effect occurs because of cultural differences in emotion dialects—specific ways in which people of different cultures express emotions—but so far there has been no evidence that supports this interesting speculation.

Researchers have also documented interesting cultural differences in inferences about emotional experiences underlying facial expressions of emotion. Matsumoto et al. (1999) compared American and Japanese ratings of how strongly expressions were displayed and how strongly the expresser was actually feeling the emotion. Americans rated external display more intensely than did the Japanese; the Japanese, however, rated internal experience more intensely than did the Americans. Within-culture analyses indicated no significant differences between the two ratings for the Japanese. Significant differences were found, however, for the Americans, who consistently rated external display more intensely than subjective experience. Although previous American–Japanese differences in judgments and expressions were interpreted to have occurred because the Japanese suppressed their intensity ratings, these findings indicated that in fact it was the Americans who exaggerated their external display ratings relative to subjective experience, not the Japanese who suppressed. Not only are such findings wake-up calls to experienced cross-cultural researchers; they also force us to consider how culture produces these tendencies, and why.

Cultural Differences in the Concept and Social Meaning of Emotion

The Concept of Emotion   Throughout this chapter, we have been discussing emotion as if it means the same thing to all people. But does it? In the United States, we place a premium on feelings. We all recognize that each of us is unique and that we have our own individual feelings about the things, events, situations, and people around us. We consciously try to be aware of our feelings, to be "in touch" with them, as we say. To be in touch with our feelings and to understand the world around us emotionally is to be a mature adult in our society.

We place importance and value on feelings and emotions throughout the life span. We cherish our feelings as adults, and we actively try to recognize the feelings of our children and of other young people around us. It is not uncommon for parents to ask their young children how they feel about their swimming lessons, their piano lessons, their teachers at school, or the broccoli on their plates. Parents often give considerable weight to the feelings of their children in making decisions that affect them. "If Johnny doesn't want to do it, we shouldn't make him do it" is a common sentiment among parents in the United States. Indeed, children's emotions are afforded almost the same status as the emotions of adults and the older generations.

Much therapeutic work in psychology centers around human emotions. The goal of individual psychotherapy systems is often to get people to become more aware of their feelings and emotions and to accept them. Much psychotherapeutic work is focused on helping individuals freely express the feelings and emotions they may have bottled up inside. In group therapy, the emphasis is on communicating feelings toward others in the group and listening to and accepting the expressions of feelings by others. This emphasis is also prevalent in workgroups. Industrial and organizational interventions are common, and much time, effort, and energy are spent establishing better lines of communication among employees and recognizing the feelings and emotions of individuals.

How American society values and structures people's feelings and emotions is directly related to the values fostered by American culture. In the United States, rugged individualism has been a cornerstone of the dominant culture, and part of that rugged individualism means that we recognize and value the unique aspects of each and every person. Diversity of feelings and emotions is part of this package; in fact, it may be the most important part in identifying individuals because emotions themselves are highly personalized and individual. Children are valued as separate entities, and their feelings are valued.

The way American culture understands and defines emotion may not be the same in other cultures. First of all, not all cultures have a word for *emotion*. Levy (1973, 1983) reports that Tahitians do not have a word for emotion; nor, according to Lutz (1980, as reported in Russell, 1991; Lutz, 1983), do the Ifaluks of Micronesia. The fact that some cultures do not even have a word that corresponds to our word *emotion* is important; clearly, in these cultures, the concept of emotion is different from ours. Perhaps it is not as important to these cultures as it is to ours. Or perhaps what we know as emotion is labeled differently, in an untranslatable way, and refers to something other than internal, subjective feelings. In this case, too, their concept of emotion would be quite different from ours.

But most cultures of the world do have a word or concept for what we call emotion. Brandt and Boucher (1986) examined the concepts of depression in different cultures, whose languages included Indonesian, Japanese, Korean, Malaysian, Spanish, and Sinhalese. Each of the languages had a word for emotion, suggesting the cross-cultural existence of this concept. But even if a culture has a word for emotion, that culture's word may have different connotations, and thus different meanings, than our English word. For example, Matsuyama, Hama, Kawamura, and Mine (1978) analyzed emotional words from the Japanese language, which included some words that are typically considered emotions (for example, *angry, sad*) but also some words that Americans would not consider to be emotions (for example, *considerate, lucky*). Samoans do not have a word for emotion but do have a word (*lagona*) that refers to feelings and sensations (Gerber, 1975, as reported in Russell, 1991).

In summary, not all cultures of the world have a word or concept for what we label *emotion* in English, and even among those that do, it may not mean the same thing as the English word. These studies suggest that the class of events—expressions, perceptions, feelings, situations—that we call emotion does not necessarily represent the same class of phenomena in other cultures.

The Categories of Emotion   Also, many English words have no equivalent in another culture, and emotion words in other languages may have no exact English equivalent. The German language, for example, contains the word *Schadenfreude,* which refers to pleasure derived from another's misfortunes. There is no exact English translation for this word. The Japanese language contains words such as *itoshii* (longing for an absent loved one), *ijirashii* (a feeling associated with seeing someone praiseworthy overcoming an obstacle), and *amae* (dependence), which also have no exact English translation. Conversely, some African languages have a word that covers what English suggests are two emotions: anger and sadness (Leff, 1973). Likewise, Lutz (1980) suggests that the Ifaluk word *song* can be described sometimes as anger and sometimes as sadness. And some English words have no equivalents in other languages. The English words *terror, horror, dread, apprehension,* and *timidity* are all referred to by the single word *gurakadj* in Gidjingali, an Australian aboriginal language (Hiatt, 1978). This aboriginal word also refers to the English concepts of shame and fear. *Frustration* may be a word with no exact equivalent in Arabic languages (Russell, 1991).

Just because a culture does not have a word for something that we consider an emotion certainly does not mean that people of that culture do not have those feelings. The fact that there is no exact equivalent in some Arabic languages for our word *frustration* does not mean that people of these cultures never feel frustrated. Similarly, just because our English language does not have a translation equivalent for the German word *Schadenfreude* does not mean that people in the United States do not sometimes derive pleasure from someone else's misfortunes. (Just watch an episode of *America's Funniest Videos!*) Certainly, in the world of subjective, emotional feeling, there must be considerable overlap in the emotions we feel, regardless of whether different cultures and languages have translation equivalents for those feeling states.

The fact that translation differences exist in the exact meaning and labeling of diverse emotional states across languages and cultures does suggest, however, that various cultures divide their world of emotion differently. The fact that German culture, for example, contains the word *Schadenfreude* must mean that identification of that feeling state or situation has some importance in that language and culture that it does not have in American culture or the English language. The same can be said of English words that find no exact translation equivalent in other languages. The types of words that different cultures use to identify and label the emotion worlds of their members give us yet another clue about the way different cultures structure and mold the emotional experiences of their people. Not only are the concepts of emotion culture-bound, but so also are the ways each culture attempts to frame and label its emotion world.

The Location of Emotion   To Americans, perhaps the single most important aspect of emotion is feelings—that is, subjective experience. Emotion words in the languages of several Oceanic peoples, such as the Samoans (Gerber, 1975), Pintupi aborigines (Myers, 1979), and Solomon Islanders (White, 1980), are statements about relationships among people or between people and events. Likewise, Riesman (1977) suggests that the African Fulani concept *semteende*, which is commonly translated as shame or embarrassment, refers more to a situation than to a feeling. That is, if the situation is appropriate to *semteende*, then someone is feeling it, regardless of what any one individual actually feels (Russell, 1991).

In the United States, we place emotion and inner feelings in the heart. Even cultures that locate emotions within the body differ in that exact location. The Japanese identify many of their emotions in the *hara*—the gut or abdomen. The Chewong of Malay group feelings and thoughts in the liver (Howell, 1981). Levy (1984) reports that Tahitians locate emotions as arising from the intestines. Lutz (1982) suggests that the closest Ifaluk word to the English word *emotion* is *niferash,* which she translates as "our insides."

That different cultures locate emotions in different places informs us that emotions are understood differently and have different meanings for different peoples. Locating emotions in the heart is convenient and important for American culture, as it speaks to the importance of feelings as something unique to oneself, that no one else can share. By identifying emotion with the heart, Americans identify it with the most important biological organ necessary for survival. The fact that other cultures identify and locate emotions outside the body, such as in social relationships with others, speaks to the importance of relationships in those cultures, in contrast to the individualism of American culture.

The Meaning of Emotions to People and to Behavior   All the differences we have discussed in the concept and meaning of emotion point to differences in the ways different cultures attribute meanings to emotional experiences. In the United States, emotions have enormous personal meaning, perhaps because

Americans typically view inner, subjective feelings as the major defining characteristic of emotion. Once emotions are defined in such a way, a major role of emotion is to inform oneself about the self. Our self-definitions are informed by our emotions, which are personal, private, inner experiences.

Cultures differ in the role or meaning of emotions. Many cultures, for example, consider emotions as statements of the relationship between people and their environment, be it objects in the environment or social relationships with other people. Emotions for both the Ifaluks of Micronesia (Lutz, 1982) and the Tahitians (Levy, 1984) denote statements of relationships with others and with the physical environment. The Japanese concept *amae,* a central emotion in Japanese culture, specifies an interdependent relationship between two people. Thus, the very concept, definition, understanding, and meaning of emotion can differ across cultures. Therefore, when talking to others about our feelings, we cannot simply assume that they will understand us in the way we expect, even though we are speaking of something as "basic" as human emotion. And we certainly cannot assume that we know what someone else is feeling, and what it means, just on the basis of knowing about emotions from our own limited perspective.

Cultural Constructionist Approaches to Emotion

Based largely on the findings above concerning cultural differences in the concept and social meaning of emotion, a host of other researchers, led by Kitayama and Markus (1991, 1994, 1995), Wierzbicka (1994), and Shweder (1994), have taken a different approach in describing cultural influences on emotional experiences. Using a constructionist approach, these researchers view emotion as a set of "socially shared scripts" composed of physiological, behavioral, and subjective components. They suggest that these scripts develop as individuals are enculturated, and that they are inextricably linked to the culture in which they are produced and with which they interact. Emotion, therefore, reflects the cultural environment in which individuals develop and live, and are as integral a part of culture as morality and ethics are. Markus and Kitayama (1991b; see also Chapter 13 for a review) cite evidence from a variety of sources to support this view, including studies that demonstrate a difference between cultures in the experience of socially engaged versus disengaged emotions, and in cultural patterns of feeling good and happiness.

In this view, culture shapes emotion. Because different cultures have different realities and ideals that produce different psychological needs and goals, they produce differences in habitual emotional tendencies. This model of the "cultural construction of emotion" is summarized in Figure 8.4. This view challenges universality and any claims concerning the biological innateness of emotion, arguing that precisely because of the inextricably intertwined relationship between culture and emotion, emotion could not possibly be biologically "fixed" for all people. They suggest that the universality of emotion is a misnomer, and that supportive findings derive from the experimental and theoretical biases of the researchers that have reported them.

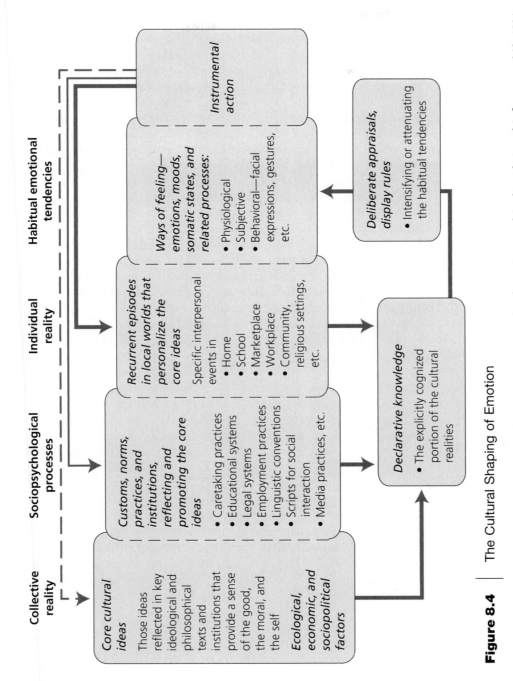

Figure 8.4 | The Cultural Shaping of Emotion

Kitayama, Shinobu, and Hazel Rose Markus (eds). From *Emotion and Culture: Empirical Studies of Mutual Influence*, p. 342, 1994. Published by the American Psychological Association. Reprinted with permission.

CONCLUSION

In this chapter, we have reviewed the evidence for the universality and biological innateness of a set of basic emotions. They are elicited by the same psychological themes around the world, and when elicited, trigger a coordinated set of responses that include expressive behavior, physiology, and action potential. They have important meaning not only to oneself but to others. Because they are universally expressed, emotions are also universally recognized.

Cultures influence emotions by influencing the relative frequencies by which antecedent events bring forth emotions, and the specific dimensions by which emotions are appraised. Cultures can influence expressive behavior via cultural display rules, and can influence how we judge emotions in others via cultural decoding rules. There are also interesting and important cultural differences in the concept and social meaning of emotion around the world.

The coexistence of universal and culture-specific aspects of emotion has been a source of debate for many years. We believe that these are not necessarily mutually exclusive positions; that is, universality and cultural relativity can indeed coexist. It appears that universality may be limited to a rather small set of basic emotions, which serve as a platform for interactions with learned rules, social mores, and shared social scripts, resulting in a variety of more complex culture-specific emotions and emotional meanings. The mere fact that universality exists does not negate the potential for cultural differences. Likewise, the mere fact that cultural differences exist does not negate the potential for universality. They are two sides of the same coin, and both need to be incorporated into future theories and research on emotion, whether within or across cultures.

Also, it is important to keep in mind that researchers often study different emotions. The universality position is limited to a small set of discrete emotions—or more precisely emotion families—that have a corresponding unique facial expression. Studies conducted by the functionalists have incorporated a broad range of emotional experience that goes well beyond this limited set of universal emotions. Also, these researchers have studied different aspects of emotion. The universality of emotion is based on the existence of pancultural signals of emotional expression in the face. Much of the research on the cultural construction of emotion is based on the **subjective experience of emotion,** and the emotion lexicons in language that are used to describe and represent those experiences. It is not inconceivable that one component of emotion may be universal while the other is culturally relative. Finally, the existence of universals and innate biological substrates of emotion does not preclude the possibility that cultures can also construct much of their experience. As mentioned earlier, the universal bases of emotion may provide a standard platform on which such construction may take place. It seems, therefore, that cultural construction of emotional experience can occur above and beyond the baseline that is provided by basic emotions with universal expressions. Future research in this area may be guided by such complementary viewpoints rather than driven by arbitrarily antagonistic positions.

Indeed, the incorporation of underlying, universal, psychobiological processes into a model of cultural construction of emotion is a challenge that lies ahead in this area of research. Scientists in this area of psychology will need to take up the greater challenge of how biology interacts with culture to produce the individual and group psychologies we see around the world. If nothing else, at least our recognition of emotions as a universal process can help bring people together, regardless of culture, race, ethnicity, or gender. As we continue our study of human feelings and emotions across cultures, perhaps it is most important to recognize how these boundaries mold our emotions. Although we all have emotions, they mean different things to different people and are experienced, expressed, and perceived in different ways. One of our first tasks in learning about emotions across cultures is to recognize and respect those differences. But an equally important task is to recognize our similarities as well.

GLOSSARY

basic emotions A small set of emotions, or family of emotions, that are considered to be universal to all humans, biologically based and genetically coded, and evolutionarily based. Humans come into the world with programs for these basic emotions; social and cultural learning then influences how they are used in life.

cultural display rules Culturally prescribed rules that govern how universal emotions can be expressed. These rules center on the appropriateness of displaying emotion, depending on social circumstances. Learned by people early in their lives, they dictate how the universal emotional expressions should be modified according to the social situation. By adulthood, these rules are quite automatic, having been very well practiced.

decoding rules Rules that govern the interpretation and perception of emotion. These are learned, culturally based rules that shape how people of each culture view and interpret the emotional expressions of others.

emotion antecedents The events or situations that elicit an emotion.

emotion appraisal The process by which people evaluate the events, situations, or occurrences that lead to their having emotions.

emotion response system coherence The idea that the various response components of an emotion—facial expressions, voice, physiological reactions, movements, etc.—are related to each other in a coordinated fashion that prepares individuals to do something vis-à-vis the emotion aroused.

ingroup advantage The ability of individuals from a certain culture to recognize emotions of others of the same culture relatively better than of those from a different culture.

self-conscious emotions Emotions that focus on the self, such as shame, guilt, pride, or embarrassment. They are important in studies of culture because we believe that humans universally have a unique knowledge of self that is different from that of other animals, thus giving rise to self-conscious emotions.

subjective experience of emotion An individual's inner feelings or experiences of an emotion.

universality studies A series of studies conducted by Ekman and Friesen and by Izard that demonstrated the pancultural universality of facial expressions of emotion.

9 CHAPTER | # Culture, Language, and Communication

CHAPTER CONTENTS

THE DUAL EVOLUTION OF LANGUAGE AND HUMAN CULTURE

As we discussed in Chapter 1, the evolution of human cultures is probably associated with the evolution of the ability for verbal language in humans. Language probably evolved in humans in order to help us create large social networks, larger than those found in nonhuman primates; to navigate those social networks quickly and efficiently; and to solve complex social coordination problems when they occur. Language is an incredibly important ability that allows us to do all these tasks and activities.

With the advent of language in humans, we were able to create meaning about the world around us in terms of symbols. Humans are intentional agents, having the ability to infer intentions in others, and language aids in our ability to communicate intentions, and our beliefs about the intentions of others, to each other quickly and efficiently. These abilities come together to help humans form human cultures. As we defined in Chapter 1, we believe human cultures are unique meaning and informational systems communicated across generations. This definition, which focuses on meaning and information systems, makes it clear that it is impossible to consider and understand human cultures without acknowledging the contribution that language makes to it. In short, human cultures exist precisely because of the ability to have language.

For this reason, language is a universal psychological ability in humans. All individuals have the capacity to develop language, and the vast majority of people all over the world indeed do so, with the exception of a very few individuals who are raised from childhood virtually in the total absence of other humans. All humans have an innate ability to acquire language, and although the exact mechanisms are not well understood, language acquisition does occur in all individuals.

Thus, all human societies have language, and language forms the basis for the creation and maintenance of human cultures. Now it is true that there are great differences among cultures in the type and use of language; some cultures, for example, have only an oral culture with no writing; many others, like the American culture, are heavily dependent on written language. Regardless of these great differences, however, language is universal to all humans.

At the same time, although the ability to have language is universal to humans, each culture creates its own unique language. And in fact, language differences reflect important differences between cultures, and they also help to reinforce culture. In the next section, therefore, we begin to explore how languages are different across cultures.

CULTURAL INFLUENCES ON VERBAL LANGUAGE

The Structure of Language

In order to examine the relationship between culture and language, it is useful first to identify the basic structure and features of language to build a vocabulary. Linguists typically describe language using the following five critical features, which appear to apply to all languages in all cultures:

1. The **lexicon,** or vocabulary, refers to the words contained in a language. For example, the words *tree, eat, how,* and *slowly* are each part of the English lexicon.
2. The **syntax and grammar** of a language refer to the system of rules governing word forms and how words should be strung together to form meaningful utterances. For example, English has a grammatical rule that says we add *s* to the end of many words to indicate plurality (*cat* becomes *cats*). English also has a syntactic rule that we generally place adjectives before nouns, not after (for example, *small dog,* not *dog small*).
3. **Phonology** refers to the system of rules governing how words should sound (pronunciation) in a given language. For instance, in English, we do not pronounce the word *new* the same way we do *sew*.
4. **Semantics** refers to what words mean. For example, *table* refers to a physical object that has four legs and a flat horizontal surface.
5. **Pragmatics** refers to the system of rules governing how language is used and understood in given social contexts. For example, the statement "It is cold" could be interpreted as a request to close a window or as a statement of fact about the temperature. How it is interpreted depends on the social and environmental context.

Linguists use two other concepts to help explain the structure of language. **Phonemes** are the smallest and most basic units of sound in a language, and **morphemes** are the smallest and most basic units of meaning in a language. Phonemes thus form the base of a language hierarchy in which language gains in complexity as sounds gain meaning, which in turn produces words, which are strung together in phrases and, finally, sentences.

Cultural Influences on Language Acquisition

As we mentioned above, all humans have the universal ability to acquire language. Although the precise mechanisms by which language acquisition occurs are still unknown, it appears that all human infants are born with the ability to make the same range of sounds. Thus, human infants produce the same range of phonemes across cultures. Through interactions with others, infants' sound production is then shaped and reinforced so that certain sounds are encouraged while certain others are discouraged. These elemental sounds become associated with meanings (morphemes) and gradually are combined into words (lexicons) and sentences. In fact, the ability to create an almost infinite number of meaningful expressions from a finite set of elemental sounds is one of the characteristics that differentiate humans from nonhuman animals (Fitch & Hauser, 2004).

Culture, therefore, influences language acquisition from a very early stage, helping to shape the morphemes of a language and the creation of words. Culture provides the rules by which words are said (phonology), and strung

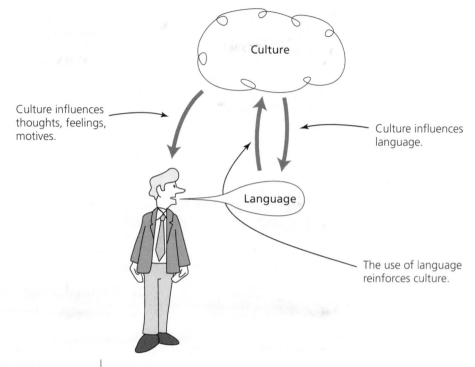

Culture influences thoughts, feelings, motives.

Culture influences language.

The use of language reinforces culture.

Figure 9.1 | The Reciprocal Relation between Culture and Language

together to form meaningful statements (syntax and grammar). Culture also provides the rules by which meaning is derived from words and statements (semantics), and the rules by which language is used in different social contexts (pragmatics). The influence of culture on language, therefore, is pervasive.

Thus, through the use of language, an individual is transformed into an agent of the culture. Thus, the feelings, associations, connotations, and nuances of language both influence and are influenced by the culture. Over time, an individual embodies the very essence of culture via language, and in using the language, he or she reinforces that language's concepts of culture (see Figure 9.1). By this token we would hypothesize that students of language may learn a language better if part of their training involves training about the culture from which the language originates, compared to language training by itself.

Language Differences across Cultures

Research has documented a number of ways in which cultures differ in their languages. Here we focus on two: cultural differences in lexicons, and cultural differences in pragmatics.

Culture and Lexicons One way in which cultures influence the language lexicon is in what is known as **self–other referents**—that is, what we call ourselves and others. In American English, for example, we generally use one of two words, and their derivatives, to describe ourselves when talking to others: *I* and *we*. We use these words irrespective of whom we are talking to or what we are talking about. If we are talking to a university professor, we use the word *I* to refer to ourselves. If we are talking to our parents, we use the same word *I*. And we use the same word *I* when referring to ourselves with friends, family, neighbors, acquaintances, bosses, or subordinates. Likewise, we generally use a single word in English to refer to another person or group of people: *you*. In conversation with our parents, bosses, friends, lovers, strangers, children, and just about anyone, we use *you* or one of its derivatives to refer to the other person or persons.

Many languages in the world, however, have much more elaborate systems of reference that depend on the nature of the relationship between people. The Japanese language, for instance, does have translation equivalents of the English words *I*, *we*, and *you*, but these words are used much less frequently in Japanese than in English. In Japanese, what you call yourself and others is dependent on the relationship between you and the other person. Often, the decision about what is appropriate to call yourself and another person depends on the status differential between the two people. For example, if you are of a higher status than the other person, in Japan you would refer to yourself by position or role rather than by the English equivalent of *I*. In Japan, teachers use the word *teacher* to refer to themselves when talking to students. Doctors may use the term *doctor*, and parents use the word *mother* or *father* when referring to themselves while speaking to their children.

In the Japanese language, if you are of a lower status than the person to whom you are speaking, you refer to yourself using one of several pronoun equivalents of *I*, such as *watashi, watakushi, boku,* or *ore*. The use of these different terms for *I* depends on your sex (women cannot say *boku* or *ore*), degree of politeness, and degree of familiarity with the other person. When speaking to someone of higher status, for example, people generally use *watashi* to refer to themselves. When speaking to friends or colleagues, men usually refer to themselves as *boku* or *ore*.

Likewise, if you are speaking to someone of higher status, you generally refer to that person by role or title. When speaking to your teachers, you refer to them as *teacher*, even when addressing them directly. You would call your boss by his or her title, such as *section chief* or *president*. You would definitely not use a personal pronoun such as our English *you* in addressing a person of higher status. When speaking to a person of lower status, you would generally use a personal pronoun or the person's actual name. As with personal pronouns for *I*, the Japanese language contains several pronouns for *you*—among them, *anata, omae,* and *kimi*. Again, the appropriate use of each depends on the relationship; generally, *omae* and *kimi* are used when speaking to someone of lower status or to someone with whom you are very familiar and intimate. Indeed, the Japanese language system of self- and other-referents is very complicated, especially when compared with American English (see Figure 9.2).

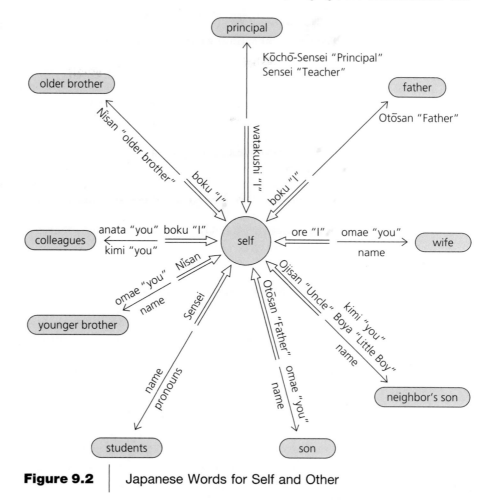

Figure 9.2 | Japanese Words for Self and Other

Source: Suzuki, T. (1973). *Words in context.* Tokyo: Kodansha International. ©Copyright 1973. Reprinted with permission.

These differences between the English and Japanese languages reflect important cultural differences. In the Japanese culture, language, mannerisms, and other aspects of behavior must be modified according to the relationship and context in which the communication is occurring. The most important dimensions along which behavior and language are differentiated in Japan are status and group orientation. All aspects of behavior differ depending on whether one person is higher or lower in status than the other person in the conversation. Also, behavior and language differ depending on whether the other person is a member of your ingroup or not. Thus, the choice of appropriate self and other referents in the Japanese language reflects important aspects of Japanese culture, and this is true of many other languages around the world as well.

Counting systems provide yet another example of how culture influences the structure of a language. In the Japanese language, for example, different words are used to denote different things being counted. Round, cylindrical objects are counted by the suffix *hon* (*ippon, nihon, sanbon,* and so on); flat objects are counted by *mai* (*ichimai, nimai, sanmai,* and so on). Japanese has many such counters, as do many other languages. In English, however, all objects are simply counted by the number, with no such prefix or suffix to denote the type of object being counted.

In addition, the Japanese language, like many other languages, bases all numbers on the words for one through ten. Eleven is literally ten-one (*ju-ichi*), 12 is ten-two (*ju-ni*), 20 is two-ten (*ni-ju*). In English, however, numbers 1 through 19 are unique, and an additive system similar to Japanese numbers starts at 20. These linguistic differences are thought to contribute to differences in math achievement between the United States and Japan (see Stigler & Baranes, 1988).

Culture and Pragmatics   Culture affects not only the language lexicons, but also pragmatics—that is, the rules governing how language is used and understood in different social contexts. Kashima and Kashima (1998), for example, examined 39 languages used in 71 countries, obtaining both cultural and linguistic data from each country. The cultural scores included Hofstede's (1980, 1983) four dimensions—individualism, power distance, uncertainty avoidance, and masculinity—and 15 other culture-related dimensions. The linguistic data included an analysis of the use of first- and second-person pronouns, and whether the language permitted dropping these pronouns in conversation. The correlations between these two sets of data were analyzed in two ways to examine the relationship between culture and pronoun usage. Kashima and Kashima found that cultures whose languages allowed pronouns to be dropped tended to be less individualistic, which they interpreted as reflecting different cultural conceptualizations of self and others.

Gudykunst and his colleagues have also done a number of studies that demonstrate cultural variability in language use and communication styles. Gudykunst and Nishida (1986b), for example, asked participants in the United States and Japan to make intimacy ratings of 30 relationship terms (such as brother, employer, stranger) and, in another study, to rate communication styles in six relationships on personalization, synchrony, and difficulty. The results indicated that the Japanese rated ingroup relationships—coworkers and university colleagues—as more intimate than did the Americans, and that the Japanese perceived more personalization but less synchrony across relationship terms. In a subsequent study, Gudykunst, Yoon, and Nishida (1987) tested participants from the United States, Japan, and Korea, asking them to rate the same three dimensions of communicative behavior in ingroup and outgroup relationships. They found that the Americans had the lowest personalization and synchronization scores, the Koreans the highest, and the Japanese in the middle, but only for ingroup communication. These researchers suggested that members of collectivistic cultures use a principle of equity involving greater social penetration when communicating with ingroup members than do members of individualistic cultures.

Cultural differences have also been documented in a number of other communication areas, such as apologies (Barnlund & Yoshioka, 1990), children's personal narratives (Minami & McCabe, 1995), self-disclosure (Chen, 1995), compliments (Barnlund & Araki, 1985), and interpersonal criticism (Nomura & Barnlund, 1983). Chen, for example, asked American and Taiwanese participants to complete a measure of self-disclosure in relation to four target persons and six conversational topics. The results indicated that Americans had a significantly higher level of self-disclosure than did the Taiwanese Chinese across all topics and target persons. Barnlund and Yoshioka reported that Japanese participants preferred more direct, extreme forms of apology, while Americans preferred indirect, less extreme forms. Also, Americans tended to favor explanation as a form of apology, whereas the Japanese preferred compensation.

Many of these cultural differences in pragmatics can be summarized in terms of communication style. Some languages are very direct; others very indirect. Some languages are very succinct and precise; others very elaborate and extended. Some cultures are very contextual, that is, important meanings are conveyed in the context within which language occurs, or in the way in which it is delivered, relative to the actual content of the speech. Consequently, some cultures are **high-context cultures** with high-context languages, while others are **low-context** (Hall, 1966, 1973). Some languages have specific forms for **honorific speech,** which are specific language forms that denote status differences among interactants, conferring higher status to others while at the same time acknowledging one's lower status when appropriate, and vice versa.

Language and Thought: The Sapir–Whorf Hypothesis

One of the most important and long-standing debates in studies of language and behavior involves the relationship between language and thought processes. This relationship is particularly important to the cross-cultural study of language, because each culture is associated with a given language as a vehicle for its expression. How does culture influence language? And how does language influence culture?

The **Sapir–Whorf hypothesis,** also referred to as *linguistic relativity,* suggests that speakers of different languages think differently, and that they do so because of the differences in their languages. Because different cultures typically have different languages, the Sapir–Whorf hypothesis is especially important for understanding cultural differences (and similarities) in thought and behavior as a function of language.

If the Sapir–Whorf hypothesis is correct, it suggests that people of different cultures think differently, just by the very nature, structure, and function of their language. Their thought processes, their associations, their ways of interpreting the world—even the same events we perceive—may be different because they speak a different language and this language has helped shape their thought patterns. This hypothesis also suggests that people who speak more than one language may actually have different thought patterns when speaking different languages.

In Support of Sapir-Whorf   Many studies have looked at language–cognition issues since Edward Sapir and Benjamin Whorf first proposed their hypothesis in the 1950s. In one of the earliest language studies, Carroll and Casagrande (1958) compared Navajo and English speakers. They examined the relationship between the system of shape classification in the Navajo language and the amount of attention children pay to shape when classifying objects. Similar to the Japanese language described earlier in this chapter, the Navajo language has the interesting grammatical feature that certain verbs of handling (for example, "to pick up," "to drop") require special linguistic forms depending on what kind of object is being handled. A total of 11 such linguistic forms describe different shapes—round spherical objects, round thin objects, long flexible things, and so forth. Noting how much more complex this linguistic feature is in Navajo than in English, Carroll and Casagrande suggested that such linguistic features might play a role in influencing cognitive processes. In their experiment, they compared Navajo- and English-dominant children to see how often they used shape, form, or type of material to categorize objects. The Navajo-dominant children were significantly more likely to categorize by shape than were the English-dominant children. In the same study, Carroll and Casagrande also reported that the performance of low-income African American English-speaking children was similar to that of European American children. This finding is particularly important, because the African American children, unlike the European Americans, were not accustomed to blocks and form-board toys. The results of this study—along with the observations concerning the relationship between culture and language lexicons, and culture and pragmatics reviewed earlier—provided early support for the idea that the language we speak influences the kind of thoughts we have. Language, that is, may act in a mediating role, helping to determine the ways in which children conceive of some aspects of their world.

Later studies also provided support for linguistic relativity. For instance, Kay and Kempton (1984) compared the thought processes of speakers of English with those of speakers of Tarahumara, a language indigenous to northern Mexico that does not distinguish between blue and green. Bloom (1981) reported that Chinese speakers are less likely than English speakers to give hypothetical interpretations to a hypothetical story. Lucy (1992), comparing American English with the language of the Yucatec Maya in southeastern Mexico, identified distinctive patterns of thought relating to differences in the two languages. Hoosain (1986, 1991) has shown how unique aspects of the Chinese language influence the ease of processing information. Garro (1986), comparing American English and Mexican Spanish, demonstrated that language influenced memory for colors. Santa and Baker (1975) provided evidence in favor of the Sapir–Whorf hypothesis in their study of language effects on the quality and order of visual reproduction of figures. Lin and

Schwanenflugel (1995), comparing English and Taiwanese Chinese, demonstrated that language structure was related to the structure of category knowledge in American and Chinese speakers. Most recently, Gordon (2004) demonstrated that the lack of counting words above the number three in the Piraha tribe of the Amazonia was associated with difficulties in counting tasks for these individuals, which also argued in favor of the Sapir–Whorf hypothesis.

Challenging Sapir–Whorf   At the same time, however, findings from other studies challenge the Sapir–Whorf hypothesis. For instance, Berlin and Kay (1969) tested Gleason's (1961) earlier claims that "The continuous gradation of color which exists in nature is represented in language by a series of discrete categories. . . . There is nothing inherent either in the spectrum or the human perception of it which would compel its division in this way. The specific method of division is part of the structure of English" (p. 4). To test this claim, Berlin and Kay undertook a study of the distribution of color terms in 20 languages. They asked international university students in the United States to list the "basic" color terms in each of their native languages. They then asked these foreign students to identify from an array of glass color chips the most typical or best examples of a basic color term the researchers specified. Berlin and Kay found a limited number of basic color terms in any language. They also found that the color chips chosen as best examples of these basic terms tended to fall in clusters they termed "focal points." In languages that had a basic term for bluish colors, the best example of the color was found to be the same "focal blue" for speakers of all the languages. These findings suggested that people in different cultures perceive colors in much the same way, despite radical differences in their languages.

Berlin and Kay's findings were later confirmed by a series of experiments conducted by Rosch. In her experiments, Rosch (for example, 1973) set out to test just how culturally universal these focal points were. She compared two languages that differ markedly in the number of basic color terms: English, with multiple color terms, and Dani, which has only two color terms. Dani is the language spoken by a Stone Age tribe living in the highlands of Irian Jaya, Indonesian New Guinea. One color term, *mili*, was found to include both "dark" and "cold" colors (for example, black, green, and blue), while the second color term, *mola*, included both "light" and "warm" colors (for example, white, red, and yellow). Rosch also explored the relationship between language and memory. She argued that if the Whorfian position were correct, Dani's lack of a rich color lexicon would inhibit Dani speakers' ability to discriminate and remember colors. As it happened, Heider and Oliver (1972) found that Dani speakers did not confuse color categories any more than did speakers of English. Nor did Dani speakers perform differently from English speakers on memory tasks.

Berlin and Kay (1969) also examined 78 languages and found that 11 basic color terms form a universal hierarchy. Some languages, such as English and German, use all 11 terms; others, such as Dani (New Guinea), use as few as two. Further, they noticed an evolutionary order in which languages encode these universal categories. For example, if a language has three color terms, those three terms describe black, white, and red. This hierarchy of color names in human language is as follows:

1. All languages contain terms for white and black.
2. If a language contains three terms, it also contains a term for red.
3. If a language contains four terms, it also contains a term for either green or yellow (but not both).
4. If a language contains five terms, it contains terms for both green and yellow.
5. If a language contains six terms, it also contains a term for blue.
6. If a language contains seven terms, it also contains a term for brown.
7. If a language contains eight or more terms, it also contains a term for purple, pink, orange, gray, or some combination of these.

Studies have also challenged Bloom's (1981) earlier claim of linguistic relativity with Chinese and English speakers. Au (1983), for example, reported five studies intending to replicate Bloom's (1981) study, using Chinese and English versions of stories used by Bloom. Au concluded that the use of hypothetical interpretations was probably not related to the use of the subjunctive, or to counterfactual reasoning in the Chinese (see also critique of Au's study by Bloom, 1984). Liu (1985) also failed to replicate Bloom's study. Takano (1989) discussed both conceptual and methodological problems with Bloom's study, and suggested that the positive findings obtained by Bloom may have been an artifact of methodological flaws. He conducted three studies investigating the nature of those flaws, and concluded that differences in the amount of mathematical training, not linguistic differences, may have produced the differences Bloom originally reported.

In a review concerning the Sapir–Whorf hypothesis, Pinker (1995) concluded that many of the earlier studies claiming linguistic relativity are severely flawed (such as Bloom's). He then pointed to the fact that we can think *without* words and language, suggesting that language does not necessarily determine our thoughts. He cited evidence of deaf children who clearly think while lacking a language, but soon invent one; of isolated adults who grew up without language but still could engage in abstract thinking; how babies, who have no words, can still do very simple forms of arithmetic (Wynn, 1992); and how thought is not just made up of words and language, but is also visual and nonverbal.

Sapir–Whorf: What's the Bottom Line?   Perhaps the best way to make sense of this area of study comes from an analysis of the basic Sapir–Whorf hypothesis published by Fishman in 1960. Many studies of the Sapir–Whorf hypothesis read as if it were only one hypothesis; actually, there are several Sapir–Whorf hypotheses. Fishman published a comprehensive breakdown of the most important ways the Sapir–Whorf hypothesis has been discussed (see Table 9.1). In his description, these different approaches are ordered in

Table 9.1 | Fishman's Sapir–Whorf Hypothesis Schema

Data of Language Characteristics	Data of Cognitive Behavior	
	Linguistic Data	Nonlinguistic Data
Lexical/Semantic	Level 1[*]	Level 2
Grammatical	Level 3	Level 4[**]

[*]Least sophisticated
[**]Most sophisticated

increasing levels of complexity. Two factors determine the level at which a given version of the hypothesis might fall. The first factor relates to the particular aspect of language that is of interest—for example, the lexicon or the grammar. The second factor relates to the cognitive behavior of the speakers of a given language—for example, cultural themes or nonlinguistic data such as a decision-making task. Of the four levels, Level 1 is the least complex; Level 4 is the most complex. Levels 3 and 4 are actually closer to Whorf's original ideas in that they concern the grammar or syntax of language as opposed to its lexicon.

In reviewing the literature on the Sapir–Whorf hypothesis, it is important to keep in mind exactly which level of the hypothesis is being tested. Few research studies test the Sapir–Whorf hypothesis at Fishman's Level 3 or 4. A considerable amount of research compares lexical differences and linguistic behavior (Fishman's Level 1) or nonlinguistic behavior (Fishman's Level 2). Most of this research is at Level 2, comparing lexical differences with non-linguistic behaviors. When such comparisons have shown differences, language is assumed to have caused these differences.

Viewed according to Fishman's classifications, the best-studied area is lexical differences between languages, which provides some of the weaker support for the hypothesis. This makes sense, because the lexicon seems to be only minimally related to thought processes, which may account for some skepticism about the Sapir–Whorf hypothesis. A less-studied area, however—that of syntactic and grammatical differences between languages—provides some evidence for the claim that language influences cognition. Perhaps stronger evidence will be found in future studies of how the pragmatic systems of different languages influence speakers' thought processes.

CULTURAL INFLUENCES ON NONVERBAL COMMUNICATION

As we have been discussing, verbal language is indeed a large component of communication. Indeed, we attend to the words and the language that people use. Our formal educational experiences, from elementary school on, center

These American servicemen were taken captive when North Korea seized the U.S. ship *Pueblo* in 1968. Can you find the nonverbal behavior displayed by some of these men, sending a message that their captors were unaware of? (Look at the position of their fingers.) Courtesy, AP/Wide Word Photos

around language—words, grammar, spelling, and punctuation. We spend much of our time thinking about just the right words to use to express ourselves—our ideas, our thoughts, our opinions. We think about just the right thing to say to our boyfriends and girlfriends, business associates, acquaintances, work colleagues, or the police. We concentrate on the words and language when we speak.

But verbal language is not the only component. Communication also involves nonverbal behaviors as well. **Nonverbal behaviors** are all of the behaviors that occur during communication that do *not* include verbal language. These include facial expressions, nonverbal vocal cues (tone of voice, pitch, intonation, pauses, silence), gestures, body postures, interpersonal distance, touching behaviors, gaze and visual attention, and the like. In short, all our nonverbal behaviors form important channels of communication as well (see Photo 9.1).

There is an interesting paradox with regard to communication. Research has shown, for example, that the bulk of messages that occur in communication are carried nonverbally, not verbally. Thus, the nonverbal channels are actually more important in understanding meaning and especially the emotional states of the speakers. Yet research has also demonstrated that most people consciously attend to the verbal language, not the nonverbal behaviors, when interacting with and judging others (Ekman, Friesen, O'Sullivan, & Scherer, 1980; O'Sullivan, Ekman, Friesen, & Scherer, 1985). For this reason, it may be important to be more attentive to the nonverbal cues that occur in communication.

The Types of Nonverbal Behaviors

In Chapter 8 we discussed at length how cultures influence facial expressions of emotion via display rules. Here we'll discuss how cultures influence other aspects of nonverbal communication.

Culture and Gestures   Gestures are nonverbal behaviors that have meaning on their own, like a phrase or sentence. The study of culture and gestures has its roots in the study by David Efron (Boas & Efron, 1936; Efron, 1941), who examined the gestures of Sicilian and Lithuanian Jewish immigrants in New York City. Efron found that there were distinct gestures among traditional Jews and Italians, but that the traditional gestures disappeared as people were more assimilated into the larger American culture. This work was followed initially by that of Ekman and his colleagues (Ekman, 1976; Friesen, Ekman, & Wallbott, 1979), who documented cultural differences in emblematic gestures between Japanese, American, and New Guinean participants. Morris, Collett, Marsh, and O'Shaughnessy (1980) have also documented many cultural differences in gestures. The American A-OK sign, for example, is an obscene gesture in many cultures of Europe, having sexual implications. Placing your hands at the sides of your head and pointing upward with the forefingers signals one is angry in some cultures; in others, however, it means that one wants sex.

Culture and Gaze   Research on humans and nonhuman primates has shown that gaze is associated with dominance, power, or aggression (Fehr & Exline, 1987) and affiliation and nurturance (Argyle & Cook, 1976). Fehr and Exline suggested that the affiliative aspects of gazing begin in infancy, because infants are very attentive to adults as their source of care and protection. Cultures create rules concerning gazing and visual attention because both aggression and affiliation are behavioral tendencies that are important for group stability and maintenance. Cross-cultural research has documented differences in these rules. People from Arabic cultures, for example, gaze much longer and more directly at their partners than do Americans (Hall, 1963; Watson & Graves, 1966). Watson (1970) classified 30 countries as either a "contact" culture (those that facilitated physical touch or contact during interaction) or a "noncontact" culture, and found that contact cultures engaged in more gazing and had more direct orientations when interacting with others, less interpersonal distance, and more touching. Within the United States, there are differences in gaze and visual behavior between different ethnic groups (Exline, Jones, & Maciorowski, 1977; LaFrance & Mayo, 1976).

Culture and Interpersonal Space   Hall (1966, 1973, 1976) specified four different levels of interpersonal space use depending on social relationship type: intimate, personal, social, and public. Although people of all cultures make these distinctions, they differ in the spaces they attribute to them. Arab males, for example, tend to sit closer to each other than do American males, with more direct, confrontational types of body orientations (Watson & Graves, 1966).

They also had greater eye contact and tended to speak in louder voices. Hall (1963, 1966) concluded that people from Arab cultures generally learn to interact with others at distances close enough to feel the other person's breath. Forston and Larson (1968) cited anecdotal evidence of how Latin American students tended to interact more closely than did students of European backgrounds. Noesjirwan (1977, 1978) reported that Indonesian subjects tended to sit closer than did Australians. Shuter (1977) reported that Italians interacted more closely than did either Germans or Americans. Shuter (1976) also reported that people from Colombia generally interacted at closer distances than did the subjects from Costa Rica.

Culture and Other Nonverbal Behaviors   Other studies have documented cultural differences in other nonverbal behaviors as well, such as in the semantic meanings attributed to body postures (Kudoh & Matsumoto, 1985; Matsumoto & Kudoh, 1987), and vocal characteristics and hand and arm movements (Vrij & Winkel, 1991, 1992). Collectively, the evidence provides more than ample support for the notion that culture plays a large role in molding all of our nonverbal behaviors, which comprise an important part of the communication process.

The Functions of Nonverbal Behaviors

Nonverbal behaviors play a large role in the communication process by serving several important functions (Ekman & Friesen, 1969). First, they serve as **emblems;** that is, they carry messages just like a phrase or sentence. The thumbs up and A-OK gestures, for instance, are emblems. Second, they serve as **speech illustrators.** For example, people often raise their brows when they raise their voice, and lower their brows when they lower their voice. Third, nonverbal behaviors serve as **conversation regulators.** That is, they manage the flow of conversation, telling others than one is finished speaking and inviting others to speak. Fourth, they convey emotion, as we discussed in Chapter 8.

INTRACULTURAL AND INTERCULTURAL COMMUNICATION

Communication is a complex and intricate process that involves the exchange of messages between interactants. It is complex because there are actually two languages occurring in any communication episode—verbal and nonverbal. In addition, there are many other processes occurring simultaneously or sequentially. In order to understand the complexity of the communication process, we need to build a vocabulary of its elemental units.

- **Messages** are the information and meanings that are exchanged when two or more people communicate. These may be knowledge, ideas, concepts, thoughts, or emotions.

- **Encoding** refers to the process by which people select, consciously or unconsciously, imbed messages in signals, and send those message-laden signals to others.
- **Signals** are observable behaviors that do not necessarily have inherent meaning, but carry messages that are encoded during communication. That is, these are the specific verbal language and nonverbal behaviors that are encoded when a message is sent.
- **Channels** refer to the specific sensory modalities by which signals are sent and messages are retrieved, such as sight or sound. The most widely used channels of communication are visual—seeing facial expressions, body postures, gestures, and the like—and auditory—hearing words, tone of voice, and so on. However, all the other senses are used in communication, including touch, smell, and taste.
- **Decoding** refers to the process by which a person receives signals from an encoder and translates those signals into meaningful messages.

The process of communication, therefore, can be described as one in which a sender encodes a message into a set of signals. These signals are conveyed through a variety of channels. The receiver decodes the signals to interpret the message. Once a message is interpreted, the decoder then becomes the encoder, relaying back his or her own messages via the same process. The original encoder then becomes the decoder. This complex process of exchange, with switching roles and encoding and decoding of messages, constitutes the process of communication. It is akin to playing catch with messages (Matsumoto, in press). And we do this amazingly quickly.

Cultural Influences on Encoding

Of course, culture influences our verbal language. It influences the language lexicons and vocabulary, and the rules by which words are put together to form meaningful phrases and sentences. Culture also influences our thoughts, feelings, and actions via language.

Culture also influences our nonverbal behaviors. People of all cultures learn to use nonverbal behaviors—facial expressions, gestures, distance, gaze, and postures—as part of their communication repertoire, but people in each culture learn to use them in very specific ways. All humans are born with the capacity to form all types of sounds; culture dictates how we shape and mold those sounds into particular languages. In the same way, culture shapes and molds nonverbal behaviors into each culture's nonverbal language.

Consider, for example, American culture. When we speak to people, we look them straight in the eye. Our faces and gestures often become animated, highlighting specific, important parts of our speech. We learn to sit or stand at a certain distance when we interact, depending on with whom we are interacting and the specific context or situation in which that interaction is occurring. We learn how to signal when we are finished speaking and when we want to continue speaking. In short, we learn a very specific, American system of nonverbal behaviors to aid in our communication process, just as we have learned American English as a verbal language.

Cultural Influences on Decoding

As with cultural decoding rules regarding the perception and interpretation of emotion, discussed in Chapter 8, we learn rules from early childhood that aid us in deciphering the cultural codes inherent in speech and all other aspects of interaction. These decoding rules develop in conjunction with display or encoding rules, and are a natural part of the development of communication skills.

Culture also influences the decoding process through ethnocentrism, cultural filters, emotions, value judgments, stereotypes and expectations, and social cognitions. As we grow, we learn how to perceive signals and interpret messages; that is, we learn cultural rules of appropriate decoding as well. Because we share a set of encoding and decoding rules with people of our culture, we develop a set of expectations about communication. These expectations are often based on implicit stereotypes we hold about how communication "ought to be." These rules and expectations form a basis of tacit understanding that need not be spoken each time we, as adult members of the same culture, communicate with one another.

Not only do we have certain expectations about the communication process; we have also learned emotional reactions associated with those expectations. These reactions can range from acceptance and pleasure to outrage, hostility, and frustration. Our emotions, in turn, are intimately tied to value judgments and attributions, which we often make without a second thought. These judgments seem only natural because they are rooted in our upbringing; they are the only types of judgments we have learned to make. Emotions and values serve as guidelines in helping us form opinions about others and ourselves.

Thus, decoding rules, and their associated emotions and value judgments, form the basis of the "filters" that we use in seeing the world. As we become more enculturated, we add more layers to those filters. These filters are like lenses that allow us to perceive the world in a certain way. By the time we are adults, we share the same filters with others in our cultural group. They become part of our self, inseparable and invisible, and are a normal part of our psychological composition because of the way we have been enculturated.

Intracultural Communication

Intracultural communication refers to communication among people of the same cultural background. Intracultural communications works because interactants implicitly share the same ground rules. Thus, the coded "packages" we send when we are encoders, and those that we receive and open when we are decoders, are familiar to us because we generally share the same type of wrapping and box. When people communicate within the boundaries of accepted ground rules, they can focus on the content of the messages that are being exchanged. They encode and decode messages using the same cultural codes. When we communicate within the shared boundaries of culture, we make an implicit judgment that the other person is a member of our culture or is engaging in socially appropriate behavior. We may consider the individual to have been socialized "well" into our culture, and we make value judgments about the process and the person's ability to engage in that accepted process.

This does not mean that all intracultural communication is positive. When we interact with people who transgress what we view as "normal" or "socially appropriate," we often have negative reactions. We sometimes have trouble interpreting the signals they are trying to send because they do not conform to the cultural rules of "packaging" that we expect of members of our culture. We react negatively because we have learned that such transgressions are not appropriate, and we may make negative dispositional attributions such as "bad," "stupid," "had a bad upbringing," or "has no common sense." In these situations, negative stereotypes can easily develop. Because our cultural filters and ethnocentrism create a set of expectations about others, communicating with people whose behaviors do not match our expectations often leads to negative attributions. Such unanticipated events require substantive processing (Forgas, 1994), which is most affected by induced emotion. If the emotion induced is negative, then it will contribute to negatively valenced attributions about others. These attributions form the core of a stereotype of such people, and reinforce the value and expectation system originally held. These processes are common even within intracultural communication episodes.

Intercultural Communication

Intercultural communication refers to communication between people of different cultural backgrounds. Consider a situation in which you are interacting with someone from a different culture. People from another culture bring with them their own verbal language. A person from Israel, for example, will bring the ability to speak Hebrew. A person from India will bring the ability to speak Hindi or a provincial dialect of India. But beyond the culture-specific verbal language that people bring with them, they also bring a culture-specific nonverbal language. Thus, people from Israel will bring with them the Israeli- or Jewish-specific language of nonverbal behaviors; people from India will bring with them the India-specific (or Hindu- or Muslim- or Brahmin-specific) language of nonverbal behaviors. Any type of interaction always involves two languages—one verbal and the other nonverbal.

When we examine intercultural communication in micromomentary detail, we find much the same process as with intracultural communication. But one big difference is that during intercultural communication, interactants do not necessarily share the same ground rules. It becomes more difficult to focus on the content of the messages that are being exchanged, as people may be encoding and decoding messages using different cultural codes. If this happens, if communication does not proceed smoothly and misunderstandings occur, we may tend to make implicit judgments that the other person does not know how to act appropriately, is rude, or is not a good person.

The message that one person wants to send is packaged in this person's cultural code. The packaged signals are received by the other person, and the second person has trouble opening the package because his or her cultural codes differ from the first. As a result, the message may be unclear, distorted, or ambiguous.

Because intercultural communication occurs under these circumstances, it is associated with a host of additional psychological issues that do not normally occur in intracultural communication. Here we will discuss two issues that have gained widespread attention in the intercultural research literature: uncertainty and ambiguity, and conflict.

Uncertainty and Ambiguity   One characteristic that sets intercultural communication apart from intracultural communication is uncertainty or ambiguity concerning the ground rules by which the interaction will occur. Because of the widespread and pervasive influence of culture on all aspects of the communication process, we cannot be sure that the rules by which two people from different cultures operate are similar. This uncertainty is inherent in both verbal and nonverbal behaviors, in both coding and decoding modes: how to package messages into signals that will be interpreted according to one's intentions, and how to open packages according to the sender's original intentions.

Intercultural interactants often engage with each other in a verbal language that is not a native language for at least one of them, and sometimes both. Thus, there is inherent uncertainty in the meaning of the words. Cultural differences in the use of all nonverbal channels add to the uncertainty. Decoders can never be as sure in intercultural situations as they are in intracultural ones that they are interpreting signals and messages as originally intended by encoders.

Gudykunst and his colleagues have documented how interactants work to reduce uncertainty in intercultural interactions, at least in initial encounters. Their work is based on Berger (1979) and Berger and Calabrese (1975), who suggested that a primary concern of strangers in initial encounters is to reduce uncertainty and increase predictability in themselves and others. Gudykunst and Nishida (1984) tested 100 American and 100 Japanese participants, assigning them to one of four experimental conditions: cultural similarity (intracultural communication) and attitude similarity, cultural dissimilarity (intercultural communication) and attitude similarity, cultural similarity and attitude dissimilarity, and cultural dissimilarity and attitude dissimilarity. Cultural similarity or dissimilarity was manipulated by having participants interact with a stranger from either their own culture or the other culture. Attitude similarity or dissimilarity was manipulated through a description of similar or dissimilar attitudes when introducing the stranger. For each participant, the researchers assessed intent to self-disclose, intent to interrogate, nonverbal affiliative expressions, attributional confidence, and interpersonal attraction. The results indicated that intent to interrogate, intent to self-disclose, and nonverbal affiliative expressiveness were all higher in the cultural dissimilarity condition than in the cultural similarity condition. Uncertainty reduction theory predicts that these strategies would be used more extensively in communication contexts with higher levels of uncertainty. Gudykunst, Sodetani, and

Sonoda (1987) extended these findings to include members of different ethnic groups as well, demonstrating that differences in ethnicity and stage of relationship are also related to differences in communicative behaviors designed to reduce uncertainty.

In another study, Gudykunst and Shapiro (1996) asked students at a large university to record their perceptions of communication episodes with other students. The researchers found that students rated intracultural episodes higher than intercultural episodes in quality of communication and positive expectations, and rated intercultural episodes higher in anxiety, uncertainty, and social identity. Likewise, students rated intraethnic encounters as higher in quality and satisfaction, and interethnic encounters as higher in anxiety and uncertainty. These data support the notion that intercultural communication episodes are marked by greater uncertainty than intracultural encounters.

Conflict   A second characteristic of intercultural communication is the inevitability of conflict and misunderstandings. During intercultural encounters, chances are great that people's behaviors will not conform to our expectations. We often interpret those behaviors as transgressions against our value system and morality. They produce negative emotions, which are upsetting to our self-concepts. These conflicts arise in intercultural episodes not only with people but also with other agents of a cultural system (such as public transportation, the post office, shops, businesses). These interactions are bound to accentuate differences in process, which inevitably lead to conflict or misunderstanding.

Figure 9.3 illustrates why this conflict is inevitable. Because interactants cannot send or receive signals unambiguously, as they are accustomed to doing in intracultural situations, the intercultural communication episode can be frustrating and patience-testing. Tempers are quick to flare in such situations, and people can easily become distraught or turned off by the extra effort such interactions require. Even if interactants are somewhat successful in unpackaging signals, the messages interpreted may be partial, ambiguous, or misunderstood. Messages may not be deciphered according to the sender's original intent, leading to miscommunication gaffes and problems later on.

Of course, uncertainty contributes to this conflict. People may become impatient with or intolerant of the ambiguity, leading to anger, frustration, or resentment. Even after uncertainty is reduced, however, conflict is inevitable because of the differences in meaning of verbal language and nonverbal behaviors across cultures, and the associated emotions and values inherent in the cultural system. The result is often differences in the interpretation of underlying intent among interactants—which can sometimes occur in intracultural communication as well.

Research highlights how intercultural interactions may be difficult. In one study (Pekerti & Thomas, 2003), East Asian and Anglo-European students in New Zealand participated in a task with either another East Asian or Anglo-European student in which they had to rate the severity of crimes. Their actual communication behaviors during the 15-minute task were coded by research assistants and categorized according to an individualistic or collectivistic style.

Figure 9.3 | A Micromomentary Analysis of Intercultural Communication

The results indicated that in the intercultural communication situation, the Anglo Europeans actually communicated in more individualistic ways than in the intracultural situation, and the East Asian students actually communicated in more collectivistic ways than in the intracultural situation. These findings suggest that in intercultural situations, cultural differences in communication actually become more pronounced, as compared with intracultural situations.

Together, uncertainty and conflict make intercultural communication a complex yet fascinating process that challenges even the most practiced and interculturally sensitive of people. Given these challenges, how can we develop our skills at intercultural communication and improve intercultural relationships?

Barriers to Effective Intercultural Communication

Barna (1996) has outlined six major obstacles to effective intercultural communication:

1. *Assumptions of similarities.* People may naively assume that others are the same as they are, or at least are similar enough to make communication easy.
2. *Language differences.* When people are trying to communicate in a language in which they are not entirely fluent, people often think that a word, phrase, or sentence has one and only one meaning—the meaning they intend to convey. To make this assumption is to ignore all the other possible sources of signals and messages discussed in the previous two chapters, including nonverbal expressions, tone of voice, body orientation, and many other behaviors.
3. *Nonverbal misinterpretations.* Misunderstandings in relation to the interpretation of nonverbal behaviors can easily lead to conflicts or confrontations that break down the communication process.
4. *Preconceptions and stereotypes.* Overreliance on stereotypes can prevent us from viewing others and their communications objectively, and from searching for cues that may help us interpret their communications in the way they were intended.
5. *Tendency to evaluate.* Different cultural values may generate negative evaluations of others.
6. *High anxiety or tension.* Intercultural communication episodes are often associated with greater anxiety and stress than are more familiar intracultural communication situations. Too much anxiety and stress can lead to dysfunctional thought processes and behaviors. Stress and anxiety can exaggerate all the other stumbling blocks, making it more likely that people will cling dogmatically to rigid interpretations, hold onto stereotypes despite objective evidence to the contrary, and make negative evaluations of others.

Improving Intercultural Communication

Mindfulness and Uncertainty Reduction Effective conflict management requires knowledge of and respect for cultural differences in worldviews and behaviors, as well as sensitivity to differences between high- and low-context communication patterns and differences in cultural perceptions of time. Ting-Toomey (1996) stresses the importance of **mindfulness** in dealing with conflict in intercultural communication. According to Langer (1989; cited in Ting-Toomey, 1996), mindfulness allows people to be conscious of their own habits, mental scripts, and cultural expectations concerning communication. Mindfulness allows one to continually create new mental categories, remain open to new information, and be aware of multiple perspectives. In short, mindfulness allows one to be conscious and conscientious about the various characteristics that are associated with ethnorelativism.

Gudykunst (1993) also suggests ways to improve intercultural communication that include mindfulness. His model of intercultural competence has three main components: motivational factors, knowledge factors, and skill factors. Motivational factors include the specific needs of the interactants, attraction between the interactants, social bonds, self-conceptions, and openness to new information. Knowledge factors include expectations, shared networks, knowledge of more than one perspective, knowledge of alternative interpretations, and knowledge of similarities and differences. Skill factors include the ability to empathize, tolerate ambiguity, adapt communication, create new categories, accommodate behavior, and gather appropriate information. Gudykunst suggests that these three types of factors influence the amount of uncertainty in a situation and the degree of anxiety or stress interactants actually feel. Finally, these components influence the degree to which interactants are "mindful" of the communication episode—that is, the degree to which they take conscious and deliberate steps to think through their own and others' behaviors and to plan and interpret the interaction appropriately as it unfolds. According to this model, a high degree of mindfulness offsets uncertainty and anxiety, resulting in effective communication.

Thus, **uncertainty reduction** is one of the major goals of initial intercultural encounters. Without uncertainty reduction, it is impossible for interactants to begin processing the content of signals and interpreting messages properly, because uncertainty renders messages inherently ambiguous. If uncertainty is reduced, interactants can then focus on the content of the signals and messages that are being exchanged. Intercultural communication is like deciphering coded language: The first step is to decipher the code (reduce uncertainty); the second is to interpret and respond to the content, once deciphered.

Face   People of individualistic cultural tendencies who have to deal with conflicts in a collectivistic culture should be mindful of the importance of **face** (the public appearance or image of a person) and the maintenance of face in the collectivistic culture (Ting-Toomey, 1996); be proactive in dealing with low-grade conflict situations; not be pushy; be sensitive to the importance of quiet, mindful observation; practice attentive listening skills, especially in relation to the feelings of others; discard the model of dealing with problems directly; and let go of conflict situations if the other party does not want to deal with them directly. Collectivistic people who must deal with conflicts in an individualistic context should be mindful of individualistic problem-solving assumptions;

focus on resolving major issues and expressing their feelings and opinions openly; engage in assertive conflict behavior; take individual responsibility for dealing with conflict; provide verbal feedback; use direct verbal messages; and commit to working out the problem directly with the other person.

In sum, according to Ting-Toomey (1996), people from both individualistic and collectivistic cultures need to be mindful of the cognitive, affective, and behavioral biases and framework within which they normally operate, and of the blinders that they often bring to communication and conflict-mediation situations. They need to be open to learning and trying new communication skills, and to create new mental categories to build more successful intercultural relationships. Finally, they need to be conscious of important cultural concepts such as face in order to communicate effectively.

Emotion Regulation   Effective intercultural communication is not always easy, and research has demonstrated a key role for a psychological process known as emotion regulation (Matsumoto & LeRoux, 2003; Matsumoto, LeRoux, Bernhard, & Gray, 2004; Matsumoto, LeRoux, Iwamoto, Choi, Rogers, Tatani, et al., 2003; Matsumoto, LeRoux, Ratzlaff, Tatani, Uchida, Kim, et al., 2001; Matsumoto, Yoo, & LeRoux, in press). Conflict and misunderstandings are inevitable, and our normal ethnocentric and stereotypic ways of thinking often lead us to make negative value judgments about those differences, conflicts, and misunderstandings. Negative emotions are often associated with these judgments. These negative reactions make it difficult for us to engage in more constructive methods of interacting; they keep us from appreciating differences and integrating with people who are different. Because conflict is inevitable in intercultural communication, it becomes extremely important to be able to control our negative emotional reactions. Those who can control their emotions will be able to engage in a more constructive intercultural process, opening the door to more successful intercultural interactions. Those who cannot will have that door closed to them. Emotions, therefore, hold the key to successful intercultural experiences.

When faced with cultural differences and conflict in intercultural communication, individuals who can somehow control their negative feelings—putting them on hold and not acting directly on them or allowing them to overcome their thinking, acting, and feeling—will be able to engage in other processes that will help them broaden their appraisal and attribution of the causes of those differences. Once emotions are held in check, individuals can then engage in critical thinking about the origins of those differences, hopefully going beyond their own cultural framework to consider causes of which they may not have even been aware. If this type of critical thinking can occur, individuals can be open to alternative hypotheses concerning the causes of those differences, and have the flexibility to accept or reject them.

Regulating or controlling negative emotions, therefore, is a gatekeeper ability that allows us to become more mindful of our communication and style and to engage in more constructive and open creation of new mental categories. Having the most complex mental model of effective intercultural communication will not help us unless we are able to deal with the negative emotions that are bound to occur in intercultural communication episodes—to put them aside for the time being so that we can engage in more constructive thought processes that involve the creation of new mental categories via critical thinking. Regulating emotions is the key that allows us to open the door to these more advanced complex processes.

In addition to emotional regulation, being a critical thinker when confronted with cultural differences and being open to new ideas and perspectives are also key ingredients to becoming an effective intercultural communicator. Critical thinking requires an understanding of your own cultural filters and ethnocentrism and a recognition that cultural differences are legitimate. Being open and flexible to accept, or at least attempt to understand, cultural differences is also necessary. In general, the literature suggests that knowledge and skills are necessary components of effective intercultural communication, but that they are not sufficient. Knowledge and skills must be combined with openness and flexibility in one's thinking and interpretations, and with the motivation to communicate effectively and build a successful relationship.

BILINGUALISM AND CULTURE

Psychological Differences as a Function of Language

One important fact that many American students should realize about the world is that although English is one of the most widely spoken languages in the world, the majority of individuals who speak English also speak at least one other language fluently. That is, individuals who speak English and only English are actually a minority in the world of English speakers.

The fact that there are so many bilingual and multilingual individuals in the world raises interesting questions concerning the relationship between language and culture in these individuals. If, as we have discussed throughout this chapter, language is a symbol system of a culture, and if people can speak two or more languages fluently, that would suggest that bilinguals have two mental representations of culture—two different meaning systems—encoded in their minds. Thus, when speaking one language, speakers may access one culturally based meaning system, but when the same person speaks another language, he or she may access a different meaning system.

This issue has actually been examined for years. Ervin (1964), for example, compared responses from a sample of English/French bilinguals to pictures from the Thematic Apperception Test (a common test used in many cross-cultural studies). The subjects told their stories in response to the pictures once in English and then in French. Ervin found that subjects demonstrated more aggression, autonomy, and withdrawal in French than they did in English, and that females demonstrated a greater need for achievement in English than in French. Ervin attributed these differences to the higher value French culture places on verbal prowess and to greater sex-role differences.

How might the issue of bilingualism and culture be important for immigrants to the United States? Consider, for example, a Chinese/English bilingual raised in a monolingual Chinese-speaking home who learned English naturally only after migrating to the United States from China at age 8. She is now a 20-year-old college student living with her parents. She uses Chinese as the only language in the home, but English at school and with most of her peers. We might predict that when using Chinese she would be likely to behave in ways appropriate to Chinese cultural norms in the home. In English, however, she might be more likely to behave in ways that are closer to European American norms.

Hull (1987) and Dinges and Hull (1992) have also reported such differences with immigrant bilinguals. Immigrants are believed to have two clearly distinct cultural affiliations, accessible through the language in which much of this cultural knowledge was learned or is associated. In their studies, Chinese/English and Korean/English immigrant bilinguals were given the California Psychological Inventory (CPI), a widely used personality test. The immigrant bilinguals completed the CPI twice—once in their native language and once in English. The central question was, would a dual self or dual personality emerge, showing up as between-language, within-group differences in CPI scores? The answer was a resounding yes. In other words, these bilinguals presented different personalities depending on whether they were responding in their first language (Chinese or Korean) or in English (their second language). In a second study, Hull (1990a, b) confirmed these earlier findings using a different measure of personality.

These findings are not limited to paper-and-pencil personality questionnaires. Matsumoto and Assar (1992) asked bilingual observers in India (Hindi and English) to view a set of 40 facial expressions of emotion. The observers were asked to judge which emotion was being portrayed in the faces, and how intensely. The observers made these judgments twice, a week apart, the first time in English and the second time in Hindi. The results showed that judgments of which emotion was being portrayed were more accurate when the judgments were made in English. But the emotions were perceived more intensely when the ratings were made in Hindi. The same people, viewing the same facial expressions, made different judgments of those expressions depending on which language they used to make those judgments.

Two explanations have been offered for the mechanisms that underlie such language-related shifts in personality. They are known as the culture-affiliation hypothesis and the minority group–affiliation hypothesis. The **culture-affiliation hypothesis** is simply that immigrant bilinguals will tend to affiliate themselves with the values and beliefs of the culture associated with the language in which they are currently operating. When the language is switched, so are the cultural values with which they affiliate. The **minority group–affiliation hypothesis,** in contrast, suggests that immigrant bilinguals will tend to self-identify as members of an ethnic minority group and adopt the behavioral stereotypes of the majority culture about their minority as their own when they are operating in the language associated with their minority group. To the extent that such stereotypes are accurate, the minority group–affiliation hypothesis will make the same predictions as does the culture-affiliation hypothesis; that is, when interacting in their first language, people will behave in ways more typical of their ancestral culture, which may also be consistent with majority culture stereotypes of that culture. Language context would predict differences in behavior, and also in personality.

A series of interesting studies by Benet-Martinez and her colleagues have shed even more light on this important issue. They propose that bilinguals are bicultural, and must navigate between their multiple cultural identities based on the contextual cues afforded them in their environment (e.g., where they are, with whom they are interacting, etc.). Benet-Martinez and colleagues propose that bilinguals engage in **code frame switching** when engaging in this navigation, switching back and forth from one cultural meaning system to the other when accessing one language or another. In one of their studies (Hong, Morris, Chiu, & Benet-Martinez, 2000), for instance, Chinese American bicultural individuals were exposed to either stereotypically American images (e.g., Superman, the U.S. flag) or Chinese images (Chinese dragon, the Great Wall), were then shown some innocuous pictures, and were asked to make attributions about causality for the events in the pictures. For example, the students saw the scene depicted in Figure 9.4 (a group of fish). They then rated statements that reflected either internal or external motives of the fish. For example, if a student judged that one fish was leading the other, this reflected more of an

Figure 9.4 | Stimulus Material Used as the Attributional Stimulus

Reprinted from Hong, Y. Y., Morris, M., Chiu, C.-Y., & Benet-Martinez, V. (2000). Multicultural minds: A dynamic constructivist approach to culture and cognition. *American Psychologist, 55,* 709–720.

internal orientation. If a student judged the one fish to be chased by the others, this reflected more of an external orientation.

The results indicated that when they were primed with American images, the students tended to make more internal attributions, a typically American attributional style (Figure 9.5). When primed with the Chinese images, however, the students tended to make more external attributions, a more typically East Asian attributional style. In their most recent studies, Benet-Martinez and colleagues (Benet-Martinez, Leu, Lee, & Morris, 2002) have shown that code frame switching actually occurs more with bicultural individuals who perceive themselves to be better integrated in both cultures.

Perceptions of Bilinguals

The research described here demonstrates how closely language and culture are intertwined. It also demonstrates the importance of language in everyday experience. In addition, these findings help to dispel the misconception that the existence of two personalities within an individual means that the individual is suffering from a mental disorder. Such a situation is clearly a natural and healthy part of the bilingual/bicultural experience.

Other misconceptions persist, however. For example, negative impressions and stereotypes, particularly about intelligence, can occur when communicating with people in their second language because they may take more time in responding and appear to have cognitive difficulties while processing information. These difficulties, known as **foreign language processing difficulties**, arise because of nonfamiliarity or lack of fluency in speaking a language, and because of uncertainty or ambiguity about the intended meaning of messages when received in a foreign language. These difficulties are a normal part of learning a language, and should not be used as a basis for negative inferences about intelligence or other dispositional characteristics of individuals who may be communicating in a second (or third) language.

Bilinguals may also experience difficulties in nonlinguistic thinking tasks; such difficulties are known as the **foreign language effect** (Takano & Noda, 1993). This term refers to a temporary decline in the thinking ability of people who are using a foreign language in which they are less proficient than their native language. The foreign language effect, seen in nonlinguistic thinking tasks, is a by-product of the foreign language processing difficulty seen in linguistic tasks. Takano and Noda demonstrated the existence of this effect in two studies involving Japanese/English bilinguals. In the first study, Japanese Japanese/English and American English/Japanese bilinguals performed a calculation task and responded to a question-and-answer task in either their first (native) or second (foreign) language. Performance for both groups of participants was lower when the question-and-answer task was in the foreign language. In the second study, basically the same methods were used with a different thinking task (nonverbal spatial reasoning tasks) and a different linguistic task (sentence verification), producing the same results.

Takano and Noda (1995) reported two additional studies showing that the foreign language effect was larger when the discrepancy between the native and

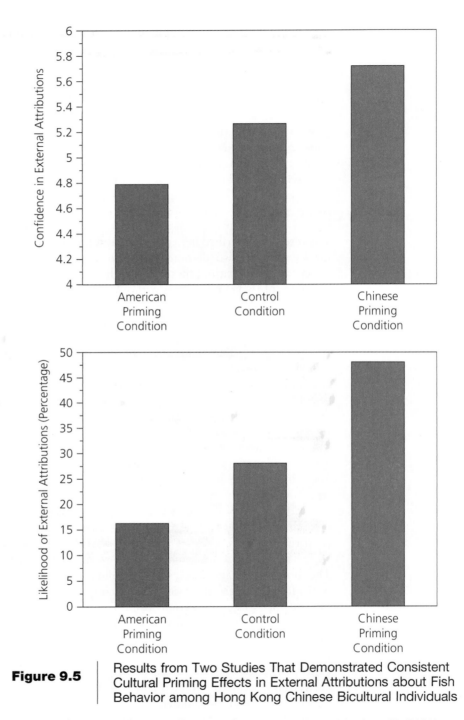

Figure 9.5 | Results from Two Studies That Demonstrated Consistent Cultural Priming Effects in External Attributions about Fish Behavior among Hong Kong Chinese Bicultural Individuals

Reprinted from Hong, Y. Y., Morris, M., Chiu, C.-Y., & Benet-Martinez, V. (2000). Multicultural minds: A dynamic constructivist approach to culture and cognition. *American Psychologist, 55,* 709–720.

foreign languages was greater, and smaller when the difference between the native and foreign languages was smaller. Their first study used the same methods as the first study in Takano and Noda (1993), using native speakers of German and Japanese with English as a common foreign language. They found that the foreign language effect was larger for the Japanese. They explained this finding in terms of the greater difference between Japanese and English than between German and English. Their second study replicated the findings from the first, this time using native Korean and English speakers, with Japanese as the common foreign language.

Collectively, these studies indicate that interference in both linguistic (foreign language processing difficulty) and nonlinguistic (foreign language effect) tasks is a normal and expected occurrence in bilinguals. These interferences occur in the same way as interferences between any two cognitive tasks asked of the same person. Seen as normal cognitive interferences, these difficulties should not be used as a basis to form negative impressions or stereotypes of bilinguals. As discussed later in this book (see Chapter 14), it is easy to fall into this trap, allowing our perceptions to be driven by ethnocentrism and, in some cases, by an unconscious wish to validate preexisting stereotypes. The research clearly shows, however, that such perceptions have little basis in fact.

Monolingualism and Ethnocentrism

Recognition of the special relationship among language, culture, and behavior is especially important for students in the United States. Americans are notoriously ignorant of languages other than English, and this ignorance is often accompanied by an ethnocentric view rejecting the need to learn, understand, and appreciate other languages, customs, and cultures. Given that Americans are the most monolingual of all peoples of the world, that language is intimately tied to culture, and that multilingualism is associated with an appreciation of different cultures, it may be that Americans are actually the most ethnocentric of all people. The fact that the United States is relatively geographically isolated from Europe and Asia, and is so economically and militarily powerful, produces a situation in which many of us do not feel the need to understand other points of view or interact with others. Our ignorance of languages other than English, and the unfortunate ethnocentrism that often accompanies this ignorance, may be the root of our future downfall. For many of us who have little exposure to these issues in our everyday lives, now is the time to begin our study of language and culture for a better understanding of the partners in our global village.

CONCLUSION

Language is the primary way we communicate with one another. It plays a critical role in the transmission, maintenance, and expression of our culture. In turn, culture has a pervasive influence on language, and language symbolizes what a culture deems important in our world. Both culture and language affect the structure of our thought processes. Thus, understanding the culture–language relationship is an important step in becoming skillful intercultural communicators.

But language is just one part of communication—and perhaps not the most important part. We use many other vehicles of expression to communicate our thoughts, feelings, desires, and wishes to others. These other means of communication are nonverbal.

Communication in its broadest sense occurs both verbally (via language) and nonverbally. We have discussed how nonverbal behaviors contribute the bulk of the messages received and interpreted in communication, and that this effect appears to be pancultural. Despite the importance of nonverbal behaviors, however, we often take them for granted. Although we receive no formal training in how to send or receive nonverbal messages and signals, by adulthood we have become so skilled at it that we do so unconsciously and automatically. Nonverbal behaviors are just as much a language as any other. Just as verbal languages differ from culture to culture, so do nonverbal languages. Because we are aware of the differences between verbal languages, we do not hesitate to use dictionaries and other resources to help us understand different languages. But when it comes to nonverbal language, we often mistakenly assume that our systems of communicating nonverbally are all the same.

Understanding cultural differences in nonverbal behavior is the first step in the process of truly appreciating cultural differences in communication. We must learn to recognize the central role that nonverbal behaviors play in the communication process and then realize how our own cultural background influences the ways we engage and interpret the nonverbal world around us. Although these processes are usually unconscious and automatic, we can work consciously to make them more flexible and inclusive of different cultural systems.

Finally, we have seen that communication is a rich and complex process that involves multiple messages sent via multiple signal systems. Culture has a pervasive influence on the encoding of both verbal and nonverbal signals and on the decoding of those signals. Because of this influence, conflict and misunderstanding are inevitable in intercultural communication. To overcome these obstacles, scholars have proposed a personal growth model focusing on emotion regulation and mindfulness. Individuals who can engage in these processes can enhance their intercultural sensitivity, creating new mental categories, being respectful of and open to cultural differences, and empathizing with others. Research on intercultural communication has made considerable progress in specifying the unique components of the intercultural communication process.

It is our hope that the information presented in this chapter has allowed you to examine what kinds of blinders and cultural scripts you may have when communicating and interacting with others, and has given you an idea of how to move from an ethnocentric base of interaction to an ethno-relative one.

GLOSSARY

channels The specific sensory modalities by which signals are sent and messages are retrieved.

code frame switching The process by which bilinguals switch between one cultural meaning system and another when switching languages.

conversation regulators Nonverbal behaviors we engage in to regulate the flow of speech during a conversation.

culture-affiliation hypothesis The hypothesis that immigrant bilinguals will tend to affiliate themselves with the values and beliefs of the culture associated with the language in which they are currently operating. When the language is switched, so are the cultural values with which they affiliate.

decoding The process by which a person receives signals from an encoder and translates these signals into meaningful messages.

emblems Nonverbal gestures that carry meaning, like a phrase or sentence.

encoding The process by which people select, consciously or unconsciously, a particular modality and method by which to create and send a message to someone else.

face The public appearance or image of a person.

foreign language effect A temporary decline in the thinking ability of people who are using a foreign language in which they are less proficient than their native tongue.

foreign language processing difficulties Problems associated with communicating and learning in a foreign language, such as taking more time to respond and experiencing cognitive difficulties while processing information.

gestures Movements of the body, usually the hands, that are generally reflective of thoughts or feelings.

high-context cultures Cultures that promote communication in which many messages are conveyed indirectly in context rather than directly in verbal language.

honorific speech Speech styles in certain languages that denote status differences among interactants.

intercultural communication The exchange of knowledge, ideas, thoughts, concepts, and emotions among people of different cultural backgrounds.

intracultural communication Communication that occurs among people of the same cultural background.

lexicon The words contained in a language, the vocabulary.

low-context cultures Cultures that promote direct communication in which messages are conveyed primarily and directly in verbal languages and the effects of context are minimized.

messages The meanings that encoders intend to convey and decoders interpret.

mindfulness A strategy to improve intercultural communication that allows people to be conscious of their own habits, mental scripts, and cultural expectations concerning communication.

minority group–affiliation hypothesis The hypothesis that immigrant bilinguals will tend to self-identify as members of an ethnic minority group and adopt the behavioral stereotypes of the majority culture about their minority as their own when they are operating in the language associated with their minority group.

morphemes The smallest and most basic units of meaning in a language.

nonverbal behaviors All the behaviors, other than words, that occur during communication, including facial expressions; movements and gestures of hands, arms, and legs; posture; vocal characteristics such as pitch, rate, intonation, and silence; interpersonal space; touching behaviors; and gaze and visual attention.

phonemes The smallest and most basic units of sound in a language.

phonology The system of rules governing how words should sound (pronunciation, "accent") in a given language.

pragmatics The system of rules governing how language is used and understood in given social contexts.

Sapir–Whorf hypothesis The proposition that speakers of different languages think differently, and that they do so because of the differences in their languages. Also referred to as *linguistic relativity*.

self–other referents The words used in a language to refer to oneself and others.

semantics What words mean.

signals The specific words and behaviors that are sent during communication.

speech illustrators Nonverbal behaviors used to illustrate or highlight speech.

syntax and grammar The system of rules governing word forms and how words should be strung together to form meaningful utterances.

uncertainty reduction One of the major goals of initial intercultural encounters—to reduce the level of uncertainty and anxiety that one feels when attempting to decode intercultural messages.

Culture and Personality

CHAPTER **10**

CHAPTER CONTENTS

One of the most important and widely studied areas in cross-cultural psychology is personality. Indeed, the search for the underlying bases of individual differences, which serve as the backbone of understanding personality, shares a close conceptual and empirical connection with culture in any cultural milieu.

We begin this chapter by first defining personality, and discussing briefly the major perspectives that have been used to study it. We discuss the measurement of personality across cultures, as well as the use of some personality scales to assess psychopathology across cultures. Then, we review major cross-cultural research on a view of personality known the Five-Factor Model (FFM), which suggests that five personality dimensions are universal to all humans. We discuss two theories that account for such universality in personality structure, and more recent research that goes beyond the FFM. We also discuss indigenous approaches to personality, and some of the research that has been conducted in this area. Although culture-specific aspects of personality and universal notions of personality may seem contradictory, we will seek ways of understanding their mutual coexistence and conceptualizing and studying their duality.

DEFINING PERSONALITY

Definitions

The first thing we need to do is define what we mean by personality. In psychology, **personality** is generally considered to be a set of relatively enduring behavioral and cognitive characteristics, traits, or predispositions that people take with them to different situations, contexts, and interactions with others, and that contribute to differences among individuals. They are the qualities or collection of qualities that make a person a distinctive individual, or the collective aggregate of behavioral and mental characteristics that are distinctive of an individual. Personality is generally believed to be relatively stable across time and consistent across contexts, situations, and interactions.

Over the years there have been many different approaches to understanding personality. The psychoanalytic work of Freud and the neoanalytic approaches of Jung and Adler, for instance, view personality as being constituted by defense mechanisms, such as denial, projection, or reaction formation; these originate from the ways in which individuals deal with unresolved conflicts in early childhood that arise because of unconscious drives and instincts. Skinner viewed personality as the sum total of all learned behaviors, shaped from early infancy and childhood through reinforcement and punishment. Maslow and Rogers brought a humanistic approach to personality, suggesting that personality was constituted on the basis of the degree of unconditional positive regard people experienced, and whether their environments allowed them to achieve self-actualization.

Perspectives

Over the course of the 20th century, several different approaches and methods have been used to elucidate the relationship between culture and personality.

Some of the earliest contributions to our understanding of this relationship came from anthropologists who were interested in human psychology within their anthropological discipline. Through mostly ethnographic fieldwork, these individuals—such as Margaret Mead, Edward Sapir, Weston Labarre, and Ruth Benedict—developed ideas and theories about culture and personality that served as a basis for cross-cultural comparison of personalities and today's cultural psychology (see review in Piker, 1998). Many of these works formed the basis for the notion of "national character," which is still popular today. A **national character** refers to the perception that each culture has a modal personality type, and that most persons in that culture share aspects of it. Although many cultural and psychological anthropologists recognize the important contributions of biologically innate factors to personality and psychology, the main thrust of the anthropological contribution is its view of personality as culturally specific, formed by the unique forces each culture deals with in its milieu. The anthropological view of personality, therefore, attributes more importance to the learning of psychological mechanisms and personality in the environment through cultural practices than to biological and evolutionary factors.

The dominant approach to understanding personality today, however, is known as trait psychology. A **trait** is a characteristic or quality distinguishing a person. It refers to a consistent pattern of behavior that a person would usually display in relevant circumstances. For example, if we describe someone as "outgoing," that would generally refer to a specific pattern of behavior in which this person is likely to engage. A person who is outgoing will likely strike up conversations, meet comfortably with strangers, and be expressive. A person who is "shy" would not.

Whereas psychological anthropology made major contributions in the first half of the 20th century, the second half was dominated by the cross-cultural psychological approach, which focused on traits (see review by Church & Lonner, 1998). This approach generally views personality as something discrete and separate from culture, and as a dependent variable in research. Thus, two or more cultures are treated as independent variables, and they are compared on some personality traits or dimensions. In contrast to the cultural or psychological anthropological approach, the cross-cultural approach tends to see personality as an etic or universal phenomenon that is equivalently relevant and meaningful in the cultures being compared. To the extent that personality does exhibit universal aspects, how did they originate? Two separate but not mutually exclusive possibilities are: (1) the existence of biologically innate and evolutionarily adaptive factors that create genetic predispositions to certain types of personality traits and (2) the possibility of culture-constant learning principles and processes (see also the discussion by MacDonald, 1998).

Cross-cultural research on personality, however, has also been concerned with the discovery of culture-specific personality traits. Cross-cultural psychologists describe culture-specific **indigenous personalities** as constellations of personality traits and characteristics found only in a specific culture (for more information, see reviews by Ho, 1998; Diaz-Loving, 1998). These types of studies, though psychological in nature, are heavily influenced in approach and understanding by the anthropological view of culture and personality.

Another approach to understanding the relationship between culture and personality that has emerged in recent years is that of *cultural psychology* (for example, Shweder, 1979a, 1979b, 1980, 1991, 2000; Markus & Kitayama, 1998). This approach sees culture and personality not as separate entities, but as a mutually constituted system in which each creates and maintains the other.

> The cultural perspective assumes that psychological processes, in this case the nature of functioning of personality, are not just influenced by culture but are thoroughly culturally constituted. In turn, the cultural perspective assumes that personalities behaving in concert create the culture. Culture and personality are most productively analyzed together as a dynamic of mutual constitution . . . ; one cannot be reduced to the other. . . . A cultural psychological approach does not automatically assume that all behavior can be explained with the same set of categories and dimensions and first asks whether a given dimension, concept, or category is meaningful and how it is used in a given cultural context. (Markus & Kitayama, 1998, p. 66)

The cultural psychological viewpoint has been heavily influenced by the cultural anthropologists, as well as by the cross-cultural work on indigenous psychologies (see Kim, 2001) and personalities. It is inherently antithetical to the cross-cultural psychological search for universals and rejects the possibility of biological and genetic mechanisms underlying universality. Instead, it suggests that just as no two cultures are alike, the personalities that comprise those cultures should be fundamentally different because of the mutual constitution of culture and personality within each cultural milieu.

The tension between the cross-cultural psychology school and the cultural psychology school, in terms of universality versus culture-specificity in personality, can be seen in the literature reviewed in this chapter. Although considerable evidence points to the universality of some aspects of personality, a considerable amount of evidence also documents the existence of indigenous personalities, as well as cultural differences in supposedly etic personality domains. How to make sense of this all is perhaps the greatest challenge facing this area of cross-cultural psychology in the near future. Some theorists, such as Church (2000), have taken up this challenge by arguing for an integrated *cultural trait psychology* that incorporates both cross-cultural psychology and cultural psychology in studies of personality.

MEASURING PERSONALITY ACROSS CULTURES

One of the most serious issues in all cross-cultural research on personality is whether personality can be measured reliably and validly across different cultures. If methods of assessing personality are not reliable or valid across cultures, then the results of research using these methods cannot be trusted to give accurate portrayals of personality similarities or differences across cultures.

Most personality measures used in cross-cultural research were originally developed in a single language and single culture, and validated in that language and culture. The psychometric evidence typically used to demonstrate a measure's reliability and validity in a single culture involves examination of internal, test–retest, and parallel forms reliabilities, convergent and predictive validities, and replicability of the factor structures that comprise the various scales of the test. To obtain all these types of psychometric evidence for the reliability and validity of a test, researchers must literally spend years conducting countless studies addressing each of these specific concerns. The best measures of personality—as well as all other psychological constructs—have this degree of psychometric evidence backing them.

A common practice in many of the early cross-cultural studies on personality was to take a personality scale that had been developed in one country or culture—most often the United States—and simply translate it and use it in another culture. In effect, the researchers simply assumed that the personality dimension measured by that scale was equivalent between the two cultures, and that the method of measuring that dimension was psychometrically valid and reliable. Thus, many studies imposed an assumed etic construct upon the cultures studied (Church & Lonner, 1998). Realistically, however, one cannot safely conclude that the personality dimensions represented by an imposed etic are equivalently and meaningfully represented in all cultures included in a study.

The mere fact that personality scales have been translated and used in cross-cultural research is not sufficient evidence that the personality domains they measure are indeed equivalent in those cultures. In fact, when this type of research is conducted, one of the researchers' primary concerns is whether the personality scales used in the study can validly and reliably measure meaningful dimensions of personality in all the cultures studied. As discussed in Chapter 2, the equivalence of a measure in terms of its meaning to all cultures concerned, as well as its psychometric validity and reliability, is of prime concern in cross-cultural research if the results are to be considered valid, meaningful, and useful.

To validate personality measures cross-culturally requires psychometric evidence from all cultures in which the test is to be used. In the strictest sense, therefore, researchers interested in cross-cultural studies on personality should select instruments that have been demonstrated to have acceptable psychometric properties. This is a far cry from merely selecting a test that seems to be interesting and translating it for use in another culture. At the very least, equivalence of its psychometric properties should be established empirically, not assumed or ignored.

Data addressing the psychometric evidence necessary to validate a test in a target culture would provide the safest avenue by which such equivalence can be demonstrated. If such data exist, they can be used to support contentions concerning psychometric equivalence. Even if those data do not offer a high degree of support (reliability coefficients are lower, or factor structures are not exactly equivalent), that does not necessarily mean that the test as a whole is not equivalent. There are, in fact, multiple alternative explanations of why such data may not be as strong in the target culture as in the culture in which the test was originally developed. Paunonen and Ashton (1998) outline and describe 10 such possible interpretations, ranging from poor test translation and response style issues to different analytic methods. Thus, if a test is examined in another culture for its psychometric properties and the data are not as strong as they were in the original culture, each of these possibilities should be examined before concluding that the test is not psychometrically valid or reliable. In many cases, the problem may be minor and fixable.

Given these issues, how have the various personality tests used in cross-cultural research fared? Many of the more recent studies in this area have been sensitive to this issue, and researchers have taken steps to ensure some degree of psychometric equivalence across cultures in their measures of personality. In their study of the Eysenck Personality Questionnaire (EPQ) in Hong Kong and England, for example, Eysenck and Chan (1982) included only those items that were common to scoring keys derived separately in both cultures, thus ensuring some comparability in the scale scores used in their comparison. Likewise, Tafarodi and Swann (1996) tested cross-cultural equivalence in their measure of self-esteem by conducting a confirmatory factor analysis on the items measured in their scales in both cultures before testing for differences. In testing for cultural differences in locus of control, Hamid (1994) back-translated his measures, administered both original and translated measures to bilinguals, and assessed the parallel forms correlation of the two questionnaires before using them in the main study. Munro (1979) established equivalence in the factor structures of his locus of control questionnaires before testing for cultural differences between blacks and whites in Africa, and Smith, Dugan, and Trompenaars (1997) conducted a pancultural factor analysis on their locus of control measure before testing for differences. This procedure allowed them to derive scale scores after eliminating individual and cultural differences in the ratings of the individual items included in the scale.

Support for the notion that cross-cultural comparisons of personality are meaningful comes from other sources as well. First, the findings derived from many of these studies "make sense"; that is, they are interpretable to a large degree and match predictions based on what we might reasonably expect based on our knowledge of culture and its probable influence on personality. Findings that were uninterpretable based on available knowledge of the cultures tested would raise questions about the psychometric validity of the scales being used. That many studies provide interpretable findings, however, suggests that the scales do measure something that is meaningful.

Another source of support comes from the data analyses used to compare cultures. Although significant differences in mean values reflect between-culture differences in averages, they do not necessarily reflect the degree of overlap among individuals within the samples comprising the various cultures in the comparison. In most cases, the degree of individual variation is many times larger than the degree of difference between cultures. Analysis of such effects would surely lead one to suspect a considerable degree of individual similarity in the personality constructs being measured (see Matsumoto, 2001, for a critique and discussion of the usefulness of cultural differences on mean scores and effect sizes).

Paunonen and Ashton (1998) reviewed the data concerning the California Psychological Inventory, the Comrey Personality Scales, the 16 Personality Factors Questionnaire, the Pavlovian Temperament Survey, the Personality Research Form, and the Nonverbal Personality Questionnaire. After reviewing each test's reliability, convergent validity, predictive validity, and factor structure invariance, these writers conclude that "(a) structured tests of personality can readily be adapted for use in a wide variety of cultures, and (b) there is an organization to many Western-derived personality traits that appears to be universal, or at least general to many of the world's cultures" (p. 165). Clearly, this conclusion is consonant with the notion of personality structure as universal in humans. Other studies (for example, Benet-Martinez & John, 1998) have also provided evidence for the psychometric equivalence of measures of the Five-Factor Model. These data provide some degree of reassurance that the cross-cultural studies reviewed in this chapter have measured personality in psychometrically acceptable ways.

A final source of support for the notion that many of the personality scales used in previous cross-cultural studies are valid comes from studies of the possible link between genetics and personality. Indeed, an increasing number of studies in recent years have begun to show that personality has some direct relationship to genes (for example, Berman, Ozkaragoz, Young, & Noble, 2002; Brummett, Siegler, McQuoid, Svenson, Marchuk, & Steffens, 2003; Eley, 1997; Jang, McCrae, Angleitner, Riemann, & Livesley, 1998; Joensson et al., 2003; Riemann, Angleitner, & Strelau, 1997; Saudino, 1997). To the extent that genetic and biological factors contribute to personality, they provide the basis on which stability in personality can be conceptualized, measured, and studied not only across individuals within a culture, but across cultures as well. Should such stability exist, and if this stability is related to biological factors that are in turn related to evolutionary factors and adaptive functions, it supports the argument that some aspects of personality may indeed be universal. This argument does not preclude the possibility of cultural specificity in some aspects of personality, in the manifestations of personality, or even in the emergence and existence of indigenous personalities; it merely suggests that some aspects of personality may be universal to all humans.

CROSS-CULTURAL STUDIES OF PERSONALITY TRAITS: THE FIVE-FACTOR MODEL OF PERSONALITY

Evidence for the Five-Factor Model

The trait approach in psychology has a long and rich history, dating to the work of Allport (1936). In the past two decades, trait approaches to personality have become extremely important in understanding the relationship between culture and personality, and it is the dominant view today. This work has culminated in what is known today as the Five-Factor Model (FFM) of personality, which we now describe.

The FFM is a conceptual model built around five distinct and basic personality dimensions that appear to be universal for all humans. The five dimensions are Openness, Conscientiousness, Extroversion, Agreeableness, and Neuroticism (OCEAN). The FFM was conceived after a number of researchers noticed the similarities in the personality dimensions that had emerged across many studies, both within and between cultures. Most notably, support for the FFM arose out of factor analyses of trait adjectives from the English lexicon that were descriptive of self and others (Juni, 1996). The factors that emerged from these types of analyses were similar to dimensions found in the analysis of questionnaire scales operationalizing personality. Further inquiry across cultures, using both factor analysis of descriptive trait adjectives in different languages and personality dimensions measured by different personality questionnaires, lent further credence to the FFM. Eysenck's (1983) many studies using the EPQ, for example, provided much support for Extroversion and Neuroticism as stable, universal personality scales. In early studies of the FFM, those factors were reported in German (Amelang & Borkenau, 1982), Dutch (De Raad, Hendriks, & Hofstee, 1992), French (Rolland, 1993), and Japanese, Chinese, and Filipino samples (Bond, 1979; Bond, Nakazato, & Shiraishi, 1975; Guthrie & Bennett, 1971; all cited in McCrae, Costa, Del Pilar, & Rolland, 1998).

Cross-cultural research of the past decade on the validity of the FFM in different countries and cultures has continued to support claims of universality. De Fruyt and Mervielde (1998), for example, confirmed the validity of the FFM in the Dutch language, Trull and Geary (1997) in Chinese, and Benet-Martinez and John (2000) in Castilian Spanish. De Raad, Perugini, and Szirmak (1997) reported support for the FFM in Dutch, Italian, Hungarian, American English, and German; Hofstee, Kiers, De Raad, Goldberg et al. (1997) also provided support for the FFM in Dutch, American English, and German. McCrae, Costa, and Yik (1996) provided support for the FFM in the Chinese personality structure, and Digman and Shmelyov (1996) documented its utility in Russia. Other studies have documented its validity in other countries and cultures, including Italy (Caprara, Barbaranelli, & Comrey, 1995; Caprara & Perugini, 1994); Australia and South Africa (Heaven, Connors, & Stones, 1994); Hong Kong (Ng, Cooper, & Chandler, 1998); Canada, Finland, Poland, and Germany (Paunonen, Jackson, Trzebinski, & Forsterling, 1992); Germany, Portugal, Israel, China, Korea, and Japan (McCrae & Costa, 1997); the Philippines (Katigbak, Church, Guanzon-Lapena, Carlota, & Del Pilar, 2002); Muslim Malaysia (Mastor, Jin, & Cooper, 2000), and others (McCrae, 2001; also see review in McCrae et al., 1998). Collectively, these studies provide convincing and substantial evidence to support the claim that the FFM—consisting of Extroversion, Neuroticism, Openness, Conscientiousness, and Agreeableness—represents a universal taxonomy of personality that is applicable to all humans.

One of the most widely used measures of the FFM is the Revised NEO-Personality Inventory (NEO-PI-R) (Costa & McCrae, 1989). It is a 240-item instrument in which respondents rate the degree to which they agree or disagree that the item is characteristic of them. This instrument has been used in many studies across many different cultures. It produces scores on the five major personality traits, as well as six subscores for each major trait. These give a good idea of the traits that are associated with the FFM (Table 10.1).

Today, two of the leading researchers on personality in the tradition of the FFM are Robert McCrae and Paul Costa. In one of their latest studies on

Table 10.1	Traits Associated with the Five-Factor Model
Major Trait	**Subtrait**
Openness	Fantasy
	Aesthetics
	Feelings
	Actions
	Ideas
	Values
Conscientiousness	Competence
	Order
	Dutifulness
	Achievement striving
	Self-discipline
	Deliberation
Extroversion	Warmth
	Gregariousness
	Assertiveness
	Activity
	Excitement seeking
	Positive emotions
Agreeableness	Trust
	Straightforwardness
	Altruism
	Compliance
	Modesty
	Tender-mindedness
Neuroticism	Anxiety
	Angry hostility
	Depression
	Self-consciousness
	Impulsiveness
	Vulnerability

the FFM (McCrae, Terracciano, Leibovich, Schmidt, Shakespeare-Finch, Neubauer et al., 2005), they and their colleagues in 51 cultures around the world asked student respondents to complete the NEO-PI-R. They conducted a statistical technique known as **factor analysis** in order to determine whether the items grouped around the five major traits. They found that indeed they did. They then computed scores for each of the cultures on each of the traits.

Two of the most important traits for describing behavioral differences are Extroversion and Neuroticism. The former refers the degree to which an individual is outgoing, expressive, and sociable or shy, introverted, and avoids contact; the latter refers to the degree of emotional stability in an individual. McCrae et al. (2005) graphed the cultural groups they studied along these two dimensions in order to create a useful visual aid in distinguishing among the cultures in terms of their personality (Figure 10.1).

Examining this graph provides some ideas about the average personality traits of individuals in these cultural groups. Americans, New Zealanders, and

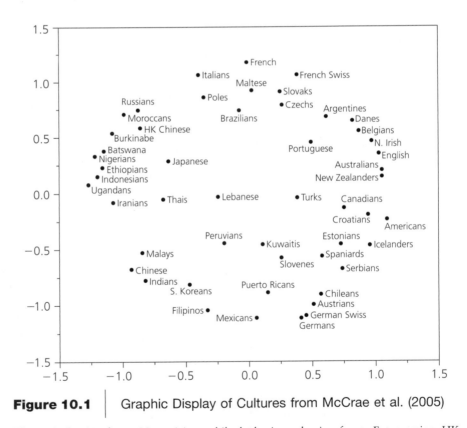

Figure 10.1 | Graphic Display of Cultures from McCrae et al. (2005)

The vertical axis refers to Neuroticism, while the horizontal axis refers to Extroversion. HK Chinese = Hong Kong Chinese; N. Irish = Northern Irish; S. Koreans = South Koreans.

Australians, for instance, tend to be high on Extroversion and in the middle of the scale for Neuroticism.

One of the concerns with findings generated with scales like the NEO-PI-R is that the findings may reflect bias on the part of the respondent to answer in a socially desirable way (see Chapter 2 to review response biases). These concerns are especially noted in cross-cultural work. McCrae and colleagues, therefore, conducted a follow-up study in which they asked samples of adults and college students in 50 cultural groups to rate someone they know well on the NEO-PI-R. The scale was modified so that the ratings were done in the third person. Analyses revealed that the same five-factor model emerged, indicating that the previous results were not dependent on ratings of oneself. In another interesting study, Allik and McCrae (2004) showed that the personality traits were *not* related to geographic location (defined as distance from the equator or mean temperature); but, geographically close cultures had more similar personality traits. Collectively, the results to date provide strong evidence that the FFM is a universal model of personality structure.

Do Perceptions of National Character Correspond to Aggregate Personality Traits?

The work by McCrae and others described above has been important because they have measured the actual personality traits of large numbers of individuals in a wide range of cultures. Thus, there are reliable data on what the actual personalities of individuals in these cultures are like. One of the things that these data allow us to do is to compare those actual personality profiles with our perceptions of national character. As described above, national character are perceptions of the average personality of people of different cultures. Perceptions of national character are, in fact, stereotypes about average personalities of people of different cultures.

But are they accurate? Terraciano et al. (2005) asked approximately 4,000 respondents in 49 cultures to describe the "typical member" of a culture using 30 bipolar scales with two or three trait adjectives on the poles of each scale. They found that there was relatively high agreement about the national character perceptions of the various cultures; but, these perceptions were *not* correlated with the actual personality trait levels of the individuals of those very same cultures. In other words, perceptions of national character were not correlated with the actual, aggregate personality levels of individuals of those cultures. These findings suggested, therefore, that perceptions of national character may actually be unfounded stereotypes of the personalities of members of those cultures.

If perceptions of national character are inaccurate, why do we have them? Terraciano and colleagues suggest that one of the functions of these unfounded stereotypes is the maintenance of a national identity. That is, one of the functions of stereotypes about other groups is to affirm, or reaffirm, the perceptions, and often the self-worth, of one's own group. Sometimes, these functions are dangerous; when perceptions of others are unfavorable, they often lead to prejudice, discrimination, and violence.

WHERE DO THESE TRAITS COME FROM?

The Five-Factor Theory of Personality

It is important to distinguish between the Five-Factor Model (FFM) of personality, which is a model of the number of traits that are universal to all people in their personality structure, and the Five-Factor Theory (FFT) of personality, which is a theory about the source of those traits. One is not entirely dependent on the other; the model of the traits may be entirely correct while the theory about where they come from entirely wrong. Alternatively, future research may show that there are more than five universal traits, while the theory that explains them is correct. Here we discuss the FFT, which attempts to account for where the universal personality traits come from.

The major proponents of the FFT are, not surprisingly, McCrae and Costa (1999). According to them, the core components of the FFT are Basic Tendencies, Characteristic Adaptations, and the Self-Concept, which is actually a subcomponent of Characteristic Adaptations.

The traits correspond to the Basic Tendencies; they refer to internal dispositions to respond to the environment in certain, predictable ways. The FFT suggests that personality traits that underlie basic tendencies are biologically based. Several sources of evidence support this idea. As described earlier, the same personality traits have been found in all cultures studied, and using different research methods (McCrae, Terracciano, Khoury, Nansubuga, Knezevic, Djuric Jocic et al., 2005; McCrae et al., 2005). Parent–child relationships have little lasting effect on personality traits (Rowe, 1994); and traits are generally stable across the adult lifespan (McCrae & Costa, 2003), although there are some developmental changes (Roberts, Walton, & Viechtbauer, 2006). Studies of twins demonstrate that the personalities of identical twins reared apart are much more similar than those of fraternal twins reared together (Bouchard & Loehlin, 2001; Bouchard, Lykken, & McGue, 1994). The FFM can predict variations in behavior among individuals in longitudinal studies (Borkenau & Ostendorf, 1998), and some evidence suggests that the FFM may apply to nonhuman primates as well (Alexander, Weiss, King, & Perkins, 2006; King & Figueredo, 1997).

The FFT suggests that the universal personality traits representing basic tendencies are expressed in characteristic ways; these characteristic ways can be largely influenced by the culture in which one exists, and here is where culture has important influences on personality development and expression. Characteristic Adaptations include habits, attitudes, skills, roles, and relationships. They are *characteristic* because they reflect the psychological core personality trait dispositions of the individual; they are also *adaptations* because they help the individual fit into the ever-changing social environment (McCrae & Costa,

1999). Culture can substantially influence these characteristic adaptations through the resources, social structures, and social systems available in a specific environment to help achieve goals. Culture can influence values about the various personality traits. Culture defines context and provides differential meaning to the components of context, including who is involved, what is happening, where it is occurring, and the like. Culture, therefore, plays a substantial role in producing the specific behavioral manifestations—the specific action units—that individuals will engage in to achieve what may be universal affective goals. Culture is "undeniably relevant in the development of characteristics and adaptations that guide the expression of personality in thoughts, feelings, and behaviors" (McCrae et al., 1998), and the characteristic adaptations vary greatly across cultures. The Basic Tendencies representing the universal personality traits, however, are not culturally variable, and a universal personality structure is the mechanism by which such goals are achieved through a balance and interaction with culture.

The characteristic adaptations help to produce a self-concept, as well as specific behaviors. For example, a person low in Depression, a facet of Neuroticism (Basic Tendency), may develop a low self-esteem, irrational perfectionistic beliefs, and pessimistic or cynical attitudes about the world (Characteristic Adaptations and Self-Concept). He or she may thus feel guilty about work or unsatisfied with his or her life (behavior). A person high on Gregariousness, however, which is part of Extroversion (Basic Tendency), may be outgoing, friendly, and talkative (Characteristic Adaptations). This person is likely to have numerous friendships and be a member of various social clubs (behaviors).

To be sure, one of the most contentious parts of the FFT is its suggestion that the origin of the personality traits are almost entirely, if not entirely, biologically determined. An alternative perspective suggests a role of culture or environment in the shaping of the personality traits underlying Basic Tendencies of behavior (Roberts, Caspi, & Moffitt, 2003; Roberts & Helson, 1997; Roberts, Helson, & Klohnen, 2002). There is little debate that culture can influence the Characteristic Adaptations and Self-Concepts associated with underlying personality traits. Debate continues concerning the origins of the traits, and future research in this area will undoubtedly need to explore many possibilities.

An Evolutionary Approach

To explain the universality of the FFM, some (for example, MacDonald, 1998) have suggested an evolutionary approach. This approach posits a universality both of human interests and of the neurophysiological mechanisms underlying trait variation. Personality structure is viewed as a universal psychological mechanism, a product of natural selection that serves both social and nonsocial functions in problem solving and environmental adaptation. Based on this theory, one would expect to find similar systems in animals that serve similar adaptive functions, and one would expect personality systems to be organized within the brain as discrete neurophysiological systems.

In this view, traits such as Conscientiousness (emotional stability), Neuroticism (affect intensity), and the other components of the FFM are considered to reflect stable variations in systems that serve critical adaptive functions. Conscientiousness, for example, may help individuals to monitor the environment for dangers and impending punishments, and to persevere in tasks that are not intrinsically rewarding (MacDonald, 1998). Affect intensity, measured by Neuroticism, is adaptive in that it helps mobilize behavioral resources by moderating arousal in situations requiring approach or avoidance.

According to MacDonald (1991, 1998), this evolutionary approach suggests a hierarchical model in which "behavior related to personality occurs at several levels based ultimately on the motivating aspects of evolved personality systems" (p. 130). In this model, humans possess evolved motive dispositions—for example, intimacy, safety—that are serviced by a universal set of personality dispositions that help individuals achieve their affective goals by managing personal and environmental resources. This resource management leads to concerns, projects, and tasks, which in turn lead to specific action units or behaviors through which the individual achieves the goals specified by the evolved motive dispositions (see Figure 10.2).

Level 1   EVOLVED MOTIVE DISPOSITIONS
                    (Domain-Specific Mechanisms)
Level 2   PERSONAL STRIVINGS
                    (Direct Psychological Effects of Domain-Specific Mechanisms)
Level 3   CONCERNS, PROJECTS, TASKS
                    (Utilize Domain-General Mechanisms)
Level 4   SPECIFIC ACTION UNITS
                    (Utilize Domain-General Mechanisms)

EXAMPLE:

Evolved Motive Disposition		INTIMACY	
Personal Striving		INTIMATE RELATIONSHIP WITH A PARTICULAR PERSON	
Concern, Project, Task	Arrange meeting	Improve appearance	Get promotion
Action Units	Find phone number	Begin dieting	Work on weekends

Figure 10.2 | Hierarchical Model of Motivation Showing Relationships between Domain-Specific and Domain-General Mechanisms

Source: Pervin, L. (Ed.). (1989). Goal concepts in personality and social psychology. Mahwah, NJ: Lawrence Erlbaum. Reprinted with permission.

Note that this model—and the assumptions about universality of the FFM made by McCrae and Costa and others (for example, McCrae & Costa, 1997)—does not minimize the importance of cultural and individual variability. Culture can substantially influence personality through the resources, social structures, and social systems available in a specific environment to help achieve goals. Culture can therefore influence mean levels of personality and values about the various personality traits. As stated earlier, culture is "undeniably relevant in the development of characteristics and adaptations that guide the expression of personality in thoughts, feelings, and behaviors" (McCrae et al., 1998). Culture defines context and provides differential meaning to the components of context, including who is involved, what is happening, where it is occurring, and the like. Culture, therefore, plays a substantial role in producing the specific behavioral manifestations—the specific action units—that individuals will engage in to achieve what may be universal affective goals. A universal personality structure, however, is considered to be the mechanism by which such goals are achieved through a balance and interaction with culture.

ARE THERE MORE THAN FIVE MAJOR PERSONALITY TRAITS?

Research documenting the robustness of the FFM of personality traits around the world has clearly made a major contribution to our understanding of personality organization and culture. Still, there are several lines of research that challenge whether five factors are enough. One of the claims made by authors of these challenges is that, because the FFM was essentially created in the United States by American researchers, it may be the case that its measurement is missing other important factors not intended to be measured in the first place.

Interpersonal Relatedness

The FFM may be missing other important personality traits, as suggested by several important lines of research. One has been led by Fanny Cheung and colleagues. They began their work with the idea that the FFM might be missing some important features of personality in Asia, and specifically China. Specifically, they reckoned that none of the FFM traits dealt well with issues of relationships, which are central in China. Thus, they developed what they initially considered an indigenous scale designed to measure personality in China that included the following traits:

- Harmony, which refers to one's inner peace of mind, contentment, interpersonal harmony, avoidance of conflict, and maintenance of equilibrium;
- *Ren Qing* (relationship orientation), which covers adherence to cultural norms of interaction based on reciprocity, exchange of social favors, and exchange of affection according to implicit rules;

- Modernization, which is reflected by personality change in response to societal modernization and attitudes toward traditional Chinese beliefs;
- Thrift v. Extravagance, which highlights the traditional virtue of saving rather than wasting and carefulness in spending, in contrast to the willingness to spend money for hedonistic purposes;
- *Ah-Q* Mentality (defensiveness), which is based on a character in a popular Chinese novel in which the defense mechanisms of the Chinese people, including self-protective rationalization, externationalization of blame, and belittling of others' achievements, are satirized;
- Face, which depicts the pattern of orientations in an international and hierarchical connection and social behaviors to enhance one's face and to avoid losing one's face. (Cheung, Leung, Zhang, Sun, Gan, Song et al., 2001) (p. 408)

Collectively, Cheung and colleagues have named these dimensions "Interpersonal Relatedness." Although they originally found support for the existence of this dimension in their studies of mainland and Hong Kong Chinese, they have also created an English version of their scale and documented the existence of the Interpersonal Relatedness dimension in samples from Singapore, Hawaii, the Midwestern United States, and with Chinese and European Americans (Cheung, Cheung, Leung, Ward, & Leong, 2003; Cheung et al., 2001; Lin & Church, 2004). Clearly, much more research needs to be done in many different cultures, but the data to date are promising.

Filipino Personality Structure

A second major line of research that challenges whether the FFM is enough comes from studies on the personality structures of Filipinos. This line of research has been headed by Tim Church and colleagues. In early research, they identified as many traits as they could that existed in the Filipino language, and asked Filipino students to rate them, just as they would on any personality test. Early studies using the same statistical techniques that have been used to test the FFM were used, and demonstrated that seven, not five, dimensions were necessary to describe the Filipino personality adequately (Church, Katigbak, & Reyes, 1998; Church, Reyes, Katigbak, & Grimm, 1997). In fact, similar types of findings were found previously with Spanish-speaking samples in Europe as well (Benet-Martinez & Waller, 1995, 1997).

In one of their latest studies, Church and colleagues (Katigbak, Church, Guanzon-Lapena, Carlota, & del Pilar, 2002) used two Filipino indigenous personality scales encompassing a total of 463 trait adjectives, and a Filipino version of the NEO-PI-R to measure the FFM, and asked 511 college students in the Philippines to complete these measures. Statistical analyses indicated that there was considerable overlap in the personality dimensions that emerged from the Filipino scales and the FFM measured by the NEO-PI-R. Still, several indigenous factors emerged, including Pagkamadaldal (Social Curiosity), Pagkamapagsapalaran (Risk-Taking), and Religiosity. These latter traits were especially important in predicting behaviors such as smoking, drinking, gambling, praying, tolerance of homosexuality, and tolerance of premarital and extramarital relations, above and beyond what could be predicted by the FFM.

Dominance

In the mid-20th century, European psychologists suggested the existence of an "authoritarian personality," and developed scales to measure it (Adorno, Frenkel-Brunswik, & Levinson, 1950). This dimension is related to the concept of dominance, and refers to the fact that people differ in their dependence on authority and hierarchical, status differences among interactants. Hofstede, Bond, and Luk (1993) analyzed data from 1,300 individuals in Denmark and the Netherlands, and found six personality dimensions. Five of these were related to the FFM; the sixth, however, was not. The researchers labeled this "Authoritarianism."

Actually, Dominance is a trait that emerges in studies of the personalities of animals. King and Figueredo (1997), for instance, presented 43 trait adjectives with representative items from the FFM to zoo trainers who work with chimpanzees in 12 zoos. The trainers were asked to describe the chimpanzees in terms of the adjectives provided. The results showed no differences between the zoos, and the interrater reliability among the raters was high. Factor analysis of the ratings produced six factors, five of which corresponded to the FFM; the sixth corresponded to dominance. The same findings have been reported in studies of orangutans and chimpanzees (Pederson, King, & Landau, 2005; Weiss, King, & Enns, 2002; Weiss, King, & Figueredo, 2000), and suggest that Dominance is an inherited trait among animals.

Summary

The development of indigenous personality constructs and measures is a healthy and important activity in cross-cultural studies of personality, and should continue into the future. To date, the findings appear not to contradict the FFM, but instead add to it. The unresolved question concerns exactly what other dimensions, if any, reliably exist across cultures. The findings reported above are indeed promising, but certainly much more research is necessary across a wider range of cultures to gauge its comparability with the FFM. Other indigenous approaches to studying traits also have been developed in countries such as India, Korea, and Greece (Cheung, Cheung, Wada, & Zhang, 2003; Saucier, Georgiades, Tsaousis, & Goldberg, 2005). These, and other approaches, will hopefully shed more light on this important topic in the future.

To be sure, we need to be clear about the difference between the FFM, which is a model of the universal personality traits, and FFT, which is a theory about the source of those traits. It is entirely possible that the FFM will be amended in the future to allow for the possibility of other traits, but for the theory underlying them to be the same. Or it could be that the FFM will turn out to be the most reliable but that the theory accounting for the source is entirely wrong. The number of traits that are universal and where they come from are two issues we need to keep separate in our minds.

CROSS-CULTURAL RESEARCH ON OTHER ASPECTS OF PERSONALITY

Internal versus External Locus of Control

One of the most widely studied personality concepts across cultures is **locus of control.** This concept was developed by Rotter (1954, 1966), who suggested that people differ in how much control they believe they have over their behavior and their relationship with their environment and with others. According to this schema, locus of control can be perceived as either internal or external to the individual. People with an internal locus of control see their behavior and relationships with others as dependent on their own behavior. Believing that your grades are mostly dependent on how much effort you put into study is an example of internal locus of control. People with an external locus of control see their behavior and relationships with the environment and others as contingent on forces outside themselves and beyond their control. If you believed your grades were mostly dependent on luck, the teacher's benevolence, or the ease of the tests, you would be exemplifying an external locus of control.

Research examining locus of control has shown both similarities and differences across cultures. In general, Americans have higher internal locus of control scores, whereas non-Americans tend to have higher external locus of control scores. A number of studies have found this pattern in comparisons of Americans with Asians, especially Chinese and Japanese (for example, Hamid, 1994; see also, however, Spadone, 1992, for no difference in an American–Thai comparison). Lee and Dengerink (1992) found higher internal locus of control scores among Americans than Swedes, and Munro (1979) found that Americans had higher internal locus of control scores than participants in Zambia and Zimbabwe (then Rhodesia). In a review of cross-cultural studies on locus of control, Dyal (1984) concluded that European Americans appear to be characterized by a more internal locus of control than African Americans. Locus of control differences have also been documented in children; Paguio, Robinson, Skeen, and Deal (1987), for example, showed that American children had higher internal locus of control scores than Filipino and Brazilian children.

These findings have often been interpreted as reflecting the American culture's focus on individuality, separateness, and uniqueness, in contrast to a more balanced view of interdependence among individuals and between individuals and natural and supernatural forces found in many other cultures. People of non-American cultures may be more likely to see the causes of events and behaviors in sources that are external to themselves, such as fate, luck, supernatural forces, or relationships with others. Americans, however, prefer to take more personal responsibility for events and situations, and view themselves as having more personal control over such events.

Although such interpretations are interesting and provocative, they still leave some gaps to be filled. For example, they do not account for phenomena such as self-serving bias or defensive attributions, in which Americans tend to place the responsibility for negative events on others, not themselves (see Chapter 13 on self-enhancement). Also, some researchers have suggested that locus of control is really a multifaceted construct spanning many different domains—academic achievement, work, interpersonal relationships, and so on—and that separate assessments of each of these domains are necessary to make meaningful comparisons on this construct. Finally, Smith, Dugan, and Trompenaars (1997), in their 14-country study of locus of control and affectivity, found some cross-national differences in locus of control, but larger differences by gender and status across countries. Thus, the search for cross-cultural differences may obscure larger differences based on other social constructs. Future research needs to address all these concerns to further elucidate the nature of cultural influences on locus of control.

Direct, Indirect, Proxy, and Collective Control

Yamaguchi (2001) has offered another interesting way of understanding control across cultures. He distinguishes between direct, indirect, proxy, and collective control. In **direct control,** the self acts as an agent, and individuals feel themselves to be more self-efficacious when their agency is made explicit, leading to greater feelings of autonomy and efficacy. Direct control may be the preferred mode of behavior in cultural contexts that promote independence or autonomy, such as in the United States.

Other cultural contexts, however, may encourage other modes of control, primarily because of their focus on interpersonal harmony. For instance, in **indirect control,** one's agency is hidden or downplayed; people pretend as if they are not acting as an agent even though in reality they are doing so. Yamaguchi (2001) tells of an example in which a rakugo (comic master) was annoyed at his disciple's loud singing. Instead of directly telling him to stop, he instead praised him with a loud voice. Although at first it sounded as if the comic master was praising the disciple, in reality he was telling him to be quiet; thus, the disciple stopped singing.

Proxy control refers to control by someone else for the benefit of oneself. This is a form of control that can be used when personal control—either direct or indirect—is not available or inappropriate. These are third-party interventions, when intermediaries are called in to regulate or intervene in interpersonal relationships or conflicts between parties with potential or actual conflicts of interest. This type of control is essential for survival for those in weaker positions and thus unable to change their environments by themselves.

Finally, in **collective control,** one attempts to control the environment as a member of a group, and the group serves as the agent of control. In this situation individuals need to worry about interpersonal harmony less because the group shares the goal of control.

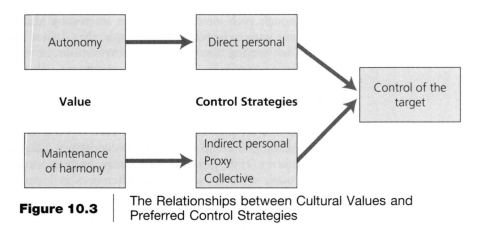

Figure 10.3 | The Relationships between Cultural Values and Preferred Control Strategies

Source: Yamaguchi, S. (2001). Culture and control orientations. In D. Matsumoto (Ed.), *The handbook of culture and psychology* (pp. 223–243). New York: Oxford University Press.

Yamaguchi (2001) suggests that direct, personal control may be the strategy of choice in cultures that value autonomy and independence, such as the United States. In cultures that value the maintenance of interpersonal harmony, however, indirect, proxy, and collective control strategies may be more prevalent (Figure 10.3).

Autonomy

Deci and Ryan (Deci & Ryan, 1985; Ryan & Deci, 2000) have posited a *self-determination theory,* which states that people from all cultures share basic psychological needs for autonomy, competence, and relatedness, but that the specific ways in which these needs are met and expressed differ according to context and culture. Meeting these needs, in whatever form or by whatever means, should be related to greater well-being of people in all cultures.

Of these claims, perhaps the most controversial is the one concerning autonomy. Contemporary thinking about cultures that focus on individualism versus collectivism, and particularly those rooted in Markus and Kitayama's (1991b) framework of independent versus interdependent self-construals (Chapter 13), suggests that people of collectivistic cultures are not autonomous. Deci and Ryan suggest, however, that there is a large distinction among autonomy, individualism, independence, and separateness. According to self-determination theory, people are autonomous when their behavior is experienced as willingly enacted and when they fully endorse the actions in which they are engaged or the values expressed by them (Chirkov, Ryan, Kim, & Kaplan, 2003). Thus, people are autonomous whenever they act in accord with their interests, values, or desires. The opposite of autonomy in this perspective is not dependence, but heteronomy, in which one's actions are perceived as controlled by someone else or are otherwise alien to oneself. Thus, one can be either autonomously independent or dependent; they are separate constructs.

These ideas have received support in several studies involving participants from South Korea, Turkey, Russia, Canada, Brazil, and the United States (Chirkov et al., 2003; Chirkov, Ryan, & Willness, 2005). In all cultures tested to date, their studies have shown that individuals tend to internalize different cultural practices, whatever those practices may be, and that despite those different practices, the relative autonomy of an individual's motivations to engage in those practices predicts well-being. Autonomy, therefore, appears to be a universal psychological need and phenomenon, although the way in which it is practiced and expressed is different in different cultures. This idea is bolstered by findings demonstrating the universality of self-efficacy—an optimistic sense of personal competence—a construct related to autonomy (Scholz, Hutierrez Dona, Sud, & Schwarzer, 2002).

INDIGENOUS APPROACHES TO PERSONALITY

As stated earlier in the chapter, **indigenous personalities** are conceptualizations of personality developed in a particular culture that are specific and relevant only to that culture. In general, not only are the concepts of personality rooted in and derived from the particular cultural group under question, but the methods used to test and examine those concepts are also particular to that culture. Thus, in contrast to much of the research described so far, in which standardized personality measures are used to assess personality dimensions, studies of indigenous personalities often use their own nonstandardized methods.

Indigenous conceptions of personality are important because they give us a glimpse of how each culture believes it is important to carve up their psychological world. By identifying indigenous concepts, each culture pays tribute to a specific way of understanding their world, which is an important part of each cultural worldview. By giving these concepts names, each culture is then allowed to talk about them, thereby ensuring each indigenous concept's special place in their culture.

Evidence

Over the years, many scientists have been interested in indigenous conceptions of personality, and have described many different personality constructs considered to exist only in specific cultures. Berry, Poortinga, Segall, and Dasen (1992) examined three such indigenous personality concepts, each of which is fundamentally different from American or Western concepts. The African model of personality, for example, views personality as consisting of three layers, each representing a different aspect of the person. The first layer, found at the core of the person and personality, embodies a spiritual principle; the second layer involves a psychological vitality principle; the third layer involves a physiological vitality principle. The body forms the outer framework that houses all these layers of the person. In addition, family lineage and community affect different core aspects of the African personality (Sow, 1977, 1978, cited in Berry et al., 1992; see also Vontress, 1991).

Doi (1973) has postulated *amae* as a core concept of the Japanese personality. The root of this word means "sweet," and loosely translated, *amae* refers to the passive, childlike dependence of one person on another. It is said to be rooted in mother–child relationships. According to Doi, all Japanese relationships can be characterized by *amae,* which serves as a fundamental building block of Japanese culture and personality. This fundamental interrelationship between higher- and lower-status people in Japan serves as a major component not only of individual psychology but of interpersonal relationships, and it does so in ways that are difficult to grasp from a North American individualistic point of view.

Early work in this area produced findings of many other personality constructs thought to be culture-specific. Such constructs have included the national character or personality of Arab culture (Beit-Hallahmi, 1972), North Alaskan Eskimos (Hippler, 1974), the Japanese (Sakamoto & Miura, 1976), the Fulani of Nigeria (Lott & Hart, 1977), the Irulas of Palamalai (Narayanan & Ganesan, 1978), Samoans (Holmes, Tallman, & Jantz, 1978), South African Indians (Heaven & Rajab, 1983), and the Ibo of Nigeria (Akin-Ogundeji, 1988).

Other indigenous personality descriptions from various cultures include the Korean concept of *cheong* (human affection; Choi, Kim, & Choi, 1993); the Indian concept of *hishkama karma* (detachment; Sinha, 1993); the Chinese concept of *ren qin* (relationship orientation; Cheung, Leung, Fan, Song, Zhang, & Zhang, 1996); the Mexican concept of *simpatia* (avoidance of conflict; Triandis, Marin, Lisansky, & Betancourt, 1984); and the Filipino concepts of *pagkikipagkapwa* (shared identity), *pakikiramdam* (sensitivity, empathy), and *pakikisama* (going along with others; Enriquez, 1992) (all cited in Church, 2000, p. 654).

To be sure, evidence for indigenous conceptions of personality are not necessarily antithetical to the existence of universal personality traits such as the FFM described earlier in this chapter. Both the FFM and indigenous personality concepts are theoretical constructs—they are inferences scientists make about the psychological underpinnings of a person's personality. The existence of one way of viewing personality does not necessarily argue against the existence of another. The two may exist simultaneously. Trait approaches such as the FFM refer more to the universal aspects of personality that are true of all people regardless of culture, while indigenous aspects of personality refer to those aspects of personality that are culture-specific. Both may be accurate.

Indigenous Concepts of Personality and the Cultural Psychology Perspective

Much of the work on indigenous personality has provided fuel for those who subscribe to the cultural psychology school—the view that culture and personality are mutually constituted. In this view, it makes no sense to consider personality as a universal construct; instead, it makes more sense to understand each culture's personalities as they exist and have developed within that culture (see description of this approach at the beginning of this chapter).

The cultural psychology viewpoint rejects the notion of a universal organization to personality that may have genetic, biological, and evolutionary components. Its proponents argue that the research supporting universality and its possible biological substrates may be contaminated by the methods used. These methods, the argument goes, have been developed in American or European research laboratories by American or European researchers; because of this cultural bias, the findings support the FFM as a default by-product of the methods. Indigenous approaches, it is claimed, are immune from such bias because their methods are centered around concepts and practices that are local to the culture being studied (see, however, the replication of the FFM using nontraditional methods of assessing taxonomies of trait adjectives in multiple languages; De Raad, Perugini, Hrebickova, & Szarota, 1998).

Is there a middle ground? We believe there is. In the past, scientists interested in cross-cultural psychology have tended to think about universal and culture-specific aspects of psychological phenomena—personality, emotion, language, and the like—as mutually exclusive, dichotomous categories. Thus, personality is either universal or indigenous. A better and more fruitful approach might be to consider the question not of whether personality is universal or indigenous, but rather how personality is *both* universal and culture-specific. It is entirely possible that some aspects of personality may be organized in a universal fashion, either because of biological or genetic factors or because of culture-constant learning and responses to the environment. The fact that some aspects of personality may be organized universally, however, does not necessarily argue against the possibility that other aspects of personality may be culturally unique. It may be these culturally unique aspects that give personality its own special flavor in each specific cultural milieu, and allow researchers the possibility of studying aspects of personality that they might not observe in other cultures. This is, in fact, the major premise underlying Five-Factor Theory that we discussed earlier. Thus, a more beneficial way of understanding the relationship between culture and personality may be to see indigenous and universal aspects of personality as two sides of the same coin, rather than as mutually exclusive. If we come to understand the relationship between culture and personality (and biology, for that matter) in ways that allow for the coexistence of universality and indigenization, then we can tackle the problem of exactly how to conceptualize and study this coexistence.

CONCLUSION

In this chapter, we have discussed the major approaches to understanding and studying the relationship between culture and personality, and have examined many different types of studies on this topic. We began by defining personality and briefly describing major approaches to the topic. We spent a considerable amount of time discussing research on the FFM, which suggests that there is universality in personality organization around a small set of basic personality traits. Additional studies in this genre have suggested that there may be a sixth or even seventh personality trait that is universal; future research is necessary to test this idea more fully.

We also discussed the FFT, a theory about where the universal personality traits come from. FFT suggests that the underlying traits reflect biologically based, inherited dispositions for behavior. But, how these traits are expressed may be culturally variable, as each person develops characteristic adaptations to address each of the traits.

In addition, we discussed interesting new cross-cultural research on control and autonomy. These studies are important because they inform us about personality organization from a different perspective. The evidence to date suggests that autonomy is a universal personality construct, and that all individuals of all cultures are autonomous. How we exert control over the environment in managing that autonomy, however, may differ in different contexts. That is, how we exert our personalities may be tactical.

Research on indigenous approaches to personality has demonstrated culturally specific aspects of personality that cannot be accounted for by the FFM. These two seemingly disparate sets of findings suggest a conflict in our understanding of the relationship between culture and personality, represented by the cross-cultural psychology versus cultural psychology schools of thought. We have suggested that these two seemingly opposing viewpoints need not be seen as mutually exclusive; rather, it may be more beneficial to view them as different, coexisting aspects of personality. The challenge for future research is to capture this coexistence, examining the relative degree of contribution of biological and cultural factors in the development and organization of personality.

In our quest to understand the relationship among culture and personality, one of the biggest issues we will need to tackle concerns the influence of context, and the effects of context on that understanding. As we have seen, context is a major dimension of culture (Hall, 1966). High-context cultures place little value on cross-context consistency, allowing (and necessitating) behaviors and cognitions that differ according to context or situation. Low-context cultures, in contrast, discourage cross-context differences, emphasizing instead consistency and stability across contexts. American culture is relatively low-context, emphasizing stability. It is only within this type of cultural context that we can even conceive of personality as a set of enduring characteristics with stability and consistency across cultures. Thus, a person in this cultural context should exhibit similar personality characteristics despite considerable differences in context.

It is relatively easy to demonstrate the existence of context specificity effects in assessments of personality. In one study, participants were randomly assigned to fill out a personality test under several conditions (Schmit, Ryan, Stierwalt, & Powell, 1995). The personality test was the NEO Five-Factor Inventory (Costa & McCrae, 1989). One group completed the measure in the usual way with general directions. Another group completed the measure as if they were applying for a customer service representative job in a department store, a job they really wanted. Even with this simple context manipulation, an analysis of the data indicated that students' responses differed substantially under the two conditions. Compared to students in the general condition, participants in the work-related condition gave significantly lower ratings on neuroticism and significantly higher ratings on extroversion, agreeableness, and conscientiousness. Thus, context specificity in personality assessment can be obtained with American participants as well, further challenging our traditional notions of personality, and the very definition of personality. Ultimately, these concerns need to be addressed in future work.

GLOSSARY

collective control A type of control in which one attempts to control the environment as a member of a group, and the group serves as the agent of control.

direct control A type of control in which the self acts as an agent, and individuals feel themselves to be more self-efficacious when their agency is made explicit, leading to greater feelings of autonomy and efficacy. Direct control may be the preferred mode of behavior in cultural contexts that promote independence or autonomy, such as in the United States.

factor analysis A statistical technique that allows researchers to group items on a questionnaire. The theoretical model underlying factor analysis is that groups of items on a questionnaire are answered in similar ways because they are assessing the same, single underlying psychological construct (or trait). By interpreting the groupings underlying the items, therefore, researchers make inferences about the underlying traits that are being measured.

indigenous personalities Conceptualizations of personality developed in a particular culture that are specific and relevant only to that culture.

indirect control A type of control in which one's agency is hidden or downplayed; people pretend as if they are not acting as an agent even though they are doing so in reality.

locus of control People's attributions of control over their behaviors and relationships as internal or external to themselves. People with an internal locus of control see their behavior and relationships with others as dependent on their own behavior. People with an external locus of control see their behavior and relationships as contingent on forces outside themselves and beyond their control.

national character The perception that each culture has a modal personality type, and that most persons in that culture share aspects of it.

personality A set of relatively enduring behavioral and cognitive characteristics, traits, or predispositions that people take with them to different situations, contexts, and interactions with others, and that contribute to differences among individuals.

proxy control Refers to control by someone else for the benefit of oneself. This is a form of control that can be used when personal control—either direct or indirect—is not available or inappropriate. These are third-party interventions.

trait A characteristic or quality distinguishing a person. It refers to a consistent pattern of behavior that a person would usually display in relevant circumstances.

11 CHAPTER | Culture and Abnormal Psychology

CHAPTER CONTENTS

One important goal of psychology is to use the knowledge gained through research to help people suffering from psychological disorders to rid themselves of symptoms and lead more effective, productive, and happy lives. Several themes have guided research and practice in this area of psychology. First and foremost are questions concerning definitions of abnormality—what is abnormal behavior? A second set of questions relates to the expression of abnormal behavior and our ability to detect it and classify it when it is expressed (assessment and diagnosis). A third question concerns how we should treat abnormal behavior when it is detected. This chapter will address the first two questions; the next chapter will address the treatment of abnormal behavior.

Culture adds an important dimension to these basic questions. Incorporating culture into our psychological theories and concepts raises a number of important issues with regard to abnormal behaviors (Marsella, 2000):

- Do definitions of normality and abnormality vary across cultures, or are there universal standards of abnormality?
- Do cultures vary in rates of abnormal behavior?
- Is abnormal behavior expressed in the same way across cultures, or can we identify culturally distinct patterns of abnormal behavior?
- Can the field develop cross-culturally reliable and valid ways of measuring, classifying, and diagnosing abnormal behaviors?
- How do psychotherapeutic approaches need to be modified in order to deal effectively with cultural influences on abnormality?

The answers to these questions have important implications for how we identify abnormal behavior and intervene to effect change. A poor understanding of the ways in which abnormal behavior is bound within the context of culture may lead to overdiagnosis, underdiagnosis, and/or misdiagnosis of distress symptoms (Paniagua, 2000), with potentially harmful consequences to the individual.

This chapter is devoted to the considerable amount of research and writing that seeks to address these questions and concerns. First, we will discuss the role of culture in defining abnormality, review studies of the prevalence and course of schizophrenia and depression across cultures, and describe a number of culture-specific psychological disorders. As you will see, culture plays a major role in shaping people's experience of psychological disorders. Second, we will discuss the role of culture in the assessment of abnormal behaviors, examine the classification schemes currently in use, and explore some issues surrounding the actual measurement of abnormality. Third, we will look at how the measurement of personality has been used in assessing psychopathology across cultures. Finally, we will cover a topic of increasing interest in the field of culture and mental health: the potentially psychologically stressful experiences of migrant populations.

DEFINING ABNORMALITY: SOME CORE ISSUES

Psychologists and other social scientists have long been interested in the influence of culture on psychopathology, or abnormal behaviors. Historically, the literature has been somewhat divided between two points of view (for a more detailed review, see Draguns, 1997). One view suggests that culture and psychopathology are inextricably intertwined, and that abnormal behaviors can be understood only in the cultural framework within which they occur. This perspective is known as **cultural relativism.** The contrasting view suggests that although culture plays a role in determining the exact behavioral and contextual manifestations of abnormal behavior, there are cross-cultural similarities, even universalities, in the underlying psychological mechanisms and subjective experiences of many psychological disorders.

Consider, for example, the following scenario:

> A woman is in the midst of a group of people but seems totally unaware of her surroundings. She is talking loudly to no one in particular, often using words and sounds the people around her find unintelligible. When questioned later about her behavior, she reports that she had been possessed by the spirit of an animal and was talking with a man who had recently died.

Is this woman's behavior abnormal?

In defining abnormal behavior, American psychologists often use a statistical approach or apply criteria of impairment or inefficiency, deviance, or subjective distress. Using a statistical approach, for example, we could define the woman's behavior as abnormal because its occurrence is rare or infrequent. Being out of touch with your surroundings, having delusions (mistaken beliefs) that you are an animal, and talking with the dead are not common experiences.

One problem with this approach to abnormality, however, is that not all rare behavior is disordered. Nor is all disordered behavior rare! Composing a concerto and speaking four languages are uncommon behaviors, yet we generally view them as highly desirable. Conversely, drinking to the point of drunkenness occurs quite frequently in the United States (and in many other countries of the world). Nevertheless, drunkenness is widely recognized as a sign of a possible substance-abuse disorder.

Another traditional approach to defining abnormality focuses on whether an individual's behavior is associated with impairment or inefficiency when carrying out customary roles. It is hard to imagine the woman described here carrying out normal day-to-day functions, such as caring for herself and working, while she believes herself to be an animal. In many instances, psychological disorders do involve serious impairments or a reduction in an individual's overall functioning. However, this is not always the case. Some people suffering from bipolar disorder (manic depression), for example, report enhanced productivity during manic episodes.

If we examine the woman's behavior in terms of deviance, we might also conclude that it is abnormal because it seems to go against social norms. But not all behavior that is socially deviant can be considered abnormal or psychologically disordered. For example, many people continue to believe that homosexuality is deviant, although it is no longer classified as a mental disorder in the United States (American Psychiatric Association, 1987). Although some Americans may view homosexuality as abnormal, in other cultures and at various periods in history homosexuality has been widely practiced. Lee (2001) has reported that homosexuality is still considered pathological in China, partly because sexual minorities are not as organized as they are in the United States and thus do not have the power and influence to challenge social norms on this issue. He believes that with time, however, homosexuality will no longer be classified as a mental disorder. Thus, using societal norms as a criterion for abnormality is difficult not only because norms change over time but because they are subjective. What one member of a society or culture considers deviant, another may accept as normal.

Reliance on reports of subjective distress to define abnormal behavior is also problematic. Whether a person experiences distress as a consequence of abnormal behavior may depend on how others treat him or her. For example, if the woman just described is ridiculed, shunned, and viewed as "sick" because of her behavior, she may well experience distress. Conversely, if she is seen as having special powers and is part of an accepting circle, she may not be distressed at all. Furthermore, there is some indication that cultural groups vary in the degree of distress they report experiencing in association with psychological disorders. Kleinman (1988) describes research indicating that depressed Chinese and African participants report feeling less guilt and shame than do depressed European American and European participants. The Chinese and African participants, however, report more somatic symptoms. These findings may reflect a cultural response bias (see Chapter 2). Some cultural groups may have values that prohibit reporting or focusing on subjective distress, in contrast to Western notions of the importance of self-disclosure.

Each of these more or less traditional ways of defining abnormality has advantages as well as disadvantages. These issues become even more complex when culture is considered. Definitions of abnormality may vary both within and across cultures.

As an alternative to these traditional approaches, many cross-cultural scholars argue that we can understand and identify abnormal behavior only if we take the cultural context into account. This viewpoint suggests that we must apply the principle of cultural relativism to abnormality. For example, the woman's behavior might appear disordered if it occurred on a street corner in a large city in the United States. It could, however, appear appropriate and understandable if it occurred in a shamanistic ceremony in which she was serving as healer. Cultures that believe in supernatural interventions are able to clearly distinguish when trance states and talking with spirits are an acceptable part of a healer's behavioral repertoire and when the same behaviors would be considered a sign of disorder (Murphy, 1976). Examples of such cultures include the Yoruba in Africa and some Eskimo tribes in Alaska. Along the same lines, behaviors associated with some religions (for example, revivalist Christian groups in the United States), such as speaking in tongues (glossolalia) and seeing visions, are widely practiced and accepted and may not necessarily indicate a mental disorder (Loewenthal, 1995).

Abnormality and normality, then, are to some extent culturally determined concepts (Kleinman, 1988; Marsella, 1979, 1980, 2000). Nonetheless, whether to accept universal or culturally relative definitions of abnormality is a source of continuing controversy in psychology. Examination of the cross-cultural literature may help provide clues on how to understand the role of culture in contributing to abnormality.

CROSS-CULTURAL RESEARCH ON ABNORMAL BEHAVIORS

Cross-cultural research over the years has provided a wealth of evidence suggesting that abnormal behaviors and psychopathology have both universal and culture-specific aspects. In this section, we will look at schizophrenia, depression, somatization, attention-deficit/hyperactivity disorder (ADHD), and a number of apparently culture-specific disorders.

Schizophrenia

Schizophrenia is characterized by "gross distortions of reality; withdrawal from social interaction; and disorganization of perception, thought, and emotion" (Carson, Butcher, & Coleman, 1988, p. 322). The prevalence rate has been estimated to be 1.1 percent in the general U.S. population (Regier, Narrow, Rae, Manderscheid, Locke, & Goodwin, 1993b). Some theories concerning the causes of schizophrenia give primacy to biological factors (for example, excess dopamine or other biochemical imbalances). Other theories emphasize family dynamics (for example, expression of hostility to the ill person). The diathesis–stress model of schizophrenia suggests that it may develop in individuals with a biological predisposition to the disorder (diathesis) following exposure to environmental stressors.

The World Health Organization (WHO; 1973, 1979, 1981) sponsored the International Pilot Study of Schizophrenia (IPSS) to compare the prevalence and course of the disorder of 1,202 patients in nine countries: Colombia, Czechoslovakia, Denmark, England, India, Nigeria, the Soviet Union, Taiwan, and the United States. Following rigorous training in using the research assessment tool, psychiatrists in each of the countries achieved good reliability in diagnosing schizophrenia in patients included in the study. As a result, WHO investigators were able to identify a set of symptoms present across all cultures in the subjects with schizophrenia. These symptoms include lack of insight, auditory and verbal hallucinations, and ideas of reference (assuming one is the center of attention) (Leff, 1977). The WHO studies are widely cited to bolster arguments for the universality of schizophrenia.

But some important cross-cultural differences emerged as well. In a finding that took the investigators by surprise, the course of the illness was shown to be more positive for patients in developing countries compared with those in highly industrialized countries. Patients in Colombia, India, and Nigeria recovered at faster rates than did those in England, the Soviet Union, and the United States. These differences were attributed to cultural factors such as the presence of extended kin networks, community support, and the tendency in developing countries to return to work.

The researchers also noted differences in symptom expression across cultures. Patients in the United States were less likely to demonstrate lack of insight and auditory hallucinations than were Danish or Nigerian patients. These findings may be related to cultural differences in values associated with insight and self-awareness, which are highly regarded in the United States but less well regarded in the other countries. Also, cultures may differ in their tolerance for particular symptoms; the Nigerian culture as a whole is more accepting of the presence of voices. Nigerian and Danish patients, however, were more likely to demonstrate catatonia (extreme withdrawal or agitation). More recently, the International Study of Schizophrenia (ISOS) followed up on samples (13 to 26 years later) in the original WHO studies. Some of the findings suggest that prognoses were still better for those from developing countries compared with developed countries (Hopper & Wanderling, 2000).

Kleinman (1988) and Leff (1981) have discussed some of the methodological problems that plagued the WHO studies—among them, an assessment tool that failed to tap culturally unique experiences and expressions of disorder. Kleinman also noted that the samples were made artificially homogeneous because of the selection criteria. He argued that the findings of cross-cultural differences might have been greater still had not the heterogeneity of the sample been reduced. Because the conclusions of the study emphasized the similarities and not the differences of schizophrenia across the various cultures, Kleinman (1995) states that we may have focused on and exaggerated the universal aspects of psychological disorders at the expense of revealing what is culturally-specific. In other words, the biases of the investigators may have led them to search for cultural commonalities while overlooking important cultural differences.

Other cross-cultural comparisons of schizophrenia have found evidence of cultural variations in symptoms. For example, a study of different ethnic groups in Britain found that Bangladeshis were less likely to view suspiciousness or hallucinatory behavior as symptoms of schizophrenia, as compared with white British persons (Pote & Orell, 2002). A study of Japanese schizophrenics indicated that they are more likely than their European American counterparts to be withdrawn and passive, conforming to cultural values (Sue & Morishima, 1982).

Studies of patients with schizophrenia have tested the theory that expressed emotion—family communication characterized by hostility, criticalness, and overinvolvement—increases the risk of relapse. The expressed-emotion construct is important because it suggests that family and social interactions influence the course of schizophrenia. These interactions are influenced, in turn, by cultural values. Research indicates that expressed emotion predicts relapse in Western samples (Butzlaff & Hooley, 1998; Mintz, Mintz, & Goldstein, 1987). Expressed emotion also predicts relapse in Mexican Americans (Lopez, Hipke, Polo, Jenkins, Karno, Vaughn, & Snyder, 2004). However, contrary to these studies, one study conducted in Malaysia found that a high level of expressed emotion was not a cause of relapse (Azhar & Varma, 1996). Kleinman (1988) notes the difficulties in using this construct in different cultures, particularly those that emphasize nonverbal communication. Kleinman questions whether measures of expressed emotion developed in one cultural context have validity in another.

Reports of cultural differences in diagnosis have also raised questions about the validity of assessment techniques used in cross-cultural comparisons of schizophrenia and other disorders (Kleinman, 1988; Leff, 1977). Paniagua (2000) states that cultural variations in language, style of emotional expressions, body language, and eye contact should all be considered when diagnosing disorders. In a reanalysis of some of the early WHO data, Leff (1977) found that U.S. psychiatrists were more likely to give diagnoses of schizophrenia than were psychiatrists in England, and less likely to give diagnoses of depression. A recent analysis of 134,523 patients in the United States demonstrated ethnic disparities in the diagnosis of serious mental illnesses (Blow, Zeber, McCarthy, Valenstein, Gillon, & Bingham, 2004). In this study, African Americans were more than four times as likely and Hispanics more than three times as likely as European Americans to be diagnosed with schizophrenia. The authors also concluded that differences in socioeconomic status, drug addiction, and other variables could not explain the disparity in diagnoses. African American adolescents were also more likely than European American adolescents to receive diagnoses of schizophrenia, even when the symptom picture was similar (DelBello, Lopez-Larson, Soutullo, & Strakowski, 2001). Finally, Afro-Caribbeans in the United Kingdom were also more likely to be diagnosed with schizophrenia than were whites (King, Nazroo, Weich, McKenzie, Bhui, Karlsen, Stansfeld, Tyrer, Blanchard, Lloyd, McManus, Sproston, & Erens, 2005). Racial bias seems to account for some of the differential pattern and cultural differences in expression of symptoms may also be important.

In summary, the WHO studies provide ample evidence of a universal set of core symptoms that may be related to schizophrenia. Other studies, however, help to temper this interpretation by documenting specific cultural differences in the exact manifestations, experience, and diagnosis of schizophrenia in different cultural contexts.

Depression

All of us have experienced moods of depression, sadness, or the blues in our lives. We may have these feelings in response to a death in the family, the breakup of a relationship, falling short of a goal, and other stresses or disappointments. The presence of a depressive disorder, however, may involve symptoms of "intense sadness, feelings of futility and worthlessness, and withdrawal from others" (Sue, Sue, & Sue, 1990, p. 325). Depression is often characterized by physical changes (such as sleep and appetite disturbances) and motivational changes (such as apathy and boredom), as well as emotional and behavioral changes (such as feelings of sadness, hopelessness, and loss of energy) (Berry, Poortinga, Segall, & Dasen, 1992).

By 2020, major depression is projected to be the second leading cause of illness-related disability affecting the world's population (World Health Organization, 2006). Women are two times more likely to experience depression than men, and this gender difference has held up across race, ethnicity, socioeconomics, and culture (Weissman, Bland, Canino, Faravelli, Greenwald, Hwu, Joyce, Karam, Lee, Lellouch, Lepine, Newman, Rubin-Stiper, Wells, Wickramaratne, Wittchen, & Yeh, 1996). In the United States, depression is currently the leading cause of disability for people ages 15 to 44 (World Health Organization, 2004). About 3.3 percent and 6.5 percent of the adult male and female U.S. population are currently diagnosed with major depression (National Institutes of Health, 2000). Lifetime prevalence rates for depression is about 16 percent (Kessler, Berglund, Demler, Jin, Koretz, Merikangas, Rush, Walters, & Wang, 2003), or 20 percent for women and 10 percent for men (Weissman & Olfson, 1995). There is also some evidence to suggest that the incidence of depression has risen over the past few decades (World Health Organization, 2006), especially among adolescents (Farmer, 2002). Developmentally, the incidence of depression increases dramatically around the time of puberty, at least in the United States, and more so for females than for males (Cyranowski, Frank, Young, & Shear, 2000). This gender difference remains throughout adulthood.

A landmark study by the WHO (1983) investigated the symptoms of depression in four countries—Canada, Switzerland, Iran, and Japan—and found that the great majority of patients (76 percent of the 573 cases) reported cross-culturally constant symptoms, including "sadness, joylessness, anxiety, tension, lack of energy, loss of interest, loss of ability to concentrate, and ideas of insufficiency" (p. 61). More than half of this group (56 percent) also reported suicidal ideation. Based on these findings, Marsella (1980; Marsella, Sartorius, Jablensky, & Fenton, 1985) suggested that vegetative symptoms such as loss of enjoyment, appetite, or sleep are cross-culturally constant ways in which people experience depression. Other studies—for example, comparing Hungarians with Americans and Canadians (Keitner, Fodor, Ryan, Miller, Epstein, & Bishop, 1991); of Iranians (Haghighatgou & Peterson, 1995); and of children in six countries (Yamamoto, Soliman, Parsons, & Davies, 1987)—have tended to support this viewpoint.

Other cross-cultural studies of depression, however, document wide variations in expression of symptoms of this disorder. Some cultural groups (for example, Nigerians) are less likely to report extreme feelings of worthlessness and guilt-related symptoms. Others (for example, Chinese) are more likely to report somatic symptoms (Kleinman, 2004). Indigenous expressions of depression for Hopi Indians include worry, sickness, and heartbrokenness (Manson, Shore, & Bloom, 1985). Ugandans conceptualize depressive symptoms in more cognitive terms (thinking too much, or "illness thoughts") rather than emotional (sadness) (Okello & Ekblad, 2006). As with schizophrenia, rates of depression also vary from culture to culture, with reports of 3.3 percent in South Korea, 4.9 percent in Lebanaon, 6.2 percent in Iran, and 12.6 percent in New Zealand (Hwu & Compton, 1994; Karam et al., 2006; Mehrabi,

Bayanzadeh, Atef-Vahid, Bolhari, Shahmohammadi, & Vaezi, 2000). How-ever, different assessments and manifestations of the disorder render it difficult to obtain comparable prevalence rates.

Leff (1977) argues that cultures vary in terms of their differentiation and communication of emotional terminology and, hence, in how they experience and express depression. Also, some cultures have few words to convey emotions such as sadness or anger (see Chapter 8).

Kleinman (1978) takes the position that depressive disease reflects a biologically based disorder, whereas depressive illness refers to the personal and social experience of depression. In arguing for a culturally relative definition of depression, Kleinman (1988) writes that:

> depression experienced entirely as low back pain and depression experienced entirely as guilt-ridden existential despair are such substantially different forms of illness behavior with distinctive symptoms, patterns of help seeking, and treatment responses that although the disease in each instance may be the same, the illness, not the disease, becomes the determinative factor. And one might well ask, "is the disease even the same?" (p. 25)

Although Kleinman accepts the idea that depressive disease is universal, he argues that the expression and course of the illness are culturally determined.

Marsella (1979, 1980; Marsella, Kaplan, & Suarez, 2002) also argues for a culturally relative view of depression, suggesting that depression takes a primarily affective form in cultures with strong objective orientations (that is, individualistic cultures). In these cultures, feelings of loneliness and isolation dominate the symptom picture. In subjective cultures (those having a more communal structure), somatic symptoms such as headaches are dominant. Marsella has also proposed that depressive symptom patterns differ across cultures because of cultural variations in sources of stress as well as in resources for coping with the stress.

Other researchers also highlight the need to consider the current social and cultural environment of the disorder. For instance, the criteria for major depression in earlier editions of the *Chinese Classification of Mental Disorders* (CCMD) included a duration of symptoms for 4 weeks (in the most recent edition, it is 2 weeks). Earlier editions used 4 weeks because mental health professionals in China argued that "2 weeks of depressive symptoms could be difficult to distinguish from social suffering, which was common in China's history of wars, turmoil, and rapid social change" (Lee, 2001, p. 423). Thus, taking into account the broader social and historical context is important in defining disorders.

In sum, as with the cross-cultural work on schizophrenia, the literature on depression points to both universal and culture-specific ways in which the disorder may occur and be experienced across cultures.

Somatization

Many cross-cultural psychologists, psychotherapists, and counselors are sensitive to the issue of **somatization**—essentially, bodily symptoms as expressions of psychological distress. Some studies have suggested that members of certain cultural groups, such as Hispanics (Koss, 1990), Japanese (Arnault, Sakamoto, & Moriwaki, 2006), Chinese (Kleinman, 1982), and Arabs (El-Islam, 1982) tend to somaticize more than Europeans or Americans do. In fact, it has been commonly thought that such reports of somatic symptoms (for example, low-back pain or intestinal problems) are just a code or camouflage for psychological symptoms.

More recent cross-cultural studies, however, challenge this viewpoint. Kirmayer (2001), for example, reviewed the available evidence and concluded that there was little support for the notion that the degree and amount of somatization vary across cultures. Moreover, although Kleinman (1982) concluded that Chinese diagnoses of neurasthenia were really cases of depression, this view was not shared by the mainland Chinese psychiatrists (reported in Draguns, 1997). According to Lee (2001), Chinese psychiatrists believe that Chinese people do not camouflage, but readily reveal, psychological symptoms within the context of a trusting doctor–patient relationship and that "the coexistence of psychologic symptoms with the presenting physical symptoms is consonant with Chinese philosophy. This is because the development of the somatoform category is grounded in the Western intellectual legacy of mind–body dichotomy, which differs from the Oriental notions of balance of holism" (p. 423). Not only Chinese but Japanese psychiatrists also disagree that the concept of somatization is more accepted in Asian cultures. (Yamashita & Koyama, 1994). Isaac, Janca, and Orley (1996), on the other hand, have reported that somatic expression of psychological distress is a universal phenomenon and that the presence of large numbers of somatic symptoms is strongly related to the overt expression of psychological distress in European and American cultures, too.

Thus, the available research tends to suggest that, although previously considered a culture-specific phenomenon, somatization may be a universal phenomenon with culture-specific meanings and expression modes.

Attention-Deficit/Hyperactivity Disorder

Up until now we have discussed disorders affecting primarily adults. We now focus on one of the disorders most commonly diagnosed in childhood—attention–deficit/hyperactivity disorder (ADHD). ADHD was first described by a German psychiatrist, Dr. Heinrich Hoffman in 1845 (National Institute of Mental Health, 2006). Despite recognition of this disorder over a century ago, ADHD became more widely known only relatively recently. It has been recognized and diagnosed in different cultures (Faraone & Biederman, 2004). Some main features of ADHD are inattentiveness (difficulty paying attention, easily distracted), impulsivity (having trouble waiting turns, interrupts others), and hyperactivity (fidgeting, can't sit still). Importantly, these symptoms must interfere with social and academic functioning to be considered a disorder. Three subtypes have been identified: ADHD with symptoms of inattention, symptoms of hyperactivity and impulsivity, and symptoms of all three—inattention, hyperactivity, and impulsivity (*Diagnostic and Statistical Manual of Mental Disorders,* 4th edition, text revision [DSM IV-TR], 2000). In contrast, according to the criteria for the *International Classification of Diseases,* 10th edition (ICD-10 Revised), all three types of symptoms must be present to diagnose ADHD. Thus, depending on the criteria used, prevalence rates are difficult to compare across different cultures. However, one consistent finding across different cultures is that boys are more likely to be diagnosed than girls (Cantwell, 1996).

The prevalence rates of ADHD across cultures has been reported as 5.8 percent in Brazil (Rohde, Szobot, Polanczyk, Schmitz, & Martins, 2005), 7.8 percent in the United States (Centers for Disease Control, 2005), 8.1 percent in Turkey (Erşan, Doğan, Doğan, & Sümer, 2004), 8.9 percent in China (Leung, Luk, Ho, Mak, Bacon-Shone, 1996), and 14.9 percent in the United Arab Emirates (UAE) (Bu-Haroon, Eapen, & Benner, 1999). Across these studies, parents, teachers, and children themselves provide reports on their behaviors as a basis for ADHD classification. The importance of the source of information is highlighted by the fact that correlations between sources is rather low (Pierrehumbert, Bader, Thévoz, Kinal, & Halfon, 2006). The higher prevalence rate found in the UAE could be due to the fact that Bu-Haroon et al.'s (1999) study had only one reporting source, the teacher. To date, no large-scale comparative cross-cultural studies have been conducted on ADHD as has been done with depression and schizophrenia. Such studies are needed to establish that ADHD is indeed a universally experienced disorder.

Some argue that ADHD is solely a cultural construct. For instance, Timimi (2004) contends that the stresses of modern Western culture (loss of extended family support, a busy and hyperactive family life) has set the stage for the emergence of the construct and higher rates of ADHD in recent years. Others acknowledge that ADHD may indeed be universal but that there are culture-specific variations. For instance, Norvilitis and Fang (2005) found both similarities and differences in the perception of ADHD among teachers in China and the United States. Both samples rated the importance of symptoms similarly to include both hyperactivity/impulsivity and inattentiveness. Where they differed was in their beliefs in the causes and treatment of ADHD. For instance, 60 percent of Chinese and 45 percent of U.S. teachers agreed with the statement that "ADHD is biologically based" and 71 percent of Chinese and 13 percent of U.S. teachers agreed with the statement that "Children with ADHD are just bored and need more to do." The authors conclude that symptoms characterizing the disorder may be similar, yet the causes and treatment of the disorder may differ between the two countries. Nonetheless, these are preliminary findings, and more studies, especially involving psychiatrists and psychologists who are making the diagnoses, are needed.

An ADHD Working Group consisting of clinicians and researchers from different nations (Australia, Brazil, France, Germany, South Korea, Mexico, the Philippines, the United Kingdom, and the United States) met to discuss the science, diagnosis, and treatment of ADHD (Remschmidt, 2004). As a result of this meeting a consensus statement was published, arguing that ADHD is a valid disorder found in both developed and developing cultures, that it has a neurobiological basis, and that it is unrecognized, underdiagnosed, and subsequently, left untreated in many countries (Remschmidt, 2004). Nonetheless, future studies including more representative samples of children from different parts of the world are needed to offer more conclusive evidence of ADHD as a universal disorder.

CULTURE-BOUND SYNDROMES

The approach used in cross-cultural studies of depression and schizophrenia can be characterized as etic; that is, it assumes universally accepted definitions of abnormality and methodology (review Chapter 2 for definitions of *etic* and *emic*). In contrast to this etic approach are various ethnographic reports of culture-bound syndromes—forms of abnormal behavior observed only in certain sociocultural milieus. Findings concerning differential rates and courses of a disorder across cultures, and of culturally distinct forms of the disorder, suggest the importance of culture in shaping the expression of abnormal behavior. In fact, ethnographic reports of **culture-bound syndromes** provide perhaps the strongest support for cultural relativism in understanding and dealing with abnormality.

Using primarily emic (culture-specific) approaches involving ethnographic examinations of behavior within a specific cultural context, anthropologists and psychiatrists have identified several apparently unique forms of psychological disorders. Some similarities between symptoms of these culture-specific disorders and those recognized across cultures have been observed. The particular pattern of symptoms, however, typically does not fit the diagnostic criteria of psychological disorders recognized in Western classification schemes. A case study of a Korean woman (P. M.) reported by a Korean anthropologist (Harvey, 1979) illustrates the kinds of symptoms that are attributed to *sinbyong* (spirit sickness), which occurs when a woman is believed to be recruited to become a shaman.

> She was not only hearing things but seeing things as well. Her ears rang a lot and she could hear voices whispering in them; and when she yielded to the urge to talk she uttered prophetic statements. Neighbors and relatives began to speculate that she had been "caught by the spirit" and was possessed. She suffered from terrible palpitations of the heart, indigestion, and dizzy spells, sometimes alternately and sometimes in combinations. She was constantly afraid of being caught hallucinating by her husband or his family. She was determined to overcome these symptoms and began to read a lot of novels as a way of fighting off the hallucinations. (p. 105)

However, after experiencing several more episodes of *sinbyong,* Harvey reports that P. M. ultimately decided to accept her calling as a shaman, became quite successful, and made a good living.

Other culture-bound disorders have been documented by various writers. *Amok,* the most widely observed culture-bound syndrome, has been identified in several countries in Asia (Malaysia, Philippines, and Thailand). The disorder is characterized by sudden rage and homicidal aggression. It is thought to be brought on by stress, sleep deprivation, and alcohol consumption (Carson et al., 1988) and has been observed primarily in males. Several stages of the disorder have been identified, ranging from extreme withdrawal prior to the assaultive behavior to exhaustion and amnesia for the rage. The phrase *running amok* derives from observations of this disorder.

Anorexia nervosa is a disorder identified in the West but not at first observed in Third World countries (Swartz, 1985). The disorder is characterized by a distorted body image, fear of becoming fat, and a serious loss of weight associated with restraining from eating food or purging after eating. Several factors have been cited as possible causes of this disorder, including a cultural emphasis on thinness as an ideal for women, constricted sex roles, and an individual's fear of being out of control or of taking on adult responsibilities. In countries where attention is not drawn to the female figure and the female body is usually entirely covered, such as in Saudi Arabia, eating disorders have not been mentioned in psychiatric literature until recently (Al-Subaie & Alhamad, 2000). Research has suggested that anorexia nervosa is no longer limited to Europe and North America, but may now be found in many urbanized parts of the world such as Hong Kong, Korea, Singapore, and China (for example, Goh, Ong, & Subramaniam, 1993; Gordon, 2001; Hoek, van Harten, van Hoeken, & Susser, 1998; Lee, 1995). However, the particular criteria for being anorexic may differ slightly among different cultural groups. For instance, distinctive reasons for forced starvation in China is not a fear of getting fat, but having an "extreme distaste for food" or being "intolerably full" (Lee-Sing, Leung, Wing, & Chiu, 1991). Newer studies of immigrants have also found differences. For instance, a comparison of white British and Southeast Asian British adolescent females diagnosed with anorexia, found that fear of fat was not part of the anorexia profile for Southeast Asian British adolescents (Tareen, Hodes, & Rangel, 2005). Interestingly, some disorders that were once labeled "culture-bound" may become less so as more and more individuals immigrate to countries and bring with them their culture-specific disorders.

Ataque de nervios is observed in Latin American groups (Febo San Miguel, Guarnaccia, Shrout, Lewis-Fernandez, Canino, & Ramirez, 2006). Symptoms include trembling, uncontrollable shouting, intense crying, heat in the chest rising to the head, and dizziness. This disorder tends to surface during stressful family events, such as funerals, divorce or separation, or witnessing an accident including a family member.

Zar is an altered state of consciousness observed among Ethiopian immigrants to Israel (Grisaru, Budowski, & Witztum, 1997). The belief in possession by Zar spirits, common in Africa, is expressed by involuntary movements, mutism, and incomprehensible language.

Whakama is a New Zealand Maori construct that includes shame, self-abasement, feelings of inferiority, inadequacy, self-doubt, shyness, excessive modesty, and withdrawal (Sachdev, 1990). It does not have an exact equivalent in European or American societies.

"Sinking heart" is a condition of distress in the Punjabi culture (Krause, 1989). It is experienced as physical sensations in the heart or chest, and is thought to be caused by excessive heat, exhaustion, worry, or social failure. It has some characteristics of depression but also resembles a cardiovascular disorder.

Avanga is actually a constellation of other, more specific forms of disorder, all of which include a vivid, imaginary companionship with a single external spirit. Originating in Tongan culture, its incidence is on the rise as people move toward cities and urbanization (Puloka, 1997).

Other culture-bound syndromes, cited by Kiev (1972) and Yap (1974), include *latah* (characterized by hysteria and echolalia, observed primarily in women in Malaysia); *koro* (extreme fear that the penis is shrinking or retracting, observed in Southeast Asian men, or extreme fear that the nipples are retracting, observed in Southeast Asian women); and *susto* (characterized by depression and apathy thought to reflect "soul loss," observed in Indians of the Andean highlands). Many other such culture-bound syndromes have been documented around the world.

How do these culturally unique disorders arise? Pfeiffer (1982) has identified four dimensions for understanding culture-bound syndromes. First, he cites culture-specific areas of stress, including family and societal structure and ecological conditions. For example, *koro* might be best understood as resulting from the unique emphasis on potency in certain cultures that emphasize paternal authority. Then, culture-specific shaping of conduct and interpretations of conduct may mean that certain cultures implicitly approve patterns of exceptional behavior. An example is *amok,* in which aggression against others "broadly follows the patterns of societal expectations" (p. 206). Finally, Pfeiffer argues that how a culture interprets exceptional behavior will be linked to culture-specific interventions. For example, interventions to heal the soul loss associated with *susto* will involve sacrifices carried out by a native healer to appease the earth so that it will return the soul.

Thus far, we have learned that culture plays a prominent role in shaping the experience of psychological disorder, both in determining the expression of symptoms of universal disorders and in contributing to the emergence of culture-specific disorders. In a sense, all disorders may be "culture-bound," disorders "since no disorder can escape cultural encoding, shaping, and presentation" (Marsella, 2000). Recognizing the important role of culture in shaping abnormal behavior requires that we take the next step and reexamine the way we assess and treat individuals with psychological disorders.

Paniagua (1998, 2000) offers four assessment guidelines for practitioners to distinguish psychopathology and culture-related conditions: (1) They should familiarize themselves with the cultural background of the client by consulting with family members, peers, and folk healers (such as medicine men and women for Native Americans). (2) Practitioners should check their own cultural biases and prejudice before attempting to evaluate clients who are culturally different. (3) Practitioners should not immediately jump to the conclusion that the client's symptoms are manifestations of a culture-bound syndrome simply because the client is of that culture. (4) Practitioners should ask culturally appropriate questions that would allow the client and family members to elaborate on possible cultural factors that may help explain the disorder under consideration.

Guarnaccia and Rogler (1999) have called for more rigorous research on culture-bound syndromes that focuses on the nature of the phenomenon, the sociocultural location of the sufferers, the relationship of culture-bound syndromes to psychiatric disorders, and the social and psychiatric history of the sufferer. An important lesson is to be learned from studying culture-bound syndromes—that it is necessary to consider cultural values, beliefs, practices, and social situations in determining how to help someone who is suffering.

Summary

The material reviewed in this section suggests that there are universal aspects of symptoms and disease expression for at least some of the major psychopathologies such as depression and schizophrenia. At the same time, however, it also suggests that psychopathologies are heavily influenced by culture, especially in terms of the specific behavioral and contextual manifestations of the abnormal behavior, and the meaning of the behavior to the lifestyles and lives of individuals. The existence of culture-bound syndromes—disorders that appear to occur only in specific cultural milieus—reinforces the position of the cultural relativists.

We began this section by positing two viewpoints about the relationship between culture and abnormal behavior: the universalist position and the cultural-relativist position. The research reviewed here provides ample evidence for both positions, indicating that psychopathology across cultures contains both universal and culturally specific components. Other writers who have reviewed the field in far more depth—including Al-Issa (1995), Draguns (1997), Pfeiffer (1994), Tanaka-Matsumi and Draguns (1997), and Guarnaccia and Rogler (1999)—have reached the same conclusion. Draguns, for example, concludes that "neither [position] should be disregarded or exaggerated and both should be sensitively and realistically blended in providing service across cultural lines" (p. 230). We still have a long way to go in infusing both etic and emic perspectives on mental disorders.

CULTURE AND THE ASSESSMENT OF ABNORMAL BEHAVIOR

Assessment of abnormal behavior involves identifying and describing an individual's symptoms in the broader context of his or her overall functioning, life history, and environment (Carson et al., 1988). The tools and methods of assessment should be sensitive to cultural and other environmental influences on behavior and functioning. Although considerable progress had been made in the field over the years, the literature on standard assessment techniques indicates that there may be problems of bias or insensitivity when psychological tests and methods developed in one cultural context are used to assess behavior in a different context.

Culture and Psychiatric Diagnoses

In assessing abnormal behavior, psychologists seek to classify abnormal behaviors into categories—diagnoses—that are both reliable and valid. *Reliability*, as you will recall, has to do with the degree to which the same diagnoses would be made consistently over time and by different clinicians; *validity* refers to the degree to which the diagnosis accurately portrays the clinical disorder it is supposed to describe.

Because culture exerts some degree of influence on the creation, maintenance, and definition of abnormal behaviors, cross-cultural issues arise concerning the reliability and validity of diagnoses, and even of the diagnostic categories used. If all abnormal behaviors were entirely etic in their expression and presentation—that is, entirely the same across cultures—then creating reliable and valid diagnostic categories would not be a problem. But just as individuals differ in their presentation of abnormality, cultures also vary; indeed, some culture-bound syndromes appear to be limited to only one or a few cultures. Thus, developing diagnostic systems and classifications that can be reliably and validly used across cultures around the world, or across different cultural groups within a single country, becomes a challenge.

One of the most widely used systems of classification is the American Psychiatric Association's *Diagnostic and Statistical Manual of Mental Disorders* (DSM). The DSM, originally published in 1952, has undergone several major revisions and is now in its fourth edition (DSM-IV). Some of the changes from DSM-III to DSM-IV represent the field's response to heavy criticism by cross-cultural psychiatrists.

> A large number of disorders described in the manual were different or simply did not exist in societies and cultures beyond the Western world. It was repeatedly noted that, after all, 80 percent of the world population does not belong to the Western cultural sphere, and that the manual could lose credibility, its international popularity notwithstanding.
>
> Diagnosis does not mean to drive an individual into a particular slot; ethnicity, diversity, and pluralism should be duly recognized as politically important. . . . For culture to be built into the DSM-IV, diagnosticians always should be reminded that their task is essentially cultural: The patient and the clinician each bring his or her own culture, and the clinician–patient encounter realizes culture (Alarcon, 1995, pp. 452, 455).

To address these criticisms, several modifications were made to the DSM-IV to increase its cultural sensitivity: (1) incorporating information on how the clinical manifestations of the disorders can vary by culture; (2) including 25 culture-bound syndromes in an appendix (some of which have been mentioned in this chapter); and (3) adding guidelines for in-depth assessment of the individual's cultural background, including cultural expressions of the individual's disorder, cultural factors related to psychosocial functioning in the individual's specific cultural context, and cultural differences between the clinician and the individual (American Psychiatric Association, 1994). Thus, the DSM-IV has taken considerable steps to incorporate the role of culture in the expression and reliable classification of psychological disorders. However, the DSM-IV does not go so far as to *require* an assessment of cultural elements that may be necessary to recognize and classify a culture-bound syndrome (Paniagua, 2000). Subsequently, challenges to the DSM-IV remain, especially concerning its difficulty in classifying culture-bound syndromes.

Another well-known and often used classification system is the *International Classification of Diseases,* 10th edition (ICD-10). Its section on mental health includes 100 major diagnostic categories encompassing 329 individual clinical classifications. It is intended to be descriptive and atheoretical. Unfortunately, reviews of ICD-10 (for example, Alarcon, 1995) have suggested that it fails to recognize the importance of culture in influencing the expression and presentation of disorder.

To address the problem of the lack of cultural considerations in the assessment of mental disorders, local diagnostic systems have been created. The *Chinese Classification of Mental Disorders* (CCMD), for example, has been heavily influenced by the DSM-IV and ICD-10 but has culture-specific features that do not exist in the international systems. The most recent edition, the CCMD-3, was revised in 2001. This manual includes disorders distinctive to Chinese culture and excludes irrelevant disorders (such as sibling rivalry, because of the one-child policy). In the mid-1980s, three African psychiatrists developed a handbook for North African practitioners (Douki, Moussaoui, & Kacha, 1987). Surely, we will see more and more indigenously created manuals to classify mental disorders across cultures.

Having a reliable and valid classification system of diagnoses would be a major plus for all health professionals and the people they seek to help. The DSM-IV seems to have made major strides toward creating such a system. Still, work in this area is continually evolving, and we are sure to see changes in this and other classification systems in the future. Hopefully, those changes will be informed by meaningful and relevant cross-cultural research. One such attempt to develop more culturally sensitive, valid, and reliable diagnoses can be found in the research journal *Culture, Medicine and Psychiatry,* which devotes a special "Clinical Cases Section" to case studies of individuals within their specific cultural context (Tanaka-Matsumi, 2001). The case narratives include a clinical case history, cultural formulation, cultural identity, cultural explanation of the illness, cultural factors related to psychosocial environment and levels of functioning, cultural elements of the clinician–patient relationship, and overall cultural assessment. Attempts such as this should benefit the development of more culturally valid classification manuals of disorders.

Cross-Cultural Assessment of Abnormal Behavior

Not only is it important to have a reliable and valid system of classification of abnormal behaviors; it is also important to have a set of tools that can reliably and validly measure behaviors, feelings, and other psychological parameters related to mental illness. Those tools may include questionnaires, interview protocols, or standardized tasks that require some sort of behavior on the part of the test taker.

Needless to say, many of the issues that concern the valid and reliable measurement of any psychological variable cross-culturally for research purposes are also relevant to discussions of measurement tools for abnormality. For instance, it may be difficult to adequately transfer and use a psychological assessment that has been developed in one culture to another because of culture-specific expressions of distress. Kleinman (1995) points out that many items of an assessment instrument may use wording that is so culture-specific (for example, "feeling blue") that directly translating them to another culture would be nonsensical. Draguns (1997) reviewed a number of issues in this area of psychological measurement, including stimulus equivalence, sample characteristics, comparability of constructs, structured self-reports, personal interviews, experimental apparatuses, and the impact of the examiner. These issues, and others, make valid and reliable measurement of pathology across cultures very difficult and complex.

A critical examination of how the tools in use fare across cultures provides a stark glimpse of reality. Traditional tools of clinical assessment in psychology are generally based on a standard definition of abnormality and use a standard set of classification criteria for evaluating problematic behavior. Therefore, the tools may have little meaning in cultures with varying definitions, however well translated into the native language, and they may mask or fail to capture culturally specific expressions of disorder (Marsella, 1979). The assessment problems encountered in studying schizophrenia and depression across cultures illustrate the limitations of traditional assessment methods.

The WHO studies described earlier, for example, used the Present State Examination (PSE) to diagnose schizophrenia. Leff (1986) has commented on the ethnocentric bias of procedures such as the PSE and the Cornell Medical Index. In a psychiatric survey of the Yoruba in Nigeria, investigators had to supplement the PSE to include culture-specific symptoms such as feeling "an expanded head and goose flesh."

Standard diagnostic instruments to measure depressive disorder may also miss important cultural expressions of the disorder in Africans (Beiser, 1985) and Native Americans (Manson et al., 1985). In an extensive study of depression among Native Americans (Manson & Shore, 1981; Manson et al., 1985), the American Indian Depression Schedule was developed to assess and diagnose depressive illness. The investigators found that depression among the Hopi includes symptoms not measured by standard measures of depression such as the Diagnostic Interview Schedule and the Schedule for Affective Disorders and Schizophrenia. These measures, based on diagnostic criteria found in the DSM-III

(American Psychiatric Association, 1987), failed to capture the short but acute dysphoric moods sometimes reported by the Hopi (Manson et al., 1985).

Concerning children, the Child Behavior Checklist (CBCL; Achenbach, 2001) has been used to assess emotional and behavioral problems of children in various parts of the world, including Thailand, Kenya, and the United States (Weisz, Sigman, Weiss, & Mosk, 1993; Weisz, Suwanlert, Chaiyasit, Weiss, Walter, & Anderson, 1988); China (Su, Yang, Wan, Luo, & Li, 1999); Denmark (Petersen, Bilenberg, Hoerder, & Gillberg, 2006); Israel and Palestine (Auerbach, Yirmiya, & Kamel, 1996); and Australia, Jamaica, Greece, and nine other countries (Crijnen, Achenbach, & Verhulst, 1999). In general, studies have found that U.S. children tend to exhibit higher levels of undercontrolled behaviors ("externalizing behaviors" such as acting out and aggression) and lower levels of overcontrolled behaviors ("internalizing" behaviors such as fearfulness and somaticizing) compared with children of other, particularly collectivistic, cultures. Thus, the CBCL (sometimes slightly modified) has been widely used in many cultures to assess problematic behaviors. However, a study that recruited American Indian (Dakota/Lakota) parents to assess the accept-ability and appropriateness of using the CBCL in their culture found that some questions were difficult for the parents to answer because the questions did not take into account Dakotan/Lakotan cultural values or traditions, and because the parents believed their responses would be misinterpreted by members of the dominant culture, who did not have a good understanding of the Dakotan/Lakotan culture (Oesterheld, 1997). This underscores again the importance of critically examining assessment tools for use cross-culturally.

Several researchers (Higginbotham, 1979; Lonner & Ibrahim, 1989; Marsella, 1979) have offered guidelines for developing measures to use in cross-cultural assessment of abnormal behavior. They suggest that sensitive assessment methods examine sociocultural norms of healthy adjustment as well as culturally based definitions of abnormality. Higginbotham also suggests the importance of examining **indigenous healing systems,** or systems of cure, such as folk healers, particular to a certain culture. An assessment of indigenous healing systems should also enhance planning for treatment strategies, one of the primary goals of traditional assessment (Carson et al., 1988).

Other research has found that the cultural backgrounds of therapist and client may contribute to the perception and assessment of mental health. For instance, Li-Repac (1980) conducted a study to evaluate the role of culture in the diagnostic approach of therapists. In this study, Chinese American and European American male clients were interviewed and videotaped, then rated by Chinese American and European American male therapists on their level of psychological functioning. The results showed an interaction effect between the cultural backgrounds of therapist and client on the therapists' judgment of the clients. The Chinese American clients were rated as awkward, confused, and nervous by the European American therapists, but the same clients were rated as adaptable, honest, and friendly by the Chinese American therapists. In contrast, European American clients were rated as sincere and easygoing by European American therapists, but aggressive and rebellious by the Chinese

American therapists. Furthermore, Chinese American clients were judged to be more depressed and less socially capable by the European American therapists, and European American clients were judged to be more severely disturbed by the Chinese American therapists. These findings illustrate how judgments of appropriate, healthy psychological functioning may differ depending on the cultural background and notions of normality of the person making the assessment.

In making clinical assessments two types of errors are possible: overpathologizing and underpathologizing (Lopez, 1989). **Overpathologizing** may occur when the clinician, unfamiliar with the client's cultural background, incorrectly judges the client's behavior as pathological when in fact the behaviors are normal variations for that individual's culture. For instance, in some cultures, hearing voices from a deceased relative is considered normal. A clinician unaware of this feature of his or her client's culture may overpathologize and mistakenly attribute this behavior to a manifestation of a psychotic disorder. **Underpathologizing** may occur when a clinician indiscriminately explains the client's behaviors as cultural—for example, attributing a withdrawn and flat emotional expression to a normal cultural communication style when in fact this behavior may be a symptom of depression.

Finally, one interesting topic concerns language issues in psychological testing. In more and more cases today, test takers (such as patients or clients) have a first language and culture that differ from the diagnostician's or clinician's. Some researchers (for example, Oquendo, 1996a, b) have suggested that evaluation of such bilingual patients should really be done in both languages, preferably by a bilingual clinician or with the help of an interpreter trained in mental health issues. The reason, as was discussed in Chapter 9, is that cultural nuances may be encoded in language in ways that are not readily conveyed in translation. That is, translations of key psychological phrases and constructs from one language to another may give the closest semantic equivalent, but may not have exactly the same nuances, contextualized meanings, and associations. Administration of tests and therapy bilingually may help to bridge this gap.

Measurement of Personality to Assess Psychopathology

One of the interesting ways in which personality tests are used cross-culturally involves the assessment not only of personality but also of clinical states and psychopathology. The most widely used scale in such cross-cultural assessments is the Minnesota Multiphasic Personality Inventory (MMPI). Butcher, Lim, and Nezami (1998) reviewed the use of the MMPI in various countries and cultures, including six Asian cultures, six Spanish-speaking cultures, eight European cultures, and three cultures in the Middle East. They reported on the procedures most researchers used in adapting the MMPI for use in their particular cultural milieu, including translation and back-translation, bilingual test–retest evaluation, study of equivalency, and the like. They concluded:

> Clinical case studies involving the assessment of patients from different cultures have shown that MMPI-2 interpretations drawn from an American perspective generally

produce congruent conclusions about clinical patients tested in other countries. . . . Computer-based MMPI-2 interpretations appear to have a high degree of accuracy when applied to patients from other countries. Computer-based reports derived on interpretive strategies developed for the United States were rated as highly accurate by clinicians when they were applied in Norway, Australia, and France. (p. 207)

Thus, clinical studies across cultures involving personality scales such as the MMPI have been shown to be quite reliable and valid in assessing psychopathology and abnormal behavior in other cultures as well. This finding is once again consistent with the premise of a universal underlying personality structure that can be reliably and validly assessed by methods typically developed and refined in the United States or Europe. If such a universal personality structure exists and can be measured by some means, then deviations from that personality structure in the form of psychopathology should also be measurable using those same means.

However, others argue that some of the items of the MMPI simply do not mean the same thing in other cultures. For instance, answering "yes" to items such as "Evil spirits possess me at times" may not be a marker of pathology for Puerto Rican individuals, as spiritism is widely practiced in that culture (Rogler, Malgady, & Rodriguez, 1989). To address these problems, there have been attempts at developing culture-specific measures of personality, such as the Chinese Personality Assessment Inventory (CPAI) by Cheung, Kwong, and Zhang (2003) (see Chapter 10 for a more detailed description). Based on a combined etic–emic approach that included indigenous concepts from Chinese culture, this personality measure was created for use specifically with Chinese individuals. The CPAI measure may be more valid and useful in assessing mental health with this population than purely imported assessments.

MENTAL HEALTH OF ETHNIC MINORITIES AND MIGRANTS

Currently, we have an inadequate understanding of the prevalence of mental disorders among ethnic minority groups in the United States. One reason is that in the past, institutional populations, in which minority groups are disproportionately represented, were overlooked in national studies on the epidemiology of mental disorders (U.S. Department of Health and Human Services, 1999). More recently, efforts have been made to address this gap in knowledge. In this final section of the chapter, we will first discuss rates of psychopathology among four ethnic minority groups that have been a focus of recent research: African Americans, Asian Americans, Latino Americans, and Native Americans. Because most research has focused on primarily European American samples, prevalence rates are usually compared to this group. Second, we will discuss the mental health of immigrants and refugees both within and outside the United States.

African Americans

A study by Regier and colleagues (1993a), involving 18,571 adults from five U.S. cities, examined the prevalence of a variety of mental disorders (including schizophrenia, depression, anxiety disorders, somatization disorders, and antisocial personality disorders) and found that the prevalence of mental disorders was higher among African Americans than among European Americans. Similarly, other studies report that African Americans are more often diagnosed with schizophrenia than are European Americans (Lindsey & Paul, 1989; McCracken, Matthews, Tang, & Cuba, 2001). In contrast, other national epidemiological surveys have found that although African Americans report lower lifetime and 12-month prevalence rates of major depression and panic disorder as compared with European Americans, African Americans report higher lifetime prevalence rates of bipolar disorder (Breslau, Kendler, Su, Aguilar-Gaxiola, & Kessler, 2005; Smith et al., 2006). Differences in prevalence may be due not to inherent cultural differences but rather, to some extent, to socioeconomic (SES) disparities. For instance, when Regier et al. took socioeconomic factors into account, the prevalence differences between African Americans and European Americans disappeared. Regier and colleagues argue that the enormous SES disparities among different ethnic groups in the United States may place those at the lower SES level at higher risk for mental disorders. Other researchers argue that ethnic minorities may also be more likely to be misdiagnosed with disorders such as schizophrenia as a result of bias and stereotyping (Lewis, Croft-Jeffreys, & Anthony, 1990).

Asian Americans

It is difficult to paint an accurate picture of the prevalence of mental illness in Asian Americans because, until recently, they have not been included in epidemiological studies (U.S. Department of Health and Human Services, 1999). Furthermore, being stereotyped as a "model minority" masks the fact that Asian Americans may also be at risk for poor mental health (Uba, 1994). Thus, although Asian Americans are the fastest-growing ethnic group in the United States, there is very limited information on the mental health of this population.

Some studies indicate that Asian Americans report higher rates of mental illness (such as depressive symptoms and social phobia) than European Americans (Greenberger & Chen, 1996; Okazaki, 2000). However, these studies are limited by their small samples. A more recent survey with a nationally representative sample found that overall, compared to other ethnic groups, Asian Americans report the lowest 12-month prevalences of disorders including major depression, mania, panic disorder, and anxiety disorders (Smith et al., 2006). One drawback of this large study, however, was that it did not distinguish between the different Asian ethnic groups. This is a critical oversight, as there is great variation within the Asian American population depending on the specific ethnic background, generational status, and immigrant or refugee status. For instance, Kuo's (1984) study found that Korean Americans had higher incidences of depression, followed by Filipino Americans, Japanese Americans, and Chinese Americans. Kuo argued that part of the reason may be that Korean immigrants have been in the United States for shorter periods of time and have lower-status jobs and more difficulty adjusting to the United States. Among Southeast Asians, Hmongs are more likely to report depression than are Laotians, Cambodians, Vietnamese, and Chinese Vietnamese (Ying, Akutsu, Zhang, & Huang, 1997). Because Southeast Asians have a greater likelihood of being from a lower SES and to have refugee status, they may be more likely to be at risk for poorer mental health than other Asian groups such as Chinese Americans (Uehara, Takeuchi, & Smukler, 1994). Clearly, the wide variation within an ethnic group demonstrates that sweeping generalizations in discussions of possible ethnic groups differences in mental health are not entirely accurate.

Latino Americans

Latino Americans are the fastest-growing population in the United States. Several epidemiological studies report few differences between Latino Americans and European Americans in lifetime rates of psychiatric disorders (Robins & Regier, 1991; Report of the Surgeon General, 2001). As with Asian Americans, there are also significant within-group differences in rates of psychopathologies depending on the specific Latino group and generational status. For instance, one study found that Puerto Ricans have higher rates of major depression than Cuban and Mexican Americans (Cho, Moscicki, Narrow, Rae, Locke, & Regier, 1993). Another study found that foreign-born Mexican Americans were at significantly lower risk for mood and anxiety disorders as compared with U.S.-born Mexican Americans (Grant, Stinson, Hasin, Dawson, Chou, & Anderson, 2004).

The National Latino and Asian American Study (Alegria et al., 2004) headed by Maria Alegria and David Takeuchi, was launched in 2002. It is the first comprehensive national study in the United States examining the prevalence of psychiatric disorders and service use among various Latino and Asian American groups. Preliminary analyses support previous study findings that there are variations in rates of mental illness among different Latino groups (e.g., higher among Puerto Ricans compared with Cuban, Mexican, and other Latinos). A review of Latino mental health in the United States indicates that factors such as reception of immigration (being hostile or supportive), history of immigration (experiencing colonization or not), varying SES, experiences with discrimination, and strength of ethnic community may explain differing rates among Latino groups (Guarnaccia, Martinez, & Acosta, 2005). For instance, to explain why Cubans are less likely to report psychological distress, these authors suggest that their unique immigration experiences, such as receiving strong support from the United States (e.g., loans to start businesses, easy transfer of professional credentials for doctors and lawyers), having access to a vibrant ethnic enclave in Miami with political and cultural status and power, and enjoying relatively high SES, have reduced potential life stressors and, subsequently, reduced their risk for psychological disorders compared with other, less well-supported Latino groups. The review highlights how variations in contexts and policies have implications for adaptation, and, subsequently, one's mental health.

Native Americans

The lives of some Native Americans are characterized by socioeconomic difficulties, segregation, and marginalization, which may translate into greater risk for mental health problems (Organista, Organista, & Kurasaki, 2003). Until recently, very few epidemiological surveys of mental health and mental disorders have included this ethnic group. The few studies that have included this population suggest that depression is a significant problem in many Native American communities (Kinzie, Leung, Boehnlein, Matsunaga, Johnson, Manson, et al., 1992; Nelson, McCoy, Stetter, & Vanderwagen, 1992). Moreover, rates of alcohol abuse and suicide among Native Americans are significantly higher than U.S. national statistics (Boehnlein, Kinzie, & Leung, 1992; Indian Health Service, 2006). A national epidemiological study indicates that Native Americans report the highest 12-month prevalence for mood and anxiety disorders compared with other ethnic groups (African American, Asian, White, and Latino) (Smith et al., 2006). Nonetheless, as with other ethnic groups, variations within the Native American community should not be ignored. One large epidemiological study—the American Indian Service Utilization, Psychiatric Risk, and Protective Factors Project (Beals, Novins, Whitesell, Spicer, Mitchell, & Manson, 2005)—involve two Native American tribes. This study reports that the Southwest Tribe and Northern Planes Tribe differed significantly in 12-month prevalences of mood and anxiety disorders. Thus, we must be sensitive to the fact that the prevalence and correlates of psychiatric disorders may differ within ethnic groups as a whole. Gathering more accurate information on ethnic differences in prevalence rates of psychiatric disorders is needed in order to inform public policy and treatment services for these traditionally underserved populations.

Migrants

Immigration (or migration to a country) has become increasingly common across the globe. There has been an increased interest in the mental health of migrants in recent years (Tanaka-Matsumi, 2001). Migrants adapting to a new cultural environment are confronted with many challenges, such as learning the customs and language of the host culture while at the same time maintaining aspects of their traditional culture (Berry & Kim, 1988). This process of adapting to, and in many cases adopting, a different culture from the one in which a person was enculturated is called **acculturation.** Berry and Sam (Berry & Sam, 1997; Sam, 2000) report that depression, anxiety, and psychosomatic problems are common among individuals undergoing acculturation. Thus, Berry and others have hypothesized that experiencing stresses associated with acculturation may lead to poorer mental health.

Interestingly, some studies report that immigrants in the United States (such as those originating from Mexico) actually report fewer physical and mental health problems than their U.S.-born counterparts (Alderete, Vega, & Kolody, 2000; Grant, Schell, Elliot, Berthold, & Chun, 2005; Vega, Koloy, Aguilar-Gaxiola, Alderete, Catalano, & Caraveo-Anduaga, 1998). Sam (1994) has also reported that acute psychiatric disorders are less prevalent in immigrant children in Norway. This has been termed the "immigrant paradox" (Berry, Phinney, Sam, & Vedder, 2006). The paradox refers to the counter-intuitive finding that immigrants report better health and mental health outcomes compared to their U.S.-born peers despite the fact that immigrants are, in general, more likely to experience poorer socioeconomic conditions have less education, and are unfamiliar with the new environment. Some researchers have suggested that factors such as strong ties to the family and access to a supportive ethnic community may account for positive physical and mental health among immigrants (e.g., Eschbach, Ostir, Patel, Markides, & Goodwin, 2004).

Concerning the acculturation process related to immigration, some studies have found that poor mental health is predicted by low assimilation to the host culture (Padilla, Wagatsuma, & Lindholm, 1985; Szapocznik, Scopetta, & Tillman, 1979), whereas others have found poor mental health to be predicted by high assimilation to the host culture (for example, Oh, Koeske, & Sales, 2002; Sodowsky & Carey, 1987). Furthermore, a study by Nguyen, Messe, and Stollack (1999) of Vietnamese immigrant adolescents living in a Midwestern U.S. city found that those reporting themselves to be more Vietnamese in their attitudes and behaviors also reported higher levels of behavioral symptoms and depression. In sum, findings are inconsistent concerning whether immigrants are indeed at higher risk for mental health problems as a result of undergoing the acculturation process.

To reconcile these divergent findings regarding acculturation's link to mental health, an ecological perspective on acculturation has been proposed. In other words, taking into account important aspects of the community, societal, and cultural contexts—such as the tolerance for and acceptance of cultural diversity, policies that may prevent the acculturating group from participating fully in the larger society, and the existence of a network of supports—may help clarify how acculturation relates to the mental health of immigrants and their children (Berry, Kim, Minde, & Mok, 1987; Nguyen et al., 1999, Oppedal, Roysamb, & Sam, 2004). For example, Nguyen et al.'s study suggests that Vietnamese teenagers living in a culturally nonsupportive environment were at greater risk for emotional and behavioral distress if they were highly involved in Vietnamese culture. However, in a culturally diverse environment such as the city of San Francisco in northern California, where many cultural traditions are supported, encouraged, and even celebrated, Vietnamese teenagers who strongly maintained the attitudes, values, and behaviors of their traditional culture may be less at risk for emotional and behavioral distress.

In addition to relating to levels of distress, an individual's level of acculturation may also contribute to the content and expression of his or her distress, with implications for the assessment, diagnosis, and treatment of acculturating individuals at risk for mental disorders. If it is assumed that highly acculturated individuals are culturally similar to members of the dominant society, then they may also be similar in the way they express psychological distress. However, psychological symptoms among less acculturated individuals may not follow this pattern. By definition, less acculturated individuals are culturally different from the groups for whom conventional symptom scales have been developed. Thus, the question of whether standard measures of psychological symptoms fit the realities of ethnic minority groups remains unanswered (Cortes, 2003, p. 208).

Refugees

The acculturation, adaptation, and mental health of refugees—migrants who are forced to flee from their countries because of political violence, social unrest, war, or civil conflicts—has also been studied. Alarmingly, about 24 million people worldwide were displaced as of 2005 (International Displacement Monitoring Centre, 2006). Not surprisingly, because of their traumatic experiences marked by profound losses and upheavals, refugees tend to show higher rates of posttraumatic stress disorder (PTSD), depression, and anxiety (Bhui, Craig, & Mohamud, 2006; Kinzie & Sack, 2002; Liebkind, 1996; van Ommeren, Sharma, Sharma, Komproe, Cardena, & de Jong, 2002) than those who migrated voluntarily. Using in-depth interviews and surveys, a study of Cambodian refugees found long-lasting effects on their mental health (Marshall, Schell, Elliott, Berthold, & Chun, 2005). Even after two decades of being in the United States, many refugees were still suffering; 51 percent had major depression, compared with the general rate of 9.5 percent of U.S. adults with major depression. Furthermore, 62 percent had had PTSD in the past year, compared with 3.6 percent in the general U.S. population. Not surprisingly, the greater the trauma experienced before arriving in the United States, the greater the toll on their mental health. Work with Vietnamese refugees in Finland (Liebkind, 1996) and Bosnian refugees living in Chicago (Miller, Worthington, Muzurovic, Tipping, & Goldman, 2002), suggests that postmigration factors are just as important in predicting a refugee's emotional distress and psychopathology as premigration traumatic experiences. For example, based on intensive, in-depth narrative interviews with Bosnian refugees, Miller et al. found that postmigration factors such as social isolation and loss of community, the loss of life projects such as building a home or running a business, and the loss of social roles and meaningful activity all contributed to refugees' posttraumatic stress reactions and emotional and physical distress.

Morton Beiser and colleagues (Beiser, 2006; Beiser & Hou, 2001; Simich, Beiser, Stewart, & Mwakarimba, 2005) have followed the adjustment of Chinese, Vietnamese, and Laotian refugees in Canada. This project is one of the few longitudinal studies of refugee adaptation and mental health. Using a longitudinal perspective has proved invaluable, as predictors of mental health may change across time. For instance, they found that learning the language of the new country did not have immediate mental health benefits but did yield benefits in the long term, predicting less depression. Refugees who learned the new culture's language well were less likely to be diagnosed with depression. The researchers also found that having the strong social support of members of the same ethnic group helped in the early years of resettlement (acting as a springboard for adaptation). However, social support was also associated with a complex set of outcomes in the long-term, such as becoming isolated from the larger society. As the number of refugees increases around the world, research that can inform treatment and policies to prevent psychiatric disorders and promote positive adaptation among this population is sorely needed.

Summary

In recent years, studies have finally included ethnic minority and immigrant groups in studying the prevalence of mental illness in the United States. To understand ethnic differences in rates of mental disorders, contextual factors such as poverty, discrimination, and stresses associated with immigrating to a new country need to be taken into account (Nazroo, 2003). For example, people at the lowest level of SES are about two and a half times more likely than those at the highest level of SES to experience a mental disorder (Regier et al., 1993b). Because ethnic minorities in the United States are disproportionately exposed to poverty and the stresses associated with it, they may be more at risk for poor mental health (Miranda & Green, 1999). However, it must also be emphasized that there is great diversity among and within ethnic groups in the prevalence of mental disorders. The strong ties to family and community that characterize African American, Latino American, Asian American, and Native American communities is an asset that can contribute to the development of positive mental health. Future research should not only continue to examine the prevalence of mental illnesses in more diverse populations, but also move beyond adopting a merely comparative approach to explore which protective factors, such close family ties, ethnic identification, and religious participation may help prevent these illnesses (Mossakowski, 2003; Newberg & Lee, 2006).

CONCLUSION

Psychiatric diagnoses, classification schemes, and measurement of abnormality are complex and difficult issues. To the extent that there are both etic and emic aspects of psychopathology, classification systems and assessment methods need to contain both etic and emic elements. Where to draw the lines, and how to measure psychological traits and characteristics within this fluid, dynamic, and ever-changing system, is the challenge that faces this area of psychology today. Although the field has made vast improvements in this area in the past few years, future research will need to elaborate even further on these issues so that classification and measurement can be more precise, meaningful, and relevant.

Inclusion of more diverse populations in pluralistic countries such as the United States is also needed in this area of research. The significance of this is not trivial, as the proper understanding, assessment, and diagnosis of mental disorders is a necessary step to develop effective preventions and treatments that improve and enhance people's lives.

GLOSSARY

acculturation The process of adapting to, and in many cases adopting, a different culture from the one in which a person was enculturated.

cultural relativism A viewpoint that suggests that the unique aspects of a particular culture need to be considered when understanding and identifying behavior.

culture-bound syndromes Forms of abnormal behavior observed only in certain sociocultural milieus.

indigenous healing systems Systems of cure, such as folk healers, particular to a certain culture.

overpathologizing Misinterpreting culturally sanctioned behavior as expressions of pathological symptoms.

somatization Bodily symptoms as expressions of psychological distress.

underpathologizing Attributing pathological symptoms to normative cultural differences.

Culture and the Treatment of Abnormal Behavior

One of the primary goals of psychology is to use the knowledge generated by research to help people improve their lives. In Chapter 11, we discussed the important role that culture plays in defining abnormality, influencing its expression and presentation in individuals and our ability to reliably and validly assess and diagnose it. The proper assessment and diagnosis of psychopathology is a necessary step toward helping people with mental disorders improve their lives. In this chapter, we discuss issues related to the treatment of abnormal behavior. We begin our discussion by reviewing a common approach to addressing psychopathology—namely, psychotherapy. In doing so, we will address the question of whether psychotherapy, which emerged from Western European culture, is applicable and useful in other cultures. Next, we discuss treatment across diverse cultures within the United States and talk about various issues, such as why some ethnic minorities are less likely to seek treatment and more likely to end treatment prematurely. Then, we discuss treatment in cultures outside the United States and talk about the relatively new field of community-clinical psychology, which offers an alternative approach to treatment. Finally, we end with a discussion of culture and clinical training.

CULTURE AND PSYCHOTHERAPY

Among the many ways in which practicing or applied psychologists pursue the goal of improving people's lives is through psychological interventions with people who have abnormal behavior disorders, and whose lives are dysfunctional because of those disorders. The primary vehicle for delivering such intervention is psychotherapy.

Traditional Psychotherapy

Traditional psychotherapy has its origins in Western Europe and can be traced to Sigmund Freud, the father of psychoanalysis. In Vienna, Freud discovered that patients under the influence of hypnosis would talk more freely and emotionally about their problems, conflicts, and fears. Moreover, recalling and reliving earlier traumatic experiences appeared to alleviate some of the patients' symptoms. Through individual therapy sessions, he encouraged his patients to explore their memories and unconscious thoughts, much as an archaeologist explores a buried city (Hothersall, 1990). His observations led him to develop the psychoanalytic model, a comprehensive theory on the structure of personality that contributes to our knowledge about the origins of psychopathology.

Freud's theory caught the attention of American psychologists, and psychotherapy was introduced to the United States in the early 1900s. Carl Rogers (1942), an American psychologist, later modified Freud's psychoanalysis techniques and developed a client-centered approach to psychotherapy. Rogers moved away from the role of the therapist as the interpreter of the patient's troubles to emphasize the client's self-propelled growth while the therapist remained empathically sensitive to the feelings and emotions of the client. Despite these modifications, traditional psychotherapy clearly stems from and is bound by a uniquely Western cultural perspective on the understanding and treatment of individuals.

Contemporary Psychotherapy

Over the course of the past century, traditional psychoanalytic psychotherapy has been transformed and evolved into many different forms and types of psychotherapeutic approaches. These approaches may differ in their theoretical perspective, activity/passivity of the therapist, guidance, focus of treatment on actual behaviors or underlying psychology, and a host of other factors. They are all similar, however, in their goal of improving the patient/client's life, their one-on-one approach, and the use of psychological principles to effect behavioral change.

Modified psychotherapeutic approaches that have developed since Freud's time include cognitive and cognitive–behavioral therapies (Beck, 1967, 1976; Ellis, 1962). In these therapies, what a person believes is more important than what a person thinks or sees. One difference between cognitive and cognitive–behavioral therapy is that cognitive interventions have traditionally focused on examining the rationality or validity of one's beliefs, whereas cognitive–behavioral interventions emphasize the development of strategies for teaching cognitive skills (Hollon & Beck, 1994). Underlying these types of therapy is an assumption that by changing our thinking we can change our behaviors, and vice versa. These therapeutic approaches originated in the treatment of depression, in which depressed individuals presumably maintain negative thoughts and evaluations of themselves, the world, and the future. Helping such individuals to understand and control their thought patterns and emotions, and changing their maladaptive views to become more adaptive, can help them to recover.

Again, these contemporary psychotherapeutic techniques are infused with cultural assumptions, such as the inherent separation of thoughts and behaviors. The recognition that psychotherapy, the most widely used form of treatment for psychopathology in the United States, is a distinctively Western approach, has led some psychologists to challenge the use of psychotherapy with individuals of non-Western backgrounds. In the next section, we will discuss some of the cultural limitations of psychotherapy.

Cultural Limitations of Psychotherapy

In a diverse world, many psychologists have come to see these "traditional" psychotherapeutic approaches as effective for some people, but less so for others, particularly those of non-European descent. Some authors (for example, Alarcon & Leetz, 1998; Wohl, 1989) have proposed that psychotherapy itself is inescapably bound to a particular cultural framework. This notion may make sense for several reasons. First, as we have seen, expressions of abnormality, and their underlying psychological causes, are at least partly bound to culture. Second, the ability of the therapist or clinician to assess and deal with such behaviors is intimately related to his or her knowledge, understanding, and appreciation of the cultural context within which the behaviors occur. Third, if the goal of psychotherapy is to help people to become more functional within their society, then functionality itself is culturally determined; that is, different cultures and societies would necessitate different outcomes.

In examining the roots and history of the development of psychotherapy, some writers have suggested that psychoanalysis—the basis for contemporary psychotherapy—was developed specifically within a Jewish cultural framework, and that it shares features with Jewish mysticism (Langman, 1997). In fact, the development of other psychotherapeutic approaches, such as behavioral or humanistic approaches, could be considered a "culturalization" of traditional psychoanalysis to American culture and society. Viewed in this fashion, psychotherapy can be considered a cultural product, reflecting and reproducing a cultural context. Because cultural context is in part composed of moral traditions embedded in political structures, psychotherapy is itself unavoidably a moral practice with political consequences embedded within a cultural framework. In this sense, there can be no value-free psychotherapy, because all psychotherapy is bound to a particular cultural framework, and cultures are inextricably tied to moral values and systems. It is useful to take a step back and examine how our approaches to treatment are bound to our cultural norms, values, and beliefs (Sue & Sue, 1999).

In traditional and contemporary psychotherapy, for instance, the focus is on the individual. The individual is expected to express verbally his or her emotions, thoughts, and feelings and to engage in self-reflection and self-disclosure in order to arrive at insights into the individual's own behavioral and thought patterns underlying the mental illness. Thus, for Western psychologists, focusing on yourself, talking about your feelings, openly expressing your emotions, and being in touch with your inner self are important to understanding and treating distressed individuals. In other cultures, however, this approach may run exactly counter to what is considered constructive for treating a mental disorder. In some Asian cultures, for example, dwelling on one's thoughts, especially if they are painful, unpleasant, or upsetting, is strongly avoided and believed to exacerbate the existing problem. Furthermore, persons from collectivistic cultures might find this focus on the self unusual and uncomfortable. Consequently, using this type of therapy may be inappropriate. Nonetheless, the use of psychotherapy has been, and continues to be, implemented with culturally diverse populations within the United States, as well as in other countries.

Psychotherapy in Cultures Outside the United States

Psychotherapy has been exported to other parts of the world such as Singapore (Devan, 2001), Malaysia (Azhar & Varma, 2000), India (Prasadaro & Matam, 2001), and China (Zhang, Young, & Lee, 2002). Psychologists in these cultures have attempted to incorporate essential elements of their culture to make psychotherapy useful. In Malaysia, for example, religion has been incorporated into psychotherapy (Azhar & Varma, 2000). Integrating religious beliefs and behaviors, such as prayer and focusing on verses of the Koran that address "worry," are some techniques to make psychotherapy more culturally relevant. Studies comparing patients with a variety of disorders, including anxiety disorder and depression, suggest that religious psychotherapy is more effective and encourages more rapid improvement compared to supportive psychotherapy (Azhar, & Varma, 1995; Azhar, Varma, & Dharap, 1994). In China, Taoist and Confucian principles are embedded in psychotherapy techniques. For instance, verses from Taoist writings that highlight main principles, such as restricting selfish desires, learning how to be content, and learning to let go, are read and reflected on by the patient. One study found that this approach, called Chinese Taoist cognitive psychotherapy, was more effective in the long term in reducing anxiety disorders than treating the patient with medications (Zhang et al., 2002).

In addition to one-on-one psychotherapy, group psychotherapy has been exported to countries outside the United States and Europe, including countries in the Middle East. Al-Mutlaq and Chaleby (1995), however, identified several problems when conducting group therapy in Arab cultures. They discovered that the Arabs in their groups had a difficult time viewing the group as therapeutic and not just as a social activity; that because of the strict gender roles in Arab society, mixed-sex group therapy was highly criticized; and that differences in tribal status made it difficult for some individuals to communicate with others in the group who were of a different tribal status. Thus, understanding the usefulness of psychotherapy in treating people with mental illnesses in different cultures is still in its infancy.

Summary

Psychotherapy is widely used within the United States and, to a (much) lesser extent, in other parts of the world. Because of its roots in Western notions of the self, distress, and healing, the usefulness of treating with psychotherapy individuals who do not originate from this cultural group is not well established. Although practitioners working with diverse cultures within the United States, as well as in other parts of the world, use modified versions of psychotherapy in their mental health services, very few studies provide empirical support for the effectiveness of this approach. Some clinical psychologists have been advocating strongly for studies of empirically supported treatments (EST)—treatments that have been shown, through empirical studies, to be effective (for recent reviews on EST research with ethnic minority populations, see Bernal & Scharrón-Del-Río, 2001, and Miranda, Bernal, Lau, Kohn, Hwang, & LaFromboise, 2005). Only by evaluating the efficacy of our treatments can we determine whether we are truly helping, and not harming, individuals by importing culturally bound psychotherapeutic interventions.

TREATMENT OF ABNORMAL BEHAVIOR ACROSS DIVERSE CULTURES IN THE UNITED STATES

Psychotherapy with Diverse Cultures in the United States

As stated previously, there is a paucity of research addressing whether psychotherapy is effective with people of diverse cultural backgrounds within the United States. Several reviews have found that rigorous research (in which participants are randomly assigned to control and treatment groups, outcomes are assessed over time, and findings are replicated) involving culturally diverse groups is rare (Chambless et al., 1996; Sue, Zane, & Young, 1994). Most research on treatments and their outcomes can be generalized only to European American, middle-class, English-speaking females (Rosselló & Bernal, 1999). More studies that rigorously test psychotherapy effectiveness in diverse samples should include comparisons within as well as between ethnic groups, adequate sample sizes, and various cross-culturally valid outcome measures (Kurasaki, Sue, Chun, & Gee, 2000).

To date, the handful of studies that have been conducted with diverse groups have focused on four major ethnic groups in the United States. These few studies report conflicting results for some cultural groups. For instance, earlier studies with African Americans found no differences in outcomes as compared with other ethnic groups (Jones & Matsumoto, 1982; Lerner, 1972), but other studies found treatment outcomes to be poorer (Sue, Fujino, Hu, Takeuchi, & Zane, 1991; Sue, Zane, & Young, 1994). However, a clinical trial of low-income African American and Latino women found psychotherapy to be an effective treatment for depression, even 1 year later (Miranda, Green, & Krupnick, 2006). Outcomes for Asian Americans have found that psychotherapy can be used successfully, for instance, with Southeast Asian Americans dealing with posttraumatic distress disorder or depression (Kinzie, Leung, & Bui, 1988). In a large-scale study in the Los Angeles area, Sue et al. (1991) found that, compared with other ethnic groups, Latinos were most likely to improve after psychotherapy treatment. It is still premature, however, to arrive at definitive conclusions about the effectiveness of psychotherapy with culturally diverse populations. Rigorous and systematic studies are needed to identify which elements of psychotherapy may be universally effective, and which elements may be culture-specific. The journal *Psychotherapy: Theory, Research, Practice, Training* published a special issue in 2006 (entitled "Culture, Race, and Ethnicity in Psychotherapy") to address these very issues.

With increasing recognition that our current approaches must include a cultural understanding of how clients respond to this type of treatment, researchers and practitioners have advocated for the infusion of cultural elements to promote successful treatment. For example, the American Psychological Association (2002) has created guidelines for providing mental health services to ethnic minority groups. Others researchers and clinicians are developing culturally driven theoretical approaches to treatment, such as the theory of multicultural counseling and therapy (Sue, Ivey, & Pedersen, 1996; Sue & Sue, 2003).

Seeking Treatment

In a pioneering study of ethnic differences in response to standard mental health services in the Seattle area, Sue (1977) found lower rates of utilization of services by Asian Americans and Native Americans than by European Americans and African Americans. More dramatically, he found that all other groups had higher dropout rates and poorer treatment outcomes relative to those of European Americans. A later study in the Los Angeles area produced similar findings (Sue, 1991).

Other large-scale studies have found similar utilization patterns with adolescents. For instance, in a study of utilization rates of mental health services by 853 African American, 704 Asian American, 964 Latino American, and 670 European American adolescents (ages 13 to 17) in Los Angeles over a five-year period, patterns of utilization reflected earlier studies involving adults. Namely, after controlling for sex, age, and poverty status, results showed that African American adolescents used services more often than European American and Asian American adolescents, and that Latino American adolescents used these services less often than European Americans (Bui & Takeuchi, 1992). Unlike studies with adult populations, Bui and Takeuchi did not find ethnic differences in dropout rates. However, they did find that Asian American adolescents were more likely to remain in treatment longer than European American adolescents, and that African American adolescents remained in treatment for the shortest time. Length of treatment is a critical variable to look at because studies have shown that the more time is spent in treatment, the more likely it is that change will occur (Orlinsky, Grawe, & Parks, 1994).

Asian Americans are distinguished by extremely low levels of soliciting treatment for mental health problems (Leong & Lau, 2001). However, we must also keep in mind that there is much variation within this ethnic group (as with others). Findings from studies with Southeast Asians in particular have been mixed, with some suggesting higher rates of utilization (Ying & Hu, 1994) and others finding lower rates (Barreto & Segal, 2005; Zane, Hatanaka, Park, & Akutsu, 1994) compared with the Asian American population as a whole. One consistent finding, however, is that Southeast Asian groups do not seem to improve with treatment as much as other Asian groups (Ying & Hu, 1994). Because Southeast Asians are more likely to be refugees who have been exposed to war trauma and are more likely to fall into lower socioeconomic categories, which may exacerbate the severity of a mental illness, treatment success may be more difficult to achieve.

Researchers have found that characteristics of mental health services, such as whether they are ethnic-specific (defined as having more than 50 percent of clients from a specific minority group) or mainstream, may contribute to variation in utilization rates. Yeh, Takeuchi, and Sue's (1994) study over a five-year period of Asian American adolescents and their use of mental health services in the Los Angeles area found that ethnic-specific mental health services were more successful in providing services to Asian American youth. More specifically, Asian American adolescents who received treatment from ethnic-specific centers were less likely to terminate services prematurely, used the services more often, and were assessed to be higher functioning at the end of services than Asian Americans who sought treatment at mainstream facilities.

Takeuchi, Sue, and Yeh (1995) have expanded these findings to include African American, Asian American, and Mexican American adults. After controlling for age, sex, socioeconomic status, and whether they had a serious or nonserious mental illness, the results revealed that over a six-year period those using ethnic-specific mental health services were more likely to return for treatment and stayed in treatment for a longer time, than those using mainstream services. Thus, having access to ethnic-specific services may encourage more ethnic minorities to seek out and use these treatment centers. In general, however, members of various ethnic groups in the United States who suffer from psychological distress are not accessing available treatment services to the extent that mainstream populations are. In the next section, we explore possible reasons why.

Barriers to Seeking Treatment

One of the pioneers of research in multicultural mental health is Stanley Sue, who is the Director of Research at the National Research Center for Asian American Mental Health. Sue suggests that some of the reasons why Asian Americans underuse mental health services include shame, loss of face, active avoidance of morbid thoughts, attributions of causes of mental illness to biological factors, and fear of a system not set up to deal well with cultural differences. Sue (1994) also suggests that these reasons are more pronounced for recent immigrants. Cheng, Leong, and Geist (1993) report that some Asian Americans believe that dwelling on upsetting thoughts or events will only exacerbate the problem. If this is the case, then it makes sense that they would avoid seeking help that requires talking about and dwelling on the problem.

For other groups, such as African Americans, individuals may be encouraged to rely on their own willpower to confront problems, to be self-reliant, and to "tough out" difficult situations (Broman, 1996; Snowden, 2001). Tolman and Reedy (1998) suggest that reduced utilization of services by Native Americans may be the result of cultural beliefs that sickness comes from disharmony with oneself, one's community, and nature. Thus, seeking help from formal mental health services, which traditionally do not focus on such a holistic view of mental health, may not be desirable. Some research indicates that Chicanos associate seeking help outside the family for treatment of mental disturbances with shame, weakness of character, and disgrace (Leong, Wagner, & Tata, 1995). As with Asian Americans, the primary source of support and help during times of difficulty are the extended family and folk healers (Koss-Chioino, 2000). Hence, formal mental health professionals such as clinicians or psychiatrists may be a last resort, at least for very traditional Chicanos.

In Latino communities in general, the cause of mental disturbances may be attributed to evil spirits; consequently, it is believed that the power to cure problems lies within the church and not with mental health professionals

(Paniagua, 1998). Prayers are an important aspect of psychological and physical healing for this community, and it may be the case that only when religious and folk healers cannot help are mental health professionals acknowledged. Likewise, in Arab American families, individuals may first seek help from informal systems of support, such as the extended family or traditional healers, before turning to more conventional mental health services (Al-Krenawi & Graham, 2000). As a result, it may be wise for mental health professionals to collaborate with churches and religious organizations to provide information about services and to think about incorporating religious and spiritual values and practices into the provision of treatment.

Other more general reasons that ethnic minorities may underuse mental health services are mistrust and stigma. Sussman, Robins, and Earls (1987) found that African Americans were more likely than European Americans to voice mistrust toward formal mental health services, fearing hospitalization and treatment. A study by Takeuchi, Bui, and Kim (1993) found that African American parents fear that coming into contact with professional help may lead to the institutionalization of their child. Mistrust among African Americans may stem from their history and experiences of segregation, racism, and discrimination (Primm, Lima, & Rowe, 1996; Priest, 1991). Similarly, the history and experiences of Native Americans may also leave them feeling mistrustful of formal mental health services.

Uba's (1994) study of Asian Americans identified stigma, suspiciousness, and a lack of awareness about the availability of services as barriers to seeking treatment. For Arab Americans, using mental health services may also be stigmatizing, especially for women. For women, being involved with conventional mental health services could damage their marriageability or increase the likelihood of separation or divorce (Al-Krenawi & Graham, 2000).

In sum, reasons such as mistrust and stigma are likely explanations as to why some ethnic minority groups in the United States do not seek treatment. Other cultural groups in the United States that underuse mental health services no doubt have their own sets of culture-specific reasons that discourage and prevent them from using available resources. Research has begun to take the next step and to identify strategies to overcome these barriers to treatment. One study found that hiring bilingual and bicultural staff, increasing outreach (activities in the community to promote awareness and give referrals), having flexible hours, and increasing the number of practitioners in the community, contributed to higher utilization rates among ethnic minorities (Snowden, Masland, Ma, & Ciemens, 2006). Future research should continue to search for and evaluate strategies that can help overcome barriers to treatment.

TREATMENT ISSUES

When ethnic minorities do seek treatment, there are still many issues to consider. Contemporary mental health services must deal effectively with the emotional concerns of a wide variety of people. This section highlights some of the challenges that may arise during treatment when the clinician and patient differ with respect to their cultural backgrounds.

One issue, especially relevant when treating recent immigrants, is understanding culturally different ways of thinking about illness and expressing thoughts about illness. Moreover, when language difficulties and culturally different ways of communicating are thrown into the picture, it can be a challenge for the clinician and patient to communicate effectively. Consequently, treatment may be compromised. The following exchange between a Pakistani immigrant receiving services in Britain and a British psychiatrist illustrates some of these difficulties (Rack, 1982, p. 110):

> *Psychiatrist* (English-speaking): "How is your wife getting on now?"
>
> *Husband*: "She is very well now, doctor. She is fine. She is looking after the house. She is cooking the food, she is caring for the baby. Thank you, so much. . . ."
>
> *Psychiatrist*: "Good, I am glad she is able to do those things: and is she feeling well herself?"
>
> (Brief conversation between the husband and wife)
>
> *Husband*: "She is very well now, doctor, she is able to look after the family, she is cooking the food, I am able to go back to work now. . . ."
>
> *Psychiatrist*: "Yes, yes, but please ask her how does she feel in herself? Is she happy? Is her mind clear? Is the *feeling* alright?"
>
> (A further lengthy conversation. Husband and wife both evidently perplexed, but wanting to answer the question helpfully.)
>
> *Husband*: "She is very happy now, doctor, because she is able to do the cooking, she is able to look after the family, she is able to care for the baby, she is able to clean the house. Thank you very much. . . ."

This exchange illustrates the potential difficulty for the clinician and patient to communicate properly when, for example, cultural differences in the meaning of the word "feeling" are coupled with language difficulties. In addition to being sensitive to aspects of verbal communication, interpreting nonverbal aspects of communication correctly is also important. In some cultures, making direct eye contact is disrespectful, such as in traditional Native American (Everett, Proctor, & Cartmell, 1983) and Arab cultures (Al-Krenawi & Graham, 2000). Thus, if the therapist is not familiar with this cultural norm, he or she might falsely assume that the client is showing a lack of interest, resisting treatment, or even being rude.

Taking into account how cultures vary on the importance of hierarchy in interpersonal relationships is also important. Wilson, Kohn, and Lee (2000) highlight the importance of showing respect for traditional family roles with Asian families, for instance by initially reinforcing the father's role as head of the family. This is also true for many Arab families. Jalali (1982) writes that the patriarchal organization of the family in Arab cultures should be recognized and respected, by addressing the father first and as the head of the family. If the therapist tries to alter power hierarchies or role patterns, this may well alienate the family. Likewise, if a child is brought in for help and the therapist treats the child and his or her parents similarly, in an egalitarian way, this may be upsetting for families from cultures in which hierarchy, respect, and obedience are highly valued. Parents may feel that the therapist is undermining their authority.

Treatment expectations may also differ across cultures. For instance, in many cultures, the therapist is the authority and is expected to be directive, to make suggestions, and to give reassurance. For instance, a study of Puerto Rican patients found that they expected their doctor to be active and concrete in dispensing advice or prescribing medication. Following a traditional psychological approach, in which the client is expected to discuss and reflect on problems while the therapist assumes a more passive role, may result in the Puerto Rican client's prematurely terminating treatment (Abad, Ramos, & Boyce, 1974). Similarly, insight-oriented therapies, in which clients engage in deep self-reflection, may not work with traditional Native American clients (Atkinson, Morten, & Sue, 1989). LaFromboise, Trimble, and Mohatt (1990) report that for Native Americans, more directive and strategic interventions are preferred over client-centered or reflective therapy. The introspective approach may lead to impatience and dropping out of therapy. Other studies have also found that Latino and Asian Americans (Atkinson, Maruyama, & Matsui, 1978; Ponce & Atkinson, 1989) and Arab Americans (Al-Krenawi & Graham, 2000) prefer directive over nondirective therapists.

Asian families may tend to wait a long time to seek formal treatment because of their reluctance to call for help outside the family. When they do finally reach out to more formal mental health services, it may be their last resort because the problem has reached a crisis level (Lin, Inui, Kleinman, & Womack, 1992). Consequently, more directive and solution-oriented approaches to treatment may be more appropriate than insight- and growth-oriented approaches (Wang, 1994). In sum, a large body of research on preferences for therapeutic approaches in ethnically different populations in the United States indicates that non–European American clients tend to prefer action-oriented therapy to nondirective approaches such as psychoanalytic or humanistic therapy (Sue & Zane, 1987).

Finally, in many cultures, the extended family is a primary source of support in times of distress. Recognizing and involving members of the extended family instead of focusing on the individual and nuclear family may be useful and may present a more familiar approach to problem solving. It is also important to note that with many ethnic families, non–blood kin may also be considered family, such as neighbors and ministers in African American families, godparents in Latino families, and elders in Asian communities (Porter, 2000).

We have highlighted just some of the many issues that come into play when counseling clients from diverse cultural origins. Hopefully, this brief discussion has illustrated how what may work best in treating one population may not necessarily work for another. Developing responses to psychological distress that are sensitive to each individual's cultural outlook, beliefs, and practices is the goal for many psychologists working with diverse populations. There is much to be done to improve our services to these culturally diverse groups (Sue et al., 1994). In the next section, we discuss some ways that researchers and mental health professionals are promoting more culturally appropriate treatment and services.

CULTURALLY COMPETENT SERVICES

A growing body of literature by researchers and practitioners has prompted mental health professionals to stress the need for culturally competent services in order to improve utilization and effectiveness of treatment for individuals from diverse cultural backgrounds. Understanding and respecting the histories, traditions, beliefs, and value systems of various cultural groups underlies culturally competent services.

To fashion more culturally sensitive services, Sue and others (Comas-Diaz & Jacobsen, 1991; Sue & Sue, 2003; Sue & Zane, 1987; Tseng & McDermott, 1981) suggest that treatment methods should be modified to improve their fit with the worldviews and experiences of culturally diverse clients. For example, psychoanalytic approaches are derived from a worldview that assumes that unconscious conflicts (probably sexual) give rise to abnormal behavior. This worldview may reflect the experience of the well-to-do Austrian women Freud treated and on which he based many of his theoretical assumptions. However, a therapeutic approach based on such a worldview may prove inappropriate for cultures that attribute abnormality either to natural factors (for example, physical problems or being out of harmony with the environment) or supernatural causes (for example, spirit possession). Cultural systems of cure and healing may be effective precisely because they operate within a particular culture's worldview (Tseng & McDermott, 1981). For example, a spiritual ceremony performed by a native shaman (priest or healer) may prove to be a more effective treatment of the culture-bound syndrome *susto* than the cognitive–behavioral approach typically used in the United States.

There is also some indication that culturally diverse clients prefer to see therapists who are similar to them in cultural background and gender. But more recent research indicates that similarity of worldviews and attitudes to treatment between client and therapist may be more important than simply ethnic similarity (Sue & Sue, 2003). For instance, matching a Korean American client who does not consider herself to be very Korean (she does not speak Korean and does not identify herself with Korean values and attitudes) with a Korean therapist may not make much difference compared with pairing her with a therapist of another ethnicity. Thus, acculturation status and ethnic identity may be more important determinants of client responses to treatment (Atkinson, Casa, & Abreu, 1992). Indeed, a study with African Americans found that those who identified strongly with African American culture preferred an ethnically similar therapist, compared with those who did not identify strongly with African American culture (Ponterotto, Alexander, & Hinkston, 1988). In a study with Chicano college students, only those who expressed a strong commitment to Chicano culture desired an ethnically matched counselor. Chicano students who primarily identified themselves with the majority culture were not concerned that their counselor be of the same ethnicity (Sanchez & Atkinson, 1983).

Thus, although such matching may be beneficial in the therapy process, it may not be essential for effective counseling. A meta-analysis of seven studies conducted in the 1990s on ethnic matching found that the effect sizes were very small (ranging from $r = .01$ to $r = .04$) for outcomes such as dropping out, number of treatment sessions, and assessment of client functioning at the end of treatment (Maramba & Nagayama Hall, 2002). Another meta-analysis of studies since the 1990s focused on ethnic matching for African American and Caucasian American clients and clinicians (Shin, Chow, Camacho-Gonsalves, Levy, Allen, & Leff, 2005). Similar to the previous meta-analysis, the researchers found that ethnic matching did not predict better overall functioning, dropout rate, and number of treatment sessions. Thus, other factors such as cultural matching (as in worldviews, cognitive styles, and language) and the level of cultural sensitivity of the therapist may be more crucial (S. Sue, 1998).

In sum, providing clinicians who are sensitive to the client's cultural background and who take the time and effort to understand the client within his or her cultural context can be more beneficial than simply matching ethnicities. Culture-sensitive counselors have been rated as being more credible and competent to conduct treatment across cultures by African Americans (Atkinson, Furlong, & Poston, 1986), Asian Americans (Gim, Atkinson, & Kim, 1991), and Mexican Americans (Atkinson et al., 1992).

Not only do client views of the therapist differ depending on the match between therapist and client; therapist views of the client also differ. In one study, for example, the records of thousands of African, Asian, Mexican, and European American outpatient clients in the Los Angeles County mental health system were examined for ethnic match with their therapist (Russell, Fujino, Sue, Cheung, & Snowden, 1996). In this study, a black therapist–black client dyad or Chinese therapist–Chinese client dyad was considered an ethnic match. However, for Asian Americans, a Chinese therapist–Japanese client was not a match. Results indicated that ethnically matched therapists tended to judge clients to have higher mental functioning than did mismatched therapists. This finding held even after controlling for variables such as age, gender, marital status, and referral source. Thus, how the therapist perceived the client differed according to whether the therapist was of the client's ethnic group or not.

Several authors have outlined the competencies and knowledge base necessary for therapists to conduct sensitive and effective treatment across cultures. Sue and Sue (2003) suggest that the culturally sensitive therapist will have acquired: (1) knowledge of diverse cultures and lifestyles, (2) skill and comfort in using innovative treatment methods, and (3) actual experience working with culturally diverse clients. It is also critically important that the therapist be aware of his or her own cultural background and its influences on definitions and perceptions of abnormal behavior. Furthermore, the therapist must be aware of how cultural beliefs and experiences influence the course of treatment. Paul Heppner, the current president of the Society for Counseling Psychology of the American Psychological Association, wrote about the increasing importance of training cross-culturally competent psychologists. He argues that

> Developing cross-cultural competence is a lifelong journey, replete with many joys and challenges, that will (a) increase the sophistication of our research, (b) expand the utility and generalizability of the knowledge bases in counseling psychology, (c) promote a deeper realization that counseling occurs in a cultural context, and (d) increase not only counseling effectiveness but also the profession's ability to address diverse mental health needs across different populations around the globe. (2006, p. 147)

Only with a deep understanding of how people's conceptions of the cause and course of illness are embedded and shaped by their cultural upbringing and outlook can psychologists begin to offer effective ways to alleviate and improve their situation.

INDIGENOUS HEALING

A focus in recent discussions of cross-cultural treatment of abnormal behavior has been culture-specific interventions, or **indigenous healing.** Indigenous healing encompasses therapeutic beliefs and practices that are rooted within a given culture. In other words, these beliefs and practices are not imported from outside cultures but are indigenously developed to treat the native population (Sue & Sue, 1999).

Many indigenous methods of healing differ widely from Western notions of healing. For instance, many indigenous treatments are rooted in religion and spirituality, not biomedical science (Sue & Sue, 1999; Yeh, Hunter, Madan-Bahel, Chiang, & Arora, 2004). A study of indigenous healing in 16 non-Western countries identified several commonalities among indigenous practices (Lee, Oh, & Mountcastle, 1992). One was the heavy reliance on family and community networks as both the context and instrument for treatment. For instance, family and community were used in Saudi Arabia to protect the disturbed individual, in Korea to reconnect and reintegrate the individual with members of the family, and in Nigeria to solve problems in the context of a group. Another commonality was the incorporation of traditional, spiritual, and religious beliefs as part of the treatment—for instance, reading verses from the Koran, opening treatment with a prayer, or conducting treatment in religious houses or churches. Finally, another commonality was the use of shamans in treatment.

A review by a group of counseling psychologists has identified several indigenous treatments such as Reiki, Qigong, and pranic healing (Yeh et al., 2004). *Reiki* refers to a "universal life energy" and is a Japanese practice used for relaxation, reducing stress, and promoting healing. In Reiki therapy this life energy is used for healing by balancing the physical, emotional, mental, and spiritual elements of our bodies. *Qigong* refers to "flow of air" or "vital energy" and is a Chinese method that emphasizes breathing, movement, and physical postures for maintaining and improving one's health. *Prana* refers to "life force" and pranic healing is based on the principle that healing is possible by increasing the life force on the unhealthy part of the physical body. All three of these indigenous therapies endorse the holistic notion that our physical health is intertwined with our emotional, mental, and spiritual health. Further, it is only by connecting these various energies that we can begin to heal.

Psychological interventions in other cultures are not limited to culture-specific interventions. In fact, there is a considerable movement in many other countries and cultures to merge aspects of traditional psychotherapy with culture-specific methods and beliefs to produce unique systems of healing. For example, Sato (1998) suggests that culturally indigenous therapies can be augmented successfully with aspects of contemporary cognitive and behavioral therapies. Writers have pointed to a variety of ways in which traditional methods of psychotherapy need to blend with and accommodate culture-specific issues, such as the discouragement of egoistic and individualistic strivings, and the doctrine of karma and reincarnation in India (Hoch, 1990); issues of deculturation, outmigration, alienation, distrust, and despair among Native American and Alaska Native cultures (Rodenhauser, 1994); issues of guardianship, social network, and social support in Shanghai (Zhang, Yan, & Phillips, 1994); and the interaction of spiritual, emotional/mental, physical, and family health in Maori New Zealand (Durie, 1997).

Prince (1980) argues that what is common to treatment across cultures is the mobilization of healing forces within the client. If, for example, Native Americans believe that illness results from disharmony among self, community, and nature, treatment should revolve around resolving the disharmony and restoring a state of balance and integration (Tolman & Reedy, 1998). Several others (for example, Torrey, 1972; Tseng & McDermott, 1981) have also attempted to determine universal features of culture-specific systems of treatment. Viewed in this fashion, culture-specific systems of treatment share the common characteristic of mobilizing healing forces within the client, but cultures (and psychotherapeutic approaches) differ in the exact ways in which the mobilization of healing forces occurs. Although selecting an approach may be as much an art as it is a science, cross-cultural research in the future should play an important role in evaluating the effectiveness of different approaches to mobilizing those healing forces within the client, and hence in the overall effectiveness and outcomes of treatment.

Examples of Blending Traditional Western-Based Treatment Approaches with Indigenous Healing Practices

Vang was a Hmong refugee who resettled in Chicago with his family. On the first several nights in Chicago, he reported severe sleep disturbances, including a severe shortness of breath and extreme panic. He reported that he was pinned down and rendered immobile the first night by a cat sitting on his chest, the second night by a figure like a large black dog, and the third night by a tall, white-skinned spirit. He awoke screaming, out of breath, and feared he was going to die during the night or that the spirit would make his wife infertile (Tobin & Friedman, 1983). As Vang explains it:

> The most recent attack in Chicago was not the first encounter my family and I have had with this type of spirit, a spirit we call Chia. . . . We are susceptible to such attacks because we didn't follow all of the mourning rituals we should have when our parents died. Because we didn't properly honor their memories we have lost contact with their spirits, and thus we are left with no one to protect us from evil spirits. (p. 444)

From a Western perspective, Vang's symptoms of sleeplessness, extreme anxiety, and depression could be seen as a result of the trauma and stress of his experiences as a refugee, perhaps leading to a diagnosis of posttraumatic distress disorder. Therapists in the United States most likely would not attribute his disturbances to spirits, as Vang does. Considering these two perspectives, what kind of treatment would be effective in this case? Would traditional psychotherapy be effective? Or would an indigenous healing method be more effective? In this particular case, the mental health workers treating Vang were sensitive to his cultural background and to his beliefs as to the origins of his extreme distress. Both Western (psychotherapeutic counseling) and non-Western healing methods indigenous to the Hmong culture (involving a shaman to perform a spirit cleansing ritual) were used to treat him, with success.

Another case study is described by Zuniga (1997, cited in Sue & Sue, 1999, p. 149):

> Mrs. Lopez, age 70, and her 30-year-old daughter sought counseling because they had a very conflictual relationship. The mother was not accustomed to a counseling format. At a pivotal point in one session, she found talking about emotional themes overwhelming and embarrassing. In order to reengage her, the counselor asked what resources she used when she and her daughter quarreled. She prayed to Our Lady of Guadalupe.

The counselor consequently used a culturally sensitive strategy of having Mrs. Lopez use prayer to understand her daughter and to find solutions for the conflicting relationship that they could discuss in the counseling sessions. Acknowledging and incorporating religion, a central guiding element in Mrs. Lopez's life, into the treatment allowed Mrs. Lopez to discuss spiritual guidance and possible solutions to the problems.

Other researchers have advocated treatment that combines and integrates traditional cultural healing practices (Kurasaki et al., 2000; Sue & Sue, 1999). In the United States, some Native American communities recognize and fund traditional healing in mental health services. However, little is known regarding how the individual or family connects indigenous approaches with conventional mental health services (Tata & Leong, 1994). Better research is needed to uncover the effectiveness of a combination of indigenous and conventional treatments (Cauce, Domenech-Rodírigues, Paradise, Cochran, Shea, et al., 2002).

AN ALTERNATIVE APPROACH TO TREATMENT

Much of our discussion in this chapter has focused on a particular treatment based on a medical model—namely, psychotherapy. Even with modifications to traditional psychotherapy, this type of treatment may still not be wholly appropriate with people of many cultures. In the medical model, treatment is designed and directed at the individual. Some assumptions of this model are that the problem resides in the individual and that highly trained professionals such as clinicians should provide the treatment. Recognizing the limitations of the medical model, the field of community psychology, led by researchers such as Kelly (1990) and Trickett (1996), combines traditional principles of clinical psychology with an emphasis on the multiple and diverse ecologies of individuals to create alternative conceptual frameworks for understanding abnormal behavior. Community psychologists go beyond the traditional focus of responding to a person's distress on an individual level to include an analysis of mental health at the community level. In other words, understanding how to treat individuals successfully requires a recognition of the relationship between the individual and his or her daily interactions within diverse social settings and contexts in the community.

Based on these considerations, some community-oriented psychologists describe an entirely different approach to the treatment of emotional distress. For example, Miller (1999; Miller & Rasco, 2004) proposes a community-based treatment to complement traditional psychotherapy:

> In contrast to the medical model, which focuses on the individual as the unit of analysis and intervention, and which emphasizes the treatment of pathology by highly trained experts, the ecological model emphasizes the relationships between people and the settings they live in; the identification of naturally occurring resources within communities that can promote healing and healthy adaptation; the enhancement of coping and adaptational strategies that enable individuals and communities to respond effectively to stressful events and circumstances; and the development of collaborative, culturally grounded community interventions that actively involve community members in the process of solving their own problems. (1999, p. 288)

Community-based treatments may be especially relevant for helping populations such as immigrants and refugees, who are unfamiliar with the host culture, who tend not to seek out professional help, and who tend to underuse mental health services. Such approaches can also be a useful alternative in developing countries, where access to professional mental health services and resources are scarce. Successful community interventions have been developed in diverse parts of the world, including Angola (Wessells & Monteiro, 2001), Sri Lanka (Tribe & DeSilva, 1999), and Mozambique (Boothby, 1994).

In sum, researchers and clinicians are just beginning to learn how various cultural communities can use cultural informants and community structure to provide mental health services in ways that differ from traditional psychotherapy. We see this as an evolution in psychotherapeutic methods in which healing, drawing on and using the strengths and resources of the community, is aimed not only at individuals but toward the health of the community as a whole. This offers a promising and potentially powerful alternative to the medical model of clinical psychology for understanding and responding to psychological distress in culturally diverse populations.

CULTURE AND CLINICAL TRAINING

Because of all the issues discussed in this chapter, and throughout the book, all accredited programs of clinical training in the United States have, for some time now, been mandated to incorporate culture and diversity in their training programs. Clinical psychologists who will be in the field actually applying psychological knowledge and principles to people who seek help need to have a base for understanding the role of culture in the expression and presentation of mental illness, the difficulties and complexities involved in psychological assessment, and the issues regarding culturally sensitive yet effective treatment. Beyond these factors, however, contemporary clinicians and therapists receive training in the broad base of culture's influence on all aspects of psychology, from perception and sensation through development to social behavior and personality. It is only with this broad base of training that contemporary psychologists can gain the perspective necessary to work effectively with their clients and patients to help them improve their lives. Of course, this need for a broad understanding of the influence of culture on psychology applies to the training and practice of psychologists outside the United States as well. Moreover, the implications of psychologists' training in other cultures, learning culturally bound methods of treatment, and then returning home to practice has not been studied.

Issues regarding culture and diversity also arise in areas outside of traditional one-on-one psychotherapy—for example, the role of culture in the development and treatment of children (Tharp, 1991) and ethnic and cultural diversity in group therapy (Brook, Gordon, & Meadow, 1998).

Finally, the increasing number of bilingual/bicultural individuals seeking help raises its own set of special issues, including the language and cultural framework within which psychotherapy and healing will occur. A number of writers have suggested that language proficiency, level of acculturation, and the degree to which cultural expressions represent symptoms should be considered in the development of an effective treatment plan (see, for example, Altarriba & Santiago-Rivera, 1994; Ben-David, 1996; Santiago-Rivera & Azara, 1995). The need for fluency in multiple languages and cultures adds to the growing list of requirements for culturally competent therapists.

These issues are not relevant only to people of different ethnicities, races, or nationality. Given that psychotherapy is inescapably bound to a particular cultural framework, perhaps *all* psychotherapy can be seen as essentially cross-cultural, in that no two people have internalized identical constructions of their cultural worlds (Wohl, 1989); this view is consistent with the emphasis in this book on culture as a psychological phenomenon. Perhaps sound principles and concepts of psychotherapy can be applied cross-culturally as long as cultural differences are taken into account; this notion is consistent with the view that cross-cultural research methods are nothing more than good traditional research methods applied cross-culturally. Although some issues (such as language) are specific to applying research methods or therapeutic approaches across cultural lines, the coming together of traditional and cross-cultural approaches could provide the basis for a fundamental revision in the training of psychotherapists and clinicians in the future.

CONCLUSION

In this chapter, we have discussed the important role culture plays in attempting to help people with mental disorders improve their lives. The material in this chapter is not only relevant on its own, but is informed by material in the entire book, showing the pervasive influence of culture on all aspects of our psychological composition. It is only within this larger perspective of the influence of culture that we can begin to truly grasp and appreciate the difficulties and complexities of diagnosing and treating abnormal behavior in a diverse world.

The difficulties presented, however, should be viewed as challenges, not obstacles. Through the study of culture, psychopathology, assessment, and psychotherapy, we are afforded the chance to expand our theoretical and conceptual horizons regarding abnormality and treatment, and to help our treatment systems evolve into bigger and better systems effectively serving larger and larger groups of people. We are currently engaged in the search for principles and knowledge that will help us achieve those goals.

Continued cross-cultural research on clinical issues—such as defining and assessing abnormality and designing treatment approaches that effectively mobilize healing forces within clients—is a must. But research on these major issues of definition, assessment, and treatment should proceed cautiously and systematically. Future research will need to explore the efficacy of different treatment approaches that address both etic and emic concerns, blending traditional and culture-specific methods in an overall, comprehensive fashion.

GLOSSARY

indigenous healing Helping beliefs and practices that originate within a given culture or society, are not transported to or from other regions, and are designed for treating the inhabitants of the given group.

Culture and Social Behavior, I

Self and Identity

In this chapter we begin our exploration of the relationship between culture and social behavior. Here, we focus on the notion of the self. We define the self and explore where it comes from, then we examine how the notion of the self may differ across cultures. The concept of self is an important first step to exploring social behavior because it organizes information about oneself. Moreover, the concept of self is intimately related to our concepts of others. In fact, we cannot create a sense of self without being able to discriminate ourselves from others. It is in recognizing that we are part of a social group, living with others, that we first differentiate what our own sense of self is.

A topic related to self is that of identity. We will define and discuss identity, and focus on cultural and multicultural identities. An important topic in this area will be cultural code frame switching. We will also explore the implicit nature of who is an American.

We then discuss a very important topic in the research literature—self-esteem, and its relative, self-enhancement. We will discuss a theoretical framework that suggests that self-enhancement is a universal process, but that people of different cultures do it in different ways. This is called "tactical self-enhancement."

Finally we will discuss the nature of attributions, which are the causal reasons we come up with to explain behaviors and events. We will discuss biases in our attributional styles, called "self-serving biases"; these are related to self-enhancement. We will explore how research has demonstrated cultural differences in attributional styles, and introduce you to the concept of universality of self-serving biases in attributions. Like self-enhancement, people of different cultures appear to differ in the specific ways in which they exhibit their self-serving biases.

CULTURE AND THE CONCEPT OF SELF

Defining the Concept of Self

One of the most powerful and pervasive concepts in the social sciences is the **self-concept.** Other terms that denote the same concept are self-image, self-construal, self-appraisal, or just self. In this book we define self-concept to be *the idea or images that one has about oneself and how and why one behaves as one does.*

To be sure, the self is a psychological construct that people create in order to help themselves understand themselves and their world better. We may not consciously think about our self very much; yet how we understand or construe our sense of self is intimately and fundamentally tied to how we understand the world around us and our relationships with others in that world. Whether conscious or not, our concept of self is an integral and important part of our lives.

Think about some descriptions of yourself. You may believe you are an optimist or a pessimist, extroverted or introverted. We use these labels as shorthand descriptions to characterize ourselves. Suppose a young woman tells you she is "sociable." An array of underlying meanings is attached to this one-word description. Descriptive labels such as this usually imply: (1) that we have this attribute within us, just as we possess other attributes such as abilities, rights, or interests; (2) that our past actions, feelings, or thoughts have close connections with this attribute; and (3) that our future actions, plans, feelings, or thoughts will be controlled or guided by this attribute and can be predicted more or less accurately by it. In short, if someone describes herself as "sociable," we know that her concept of self is rooted in, and supported and reinforced by, a rich repertoire of specific information concerning her own actions, thoughts, feelings, motives, and plans. The concept of self as "sociable" may be central to one's self-definition, enjoying a special status as a salient identity (Stryker, 1986) or self-schema (Markus, 1977).

A sense of self is critically important and integral to determining our own thoughts, feelings, and actions, and to how we view the world and ourselves and others in that world, including our relationships with other people, places, things, and events. In short, our sense of self is at the core of our being, unconsciously and automatically influencing our every thought, action, and feeling. Each individual carries and uses these internal attributes to guide his or her thoughts and actions in different social situations. A noted anthropologist, Clifford Geertz (1975), described the self as "a bounded, unique, more or less integrated motivational and cognitive universe, a dynamic center of awareness, emotion, judgment, and action organized into a distinctive whole and set contrastively both against other such wholes and against a social and natural background" (p. 48).

Where Does the Self-Concept Come From?

The concept of self is an important product of human cultures. You might remember that in Chapter 1, we made a distinction between cultural practices and cultural worldviews. *Cultural practices,* on one hand, refer to the discrete, observable, objective, and behavioral aspects of human activities in which people engage related to culture. For example, parent–child sleeping arrangements are an example of a cultural practice, as would be the specific ways in which people of a culture manage their emotional expressions in a social context. Cultural practices refer to the *doing* of culture.

Cultural worldviews, on the other hand, are belief systems about one's culture. They are cognitive generalizations about how one's culture is or should be, regardless of whether or not those generalized images are true. They are produced because verbal language is a unique characteristic of humans, and because people talk about their own and other cultures. These verbal descriptions can be oral or written, and are social constructions of reality expressed in consensual ideologies about one's culture.

The concept of self is part of one's cultural worldviews because how one sees oneself in relation to the rest of the world is an intimate part of one's culture. Like cultural worldviews, the concept of self is also a cognitive generalization about one's nature, whether or not that belief is grounded in reality.

Cultural worldviews influence the construction of the self as a cognitive generalization derived from past experiences that organize and guide the processing of social experiences (Markus, 1977). They aid in addressing needs for affiliation and uniqueness, and explain the importance of understanding values as guiding principles as an important part of culture (Schwartz, in press; Schwartz & Bardi, 2001). They are social constructions "that consist of viewing oneself as living up to specific contingencies of value . . . that are derived from the culture at large but are integrated into a unique individualized worldview by each person" (Pyszczynski, Greenberg, Solomon, Arndt, & Schimel, 2004).

One popular theory about the origin of the self-concept is known as **terror management theory** (Becker, 1971, 1973). This theory suggests that, because humans have unique cognitive abilities, we are the only animals aware of the fact that we will die eventually, and we are afraid, terrified in fact, of that inevitable death. Because inevitable death is terrifying to us, we create psychological phenomena as a buffer against the terror of dying (Greenberg, Solomon, & Pyszczynski, 1997). We fabricate and give meaning to our existence in order to raise our human existence above nature so that meaning can be drawn from life (Becker, 1971). This meaning is not physical in nature, nor does it exist as an objective element (Triandis, 1972) of culture. Rather the meanings afforded in cultural worldviews and the self-concept arise because humans must balance a propensity for life with an awareness of the inevitability of death.

> From this perspective, then, each individual human's name and identity, family and social identifications, goals and aspirations, occupation and title, are humanly created adornments draped over an animal that, in the cosmic scheme of things, may be no more significant or enduring than any individual potato, pineapple, or porcupine. But it is this elaborate drapery that provides us with the fortitude to carry on despite the uniquely human awareness of our mortal fate. (Pyszczynski, Greenberg, Solomon, Arndt, & Schimel, 2004)

According to this view, therefore, humans create cultural worldviews, and thus concepts of the self, partially as a reaction to the terror we feel because of our awareness of our mortality.

CULTURAL DIFFERENCES IN SELF-CONCEPT

The Independent versus Interdependent Self-Construal Theory

Given that self-concepts are rooted in cultural worldviews, and given that cultural worldviews should differ in different cultures, it thus follows that the concept of self should also differ in different cultures. These differences in self-concepts occur because different cultures are associated with different systems of rules of living, and exist within different social and economic environments and natural habitats. The different demands that cultures place on individual members mean that individuals integrate, synthesize, and coordinate their worlds differently, producing differences in self-concepts.

Markus and Kitayama (1991b) used these ideas to describe two fundamentally different senses of self, contrasting the Western or individualistic construal of self as an independent, separate entity with a composite construal of self more common in non-Western, collectivistic cultures, in which the individual is viewed as inherently connected or interdependent with others and inseparable from a social context. They argued that in the United States, standing out and asserting yourself is a virtue: "The squeaky wheel gets the grease." American politicians routinely credit their success to self-confidence, trusting their instincts, and the ability to make decisions and stick by them. In many individualistic cultures like ours, there is a strong belief in the separateness of individuals. The normative task in these cultures is to maintain the independence of the individual as a separate, self-contained entity.

In American society, many of us have been socialized to be unique, to express ourselves, to realize and actualize the inner self, and to promote our personal goals. These are the tasks the culture provides for its members. These cultural tasks have been designed and selected throughout history to encourage the independence of each separate self. With this set of cultural tasks, our sense of self-worth or self-esteem takes on a particular form. When individuals successfully carry out these cultural tasks, they feel satisfied with themselves, and self-esteem increases accordingly. Under this **independent construal of self,** individuals focus on personal, internal attributes—individual ability, intelligence, personality traits, goals, or preferences—expressing them in public and verifying and confirming them in private through social comparison. This independent construal of self is illustrated graphically in Figure 13.1a. Self is a bounded entity, clearly separated from relevant others. Note that there is no overlap between the self and others. Furthermore, the most salient self-relevant information (indicated by bold Xs) relates to

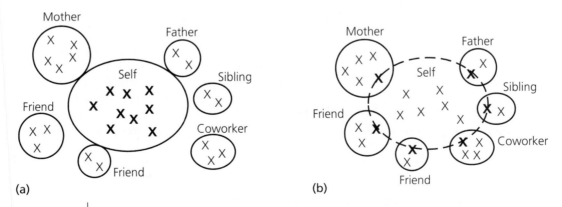

(a)   (b)

Figure 13.1 | (a) Independent Construal of Self (b) Interdependent Construal of Self

attributes thought to be stable, constant, and intrinsic to the self, such as abilities, goals, and rights.

In contrast to the individualistic, independent self-construal, Markus and Kitayama (1991b) suggested that many non-Western, collectivistic cultures neither assume nor value overt separateness. Instead, these cultures emphasize what may be called the "fundamental connectedness of human beings." The primary normative task is to fit in and maintain the interdependence among individuals. Individuals in these cultures are socialized to adjust themselves to an attendant relationship or a group to which they belong, to read one another's minds, to be sympathetic, to occupy and play their assigned roles, and to engage in appropriate actions. These cultural tasks have been designed and selected throughout history to encourage the interdependence of the self with others.

Given this construal of the self, self-worth, satisfaction, and self-esteem can have very different characteristics from those familiar to us. The self-esteem of those with interdependent construals of the self may depend primarily on whether they can fit in and be part of a relevant ongoing relationship. Under this construal of self, individuals focus on their interdependent status with other people and strive to meet or even create duties, obligations, and social responsibilities. The most salient aspect of conscious experience is intersubjective, rooted in finely tuned interpersonal relationships. The **interdependent construal of self** is illustrated graphically in Figure 13.1b. The self is unbounded, flexible, and contingent on context. Note the substantial overlapping between the self and relevant others. The most salient aspects of the self (shown by bold Xs) are defined in relationships—that is, those features of the self related to and inseparable from specific social contexts. This does not mean that those with interdependent selves have no knowledge of their internal attributes, such as personality traits, abilities, and attitudes. They clearly do. However, these internal attributes are relatively less salient in consciousness and thus are unlikely to be the primary concerns in thinking, feeling, and acting.

Because of their collectivistic nature, many Asian cultures foster interdependent construals of self. In these cultures, if you stand out, you will most likely be punished: "The nail that sticks up shall get pounded down." In Japan, for example, political rhetoric sounds very different from that in the United States. A former vice prime minister of Japan once said that in his 30-year career in national politics, he had given the most importance and priority to interpersonal relations. Similarly, "politics of harmony" was the sound bite a former Japanese prime minister used to characterize his regime in the 1980s.

An Example of the Independent versus Interdependent Self: Consequences for Self-Perception

Markus and Kitayama (1991b) used the independent versus interdependent self-construal framework to explain many cross-country differences in psychological processes, especially between the United States and Asian countries. One of these processes was self-perception. Markus and Kitayama contended that, with an independent construal of self, one's internal attributes such as abilities or personality traits are the most salient self-relevant information. These internal attributes should be relatively less salient for those with interdependent selves, who are more likely to think about the self in particular social relationships (for example, "me" with family members, "me" with my boyfriend) or in specific contexts ("me" in school, "me" at work). In cultures that foster an interdependent self-construal, however, internal attributes are not the most salient self-relevant information; instead, information concerning one's social roles and relationships with others are more salient and important.

Several studies (Bond & Tak-Sing, 1983; Shweder & Bourne, 1984) have supported these notions. In these studies, subjects wrote down as many of their own characteristics as possible. Subjects typically generated several types of responses. One response type was the abstract, personality-trait description of the self, such as "I am sociable." Another response type was the situation-specific self-description, such as "I am usually sociable with my close friends." Consistent with the theory of independent and interdependent selves, these studies show that American subjects tend to generate a greater number of abstract traits than do Asian subjects. These data have been interpreted that people with an independent construal of self view their own internal attributes, such as abilities or personality traits, as the most salient self-relevant information. Internal attributes are relatively less salient for those with interdependent selves, who are more likely to think about the self in particular social relationships or contexts.

Consistent with this analysis, Triandis and colleagues (see Triandis, 1989, for a review) have shown that individuals from interdependent cultures (for example, China, Japan, and Korea) generate many more social categories, relationships, and groups to which they belong. Indeed, in a study done in the People's Republic of China, as many as 80 percent of all the responses given to the self-description task were about their memberships in a variety of different groups. Dhawan, Roseman, Naidu, Komilla, and Rettek (1995) reported similar tendencies in self-perception in a study comparing American and North Indian participants.

Another study by Bochner (1994) compared self-perception statements made by Malaysian, Australian, and British participants. The responses were coded according to whether they were idiocentric (individualistic), allocentric (collectivistic), or group self-references, and weighted according to the order in which they were reported. As predicted, Malaysians produced more group and fewer idiocentric references. This is a strong indication that specific relationships are very important for self-definition in this culture. The data also indicated that cultural variations in self-concept are not categorically different across cultures; that is, all people seem to identify themselves according to both personal attributes and group membership. Rather, what differentiates among people in different cultures is the relative salience of either type of self-reference when describing oneself.

An Empirical Assessment of the Independent versus Interdependent Self-Construal Theory

The theory of independent versus interdependent self-construals has been an extremely important one in cross-cultural psychology. This framework spurred a new generation of cultural psychological research that comprised what we called Phase III research (see Chapter 2 for a refresher). Among these, a considerable number of studies have now been conducted that allows for an objective, empirical assessment of the validity of the Markus and Kitayama (1991b) framework, to which we now turn.

Data Regarding Assumptions Concerning Culture and Self   The theory starts with the idea that American culture is individualistic and Asian cultures, especially in Japan, are collectivistic. As mentioned in Chapters 1 and 2, recent years have seen a large increase in the number of valid instruments that have been developed to measure individualism and collectivism. When these studies have compared scores between Americans and Asians, especially Japanese, however, they often do *not* find that Americans are more individualistic and Japanese are more collectivistic. For instance, Matsumoto, Kudoh, and Takeuchi (1996) administered an individualism–collectivism test to Japanese university students, and based on their scores classified the participants as either individualists or collectivists. They reported that over 70 percent of the Japanese respondents were actually classified as individualists (Figure 13.2).

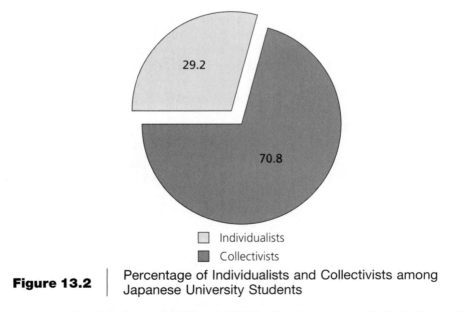

Individualists
Collectivists

Figure 13.2 | Percentage of Individualists and Collectivists among Japanese University Students

Matsumoto, D., T. Kudoh, and S. Takeuchi (1996). Changing patterns of individualism and collectivism in the United States and Japan. *Culture and Psychology*, 2, 77–107.

More recently, Oyserman, Coon, and Kemmelmeier (2002) conducted a meta-analysis involving 83 studies in which individualism and collectivism was measured, and in which North Americans (Americans and Canadians) were compared with people from other countries and other ethnic groups within the United States. Their results demonstrated that European Americans were, in general, more individualistic and less collectivistic than, for instance, Chinese, Taiwanese, Indians, and Asian Americans. However, European Americans were not more individualistic than African Americans or Latinos, and not less collectivistic than Japanese or Koreans. These findings raise questions about the assumptions about culture underlying American–Japanese cross-cultural comparisons in the literature.

As a result of Markus and Kitayama's (1991b) theory, several scales measuring independent and interdependent self-construals were developed (Gudykunst, Matsumoto, & Ting-Toomey, 1996; Singelis, 1994). Unfortunately, however, when these scales are used to measure self-construals in American–Japanese comparisons, they do not show they predicted effects. For instance, Kleinknecht, Dinnel, Kleinknecht, Hiruma, and Harada (1997) administered such a scale to American and Japanese students and found that there were no cultural differences on independent self-construals. There were differences on interdependent self-construals; but the Americans were *more* interdependent than the Japanese (Figure 13.3).

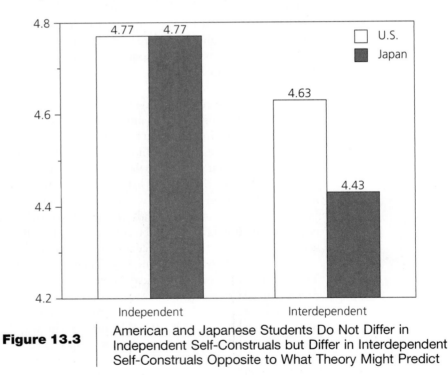

Figure 13.3 | American and Japanese Students Do Not Differ in Independent Self-Construals but Differ in Interdependent Self-Construals Opposite to What Theory Might Predict

Kleinknecht, R. A., D. Dinnel, E. E. Kleinknecht, N. Hiruma, and N. Harada (1997). Cultural Factors in Social Anxiety: A Comparison of Social Phobia Symptoms and Taijin Kyofusho. *Journal of Anxiety Disorders, 11,* 157–177.

These contradictory findings do not occur only with typical scales that involve ratings of single sentences. Li (2003) used ethnographic, qualitative, and quantitative methods to explore differences between Anglo-Canadians and mainland Chinese in their self-construals and self-other boundaries, and reported findings contrary to those predicted by the theory of independent versus interdependent self-construals.

Levine, Bresnahan, Park, Lapinski, Wittenbaum, Shearman et al. (2003) conducted a meta-analysis of studies that measured self-construals in different countries and examined whether the findings occurred in the predicted direction. They concluded that "the evidence for predicted cultural differences is weak, inconsistent, or non-existent" (p. 210). Moreover, the two-factor structure (i.e., independent versus interdependent) of the scales were meta-analyzed, and the authors concluded that the scales were "radically multi-dimensional and highly unstable within and across cultures" (p. 210). Other studies have also called into question the structure of the self-construal scales, indicating that there is no support for a two-factor, independent versus interdependent self-construal model, but in fact that there is support for a multi-dimensional model (Hardin, 2006; Hardin, Leong, & Bhagwat, 2004).

Methodological Issues?   Another issue to consider is the degree to which previous findings showing country differences are associated with the research methods used to test for those differences in the first place. Take, for instance, the research on cultural differences on self-perception described above as an example of the possible consequence of cultural differences in self-concept. Those findings do not mean that Americans have more knowledge about themselves than Asians do, or vice versa. Because the most salient information about self for the interdependent selves is context-specific, these individuals generally find it difficult or unnatural to state anything in abstract, non-contextual terms. Instead, those with interdependent selves are culture-bound to define themselves in relation to context. The studies cited above suggested that Asians found it difficult to describe themselves in terms of abstract internal attributes; that is, they find it artificial and unnatural to make abstract statements such as "I am sociable" without specifying a relevant context. Whether a person is sociable or not depends on the specific situation. If this interpretation is correct, then Asians should be comfortable describing themselves in terms of abstract internal attributes once a context has been specified.

Cousins (1989) has provided evidence to support this analysis. Using the Twenty Statements Test he asked American and Japanese respondents to write down who they were in various specific social situations (for example, at home, in school, or at work). This instruction supposedly helped respondents to picture a concrete social situation, including who was there and what was being done to whom. Once the context was specified, the Japanese respondents actually generated a *greater* number of abstract internal attributes (for example, I am hardworking, I am trustworthy, I am lazy) than did the Americans. American respondents tended to qualify their descriptions (I am more or less sociable at work, I am sometimes optimistic at home). It was as if they were saying "This is how I am at work, but don't assume that this is the way I am everywhere." With this more contextualized task, the Americans may have felt awkward providing self-descriptions because their self-definitions typically are not qualified by specific situations. Thus, the previous differences were specific to the certain way in which the data were collected in the first place (i.e., in a noncontextualized, general task).

Going beyond Independent and Interdependent Self-Construals: Multiple Selves in Cultural Contexts

The most recent findings involving measures of self-construals described above are consistent with the notion that independent and interdependent self-construals are not mutually exclusive dichotomies, but instead coexist simultaneously within individuals. Actually, the concept of independent versus interdependent selves is not unlike other dualities of self and human nature proposed throughout the history of psychology, including Freud's (1930/1961) union with others versus egoistic happiness, Angyal's (1951) surrender and autonomy, Balint's (1959) ocnophilic and philobatic tendencies, Bakan's (1966) communion and agency, Bowen's (1966) togetherness and individuality, Bowlby's (1969) attachment and separation, Franz and White's (1985) individuation and attachment, Stewart and Malley's (1987) interpersonal relatedness and self-definition, and Slavin and Kriegman's (1992) mutualistic and individualistic urges (all cited in Guisinger & Blatt, 1994). Many theorists, including Doi (1973), Kim and Berry (1993), Heelas and Lock (1981) and, Singelis (2000), have noted the difference between conceptualization of self in mainstream American psychology and in other cultures. Sampson (1988) has referred to the sense of self in mainstream approaches as "self-contained individualism," contrasting it with what he termed "ensembled individualism," in which the boundary between self and others is less sharply drawn and others are part of oneself.

Guisinger and Blatt (1994) suggest that mainstream American psychology has traditionally emphasized self-development, stressing autonomy, independence, and identity over the development of interpersonal relatedness. They also suggest, however, that evolutionary pressures of natural selection have fostered two basic developmental approaches—one involving self-definition as described in mainstream psychology, the other focusing on the development of interpersonal relatedness. They cite evidence from observational research as well as social biology to support their claims that cooperation, altruism, and reciprocation are aspects of self-development equally as important as autonomy and individual definition. Moreover, they suggest that these dual developmental processes are not mutually exclusive, as they are often depicted. Rather, they are fundamentally and basically intertwined, with the development of a mature sense of self in one aspect depending, in part, on the development of a mature self in the other.

Niedenthal and Beike (1997) have carried these concepts a step further, proposing the existence of both interrelated and isolated self-concepts. Whereas previous theories of self distinguished different types of self on the level of personality, motivation, and culture, their view focuses on the level of cognitive representation. Specifically, they suggest that "some concepts derive their meaning through mental links to concepts of other people, whereas other concepts of self have an intrinsic or cognitively isolated characterization" (p. 108). Like Guisinger and Blatt (1994), they suggest that these concepts exist not as dichotomies, but rather as interrelated dualities. Referring mainly to the cognitive structures characteristic of these two tendencies, Niedenthal and Beike (1997) suggest that individuals represent the self with a variety of more or less interrelated structures at the same time, and that one person can have separate interrelated and isolated self-concepts in the same domain. Likewise, Kagitcibasi (1996a, 1996b) proposes an integrative synthesis of the self that is both individuated and, at the same time, relational.

Actually, before Markus and Kitayama (1991b) proposed their theory of independent and interdependent self-construals, Triandis (1989) proposed the existence of three types of selves—the private, public, and collective—that coexist in everyone. Triandis suggested that individuals sampled different self-construals depending on the specific context they were in. Thus, people in individualistic settings may sample their private self more than their public or collective self, whereas people in collectivistic settings may sample their collective self more than their private or public self. This characterization is consistent with that of other writers who have suggested the existence of other, multiple types of self-construals, such as the independent, relational, and collective self (Cross & Morris, 2003; Cross, Morris, & Gore, 2002; Greenwald & Pratkanis, 1984; Kosmitzki, 1996; Oyserman, 1993; Oyserman, Gant, & Ager, 1995).

Most importantly, cross-cultural research has shown that these different self-construals exist in people of different cultures (E. S. Kashima & Hardie, 2000; Y. Kashima, Yamaguchi, Kim, & Choi, 1995; Uleman, Rhee, Bardoliwalla, Semin, & Toyama, 2000), and even to different degrees within cultures depending on area (Y. Kashima, Kokubo, Kashima, Boxall, Yamaguchi, & Macrae, 2004). Moreover, the cultural values of people of different cultures differ depending on the specific context they are in (Matsumoto, Weissman, Preston, Brown, & Kupperbusch, 1997; Rhee, Uleman, & Lee, 1996); people switch from one mode to the other depending on context (Bhawuk & Brislin, 1992); and different behaviors can be elicited in the same individuals if different self-construals are primed (Gardner, Gabriel, & Lee, 1999; Kemmelmeier & Cheng, 2004; Trafimow, Silverman, Fan, & Law, 1997; Trafimow, Triandis, & Goto, 1991; Verkuyten & Pouliasi, 2002; Ybarra & Trafimow, 1988). (Recall the priming experiment that was described in Chapter 2.) Individuals can clearly balance the need to belong with the need to be different (Brewer, 2004; Hornsey & Jetten, 2004). Thus, the notion that cultures are associated with a single sense of self, or even *primarily* with one sense of self, is not commensurate with the literature, and is a cultural dichotomization based on the erroneous assumption that cultures are homogeneous, externally distinctive, and geographically located, all of which were not true in the past, and are increasingly less true in today's world (Hermans & Kempen, 1998).

CULTURE AND IDENTITY
Cultural Identity

Identity refers to the social groups of which an individual sees himself or herself to be a part. All individuals have multiple identities because of the multiple social roles we play—parent, teacher, student, brother or sister, worker, etc.—one particularly interesting type of identity is our **cultural identity.** This refers to individuals' psychological membership in a distinct culture.

An identity, and especially a cultural identity, is important because it fulfills a universal need to belong to social groups. As we discussed in Chapter 1, humans probably have a universal need for affiliation. Addressing this need helps us create meaningful and lasting relationships. These relationships, in turn, help us reproduce, ensuring survival; they also help us in living longer, healthier, and happier lives. Multiple studies, in fact, have shown that individuals accepted into social groups have better physical and psychological consequences; those rejected by social groups have more negative consequences (Baumeister, Ciarocco, & Twenge, 2005). Ostracized and isolated individuals exhibit a wide range of distress behaviors (see also Chapter 7).

In the United States, one salient category of identity is that of being "American." But what exactly is this category, and who identifies themselves as being American? Of course, anyone born and raised in the United States is technically an American in nationality, as are those who are naturalized citizens. Yet some research provides strong evidence for an implicit assumption that being "American" equals being "white." Devos and Banaji (2005), for instance, conducted six studies with African Americans, Asian Americans, and white Americans in which they showed that, although all participants expressed strong principles of egalitarianism—a founding value in American culture—both African Americans and Asian Americans were less associated with the category "American" than were whites. This nonattribution of being American to non-whites occurred for both white and Asian American participants, but not for the African Americans. In fact, African Americans and Asian Americans were explicitly reported to be even more American than white Americans, but implicitly the opposite pattern was found.

The nonattribution of being American for Asian Americans is interesting. Many Asian Americans experience this dialogue, or a version of it:

A new acquaintance: "So where are you from?"

Typical Asian American answer: "San Francisco." (Or New York, or Chicago, or anywhere.)

Typical new acquaintance response: "No, where are you *really* from?"

One of us (D. M.) was born and raised in Hawaii, which, of course, is one of the states in the United States. When I went to a university in the Midwest (many years ago!), many of my new dorm friends asked me where I came from. When I told them I came from Hawaii, they would then ask, "When did you come to the United States?" These kinds of events happen today as well. Recently

I was a guest at a local elementary school in Indianapolis. I met one of the young students—perhaps a 4th-grader—in the hallway, and was actually having a conversation with him when he asked "Do you speak English?" It was very humorous, especially because we had already been conversing in English.

These are examples of **identity denial,** in which an individual is not recognized as a member of a group with which he or she identifies. Cheryan and Monin (2005) have shown that Asian Americans experience identity denial more frequently than do other ethnic groups in the United States, and in reaction to this, they tend to demonstrate knowledge of American culture and greater participation in American cultural practices (e.g., watching TV, listening to music, having American friends).

Multicultural Identities

As culture is a psychological construct—a shared system of rules—it is conceivable that people have not just a single cultural identity but, in some circumstances, have two or more such identities. These multicultural identities are becoming increasingly commonplace in today's world, with borders between cultural groups becoming less rigid, increased communication and interaction among people of different cultural groups, and more intercultural marriages. If culture is defined as a psychological construct, the existence of multicultural identities suggests the existence of multiple psychocultural systems of representations in the minds of multicultural individuals.

In fact, there is a growing literature on this important topic, all of which documents the existence of such multiple psychological systems in multicultural individuals. Oyserman (1993), for example, conducted four studies testing Arab and Jewish Israeli students in Israel. Although social, collectivistic types of identities had long been considered central to many cultures of that region, Oyserman suggested that these cultures would include considerable individualistic aspects as well, given the history of the region and the influence of the British. In Oyserman's studies, participants completed a battery of tests, including assessments of individualism, collectivism, public and private self-focus, and intergroup conflicts. Across all four studies, the results indicated that individualism as a worldview was related to private aspects of the self and to distinguishing between self and others, while collectivism was related to social identities, public aspects of the self, and increased awareness of intergroup conflict. Both cultural groups endorsed both types of cultural tendencies, suggesting that members of these groups use both individualistic and collectivistic worldviews in organizing perceptions of self and others.

Another study, by Oyserman, Gant, and Ager (1995), also supported the existence of multiple concepts of self. In this study, the researchers examined the effects of multiple, contextualized concepts of the self on school persistence in European American and African American youths. They found that different self-concepts were predictive of achievement-related strategies for European Americans and African Americans. More important, balance between different achievement-related self-construals predicted school achievement, especially for African American males.

Some studies (described also in Chapter 9) demonstrate that bicultural individuals have multiple cultural systems in their minds, and access one or the other depending on the context they are in. This is known as **cultural frame switching** (Benet-Martinez, Leu, Lee, & Morris, 2002; Hong, Morris, Chiu, & Benet-Martinez, 2000).

Studies have also documented a **cultural reaffirmation effect** among multicultural individuals living in multicultural societies. For example, Kosmitzki (1996) examined monocultural and bicultural Germans and Americans who made trait–attribute ratings of themselves, their native cultural group, and their adoptive cultural group. Compared with monoculturals, bicultural individuals identified more closely with their native culture, evaluated it more positively, and evaluated the two cultures as less similar to each other. In short, the bicultural individuals appeared to endorse even more traditional values associated with their native culture than did native monocultural individuals in those native cultures.

This curious finding is well supported in other studies. For example, Matsumoto et al. (1997) compared ratings of collectivistic tendencies in interpersonal interactions of Japanese Americans with those of Japanese nationals in Japan. They found that the Japanese Americans were more collectivistic than the Japanese nationals in the native culture. Sociological studies involving immigrants to the United States, including those from China, Japan, Korea, and the Philippines, also suggest that the immigrant groups in the United States from other Asia–Pacific countries appear to be more traditional than people from the native cultures from which they immigrated (for example, Takaki, 1998). Anecdotally, strong cultural traditions, customs, heritage, and language seem to continue among Chinese American immigrant populations throughout the United States.

What may account for such findings? We would speculate that when immigrant groups arrive in the United States, they bring with them the culture of their native group at that time. As they are immersed within a multicultural society, the stress of multicultural life in a different world contributes to the cultural reaffirmation effect, as documented by Kosmitzki (1996) and others. The immigrant group thus crystallizes the sense of culture they brought with them, and it is this psychological culture that is communicated across generations of immigrant groups. As time passes, the native culture itself may undergo change, but the immigrant group continues to transmit their original cultural system. After some time, if you compare the immigrant group with the native cultural group, you will find that the immigrant group actually conforms more to the original cultural stereotype than does the native group, because the immigrant culture has crystallized while the native culture has changed. Thus, although individual members of immigrant groups often grow up with multicultural identities, the identity of their native culture is often one of long-standing tradition and heritage.

In defence of multiculturalism: A polycultural society can flourish if all its members play a role in establishing its core values

Multiculturalism has always been an embattled idea, but the battle has grown fiercer of late. In this, as in so many other things, it is terrorism that is setting the agenda, goading us and forcing us to respond—terrorism, whose goal it is to turn the differences between us into divisions and then to use those divisions as justifications. No question about it: It's harder to celebrate the virtues of polyculture when even Belgian women are being persuaded by Belgians of North African descent to blow up themselves and other people. Comedians, among others, have been trying to defuse—wrong verb—people's fears by facing up to them: "My name's Shazia Mirza, or at least that's what it says on my pilot's licence." But it will take more than comedy to calm things down. Britain, the most determinedly "multiculturist" of European nations, is at the heart of the debate. According to some opinion polls, the British people avowed their continued support for multiculturalism even in the immediate aftermath of the July 7 bombings. Many commentators, however, have been less affirmative. David Goodhart, editor of *Prospect* magazine, asks the old philosophical question "Who is my brother?" and suggests that an overly diverse society may become an unsustainable one. Britain's first black archbishop, the Rt. Rev. John Sentamu, accuses multiculturalism of being bad for English national identity. And the British government has announced that new citizens will have to pass a "Britishness test" from now on. A passport will be a kind of driver's licence proving that you've learned the new rules of the nationalist road. At the other end of the spectrum, Karen Chouhan of the 1990 Trust, a "black-led" human-rights organization, insists "We need to move forward with a serious debate about how far we have to go in tackling race discrimination in every corner of society, not move it back by forcing everyone to be more (white) British." And professor Bhikhu Parekh redefines multiculturalism as the belief that "no culture is perfect or represents the best life, and that it can therefore benefit from a critical dialogue with other cultures. . . . Britain is and should remain a vibrant and democratic multicultural society that must combine respect for diversity with shared common values." It's impossible for someone like me, whose life was transformed by an act of migration, to be entirely objective about the value of such acts. I have spent much of my writing life celebrating the potential for creativity and renewal of the cultural encounters and frictions that have become commonplace in our much-transplanted world. Then again, as people keep pointing out, I have a second axe to grind, because the *Satanic Verses* controversy was a pivotal moment in the forging of a British Muslim identity and political agenda. I did not fail to note the ironies: a secular work of art energized powerful communalist, anti-secularist forces, "Muslim" instead of "Asian." And, yes, as a result the argument about multiculturalism, for me, has become an internal debate, a quarrel in the self. Nor am I alone. The melange of culture is in us all, with its irreconcilable contradictions. In our swollen, polyglot cities we are all cultural mestizos, and the argument within rages to some degree in us all. So it is important to make a distinction between multifaceted culture and multiculturalism. In the age of mass migration and the Internet, cultural plurality is an irreversible fact, like globalization. Like it or dislike it, it's where we live, and the dream of a pure monoculture is at best an unattainable, nostalgic fantasy, and at worst a life-threatening menace—when ideas of racial purity, religious purity or cultural purity turn into programs of "ethnic cleansing," for example, or when Hindu fanatics in India attack the "inauthenticity" of Indian Muslim experience, or when Islamic ideologues drive young people to die in the service of "pure" faith, unadulterated by compassion or doubt. "Purity" is a slogan that leads to segregations and explosions. Let us have no more of it. A little more impurity, please, a little less cleanliness, a little more dirt. We'll all sleep easier in our beds. Multiculturalism, however, has all too often become mere cultural relativism, a much less defensible proposition, under cover of which much that is reactionary and oppressive—of women, for example—can be justified. The British multiculturalist idea of different cultures peacefully coexisting under the umbrella of a vaguely defined pax Britannica was seriously undermined by the July bombers and the disaffected ghetto culture from which they sprang. Of the other available social models, the one-size-fits-all homogenizing of "full assimilation" seems not only undesirable but unachievable. What remains is the "core values" approach to which Parekh alludes, and of which the "Britishness test" is, at least as currently proposed, a grotesque comic parody. When we, as individuals, pick and mix cultural elements for ourselves, we do not do so indiscriminately, but according to our natures. Societies, too, must retain the ability to discriminate, to reject as well as to accept, to value some things above others, and to insist on the acceptance of those values by all their members. This is the question of our time: How does a fractured community of multiple cultures decide what values it must share in order to cohere, and how can it insist on those values even when they clash with some citizens' traditions and beliefs? The beginnings of an answer may be found by asking the question the other way around: What does a society owe to its citizens? The French riots demonstrate a stark truth. If people do not feel included in the national idea, their alienation will eventually turn to rage. Chouhan and others are right to insist that issues of social justice, racism and deprivation need urgently to be addressed. If we are to build a plural society on the foundation of what unites us, we must face up to what divides. But the questions of core freedoms and primary loyalties can't be ducked. No society, no matter how tolerant, can expect to thrive if its citizens don't prize what their citizenship means—if, when asked what they stand for as Frenchmen, as Indians, as Americans, as Britons, they cannot give a clear reply.

Rushdie, S. In defense of multiculturalism: A polycultural society can flourish if all its members play a role in establishing its core values. *Toronto Star*, p. A27. Dec. 15, 2005.

Salman Rushdie is the author of *The Satanic Verses, Fury,* and many other books.

SELF-ESTEEM AND SELF-ENHANCEMENT
What Are These, and Where Do They Come From?

Self-esteem refers to the cognitive and affective evaluations we make about ourselves. One way of understanding the origin of self-esteem is through cultural worldviews. As described earlier in this chapter, cultural worldviews are ideological belief systems about the world. The concept of self is a cognitive generalization about how one believes one is, and is an important and integral part of one's cultural worldviews. Self-esteem is a psychological phenomenon created by humans as a buffer against the terror that is associated with the knowledge of the inevitability of one's death (terror management theory) (Becker, 1971, 1973). Self-esteem, therefore, is "a culturally based construction that consists of viewing oneself as living up to specific contingencies of value . . . that are derived from the culture at large but are integrated into a unique individualized worldview by each person" (Pyszczynski, Greenberg, Solomon, Arndt, & Schimel, 2004). In this theory, cultural worldviews are also fabricated and given meaning by people's minds (Becker, 1971). One of the goals of these cultural worldviews is to raise human existence above nature so that meaning can be drawn from life.

Self-enhancement refers to the collection of psychological processes by which we bolster our self-esteem. Terror management theory would suggest that self-enhancement is a universal psychological process, and that individuals will universally work to bolster their self-esteem. Self-esteem is often not correlated with objective standards of competence or performance (Baumeister, Campbell, Krueger, & Vohs, 2003; Pyszczynski et al., 2004; Rodriguez, Wigfield, & Eccles, 2003), which suggests that people create uniqueness about themselves regardless of objective reality. As a part of one's self-concept, cultural worldviews likewise are subject to the same need for uniqueness. That is why people often report with pride what their cultures are like, saying that is what makes their cultures unique, even though in many instances people of different cultures report the same content (e.g., "the emphasis in my culture is in the importance of family"). And even though people of Asian cultures say that they do not boast, they often take pride in their humility and supposed collectivism.

Cultural worldviews, then, are uniquely human products. The expression of cultural ideologies may serve a function of enhancing or reinforcing self-esteem as derived from cultural issues, thus contributing to the feeling of one's uniquely human existence. And just as self-esteem is an abstract, supernatural construct that may in reality have little to do with behaviors, happiness, lifestyles, and relationships, ideological cultural worldviews may also have little to do with reality on the level of behavior and mental processes among members of culture. Instead it may be that the *expression* of those ideologies serves a social, psychological, self-esteem–striving function that in reality may not be reflective of actual ways of being, but rather are indicators of conformity to social demands or social intelligence. Ideological cultural worldviews, then, like self-esteem, serve as a psychological defense against the anxieties of living and provides humans with the ability to achieve a sense of value (Salzman, 2001).

Cultural Differences in Self-Esteem and Self-Enhancement

Early cross-cultural research on self-esteem and self-enhancement reported that members of individualistic cultures, such as Americans and Canadians, self-enhanced, while members of collectivistic cultures, such as Asians, did not. This research implied that European Americans in particular have a pervasive tendency to maintain their feelings of self-esteem and self-worth. Wood, Hillman, and Sawilowsky (1995), for example, found that American adolescents had significantly higher self-esteem scores than their Indian counterparts. Americans also report higher self-esteem scores than Japanese or Chinese (Heine, Lehman, Markus, & Kitayama, 1999). Studies with children have also found differences in Asian versus European countries on individual self-esteem. Chan's (2000) study of 1,303 children compared Anglo and Chinese children in Britain and Chinese children in Hong Kong. As predicted, he found that Hong Kong Chinese children reported significantly lower levels of self-esteem than did Anglo British children. In addition, several studies in North America have found that Asian Americans report lower self-esteem scores than European Americans (Crocker & Lawrence, 1999; Mintz & Kashubeck, 1999; Porter & Washington, 1993). Radford, Mann, Ohta, and Nakane (1993), comparing self-esteem related to decision making in Australian and Japanese students, found that Australians had higher self-esteem scores than did the Japanese.

Another method for enhancing self-esteem, in the United States, is the **false uniqueness effect.** Wylie (1979) found that American adults typically consider themselves to be more intelligent and more attractive than average. This effect appears to be stronger for males than for females in the United States (Joseph, Markus, & Tafarodi, 1992). In a national survey of American students, Myers (1987) found that 70 percent of the students thought they were above average in leadership ability; with respect to the ability to get along with others, 0 percent thought they were below average, and 60 percent thought they were in the top 10 percent. This type of study clearly shows that there is a tendency to view oneself and one's ability and traits more positively in comparison to others, at least in the United States. Early studies of the false uniqueness effect in countries and cultures outside the United States, however, demonstrated that these biases did not exist. For example, when Japanese students were asked to rate themselves in comparison to others on a number of abilities and traits, they claimed that about 50 percent of students would be better than they are (see Figure 13.4; Markus & Kitayama, 1991a; Markus, Mullally, & Kitayama, 1997). In other words, the false uniqueness effect was nonexistent in this sample. Furthermore, Japanese participants are more likely to say that successful things have occurred because of good luck or effort and that failures have occurred because of insufficient abilities (Shikanai, 1978).

Early studies suggested that not only did collectivistic Asians not self-enhance, they also engaged in more of the opposite tendency, that is to self-efface. **Self-effacement** refers to the tendency to downplay one's virtues. Some researchers have suggested that Asians, such as Chinese and particularly Japanese, not only are more self-effacing; they are downright more negative about

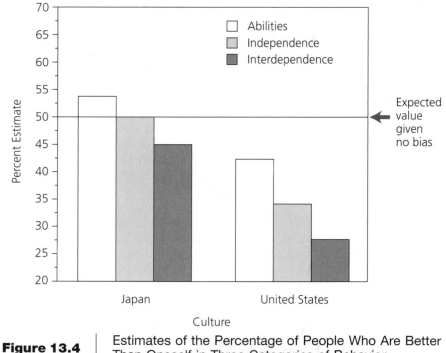

Figure 13.4 | Estimates of the Percentage of People Who Are Better Than Oneself in Three Categories of Behavior

Markus, H. R., and S. Kitayama, (1991). Cultural Variation in Self-Concept. In G. R. Goethals & J. Strauss (Eds.), *Multidisciplinary Perspectives on the Self*. New York: Springer Verlag. Reprinted with permission.

themselves, and are more attuned to negative than to positive self-evaluations, in both private and public settings (Kitayama, Matsumoto, Markus, & Norasakkunkit, 1997; Leung, 1996).

Despite the fact that some psychologists have concluded that North Americans and Western Europeans self-enhance while Asians do not (Heine, 2005; Heine et al., 1999), the most recent research strongly suggests that people of all cultures self-enhance, but they just do so in different ways. For example, it could be that individualism fosters a *certain type* of self-esteem—one that is often measured in psychological research—whereas collectivism fosters a different type. Tafarodi and Swann (1996) tested this "cultural trade-off" hypothesis in a study of Chinese and American college students. They hypothesized that highly collectivistic cultures promote the development of global self-esteem, which is reflected in generalized self-liking, while at the same time challenging the development of another dimension of self-esteem, reflected in generalized self-competence; individualistic cultures, they hypothesized, foster the opposite tendencies. As predicted, they found that the Chinese were lower in self-competence but higher in self-liking than the Americans. These findings support the notion that self-esteem may have multiple facets, and that different cultural milieus either support or challenge the development of different facets. For instance, although self-enhancement may not occur in other cultures when people are asked to focus on their own individual traits and attributes, when people are asked about relational and community-related traits, self-enhancement does indeed take place (Kurman, 2001).

This notion also received some support in a study by Kitayama and Karasawa (1997). This study examined implicit rather than explicit self-esteem in a sample of Japanese individuals by examining their preference for certain Japanese alphabetical letters and numbers over others. The results indicated that letters included in one's own name and numbers corresponding to the month and day of one's birth were significantly better liked than other letters and numbers. The authors interpreted these findings to suggest a dimension of self-esteem that may be fostered in a collectivistic cultural milieu, but not necessarily within an individualistic one.

Sedikides, Gaertner, and Toguchi (2003) provided very strong evidence for what they call **tactical self-enhancement.** They tested American and Japanese participants and showed that Americans self-enhanced on individualistic attributes, while Japanese self-enhanced on collectivistic attributes. Sedikides and colleagues conducted a meta-analysis of cross-cultural studies on self-esteem and self-enhancement conducted to date, and provided more evidence that both Westerners and Easterners self-enhanced, but they did so in tactically different ways. Their conclusions are supported by other independent researchers (Schmitt & Allik, 2005; Zhang, 2005).

These most recent findings are consistent with the view described earlier, that self is a universal part of cultural worldviews, and that all humans have the tendency to enhance their sense of self because of their unique cognitive abilities, including the need to seek meaning, and knowledge of themselves. These findings also highlight the importance of context in understanding psychological processes. In one context, members of some cultures may be very likely to self-efface; in others, however, these very same individuals may self-enhance. These differences are probably related to differences in *socially appropriate responding,* which we discussed in Chapter 2.

CULTURE AND ATTRIBUTIONS

What Are Attributions, and Where Do They Come From?

Attributions are the inferences people make about the causes of events and their own and others' behaviors. Attributions represent the ways we understand the world around us and the behavior of others. You might attribute a friend's failure to show up for a date to irresponsibility, too much traffic, or just forgetting. You might attribute your success on an exam to your effort or to luck.

You might remember, in Chapter 1 we discussed some of the unique cognitive abilities that humans have that allow us to create human cultures. One of these was the ability to infer agency in oneself and others—that is, to know that other people have intentions and that they do things because they are *intentional agents.* People have needs, motives, desires, and goals, and their behaviors are often the direct result of these. Knowing that this is true for oneself and others, and especially that others make that inference about oneself, is one of the most important cognitive building blocks of human culture.

This same cognitive ability enables humans to create attributions. Attributions allow us to explain things, to put things in order, and to make sense of the world. Attributions are based on the unique human cognitive ability to understand that oneself and others are intentional agents. And because these are cognitive abilities that are universal to humans, the process of making attributions is a universal psychological process. That is, all people of all cultures make attributions. There is, in fact, probably a universal need to know—a universal motive for humans to derive meaning from events and behaviors. This would explain why humans personalize inanimate objects or random acts of nature (e.g., hurricanes) and make causal inferences—attributions—about them. By creating attributions about such things, we exert psychological control over the world.

The study of attributions has a rich history in social psychology. Researchers distinguish among the types of attributions people make. For instance, an important concept in attribution research is the distinction between internal and external attributions. Internal attributions specify the cause of behavior within a person; these are also known as **dispositional attributions,** because they are attributions about people's dispositions. External attributions locate the cause of behavior outside a person, such as other people, nature, or acts of God; these are also known as **situational dispositions.**

Cultural Differences in Attributional Styles?

Because attributions are creations of the mind, they may or may not be rooted in an objective reality, and are influenced by culture. Thus, attributions are subjected to many possible biases in ways of thinking. One of these is called **self-serving bias.** This is the tendency to attribute one's successes to personal factors and one's failures to situational factors (Bradley, 1978). If you fail an exam, for instance, you may attribute your failure to a poorly constructed test, lousy teaching, distractions, or a bad week at home (situational causes). If you ace an exam, however, you are more likely to attribute your success to effort, intelligence, or ability (dispositional causes).

Research for many decades has shown that Americans often exhibit a self-serving bias in their attributional styles. One of the earliest studies to show this, in fact, was Jones and Harris's (1967) study of attributions about an essay supporting Fidel Castro in Cuba. Participants inferred that the author must have a favorable attitude toward Castro. Furthermore, such dispositional inferences occurred even when obvious situational constraints were present. The subjects in this study inferred a pro-Castro attitude even when they were explicitly told that the person was assigned to write a pro-Castro essay and no choice was given. The subjects ignored these situational constraints and erroneously drew inferences about the author's disposition. This bias toward inference about the actor's disposition even in the presence of very obvious situational constraints has been termed **fundamental attribution error** (Ross, 1977). Fundamental attribution error is also known as "correspondence bias."

Fundamental attribution error has been replicated many times in American psychological experiments. Early cross-cultural research, however, suggested that it may not be as robust or pervasive, however, among people of other cultures. For example, J. G. Miller (1984) examined patterns of social explanation in Americans and Hindu Indians. Both Hindu and American respondents were asked to describe someone they knew well who either did something good for another person or did something bad to another person. After describing such a person, the respondents were asked to explain why the person committed that good or bad act. American respondents typically explained the person's behavior in terms of general dispositions (for example, "She is very irresponsible."). The Hindus, however, were much less likely to offer dispositional explanations. Instead, they tended to provide explanations in terms of the actor's duties, social roles, and other situation-specific factors (see also Shweder & Bourne, 1984).

Much of the early cross-cultural research on attributions focused on attributions concerning success and failure in academic achievement situations, and many studies have found considerable differences across cultures in the nature of attributions about academic performance. These findings often differ from what has typically been found to be true of Americans. Hau and Salili (1991), for example, asked students in junior and senior high school in Hong Kong to rate the importance and meaning of 13 specific causes of academic performance. Effort, interest, and ability—all internal attributions—were rated the most important causes, regardless of success or failure. Research from the United States would have predicted that these dimensions would be important in making attributions of success but not failure, because of self-serving bias.

Two studies with Taiwanese subjects also challenge our notions about self-serving attributions. Crittenden (1991) found that Taiwanese women used more external and self-effacing attributions about themselves than did American women. Crittenden suggested that the Taiwanese women did this to enhance their public and private self-esteem by using an attributional approach that conformed to a feminine gender role. Earlier, Bond, Leung, and Wan (1982) found that self-effacing Chinese students were better liked by their peers than those who adopted this attributional style less often.

Other cross-cultural studies on attributions concerning academic performance pepper the literature with findings that challenge American notions of attribution. Kashima and Triandis (1986) showed that Japanese people use a much more group-oriented, collective approach to attribution with regard to attention and memory achievement tasks. Compared with their American counterparts, Japanese subjects attributed failure to themselves more and attributed success to themselves less. Kashima and Triandis interpreted this finding as suggestive of American and Japanese cultural differences in degree of responsibility taking.

There are many cross-cultural studies of attributions in nonacademic areas as well that also show many cultural differences. For example, Moghaddam,

Ditto, and Taylor (1990) examined the attributional processes of Indian female immigrants to Canada who experienced varying levels of distress in relation to the degree to which they have adjusted to life in Canada. They found that the Indian women were more likely to attribute both successes and failures to internal causes. American research would have hypothesized that the subjects would attribute only successes to internal causes and attribute failures to external causes, again because of self-serving bias.

Forgas, Furnham, and Frey (1989) documented broad cross-national differences in the importance of different types of specific attributions for wealth. Their study included 558 subjects from the United Kingdom, Australia, and the Federal Republic of Germany. The British considered family background and luck to be the most important determinants of wealth. The Germans also considered family background to be the most important determinant. The Australians, however, rated individual qualities as the most important determinant of wealth. Romero and Garza (1986) reported differences between Hispanic and Anglo women in their attributions concerning occupational success and failure. In their study, Chicanas and Anglo American female university students provided data concerning their attributions about an Anglo, African American, or Chicana female's success or failure in a teaching job. They found that Chicanas tended to make more attributions on the basis of luck, ethnicity, or gender. In making attributions about failure, Anglo females tended to attribute less competence to the actor than did the Chicanas.

Several studies have examined newspaper articles to investigate whether attributions about certain "real-life" behaviors (as opposed to filling out a questionnaire about imaginary behaviors in someone's research lab) may differ across cultures. For example, Morris and Peng (1994) found that U.S. newspaper articles were more likely to attribute the cause of a murder to an individual's personality traits, attitudes, and beliefs (such as "bad temper," "psychologically disturbed"), but Chinese newspapers were more likely to attribute the cause to situational factors (such as "didn't get along with his advisor," "isolated from his community"). Lee, Hallahan, and Herzog (1996) coded Hong Kong and U.S. newspaper articles concerning sporting events for attributional style and judged the extent to which events were attributed to personal or situational factors. As hypothesized, they found that attributions by Hong Kong reporters were more situational and less dispositional than those of U.S. reporters.

Cultural differences in the nature of attributional processes exist across a wide range of events, including occupational performance, wealth and economic success, crime, physical and psychological disorders, sports, and moral and immoral behaviors. Collectively, these studies indicate quite convincingly that attributional styles differ substantially across cultures and that they do not always conform to the attributional biases we are familiar with from research involving Americans.

Universal and Culture-Specific Features of Attributional Styles

Although many studies have demonstrated cross-cultural differences in attributional styles, one major question that arises is to what extent are attributional processes universal, and to what extent are they culturally specific? What do the cultural differences in attributional styles and processes described above mean?

Two comprehensive reviews of the literature shed some light on this topic. Choi, Nisbett, and Norenzayan (1999) reviewed the cross-cultural literature on causal attributions, and concluded that the differences obtained demonstrating that North Americans tended to make the fundamental attribution error while East Asians did not were not caused by a lack of dispositional thinking on the part of East Asians, but to a greater sensitivity to context and situationalism. To demonstrate this, these researchers conducted a study in which they asked Korean and American participants to predict the behaviors of a group of individuals based on situational information, and the behavior of a single individual based on both personality and situational information. The findings indicated that when dispositional (personality) information was not available or applicable, the Koreans used situational information more than did the American participants, suggesting a stronger belief in situational influence in the Koreans than the Americans. When both dispositional and situational information was present, however, there were no cultural differences in the attributions of the Koreans or the Americans.

Mezulis, Abramson, Hyde, and Hankin (2004) conducted a meta-analysis of 266 studies that produced 503 effects. Across all studies, they demonstrated that there was a very large effect for a self-serving bias. Moreover this bias was present in nearly all samples, indicating universality in the self-serving bias. When they analyzed their data separately for different cultures, they found that there were *no* differences in the size of the bias between European Americans, African Americans, Asian Americans, Hispanic Americans, Native Americans, and mixed Americans; they all showed the self-serving bias to a large degree. The sizes of the effects for Asian cultures were lower, but still showed evidence for the self-serving bias. Moreover, there were major differences across the Asian countries. The data for Japan, for instance, indicated almost no degree of bias. Mainland China and South Korea, however, were associated with large self-serving biases, at levels comparable to those found in the United States. These findings, therefore, suggest that simple explanations based on collectivism *cannot* account for cultural differences in self-serving bias, because many of the Asian cultures share some similarities in collectivism.

Thus, it appears that the self-serving bias in attributions, which helps to produce effects such as the fundamental attribution error, is universal. These latest findings are consistent with the view of the origin of attributions we discussed earlier, and the role that self-esteem and cultural worldviews play in maintaining our self-image. All people of all cultures appear to have a universal need to maintain their self-image and protect their self-integrity; attributions are one of the ways in which this is achieved. People of different cultures vary, however, in the specific ways in which they use the attributional process. This cultural influence probably starts early; Bornstein, Haynes, Azuma, Galperin, Maital, and Ogino and associates (1998), for example, examined attributions of mothers of 20-month-olds in Argentina, Belgium, France, Israel, Italy,

Japan, and the United States with regard to success and failure in seven parenting tasks. They found only a few cross-cultural similarities, but many differences, especially with regard to degree of competence and satisfaction in parenting. Child age could not be a factor, as it was controlled in the study, and child gender was also found not to influence the data. These types of findings provide us with ideas about how and why parents transmit valuable cultural information to their children, resulting in specific styles of attribution (among many other psychological effects).

Arab Attributions for the World Trade Center Bombing

There are many reasons that can be inferred about the September 11th bombing of the World Trade Center in 2001. Sidanius, Henry, Pratto, and Levin (2004) studied two types of attributions about the attacks by asking Arab graduate and undergraduate students in Lebanon about the attacks. The sample included both Christians and Muslims, and the participants were asked to rate eight possible attributions of the causes of the attacks. The eight attributions were grouped into two major categories: the *clash of civilizations* and the *anti–U.S. dominance* category. Both Christians and Muslims gave more importance to the antidominance category than the clash of civilizations account. In addition, antidominance attributions were more related to attitudes toward terrorist and antiterrorist activities than clash of civilization attributions. Thus, in the minds of this sample, the attack on the United States was primarily a reaction to American support for Israel, and "perceived American imperialism, arrogance, and disregard for the lives and welfare of people in the Arab world" (p. 412).

CONCLUSION

In this chapter, we have discussed the major approaches to understanding and studying the relationship between culture, self, self-esteem and self-enhancement, identity, and attributions.

GLOSSARY

attributions The inferences people make about the causes of events and their own and others' behaviors.

cultural identity An individual's psychological membership in a distinct culture.

cultural frame switching The ability of bicultural individuals to have multiple cultural systems in their minds, and to access one or the other depending on the context they are in.

cultural reaffirmation effect The amplified endorsement of home cultural values by bicultural individuals.

dispositional attributions Attributions about people's internal characteristics, traits, or personality.

false uniqueness effect The tendency for individuals to underestimate the commonality of desirable traits and to overestimate their uniqueness.

fundamental attribution error A tendency to explain the behaviors of others using internal attributions but to explain one's own behaviors using external attributions.

identity denial When an individual is not recognized as a member of a group with which he or she identifies.

independent construal of self A sense of self that views the self as a bounded entity, clearly separated from relevant others.

interdependent construal of self A sense of self that views the self as unbounded, flexible, and contingent on context. This sense of self is based on a principle of the fundamental connectedness among people.

self-concept The idea or images that one has about oneself and how and why one behaves as one does.

self-effacement The tendency to downplay one's virtues.

self-enhancement A collection of psychological processes by which individuals maintain or enhance their self-esteem.

self-esteem The cognitive and affective evaluations we make about ourselves.

self-serving bias A bias in which people tend to attribute good deeds and successes to their own internal attributes but attribute bad deeds or failures to external factors.

situational dispositions Attributions based on the situation or context.

tactical self-enhancement The idea that people of different cultures all self-enhance, but they choose to do it in different ways—i.e., tactically.

terror management theory The theory that suggests that, because humans have unique cognitive abilities, we are the only animals aware of the fact that we will die eventually, and we are afraid, terrified in fact, of that inevitable death. Because inevitable death is terrifying to us, we create psychological phenomena as a buffer against the terror of dying.

14 CHAPTER | **Culture and Social Behavior, II**

Interpersonal and Intergroup Relations

CHAPTER CONTENTS

All mankind is of one author, and is one volume; when one man dies,
one chapter is not torn out of the book, but translated into a better
language; and every chapter must be so translated. . . . As therefore
the bell that rings to a sermon, calls not upon the preacher only, but
upon the congregation to come: so this bell calls us all: but how
much more me, who am brought so near the door by this sickness. . . .
No man is an island, entire of itself; every man is a piece of the
continent, a part of the main. If a clod be washed away by the sea,
Europe is the less, as well as if a promontory were, as well as if a
manor of thy friend's or of thine own were. Any man's death
diminishes me, because I am involved in mankind; and therefore
never send to know for whom the bell tolls; it tolls for thee.

(John Dunne, 1624)

Humans are social animals, and all of us are fundamentally interconnected with each other in our lives. All individuals need others to live, work, play, and function in our societies and cultures. Without others, we can neither function effectively nor achieve our goals.

In this chapter, we will discuss how cultures affect social behaviors. Chapter 13 dealt with social behavior from the viewpoint of the individual; in this chapter we deal with how people actually interact with others, and how culture informs this process. We will begin our discussion by examining how we form impressions of others. We will then deal with a very important issue in many people's lives—that of love, sex, and marriage. We will discuss how cultures influence conformity, obedience, compliance, and cooperation. We will then turn our attention to intergroup relations, discussing ingroups versus outgroups, ethnocentrism, prejudice, stereotypes, and discrimination. We will discuss the relationship between culture and aggression, and end with a discussion of acculturation—how we adapt and adjust to new cultures.

CULTURE AND IMPRESSION FORMATION

People of all cultures have a universal need to form meaningful bonds with others, have intimate relationships, and to belong to social groups (Baumeister & Leary, 1995). As we discussed in Chapter 1, this universal need is most likely related to the fact that creating these bonds and relationships is associated with many things that aid in our survival. They help ensure reproduction by finding mates, of course; but they also aid in our caring for offspring and the elderly, and in buffering many of life's trials and tribulations. People with meaningful social relationships live longer and are healthier (Chapter 7).

Culture and Face Recognition

One of the psychological processes necessary to creating social bonds is the ability to recognize other people's faces. Early research in this field showed the existence of a same-race bias in the ability to recognize faces. Malpass and Kravitz (1969), for example, showed photographs of either African American or European American individuals to observers in either a predominantly African American or European American university. Observers recognized individuals of their own race better than they did people of the other race. These results have been replicated a number of times (for example, Malpass, 1974), using different methods (Wright, Boyd, & Tredoux, 2001), and supported in meta-analyses examining findings across multiple samples and studies (for example, Bothwell, Brigham, & Malpass, 1989; Meissner & Brigham, 2001). Research has documented this effect for Asian faces as well, comparing European and Asian American judgments of European and Asian faces (O'Toole, Deffenbacher, Valentin, & Abdi, 1994). Other studies have also demonstrated a same-race bias in discriminating between male and female faces (O'Toole, Peterson, & Deffenbacher, 1996). This bias exists in children as young as 3 months old (Bar-Haim, Ziv, Lamy, & Hodes, 2006; Kelly, Quinn, Slater, Lee, Gibson, Smith et al., 2005).

Why might this bias exist? Brigham and Malpass (1985) and Meissner and Brigham (2001), for example, suggest that attitudes toward people of same and other races, social orientation, task difficulty, and experience all contribute to this differential recognition ability. Meissner and Brigham's meta-analysis also suggests that the explanation provided by intergroup contact theories—that differential recognition stems from limited experience with members of other groups—has received only weak support in the research literature. Devine and Malpass (1985) showed that orienting strategies can affect differential face recognition. When observers in their study were told that they were participating in a reaction-time experiment and would later be asked to make differential judgments about the people they observed, no difference in recognition rates occurred. A study by Levy, Lysne, and Underwood (1995) also established conditions in which same-sex, same-age, and same-race information was not associated with better memory recall. These researchers suggested that different self-schemas held by the observers accounted for the differences. Finally, some research suggests that same-race and other-race faces may actually be perceived and classified differently, with race features being coded differentially in same-race and other-race perceptions (Levin, 1996).

Impression Formation

Person perception refers to the process of forming impressions of others. Appearance, especially physical attractiveness, influences judgments of personality. Research with North American subjects has consistently shown that people tend to ascribe desirable personality characteristics to those who are good-looking, seeing them as more sensitive, kind, sociable, pleasant, likable, and interesting than those who are unattractive (Dion, 1986; Patzer, 1985). Attractive people are also judged to be more competent and intelligent (Ross & Ferris, 1981). Attractiveness ratings are strongly correlated with social competence, adjustment, potency, and intellectual competence, and negatively with modesty (Eagly, Ashmore, Makhijani, & Longo, 1991); and are strongly correlated with social skills, sociability, mental health, dominance, intelligence, and sexual warmth, and again negatively with modesty (Feingold, 1992). These studies demonstrated quite consistent agreement in findings involving North American participants with regard to the psychological meanings attributed to attractive people.

Other aspects of appearance also influence our perceptions of others. For example, greater height, which is generally considered attractive, has been associated with leadership ability, competence, and high salary (Deck, 1968; Patzer, 1985). Adults with baby-face features tend to be judged as warm, kind, naive, and submissive; adults with more mature facial features tend to be judged as strong, worldly, and dominant (Berry & McArthur, 1985, 1986). People who are neat dressers are thought to be conscientious (Albright, Kenny, & Malloy, 1988). People with poor eye contact are often judged to be dishonest (DePaulo, Stone, & Lassiter, 1985).

Culture and Attractiveness

Although the effects of attractiveness and physical appearance on the formation of positive impressions is well documented in the mainstream psychological literature, cultures clearly differ on the meaning and definition of attractiveness. Beauty is in the eye of the beholder, or so it is said, and people of different cultures may have quite different concepts of what is beautiful and what is not. Cultural differences in the definition of attractiveness, in turn, can influence the formation of impressions. Daibo, Murasawa, and Chou (1994), for example, compared judgments of physical attractiveness made by Japanese and Koreans. They showed male and female university students in both countries slides of Japanese and Korean females and asked them to rate the attractiveness and likability of each person using 13 bipolar adjective scales. Three poses of each person were shown: front view, profile, and three-quarter view. Facial physiognomy—that is, the anatomical characteristics of the face—were also measured separately by an anatomist, and these measurements were correlated with the psychological judgments provided by the respondents. In Japan, attractiveness ratings were positively correlated with large eyes, small mouths, and small chins. In Korea, however, attractiveness ratings were correlated with large eyes, small and high noses, and thin and small faces. Koreans tended to attach other affective and psychological judgments, such as maturity and likability, to judgments of attractiveness. The Japanese, however, did not. These findings show not only that the two cultures have different standards for beauty, but that beauty has culturally specific psychological meanings.

Wheeler and Kim (1997) demonstrated similar effects. These researchers showed photos of Korean males and females to Korean university students, who made judgments of social competence, intellectual competence, concern for others, integrity, adjustment, potency, sexual interest/warmth, and modesty. Consistent with research involving North American judges, this study found that Korean students rated attractive faces as more socially and intellectually competent, better adjusted, more sexually interesting, and less modest. Contrary to previous research with North Americans, however, the Koreans did not rate attractive faces as more potent. They did rate them as having more integrity and concern for others, which was not found in previous mainstream studies. Wheeler and Kim concluded that, although all cultures appear to stereotype on the basis of physical attractiveness, the contents of the stereotypes probably depend on cultural values.

Another study also demonstrated cultural differences in the psychological meaning derived from attractive faces. Matsumoto and Kudoh (1993) asked American and Japanese subjects to judge Caucasian and Japanese faces that were either smiling or neutral on three dimensions: attractiveness, intelligence, and sociability. The Americans consistently rated the smiling faces higher on all three dimensions, congruent with our traditional notions of person perception and impression formation. The Japanese, however, only rated the smiling faces as more sociable. There was no difference in their ratings of attractiveness between smiles and neutrals, and they rated the neutral faces as more intelligent.

But there is also evidence that judgments of attractiveness are consistent across cultures. Cunningham, Roberts, Barbee, Druen, and Wu (1995) conducted three studies, all using basically the same methods. In the first, European Americans and Asian and Hispanic immigrants judged faces of Asian, Hispanic, African American, and European American women. In the second study, Taiwanese respondents rated the same stimuli. In the third study, African and European Americans rated African American female faces. The stimuli were photographs whose subjects ranged from college students to contestants in beauty contests in other cultures. In all three studies, the researchers obtained attractiveness ratings from the judges, as well as 28 separate measurements of facial features. The results across all three studies indicated extremely high correlations among the judge groups in their attractiveness ratings. Moreover, the attractiveness ratings by all groups correlated with the same facial characteristics, which included the nature of the eyes, nose, cheeks, chins, and smiles. Moreover, a meta-analysis reviewing 1,800 articles and 919 findings indicated that raters agree both within and across cultures about who is and is not attractive (Langlois, Kalakanis, Rubenstein, Larson, Hallam, & Smoot, 2000).

So, is beauty in the eye of the beholder? The findings of the studies described above, including the meta-analysis, would suggest not—that there is a universal standard for what does and does not constitute attractiveness. Of course, there may be individual differences in judgments and criteria for attractiveness, but on the average, it appears that what is attractive for one group is similarly attractive for another. On the individual level, however, beauty really is in the eye of the beholder.

LOVE, SEX, AND MARRIAGE ACROSS CULTURES

Culture and Mate Selection

So what do people look for in a mate, and is it different across cultures? In one of the best-known studies on this topic (Buss, 1989, 1994), more than 10,000 respondents in 37 cultures drawn from 33 countries completed two questionnaires, one dealing with factors in choosing a mate and the second dealing with preferences concerning potential mates. In 36 of the 37 cultures, females rated financial prospects as more important than did males; in 29 of those 36 cultures, females also rated ambition and industriousness as important than did males. In all 37 cultures, males preferred younger mates and females preferred older mates; in 34 of the cultures, males rated good looks as more important than did females; and in 23 of the cultures, males rated chastity as more important than did females. Buss (1989) concluded that females value cues related to resource acquisition in potential mates more highly than males do, whereas males value reproductive capacity more highly than do females. These findings were predicted, in fact, on the basis of an evolutionary-based framework that generated hypotheses related to evolutionary concepts of parental involvement, sexual selection, reproductive capacity, and certainty of paternity or maternity. The degree of agreement in sex differences across cultures has led Buss (1989) and his colleagues to view these mate-selection preferences as universal, arising from different evolutionary selection pressures on males and females.

Hatfield and Sprecher (1995) have replicated and extended the findings by Buss and his colleagues. In this study, male and female students in the United States, Russia, and Japan were surveyed concerning their preferences in a marital partner, using a 12-item scale. The items all referred to positive traits: physically attractive, intelligent, athletic, ambitious, good conversationalist, outgoing and sociable, status or money, skill as a lover, kind and understanding, potential for success, expressive and open, and sense of humor. Across all three cultures, the data indicated that the only scale on which men gave higher ratings than women was physical attractiveness. Women gave higher ratings than men on all the other scales except good conversationalist. There were also some interesting cultural differences. For example, Americans preferred expressivity, openness, and sense of humor more than did the Russians, who in turn preferred these traits more than did the Japanese. Russians desired skill as a lover most, while Japanese preferred it least. The Japanese gave lower ratings than the other two cultures on kind and understanding, good conversationalist, physical attractiveness, and status.

Other researchers offer an alternative explanation for interpersonal attraction based on a social construction perspective (for example, Beall & Sternberg, 1995). This perspective highlights the importance of individual and cultural, as opposed to evolutionary, factors in understanding interpersonal attraction. Indeed, social constructionists argue that there are more gender similarities than differences when it comes to choosing mates. For instance, a U.S. study of the most important traits reported by both men and women when looking for a partner are kindness, consideration, honesty, and a sense of humor (Goodwin, 1990).

A study by Pines (2001) provides evidence for both the evolutionary theory and the social construction theory of mate selection. In this study, American and Israeli students were extensively interviewed about their romantic relationships. As evolutionary theory would predict, more men than women mentioned physical appearance as a reason for attraction to their partner. However, as social construction theory would predict, culture also played an important role in determining what was considered attractive. For example, Americans were attracted to the status of their partners more than Israelis were. Also, closeness and similarity were more important factors for Americans than for Israelis.

There may also be developmentally different preferences in what one considers attractive in a partner. For instance, a study involving Dutch and German participants reports that as people get older, the stereotypical male preference for appearance and female preference for financial prospects give way to a preference for a steady relationship, home, and children (De Raad & Boddema-Winesemius, 1992).

So there are some aspects of finding a mate that are universal, and some that appear to be culture specific. But what about trying to romantically attract someone who is *already* in a romantic relationship—that is, stealing someone else's mate? This is known as **mate poaching,** and a study involving 16,954 participants in 53 countries showed that it was most common in Southern Europe, South America, Western Europe, and Eastern Europe, and relatively less frequent in Africa, South and Southeast Asia, and East Asia. In all regions studied, men were more likely to have attempted mate poaching and to be the victims of mate-poaching attempts by others. Across all regions of the world, mate poachers tended to be more extroverted, disagreeable, unconscientious, unfaithful, and erotophilic—being comfortable in talking about sex. In all regions, successful mate poachers were more open to new experiences, were sexually attractive, were not exclusive in their relationships, exhibited less sexual restraint, and were more erotophilic. And men and women in all regions who were the targets of mate-poaching attempts were more extroverted, open to experience, sexually attractive, erotophilic, and low on relationship exclusivity.

There were also some cultural differences in mate poaching. Cultures with more economic resources had higher rates of mate-poaching attempts. Also, in countries with more women than men, women were more likely to engage in mate poaching; this was not the case for men, however. And the sex differences in mate poaching tended to be smaller in cultures that were more gender egalitarian.

Thus, not only are there universal and culture-specific aspects of finding a mate; there also appear to be universal and culture-specific aspects to attracting someone else's mate. How does finding a mate, however, translate into falling in love?

Culture and Love

Love is one of the uniquely human emotions, and it is important because it aids in our finding potential mates and creating a social support system to buffer the stresses of life. Love, it is said, "is a many-splendored thing," and "love conquers all." In the United States, love seems to be a prerequisite to forming a long-term romantic relationship. But is that so in other cultures as well?

Maybe not. Many studies, in fact, have demonstrated specific cultural differences in attitudes about love. Ting-Toomey (1991), for instance, compared ratings of love commitment, disclosure maintenance, ambivalence, and conflict expression by 781 participants from France, Japan, and the United States. Love commitment was measured by ratings of feelings of attachment, belongingness, and commitment to the partner and the relationship; disclosure maintenance by ratings of feelings concerning the private self in the relationship; ambivalence by ratings of feelings of confusion or uncertainty regarding the partner or the relationship; and conflict expression by ratings of frequency of overt arguments and seriousness of problems. The French and the Americans had significantly higher ratings than the Japanese on love commitment and disclosure maintenance. The Americans also had significantly higher ratings than the Japanese on relational ambivalence. The Japanese and the Americans, however, had significantly higher ratings than the French on conflict expression.

Simmons, vom Kolke, and Shimizu (1986) examined attitudes toward love and romance among American, German, and Japanese students. The results indicated that romantic love was valued more in the United States and Germany than in Japan. These researchers explained this cultural difference by suggesting that romantic love is more highly valued in cultures with few strong, extended family ties, and less valued in cultures in which kinship networks influence and reinforce the relationship between marriage partners.

Many other studies document cultural differences in attitudes about love and romance. Furnham (1984), for instance, found that Europeans valued love more than do South Africans and Indians. Murstein, Merighi, and Vyse (1991) found that Americans tended to prefer friendships that slowly evolve into love, as well as relationships in which the lovers are caught up in an excited, panicky state, but that the French rated higher on love as characterized by altruistic generosity. Wang (1994) found that contrary to popular stereotypes, Italian males report less passionate love feelings in their relationships than American males. Landis and O'Shea (2000) studied 1,709 participants from Denmark, England, Israel, Canada, and five cities in the United States, and found that some aspects of passionate love were unique to a specific country, such as protective intimacy ("I would get jealous if I thought he/she were falling in love with someone else.") and tender intimacy ("I will love him/her forever.") for men and women in the United States, and realistic closeness ("If she/he were going through a difficult time, I would put away my concerns to help him/her out.") and idealistic closeness ("No one else could love her/him like I do.") for Danish men and women. Dion and Dion (1993a) found that Chinese and other Asian respondents were more friendship-oriented in their love relationships than were respondents from European backgrounds. Ellis, Kimmel, Diaz-Guerrero, Canas, and Bajo (1994) found that Mexicans rated love as less positive and less potent than Spaniards and Hispanic Americans.

Thus, it appears that, although love may be a universal and uniquely human emotion, it is valued differently in different cultures. Of course, there are many forms of love (Hatfield, 1988; Hatfield & Rapson, 1996; Sternberg, 1988), and we do not know exactly what kinds of cultural similarities and differences exist for what specific types of love. Future research will need to explore this interesting question.

Culture and Sex

Sex is, of course, necessary for human reproduction, and thus is a biological necessity for survival of the species. Yet it is associated with much psychological meaning, and thus with cultural meaning, especially before marriage. Many cultures of the world share some degree of normative attitudes toward sex, including a taboo on incest and a condemnation of adultery (Brown, 1991). Thus, there does appear to be some degree of universality in some types of norms regarding sex around the world.

There are also important cultural differences, especially regarding premarital sex and homosexuality. A 37-country study by Buss (1989), for instance, reported that people from many non-Western countries, such as China, India, Indonesia, Iran, and Taiwan, and Palestinian Arabs valued chastity very highly in a potential mate, whereas people in western European countries such as Sweden, Norway, Finland, the Netherlands, West Germany, and France attach little importance to prior sexual experience. And homosexuality is generally more accepted in cultures that tend to be industrialized, capitalistic, and affluent (Inglehart, 1998). Cultures also differ in how open there are about expressing sexuality in public, for example, displaying advertising for condoms (Jones, Forrest, Goldman, Henshaw, Lincoln et al., 1985).

Widmer, Treas, and Newcomb (1998) surveyed 33,590 respondents in 24 countries on their attitudes toward premarital sex, teen sex, extramarital sex, and homosexuality. Their findings indicated a widespread acceptance of premarital sex across the samples. Teen sex and extramarital sex, however, were not as accepted. And attitudes about homosexuality varied greatly across cultures. Widmer and colleagues then grouped the countries into those that had similar responses. One group was called the "Teen Permissives"; it included East and West Germany, Austria, Sweden, and Slovenia. A second group was called "Sexual Conservatives"; it included the United States, Ireland, Northern Ireland, and Poland. A third group was called "Homosexual Permissives"; it included Netherlands, Norway, Czech Republic, Canada, and Spain. And the fourth group was called "Moderates"; it included Australia, Great Britain, Hungary, Italy, Bulgaria, Russia, New Zealand, and Israel. Japan and the Philippines did not merge with any of the groups, and had their own unique attitudes toward sex.

Cultures also affect sex within marriage. Cultures with fewer resources and higher stress—especially insensitive or inconsistent parenting, physically harsh environments, or economic hardships—are associated with more insecure romantic attachments, and higher fertility rates (Schmitt, Alcalay, Allensworth, Allik, Ault, & Austers, 2004). There may be an evolutionary explanation for these findings: stressful environments may cause insecure attachments, which may be linked to short-term mating strategies—to reproduce early and often. This link may be seen today; as cultures become more affluent, birth rates tend to decline.

When extramarital sex occurs, do people of different cultures differ in their responses? Apparently not; jealousy appears to be a universal reaction to the infidelity of one's mate. There are interesting gender differences in the sources of infidelity; men appear to become jealous when they experience a loss of sexual exclusivity in their mates; women appear to become jealous when they experience a loss of emotional involvement in their mates, and this pattern has been found in a wide variety of cultures (Buss, Shackelford, Kirkpatrick, Choe, Lim, & Hasegawa, 1999; Fernandez, Sierra, Zubeidat, & Vera-Villarroel, 2006). Buss and Schmitt (1993) suggest that these universal gender differences are predictable on the basis of biological sex differences and evolutionary needs. Violations of emotional involvement for women threatens the care of offspring; violations of sexual exclusivity for men threatens their ability to reproduce and produce offspring.

Culture and Marriage

Marriage is an institutionalized relationship that publicly recognizes the long-term commitment that two people make to each other. About 90 percent of people in most societies get married, or whatever is the equivalent of married in their society (Carroll & Wolpe, 1996). And a study involving 17,804 participants in 62 cultures around the world found that 79 percent of the romantic attachments people had could be considered "secure"—that is, one in which both the self and the other are considered valuable and worthy of trust; they are characterized as being responsive, supportive, comfortable in their mutual interdependence (Schmitt et al., 2004). This suggests a large degree of normativeness around the world in the way people form romantic attachments with others. These findings should tell us that there is something universal in the fact that people need and want to make such commitments with someone else.

But there are cultural differences in the ways in which people around the world form romantic attachments and view the role of love in marriage. For example, individuals in South, Southeast, and East Asia tend to score higher on preoccupied romantic attachment, in which attachments to others are relatively more dependent on the value that they provide to others and that others provide to themselves (Schmitt et al., 2004). That is, they tend to strive more for the approval of highly valued others in romantic relationships.

In the United States today, there is decreasing pressure on people, especially women, to get married before a certain age or to have children. Yet there are many people in many other cultures of the world that still harbor many traditional values concerning marriage, including the belief that women should get married before a certain age, such as 25, and have children before 30. These values are at conflict within cultures and societies that are, at the same time, becoming more economically powerful. As the children of these cultures leave to visit and/or study in cultures such as the United States, those types of conflicts come to a head, especially for women, who on the one hand want to get an education, job, and career, and yet on the other feel the pressure from their families to get married, settle down, have children, and raise a family. Often these families who provide the financial support for their children to get an international education are perceived to not really value the education their children are receiving, especially if they insist on an early marriage and child-rearing.

Marriage also differs in different cultures on the perceived role of love. Levine, Sato, Hashimoto, and Verma (1995), for instance, asked students in India, Pakistan, Thailand, Mexico, Brazil, Japan, Hong Kong, the Philippines, Australia, England, and the United States to rate the importance of love for both the establishment and the maintenance of a marriage. Individualistic cultures were more likely to rate love as essential to the establishment of a marriage, and to agree that the disappearance of love is a sufficient reason to end a marriage. Countries with a large gross domestic product also showed this tendency—not surprising, given the high correlation between affluence and individualism. Also, countries with high marriage and divorce rates, and low fertility rates, assigned greater importance to romantic love. Divorce rates were highly correlated with the belief that the disappearance of love warranted the dissolution of a marriage.

Jankowiak and Fischer (1992) compared 186 traditional cultures on love, and showed that in every culture but one, young people reported falling passionately in love; experienced the euphoria and despair of passionate love; knew of poems, stories, and legends about famous lovers; and sang love songs. Nonetheless, this did not mean that the young people from these cultures could pursue these feelings of love and marry the person they fell in love with. Instead, in many of these cultures, arranged marriages were the norm.

Arranged marriages are quite common in many cultures of the world. In India, for instance, arranged marriages date back 6,000 years (Saraswathi, 1999). Sometimes marriages are arranged by parents far before the age at which the couple can even consider marriage. In other cases, marriage meetings are held between prospective couples, who may then date for a while to decide whether to get married or not. In these cultures, marriage is seen as more than just the union of two individuals, but rather as a union and alliance between two entire families (Dion & Dion, 1993b; Stone, 1990). Love between the two individuals is often not part of this equation but is something that should grow in the marriage relationship. People from these cultures often report that they "love the person they marry," not "marry the person they love."

In fact, Hatfield and Rapson (1996) report that getting married based on romantic love is a relatively new concept—about 300 years old in the West and much newer in non-Western cultures. With globalization, however, young people from these countries are opting for selecting their own mates. For instance, 40 percent of young people in India intend to find a marriage partner on their own (Sprecher & Chandak, 1992). This trend is currently reflected in other countries as well, such as Japan, China, Egypt, and Turkey (Arnett, 2001).

Intercultural Marriages

Marriage in any culture is not easy, because two people from two different backgrounds, and often two different cultures within a culture, come together to live, work, and play. And being together with anyone 24/7 is tough, and bound to bring about its own share of conflicts and struggles (hopefully along with the joy and love!). Any marriage requires work from both partners to be successful, regardless of how "successful" is defined.

This is especially true for intercultural marriages, in which the partners come from two different cultural backgrounds. Given the existence of cultural differences in attitudes toward love, interpersonal attraction, and marriage, and the fact that any marriage in any culture is not easy, it is no wonder that intercultural marriages bring with them their own special problems and issues. Studies of intercultural marriages (see Cottrell, 1990, for a review) have generally shown that conflicts in intercultural marriages arise in several major areas, including the expression of love and intimacy, the nature of commitment and attitudes toward the marriage itself, and approaches to child-rearing. Other potential sources of conflict include differences in perceptions of male–female roles, especially with regard to division of labor (McGoldrick & Preto, 1984; Romano, 1988), differences in domestic money management (Ho, 1984; Hsu, 1977; Kiev, 1973; McGoldrick & Preto, 1984), differences in perceptions of relationships with extended family (Cohen, 1982; Markoff, 1977), and differences in the definitions of marriage itself (Markoff, 1977).

It is no wonder that couples in intercultural marriages experience conflicts with regard to intimacy and love expression. As described in Chapter 8, people of different cultures vary considerably in their expression of basic emotions such as anger, frustration, and happiness. And as we have seen, cultures differ on the degree to which emotions such as love and intimacy are seen as important ingredients of a successful marriage. These differences arise from a fundamental difference in attitudes toward marriage. Americans tend to view marriage as a lifetime companionship between two individuals in love. People of many other cultures view marriage more as a partnership formed for succession (that is, for producing offspring) and for economic and social bonding. Love does not necessarily enter the equation for people in these cultures, at least in the beginning. And in fact many literatures, songs, and today, television and cinema dramas depict the heartbreak of the breakup of a love relationship in order for lovers to get married to someone else through an arranged marriage. With such fundamental differences in the nature of marriage across cultures, it is no wonder that intercultural marriages are often among the most difficult of relationships.

Sometimes the differences between two people involved in an intercultural marriage do not arise until they have children. Often, major cultural differences emerge around issues of child-rearing. This is no surprise, either, because of the enormous differences in socialization practices and the role of parenting in the development of culture, as discussed in Chapter 3. Although it has been a common belief that children of intracultural marriages have stronger ethnic identities than children of intercultural marriages, research does not tend to support this claim (for example, Parsonson, 1987). Children tend to develop strong or weak ethnic identities based not on their parents' similarities or differences, but on their upbringing, especially with regard to attitudes, values, and behaviors regarding their single or dual cultures. Children with stronger ethnic identities, however, are more likely to want to marry within their own ethnic group (Parsonson, 1987).

How can intercultural couples overcome these additional obstacles in their relationships to build successful marriages? Of course, communication is important in any relationship, and such communication is especially important in intercultural relationships (Atkeson, 1970). Ho (1984) has suggested that three types of adjustments help to resolve differences: capitulation, compromise, and coexistence. *Capitulation* refers to the ability and willingness to give up one's own cultural behaviors and accept the other's position occasionally. *Compromise* refers to finding a mutual point, with both partners partially giving up their positions and partially accepting each other's. *Coexistence* refers to the process by which both partners live with their respective differences by accepting each other "as they are" in their marriage.

Tseng (1977) offers some additional ways of dealing with intercultural relationships. Tseng's "alternating way" is one in which partners take turns in adapting their cultural behaviors. A "mixing way" is one in which partners take some behaviors and customs from both cultures and randomly introduce them into their marriage. "Creative adjustment" is when partners invent a completely new set of behavior patterns after deciding to give up their respective cultural norms.

There is yet another way of negotiating the trials and tribulations of intercultural marriage, which we will call the "context constructionistic" way. Cultural differences between two people will manifest themselves in specific contexts. One way for two people from different cultures to deal with these differences is to discuss the perspectives of both cultures in relation to each context in which there is a conflict or difference. The couple can then discuss the pros and cons of both perspectives in relation to their lives as a whole—work, family, children, and cultural and ethnic "balance"—and make functional decisions based on these discussions. In some cases, a couple may choose to go with one cultural perspective, in other cases, with the other perspective. The couple may choose to alternate perspectives, or to be creative and establish their own unique perspective on the situation, blending their cultural knowledge. In this fashion, the everyday negotiation of intercultural marriage is an interesting and exciting journey in which the couple as a unit must engage, rather than a "problem" to be dealt with.

In many ways, intercultural marriages are the prime example of intercultural relationships. For them to be successful, both partners need to be flexible, compromising, and committed to the relationship. If these three ingredients are in play, couples will often find ways to make their relationships work. Despite the difficulties, anecdotal evidence suggests that intercultural marriages are not necessarily associated with higher divorce rates than intracultural marriages. Perhaps it all comes down to how much both spouses are willing to work to negotiate differences, compromise, and stay together. Sounds like a good recipe for intracultural marriages as well.

CULTURE AND CONFORMITY, COMPLIANCE, AND OBEDIENCE

Conformity means yielding to real or imagined social pressure. **Compliance** is generally defined as yielding to social pressure in one's public behavior, even though one's private beliefs may not have changed. **Obedience** is a form of compliance that occurs when people follow direct commands, usually from someone in a position of authority.

Two of the best-known studies on conformity, compliance, and obedience are the Asch and Milgram studies. In his earliest experiments, Asch (1951, 1955, 1956) examined a subject's response to a simple judgment task after other "subjects" (actually experimental confederates) had all given the same incorrect response. For example, a subject would be placed in a room with others, shown objects (lines, balls, and so forth), and asked to make a judgment about the objects (such as relative sizes). The answer was often obvious, but subjects were asked to give their answers only after a number of experimental confederates had given theirs. The basic finding from these simple experiments was that, more often than not, subjects would give the wrong answer, even though it was obviously wrong, if the people answering before them had given that same wrong answer. Across studies and trials, group size and group unanimity were major influencing factors. Conformity peaked when the group contained seven people and was unanimous in its judgments (even though the judgments were clearly wrong).

In Asch's studies, compliance resulted from subtle, implied pressure. But in the real world, compliance can occur in response to explicit rules, requests, and commands. We can only imagine how forceful and pervasive group pressure to conform and comply are in the real world if they can operate in a simple laboratory environment among people unknown to the subject on a task that has relatively little meaning.

In Milgram's (1974) famous study, subjects were brought into a laboratory ostensibly to study the effects of punishment on learning. Subjects were instructed to administer shocks to another subject (actually an experimental confederate) when the latter gave the wrong response or no response. The shock meter was labeled from "Slight Shock" to "DANGER: Severe Shock," and the confederate's behaviors ranged from simple utterances of pain through pounding on the walls, pleas to stop, and then deathly silence. (No shock was actually administered.) Milgram reported that 65 percent of the subjects obeyed the commands of the experimenter and administered the most severe levels of shock.

The Asch experiments were rather innocuous in the actual content of the compliance (for example, judgments of the length of lines). The Milgram studies, however, clearly highlighted the potential negative and harmful effects of compliance and obedience. To this day, it stands as one of the best-known studies in American social psychology. Replication is unlikely to be attempted today because of restrictions based on ethics and university standards of conduct, but its findings speak for themselves on the power of group influence.

A number of cross-cultural studies do indeed show that people of other cultures view conformity, obedience, and compliance differently than Americans. Some studies have shown that Asian cultures in particular not only engage in conforming, compliant, and obedient behaviors to a greater degree than Americans, but also value conformity to a greater degree. For example, Punetha, Giles, and Young (1987) administered an extended Rokeach Value Survey to three groups of Asian subjects and one group of British subjects. The British subjects clearly valued individualistic items, such as independence and freedom, whereas the Asian subjects endorsed societal values, including conformity and obedience. Studies involving other Asian and American comparisons have generally produced the same results (Hadiyono and Hahn, 1985; Argyle, Henderson, Bond, Iizuka, and Contarello, 1986; Buck, Newton, and Muramatsu, 1984). And valuing conformity and obedience is not limited to Asian cultures. For instance, Cashmore and Goodnow (1986) demonstrated that Italians were more conforming than Anglo-Australians, and El-Islam (1983) documented cultural differences in conformity in an Arabian sample.

Bond and Smith (1996) conducted a meta-analysis of studies examining the effects of conformity across studies involving the types of tasks originally used by Asch. Analyzing 133 studies conducted in 17 different countries, they found that the magnitude of the effect of conformity was very large in some countries and very small in others, with a mean effect of moderate value. When they analyzed the relationship between the magnitude of the effect and characteristics of the studies, they found that conformity was higher when the majority that tried to influence the conforming participant was larger, and when there was a greater proportion of female participants. Conformity was also greater when the majority did not consist of outgroup members and when the stimuli were more ambiguous. Of particular note was the finding that effect size was significantly related to individualism–collectivism, with conformity higher in collectivistic countries than in individualistic ones.

Smith and Bond (1999) also reviewed nine studies that used the Milgram paradigm, conducted in the United States and eight other countries. The results of these studies indicated a broad range in the percentage of participants obeying the experimenter, ranging from a low of 16 percent among female students in Australia to a high of 92 percent in the Netherlands. These differences may reflect real cultural differences in obedience, but they may also reflect other types of differences, including differences in the meaning of the particular tasks used in the studies, the specific instructions given to the participants, and the nature of the confederate who supposedly received the shocks.

That conformity differs across cultures makes sense. Traditional American culture fosters individualistic values, endorsing behaviors and beliefs contrary to conformity. To conform in American culture is to be "weak" or somehow deficient. But many other cultures foster more conforming values; in those cultures, conformity, obedience, and compliance enjoy much higher status and a positive orientation. In these cultures, conformity is viewed not only as "good" but as necessary for the successful functioning of the culture, its groups, and the interpersonal relationships of its members. We need to ask ourselves why the best-known studies of conformity and obedience conducted in the United States are so negative in their orientation. Although the Asch studies are rather innocuous, the Milgram studies are clearly a powerful indictment of the potential negative consequences of obedience. Have any studies been conducted by American social psychologists that might show positive outcomes of conformity, compliance, or obedience? If not, perhaps we need to examine the possible biases of American social scientists in approaching these topics. We contend that conformity and obedience are important constructs in any social system as a way of reinforcing behaviors (Lachlan, Janik, & Slater, 2004); cultures, however, construct different meanings about it.

CULTURE AND COOPERATION

Cooperation refers to people's ability to work together toward common goals. Trust and cooperation are necessary for the efficient functioning and survival of any social group, human or animal. Yet humans differ from animals in important ways. Whereas cooperative behavior in nonhuman primates exists, it is generally limited to kin and reciprocating partners, and is virtually never extended to strangers; humans, on the other hand, give blood, volunteer, recycle, and are willing to incur costs to help even strangers in one-shot interactions (Silk, Brosnan, Vonk, Henrich, Povinello, Richardson, A. S., et al., 2005). Human cooperation, trust, and giving allows people to care for other people's children, even those of strangers, and to help out victims of tragedies, even if we do not know them. This does not happen in the nonhuman animal world. Human trust and cooperation appears to be based on unique cognitive abilities (see Chapter 1) that only humans have, including empathy and concern for the welfare of others (Silk et al., 2005), and memory (Pennisi, 2005); reciprocity and cooperation can be practiced only by those who can remember who was helpful and who was not.

A number of studies in the cross-cultural literature demonstrate differences between cultures in their values and attitudes about cooperation and in their cooperative behaviors. Domino (1992), for example, compared children from the People's Republic of China with children from the United States on a social values task. The task required the child to decide between two alternatives offering tokens to the child and an unspecified classmate. Basically, the choices involved receiving more tokens for oneself or receiving fewer tokens and allowing the classmate to receive more. Six different types of outcome preferences were distinguished: individualism, competition, equality, group enhancement or cooperation, competition and individualism, and equality and individualism. Across a series of trials, the most common preferences of American children were individualism (receiving many tokens for oneself) and competition (receiving as many more tokens than the other as possible). In contrast, the most common preferences of Chinese children were equality (equal division of tokens) and group enhancement (most number of tokens collectively for both individuals, irrespective of division). Domino interpreted these findings as supportive of the notion that the process of socialization in China is geared to promoting group solidarity and group consciousness.

An experiment by Wong and Hong (2005) demonstrated that differences in cooperative behavior were linked to culture. They primed Chinese American bicultural individuals with either Chinese or American cultural icons before the participants played a game called Prisoner's Dilemma, in which participants can cooperate or not (defect) with their partners. When the Chinese culture was primed, the bicultural participants cooperated more with their friends, compared with when the American culture was primed. These findings reinforce the notion that individualistic cultures such as that in the United States foster competition, while collectivistic cultures foster cooperation.

But is the source of the difference cultural? One of the most well-known lines of research on cooperation and culture is that of Yamagishi and colleagues. In one study, Yamagishi (1986) categorized Japanese participants as high and low trusters; they then participated in an experiment in which they could cooperate with others by giving money to them, either with or without a sanctioning system that provided for punishments. The conditions, therefore, were the presence or absence of the sanctioning system. The results indicated that high trusters did indeed cooperate more than low trusters without the sanctioning system; when the sanctioning system was in effect, however, low trusters cooperated more than did the high trusters. Yamagishi (1988) then replicated this study in the United States and compared the American and Japanese responses. He found the same results for Americans as he did for the Japanese; when there was no sanctioning system, high-trusting Americans cooperated more than low-trusting Americans. When there was a sanctioning system, the findings reversed. Moreover, there were no differences between the Americans and the Japanese when the sanctioning system was in effect. This suggests, therefore, that the greater cooperation observed in Japanese culture exists because of the sanctioning system within which individuals exist; when Americans were placed in that same type of system, they behaved in similar ways.

Mashima, Yamagishi, and Macy (2004) compared American and Japanese students who played Prisoner's Dilemma with both Americans and Japanese. They found no differences in cooperative behavior between American and Japanese players, and no differences as a function of ingroup (same-country partner) or outgroup (other-country partner).

But these findings may be limited to specific types of behaviors and targets. Allik and Realo (2004), for instance, examined the relationship between individualism and social capital across the states in the United States and across 42 cultures around the world. Social capital was broadly defined as interpersonal trust, civic engagement, and time spent with friends. The results were clear: both states in the United States and countries around the world that were more individualistic (less collectivistic) were associated with greater social capital; people are more trusting of others and engaged with them (see Figure 14.1). Kemmelmeier, Jambor, and Letner (2006) took this research a step further, and showed that in the United States, states that were more individualistic also had higher rates of charitable giving and volunteerism.

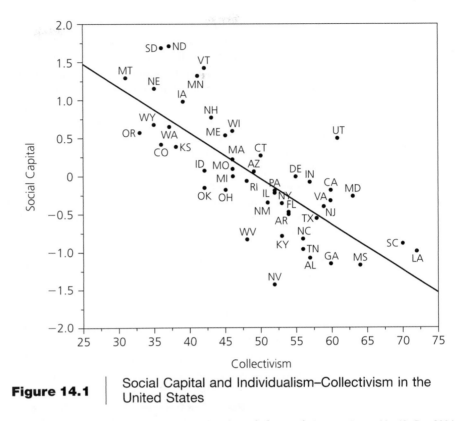

Figure 14.1 | Social Capital and Individualism–Collectivism in the United States

van de Vijver, F.J.R., *Journal of Cross-Cultural Psychology*, vol. 35, no. 1, pp. 29–49, Jan 2004.

Thus, cultural differences in cooperative behavior may exist, but these are most likely related to the specific situational constraints that individuals are in at the time when a behavior occurs. Some contexts foster some types of cooperative behavior with some people; others do not. Of course, culture provides the environment that defines the situational constraints and contexts. The effects of culture, therefore, are specific to type of behavior and context.

CULTURE AND INTERGROUP RELATIONS

Ingroups and Outgroups

Individuals in all societies make distinctions among the individuals with whom they interact; making such distinctions, in fact, is a universal necessity, because they are necessary conditions for both individual and group functioning, and ultimately for survival. Many different types of such social distinctions can and should be made; however, one type of meaningful social relationship that people of all societies make is known as ingroups and outgroups (Brewer & Kramer, 1985; Messick & Mackie, 1989; Tajfel, 1982). **Ingroup relationships** are characterized by a history of shared experiences, and an anticipated future, that produce a sense of intimacy, familiarity, and trust. Outgroup relationships lack these qualities. In all societies, enculturation involves learning who are ingroups and who are not. **Outgroup relationships,** however, are associated with greater ambiguity and uncertainty, precisely because there is no intimacy, familiarity, shared experiences or history, or an anticipated future.

Differentiating between ingroups and outgroups is important for everyone in all societies and cultures. The ability to make this differentiation is probably rooted in our evolutionary need to distinguish between friends and foes—rivals for mates, food, and other resources. This differentiation leads to interesting psychological consequences. For instance, people tend to expect greater similarities between themselves and their ingroups, relative to their outgroups (Robbins & Krueger, 2005). People also tend to attribute more uniquely human emotions, such as contentment, delight, or resignation, to their ingroups, but more primary, basic emotions such as happiness or anger to outgroups (Cortes, Demoulin, Rodriguez, Rodrigues, & Lyens, 2005), as well as values and adjectives thought to be uniquely human and to describe human essence (Haslam, Bain, Douge, Lee, & Bastian, 2005).

One of the important functions of culture is to ascribe different meanings to ingroup and outgroup relationships (Triandis, Bontempo, Villareal, Asai, & Lucca, 1988), and these differences produce many cultural differences in the specific nature and function of self–ingroup and self–outgroup relationships. Below we discuss several ways in which these differences occur.

Structure and Format of Ingroup/Outgroup Relationships   We have already touched on how people of different cultures can differ in their self–ingroup and self–outgroup relationships. Our own observations suggest that people of different cultures may not consider the same types of people and relationships when defining ingroups and outgroups. Just because we consider a certain type of person (a friend at school, a work colleague) an ingroup (or outgroup) member, we cannot assume that people from another culture will interpret and act on those relationships in exactly the same way.

Cultures differ in the formation and structure of self–ingroup and self–outgroup relationships in other ways as well. In North American culture, ingroup and outgroup membership is stable, no matter what we are talking about, to whom we are talking, or where we are talking. Our friends are our friends no matter what. But to someone in another culture, some people may constitute an ingroup in one circumstance or situation, but the same people may constitute an outgroup in another. For example, a study by Harrison, Stewart, Myambo, and Teveraishe (1995) demonstrated interesting psychological differences in how people perceive their ingroups. In this study, adolescents in Zimbabwe and the United States completed a 33-item test that measured six aspects of social relationships: (1) reliable alliance, (2) enhancement or worth, (3) affection, (4) instrumental help and guidance, (5) companionship and social integration, and (6) intimacy. The researchers added three other dimensions: (7) conflict, (8) satisfaction, and (9) discipline. The participants completed this test about their relationship with six target individuals: mother, father, favorite relative, teacher, best friend, and favorite sibling. Zimbabweans perceived social support as being provided by a variety of persons in their social network. The Americans, however, perceived social support as being provided primarily by parents and best friends. Also, the Zimbabweans perceived their social support network as providing them with intimacy; the Americans, on the other hand, perceived their social support network as basically providing them with affection. Again, these differences highlight the different ways in which people of different cultures can perceive ingroups and outgroups, and the different psychological meanings attributed to them. These differences are related to differences in cultural values: Zimbabwean culture places a higher value on relationships, whereas American culture places a higher value on individuality and uniqueness.

The Meaning of Ingroup/Outgroup Relationships   Self–ingroup and self–outgroup relationships differ in individualistic and collectivistic cultures (Triandis et al., 1988), and these differences in the meaning of ingroup and outgroup relationships produce differences in the types of behaviors people engage in when interacting with others. In individualistic cultures, such as that in the United States, people often belong to multiple ingroups. Many Americans belong to several ingroups—music groups, sports groups, church groups, social groups, and so forth. Children may belong to football teams during football season, basketball teams during basketball season, and baseball teams during baseball season. They may take swimming lessons, take piano or violin lessons, belong to Boy or Girl Scouts, and generally just be the busiest people around. In contrast, members of collectivistic cultures, including many Asian and South American cultures, belong to fewer ingroups. They do not belong to all the different sports, music, and social groups that people in individualistic cultures do.

This difference between individualistic and collectivistic cultures in ingroup membership has important consequences for the degree of commitment people have to different groups. In general, in exchange for belonging to fewer groups, people in collectivistic cultures have greater commitments to the groups to which they belong. They also identify more with the groups to which they belong; that is, the groups themselves become an integral part of each individual's self-concept and identity. This makes sense because, by definition, collectivistic cultures depend on groups to a much greater degree, and subjugating personal goals in favor of collective goals is a necessity.

Members of individualistic cultures do not necessarily identify with their ingroups as much as people from collectivistic cultures. They have fewer commitments to their ingroups and move much more easily from ingroup to ingroup. Groups take on special importance in collectivistic cultures, but the same degree of importance does not attach to group membership in individualistic cultures.

It follows that collectivistic cultures require a greater degree of harmony, cohesion, and cooperation within their ingroups and place greater burdens on individuals to identify with the group and conform to group norms. Sanctions usually exist for nonconformity. Individualistic cultures depend less on groups and more on the uniqueness of their individuals. The pursuit of personal goals rather than collective ones is of primary importance. As a result, individualistic cultures require less harmony and cohesion within groups and place less importance on conformity of individuals to group norms.

These differences in the meaning of self–ingroup relationships between individualistic and collectivistic cultures have consequences for behavior. In collectivistic cultures, for example, we would expect people to make more individual sacrifices for their ingroups in pursuit of group goals. We would expect to see people trying harder to cooperate with one another, even if it means that the individual must suppress his or her own feelings, thoughts, behaviors, or goals to maintain harmony and cohesion. We would expect people to try to find ways of agreeing with each other, downplaying and minimizing interpersonal differences for the sake of harmony.

Self–ingroup relationships in individualistic cultures have different consequences for behavior. In these cultures, we would expect people to make fewer sacrifices of their own individual goals, needs, and desires for the sake of a common good. We would expect people to be more expressive of their own feelings, attitudes, and opinions, without as much fear or worry about the consequences for group harmony or cohesion. We would expect people to bring up interpersonal concerns, problems, and conflicts more freely.

Not only do self–ingroup relationships differ between individualistic and collectivistic cultures, but self–outgroup relationships also differ. In collectivistic cultures, the primary focus of attention is on ingroup relationships. For that reason, relationships with outgroup people are marked by a relative lack of concern. To the degree that members of collectivistic cultures focus on harmony, cohesion, and cooperation in ingroup relations, they tend to exhibit distancing, aloofness, and even discrimination with regard to self–outgroup relationships. The opposite is true in individualistic cultures, in which people are more likely to treat outgroup persons more equally, with relatively less distinction between ingroups and outgroups. Members of individualistic cultures engage in positive, relationship-building behaviors with outgroup others that members of collectivistic cultures would reserve only for ingroup others. These concepts are summarized in Table 14.1.

Ethnocentrism and Prejudice

We define **ethnocentrism** as the tendency to view the world through one's own cultural filters. With this definition, and knowledge about how we acquire those filters, it follows that just about everyone in the world is ethnocentric. That is, everyone learns a certain way of behaving, and in doing so learns a certain way of perceiving and interpreting the behaviors of others. This way of perceiving and making interpretations about others is a normal consequence of growing up in society. A large goal of enculturation (Chapter 3) is learning what is normal, right, appropriate, and good. By doing so, however, we also learn what is abnormal, incorrect, inappropriate, and bad. And just as we learn

Table 14.1 | Self–Ingroup and Self–Outgroup Relationship Differences as a Function of Individualism and Collectivism

Type of Culture	Characteristics
In individualistic cultures . . .	1. People have more ingroups. 2. People are not as attached to any single ingroup, because there are numerous ingroups to which they can be attached. 3. Survival of the individuals and the society is more dependent on the successful and effective functioning of individuals rather than groups. 4. People make relatively fewer distinctions between ingroups and outgroups.
In collectivistic cultures . . .	1. People have fewer ingroups. 2. People are very attached to the ingroups to which they belong. 3. Survival of the individuals and the society is more dependent on the successful and effective functioning of the groups rather than individuals. 4. People make greater distinctions between ingroup and outgroup others.

Adapted from Triandis et al, 1988.

how to attach these labels to our own behavior, we use those same standards to judge the behavior of others. Herein lies the beginnings of ethnocentrism in all of us. In this sense, ethnocentrism per se is neither bad nor good; it merely reflects the state of affairs—that we all have our cultural filters on when we perceive others.

Ethnocentrism is closely related to the construct known as **prejudice,** which refers to the tendency to prejudge others on the basis of their group membership. Prejudice can have two components: a cognitive (thinking) component, and an affective (feeling) component. Stereotypes (more below) form the basis of the cognitive component of prejudice—the stereotypic beliefs, opinions, and attitudes one harbors toward others. The affective component comprises one's personal feelings toward other groups of people. These feelings may include anger, contempt, resentment, or disdain, or even compassion, sympathy, and closeness. Although the cognitive and affective components are often related, they need not be, and may actually exist independently of each other within the same person. That is, a person may have feelings about a particular group of people without being able to specify a stereotype about them; and a person may have stereotypic beliefs about others that are detached from their feelings.

Ethnocentrism and prejudice can be explicit or implicit. **Explicit prejudice** refers to prejudice that is verbalized and thus made public. Conducting studies on prejudice using explicit measures, however, is difficult, because respondents may be biased to respond in socially desirable or politically correct ways (see Chapter 2), thus distorting findings. Therefore, researchers who have examined studies on explicit prejudice over the past half century have concluded that explicit prejudice is actually on the decline (Wittenbrink, Judd, & Park, 1997).

But is it really? In recent years an interesting measure has been developed that supposedly measures prejudice implicitly. **Implicit prejudice** refers to prejudicial attitudes, values, or beliefs that are unspoken and perhaps even outside conscious awareness. This measure is called the Implicit Association Test (IAT) (Greenwald, McGhee, & Schwartz, 1998). Participants are generally shown pairs of stimuli, such as faces of European American or African American individuals and adjectives such as good and bad, and are asked to make a simple evaluation of the pair (such as whether the pairing is accurate or not). Implicit attitudes are measured by the amount of time respondents take to make their judgments; faster times supposedly reflect stronger implicit beliefs. Research has shown that results from both explicit measures (e.g., questionnaires) and implicit measures (like the IAT) are correlated, but to a very small degree (Hoffman, Gawronski, Gschwendner, Le, & Schmitt, 2005).

Pena, Sidanius, and Sawyer (2004) used both implicit and explicit measures to determine prejudice toward whites and blacks in four countries—the United States, Cuba, Dominican Republic, and Puerto Rico. They found that, despite the fact that there were no differences in attitudes on the explicit measure, on the implicit measure whites were judged more favorably than blacks by all groups, which included both white and black participants (see Figure 14.2). This finding is interesting because the implicit racial prejudice against blacks was found among Latin American participants with discernible African heritage as well.

Other research has demonstrated that prejudicial attitudes and judgments are quick, automatic, and often based on physical features such as in the face (Blair, Judd, & Fallman, 2004; Maddox, 2005). Individuals from racial and ethnic groups other than one's own are often associated unconsciously with fear responses, among both white and black Americans (Olsson, Ebert, Banaji, & Phelps, 2005). And ethnocentric, prejudicial attitudes are more strongly related to the strength of one's own ingroup attitudes (Duckitt, Callaghan, & Wagner, 2005).

Origins of and Factors Contributing to Prejudice   There are probably many factors that contribute to the apparent universality of ethnocentrism and prejudice. One, for example, may be that they are the outcomes of social biology and evolution (see, for example, van den Berghe, 1981). This argument suggests that sentiments about ethnicity and race are logical extensions of kinship sentiment—that is, the favoring of kin over nonkin. Kinship sentiments are biologically and evolutionarily functional, increasing the likelihood of one's own genes' being transmitted to future generations. Because racial and ethnic groups may be viewed as extensions of kin, these sentiments may predispose people to behave more favorably to such kin. If kinship sentiments do apply to

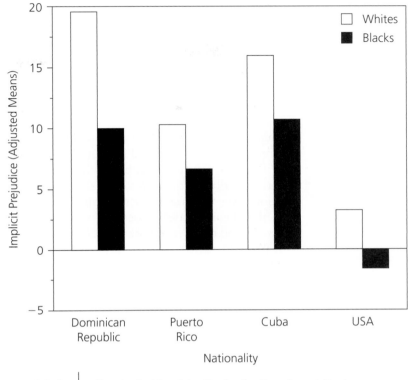

Figure 14.2 | Symbols Used to Evaluate Good and Bad

van de Vijver, F. J. R., *Journal of Cross-Cultural Psychology*, vol. 35, no. 6, Nov. 2004, p. 754. Copyright © 2004 by Fons J. R. van de Vijver. Reprinted by Permission of Sage Publications, Inc.

ethnicity and race, this argument continues, prejudice and discrimination may indeed be fundamental and inevitable.

Theories concerning intergroup conflict and power also explain ethnocentrism and prejudice (Duckitt, 1992; Healey, 1998). These suggest that the competition that naturally occurs among groups in any society—whether for power, prestige, status, or wealth—produces prejudicial and discriminatory thoughts, feelings, and actions among both those in power (the "haves") and those without (the "have-nots"). Such prejudice and discrimination on both sides, but especially on the part of the haves, can serve as a justification to exploit the have-nots. As such, prejudice and discrimination require an identifying variable or characteristic to which they can become attached, race, ethnicity, or social class is often used as that marker (see also Mirande, 1985; Moore, 1988).

Social and cultural factors also play a role, in that society may promote ideological prejudice and institutional discrimination in order to impose inferior status on some groups. This inferior status, in turn, reinforces the ideological prejudice and institutional discrimination, which themselves further reinforce the inferior status. Children growing up in such societies, whether as members of the "inferior" or the "superior" group, become enculturated in these ways of thinking, feeling, and acting, which become a part of their own operating culture, thus ensuring the reenactment of this cycle of exploitation. Jane Elliot, a schoolteacher in the 1960s, is well known for her Blue-Eyed/Brown-Eyed classroom exercises, in which she demonstrated how quickly children can learn to become discriminatory simply based on the messages they are told about a particular group. In this exercise, she divided the children into brown-eyed and blue-eyed groups and told one group they were superior, more talented, and better than the other. She found that in a short time the children actually took on the stereotypes of these groups and, furthermore, began to act in discriminatory ways toward one another.

Other theories have focused on aspects of personality that contribute to the formation and maintenance of prejudice and discrimination. Of particular note is the work on the relationship between authoritarian personality and prejudice (Adorno, Frenkel-Brunswick, Levinson, & Sanford, 1950, cited in Healey, 1998). This work suggests that prejudicial thoughts and feelings and discriminatory behaviors are an integral part of authoritarian personalities, and that people with such personalities in fact require prejudicial thoughts and feelings to function effectively in their lives and in society. More recent research, however, suggests a more precise relationship between authoritarianism and prejudice. Verkuyten and Hagendoorn (1998), for example, conducted two studies that examined the interaction of self-categorization, authoritarian personality, ingroup stereotypes, and prejudicial attitudes. Participants were instructed to focus on themselves either as unique individuals (personal identity condition) or as members of a larger group (national identity condition). They also completed an authoritarian personality questionnaire, provided data about their stereotypes regarding their own group, and rated three different outgroups in terms of prejudicial attitudes. The results indicated that authoritarian personality predicted prejudicial attitudes only when the participants focused on their personal identities. When participants focused on their national identities, their ingroup stereotypes predicted their prejudicial attitudes, but individual differences on the authoritarian measure did not. These findings suggest that personality variables may be salient only when the reference for prejudicial thought is oneself as an individual, and not as a member of a larger group.

In 1965, Campbell and Levine (cited in Seelye & Brewer, 1970) suggested that a number of psychological factors contribute to ethnocentrism. On the individual level, they cited variables such as ingroup loyalty, ethnocentric hostility, authoritarianism, rigidity, self-esteem, and extent or frequency of contact with outgroup members. They tested the relationship between these variables and acculturation in a study of Americans who were living in Guatemala. Data were collected in open-ended interviews that covered many aspects of daily life, as well as attitudes, opinions, beliefs, and behaviors. They then related all the variables collectively to acculturation to Guatemalan life. They concluded that "actual contact with the Guatemalan culture, especially to the extent that it increases the individual's sense of security within the new culture and reduces his commitment to the original ingroup, has more impact on adaptation to the culture than attitudinal variables" (p. 154). Their findings suggest the important role of emotion, self, and values in the formation of ethnocentrism discussed earlier in this chapter, as well as their role in developing flexibility in one's ethnocentrism.

Other studies, however, suggest that exposure to differences can lead to negative attitudes and emotions. Vrij and Winkel (1994), for example, showed Dutch police officers slides of either black (Surinamer) or white (Dutch) actors, supposedly being interrogated about a crime, and asked for their impressions. In addition to skin color and appearance, the researchers manipulated accent, fluency, and speech style to correspond to either the Surinamer or Dutch individual. The results indicated that speech style and fluency of the Surinamers were both related to more negative impressions of nervousness, unpleasantness, and suspiciousness. Thus, differences evoked more negative attitudes than did similarities.

Clearly there are many factors that contribute to ethnocentrism and prejudice. This fact makes dealing with them very difficult, because they are produced and reinforced by multiple sources, some of them very deep-seated, long-term, and possibly even genetically based.

Stereotypes

Stereotypes are generalized images that we have about groups of people, particularly about their underlying psychological characteristics or personality traits (Lee, Jussin, & McCauley, 1995). Stereotypes can be either positive or negative. For example, a common positive stereotype is that Asians are hardworking, the "model minority." Another positive stereotype is that Germans are industrious and scientifically minded. Stereotypes can be generally true or completely false. Stereotypes based on some degree of "factual" observation are called sociotypes (Triandis, 1994). But stereotypes can also be totally baseless. Because stereotypes can be perpetuated without direct observation of the behaviors of others, some stereotypes have no factual connection to the target group. Even when we convince ourselves that a stereotype is based on direct observations, we have to question the validity of those observations and the interpretations based on them because of the cultural and psychological biases inherent in those processes. And, people hold stereotypes about their own groups as well as about other groups. Stereotypes about one's own group are called **autostereotypes;** stereotypes about other groups are called **hetero-stereotypes.** In fact, there is often a considerable degree of overlap between a group's autostereotypes and the heterostereotypes that others hold about that group. Iwao and Triandis (1993), for example, asked Japanese and American undergraduate students to respond to three scenarios describing conflicts among individuals and to rate stereotypes of Americans and Japanese. When respondents from the two different cultures were similar in their interpretations of an episode, the relationship between autostereotypes and heterostereotypes was high; when they were dissimilar in their interpretations, the relationship was low. The Japanese viewed themselves as passively accepting inconsistencies between their public and private selves, acting according to group norms, whereas Americans tried to reduce the discrepancy between their private and public selves. Similar findings have been reported elsewhere also (Nichols & McAndrew, 1984; Walkey & Chung, 1996).

The Content of Stereotypes   A number of studies spanning many years have examined the content of stereotypes. In one of the oldest and most often cited studies, Katz and Braly (1933) gave undergraduate students at Princeton University a list of adjectives and asked them to select the traits they considered representative of 10 different racial/ethnic groups. The 12 traits most frequently assigned to each group by the students are shown in Table 14.2. This study was followed up on the same university campus in 1951 (Gilbert, 1951) and again in 1967 (Karlins, Coffman, & Walters, 1969). The researchers found a number of surprising changes over the years, both in stereotypes and in students' willingness to ascribe stereotypic traits to the various groups. Other researchers have conducted similar studies of American university students, using similar methods (for example, Clark & Person, 1982; Wood & Chesser, 1994). The most recent study replicating and extending the original Princeton study reports that most of the stereotypes of the various ethnic and national groups have changed into more favorable stereotypes. The greatest change in stereotype content was for African Americans (Madon, Guyll, Aboufadel, Montiel, Smith, Palumbo, & Jussim, 2001).

People in all cultures have stereotypes of others, and in many cases, there are many commonalities in these stereotypes, even across cultures (Nichols & McAndrew, 1984; Smith, Griffith, Griffith, & Steger, 1980; Forgas & O'Driscoll, 1984; Walkey & Chung, 1996; Williams & Best, 1994). There is often ingroup bias in one's stereotypes, with the exception of white Americans, who have been demonstrated to have ingroup derogation (Burton, Greenberger, & Hayward, 2005). Having stereotypes, therefore, many be a universal phenomenon, and the content of many stereotypes may also share some universal features. But where do stereotypes come from?

The Origins of Stereotypes   In our view, stereotypes are products of normal, everyday psychological processes, including selective attention, attribution, concept formation, and memory. For example, the *cocktail party phenomenon* illustrates how selective attention may contribute to stereotypes. People can often hear their own names across the room at a party even though myriad other sounds are occurring at the same time. One study reported that people who believe an individual's characteristics are relatively fixed traits tend to pay more attention to stereotypic-consistent information than do people who believe an individual's characteristics are malleable, which may work to reinforce stereotypic thinking in the former group and hinder revising their stereotypes (Plaks, Stroessner, Dweck, & Sherman, 2001).

Table 14.2 | The 12 Traits Most Frequently Assigned to Various Racial and National Groups by 100 Princeton Students

Trait	Frequency	Trait	Frequency	Trait	Frequency
Germans		Honest	32	Aggressive	20
Scientifically minded	78	Very religious	29	Straightforward	19
Industrious	65	Industrious	21	Practical	19
Stolid	44	Extremely nationalistic	21	Sportsmanlike	19
Intelligent	32	Superstitious	18	**Chinese**	
Methodical	31	Quarrelsome	14	Superstitious	34
Extremely nationalistic	24	Imaginative	13	Sly	29
Progressive	16	Aggressive	13	Conservative	29
Efficient	16	Stubborn	13	Tradition-loving	26
Jovial	15	**English**		Loyal to family ties	22
Musical	13	Sportsmanlike	53	Industrious	18
Persistent	11	Intelligent	46	Meditative	18
Practical	11	Conventional	34	Reserved	17
Italians		Tradition-loving	31	Very religious	15
Artistic	53	Conservative	30	Ignorant	15
Impulsive	44	Reserved	29	Deceitful	14
Passionate	37	Sophisticated	27	Quiet	13
Quick-tempered	35	Courteous	21	**Japanese**	
Musical	32	Honest	20	Intelligent	45
Imaginative	30	Industrious	18	Industrious	43
Very religious	21	Extremely nationalistic	18	Progressive	24
Talkative	21	Humorless	17	Shrewd	22
Revengeful	17	**Jews**		Sly	20
Physically dirty	13	Shrewd	79	Quiet	19
Lazy	12	Mercenary	49	Imitative	17
Unreliable	11	Industrious	48	Alert	16
Negroes		Grasping	34	Suave	16
Superstitious	84	Intelligent	29	Neat	16
Lazy	75	Ambitious	21	Treacherous	13
Happy-go-lucky	38	Sly	20	Aggressive	13
Ignorant	38	Loyal to family ties	15	**Turks**	
Musical	26	Persistent	13	Cruel	47
Ostentatious	26	Talkative	13	Very religious	26
Very religious	24	Aggressive	12	Treacherous	21
Stupid	22	Very religious	12	Sensual	20
Physically dirty	17	**Americans**		Ignorant	15
Naïve	14	Industrious	48	Physically dirty	15
Slovenly	13	Intelligent	47	Deceitful	13
Unreliable	12	Materialistic	33	Sly	12
Irish		Ambitious	33	Quarrelsome	12
Pugnacious	45	Progressive	27	Revengeful	12
Quick-tempered	39	Pleasure-loving	26	Conservative	12
Witty	38	Alert	23	Superstitious	11
		Efficient	21		

Katz & Braly, 1933.

A **concept** is a mental category we use to classify events, objects, situations, behaviors, or even people with respect to what we perceive as common properties. (Cultures differ on exactly what these common properties may be; this matter was discussed more fully in Chapter 5.) We use these common properties to aid us in classification or **categorization,** which refers to the process by which psychological concepts are grouped together. We form concepts so that we can evaluate information, make decisions, and act accordingly. It is far easier and more efficient to create concepts or categories of information and to evaluate and act on those categories than it is to process each individual item. In psychology, the study of concept formation involves examining how people classify or categorize events, objects, situations, and people into concepts. Concept formation and categorization provide us with a way to organize the diversity of the world around us into a finite number of categories. Those categories, in turn, are based on particular properties of the objects that we perceive or deem to be similar in some psychologically meaningful way. For example, we may classify all objects of a certain color together, all types of facial expressions representing a particular emotion together, and so on. Once such concepts have formed, we can access the individual stimulus through the category and gather information about that stimulus based on that category.

Social identity theory (Tajfel & Turner, 1986) is helpful in understanding stereotyping and prejudice. According to this theory, we categorize people into social groups and place ourselves within a category. We are motivated to positively evaluate our own social group (ingroup) in comparison to other groups (outgroups) in order to maintain a positive social identity. Thus, according to this perspective, stereotyping and prejudice may grow out of the desire to attain or maintain a positive social identity.

Attributions refer to this process by which we infer the causes of our own and other people's behavior (Chapter 13), and these help to create and reinforce stereotypes. For instance, in a study of junior–high-school students, girls were less likely than boys to attribute their academic success to high ability, but were more likely than boys to attribute failure to low ability (Stipek & Gralinski, 1991). These attributions could reinforce the stereotypes these adolescents have about appropriate gender roles and expectations.

Emotions are an integral and important part of our normal, everyday lives. Emotions reinforce important cultural concepts, and we have very complex emotional reactions to people of different groups (Cottrell & Neuberg, 2005). Forgas and his colleagues have reported an interesting and important line of research on the role of emotion in person perception, intergroup discrimination, and stereotype judgments. This research suggests the existence of mood-congruent bias in such judgments of others. In one study, for example, Forgas and Moylan (1991) induced happy, sad, or neutral moods in participants, who then formed impressions about Asians or Caucasians interacting with same-race or other-race partners. Participants who were happy had more positive judgments of the target persons; participants who were sad had more negative judgments. In addition, the degree of influence of mood on judgment was larger when the participants were judging mixed-race dyads. On the basis of these and similar findings (for example, Forgas & Bower, 1987; Forgas & Fiedler, 1996), Forgas has suggested that the role of emotion or mood in these types of judgments may be greatest when participants engage in substantive processing, which requires them to select, learn, and interpret novel stimuli and to relate this information to preexisting knowledge (for a review of this affect infusion model, see Forgas, 1992, 1994). Forgas (1994) also suggests, however, that stereotypic judgments of others are probably the least affected by emotion or mood because these judgments involve a direct access strategy—the direct retrieval of preexisting information.

All of the psychological processes discussed here interact to make stereotypes an inevitable aspect of our psychological life. Actually, as general categories of mental concepts, stereotypes are invaluable aids, helping us keep information about the world organized in our mental representations. We have such categorical representations about many objects in the world, and there is no way we could keep track of the world without them. Categorical representations of people happen to be called stereotypes.

As a special type of category—that is, having to do with people—stereotypes are important in helping us interact effectively with, or act as a hindrance to interaction with, others in our world. The problem is that it is relatively easy for negative stereotypes to develop, because our own cultural upbringing, cultural filters, and possibly inherent ethnocentrism and prejudice create a set of expectations in us about the behaviors and traits of others. When we observe people from a different cultural background, we are often exposed to behaviors, activities, or situations that do not match our initial expectations based on our own cultural backgrounds. These observations can lead to negative attributions about the causes of those events or the underlying intentions or psychological characteristics of the actors being observed. Because such events are unexpected, they often require what Forgas (1994) would call "substantive processing," which is the type of processing most affected by induced emotion. If the emotion induced at the time is negative, which is a natural reaction to our witnessing something outside of our expectations, then that negative emotion will be more likely to contribute to negatively valenced attributions about the other person. Such negatively valenced attributions can form the core of a mental concept that may then be placed in a category of such people. This negative attribution will also have a reinforcing effect on the value and expectation system that began the process. The result is a negative stereotype.

Once developed, stereotypes are easily reinforced. Our expectations change according to our stereotypes. We may selectively attend to events that appear to support our stereotypes, ignoring, albeit unconsciously, events and situations that challenge those stereotypes (Johnston, Hewstone, Pendry, & Frankish, 1994); that is, it is easy to vindicate our stereotypic ways of thinking. For instance, Lyons and Kashima (2001) found that when people were presented with stereotypical and nonstereotypical information about a certain group (in this case, football players), they tended to remember and communicate to other people the stereotypical information rather than the nonstereotypical. Our negative attributions may be reenacted, thus reinforcing the negative stereo-types held as categorical representations of that group of people.

Even when events occur that are contrary to our stereotypic beliefs, we selectively do not attend to them, or come up with unique attributional pro-cesses to convince ourselves that our stereotype is correct. We may suggest that the observed event was a fluke or that the person observed was not a good representative of the group to which the stereotype applies. Such dismissals can occur quickly, with little conscious thought or effort, and are resistant to infusion of emotion at the time.

Stereotypes can also be created and perpetuated in individuals merely by communication of verbal labels from generation to generation, with no actual interaction with the people who are the target of the stereotype (Brislin, 1993). Research suggests that stereotypes that are most communicable (most easily talked about) are most likely to persist over time. An understanding of the communicability of stereotypes is helpful in predicting the maintenance and modification in the contents of stereotypes of real groups in the real world (Schaller, Conway, & Tanchuk, 2002).

Stereotypes can be created and reinforced by television, movies, magazines, and other media. For example, gender and class stereotypes are reinforced in popular American television shows (Croteau & Hoynes, 2000). Men are more likely than women to be portrayed as having high-status, traditionally male jobs (such as doctors or lawyers) and are less likely to be shown in the home. Fathers in working-class families are usually portrayed as incompetent yet lovable buffoons (for example, Al Bundy, Homer Simpson), while middle-class fathers are depicted as competent at their jobs and as parents (as in *The Cosby Show* and *The Brady Bunch*) (Butsch, 1992). These portrayals may reinforce stereotypes we have of individuals from different class backgrounds. In another example, Taylor and Stern's (1997) analysis of 1,300 prime-time television advertisements shows that Asians are overrepresented in business settings and underrepresented in home settings and family or social relationships, which, they argue, feeds into the stereotype of the successful model minority.

It is important to distinguish between stereotype activation and application (Bargh, 1996; Devine, 1989; Gilbert & Hixon, 1991). Well-learned stereotypes are activated automatically (Blair, 2001), but whether people apply the stereo-type or not depends on factors such as whether they are motivated to be non-prejudiced (Monteith, Sherman, & Devine, 1998) or are encouraged to be aware of egalitarian norms and standards (Macrae, Bodenhausen, & Milne, 1998).

Stereotypes can also change depending on major events, such as war. A study by Bal-Tal and Labin (2001) of Israeli adolescents and their stereotypes of Palestinians, Jordanians, and Arabs was conducted longitudinally on three separate occasions. The researchers administered surveys at a relatively peaceful time, directly after an attack by an extreme Palestinian group, and then again a few months later. Stereotypic judgments concerning Palestinians became more negative directly after the attack, but after a few months they returned to the initial baseline level. Their results support the view of Oakes, Haslam, and Turner (1994) that stereotypes are "fluid, variable, and context-dependent" (p. 211). Thus, in addition to a recognition of the cognitive and emotional factors that contribute to stereotypical thinking, situational factors are also important.

Stereotypes may be formed through limited exposure to members of the target group or to exposure based on a "biased" sample. Thus, stereotypes can be formed and reinforced in a person on the basis of very limited exposure, or no exposure at all, to the target group. The complex interplay of these external factors with our own cultural and psychological processes make stereotypes a difficult problem to deal with.

Stereotypes of ourselves (self-stereotypes) and others are difficult to change because they become part of our self-system. They are intimately tied to our emotions, values, and core self and, as such, are difficult to change once we acquire them.

The Impact of Stereotypes   Although stereotypes are useful as categories in terms of helping us organize information, they are dangerous if applied to people uniformly without recognizing the vast number of individual differences that occur within any cultural or ethnic group. Recall, for instance, the construct of stereotype threat that we discussed in Chapter 5. Cohen and Garcia (2005) also demonstrated the existence of **collective threat**: the fear that an ingroup member's behavior can reinforce negative stereotypes about one's group. Collective threat resulted in lower self-esteem, lower academic performance, self-stereotyping, and physical distancing from the ingroup member whose behavior reinforced the negative stereotype. Even the **model minority stereotype** of Asian Americans in the United States has its drawbacks, because it has been demonstrated that this stereotype has two components: excessive competence coupled with deficient sociality (Lin, Kwan, Cheung, & Fiske, 2005).

Discrimination

Discrimination refers to the unfair treatment of others based on their group membership. The difference between prejudice and discrimination is the difference between thinking/feeling (prejudice) and doing (discrimination). Like stereotypes and prejudice, discrimination can include preferential or positive treatment as well as deferred or negative treatment. The important issue in defining discrimination revolves around the concept of fairness and treatment based on group membership.

Although prejudice and discrimination are often linked, they need not be. Merton (1968) highlighted the ways in which prejudice and discrimination may be related to each other in any single person. Those who are unprejudiced may or may not discriminate, and those who discriminate may or may not be prejudiced. Prejudice and discrimination are processes that occur on the individual level.

There have been many studies of discrimination in a variety of behaviors. Saucier, Miller, and Douct (2005) meta-analyzed 48 studies examining discrimination in helping behavior against blacks. No overall discrimination was found across all studies. But discrimination was more likely when participants could rationalize decisions not to help with reasons having nothing to do with race, such as when helping was more difficult, required more effort, took longer, or was riskier. Discrimination against blacks also occurred when there were higher levels of emergency.

When prejudice and discrimination occur on the group or organizational level, they are known as various "-isms" and institutional discrimination. Racism, classism, and sexism are just a few of the many examples of the prejudicial thoughts and feelings that can be harbored by large groups of people about other groups based on their biological, sociological, or psychological characteristics. The particular characteristic used is generally attached to the -ism suffix. Thus, racism is group-based prejudicial thought based on race, classism is prejudice based on social class, and sexism is prejudice based on sex.

Although prejudice can be either positive or negative in content, -isms are usually negative and derogatory, used to justify inferior status on the part of the people being characterized. *Prejudice* describes preferential thoughts and feelings held by an individual; *-isms* are prejudices that are held by one group of people about another. As such, they generally constitute systems of ideas, beliefs, and opinions held by a large group of people and are often woven into the social and cultural fabric of that group. Thus, they constitute an ideology that can be communicated from one generation to the next, much as other elements of culture are communicated (see Healey, 1998).

Institutional discrimination is discrimination that occurs on the level of a large group, society, organization, or institution. It is unequal or unfair patterns of behavior or preferential treatment of people by a large group or organization solely on the basis of group membership. These patterns of treatment may or may not be conscious and deliberate. Allegations concerning such institutional discrimination are all around us in the daily news, involving the educational system, places of business and work, the legal and criminal justice systems, and professional sports.

One of the most immediate and controversial issues regarding possible institutional discrimination concerns affirmative action policies in admissions to colleges and universities. Several years ago, officers of the University of California voted to repeal affirmative action admissions procedures. Proponents of the repeal point to data suggesting that, despite many years of affirmative action policies for underrepresented populations, there has been no real change in the numbers of people from these groups being educated, because many drop out or fail. They also point to the cost of remedial education needed to compensate for poor academic preparation, detracting from the university's ability to provide quality education to those students who were admitted based on non–affirmative action criteria. On the other side, opponents of the repeal point to their own data suggesting that affirmative action policies were working to educate far greater numbers of individuals from underrepresented groups. They suggest that other problems, such as the need for remediation, merely highlight the other racist and discriminatory programs and policies of the university system and society as a whole.

Patricia Gurin (1997) from the University of Michigan analyzed longitudinal data from several survey studies involving more than 10,000 students from almost 200 colleges and universities nationwide. These studies examined the relationship between the diversity of the school campus and student learning outcomes. Based on the results of these studies, she concluded that students who experienced more racial and ethnic diversity in the classroom, as measured by the proportion of minorities in the classroom and the extent and quality of interaction with students of different racial and ethnic backgrounds, "showed the greatest engagement in active thinking processes, growth in intellectual engagement and motivation, and growth in intellectual and academic skills." She argued that diversity created through affirmative action policies enhances education.

Maio and Esses's (1998) study throws an interesting light on this subject. These authors examined the degree to which knowledge about affirmative action policies may produce negative perceptions about people who benefit from such policies. They presented participants with a fictitious editorial describing an unfamiliar group in a positive manner. In one condition, the editorial indicated that the group benefited from affirmative action policies; in another condition, there was no mention of such benefit. When affirmative action was mentioned, participants expressed less favorable perceptions of and attitudes toward the group. The participants even expressed less favorable attitudes toward immigration by the group, and toward immigration in general. These findings highlight the need for us, as psychologists and concerned citizens of the world, to gather as much data as possible about the social and psychological consequences of programs and policies related to allegations of -isms or institutional discrimination and to become fully educated and informed about the issues.

CULTURE AND AGGRESSION

Aggression is any act or behavior that intentionally hurts another person, either physically or psychologically. Models of aggression suggest that it occurs when provocation leads to negative emotions, which prime a person to either fight or flee. Which response the individual chooses depends on genetics and biological predispositions, previously learned response patterns, and the specific characteristics of the context and situation (Geen, 1994).

Culture influences group-level tendencies toward aggression. Many cross-cultural psychologists and anthropologists have examined cultures such as the Yanomami of Venezuela and Brazil (for example, Sponsel, 1998)—a cultural group well known for its aggressive tendencies, both within the group and toward outsiders, and often referred to as the "fierce people." Landau (1984) compared levels of stress, social support systems, and the rates of murder and other crimes in 13 countries and found a correlation among these variables. Robbins, DeWalt, and Pelto (1972) showed that countries with hotter and more humid climates are associated with higher murder rates, and this tendency has also been documented for the states of the United States (Anderson & Anderson, 1996).

There are universal aspects to aggression across cultures. Bond (2004) has suggested that aggression is a form of coercive control that can occur in all cultures. As we discussed in Chapter 1, all cultures represent some form of solutions to a universal set of problems that humans face around the world in order to survive. Part of these problems concern how to distribute desired materials, goods, and resources among group members, while at the same time maintaining social order and harmony. In order to do this, all cultures develop norms. The norms, however, often favor some people while not favoring others. Violations of these norms by individuals or groups who are perceived as competitors for those same resources are conceptualized as aggressive; these perceptions, in turn, stimulate a process of counterattack, which further escalates violence.

One construct that has been shown to be very important in understanding aggression across cultures concerns honor. *Honor* refers to respect, esteem, or admiration, and some cultures can be characterized as **cultures of honor,** in which norms place a strong emphasis on status and reputation. In these cultures, insults, threats, and sexual infidelity can especially threaten one's honor, often resulting in anger, which leads to violence and aggression. Higher rates of violent crimes and other aggressive acts in the U.S. South, for instance, has been linked to a "Southern culture of honor" (Nisbett, 1993). In one study (Cohen, Nisbett, Bowdle, & Schwarz, 1996), for example, participants were purposefully bumped by a research confederate and called an "asshole." Individuals born and raised in the northern United States were relatively unaffected by the insult; those from the South, however, were more likely to believe that their masculinity was threatened, were more upset, more physiologically and cognitively primed for aggression, and were more likely to actually engage in aggressive behavior. These acts were interpreted as attempts to restore lost honor. Cortisol and testosterone levels were measured, and both were found to be elevated in the Southern sample.

The culture of honor is also at work in many cases of domestic violence, especially by males toward females because of actual or perceived infidelity or promiscuity. In cultures of honor, female infidelity or promiscuity is considered to bring dishonor and disgrace to a man and his family. The damage to the reputation can be restored through violence, and women in such relationships are expected to remain loyal to the man and family despite such violence (Vandello & Cohen, 2003).

But the culture of honor construct is not the only one at work in influencing aggression across cultures. Archer (2006), for example, analyzed data across 52 nations, and showed that the rates and types of physical aggression between partners differed across cultures. Cultures that were more individualistic and egalitarian had less female victimization and more male victimization.

There are also social facilitation effects occurring in many cases of culturally driving violence; that is, people in groups can be more aggressive than individuals by themselves. Jaffe and Yinon (1983), for example, showed that groups of Israeli participants were more willing to administer shocks to subjects in an experiment than were individuals. Other studies, however, have suggested that being in groups does not necessarily lead to more aggression. Rather, people are surer of themselves in groups. If the group's cultural norms favor aggression, then aggressive behaviors are more likely to occur. However, if the group's cultural norms favor nonaggression, then aggressive behaviors are more likely to be restrained (Rabbie & Horwitz, 1982).

Cultural influences on aggression may appear early in life. In one study (Farver, Welles-Nystroem, Frosch, Wimbarti, & Hoppe-Graff, 1997), for example, 4-year-olds in the United States, Sweden, Germany, and Indonesia told two stories using toys with aggressive and neutral cues. American children's narratives had significantly more aggressive content, aggressive words, unfriendly characters, and mastery of situations with aggression than did those of the other three cultures. Zahn-Waxler, Friedman, Cole, Mizuta, and Hiruma (1996) compared 4-year-old American and Japanese children, and found that American children showed more anger, more aggressive behavior and language, and greater underregulation of emotion than did Japanese children across different contexts of assessment.

Examining the influence of culture on aggression and violence can provide us with different ways of understanding why violence and wars occur around the world. Across time in history, for example, many wars can be considered clashes of culture, and the potential for such clashes to occur may increase as our world becomes a functionally smaller place with improvements in communication and transportation technologies. Hopefully recognizing the contributions of culture to this process can lead to more peaceful ways of being.

ACCULTURATION

The final topic we will explore in this chapter concerns **acculturation,** which we define as the process by which people adopt a different cultural system. Understanding the process of acculturation is important for many individuals in the world today, including not only immigrants and sojourners, but also refugees, asylum seekers, and those whose countries are overcome by war. The process of acculturation has at least two related but different components: **intercultural adaptation,** which refers to how people change their behaviors or ways of thinking in a new cultural environment; and **intercultural adjustment,** which refers to the subjective experiences people have as they adapt their behaviors and thinking.

By far the most prevalent model in the field today concerning intercultural adaptation is Berry's (Berry, Kim, & Boski, 1988; Berry & Sam, 1997). In Berry's model, immigrants and sojourners basically ask themselves two questions:

1. Do I value and want to maintain my *home* cultural identity and characteristics?
2. Do I value and want to maintain relationships with people from the *host* culture as well?

Berry calls people who answer Yes to the first but No to the second Separators, because they essentially live in their own immigrant communities, speaking their native language and interacting with their home-culture friends, with minimal contact with host-culture individuals. Individuals who answer No to the first and Yes to the second are called Assimilators; these individuals typically reject their home culture and totally assimilate to the host culture. They minimize interactions with people from their home culture, and typically speak the language of the host culture even when interacting with people from their home culture. People who answer No to both questions are known as Marginalizers. They reject both home and host cultures, and do not do well in either. They live on the fringes of both cultures, not really being able to immerse themselves in either. Finally, people who answer Yes to both questions are known as Integrators. These individuals are able to move from one cultural context to another, switching their cultural styles as they go along in accordance with the cultural system they are in. They are likely to be bilingual or multilingual as well as bicultural or multicultural (see Figure 14.3).

While Berry's model may describe how people behave, is one strategy better than another when it comes to how well people adjust in the new culture? Although it may be politically correct to suggest that Integration is the "best" pattern of adaptation, research has been equivocal in terms of whether it actually produces the best outcomes in terms of adjustment. In fact, critical reviews of the research literature examining differences in adjustment outcomes for the various adaptation strategies tend to show that Integration is not necessarily associated with the best adjustment outcomes (Rudmin, 2003). In fact, people can be relatively happy and well adjusted, at least in terms of their

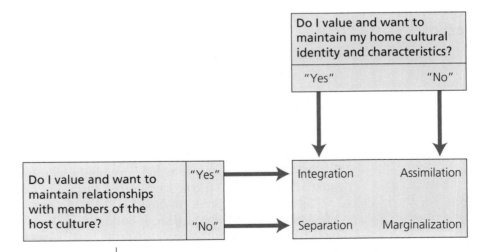

Figure 14.3 | Berry's Four Basic Acculturation Strategies

Berry, J. W., U. Kim, and P. Boski (1988). Psychological Acculturation of Immigrants. *International and Intercultural Communication Annual* (Vol. 11, pp. 62–89). Newbury Park, CA: Sage.

own self-report, regardless of what kind of adaptational strategies they may use as part of their acculturation process. Many members of immigrant groups in the United States, for instance, live happy, productive lives, not speaking very much English and not interacting very much with host Americans.

So what psychological factors may predict intercultural adaptation and adjustment? With regard to the former, certainly changing one's behaviors and ways of thinking would be helped if one knew what they would have to be changed to. Thus, knowledge of the target culture's norms, beliefs, attitudes, and values, would seem to be a prerequisite for adaptation. And in fact, this is exactly what Kurman and Ronen-Eilon (2004) found in their study of immigrants and individuals from the former Soviet Union in Israel. Another study found that knowledge of a host culture's gestures (see Chapter 9) was positively correlated with length of stay in a foreign country and negatively correlated with communication problems (Molinsky, Krabbenhoft, Ambady, & Choi, 2005).

With regard to intercultural adjustment, several factors seem to be important. One is "cultural fit," or the degree to which a person's characteristics match those of the new cultural environment in which he or she will acculturate (Ward & Chang, 1997). Ward and her colleagues have provided evidence for the cultural fit hypothesis, showing that individuals with better fits have better adjustment; those with worse fits, however, have worse adjustment, that is, they are less happy while at the same time more depressed, stressed, or anxious. We have replicated these findings as well (Matsumoto, Kouznetsova, Ray, Ratzlaff, Biehl, & Raroque, 1999).

Another factor that is important for intercultural adjustment is emotion regulation, which is defined as the ability to monitor and manage one's emotional reactions in order to achieve constructive outcomes. In a series of studies, we have demonstrated that emotion regulation is one of the keys to successful intercultural adjustment (Matsumoto, LeRoux, Bernhard, & Gray, 2004; Matsumoto, LeRoux, Iwamoto, Choi, Rogers et al., 2003; Matsumoto, LeRoux, Ratzlaff, Tatani, Uchida et al., 2001). This makes sense, because intercultural adaptation is fraught with inevitable conflicts that bring about many stresses. The ability to adjust successfully requires one to be able to handle the many inevitable stresses that occur when living in a new culture. Part of this ability requires us to not be overcome with emotions when they occur; instead, we need to be able to keep emotions in check but channel their energies toward useful goals. This process is emotion regulation.

A variable related to emotion regulation is called Need for Cognitive Closure. This refers to the desire for a definite answer to a question, rather than uncertainty, confusion, or ambiguity (Kruglanski, 1989). Need for Cognitive Closure is probably negatively related to emotion regulation, since people with low emotion regulation probably have a higher Need for Cognitive Closure because they cannot deal with the anxiety of the unknown well. Need for Cognitive Closure has been shown to be negatively correlated with adjustment in Croatian and Polish immigrants in Italy (Kosic, Kruglanski, Pierro, & Mannetti, 2004).

CONCLUSION

We began this chapter by noting that "no man is an island," and we have discussed how true that really is. No matter how we look at it, we cannot ignore the fact that we are fundamentally connected with other people in our world. Our behaviors, thoughts, and feelings are all influenced by others, and we in turn influence those around us.

As we close this chapter, we cannot help feeling that, despite the great differences across cultures in people's social behaviors, there are considerable underlying similarities as well. There are many universal psychological processes; culture produces differences in how we define goals to address universal needs and motives, and in their behavioral manifestations. Yet, at the core of it all, perhaps there is some culture-constant belief or value that we all operate on as human beings. The seminal review by Amir and Sharon (1988) on the cross-cultural validity of social psychological laws speaks to this point. Their review of studies examining social psychological principles across cultures indicated that original findings are often replicated across studies in statistical main effects—that is, in broad ways transcending culture. Somehow, cross-cultural psychology and research should attempt to engage this core, seeking similarities as well as differences at various levels of our psychological lives.

GLOSSARY

aggression Any act or behavior that intentionally hurts another person, either physically or psychologically.

acculturation The process by which people adopt a different cultural system.

autostereotypes Stereotypes you hold about your own group.

categorization The process by which psychological concepts are grouped together.

collective threat The fear that an ingroup member's behavior can reinforce negative stereotypes about one's group.

compliance Yielding to social pressure in one's public behavior, even though one's private beliefs may not have changed.

concept A mental category we use to classify events, objects, situations, behaviors, or even people with respect to what we perceive as common properties.

conformity Yielding to real or imagined social pressure.

cooperation People's ability to work together toward common goals.

cultures of honor Cultures in which norms place a strong emphasis on status and reputation.

discrimination The unfair treatment of others based on their group membership.

ethnocentrism The tendency to view the world through one's own cultural filters.

explicit prejudice Prejudice that is verbalized and thus made public.

heterostereotypes Stereotypes you hold about other groups.

implicit prejudice Prejudicial attitudes, values, or beliefs that are unspoken and perhaps even outside conscious awareness.

ingroup relationships Relationships characterized by some degree of familiarity, intimacy, and trust. We feel close to people around us we consider to be in our ingroup. Self–ingroup relationships develop through bonds that tie the ingroup together through common friendship or relationships or goals.

institutional discrimination Discrimination that occurs on the level of a large group, society, organization, or institution.

intercultural adaptation How people change their behaviors or ways of thinking in a new cultural environment.

intercultural adjustment The subjective experiences people have as they adapt their behaviors and thinking.

mate poaching Attracting someone who is already in a romantic relationship with someone else.

model minority stereotype The stereotype of Asian Americans that they are overachievers.

obedience A form of compliance that occurs when people follow direct commands, usually from someone in a position of authority.

outgroup relationships Relationships that lack the familiarity, intimacy, and trust characteristic of relationships with ingroup others.

person perception The process of forming impressions of others.

prejudice The tendency to prejudge others on the basis of their group membership.

stereotypes Generalized images we have about groups of people, particularly about their underlying psychological characteristics or personality traits.

15 CHAPTER

Culture and Organizations

We all spend a major portion of our lives in organizations. In fact, most of you reading this book are probably doing so within the educational system—an organization that plays an important part in many people's lives and is an important agent of socialization in the development and maintenance of culture. The companies that we work for are also organizations. And many of the extracurricular activities we engage in are supported by organizations, such as the YMCA, churches, sport clubs, and the like. Other organizations provide structure and services, such as government and hospitals.

In the past, it was probably easier than it is now to study organizations in relative isolation from issues of culture. Previously, the American workforce was less racially, ethnically, and culturally diverse than it is today. With less cultural diversity, the expectations of the members of any work organization were generally similar. Communication, lines of authority, and hierarchical structure were established with less conscious awareness of differences among people. Members of organizations had implicit, tacit knowledge about how to behave around one another and how to work together, because they all started with relatively similar cultural backgrounds.

Organizations were more isolated from issues of culture in yet another way, as many companies in the past were entirely or primarily domestic. Most of the work-related issues companies dealt with were confined to the United States and its culture. And most of the companies that competed or cooperated with one another were based in the same country and culture. This national work environment is now a thing of the past. Not only is the American workforce culturally diverse, but many companies today operate in an international arena.

The workplace of the world now includes unprecedented numbers of **multinational and international corporations**—work organizations that have subsidiaries, satellite offices, and work units in more than one country. Increasingly, these companies need to deal with people of diverse and varied backgrounds. Today, transfers from one business unit to another within the same company can mean a transfer from one country to another. Clearly, this internationalization of business brings with it more intercultural issues and challenges.

Even domestic companies that are not multinational in their structure must face the challenge of internationalization, with its associated intercultural issues. New trade laws and treaties, along with the Internet, have brought more business competitors from distant cultures, as well as increased opportunities for opening markets in other countries and cultures. Advances in communication and transportation allow companies and individuals to work more easily today than ever before over vast physical and cultural distances. Technological changes in communication—telephones, facsimile machines, videoteleconferencing, and electronic mail—have forced the issue of culture to the forefront of our work lives. The business world has become a global village, in which the exchange of goods, services, and resources knows few boundaries. This global village raises issues within our borders as well as across borders. Many of these issues are cultural. Our ability to deal with these issues in an ever-changing business world will determine our success or failure.

Although there are many different types of organizations in the world, this chapter will focus on one particular type—work organizations—because they have been the topic of many intercultural studies and provide the context for our knowledge of the effects of culture on organizations. The work context may be an interesting place to study the influence of culture on psychological processes because it may enhance or diminish differences. Sanchez-Burks, Lee, Choi, Nisbett, Zhao, and Koo (2003), for instance, demonstrated that American versus East Asian cultural differences in attention to indirect meaning was actually larger in work as compared with nonwork settings. The information gained in understanding the relationship between culture and work organizations can be useful in understanding other organizations as well.

In this chapter, we begin by defining organizational culture and distinguishing it from organizational climate. We examine cross-cultural research analyzing organizational culture first through work-related values, focusing on Hofstede's four major dimensions of culture. We examine culture and the meaning of work, and how culture is related to motivation and productivity, leadership and management, and decision making. We examine intercultural issues related to business and work, and discuss the important issue of sexual harassment across cultures.

ORGANIZATIONAL CULTURE AND ORGANIZATIONAL CLIMATE

An organization is a structure created by people to achieve certain objectives. Organizations are composed of people who work collectively to address the overall goals of the organization. Different people or groups may have different specific goals within the organization, but theoretically they should collectively address a common goal (for example, building a car, selling groceries). Different people or groups may be specialized according to role, objective, or task, and rank or status within a hierarchy may differentiate them from one another.

Each organization is unique, and because each contains a group of people with a way of existence, they have culture. This is known as "organizational culture" or "corporate culture" (O'Reilly, 1989; O'Reilly, Chatman, & Caldwell, 1991). Recall that in Chapter 1 we defined *culture* as a unique meaning and information system, shared by a group and transmitted across generations, that allows the group to meet basic needs of survival, pursue happiness and well-being, and derive meaning from life. Likewise, **organizational culture** can be defined as a meaning and information system shared within an organization and transmitted across successive generations of members, that allows the organization to survive and thrive.

The concept of organizational culture needs to be compared with another closely related construct, **organizational climate**. This refers to a shared perception of "the way things are around here" (Reichers & Schneider, 1990)—a shared perception of organizational policies, practices, and procedures. In addition, the term contains nuances of an emotional climate—that is, how people generally feel in their normal, everyday business practices. Climate can probably be best understood as a manifestation of organizational culture (Reichers & Schneider, 1990; Schein, 1985), which generally refers to a deeper, less consciously held set of values, attitudes, and meanings.

The concept of organizational climate is a long-standing one in the field of industrial and organizational psychology. Reichers and Schneider (1990), in their review of these two constructs, point out that writing appeared as early as 1939 on organizational climate and its relationship to work behaviors. Organizational culture, on the other hand, is a relatively new concept. It first appeared in the literature in 1979 and has currently become an important catchphrase. Most of the cross-cultural research on organizations has focused on culture, not climate, and that will be our focus in this chapter. Hopefully, future research will begin to examine in more detail how organizational climate is related to culture, and how it differs across national and social cultures.

CULTURAL DIFFERENCES IN WORK-RELATED VALUES

The primary way in which scientists have tried to understand organizational culture is by studying employees' work-related values. The best-known study of work-related values was conducted by Hofstede (1980, 1984) in the 1960s and 1970s. Hofstede's work, beginning in organizational culture, in fact, has aided scientists in understanding national cultures as well, which we discussed in Chapter 1. His study involved employees at International Business Machines (IBM), a multinational corporation with branch offices and subsidiaries in many different countries. In his original study in 1980, Hofstede reported data collected from workers in 40 different countries. In his 1984 study, he reported data from an additional 10 countries. Most recently he has reported data from 72 countries involving the responses of more than 117,000 employees of a multinational business organization, spanning over 20 different languages and seven occupational levels to his 63 work-related values items (Hofstede, 2001). Hofstede identified four major dimensions of work-related values and computed overall scores for each country on each of these four dimensions. As we discussed in Chapter 1, the four dimensions Hofstede reported were Power Distance, Uncertainty Avoidance, Individualism–Collectivism, and Masculinity–Femininity. Each of the dimensions he identified is related to concrete differences in attitudes, opinions, beliefs, and behaviors within work organizations, and each forms the basis for understanding certain societal norms in each of the countries in Hofstede's studies. These dimensions also have consequences for organizational structure and interorganizational behavior, and we focus here on what they mean in terms of organizational culture.

Power Distance

Organizations need vertical or hierarchical relationships based on status and power. Differentiating people according to their roles, functions, and positions is vital to the successful operation of an organization. The various statuses afforded to different individuals within a hierarchy come with certain benefits, rights, privileges, and power not afforded to others. The "chain of command" within a company identifies the players and their roles.

The basic hierarchical relationship is that between a boss and his or her immediate subordinate. In most cases, an employee is involved in a hierarchical relationship both with someone of higher status and with others of lower status. People within each culture develop ways of interacting with others according to the status differential that exists between the individual and the person with whom he or she is interacting. Power Distance refers to the degree to which different cultures encourage or maintain power and status differences between interactants. Organizations and cultures high on Power Distance develop rules, mechanisms, and rituals that serve to maintain and strengthen the status relationships among their members. Cultures low on Power Distance minimize those rules and customs.

According to Hofstede, cultural differences on Power Distance (PD) are related to individual differences in behaviors that have consequences for their work. Table 15.1 summarizes the Power Distance–related characteristics Hofstede gleaned from his own research and that of others. For example, managers in organizations in high-PD cultures are seen as making decisions autocratically and paternalistically, whereas managers in low-PD cultures are seen as making decisions only after more extensive consultation with their subordinates. The concrete behaviors listed in Table 15.1 are related to societal norms, which in turn have important consequences for organizational structure. In general, cultures high on PD foster organizations with greater centralization of organization and process, taller organizational pyramids, larger proportions of supervisory personnel, larger wage differentials, lower qualifications for the lower strata of employees, and greater valuation of white-collar as opposed to blue-collar jobs. All these characteristics of work organizations and of interpersonal relationships within companies can be considered as natural consequences of social and cultural differences on power distance.

Uncertainty Avoidance

Uncertainty is a fact of life. This is true for individuals, but it is especially true for companies. Today's profits can easily turn into tomorrow's losses, and vice versa. How a market will react to a new product, revisions in old products, corporate restructuring, mergers and acquisitions, and all the other changes that occur within organizations and in the business world is a major source of uncertainty. With this uncertainty can come confusion, stress, and anxiety.

Every society and organization develops its own ways of dealing with the anxiety and stress associated with uncertainty. Often, these ways involve development of rituals, informal or written, concerning a code of conduct among employees, as in intracompany policies regarding communication or interpersonal relationships. These rules may also govern behavior between companies within a society, or across cultures, as in domestic and international laws governing business and interbusiness relationships.

Table 15.1 | Summary of Connotations of Power Distance (PD) Differences Found in Survey Research

Low-PD Countries	High-PD Countries
Parents put less value on children's obedience.	Parents put high value on children's obedience.
Students put high value on independence.	Students put high value on conformity.
Authoritarian attitudes in students are a matter of personality.	Students show authoritarian attitudes as a social norm.
Managers seen as making decisions after consulting with subordinates.	Managers seen as making decisions autocratically and paternalistically.
Close supervision negatively evaluated by subordinates.	Close supervision positively evaluated by subordinates.
Stronger perceived work ethic, strong disbelief that people dislike work.	Weaker perceived work ethic, more frequent belief that people dislike work.
Managers more satisfied with participative superior.	Managers more satisfied with directive or persuasive superior.
Subordinates' preference for manager's decision-making style clearly centered on consultative, give-and-take style.	Subordinates' preference for manager's decision-making style polarized between autocratic-paternalistic and majority rule.
Managers like seeing themselves as practical and systematic; they admit a need for support.	Managers like seeing themselves as benevolent decision makers.
Employees less afraid of disagreeing with their boss.	Employees fear to disagree with their boss.
Employees show more cooperativeness.	Employees reluctant to trust each other.
Managers seen as showing more consideration.	Managers seen as showing less consideration.
Students have positive associations with "power" and "wealth."	Students have negative associations with "power" and "wealth."
Mixed feeling about employees' participation in management.	Ideological support for employees' participation in management.
Mixed feelings among managers about the distribution of capacity for leadership and initiative.	Ideological support among managers for a wide distribution of capacity for leadership and initiative.
Informal employee consultation possible without formal participation.	Formal employee participation possible without informal consultation.
Higher-educated employees hold much less authoritarian values than lower-educated ones.	Higher- and lower-educated employees show similar values about authority.

Hofstede, G. H., *Behaviors, Institutions and Organizations Across Nations* (2nd ed.), 2001. p. 98. Copyright © 2001 by Geert Hofstede. Reprinted by permission of Sage Publications.

Uncertainty Avoidance describes the degree to which different societies and different cultures develop ways to deal with the anxiety and stress of uncertainty. Cultures high on Uncertainty Avoidance develop highly refined rules and rituals that are mandated and become part of the company rubric and normal way of operating. Companies in these cultures may be considered rule-oriented. In Hofstede's survey, Greece, Portugal, Belgium, and Japan were the four countries with the highest scores on this dimension. Cultures low on Uncertainty Avoidance are less concerned with rules and rituals to deal with the stress and anxiety of uncertainty. Companies in these cultures have a more relaxed attitude concerning uncertainty and ambiguity and mandate fewer rules and rituals for their employees. In Hofstede's study, Sweden, Denmark, and Singapore had the lowest scores on Uncertainty Avoidance.

Cultural differences on Uncertainty Avoidance are directly related to concrete differences in jobs and work-related behaviors. Table 15.2 lists the characteristics of people associated with cultures high or low on Uncertainty Avoidance. For example, cultures high on Uncertainty Avoidance tend to be associated with greater job stress than cultures low on Uncertainty Avoidance.

Table 15.2 | Summary of Connotations of Uncertainty Avoidance (UA) Differences Found in Survey Research

Low-UA Countries	High-UA Countries
Lower anxiety level in population.	Higher anxiety level in population.
Greater readiness to live by the day.	More worry about the future.
Lower job stress.	Higher job stress.
Less emotional resistance to change.	More emotional resistance to change.
Less hesitation to change employers.	Tendency to stay with the same employer.
Loyalty to employer is not seen as a virtue.	Loyalty to employer is seen as a virtue.
Preference for smaller organizations as employers.	Preference for larger organizations as employers.
Smaller generation gap.	Greater generation gap.
Lower average age in higher-level jobs.	Higher average age in higher-level jobs, gerontocracy.
Managers selected on criteria other than seniority.	Managers selected on basis of seniority.
Stronger achievement motivation.	Less achievement motivation.
Hope of success.	Fear of failure.
More risk-taking.	Less risk-taking.
Stronger ambition for individual advancement.	Lower ambition for individual advancement.
Prefers manager career over specialist career.	Prefers specialist career over manager career.
A manager need not be an expert in the field he/she manages.	A manager must be an expert in the field he/she manages.
Hierarchical structures of organizations can be sidestepped for pragmatic reasons.	Hierarchical structures of organizations should be clear and respected.
Preference for broad guidelines.*	Preference for clear requirements and instructions.
Rules may be broken for pragmatic reasons.	Company rules should not be broken.

Table 15.2 | (*continued*)

Low-UA Countries	High-UA Countries
Conflict in organizations is natural.*	Conflict in organizations is undesirable.
Competition between employees can be fair and right.	Competition between employees is emotionally disapproved of.
More sympathy for individual and authoritative decisions.	Ideological appeal of consensus and of consultative leadership.
Delegation to subordinates can be complete.*	Initiative of subordinates should be kept under control.
Higher tolerance for ambiguity in perceiving others (higher LPC).	Lower tolerance for ambiguity in perceiving others (lower LPC).
More prepared to compromise with opponents.	Lower readiness to compromise with opponents.
Acceptance of foreigners as managers.	Suspicion toward foreigners as managers.
Larger fractions prepared to live abroad.	Fewer people prepared to live abroad.
Higher tolerance for ambiguity in looking at own job (lower satisfaction scores).	Lower tolerance for ambiguity in looking at own job (higher satisfaction scores).
Citizen optimism about ability to control politicians' decisions.	Citizen pessimism about ability to control politicians' decisions.
Employee optimism about the motives behind company activities.	Employee pessimism about the motives behind company activities.
Optimism about people's amount of initiative, ambition, and leadership skills.	Pessimism about people's amount of initiative, ambition, and leadership skills.

*Based on studies by Laurent (1978).

Ibid., p. 160.

This finding is ironic, given that cultures high on Uncertainty Avoidance place greater emphasis on developing ways of dealing with the stress and anxiety produced by uncertainty. Perhaps the ways that are developed are so complex that they produce increased stress in the workers who have to abide by those rules and rituals!

Individualism–Collectivism

As described throughout this book, Individualism–Collectivism has been used to explain, understand, and predict cultural differences in a variety of contexts. It is also a very important dimension in relation to work organizations. Collectivistic cultural values foster more compliance with company policies and more conformity in group, section, or unit behavior. Collectivism also fosters a greater degree of reliance on group work and group orientation to company and organizational tasks. Harmony within groups, sections, or business units is valued more in collectivistic cultures; members are more likely to engage in behaviors that ensure harmony and to refrain from behaviors that threaten harmony.

In Hofstede's study, the United States, Australia, Great Britain, and Canada had the highest scores on Individualism–Collectivism. Workers in these countries were characterized as being the most individualistic of all workers in the study. It is interesting to note that each of these countries has a strong historical link to Great Britain. Peru, Pakistan, Colombia, and Venezuela had the lowest scores on Individualism–Collectivism and were the most collectivistic.

Individualism–Collectivism differences between countries and cultures are associated with concrete differences in worker attitudes, values, beliefs, and behaviors about work and their companies. Table 15.3 summarizes the differences Hofstede gleaned from his and other people's studies. For example, people in individualistic cultures tend to regard their personal time as important and to make clear distinctions between their time and company time. People in individualistic cultures place more importance on freedom and challenge in their jobs, and initiative is generally encouraged on the job. In collectivistic cultures, freedom, independence, and initiative are normally frowned upon.

Masculinity–Femininity

Biological differences between men and women are a given. The question that every society, culture, and individual has to deal with is the degree to which the biological differences translate, or should translate, to practical differences in social roles, functions, or positions. Traditionally, American culture has expected men to be more assertive, dominant, and the primary wage earner and women to be more nurturing, caring, and primarily concerned with family and child care issues (see also Chapter 7). This picture has been changing rapidly in the United States and continues to be a source of conflict, controversy, and confusion. Values concerning equity and equality have infused the workplace, and many American companies are still in transition toward providing gender equity in the workplace.

Each culture and society must deal with the issue of sex roles and gender differences. A fourth dimension emerged in Hofstede's study, which he labeled Masculinity–Femininity. According to Hofstede, Masculinity–Femininity refers to the degree to which cultures foster or maintain differences between the sexes in work-related values. Cultures high on Masculinity–Femininity—such as Japan, Austria, Venezuela, and Italy—were associated with the greatest degree of sex differences in work-related values. Cultures low on Masculinity–Femininity—such as Denmark, the Netherlands, Norway, and Sweden—had the fewest differences between the sexes.

As with each of the other dimensions Hofstede generated, cultural differences on Masculinity–Femininity were associated with very concrete differences

Table 15.3 | Summary of Connotations of Individualism–Collectivism (IC) Differences Found in Survey and Related Research

Low-IC Countries	High-IC Countries
Importance of provisions by company (training, physical conditions).	Importance of employees' personal life (time).
Emotional dependence on company.	Emotional independence from company.
Large company attractive.	Small company attractive.
Moral involvement with company.	Calculative involvement with company.
Moral importance attached to training and use of skills in jobs.	More importance attached to freedom and challenge in jobs.
Students consider it less socially acceptable to claim pursuing their own ends without minding others.	Students consider it socially acceptable to claim pursuing their own ends without minding others.
Managers aspire to conformity and orderliness.	Managers aspire to leadership and variety.
Managers rate having security in their position more important.	Managers rate having autonomy more important.
Managers endorse "traditional" points of view, not supporting employee initiative and group activity.	Managers endorse "modern" points of view on stimulating employee initiative and group activity.
Group decisions are considered better than individual decisions.	Individual decisions are considered better than group decisions.
Duty in life appeals to students.	Enjoyment in life appeals to students.
Managers choose duty, expertness, and prestige as life goals.	Managers choose pleasure, affections, and security as life goals.
Individual initiative is socially frowned upon; fatalism.	Individual initiative is socially encouraged.
More acquiescence in responses to "importance" questions.	Less acquiescence in responses to "importance" questions.
People thought of in terms of ingroups and outgroups; particularism.	People thought of in general terms; universalism.
Social relations predetermined in terms of ingroups.	Need to make specific friendships.
More years of schooling needed to do a given job.	Fewer years of schooling needed to do a given job.
More traffic accidents per 1000 vehicles.	Fewer traffic accidents per 1000 vehicles.
More traditional time-use pattern.	More modern time-use pattern.

Ibid., p. 226.

between workers and organizations. Table 15.4 summarizes these differences. For example, managers in cultures high on Masculinity–Femininity valued leadership, independence, and self-realization; cultures low on Masculinity–Femininity placed less importance on these constructs. Employees in

Table 15.4 | Summary of Connotations of Masculinity (MA) Differences Found in Survey and Related Research

Low-MA Countries	High-MA Countries
Relationship with manager, cooperation, friendly atmosphere, living in a desirable area, and employment security relatively more important to employees.	Earnings, recognition, advancement, and challenge relatively more important to employees.
Managers relatively less interested in leadership, independence, and self-realization.	Managers have leadership, independence, and self-realization ideal.
Belief in group decisions.	Belief in the independent decision maker.
Students less interested in recognition.	Students aspire to recognition (admiration for the strong).
Weaker achievement motivation.	Stronger achievement motivation.
Achievement defined in terms of human contacts and living environment.	Achievement defined in terms of recognition and wealth.
Work less central in people's lives.	Greater work centrality.
People prefer shorter working hours to more salary.	People prefer more salary to shorter working hours.
Company's interference in private life rejected.	Company's interference in private life accepted.
Greater social role attributed to other institutions than corporation.	Greater social role attributed to corporation.
Employees like small companies.	Employees like large corporations.
Entire population more attracted to smaller organizations.	Entire population more attracted to larger organizations.
Lower job stress.	Higher job stress.
Less skepticism as to factors leading to getting ahead.	Skepticism as to factors leading to getting ahead.
Students more benevolent (sympathy for the weak).	Students less benevolent.
Managers have more of a service ideal.	Managers relatively less attracted by service role.
"Theory X" (employees dislike work) strongly rejected.	"Theory X" gets some support.
More women in jobs with mixed-sex composition.	Fewer women in jobs with mixed-sex composition.
Smaller or no value differences between men and women in the same jobs.	Greater value differences between men and women in the same jobs.
Sex role equality in children's books.	More sex role differentiation in children's books.

Ibid., p. 330.

high-Masculinity–Femininity cultures regarded earnings, recognition, advancement, and challenge as relatively more important than did employees in low-Masculinity–Femininity cultures. And fewer women were in mixed-sex jobs in organizations in high-Masculinity–Femininity cultures than in low-Masculinity–Femininity cultures.

Cultural differences on Masculinity–Femininity have interesting consequences for both organizational structure and employee relationships (Hofstede, 1980). For example, young men in high-Masculinity–Femininity cultures generally expect to make a career in their jobs, and those who do not, see themselves as failures. In high-Masculinity–Femininity cultures, organizational interests, needs, and goals are viewed as a legitimate reason to interfere in the personal and private lives of employees. High-Masculinity–Femininity cultures generally have fewer women in better-paid jobs and jobs requiring more-qualifications, and those women who are in jobs requiring more-qualifications tend to be very assertive. Job stress is generally higher in organizations located in high-Masculinity–Femininity cultures.

Long- versus Short-Term Orientation

Although Hofstede originally reported four cultural dimensions of work-related values, he recently added a fifth dimension—Long- versus Short-Term Orientation. This dimension originated from his research in Asia, where he and his collaborators found that there was an additional dimension that characterized organizational cultures there (Chinese Culture Connection, 1987; Hofstede & Bond, 1988). This dimension refers to the degree to which cultures encourage delayed gratification of material, social, and emotional needs among its members. The most long-term-oriented cultures in Hofstede's study were China, Hong Kong, and Taiwan; the most short-term-oriented were Poland, West Africa, and Spain.

Cultures with Long-Term Orientations are based on two principles:

- Unequal status relationships lead to a stable society.
- The family is typical of all social organizations.

These principles translate to abstract values that play an important role not only in interpersonal relationships in business but also as organizational goals and principles. For example, cultures and organizations high in Long-Term Orientation differentiate more between elders and youngers, and between brothers and sisters; believe that humility is a great human virtue, focus on building relationships and market position rather than bottom-line profits, integrate business and family lives, and coordinate more hierarchically and horizontally (Hofstede, 2001).

Other Research on Organizational Culture

To be sure, there have been several other large-scale attempts to measure organizational culture around the world, and these undoubtedly aid in our

Table 15.5	Four Major Sets of Dimensions of Cultural Variability Found in Studies of Work-Related Values

Framework	Dimensions
Hofstede's (2001) dimensions of work-related values	Individualism–Collectivism Power Distance Uncertainty Avoidance Masculinity–Femininity Long- vs. short-term orientation
Smith, Dugan, and Trompenaars's (1996) dimensions of values	Egalitarian commitment vs. conservatism Utilitarian involvement vs. loyal involvement
House, Hanges, Javidan, Dorfman, and Gupta's (2004) dimensions of leadership values	Performance orientation Assertiveness orientation Future orientation Human orientation Institutional collectivism Family collectivism Gender egalitarianism Power distance Uncertainty avoidance
Inglehart's (1997) dimensions of attitudes, values, and beliefs	Traditional vs. secular-rational orientation Survival vs. self-expression values

understanding of national culture as well. For example Smith, Dugan, and Trompenaars (1996) have reported two universal value orientations in their work in organizations, House, Hanges, Javidan, Dorfman, and Gupta (2004) have reported nine value orientations related to leadership, and Inglehart (1997) has reported two attitudinal-belief-value orientations (Table 15.5). Thus, in reality there is a wide range of cultural dimensions to use in developing cultural theories and accounting for between-country differences. Many of these dimensions, however, are theoretically and empirically related to each other. Hofstede (1996b), for instance, reanalyzed Trompenaars's (1993) data, and reported that Trompenaars' dimensions were statistically correlated with his own.

Some Practical Implications of Organizational Culture

Our increased awareness of the nature and function of organizational culture has brought about a growing interest in the practical implications of organizational culture in business and places of work. An increasing number of studies have examined these implications, and they provide important information concerning real-life issues involving organizational culture. Some studies, for example, have examined the role of organizational culture in producing or mitigating stress perceived by employees (for example, Peterson, 1997; Peterson & Smith, 1997; Thompson, Stradling, Murphy, & O'Neill, 1996). Peterson suggests that not only does the specific work that people do create stress, but so does the culture in which they work. Some organizational cultures may produce stress by their very nature (Thompson et al., 1996) or through the historical evolution of cultural values in the company (Peterson & Smith, 1997).

One topic that has gained prominence not only in the scientific literature but also in applied work is the issue of cultural fit between person and company. Given the work conducted in the past two decades on organizational culture, and the work that has been done for years on individual culture, a logical question concerns the match between employees and the cultures they come from, on the one hand, and a company and its organizational culture, on the other. Do "mismatches" create conflicts? Do successful "matches" lead to more productive companies?

Abrams, Ando, and Hinkle (1998) examined cross-cultural differences in organizational identification and subjective norms as predictors of workers' turnover intentions. In their study, employees of companies in Great Britain and Japan completed questionnaires related to turnover intentions, attitudes toward leaving the organization, subjective norms regarding perceived approval for leaving, and organizational identification. In the British sample, turnover intentions were predicted by organizational identification; workers with stronger identifications with the company had lower turnover intentions. In the Japanese sample, however, turnover intentions were associated with both organizational identification and subjective norms. These findings suggest that although social identity is strongly associated with employee turnover in both cultures, subjective normative aspects of group membership play a larger role in predicting turnover in Japan than they do in Great Britain.

Research has also documented positive aspects of employee–company cultural congruence. Meglino, Ravlin, and Adkins (1989), for example, questioned 191 production workers, 17 supervisors, and 13 managers on job satisfaction and organization commitment; they also collected objective data concerning attendance, performance, and efficiency. Two measures of employees' values congruence were computed and correlated with all psychological and behavioral data. Correlational analyses indicated that workers who were more satisfied and committed had values that were congruent with those of their supervisor.

These findings raise important questions concerning the nature of personnel selection in all companies and cultures today, especially in the United States with its diverse workforce population. Adding to the complexity of these issues are the cultural and ethnic differences in career choices of today's young adults (Kim, 1993) and perceived past and future barriers to career development (Luzzo, 1993). Finding an appropriate match between employer and employee is a daunting task for both individuals and organizations, as neither side profits from an unsuitable relationship or unhappy employees.

The literature of the past few years includes a number of approaches to personnel selection and training, all of which demonstrate an increasing sensitivity to cultural issues. For example, Love, Bishop, Heinisch, and Montei (1994) have described the adaptations and modifications they made to a selection system for hiring American workers in a Japanese–American joint-venture assembly plant. During the 1980s, the number of such joint ventures between the United States and Japan increased dramatically, particularly in the automotive industry. Today, there are many such ventures, not only with Japanese companies but with companies from many different cultures. In addition, an increasing number of American companies are establishing themselves in other countries and cultures, raising the same issues overseas. In their work, Love and colleagues modified job-analysis procedures and traditional selection systems to accommodate Japanese culture and management philosophy. They then engaged in a series of steps to validate their system cross-culturally to ensure compatibility with Japanese management demands regarding productivity, team orientation, quality standards, and formal employee performance evaluations. It is particularly interesting to note the reason why the selection system could not be compared with performance criteria data on individuals:

After submitting a formal proposal to develop a performance appraisal system, in part for validation purposes, and meeting with management, it quickly became obvious that Japanese management philosophy prohibits such a practice. Differentiating between employees on the basis of job performance is an affront to Japanese cultural beliefs, which prefer a homogeneous workforce (Maher & Wong, 1994). In particular, Japanese managers suggested that individual performance appraisals would damage the "team" concept, held in high esteem throughout the plant (Love et al., 1994, pg. 843).

Thus, organizational culture and the fit between employee and company are real-life issues that have important implications in our everyday lives. Organizations have begun to struggle with the issue of cultural match between employee and company, and new ways of assimilating newcomers into organizations are constantly being developed from a cultural perspective (see, for example, Hess, 1993). Although most research approaches this issue from the organization's point of view, some researchers have also addressed efforts by employees to assess the fit between themselves and the culture of the organization to which they are applying (for example, Pratt, 1993). Systematic research on these issues is still young, and we have much to learn. What constitutes a "successful" or "unsuccessful" match? How do we make these assessments? In some cultures, as Love et al. discovered, making such assessments may be counter to the prevailing cultural norms. And how valid is the suggestion that all personnel election decisions should be informed by matches? Are there optimal levels of mismatches that may spur on maximal performance? For example, although individualism is usually associated with creativity and initiative, at least one study has shown that innovation and entrepreneurship is highest under conditions of balanced individualism and collectivism, and lowest in either highly individualistic or highly collectivistic corporations (Morris, Avila, & Allen, 1993). Could such an effect exist within organizations as well?

CULTURE AND THE MEANING OF WORK

People of different cultures may construe themselves and their existence in relation to work differently across cultures, and these differences are related to meaningful dimensions of cultural variability. Some people may view their work groups and the work organizations (companies) to which they belong as a fundamental part of themselves. Work, work colleagues, and the company become synonymous with the self. The bonds between these people and their work colleagues, and between themselves and their company, are stronger and qualitatively different from those of people in individualistic cultures. Others, however, have an easier time separating themselves from their jobs. They make greater distinctions between "work time" and "personal time," and between company-based expense accounts and personal expenses. They also make greater distinctions between social and work activities, with regard to both their work colleagues and their business associates (potential clients, customers, and so forth).

Cultural differences in the meaning of work can manifest themselves in other aspects of work as well. For example, in American culture, it is easy to think of work simply as a means to accumulate money (pay or salary) and make a living. In other cultures, especially collectivistic ones, work may be seen more as fulfilling an obligation to a larger group. In this situation, we would expect to find less movement of individuals from one job to another because of the individual's social obligations toward the work organization to which he or she belongs and to the people comprising that organization. In individualistic cultures, it is easier to consider leaving one job and going to another because it is easier to separate jobs from the self. A different job will just as easily accomplish the same goals.

In understanding cultural differences in work, one cannot ignore the large influence of the socioeconomic status of the society. In many cultures of the world, people young and old alike are without work, and thus have many difficulties making a living for themselves and their families. The inability to work, related to the unavailability of work, has major consequences for individuals and societies, causing great unrest and hardship at both levels. To many around the world, having a job—any job—is a luxury. A glance at the differences in per capita gross domestic product, which is an index of the purchasing power of the average individual in each country, gives one an idea of these differences (Table 15.6).

And regardless of the type of work one does, in many cultures of the world people who have work come to perceive their work as their *lifework*. That is, people tend to ascribe important meaning to what they are doing. The ability to do so is probably unique to humans, because of the unique cognitive skills humans have, as we discussed in Chapter 1. People's views of their lifework are an important aspect of human culture.

Table 15.6 | Rank Order of GDP per capita (PPP)*

Rank	Country	GDP per capita (PPP)	Date of Information
1	Bermuda	$ 69,900	2004 est.
2	Luxembourg	$ 55,600	2005 est.
3	Equatorial Guinea	$ 50,200	2005 est.
4	United Arab Emirates	$ 43,400	2005 est.
5	Norway	$ 42,300	2005 est.
6	United States	$ 41,800	2005 est.
7	Ireland	$ 41,000	2005 est.
8	Guernsey	$ 40,000	2003 est.
9	Jersey	$ 40,000	2003 est.
10	British Virgin Islands	$ 38,500	2004 est.
11	Iceland	$ 35,600	2005 est.
12	Denmark	$ 34,600	2005 est.
13	San Marino	$ 34,600	2001 est.
14	Canada	$ 34,000	2005 est.
15	Hong Kong	$ 32,900	2005 est.
16	Austria	$ 32,700	2005 est.
17	Cayman Islands	$ 32,300	2004 est.
18	Switzerland	$ 32,300	2005 est.
19	Australia	$ 31,900	2005 est.
20	Japan	$ 31,500	2005 est.
21	Belgium	$ 31,400	2005 est.
22	Finland	$ 30,900	2005 est.
23	Netherlands	$ 30,500	2005 est.
24	Germany	$ 30,400	2005 est.
25	United Kingdom	$ 30,300	2005 est.
26	France	$ 29,900	2005 est.
27	Sweden	$ 29,800	2005 est.
28	Italy	$ 29,200	2005 est.
29	Isle of Man	$ 28,500	2003 est.
30	European Union	$ 28,100	2005 est.
31	Singapore	$ 28,100	2005 est.
32	Gibraltar	$ 27,900	2000 est.
33	Taiwan	$ 27,600	2005 est.
34	Qatar	$ 27,400	2005 est.

Table 15.6 | (*continued*)

Rank	Country	GDP per capita (PPP)	Date of Information
35	Monaco	$ 27,000	2000 est.
36	Spain	$ 25,500	2005 est.
37	New Zealand	$ 25,200	2005 est.
38	Falkland Islands (Islas Malvinas)	$ 25,000	2002 est.
39	Liechtenstein	$ 25,000	1999 est.
40	Israel	$ 24,600	2005 est.
41	Andorra	$ 24,000	2004
42	Brunei	$ 23,600	2003 est.
43	Bahrain	$ 23,000	2005 est.
44	Greece	$ 22,200	2005 est.
45	Faroe Islands	$ 22,000	2001 est.
46	Macau	$ 22,000	2004
47	Aruba	$ 21,800	2004 est.
48	Slovenia	$ 21,600	2005 est.
49	Cyprus	$ 21,500	NA
50	Korea, South	$ 20,400	2005 est.
51	Bahamas, The	$ 20,200	2005 est.
52	Greenland	$ 20,000	2001 est.
53	Malta	$ 19,900	2005 est.
54	Czech Republic	$ 19,500	2005 est.
55	Portugal	$ 19,300	2005 est.
56	Kuwait	$ 19,200	2005 est.
57	Puerto Rico	$ 18,600	2005 est.
58	French Polynesia	$ 17,500	2003 est.
59	Barbados	$ 17,000	2005 est.
60	Estonia	$ 16,700	2005 est.
61	Trinidad and Tobago	$ 16,700	2005 est.
62	Hungary	$ 16,300	2005 est.
63	Slovakia	$ 16,100	2005 est.
64	Netherlands Antilles	$ 16,000	2004 est.
65	Guam	$ 15,000	2005 est.
66	New Caledonia	$ 15,000	2003 est.
67	Virgin Islands	$ 14,500	2004 est.

(*continued*)

Table 15.6 │ (*continued*)

Rank	Country	GDP per capita (PPP)	Date of Information
68	Martinique	$ 14,400	2003 est.
69	Lithuania	$ 13,700	2005 est.
70	Poland	$ 13,300	2005 est.
71	Latvia	$ 13,200	2005 est.
72	Oman	$ 13,200	2005 est.
73	Argentina	$ 13,100	2005 est.
74	Mauritius	$ 13,100	2005 est.
75	Saudi Arabia	$ 12,800	2005 est.
76	Northern Mariana Islands	$ 12,500	2000 est.
77	Malaysia	$ 12,100	2005 est.
78	South Africa	$ 12,000	2005 est.
79	Croatia	$ 11,600	2005 est.
80	Turks and Caicos Islands	$ 11,500	2002 est.
81	Libya	$ 11,400	2005 est.
82	Chile	$ 11,300	2005 est.
83	Costa Rica	$ 11,100	2005 est.
84	Russia	$ 11,100	2005 est.
85	Antigua and Barbuda	$ 11,000	2002 est.
86	Botswana	$ 10,500	2005 est.
87	Mexico	$ 10,000	2005 est.
88	Bulgaria	$ 9,600	2005 est.
89	Uruguay	$ 9,600	2005 est.
90	World Average	$ 9,500	2005 est.
91	Saint Kitts and Nevis	$ 8,800	2002 est.
92	Brazil	$ 8,400	2005 est.
93	French Guiana	$ 8,300	2003 est.
94	Iran	$ 8,300	2005 est.
95	Tunisia	$ 8,300	2005 est.
96	Thailand	$ 8,300	2005 est.
97	Kazakhstan	$ 8,200	2005 est.
98	Turkey	$ 8,200	2005 est.
99	Romania	$ 8,200	2005 est.

Table 15.6 | (*continued*)

Rank	Country	GDP per capita (PPP)	Date of Information
100	Turkmenistan	$ 8,000	2005 est.
101	Colombia	$ 7,900	2005 est.
102	Guadeloupe	$ 7,900	2003 est.
103	Macedonia	$ 7,800	2005 est.
104	Seychelles	$ 7,800	2002 est.
105	Anguilla	$ 7,500	2002 est.
106	Algeria	$ 7,200	2005 est.
107	Panama	$ 7,200	2005 est.
108	Ukraine	$ 7,200	2005 est.
109	Cyprus	$ 7,135	NA
110	Dominican Republic	$ 7,000	2005 est.
111	Saint Pierre and Miquelon	$ 7,000	2001 est.
112	Namibia	$ 7,000	2005 est.
113	Belarus	$ 6,900	2005 est.
114	Belize	$ 6,800	2005 est.
115	Bosnia and Herzegovina	$ 6,800	2005 est.
116	Gabon	$ 6,800	2005 est.
117	China	$ 6,800	2005 est.
118	Cape Verde	$ 6,200	2005 est.
119	Reunion	$ 6,200	2005 est.
120	Lebanon	$ 6,200	2005 est.
121	Venezuela	$ 6,100	2005 est.
122	Fiji	$ 6,000	2005 est.
123	Peru	$ 5,900	2005 est.
124	American Samoa	$ 5,800	2005 est.
125	Palau	$ 5,800	2005 est.
126	Samoa	$ 5,600	2002 est.
127	Dominica	$ 5,500	2003 est.
128	Saint Lucia	$ 5,400	2002 est.
129	Philippines	$ 5,100	2005 est.
130	Cook Islands	$ 5,000	2001 est.
131	Grenada	$ 5,000	2002 est.

(*continued*)

Table 15.6 | (*continued*)

Rank	Country	GDP per capita (PPP)	Date of Information
132	Nauru	$ 5,000	2005 est.
133	Swaziland	$ 5,000	2005 est.
134	Albania	$ 4,900	2005 est.
135	Paraguay	$ 4,900	2005 est.
136	Azerbaijan	$ 4,800	2005 est.
137	El Salvador	$ 4,700	2005 est.
138	Jordan	$ 4,700	2005 est.
139	Guatemala	$ 4,700	2005 est.
140	Guyana	$ 4,600	2005 est.
141	Armenia	$ 4,500	2005 est.
142	Jamaica	$ 4,400	2005 est.
143	Serbia	$ 4,400	2005
144	Sri Lanka	$ 4,300	2005 est.
145	Ecuador	$ 4,300	2005 est.
146	Morocco	$ 4,200	2005 est.
147	Suriname	$ 4,100	2005 est.
148	Egypt	$ 3,900	2005 est.
149	Maldives	$ 3,900	2002 est.
150	Syria	$ 3,900	2005 est.
151	Micronesia, Federated States of	$ 3,900	2000 est.
152	Montenegro	$ 3,800	2005 est.
153	Wallis and Futuna	$ 3,800	2004 est.
154	Indonesia	$ 3,600	2005 est.
155	Niue	$ 3,600	2000 est.
156	Cuba	$ 3,500	2005 est.
157	Iraq	$ 3,400	2005 est.
158	Montserrat	$ 3,400	2002 est.
159	Georgia	$ 3,300	2005 est.
160	India	$ 3,300	2005 est.
161	Angola	$ 3,200	2005 est.
162	Bolivia	$ 2,900	2005 est.
163	Saint Vincent and the Grenadines	$ 2,900	2002 est.

Table 15.6 | (*continued*)

Rank	Country	GDP per capita (PPP)	Date of Information
164	Nicaragua	$ 2,900	2005 est.
165	Vanuatu	$ 2,900	2003 est.
166	Honduras	$ 2,900	2005 est.
167	Vietnam	$ 2,800	2005 est.
168	Mayotte	$ 2,600	2003 est.
169	Papua New Guinea	$ 2,600	2005 est.
170	Ghana	$ 2,500	2005 est.
171	Saint Helena	$ 2,500	1998 est.
172	Lesotho	$ 2,500	2005 est.
173	Cameroon	$ 2,400	2005 est.
174	Pakistan	$ 2,400	2005 est.
175	Marshall Islands	$ 2,300	2001 est.
176	Zimbabwe	$ 2,300	2005 est.
177	Tonga	$ 2,300	2002 est.
178	Cambodia	$ 2,200	2005 est.
179	Mauritania	$ 2,200	2005 est.
180	Bangladesh	$ 2,100	2005 est.
181	Sudan	$ 2,100	2005 est.
182	Kyrgyzstan	$ 2,100	2005 est.
183	Guinea	$ 2,000	2005 est.
184	Gambia, The	$ 1,900	2005 est.
185	Laos	$ 1,900	2005 est.
186	Mongolia	$ 1,900	2005 est.
187	Moldova	$ 1,800	2005 est.
188	Senegal	$ 1,800	2005 est.
189	Uzbekistan	$ 1,800	2005 est.
190	Uganda	$ 1,800	2005 est.
191	Burma	$ 1,700	2005 est.
192	Solomon Islands	$ 1,700	2002 est.
193	Togo	$ 1,700	2005 est.
194	Korea, North	$ 1,700	2005 est.
195	Haiti	$ 1,700	2005 est.
196	Cote d'Ivoire	$ 1,600	2005 est.
197	Chad	$ 1,500	2005 est.

(*continued*)

Table 15.6 | (*continued*)

Rank	Country	GDP per capita (PPP)	Date of Information
198	Rwanda	$ 1,500	2005 est.
199	Bhutan	$ 1,400	2003 est.
200	Nepal	$ 1,400	2005 est.
201	Nigeria	$ 1,400	2005 est.
202	Congo, Republic of the	$ 1,300	2005 est.
203	Djibouti	$ 1,300	2002 est.
204	Mozambique	$ 1,300	2005 est.
205	Burkina Faso	$ 1,300	2005 est.
206	Mali	$ 1,200	2005 est.
207	Sao Tome and Principe	$ 1,200	2003 est.
208	Tajikistan	$ 1,200	2005 est.
209	Benin	$ 1,100	2005 est.
210	West Bank	$ 1,100	2003 est.
211	Tuvalu	$ 1,100	2000 est.
212	Kenya	$ 1,100	2005 est.
213	Central African Republic	$ 1,100	2005 est.
214	Eritrea	$ 1,000	2005 est.
215	Tokelau	$ 1,000	1993 est.
216	Liberia	$ 1,000	2005 est.
217	Ethiopia	$ 900	2005 est.
218	Niger	$ 900	2005 est.
219	Zambia	$ 900	2005 est.
220	Yemen	$ 900	2005 est.
221	Madagascar	$ 900	2005 est.
222	Afghanistan	$ 800	2004 est.
223	Kiribati	$ 800	2001 est.
224	Guinea-Bissau	$ 800	2005 est.
225	Sierra Leone	$ 800	2005 est.
226	Burundi	$ 700	2005 est.
227	Tanzania	$ 700	2005 est.
228	Congo, Democratic Republic of the	$ 700	2005 est.

Table 15.6 | (*continued*)

Rank	Country	GDP per capita (PPP)	Date of Information
229	Comoros	$ 600	2005 est.
230	Somalia	$ 600	2005 est.
231	Malawi	$ 600	2005 est.
232	Gaza Strip	$ 600	2003 est.
233	East Timor	$ 400	2004 est.

* Countries for which no information is available are not included in this list.

CULTURE, MOTIVATION, AND PRODUCTIVITY

One important issue all companies, work organizations, and businesses must address is the degree to which their employees will be productive in various types of work settings. All companies want to maximize productivity while minimizing personnel costs and the expenditure of other resources, thereby ensuring the greatest profit margins. This concern has led to an important area of research on productivity as a function of group size.

Early research on group productivity in the United States typically showed that individual productivity tends to decline in larger groups (Latané, Williams, & Harkins, 1979). These findings contributed to the coining of the term **social loafing.** Two factors appear to contribute to this phenomenon. One is reduced efficiency resulting from a lack of coordination among workers' efforts, resulting in lack of activity or duplicate activity. The second factor is a reduction in effort by individuals when they work in groups as compared to when they work by themselves. Latané (1981) and his colleagues (Latané et al., 1979) conducted a number of studies investigating group size, coordination, and effort. They found that in larger groups, both lack of coordination and reduced effort resulted in decreased productivity. Latané (1981) attributed these findings to a diffusion of responsibility in groups. As group size increases, the responsibility for getting a job done is divided among more people, and group members ease up because their individual contribution is less recognizable.

Early cross-cultural research on groups and their productivity, however, found exactly the opposite phenomenon in other cultures. Earley (1989) examined social loafing in an organizational setting among managerial trainees in the United States and in the People's Republic of China. Subjects in both cultures worked on a task under conditions of low or high accountability and low or high shared responsibility. The results clearly indicated social loafing for the American subjects, whose individual performances in a group were less than when working alone, but not for the Chinese.

Shirakashi (1985) and Yamaguchi, Okamoto, and Oka (1985) conducted studies involving Japanese participants in several tasks. They found that not only did social loafing not occur, but exactly the opposite occurred. Working in a group enhanced individual performance rather than diminished it. Gabrenya, Wang, and Latané (1985) also demonstrated this **social striving** in a sample of Chinese schoolchildren. These authors have speculated that cultures such as China and Japan foster interpersonal interdependence and group collective functioning more than do the American culture, thus fostering group productivity because of increasing coordination among ingroup members. These cultures also place higher values on individual contributions in group settings.

Interestingly, this trend may also be occurring in the United States, perhaps as a result of the influence of Asian business practices that focus on teamwork, cooperation, and quality (see Ebrahimpour & Johnson, 1992; Hodgetts, Luthans, & Lee, 1994). As a result of studying successful business practices overseas, many American companies have tried to adapt and adopt some of these practices, including increasing teamwork, in their daily work behaviors. Indeed, several studies involving American participants have begun to challenge the traditional notion of social loafing (for example, Harkins, 1987; Harkins & Petty, 1982; Shepperd & Wright, 1989; Wagner, 1995; Weldon & Gargano, 1988; Zaccaro, 1984). Jackson and Williams (1985), for instance, reported that Americans working collectively improved performance and productivity. In a more recent study, Westaby (1995) asked participants in the United States and Japan to complete a paper-and-pen tracing task, either individually or in the presence of a group. Although the author expected that the Japanese would perform better in the group situation, the effect of group presence was actually the same for Americans and Japanese. Participants of both cultures had higher productivity and job quality in the presence of a group than when working alone. Further analyses indicated that although Japanese participants had higher productivity than American participants in general (regardless of social context), there was no difference in the quality of the work. Thus, our notions of social loafing and group productivity are now being challenged not only cross-culturally but also within American culture.

How does social striving work in the United States? Clearly, the same processes that work in one culture may or may not work in another. Bagozzi, Werbeke, and Gavino (2003), for instance, showed that while shame produced positive effects in Philippino employees (enhanced customer relationship building and civic virtue), it had negative effects in Dutch employees (diminished sales volume, and problems in communication and relationships). Some scholars have suggested that one way in which work groups and teams can become more productive in cultures like that in the United States is through the use of constructive thought patterns that help to transform self-managing teams into self-leading teams (for example, Manz, 1992; Neck & Manz, 1994). The idea is that employees become empowered to influence strategic issues concerning what they do and why, in addition to how they do their work. Again, these suggestions highlight the notion that different bases may underlie productivity or nonproductivity in different cultural groups.

CULTURE, LEADERSHIP, AND MANAGEMENT STYLES

Cultural Differences in the Definition of Leadership and Management

In many industrialized cultures, **leadership** can be defined as the "process of influence between a leader and followers to attain group, organizational, or societal goals" (Hollander, 1985, p. 486). Leaders may be autocratic, dictatorial, democratic, and so on. In common language, we speak of "strong" and "effective" leaders as opposed to "weak" and "ineffective" ones. In many work situations, especially in the United States, we expect leaders to have vision, authority, and power and to give subordinates tasks that have meaning in a larger picture. In American culture, leaders are expected to be decision makers—"movers and shakers" of organizations and of people.

In other cultures, leaders may share many of these same traits, but their leadership and managerial styles are not necessarily seen as dynamic or action-oriented. For example, some of the most effective leaders and managers in organizations in India are seen as much more nurturing, taking on a parental role within the company and in relation to their subordinates (Sinha, 1979). These leaders are seen as much more participative, guiding and directing their subordinates' tasks and behaviors as opposed to merely giving directives. Still, leaders and managers in India need to be flexible, at times becoming very authoritative in their work roles. Thus, the optimal leadership style in India, according to Sinha, is somewhere between a totally participative and totally authoritative style.

Another way leadership and managerial styles differ across cultures is in the boundaries of that leadership. In American culture, for example, workers make a clear distinction between work and personal life. When 5:00 P.M. arrives and the bell to end work rings, many American workers consider themselves "off" from work and on their personal time. The boundary between work and their personal lives is very clear. Leaders, bosses, and others in the company should have nothing to say about how members of the company live their personal lives (for example, where they should live or whom they should marry). In other cultures, however, the boundaries between work and personal life are less clear. In many countries, the individual's existence at work becomes an integral part of the self. Thus, the distinction between work and company, on the one hand, and one's personal life, on the other, is fuzzy and blurred. Needless to say, leaders in such cultures can request overtime work from their subordinates and expect to receive it with much less griping than in American culture.

As the distinction between work and self becomes blurred, so do the boundaries of jurisdiction for leaders. For example, leaders and managers in

India and Japan are expected to look after their subordinates in terms of their work and existence within the company; but it is not uncommon for leaders to be concerned with their subordinates' private lives as well. Subordinates in these cultures often will not hesitate to consult with their bosses about problems at home and to seek advice and help from them about those problems. Leaders, more often than not, will see helping their subordinates with this part of their lives as an integral and important part of their jobs. In India and Japan, it is not uncommon for bosses to find marriage partners for their subordinates and to look after them inside as well as outside the company. The bond between them extends well beyond the company.

Cross-Cultural Research on Leadership and Management

Given these cross-cultural differences in the definition of leadership, it is not surprising that many cross-cultural studies report differences in specific leadership behaviors (see, for example, Black & Porter, 1991, on managerial differences in the United States and Hong Kong; Okechuku, 1994, on managers' ratings of subordinates in Canada, Hong Kong, and China; Smith, Peterson, & Schwartz, 2002, on sources of guidance of managers in 47 nations). Smith, Peterson, and Misumi (1994), for instance, obtained effectiveness ratings of work teams in electronics assembly plants in Japan, Great Britain, and the United States, as well as ratings of 10 event-management processes used by superiors. The results indicated that for the Japanese, work performance depended on the relatively frequent use of manuals and procedures and on relatively frequent guidance from supervisors (related to high Uncertainty Avoidance). American and British supervisors, however, favored more contingent responses, suggesting that the preferred managerial response depends on the specific event or task they face.

Many other studies have documented cross-cultural differences in leadership and managerial style. Schmidt and Yeh (1992) found cross-national differences in leader influence strategies in Japan, Taiwan, Australia, and Great Britain. Howell, Dorfman, Hibino, Lee, and Tale (1995) found cultural differences in decision making and contingent punishment in Japan, Korea, Taiwan, Mexico, and the United States. Gerstner and Day (1994) asked students from eight countries to rate 59 traits of a business leader; they found that the ratings correlated highly with Hofstede's indices of Individualism–Collectivism, Power Distance, and Uncertainty Avoidance.

Some studies have attempted to identify culture-specific leadership and managerial styles. Many authors, for example, have tried to describe the Japanese management style (see, for example, the review by Keys, Denton, & Miller, 1994), in hopes of adapting Japanese leadership and managerial practices to American industry. Similarly, Jou and Sung (1990) have described four managerial styles prevalent in Taiwan. No doubt much of this attention to Japan and other Asian countries was due to the widespread success of Asian companies and economies, including those of South Korea, Hong Kong,

Taiwan, and mainland China. In the past ten years, however, the American economy and businesses appear to be doing relatively better in the world economy, while many Asian economies are struggling. These dynamic trends in the global economy are associated with an evolution in studies of managerial styles across cultures, and many authors are now questioning the long-term effectiveness of Asian managerial and leadership approaches of the past (see, for example, Keys, Denton, & Miller, 1994).

Not all cross-cultural research on this topic, however, has shown cultural differences; a substantial amount of literature documents cultural similarities in leadership behaviors as well. For example, Smith, Peterson, Misumi, and Bond (1992) examined work teams in Japan, Hong Kong, the United States, and Great Britain, and found that leaders who were rated high in behaviors related to task performance and group maintenance all achieved higher work quality. Smith (1998) also found consistent themes in a survey of managers' handling of day-to-day work events in Brazil, Mexico, Colombia, and Argentina. Many other studies (see review by Bond & Smith, 1996) show similar cross-cultural consistencies in some aspects of managerial behavior.

How are we to make sense of the literature that shows both similarities and differences across cultures in leadership and managerial behaviors? Misumi (1985) suggests that management involves general and universal functions that all effective leaders must carry out, but that the specific ways in which they are carried out may differ. Misumi contrasts functions related to task performance and group maintenance, and suggests that both domains involve universal leadership goals that are consistent across cultures and companies. Different specific behaviors may be used to accomplish these managerial goals, however, depending on situations, companies, and cultures these behaviors will vary. This approach invites us to examine and understand human behavior on multiple levels—one level involving cross-cultural universals or similarities in functions and goals, and the other involving differences in culture- and context-specific instrumental behaviors.

In addition to cultural explanations of differences in leadership behaviors, an emerging line of research has demonstrated the potential effects of climate and national wealth on leadership. In an interesting series of studies, Van de Vliert and his colleagues and shown that the climate of a country—whether hot, cold, or mild—is related to levels of poverty and workers' wages (Van de Vliert, 2003), motives for volunteer work (Van de Vliert, Huang, & Levine, 2004), happiness and altruism (Van de Vliert, Huang, & Parker, 2004), domestic violence (Van de Vliert, Schwartz, Huismans, Hofstede, & Daan, 1999), and leader reliance on subordinates (Van de Vliert & Smith, 2004). In one of his latest studies, Van de Vliert (2006) examined the relationship between climate and autocratic leadership, in which superiors act in more self-centered ways, make decisions unilaterally, and supervise subordinates' activities more closely. The sample included 17,370 middle managers from companies in 61 cultures. He found that autocratic leadership styles were less effective in rich countries with a demanding (very harsh hot or cold) climate, but more effective in poor countries with a demanding climate (Figure 15.1).

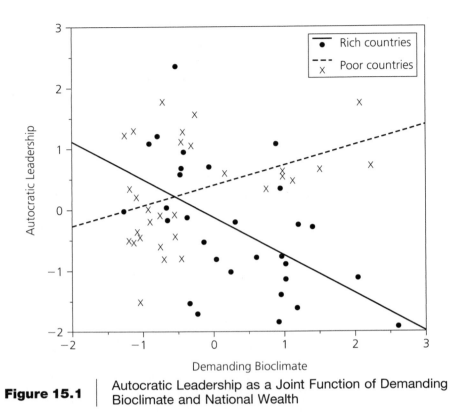

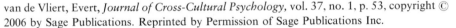

Figure 15.1 | Autocratic Leadership as a Joint Function of Demanding Bioclimate and National Wealth

van de Vliert, Evert, *Journal of Cross-Cultural Psychology*, vol. 37, no. 1, p. 53, copyright © 2006 by Sage Publications. Reprinted by Permission of Sage Publications Inc.

Intracultural and cross-cultural research has accomplished much in the way of documenting cross-cultural consistencies and differences in leadership behaviors. Less frequent in the literature, however, are studies that examine leadership and managerial effectiveness in intercultural settings. What happens, for example, when managers from other countries and cultures—Japan, Korea, Hong Kong, France, or Germany, for example—come to the United States and are placed in a situation in which they must manage and lead American subordinates? What happens when Americans are sent to other countries? Such situations occur frequently in today's global marketplace and are often central to the effective and successful functioning of companies. Yet research has been slow to address these complex questions. A study by Thomas and Toyne (1995) suggests that American subordinates may respond best when managers from other cultures demonstrate moderate levels of adaptation to the American culture and employee; high or low levels of adaptation have less positive effects on the subordinates. More research on this important topic is obviously necessary to capture the essence of effective intercultural management, a situation that promises to become even more important in the future.

CULTURE AND DECISION-MAKING PROCESSES

How is your pay determined? Is it by how much you do? Your seniority? Your degrees, certifications, or qualifications? Some combination? Are these decisions fair? These, and other, decisions are one of the most important things a company, or any organization, does. As with many other types of behaviors, culture influences how a company makes decisions.

Making Decisions

Many organizations in the United States use a democratic decision-making procedure. In a democratic procedure, every person involved has a say in the decision, usually by way of a vote; once votes are tallied, the decision of the majority prevails. This procedure has advantages and disadvantages. A major advantage to this procedure is that everyone has an equal say in the process. Democratic decision making is associated with an individualistic cultural viewpoint, which tends to see each person as a separate, autonomous being.

The democratic process can also lead to considerable red tape and bureaucracy. Many organizations, in fact, are not so much democracies as oligarchies (Ferrante, 1992). An **oligarchy** is an organizational structure characterized by rule- or decision-making power of a few. Decisions are typically made by people "at the top," who then impose their decisions on subordinates. Sometimes the sheer size of organizations necessitates that they be oligarchies if decisions are to be made at all. If everyone were to be involved in all types of decisions, the bureaucratic process would simply be too unwieldy and time-consuming. This top-down approach to business decision making is characteristic of many American companies.

Cross-cultural research and the intercultural experiences of many businesspersons reveal interesting differences in organizational decision making across cultures. One of the most studied cultures is that of Japan, because of its economic successes over the past few decades. (Similar decision-making procedures in other cultures are reviewed in Berry, Poortinga, Segall, and Dasen, 1992). The Japanese process of decision making is known as the **ringi** system. In a Japanese company, there is no formal system by which every person is ensured a vote. Instead, a proposal is circulated among all people who will be affected by it, regardless of status, rank, or position. Initiatives for proposals can come from top, middle, or lower management, or from subordinates within a business section. Even before a proposal is formally circulated among all interested parties, there is often considerable discussion and debate about the proposal. All views are taken into account, so that the proposal, when written and formally circulated, addresses concerns and negative consequences raised by as many parties as possible. There is considerable consultation about the proposal on as broad a basis as possible, and consensus is achieved before the proposal is formally implemented. This broad-based, consensus-building procedure is called **nemawashi.** If proposals do not achieve consensus by this procedure, they do not appear formally. Proposals that have gone through this procedure and have received the blessing of all those affected are then put in the form of a formal proposal on paper. A routing of the proposal involves all section chiefs and managers before it gets to the person or persons on top, who then put their formal stamp of approval on it. Needless to say, by the time something gets to that stage, it has met with the approval of many people throughout the organization.

Like all decision-making procedures, the Japanese system has advantages and disadvantages. One of the major disadvantages is the time-consuming nature of the process. In fact, the inability of Japanese managers to make a decision on the spot in international negotiations is often a source of frustration for American negotiators, who are used to dealing with single decision makers. The Japanese negotiator, however, must contact all the people within the company affected by the impending decision prior to making that decision. An advantage of the Japanese system, however, is the speed with which decisions can be implemented. Although the Japanese typically take much more time making a decision, they can usually implement it relatively quickly. No doubt, having everyone briefed in advance about the proposal aids in speedy implementation. Also, people in a collectivistic culture are more likely to get behind a decision that is for the good of the company, whatever their personal feelings about it.

Cross-cultural studies of organizational decision making point out other important and interesting differences between cultures. Yates, Lee, and Shinotsuka (1996), for example, found that people of East Asian cultures were more confident than Americans that their decisions were correct. To explain these findings, the authors suggest that people of East Asian cultures tend to select what may appear to be the first adequate solution to a problem that is identified, rather than considering a wide range of alternatives before deciding. Smith, Wang, and Leung (1997) obtained similar results in their study of 121 managers from mainland China, who reported strong reliance on widespread beliefs as a source of guidance when making decisions and handling various work events. Radford and colleagues (Radford, Nakane, Ohta, & Mann, 1991; Radford, Mann, Ohta, & Nakane, 1993) found comparable differences between Australian and Japanese students. The Australians preferred careful, individual thought when making decisions; the Japanese preferred other strategies that involved more interpersonal dimensions. On an organizational level, Hall, Jiang, Loscocco, and Allen (1993) compared decision-making patterns in small businesses in China and the United States. They found that, in general, the Chinese organizations were more centralized than their American counterparts.

Weatherly and Beach (1998) conducted four studies that examined the relationship between organizational culture and decision making involving managers and employees from a number of commercial organizations. They found that the decisions made by an organization are generally influenced by the degree to which features of the options are compatible with features of the organization's own culture; the higher the degree of compatibility, the more likely it is that the decision will endorse that option. They also found that an organization's employees are more likely to endorse a management decision if features of the decision are compatible with features of the organizational culture. This study is important because it places organizational decision making within the larger context of organizational culture at multiple levels.

One particular problem that has plagued decision making in groups is "groupthink"—a collective pattern of thinking that hinders effective group decisions. Groupthink is generally characterized by direct pressure; self-censorship; illusions of invulnerability, unanimity, or morality; mind guarding; collective rationalization; and shared stereotypes (Janis, 1983). These types of processes may underlie social loafing and general apathy toward work and productivity. Such destructive thought patterns, however, can be transformed into constructive ones, or "teamthink" (Neck & Manz, 1994). Teamthink involves the encouragement of divergent views, open expression of concerns and ideas, awareness of limitations and threats, recognition of members' uniqueness, and discussion of collective doubts. These constructive patterns lead to more effective decision making. Such a process may be critical for many organizations in many cultures, and especially for increasingly diversified companies in the United States, because it may be one way of maintaining individuality while serving the collective common good of the organization.

Fairness

Leaders often rely on being perceived as fair in order to have any sense of effectiveness. Thus, research on judgments of fairness has become an important area of study. Research in this area generally falls under one of two categories— studies on the outcomes of decisions regarding the distribution of resources such as pay (**distributive justice**), and studies on the process of making such decisions (**procedural justice**).

Morris and Leung (2000) reviewed the research in this area, and classified cross-cultural studies or distributive justice into two types: studies examining cross-cultural differences in the criteria by which decisions are made, and studies examining cross-cultural differences in the behaviors judged to match the criteria. With regard to the former, Morris and Leung noted many inconsistencies in the literature across studies in the findings, and concluded that people of different cultures apply different criteria in making allocation decisions, and that these criteria are based on situational cues. Different situations in different cultures produce different cues which, in turn, are associated with different criteria to be used in making allocating decisions.

With regard to the behaviors judged to match criteria, Americans' judgments of fairness are more likely to be tied to judgments of performance and merit, whereas many East Asians' judgments, such as South Koreans, are more tied to seniority, education, and family size (Hundley & Kim, 1997). Morris and Leung's analysis of these studies suggested that these types of judgments are not static; as cultural beliefs, values, and opinions change across time, their judgments of this aspect of fairness also shift across time. In Japan today, for example, there is a much larger concern for performance and merit-based rewards than seniority and education, as compared with 20 or 30 years ago (Matsumoto, 2002).

As with distributive justice, Morris and Leung (2000) separated studies related to procedural justice into studies examining criteria and then the behaviors associated with the criteria. The studies they reviewed suggested that in hierarchical, high-Power-Distance cultures, people in legitimate positions of authority can treat subordinates more harshly before this behavior is seen as unfair. Moreover, a meta-analysis examining 25 studies in 14 cultures (Fischer & Smith, 2003) indicated that the hierarchical nature of cultures was important in influencing reward allocation. Specifically, they found that rewards such as pay and promotions were distributed in hierarchical cultures differentially on the basis of equity and performance, whereas more egalitarian, horizontal cultures preferred equality over equity. Also importantly, Fischer and Smith found that individualism–collectivism was *not* as important in determining reward allocations as the hierarchical, power dimensions of culture were.

INTERCULTURAL ISSUES REGARDING BUSINESS AND WORK

As companies become increasingly dependent on other companies in other countries and cultures for business survival and success, people today are facing an ever-larger number of intercultural issues in the workplace. Add to these organizational developments the increasingly porous and flexible nature of national borders, and the result is a large number of people of different cultural backgrounds, lifestyles, values, and behaviors living and working together. These social trends and changes bring their own particular set of issues, challenges, and opportunities regarding intercultural interactions in the workplace and other work-related situations.

For multinational corporations, international business is not just international; it is intercultural. As we have seen throughout this chapter, business organizations are affected in many different ways by the cultures in which they reside. Organizational structures differ, organizational decision-making procedures differ, and people differ—in their definitions of work, work-related values, identification between self and company, and rules of interacting with other workers. Today's international business world requires that business organizations, and the people within them, gain intercultural competence as well as business competence.

In this section of the chapter, we will discuss three broad areas in which intercultural issues have come to the fore in recent decades: international negotiation, overseas assignments, and working with an increasingly diverse workforce population.

Negotiation

Improving communications technologies and changes in trade and tariff laws have resulted in an increasing interdependence among countries for economic and business survival. Not only multinational corporations but domestic companies too need to negotiate with companies in other countries to obtain resources, sell products, and conduct other business activities.

In the United States, Americans generally approach negotiation with a certain set of assumptions, summarized in Table 15.7 (Kimmel, 1994). In the United States, negotiation is a business, not a social activity. The objective of the negotiation is to get a job done, which usually requires a mixture of problem solving and bargaining. Communication is direct and verbal, with little deliberate or intentional use of nonverbal behaviors in the communication process.

Along with the 11 basic assumptions summarized in Table 15.7, Kimmel (1994) lists eight cultural values related to the American negotiation process:

1. *Time* is a commodity to be used efficiently to accomplish goals.
2. *Individual control.* You control your own destiny, and should do something about your life.
3. *Specialization* is desirable in work and social relationships; there is little desire for consistency or harmony.
4. *Pragmatism.* There are few absolute truths; what works is good.
5. *Democracy.* Everyone with an interest in an issue should have a say in the process.
6. *Equal opportunity.* People should have equal opportunities to develop their abilities.
7. *Independence.* Authority is resisted, and everyone has a right to privacy.
8. *Competition.* One must compete with others to get ahead; achievements are rewarded through upward mobility and income.

Negotiation processes in other cultures, however, challenge many of these traditionally American assumptions. In the arena of international negotiation, negotiators come as representatives not only of their companies but of their cultures as well. They bring all the issues of culture—customs, rituals, rules, and heritage—to the negotiating table. Factors that we are not even aware of play a role in these negotiating sessions, such as the amount of space between the people, how to greet each other, what to call each other, and what kinds of expectations we have of each other. The "diplomatic dance" that has been observed between American and Arab negotiators is but one example. People from Arab cultures tend to interact with others at a much closer distance than Americans are accustomed to. As the Arabs move closer, Americans unconsciously edge backward, whereupon the Arabs unconsciously edge forward, until they are almost chasing each other around the room.

Many studies have examined the Japanese approach to negotiation (see, for example, Allerheiligen, Graham, & Lin, 1985; Goldman, 1994; Graham, 1983, 1984, 1993; Graham & Andrews, 1987), which challenges virtually all of the American assumptions. Graham and Andrews, for example, videotaped American and Japanese participants during negotiation, then reviewed the videotapes with them to discuss negotiation processes and outcomes. One of the main concerns expressed by participants in both cultures involved language and communication processes. Indeed, even small cultural differences can have

Table 15.7 | U.S. Assumptions about Negotiating

Topic	Description
Conception of the negotiation process	Negotiation is a business, not a social activity. The object is to get a job done, which usually requires a mixture of problem-solving and bargaining activities. Most negotiations are adversarial, and negotiators are trying to get as much as possible for their side. The flow of a negotiation is from prenegotiation strategy sessions to opening sessions to give-and-take (bargaining) to final compromises to signing and implementation of agreements. All parties are expected to give up some of their original demands. Success can be measured in terms of how much each party achieves its bottom-line objectives.
Type of issues	Substantive issues are more important than social and emotional issues. Differences in positions are seen as problems to be solved.
Protocol	Negotiations are scheduled occasions that require face-to-face interactions among the parties involved. Efficiency of time centering on substantive tasks is valued over ceremony and social amenities. During negotiation, standardized procedures of interaction should be followed; social interactions are informal and should occur elsewhere.
Reliance on verbal behaviors	Communication is direct and verbal. What is said is more important than how it is said, or what is not said. Communications tend to be spontaneous and reactive after presentation of initial positions.
Nature of persuasive arguments	Tactics such as bluffing are acceptable in the bargaining process. Current information and ideas are more valid than history or tradition.
Individual negotiator's latitude	The representatives who negotiate have a great deal of latitude in reaching agreements for their companies.
Bases of trust	Negotiators trust the other parties until they prove untrustworthy. Trust is judged by the behavior of others.
Risk-taking propensities	Negotiators are open to different or novel approaches to problem issues. Brainstorming is good. Avoiding uncertainty is not important in the negotiation process. Fixed ideological positions and approaches are not acceptable.
Value of time	Time is very important. Punctuality is expected. A fixed time is allotted for concluding a negotiation.
Decision-making system	Majority voting and/or authoritative decisions are the rule. Certain team members are expected to be authorized to make binding decisions.
Forms of satisfactory agreement	Oral commitments are not binding. Written contracts that are exact and impersonally worded are binding. There is the expectation of contractual finality. Lawyers and courts are the final arbitrators in any arguments after contracts have been signed.

Kimmel, 1994.

big effects on international business. In the Japanese language, for example, the word for "yes" (*hai*) is also used as a conversation regulator, signaling to others that you are listening to what they are saying (but not necessarily agreeing). American negotiators, hearing this word used as a regulator, often interpret it to mean "yes." As you can imagine, considerable conflict can and does arise when, after using this word throughout the conversation, the Japanese take a contradictory position. To the Japanese, they were merely saying "um hmm," but to the Americans, it sounded like "yes." Such misunderstandings can lead to conflict, mistrust, the breakdown of negotiations, and the loss of business and good-faith relations (see Okamoto, 1993).

One interesting cultural difference between American and Japanese approaches to negotiation is in entertainment. American businesspeople are used to "sitting down at the table and hammering out a deal." Japanese business-people may want to have dinner, have drinks, and play golf. The Japanese are more willing to engage in these activities because they are interested in developing a relationship with their business partners as people; it also gives them a good opportunity to make judgments about the character or integrity of potential partners, which is an important aspect of their business decisions. American businesspeople are primarily concerned with "the deal" and what is right for the company's bottom line. Many American business negotiators not used to the Japanese style of negotiating become impatient with these activities, feeling as though they never get to talk business. By the same token, many Japanese negotiators, put on the spot by American negotiators, feel as though they have been thrust into a situation and forced to make a decision they cannot possibly make. Needless to say, these cultural differences in negotiation styles have led to many a breakdown in international business negotiations.

One study highlighted the difficulties associated with intercultural negotia-tion. In this study, American and Japanese business students and managers negotiated with each other either intraculturally or interculturally. Their actual behaviors were transcribed and coded. As predicted, Americans communicated more directly and avoided using social influence when negotiating with other Americans; Japanese negotiators communicated more indirectly and used more social influence when negotiating with other Japanese. When negotiating inter-culturally, the Japanese adapted to the situation, interacting more directly and using less social influence. Yet, the outcomes of the negotiation were not as successful as when negotiating intraculturally, despite the fact that adaptive behaviors had occurred.

Gelfand, Major, Raver, Nishii, and O'Brien's (2006) theoretical work on relational self-construals may explain why. They argue that relational self-construals—that is, viewing oneself as fundamentally connected with others—is an important aspect to understanding negotiation. Negotiation starts with individuals coming with their own sense of relational self, which is influenced by the culture from which they come. Over the process of negotiation, one of the goals of negotiation is to align the relational self-construal of the negotiators so that they are congruent. Congruence between the relational self-construals of the negotiators aids in the production of relational behaviors, created value, and eventually economic or relational capital. One implication of this model, therefore, is that even if behaviors are adapted to the situation, negotiation may not be as fruitful as it can be unless the relational self-construals of the negotiators are aligned through the negotiation process.

Cross-cultural research on international negotiation has spanned other countries and cultures as well, including Brazil (Allerheiligen et al., 1985; Graham, 1983, 1984), China (Allerheiligen et al., 1985), Russia (Graham, Evenko, & Rajan, 1992), Taiwan (Graham, Kim, Lin, & Robinson, 1988), Germany and Britain (Campbell, Graham, Jolibert, & Meissner, 1988), and Mexico and Canada (Adler, Schwartz, & Graham, 1987). Many of these studies, like those on the Japanese process, demonstrate how people of different cultures approach negotiation from often quite different viewpoints. For example, Tse, Francis, and Walls (1994) examined Chinese and Canadian negotiation practices. They found that the Chinese avoided conflict more than the Canadians did, and when conflict did occur, they opted for withdrawal or consultation with superiors more than the Canadians did. Context may also play an important role in the negotiation process, as people of collectivistic cultures tend to make a larger distinction between ingroup and outgroup members than do people of individualistic cultures. Thus, negotiation processes involving collectivistic cultures may differ drastically depending on the exact nature of the relationship between the negotiators (ingroup versus outgroup) and the exact context of the negotiation (formal meeting during the day at a company versus informal meeting after work in a bar).

The available research tells us little about the degree to which negotiators adjust their cultural practices depending on whom they are negotiating with, and on what parameters such adjustment occurs. Nor has cross-cultural research done much to elucidate the ingredients of a "successful" negotiation. Furthermore, a review of cross-cultural studies on negotiation (Gelfand & Dyer, 2000) suggests that factors such as proximal social conditions (deadlines, negotiator relationships), the negotiators' psychological states (implicit theories and metaphors, judgment biases), and behaviors (tactics) are also important in understanding international/intercultural discussions and negotiations. Indeed, Gelfand and Dyer's model of the influence of culture on the negotiation process identifies many important variables that indicate that the process is very complex (Figure 15.2). Future studies are needed to examine these important issues.

Overseas Assignments

Many corporations with subsidiaries and business partners in other countries are finding it increasingly necessary to send workers abroad for extended periods. Worker exchanges and overseas assignments are used to train employees and business units in another country in skills that are found only there. Such overseas assignments can give rise to myriad problems, not only because of all the cultural differences discussed in this chapter, but also because

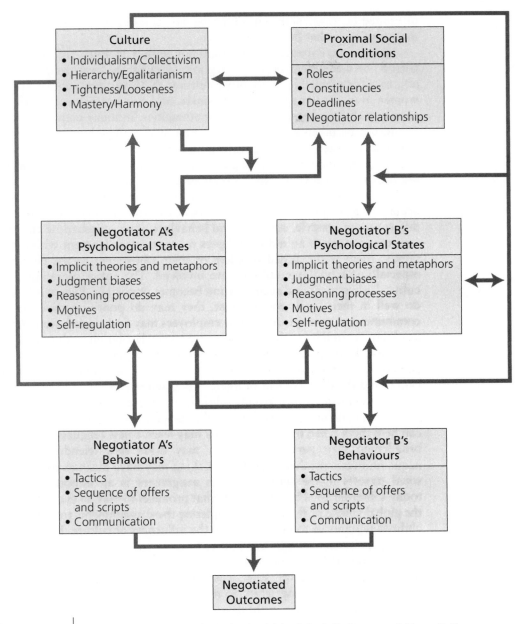

Figure 15.2 | A Dynamic and Psychological Model of Culture and Negotiation

Gelfand, Michele J. A Cultural Perspective on Negotiation: Progress, Pitfalls and Prospects, *Applied Psychology: An International Review,* vol. 49, no. 1, p. 77, 2000, Blackwell Publishing. Reprinted with permission.

of limited language skills and differing expectations of the person on assignment and his or her hosts.

American companies today would not hesitate to send "the most qualified person" on assignment, either for negotiation or for the long term, regardless of sex, race, or ethnicity. Many other cultures, however, are not accustomed to women in important positions in business, and may not be totally receptive to people of different perceived races or ethnicities. In many contexts, a woman would not be taken as seriously as a man, and racial/ethnic stereotypes may dominate interactions. Resulting frustrations might include not being looked at during a conversation and having questions directed to a man when a woman is the recognized leader or expert on an assignment team.

Many of the most pressing problems for people on overseas assignments occur not at work but in other aspects of living in a foreign country. Major differences in lifestyle, customs, and behaviors often overshadow cultural differences at work. If an individual goes on overseas assignment with his or her family, there is the added problem of their adjustment to the new culture, especially if school-age children are involved. The entire spectrum of intercultural adjustment and acculturation becomes important. Even when workers do well in their work environment, they may do poorly in their home and community adjustment. And while employees may find a safe haven during the workday in a milieu with which they are somewhat familiar, their families are often left bearing the brunt of intercultural adaptation. Interested readers should review the material presented in Chapter 9 on intercultural communication and the development of intercultural sensitivity.

On the positive side, people who go on overseas assignments have a tremendous opportunity to learn new skills and new ways of doing their work that can help them when they return. They may learn a new language and customs, broadening their perspectives. They may make new friends and business acquaintances, and this type of networking may have business as well as personal payoffs in the future. Foreign assignment is an important aspect of today's international business world that promises to play an even larger role in the global village of the future. Completing these assignments to the best of our abilities requires us to understand all the influences of culture, both inside and outside the workplace. In the future, these types of skills will be even more valuable than they are today. Little systematic, formal research exists on this topic in the published literature (despite an abundance of anecdotal and case-study data that are proprietary to many companies). Future research on this important topic will help in the design of intercultural adjustment programs for company employees, allowing them to be more effective in their overseas assignments.

Working with an Increasingly Diverse Workforce Population

Organizations all around the world are dealing with an increasingly diverse workforce population. For example, American companies are increasingly hosting workers from other countries. Joint ventures between American and

Asian and European companies have increased over the past 10 years—most visibly in automobile manufacturing, but also in computers and semiconductors, communication technology, and many other fields. One result is an influx of workers from these countries and cultures to the United States.

Many of the problems that arise when American workers go overseas also arise when foreign workers come to the United States. Often, managers from another culture come to oversee and supervise production or assembly, bringing with them all the expectations, customs, and rituals of their home country. Not surprisingly, they find that those ways of doing business do not work in the United States, because the people are different and the system is different. Similarly, many of the problems experienced by American families abroad are also experienced by the families of workers who come to the United States. To make the transition easier, many Japanese companies in the Los Angeles area have established little Japanese villages and apartments where the Japanese lifestyle and customs can be preserved. These controversial enclaves serve to maintain barriers between people, raising problems of their own.

One study highlights some of the problems and issues that may arise in these situations. In this study, Graham (1993) spent six months as a hidden participant observer at a Japanese automobile plant near Lafayette, Indiana (Subaru/Isuzu Automotive). During this time, the author was able to document worker resistance to Japanese management practices in the form of sabotage, protest, agitation, and confrontation. The results of this study brought into question the validity and worth of simply "transferring" the Japanese management model to the American milieu. The data also failed to support the contention that participation schemes (such as teamwork) automatically increase worker control or that decentralized authority structures increase worker autonomy.

Another study focused on cultural differences in ways of handling disagreement. In this study (Smith, Dugan, Peterson, & Leung, 1998), managers and supervisors from a variety of organizations in 23 countries completed a questionnaire about how they handled disagreements in their work unit. The responses were aggregated for each country, and the country mean values on the questionnaire were correlated with the country's scores on Hofstede's dimensions described earlier. The results indicated that power distance (PD) significantly predicted the frequency of disagreements between work groups. In handling disagreements, people in low-PD cultures tended to rely on subordinates and coworkers. People of individualistic countries relied more on their own personal experience and training, whereas people of collectivistic cultures relied more on formal rules and procedures. Although this study involved participants in different countries, these types of psychological differences based on Power Distance and Individualism–Collectivism may be important in understanding cultural differences within a single multicultural organization.

Despite the potential problems associated with receiving foreign workers, many of the advantages of overseas assignments also apply to receiving people from abroad. The ability to reap these benefits depends on the openness of the host organization to learn and on the goodwill and intent of the employee and the company to engage in a mutually beneficial partnership.

Even without international joint ventures and worker exchanges, many American companies are dealing with increasing diversity solely on the basis of the increasing diversity of the American population. The United States is home to people of many different races, ethnicities, and cultures. Within this "mixed salad" of cultures are generational differences, from recent immigrants to second-, third-, and multiple-generation Americans of wide-ranging ethnic and cultural backgrounds. The problems that can occur when two cultures clash can be magnified many times over when people from multiple cultures are thrust together to interact and work toward a common goal.

Many of the issues raised in dealing with people across countries and cultures are relevant for domestic work organizations dealing with an increasingly diverse American workforce as well. People come to work with different expectations, and different expectations can lead to intercultural clashes. Cultural differences in the management of time and people, in identification with work, and in making decisions all provide areas for conflict. People in the United States come to work with differences in work-related values and the degree to which they respect or minimize power and status differences between them. People come to work with different views regarding sex differences and how to manage uncertainty.

Many successful companies have met these challenges by making explicit what kinds of communication styles, decision making, productivity, and worker behaviors are important for the success of the company. Many companies today actively train their employees in intercultural issues ranging from communication to expectations (see, for example, Goldman, 1992); the most successful of these programs undoubtedly have important positive, practical implications in many areas of people's lives. Many companies have created temporary organizational cultures in which their employees can move and adapt without fear of losing themselves or their own personal cultures. They have designed ways not only of avoiding problems but also of handling problems effectively and constructively when they do arise. Negotiating all these issues requires additional work and effort by companies and people alike, but organizations that can do so successfully are likely to realize long-term benefits to the bottom line.

CULTURE AND SEXUAL HARASSMENT

You are the boss of a company that is trying to close a major deal with another company in another country. Your best negotiator is a woman, whom you trust and has been with the company for years. You have been told, however, that the people from the other company will not deal with a woman. When previous negotiating teams have been sent, their negotiators clearly ignore the woman and talk only to the male, even though the male is the woman's assistant. What would you do?

Complex issues concerning gender and sex are commonplace in organizations that work cross-culturally. One of these is sexual harassment. **Sexual harassment** is defined by the Equal Employment Opportunity Commission as unwelcome sexual advances, requests for sexual favors, or other verbal or physical conduct of a sexual nature in which submission to such behavior is a condition to employment and employment decisions affecting the individual (such as promotion), and where the behavior interferes with the individual's work environment or creates a intimidating, offensive, or hostile work environment. The past few decades have seen a dramatic increase in awareness to issues concerning sexual harassment in the U.S. workplace. The increase in the number of intercultural contacts in work organizations brought about by the creation of multinational companies and transfer of employees across borders has brought about an increase in the awareness of these issues cross-culturally as well.

To our knowledge, there is not yet formal research across a wide range of cultures documenting the incidence of sexual harassment, but we believe it is also widespread across cultures. This may be true for a variety of cultural reasons (Luthar & Luthar, 2002). For one, sex- and gender-based discriminatory actions—both in terms of behaviors and words—may be tolerated more across different cultures. Recall, for example, our discussion of cultural differences in masculinity versus femininity (Chapter 6). Cultures differ greatly in the degree to which they differentiate behaviors between men and women. One may even say that these differences are not only tolerated but also expected and natural; thus, what may be construed as sexual harassment in the United States may not been seen as such in other cultures. Moreover, there are large cultural differences in sex roles, which contribute to this situation. Differences across cultures in power and hierarchy also contribute to this state of affairs, because power differences contribute to the maintenance of sex and gender differences within a culture, and in many cultures males have more powerful roles in organizations.

When it occurs, sexual harassment may have the same effects across cultures. Studies examining the experiences of individuals have shown that there are three major types of sexual harassment-related experiences: sexist hostility, sexual hostility, and unwanted sexual advances (Fitzgerald, Gelfand, & Drasgow, 1995); these same clusters of experiences were reported by Latina women as well (Cortina, 2001). Fitzgerald and colleagues (Fitzgerald, Drasgow, Hulin, Gelfand, & Magley, 1997) demonstrated that sexual harassment in the U.S. workplace affects job satisfaction, health conditions, and psychological conditions. Subsequently, these same types of effects have been shown to occur in Turkey (Wasti, Bergman, Glomb, & Drasgow, 2000) and among Latinas (Cortina, Fitzgerald, & Drasgow, 2002).

Being the victim of sexual harassment can be stressful for anyone, and research shows that women across a wide range of cultures attempt to cope with these experiences in a variety of ways, including avoidance, denial, negotiation, advocacy seeking, and social coping (Cortina & Wasti, 2005; Wasti & Cortina, 2002). Research has demonstrated acculturation effects as well; in one study, Hispanic women with greater affiliation to mainstream American cultures experienced *more* sexual harassment than Hispanic women with less affiliation (Shupe, Cortina, Ramos, Fitzgerald, & Salisbury, 2002). Clearly, more cross-cultural research on this very important topic is needed, as well as education across many strata of society in many cultures.

CONCLUSION

The cultural differences that people bring with them to the workplace, both internationally and domestically, present us with challenges unprecedented in the modern industrialized period of history. To meet these challenges, business, government, and private organizations look to research and education about cultural diversity as it relates to work. Intercultural communication and competence training and business consulting with regard to managing diversity have become major growth industries.

Too often, the idea of managing diversity rests on the underlying assumption that diversity is an unwanted by-product of our work environment—a nuisance variable that must be dealt with in order to maximize efficiency. As we move toward a greater appreciation of cultural similarities and differences, however, we may gain a better appreciation for the different approaches to work, management, and leadership that have worked for different cultures. As we confront the challenges of diversity in the future, we need to move away from the notion of managing a nuisance variable to viewing it as a potential resource for tapping into products, services, and activities that will make companies more efficient, productive, and profitable than ever before. By tapping into diversity rather than managing it, perhaps we can increase international and intercultural cooperation not only in business but among people in general.

Finally, aside from the research we have reviewed above, other areas of cross-cultural study are just beginning to develop. For example, studies have documented cultural differences in "brand personality dimensions"; Japanese brands, for instance, may be associated with a dimension of peacefulness, Spanish brands with passion, and American brands may be associated with ruggedness and competence (Aaker, Benet-Martinez, & Garolera, 2001). Research has also begun to examine the characteristics of cultures that make songs, books, or movies popular or not (Salganik, Dodds, & Watts, 2006). These types of studies will complement well the studies in the workplace described above.

GLOSSARY

distributive justice fairness regarding the distribution of resources, such as pay, the corner office, or perks.

leadership The "process of influence between a leader and followers to attain group, organizational, or societal goals" (Hollander, 1985).

multinational and international corporations Work organizations that have subsidiaries, satellite offices, and work units in more than one country.

nemawashi The broad-based consensus-building procedure that occurs within the Japanese ringi system of decision making.

oligarchy An organizational structure characterized by rule- or decision-making power of a few. Decisions are typically made by people "at the top," who impose their decisions on subordinates.

organizational climate A shared perception of organizational policies, practices, and procedures, and how people feel about them.

organizational culture A dynamic system of rules involving attitudes, values, beliefs, norms, and behaviors that are shared among members of an organization.

procedural justice Fairness associated with the procedures and processes that organizations use to make decisions.

ringi The Japanese process of decision making, which involves circulating a proposal among all people who will be affected by it, addressing concerns and negative consequences raised by as many parties as possible, consulting on as broad a basis as possible about the proposal, and achieving consensus before the proposal is formally implemented.

sexual harassment Unwelcome sexual advances, requests for sexual favors, or other verbal or physical conduct of a sexual nature in which submission to such behavior is a condition to employment and employment decisions affecting the individual (such as promotion), and where the behavior interferes with the individual's work environment or creates an intimidating, offensive, or hostile work environment.

social loafing The common finding in research on group productivity in the United States that individual productivity tends to decline in larger groups.

social striving The opposite of social loafing; the finding in many cultures that working in a group enhances individual performance rather than diminishes it.

References

Aaker, J. L., Benet-Martinez, V., & Garolera, J. (2001). Consumption symbols as carriers of culture: A study of Japanese and Spanish brand personality constructs. *Journal of Personality and Social Psychology, 81,* 492–508.

Abad, V., Ramos, J., & Boyce, E. (1974). A model for delivery of mental health services to Spanish-speaking minorities. *American Journal of Orthopsychiatry, 44,* 584–595.

Abrams, D., Ando, K., & Hinkle, S. (1998). Psychological attachment to the group: Cross-cultural differences in organizational identification and subjective norms as predictors of workers' turnover intentions. *Personality and Social Psychology Bulletin, 24*(10), 1027–1039.

Abrams, K. K., Allen, L. R., & Gray, J. J. (1993). Disordered eating attitudes and behaviors, psychological adjustment, and ethnic identity: A comparison of black and white female college students. *International Journal of Eating Disorders, 14,* 49–57.

Abramson, R. P., & Pinkerton, D. S. (1995). *Sexual nature, sexual culture.* Chicago: University of Chicago Press.

Achenbach, T. M. (2001). *Child behavior checklist for ages 6 to 18.* Burlington: University of Vermont, Research Center for Children, Youth and Families.

Acioly, N. M., & Schliemann, A. D. (1986). *Intuitive mathematics and schooling in understanding a lottery game.* Paper presented at the Tenth PME Conference, London.

Adler, N. E., Boyce, T., Chesney, M. A., Cohen, S., Folkman, S., Kahn, R. L., & Syme, S. L. (1994). Socioeconomic status and health: The challenge of the gradient. *American Psychologist, 49*(1), 15–24.

Adler, N. J., Schwartz, T., & Graham, J. L. (1987). Business negotiations in Canada (French and English speakers), Mexico and the United States. *Journal of Business Research, 15,* 411–429.

Adorno, T. W., Frenkel-Brunswick, E., Levinson, D. J., & Sanford, R. N.

(1950). *The authoritarian personality.* New York: Harper & Row.

Adorno, T. W., Frenkel-Brunswik, E., & Levinson, D. J. (1950). *The authoritarian personality.* Oxford, England: Harpers.

Ajwani, J. K. (1982). A correlational study of Cattel's personality factor B. and I.Q. as measured by his culture fair test. *Indian Psychological Review, 22*(1), 9–11.

Akan, G. E., & Grilo, C. M. (1995). Sociocultural influences on eating attitudes and behaviors, body image, and psychological functioning: A comparison of African American, Asian American, and Caucasian college women. *International Journal of Eating Disorders, 18*(2), 181–187.

Akin-Ogundeji, O. (1988). An African perspective on personality: A case study of the Ibo. *Journal of Human Behavior and Learning, 5*(1), 22–26.

Al-Krenawi, A., & Graham, J. R. (2000). Culturally sensitive social work practice with Arab clients in mental health settings. *Health & Social Work, 25*(1), 9–22.

Al-Mutlaq, H., & Chaleby, K. (1995). Group psychotherapy with Arab patients. *Arab Journal of Psychiatry, 6*(2), 125–136.

Al-Subaie, A., & Alhamad, A. (2000). Psychiatry in Saudi Arabia. In I. Al-Junūn (Ed.), *Mental illness in the Islamic world* (pp. 205–233). Madison, CT: International Universities Press.

Alarcon, R. D. (1995). Culture and psychiatric diagnosis. *Cultural Psychiatry, 18*(3), 449–465.

Alarcon, R. D., & Leetz, K. L. (1998). Cultural intersections in the psychotherapy of borderline personality disorder. *American Journal of Psychotherapy, 52*(2), 176–190.

Albert, A. A., & Porter, J. R. (1986). Children's gender role stereotypes: A comparison of the United States and South Africa. *Journal of Cross-Cultural Psychology, 17*, 45–65.

Albright, L., Kenny, D. A., & Malloy, T. E. (1988). Consensus in personality judgments at zero acquaintance. *Journal of Personality and Social Psychology, 55*, 387–395.

Alderete, E., Vega, W. A., & Kolody, B. (2000). Lifetime prevalence of the risk factors for psychiatric disorders among Mexican migrant farmworkers in California. *American Journal of Public Health, 90*(4), 608–614.

Alegria, M., Takeuchi, D., Canino, G., Duan, N., Shrout, P. Meng, X., et al. (2004). Considering context, place and culture: the National Latino and Asian American Study. *International Journal of Methods and Psychiatric Research, 13*(4), 208–220.

Allamani, A., Voller, F., Kubicka, L., & Bloomfield, K. (2000). Drinking cultures and the position of women in nine European countries. *Substance Abuse, 21*, 231–247.

Allerheiligen, R., Graham, J. L., & Lin, C. (1985, Fall). Honesty in interorganizational negotiations in the United States, Japan, Brazil, and the Republic of China. *Journal of Macromarketing*, 4–16.

Allik, J., & McCrae, R. R. (2004). Towards a geography of personality traits: Patterns of profiles across 36 cultures. *Journal of Cross-Cultural Psychology, 35*, 13–28.

Allik, J., & Realo, A. (2004). Individualism-collectivism and social capital.

Journal of Cross-Cultural Psychology, 35, 29–49.

Allport, G. W. (1936). *Personality: A psychological interpretation*. New York: Holt.

Altarriba, J., & Santiago-Rivera, A. L. (1994). Current perspectives on using linguistic and cultural factors in counseling the Hispanic client. *Professional Psychology: Research and Practice, 25*(4), 388–397.

Amelang, M., & Borkenau, P. (1982). Ueber die faktorielle Struktur und externe Validtaet einiger Fragebogen-Skalen zur Erfassung von Dimensionen der Extraversion und emotionalen Labilitaet [The factional structure and external validity of some questionnaire scales for measurement of the dimensions of extraversion and emotional lability]. *Zeitschrift fuer Differentielle und Diagnostische Psychologie, 3*(2), 119–145.

American Psychiatric Association. (1987). *Diagnostic and statistical manual of mental disorders* (3rd ed.) [DSM-IIIR]. Washington, DC: Author.

American Psychiatric Association. (1994). *Diagnostic and statistical manual of mental disorders* (4th ed.) [DSMIV]. Washington, DC: Author.

American Psychological Association. (2002). *Guidelines on multicultural education, training, research, practice and organizational change for psychologists*. Washington, DC: Author.

Amir, Y., & Sharon, I. (1988). Are social psychological laws cross-culturally valid? *Journal of Cross-Cultural Psychology, 18*(4), 383–470.

Anderson, C. A., & Anderson, K. B. (1996). Violent crime rate studies in philosophical context: A destructive testing approach to heat and southern culture of violence effects. *Journal of Personality, 70*(4), 740–756.

Anderson, N. B., & Nickerson, K. J. (2005). Genes, race, and psychology in the genome era. *American Psychologist, 60*, 5–8.

Angyal, A. (1951). *Neurosis and treatment: A holistic theory.* New York: Wiley.

Archer, J. (2006). Cross-cultural differences in physical aggression

between partners: A social-role analysis. *Personality and Social Psychology Review, 10*, 133–153.

Argyle, M., & Cook, M. (1976). *Gaze and mutual gaze.* New York: Cambridge University Press.

Argyle, M., Henderson, M., Bond, M. H., Iizuka, Y., & Contarello, A. (1986). Cross-cultural variations in relationship rules. *International Journal of Psychology, 21*, 287–315.

Armstrong, T. L., & Swartzman, L. C. (1999). Asian versus Western differences in satisfaction with Western medical care: The mediational effects of illness attributions. *Psychology and Health, 14*, 403–416.

Armstrong, T. L., & Swartzman, L. C. (2001). Cross-cultural differences in illness models and expectations. In S. S. Kazarian & D. R. Evans (Eds.), *Handbook of cultural health psychology* (pp. 63–84). San Diego: Academic Press.

Arnault, D., Sakamoto, S., & Moriwake, A. (2006). Somatic and depressive symptoms in female Japanese and American Students: A preliminary investigation. *Transcultural Psychiatry, 43*(2), 275–286.

Arnett, J. (2001). *Adolescence and emerging adulthood: A cultural approach.* Upper Saddle River, NJ: Prentice Hall.

Arnett, J. J., & Balle-Jensen, L. (1993). Cultural bases of risk behavior: Danish adolescents. *Child Development, 64*(6), 1842–1855.

Asch, S. E. (1951). Effects of group pressure upon the modification and distortion of judgments. In H. Guetzkow (Ed.), *Groups, leadership and men: Research in human relations* (pp. 177–190). Pittsburgh: Carnegie Press.

Asch, S. E. (1955). Opinions and social pressures. *Scientific American, 193*, 31–35.

Asch, S. E. (1956). Studies of independence and conformity: A minority of one against a unanimous majority. *Psychological Monographs, 70*(9, Whole No. 416).

Atkeson, P. (1970). Building communication in intercultural marriage. *Psychiatry: Journal for the Study of Interpersonal Processes, 33*(3), 396–408.

Atkinson, D. R., Casa, A., & Abreu, J. (1992). Mexican American acculturation, counselor ethnicity and cultural sensitivity, and perceived counselor competence. *American Psychologist, 39*, 515–520.

Atkinson, D. R., Furlong, M. J., & Poston, W. C. (1986). Afro-American preferences for counselor characteristics. *Journal of Counseling Psychology, 33*, 326–330.

Atkinson, D. R., Maruyama, M., & Matsui, S. (1978). Effects of counselor race and counseling approach on Asian Americans' perceptions of counselor. *Journal of Counseling Psychology, 25*, 76–83.

Atkinson, D. R., Morten, G., & Sue, D. W. (1989). *Counseling American minorities* (3rd ed.). Dubuque, IA: Brown.

Au, T. K. (1983). Chinese and English counterfactuals: The Sapir-Whorf hypothesis revisited. *Cognition, 15*, 155–187.

Auerbach, J. G., Yirmiya, N., & Kamel, F. N. (1996). Behavior problems in Israeli Jewish and Palestinian preschool children. *Journal of Clinical Child Psychology, 25*(4), 398–405.

Azhar, M. Z., & Varma, S. L. (1996). Relationship of expressed emotion with relapse of schizophrenia patients in Kelantan. *Singapore Medical Journal, 37*, 82–85.

Azhar, M. Z., & Varma, S. L. (2000). Mental illness and its treatment in Malaysia. In I. Al-Junūn (Ed.), *Mental illness in the Islamic world* (pp. 163–186). Madison, CT: International Universities Press.

Azhar, M. Z., Varma, S. L., & Dharap, A. S. (1994). Religious psychotherapy in anxiety disorder patients. *Acta Psychiatry Scandinavica, 90*, 1–3.

Bagozzi, R. P., Werbeke, W., & Gavino Jr., J. C. (2003). Culture moderates the self-regulation of shame and its effects on performance: The case of salespersons in the Netherlands and the Philippines. *Journal of Applied Psychology, 88*, 219–233.

Bakan, D. (1966). *The duality of human existence*. Boston: Beacon Press.

Bal-Tal, D., & Labin, D. (2001). The effect of a major event on stereotyping: Terrorist attacks in Israel and Israeli adolescents' perceptions of Palestinians, Jordanians and Arabs. *European Journal of Social Psychology, 31*, 265–280.

Balint, M. (1959). *Thrills and regression*. London: Hogarth Press.

Balter, M. (2004). Seeking the key to music. *Science, 306*, 1120–1122.

Bargh, J. (1996). Automaticity in social psychology. In E. Higgins & A. Kruglanski (Eds.), *Social psychology: Handbook of basic principles* (pp. 169–183). New York: Guilford.

Bar-Haim, Y., Ziv, T., Lamy, D., & Hodes, R. M. (2006). Nature and nurture in own-face face processing. *Psychological Science, 17*, 159–163.

Barna, L. M. (1996). Stumbling blocks in intercultural communication. In L. A. Samovar & R. E. Porter (Eds.), *Intercultural communication: A reader* (8th ed., pp. 370–379). Belmont, CA: Wadsworth.

Barnlund, D. C., & Araki, S. (1985). Intercultural encounters: The management of compliments by Japanese and Americans. *Journal of Cross-Cultural Psychology, 16*(1), 9–26.

Barnlund, D. C., & Yoshioka, M. (1990). Apologies: Japanese and American styles. *International Journal of Intercultural Relations, 14*, 193–206.

Barreto, R. M., & Segal, S. P. (2005). Use of mental health services by Asian americans. *Psychiatric Services, 56*(6), 746–748.

Barry, H. (1980). Description and uses of the Human Relations Area Files. In H. C. Triandis & J. W. Berry (Eds.), *Handbook of cross-cultural psychology: Vol. 2. Methodology* (pp. 445–478). Boston: Allyn & Bacon.

Barry, H., Josephson, L., Lauer, E., & Marshall, C. (1976). Agents and techniques for child training. *Ethnology, 16*, 191–230.

Barstow, D. G. (1999). Female genital mutilation: The penultimate gender abuse. *Child Abuse and Neglect, 23*, 501–510.

Bartlett, F. C. (1932). *Remembering*. Cambridge, UK: Cambridge University Press.

Baumeister, R. F. (2005). *The cultural animal: Human nature, meaning, and social life*. New York: Oxford University Press.

Baumeister, R. F., & Leary, M. R. (1995). The need to belong: Desire for interpersonal attachments as a fundamental human motivation. *Psychological Bulletin, 117*, 497–529.

Baumeister, R. F., Campbell, J. D., Krueger, J. I., & Vohs, K. D. (2003). Does high self-esteem cause better performance, interpersonal success, happiness, or healthier lifestyles? *Psychological Science in the Public Interest, 4*, 1–44.

Baumeister, R. F., Ciarocco, N. J., & Twenge, J. M. (2005). Social exclusion impairs self-regulation. *Journal of Personality and Social Psychology, 88*, 589–604.

Baumrind, D. (1967). Child care practices anteceding three patterns of preschool behavior. *Genetic Psychology Monographs, 75*, 43–88.

Baumrind, D. (1971). Current patterns of parental authority. *Developmental Psychology Monograph, 4* (No. 1, Pt. 2).

Baumrind, D. (1991). The influence of parenting style on adolescent competence and substance use. *Journal of Early Adolescence, Special issue: The work of John P. Hill: Theoretical, instructional, and policy contributions 11*(1), 56–95.

Baydar, N., & Brooks-Gunn, J. (1998). Profiles of grandmothers who help care for their grandchildren in the United States. *Family Relations: Interdisciplinary Journal of Applied Family Studies, Special issue: The family as a context for health and well-being, 47*(4), 385–393.

Beall, A. E., & Sternberg, R. J. (1995). The social construction of love. *Journal of Social and Personal Relationships, 12*, 417–438.

Beals, J., Novins, D. K., Whitesell, N. R., Spicer, P., Mitchell, C., & Manson, S. (2005). Prevalence of mental disorders and utilization of mental health services in two American Indian reservation populations: Mental health disparities in a national context. *American Journal of Psychiatry, 162*(9), 1723–1732.

Beck, A. T. (1967). *Depression: Clinical, experimental and theoretical aspects*. New York: Harper and Row.

Beck, A. T. (1976). *Cognitive therapy and the emotional disorders*. New York: International Universities Press.

Becker, E. (1971). *The birth and death of meaning* (2nd ed.). New York: Free Press.

Becker, E. (1973). *The denial of death*. New York: Academic Press.

Behrensmeyer, A. K. (2006). Climate change and human evolution. *Science, 311*, 476–478.

Beiser, M. & Hou, F. (2001). Language acquisition, unemployment and depressive disorder among Southeast Asian refugees: A 10-year study. *Social Science & Medicine, 53*(10), 1321–1334.

Beiser, M. (1985). A study of depression among traditional Africans, urban North Americans, and Southeast Asian refugees. In A. Kleinman & B. Good (Eds.), *Culture and depression: Studies in the anthropology and cross-cultural psychiatry of affect and disorder* (pp. 272–298). Berkeley: University of California Press.

Beiser, M. (2006). Longitudinal research to promote effective refugee resettlement. *Transcultural Psychiatry, 43*(1), 56–71.

Beit-Hallahmi, B. (1972). National character and national behavior in the Middle East conflict: The case of the "Arab personality." *International Journal of Group Tensions, 2*(3), 19–28.

Bell, R. (1968). A reinterpretation of the direction of effects in studies of socialization. *Psychological Review, 75*, 81–95.

Belsky, J. (2002). Quantity counts: Amount of child care and children's socioemotional development. *Journal of Developmental & Behavioral Pediatrics, 23*(3), 167–170.

Bem, S. (1981). Gender schema theory: A cognitive account of sex-typing. *Psychological Review, 88*, 354–364.

Ben-David, A. (1996). Therapists' perceptions of multicultural assessment and therapy with immigrant families. *Journal of Family Therapy, 18*, 23–41.

Benet-Martinez, V., & John, O. P. (1998). Los Cinco Grandes across cultures and ethnic groups: Multi trait–multi method analyses of the Big Five in Spanish and English. *Journal of Personality and Social Psychology, 75*(3), 729–750.

Benet-Martinez, V., & Waller, N. G. (1995). The big-seven factor model of personality description: Evidence for its cross-cultural generality in a Spanish sample. *Journal of Personality and Social Psychology, 69*, 701–718.

Benet-Martinez, V., & Waller, N. G. (1997). Further evidence for the cross-cultural generality of the big-seven factor model: Indigenous and imported Spanish personality constructs. *Journal of Personality, 65*, 567–598.

Benet-Martinez, V., Leu, J., Lee, F., & Morris, M. (2002). Negotiating biculturalism: Cultural frame-switching in biculturals with "Oppositional" vs. "Compatible" cultural identities. *Journal of Cross-Cultural Psychology, 33*, 492–516.

Beratis, S. (1986). Suicide in southwestern Greece 1979–1984. *Acta Psychiatrica Scandinavica, 74*(5), 433–439.

Berger, C. R. (1979). Beyond initial interaction. In H. Giles & R. St. Claire (Eds.), *Language and social psychology* (pp. 122–144). Oxford, UK: Basil Blackwell.

Berger, C. R., & Calabrese, R. J. (1975). Some explorations in initial interaction and beyond: Toward a development theory of interpersonal communication. *Human Communication Research, 10*, 179–196.

Berkman, L. F., & Syme, S. L. (1979). Social networks, host resistance, and mortality: A nine-year follow-up study of Alameda County residents. *American Journal of Epidemiology, 109*, 186–204.

Berlin, B., & Kay, P. (1969). *Basic color terms: Their universality and evolution*. Berkeley: University of California Press.

Berman, S., Ozkaragoz, T., Young, R., & Noble, E. (2002). D2 dopamine receptor gene polymorphism discriminates two kinds of novelty seeking. *Personality and Individual Differences, 33*(6), 867–882.

Berry, J. W. (1969). On cross-cultural comparability. *International Journal of Psychology, 4*, 119–128.

Berry, D. S., & McArthur, L. Z. (1985). Some components and consequences of a babyface. *Journal of Personality and Social Psychology, 48*, 312–323.

Berry, D. S., & McArthur, L. Z. (1986). Perceiving character in faces: The impact of age-related craniofacial changes in social perception. *Psychological Bulletin, 100*, 3–18.

Berry, J. W. (1966). Temne and Eskimo perceptual skills. *International Journal of Psychology, 1*, 207–229.

Berry, J. W. (1976). Sex differences in behavior and cultural complexity. *Indian Journal of Psychology, 51*, 89–97.

Berry, J. W., & Kim, U. (1988). Acculturation and mental health. In P. Dasen, J. W. Berry, & N. Sortarious (Eds.), *Health and cross-cultural psychology: Towards applications* (pp. 207–236). Newbury Park, CA: Sage.

Berry, J. W., & Sam, D. (1997). Acculturation and adaptation. In J. W. Berry, M. H. Segall & C. Kagitcibasi (Eds.), *Handbook of cross-cultural psychology, vol 3: Social and behavioral applications*. Boston, MA: Allyn and Bacon.

Berry, J. W., & Sam, D. L. (1997). Acculturation and adaptation. In J. W. Berry, M. H. Segall, & C. Kagitcibasi (Eds.), *Handbook of cross-cultural psychology: Vol 3. Social behavior and applications* (2nd ed., pp. 291–326). Boston: Allyn & Bacon.

Berry, J. W., Kim, U., & Boski, P. (1988). Psychological acculturation of immigrants. In Y. Y. Kim & W. B. Gudykunst (Eds.), *Cross-cultural adaptation: Current approaches. International and intercultural communication annual* (Vol. 11, pp. 62–89). Newbury Park, CA: Sage.

Berry, J. W., Kim, U., Minde, T., & Mok, D. (1987). Comparative studies of acculturative stress. *International Migration Review, 21*, 491–511.

Berry, J. W., Phinney, J. S., Sam, D. L., & Vedder, P. (2006). *Immigrant youth in cultural transition: Acculturation, identity, and adaptation across national contexts.* New Jersey: Lawrence Erlbaum.

Berry, J. W., Poortinga, Y. H., Segall, M. H., & Dasen, P. R. (1992). *Cross-cultural psychology: Research and applications.* New York: Cambridge University Press.

Best, D., House, A., Barnard, E. A., & Spicker, S. B. (1994). Parent-child interactions in France, Germany, and Italy: The effects of gender and culture. *Journal of Cross-Cultural Psychology, 25*(2), 181–193.

Betancourt, H., & Lopez, R. S. (1993). The study of culture, ethnicity, and race in American psychology. *American Psychologist, 48*(6), 629–637.

Bhawuk, D. P. S., & Brislin, R. (1992). The measurement of intercultural sensitivity using the concepts of individualism and collectivism. *International Journal of Intercultural Relations, 16,* 413–436.

Bhui, K., Craig, T., & Mohamud, S. (2006). Mental disorders among Somali refugees: Developing culturally appropriate measures and assessing socio-cultural risk factors. *Social Psychiatry and Psychiatric Epidemiology, 41*(5), 400–408.

Binion, V. J. (1990). Psychological androgyny: A black female perspective. *Sex Roles, 22,* 487–507.

Bissilat, J., Laya, D., Pierre, E., & Pidoux, C. (1967). La notion de lakkal dans la culture Djerma-Songhai [The concept of lakkal in Djerma-Songhai culture]. *Psychopathologie Africaine, 3,* 207–264.

Black, J. S., & Porter, L. W. (1991). Managerial behavior and job performance: A successful manager in Los Angeles may not succeed in Hong Kong. *Journal of International Business Studies, 22,* 99–113.

Blair, I. V. (2001). Implicit stereotypes and prejudice. In G. B. Moskowitz (Ed.), *Cognitive social psychology: The Princeton symposium on the legacy and future of social cognition* (pp. 359–374). Mahwah, NJ: Erlbaum.

Blair, I. V., Judd, C., M., & Fallman, J. L. (2004). The automaticity of race and afrocentric facial features in social judgments. *Journal of Personality and Social Psychology, 87,* 763–778.

Blau, Z. S. (1981). *Black children–white children: Competence, socialization, and social structure.* New York: Free Press.

Block, J. (1983). Differential premises arising from differential socialization of the sexes: Some conjectures. *Child Development, 54,* 1335–1354.

Bloom, A. H. (1981). *The linguistic shaping of thought: A study in the impact of language on thinking in China and the West.* Hillsdale, NJ: Erlbaum.

Bloom, A. H. (1984). Caution—the words you use may affect what you say: A response to Au. *Cognition, 17*(3), 275–287.

Blow, F. C., Zeber, J. E., McCarthy, J. F., Valenstein, M., Gillon, L., & Bingham, C. R. (2004). Ethnicity and diagnostic patterns in veterans with psychoses. *Social Psychiatry Psychiatric Epidemiology, 39*(10), 841–51.

Boas, F., Efron, D., & Foley, J. P. A. (1936). A comparative investigation of gestural behavior patterns in "racial" groups living under different as well as similar environmental conditions. *Psychological Bulletin, 33,* 760.

Bochner, S. (1994). Cross-cultural differences in the self concept. *Journal of Cross-Cultural Psychology, 25,* 273–283.

Boehnlein, J. K., Kinzie, J. D., & Leung, P. K. (1992). The natural history of medical and psychiatric disorders in an American Indian community. *Culture, Medicine & Psychiatry, 16*(4), 543–554.

Boesch, C. (2003). Is culture a golden barrier between human and chimpanzee? *Evolutionary Anthropology, 12,* 82–91.

Bond, M. H. (1979). Winning either way: The effect of anticipating a competitive interaction on person perception. *Personality and Social Psychology Bulletin, 5*(3), 316–319.

Bond, M. H. (2004). Culture and aggression: From context to coercion. *Personality and Social Psychology Review, 8,* 62–78.

Bond, M. H. (2004, August). *The third stage of cross-cultural psychology: Some personal prescriptions for our future.* Paper presented at the 17th International Congress of the International Association for Cross-Cultural Psychology, Xian, China.

Bond, M. H., & Smith, P. B. (1996). Cross-cultural social and organizational psychology. *Annual Review of Psychology, 47,* 205–235.

Bond, M. H., & Tak-Sing, C. (1983). College students' spontaneous self concept: The effect of culture among respondents in Hong Kong, Japan, and the United States. *Journal of Cross-Cultural Psychology, 14,* 153–171.

Bond, M. H., Leung, K., & Wan, K. C. (1982). The social impact of self-effacing attributions: The Chinese case. *Journal of Social Psychology, 118*(2), 157–166.

Bond, M. H., Leung, K., Au, A., Tong, K. K., Reimel de Carrasquel, S., Murakami, F., et al. (2004). Culture-level dimensions of social axioms and their correlates across 41 cultures. *Journal of Cross-Cultural Psychology, 35,* 548–570.

Bond, M. H., Nakazato, H., & Shiraishi, D. (1975). Universality and distinctiveness in dimensions of Japanese person perception. *Journal of Cross-Cultural Psychology, 6*(3), 346–357.

Bond, M. H., & Wang, S. (1983). China: Aggressive behavior and the problems of mainstreaming order and harmony. In A. P. Goldstein & M. H. Segall (Eds.), *Aggression in global perspective* (pp. 58–74). New York: Pergamon.

Boothby, N. (1994). Trauma and violence among refugee children. In A. Marsella, T. Bornemann, S. Ekblad, & J. Orley (Eds.), *Amidst the pain and peril: The mental health and well-being of the world's refugees* (pp. 239–259). Washington, DC: American Psychological Association.

Borkenau, P., & Ostendorf, F. (1998). The Big Five as states: How useful is the five-factor model to describe intraindividual variations over time? *Journal of Research in Personality, 32*(2), 202–221.

Born, M., Bleichrodt, N., & Van der Flier, H. (1987). Cross-cultural comparison of sex-related differences on intelligence tests: A meta-analysis. *Journal of Cross-Cultural Psychology, 18,* 283–314.

Bornstein, M. H. (1989). Cross-cultural developmental comparisons: The case of Japanese-American infant and mother activities and interactions. What we know, what we need to know, and why we need to know. *Developmental Review, 9,* 171–204.

Bornstein, M. H., Haynes, O. M., Azuma, H., Galperin, C., Maital, S., & Ogino, M., et al. (1998). A cross-national study of self-evaluations and attributions in parenting: Argentina, Belgium, France, Israel, Italy, Japan and the United States. *Developmental Psychology, 34*(4), 662–676.

Bothwell, R. K., Brigham, J. C., & Malpass, R. S. (1989). Cross-racial identification. *Personality and Social Psychology Bulletin, 15*(1), 19–25.

Bouchard, T. J., & Loehlin, J. C. (2001). Genes, evolution, and personality. *Behavior Genetics, 31,* 243–273.

Bouchard, T. J., Jr., & McGue, M. (1981). Familial studies of intelligence: A review. *Science, 212,* 1055–1059.

Bouchard, T. J., Lykken, D. T., & McGue, M. (1994). Sources of human psychological differences: The Minnesota study of twins reared apart. *Science, 250,* 223–228.

Boucher, J. D., & Brandt, M. E. (1981). Judgment of emotion: American and Malay antecedents. *Journal of Cross-Cultural Psychology, 12*(3), 272–283.

Bowlby, J. (1969). *Attachment and loss: Vol. 1. Attachment.* New York: Basic Books.

Bowman, S. A., Gortmaker, S. L., Ebbeling, C. B., Pereira, M. A., & Ludwig, D. S. (2003). Effects of fast-food consumption on energy intake and diet quality among children in a national household survey. *Pediatrics, 113,* 112–118.

Boyer, P. (2000). Evolutionary psychology and cultural transmission. *American Behavioral Scientist, 43,* 987–1000.

Bradley, G. W. (1978). Self-serving biases in the attribution process:

A re-examination of the fact or fiction question. *Journal of Personality and Social Psychology, 35,* 56–71.

Bradley, R. H., & Corwyn, R. (2005). Caring for children around the world: A view from HOME. *International Journal of Behavioral Development, 29*(6), 468–478.

Bradley, R. H., Caldwell, B. M., & Corwyn, R. F. (2003). The Child Care HOME Inventories: Assessing the quality of family child care homes. *Early Childhood Research Quarterly, 18*(3), 294–309.

Brandt, M. E., & Boucher, J. D. (1985). Judgment of emotions from antecedent situations in three cultures. In I. Lagunes & Y. Poortinga (Eds.), *From a different perspective: Studies of behavior across cultures* (pp. 348–362). Lisse, Netherlands: Swets & Zeitlinger.

Brandt, M. E., & Boucher, J. D. (1986). Concepts of depression in emotion lexicons of eight cultures. *International Journal of Intercultural Relations, 10,* 321–346.

Brazelton, T. B., & Nugent, J. K. (1995). *Neonatal Behavioral Assessment Scale.* Cambridge, MA: Harvard University Press.

Breslau, J., Kendler, K. S., Su, M., Aguilar-Gaxiola, S., & Kessler, R. C. (2005). Lifetime risk and persistence of psychiatric disorders across ethnic groups in the United States. *Psychological Medicine, 35*(3), 317–327.

Brewer, M. B. (2004). Taking the origins of human nature seriously: Toward a more imperialist social psychology. *Personality and Social Psychology Review, 8,* 107–113.

Brewer, M. B., & Kramer, R. M. (1985). The psychology of intergroup attitudes and behavior. *Annual Review of Psychology, 36,* 219–243.

Brislin, R. (1970). Back translation for cross-cultural research. *Journal of Cross-Cultural Psychology, 1,* 185–216.

Brislin, R. (1993). *Understanding culture's influence on behavior.* Fort Worth, TX: Harcourt Brace Jovanovich.

Brodsky, M., & Hui, K.-K. (2006). Complementary and alternative

medicine. In D. Wedding & M. Stuber (Eds.), *Behavior and medicine* (4th ed., pp. 281–285). Ashland, OH: Hogrefe & Huber.

Broman, C. L. (1996). Coping with personal problems. In H. W. Neighbors & J. S. Jackson (Eds.), *Mental health in black America* (pp. 117–129). Thousand Oaks, CA: Sage.

Brondolo, E., Rieppi, R., Kelly, K. P., & Gerin, W. (2003). Perceived racism and blood pressure: A review of the literature and conceptual and methodological critique. *Annals of Behavioral Medicine, 25*(1), 55–65.

Bronfenbrenner, U. (1979). *The ecology of human development.* Cambridge, MA: Harvard University Press.

Bronstein, P. A. (1984). Differences in mothers' and fathers' behaviors toward children: A cross-cultural comparison. *Developmental Psychology, 20*(6), 995–1003.

Bronstein, P. A., & Paludi, M. (1988). The introductory psychology course from a broader human perspective. In P. A. Bronstein & K. Quina (Eds.), *Teaching a psychology of people: Resources for gender and sociocultural awareness* (pp. 21–36). Washington, DC: American Psychological Association.

Brook, D. W., Gordon, C., & Meadow, H. (1998). Ethnicity, culture, and group psychotherapy. *Group, 22*(2), 53–80.

Broota, K. D., & Ganguli, H. C. (1975). Cultural differences in perceptual selectivity. *Journal of Social Psychology, 95,* 157–163.

Brown, D. E. (1991). *Human universals.* Philadelphia, PA: Temple University.

Brummett, B. H., Siegler, I. C., McQuoid, D. R., Svenson, I. K., Marchuk, D. A., & Steffens, D. C. (2003). Associations among the NEO Personality Inventory, Revised and the serotonin transporter gene-linked polymorphic region in elders: Effects of depression and gender. *Psychiatric Genetics, 13*(1), 13–18.

Bruner, J. S., Oliver, R. R., & Greenfield, P. M. (1966). *Studies in cognitive growth.* New York: Wiley.

Bu-Haroon, A., Eapen, V., & Bener, A. (1999). The prevalence of hyperactivity symptoms in the United Arab Emirates. *Nordic Journal of Psychiatry, 53*(6), 439–442.

Buck, E. B., Newton, B. J., & Muramatsu, Y. (1984). Independence and obedience in the U. S. and Japan. *International Journal of Intercultural Relations, 8,* 279–300.

Buhusi, C. V., & Meck, W. H. (2005). What makes us tick? Functional and neural mechanisms of interval timing. *Nature Reviews, 6,* 756–765.

Bui, K-.T., & Takeuchi, D.T. (1992). Ethnic minority adolescents and the use of community mental health care services. *American Journal of Community Psychology, 20,* 403–417.

Burton, M. L., Greenberger, E., & Hayward, C. (2005). Mapping the ethnic landscape: Personal beliefs about own group's and other group's traits. *Cross-cultural Research, 39,* 351–379.

Buss, D. M. (1988). The evolution of human intrasexual competition: Tactics of mate attraction. *Journal of Personality & Social Psychology, 54,* 616–628.

Buss, D. M. (1989). Sex differences in human mate preferences: Evolutionary hypotheses tested in 37 cultures. *Behavioral & Brain Sciences, 12,* 1–49.

Buss, D. M. (1991). Evolutionary personality psychology. *Annual Review of Psychology, 42,* 459–491.

Buss, D. M. (1994). *The evolution of desire: Strategies of human mating.* New York: Basic Books.

Buss, D. M. (2001). Human nature and culture: An evolutionary psychological perspective. *Journal of Personality, 69,* 955–978.

Buss, D. M., & Schmitt, D. P. (1993). Sexual strategies theory: An evolutionary perspective on human mating. *Psychological Review, 100,* 204–232.

Buss, D. M., Shackelford, T. K., Kirkpatrick, L. A., Choe, J. C., Lim, H. K., & Hasegawa, M. (1999). Jealousy and the nature of beliefs about infidelity: Test of competing hypotheses about sex differences in the United States, Korea, and Japan. *Personal Relationships, 6,* 125–150.

Butcher, J. N, Lim, J., & Nezami, E. (1998). Objective study of abnormal personality in cross-cultural settings: The Minnesota Multiphasic Personality Inventory (MMPI-2). *Journal of Cross-Cultural Psychology, 29*(1), 189–211.

Butsch, R. (1992). Class and gender in four decades of television situation comedy. *Critical Studies in Mass Communication, 9,* 387–399.

Butzlaff, R. L., & Hooley, J. M. (1998) Expressed emotion and psychiatric relapse: A meta-analysis. *Archives of General Psychiatry, 55,* 547–552.

Cachelin, F. M., Phinney, J. S., Schug, R. A., & Striegel-Moore, R. M. (2006). Acculturation and eating disorders in a Mexican American community sample. *Psychology of Women Quarterly, 30*(4), 340–347.

Callister, L., Vehvilainen-Julkunen, K., & Lauri, S. (2001). Giving birth: Perceptions of Finnish childbearing women. *American Journal of Maternal/Child Nursing, 26*(1), 28–32.

Campbell, D. T., & Levine, R. A. (1965). *Propositions about ethnocentrism from social science theories.* Unpublished monograph, Northwestern University, Evanston, Illinois.

Campbell, N. C. G., Graham, J. L., Jolibert, A., & Meissner, H. G. (1988). Marketing negotiations in France, Germany, the United Kingdom and the United States. *Journal of Marketing, 52,* 49–62.

Camras, L., Oster, H., Campos, J. J., & Bakeman, R. (2003). Emotional facial expressions in European-American, Japanese, and Chinese infants. In P. Ekman, J. J. Campos, R. J. Davidson & F. B. M. de Waal (Eds.), *Emotions inside out: 130 years after Darwin's "the expression of the emotions in man and animals"* (Vol. 1000, pp. 135–151). New York: New York Academy of Sciences.

Cantwell, D. P. (1996). Attention deficit disorder: A review of the past 10 years. *Journal of the American Academy of Child and Adolescent Psychiatry, 35,* 978–987.

Caprara, G. V., & Perugini, M. (1994). Personality described by adjectives: The generalizability of the Big Five to the Italian lexical context. *European Journal of Personality, 8*(5), 357–369.

Caprara, G. V., Barbaranelli, C. & Comrey, A. L. (1995). Factor analysis of the NEO-PI Inventory and the Comrey Personality Scales in an Italian sample. *Personality and Individual Differences, 18*(2), 193–200.

Carroll, J. B., & Casagrande, J. B. (1958). The function of language classifications in behavior. In E. E. Maccoby, T. M. Newcomb, & E. L. Hartley (Eds.), *Readings in social psychology* (pp. 18–31). New York: Holt.

Carroll, J. L., & Wolpe, P. R. (1996). *Sexuality and gender in society.* New York: HarperCollins.

Carson, R. C., Butcher, J. N., & Coleman, J. C. (1988). *Abnormal psychology and modern life* (8th ed.). Glenview, IL: Scott, Foresman.

Casey, R. J. (1993). Children's emotional experience: Relations among expression, self-report, and understanding. *Developmental Psychology, 29,* 119–129.

Cashmore, J. A., & Goodnow, J. J. (1986). Influences on Australian parents' values: Ethnicity versus sociometric status. *Journal of Cross-Cultural Psychology, 17,* 441–454.

Cauce, A. M., Domenech-Rodrigues, M., Paradise, M., Cochran, B. N., Shea, J. M., et al. (2002). Cultural and contextual influence in mental health help seeking: A focus on ethnic minority youth. *Journal of Counseling and Clinical Psychology, 70,* 44–55.

Caudill, W., & Frost, L. (1974). A comparison of maternal care and infant behavior in Japanese-American, American, and Japanese families. In W. P. Lebra (Ed.), *Youth, socialization, and mental health: Vol. 3. Mental health research in Asia and the Pacific* (pp. 3–15). Honolulu: University Press of Hawaii.

Caudill, W., & Weinstein, H. (1969). Maternal care and infant behavior in Japan and America. *Psychiatry: Journal for the Study of Interpersonal Processes, 32*(1), 12–43.

Cederblad, M. (1988). Behavioral disorders in children from different cultures. *Acta Psychiatrica Scandinavia Supplementum, 344,* 85–92.

Centers for Disease Control (2005). Mental health in the United States: Prevalence of diagnosis and medication treatment for attention-deficit/hyperactivity disorder, United States, 2003. *Morbidity and Mortality Weekly, 54*(34) 842–847.

Centers for Disease Control and Prevention (2006). National Center for Injury Prevention and Control. Injuries among Native Americans: Fact Sheet. Atlanta: CDC.

Chambless, D. L., Sanderson, W. C., Shoham, V., Bennett-Johnson, S., Pope, K. S., Crits-Christoph, P., Baker, M., Johnson, B., Woody, S. R., Sue, S. Beutler, L., Williams, D. A., & McCurry, S. (1996). An update on empirically validated therapies. *Clinical Psychologist, 49,* 5–18.

Chan, Y. M. (2000). Self-esteem: A cross-cultural comparison of British-Chinese, White British and Hong Kong Chinese children. *Educational Psychology, 20*(1), 59–74.

Chandra, S. (1975). Some patterns of response on the Queensland test. *Australian Psychologist, 10*(2), 185–192.

Chao, R. (2000). Cultural explanations for the role of parenting in the school success of Asian-American children. In R. Taylor & M. Wang (Eds.), *Resilience across contexts: Family, work, culture, and community* (pp. 333–363). Mahwah, NJ: Erlbaum.

Chao, R. (2001). Extending research on the consequences of parenting style for Chinese Americans and European Americans. *Child Development, 72*(6), 1832–1843.

Chao, R. K. (1994). Beyond parental control and authoritarian parenting style: Understanding Chinese parenting through the cultural notion of training. *Child Development, 65,* 1111–1119.

Chao, R. K. (1996). Chinese and European American mothers' beliefs about the role of parenting in children's school success.

Journal of Cross-Cultural Psychology, 27(4), 403–423.

Charlesworth, W. R., & Kreutzer, M. A. (1973). Facial expressions of infants and children. In P. Ekman (Ed.), *Darwin and facial expression* (pp. 91–168). New York: Academic Press.

Chen, C., Lee, S., & Stevenson, H. W. (1996). Long-term prediction of academic achievement of American, Chinese, and Japanese adolescents. *Journal of Educational Psycholoyg, 88*(4), 750–759.

Chen, G. M. (1995). Differences in self-disclosure patterns among Americans versus Chinese: A comparative study. *Journal of Cross-Cultural Psychology, 26,* 84–91.

Chen, X., Dong, Q., & Zhou, H. (1997). Authoritative and authoritarian parenting practices and social and school performances in Chinese children. *International Journal of Behavioral Development, 21*(4), 855–873.

Cheng, D., Leong, F. T. L., & Geist, R. (1993). Cultural differences in psychological distress between Asian and Caucasian American college students. *Journal of Multicultural Counseling and Development, 21,* 182–190.

Cheryan, S., & Monin, B. (2005). "Where are you *really* from?" Asian Americans and identity denial. *Journal of Personality and Social Psychology, 89,* 717–730.

Cheung, F. M., Cheung, S. F., Leung, K., Ward, C., & Leong, F. T. (2003). The English version of the Chinese personality assessment inventory. *Journal of Cross-Cultural Psychology, 34,* 433–452.

Cheung, F. M., Cheung, S. F., Wada, S., & Zhang, J. (2003). Indigenous measures of personality assessment in Asian countries: A review. *Psychological Assessment, 15,* 280–289.

Cheung, F. M., Kwong, J. Y. Y., & Zhang, J. (2003). Clinical validation of the Chinese Personality Assessment Inventory. *Psychological Assessment, 15*(1), 89–100.

Cheung, F. M., Leung, K., Fan, R. M., Song, W. Z., Zhang, J. X., & Zhang, J. P. (1996). Develop-

ment of the Chinese Personality Assessment Inventory. *Journal of Cross-Cultural Psychology, 27,* 181–199.

Cheung, F. M., Leung, K., Zhang, J.-X., Sun, H.-F., Gan, Y.-Q., Song, W.-Z., et al. (2001). Indigenous Chinese personality constructs: Is the five-factor model complete? *Journal of Cross-Cultural Psychology, 32,* 407–433.

Chevalier-Skolnikoff, S. (1973). Facial expression of emotion in nonhuman primates. In P. Ekman (Ed.), *Darwin and facial expression* (pp. 11–89). New York: Academic Press.

Chinese Culture Connection. (1987). Chinese values and the search for culture-free dimensions of culture. *Journal of Cross-Cultural Psychology, 18,* 143–164.

Chirkov, V. I., Ryan, R. M., & Willness, C. (2005). Cultural context and psychological needs in Canada and Brazil: Testing a self-determination approach to the internalization of cultural practices, identity and well-being. *Journal of Cross-Cultural Psychology, 36,* 423–443.

Chirkov, V., Ryan, R. M., Kim, Y., & Kaplan, U. (2003). Differentiating autonomy from individualism and independence: A self-determination theory perspective on internalization of cultural orientations and well-being. *Journal of Personality and Social Psychology, 84,* 97–110.

Chiu, L. H. (1972). A cross-cultural comparison of cognitive styles in Chinese and American children. *International Journal of Psychology, 7,* 235–242.

Cho, M. J., Moscicki, E. K., Narrow, W. E., Rae, D. S., Locke, B. Z., & Regier, D. A. (1993). Concordance between two measures of depression in the Hispanic Health and Nutrition Examination Survey. *Social Psychiatry and Psychiatric Epidemiology, 28*(4), 156–163.

Choe, H. (1994). Korea. In K. Hurrelmann (Ed.), *International handbook of adolescence* (pp. 246–256). Westport, CT: Greenwood Press.

Choi, I., & Nisbett, R. (2000). Cultural psychology of surprise: Holistic theories and recognition of contradiction. *Journal of Personality and Social Psychology, 79*, 890–905.

Choi, I., Nisbett, R., & Norenzayan, A. (1999). Causal attribution across cultures: Variation and universality. *Psychological Bulletin, 125*, 47–63.

Choi, S.-C., Kim, U., & Choi, S.-H. (1993). Indigenous analysis of collective representations: A Korean perspective. In U. Kim & J. W. Berry (Eds.), *Indigenous psychologies: Research and experience in cultural context* (pp. 193–210). Newbury Park, CA: Sage.

Church, A. T. (2000). Culture and personality: Toward an integrated cultural trait psychology. *Journal of Personality, 68*, 651–703.

Church, A. T., & Katigbak, M. S. (1988). Imposed-etic and emic measures of intelligence as predictors of early school performance of rural Philippine children. *Journal of Cross-Cultural Psychology, 19*(2), 164–177.

Church, A. T., & Lonner, W. J. (Eds.). (1998). The cross-cultural perspective in the study of personality: Rationale and current research. *Journal of Cross-Cultural Psychology, 29*(1), 32–62.

Church, A. T., Katigbak, M. S., & Reyes, J. A. (1998). Further exploration of Filipino personality structure using the lexical approach: Do the big-five or big-seven dimensions emerge? *European Journal of Personality, 12*, 249–269.

Church, A. T., Reyes, J. A., Katigbak, M. S., & Grimm, S. D. (1997). Filipino personality structure and the big-five model: A lexical approach. *Journal of Personality, 65*, 477–528.

Claeys, W. (1967). The factorial intelligence structure of the Congolese at the beginning of their university studies. *Psychologica Belgica, 7*, 7–15.

Clark, M. L., & Person, W. (1982). Racial stereotypes revisited. *International Journal of Intercultural Relations, 6*, 381–392.

Clymer, E. C. (1995). The psychology of deafness: Enhancing self-concept in the deaf and hearing impaired. *Family Therapy, 22*(2), 113–120.

Cogan, J. C., Bhalla, S. K., Sefa-Dedeh, A., & Rothblum, E. D. (1996). A comparison study of United States and African students on perceptions of obesity and thinness. *Journal of Cross-Cultural Psychology, 27*, 98–113.

Cohen, D., Nisbett, R., Bowdle, B. F., & Schwarz, N. (1996). Insult, aggression, and the southern culture of honor: An "experimental ethnography." *Journal of Personality and Social Psychology, 70*, 945–960.

Cohen, G. L., & Garcia, J. (2005). "I" am "us": Negative stereotypes as collective threats. *Journal of Personality and Social Psychology, 89*, 566–582.

Cohen, N. (1982). Same or different? A problem of identity in cross-cultural marriages. *Journal of Family Therapy, 4*(2), 177–199.

Cole, M. (2006). Culture and cognitive development in phylogenetic, historical, and ontogenetic perspective. In W. Damon, R. M. Lerner, D. Kuhn, & R. S. Siegler (Eds.), *Handbook of child psychology: Vol. 2. Cognition, perception, and language* (6th ed., pp. 636–683). New York: Wiley.

Cole, M., & Scribner, S. (1974). *Culture and thought: A psychological introduction*. New York: Wiley.

Cole, M., Gay, J., Glick, J. A., & Sharp, D. W. (1971). *The cultural context of learning and thinking: An exploration in experimental anthropology*. New York: Basic Books.

Cole, T. J., Bellizzi, M. C., Flegal, K. M., & Dietz, W. H. (2000). Establishing a standard definition for child overweight and obesity worldwide: International survey. *BMJ, 320*, 1240–1243.

Coll, C. G. (1990). Developmental outcome of minority infants: A process-oriented look into our beginnings. *Child Development, 61*(2), 270–289.

Collins, W., & Laursen, B. (2004). Changing relationships, changing youth: Interpersonal contexts of adolescent development. *Journal of Early Adolescence, Special issue: Memorial Issue: Adolescence: The Legacy of Hershel and Ellen Thornburg 24*(1), 55–62.

Collins, W., Maccoby, E., Steinberg, L., Hetherington, M., & Bornstein, M. (2000). Contemporary research on parenting: The case for nature and nurture. *American Psychologist, 55*(2), 218–232.

Comas-Diaz, L. (1992). The future of psychotherapy with ethnic minorities. *Psychotherapy, 29*, 88–94.

Comas-Diaz, L., & Jacobsen, F. M. (1991). Ethnocultural transference and countertransference in the therapeutic dyad. *American Journal of Orthopsychiatry, 61*, 392–402.

Connection, C. C. (1987). Chinese values and the search for culture-free dimensions of culture. *Journal of Cross-Cultural Psychology, 18*, 143–174.

Cortes, B. P., Demoulin, S., Rodriguez, R. T., Rodrigues, A. P., & Lyens, J.-P. (2005). Infrahumanization or familiarity? Attribution of uniquely human emotions to the self, the ingroup, and the outgroup. *Personality and Social Psychology Bulletin, 31*, 243–253.

Cortes, D. E. (2003). Idioms of distress, acculturation and depression: The Puerto Rican experience. In K. M. Chun, P. B. Organista, & G. Marin (Eds.), *Acculturation: Advances in theory, measurement, and applied research* (pp. 207–222). Washington DC: American Psychological Association.

Cortina, L. M. (2001). Assessing sexual harassment among Latinas: Development of an instrument. *Cultural Diversity & Ethnic Minority Psychology, 7*, 164–181.

Cortina, L. M., & Wasti, S. A. (2005). Profiles in coping: Responses to sexual harassment across persons, organizations, and cultures. *Journal of Applied Psychology, 90*, 182–192.

Cortina, L. M., Fitzgerald, L. F., & Drasgow, F. (2002). Contextualizing Latina experiences of sexual harassment: Preliminary tests of a structural model. *Basic and Applied Social Psychology, 24*, 295–311.

Costa, P. T., & McCrae, R. R. (1989). *The Neo-PI/Neo-FFI manual supplement*. Odessa, FL: Psychological Assessment Resources.

Costa, P. T., Terracciano, A., & McCrae, R. R. (2001). Gender differences in personality traits across cultures: Robust and surprising findings.

Journal of Personality & Social Psychology, 81, 322–331.

Cottrell, A. B. (1990). Cross-national marriages: A review of literature. *Journal of Comparative Family Studies, 21*(2), 151–169.

Cottrell, C. A., & Neuberg, S. L. (2005). Different emotional reactions to different groups: A sociofunctional threat-based approach to "prejudice." *Journal of Personality and Social Psychology, 88,* 770–789.

Cousins, S. D. (1989). Culture and self-perception in Japan and the United States. *Journal of Personality and Social Psychology, 56,* 124–131.

Crandall, C. S., & Martinez, R. (1996). Culture, ideology, and antifat attitudes. *Personality and Social Psychology Bulletin, 22*(11), 1165–1176.

Crijnen, A. A. M., Achenbach, T. M., & Verhulst, F. C. (1999). Problems reported by parents of children in multiple cultures: The Child Behavior Checklist syndrome constructs. *American Journal of Psychiatry, 156*(4), 569–574.

Crittenden, K. S. (1991). Asian self-effacement or feminine modesty? Attributional patterns of women university students in Taiwan. *Gender and Society, 5,* 98–117.

Crocker, J., & Lawrence, J. S. (1999). Social stigma and self-esteem: The role of contingencies of worth. In D. A. Prentice & D. T. Miller (Eds.), *Cultural divides: Understanding and overcoming group conflict* (pp. 364–392). New York: Russell Sage Foundation.

Crook, T. H., Youngjohn, J. R., Larrabee, G. J., & Salama, M. (1992). Aging and everyday memory: A cross-cultural study. *Neuropsychology, 6*(2), 123–136.

Cross, S., & Morris, M. L. (2003). Getting to know you: The relational self-construal, relational cognition, and well-being. *Personality and Social Psychology Bulletin, 29,* 512–523.

Cross, S., Morris, M. L., & Gore, J. S. (2002). Thinking about oneself and others: The relational-interdependent self-construal and social cognition. *Journal of Personality and Social Psychology, 82,* 399–418.

Croteau, D., & Hoynes, W. (2000). *Media/society: Industries, images and audiences* (2nd ed.). Thousand Oaks, CA: Sage.

Csikszentmihalyi, M. (1999). Implications of a systems perspective for the study of creativity. In R. J. Sternberg (Ed.), *Handbook of creativity* (pp. 313–335). New York: Cambridge University Press.

Cunningham, M. R., Roberts, A. R., Barbee, A. P., Druen, P. B., & Wu, C. (1995). "Their ideas of beauty are, on the whole, the same as ours": Consistency and variability in the cross-cultural perception of female physical attractiveness. *Journal of Personality and Social Psychology, 68*(2), 261–279.

Cyranowski, J. M., Frank, E., Young, E., Shear, M. K. (2000). Adolescent onset of the gender difference in lifetime rates of major depression. *Archives of General Psychiatry, 57,* 21–27.

Daibo, I., Murasawa, H., & Chou, Y. (1994). Attractive faces and affection of beauty: A comparison in preference of feminine facial beauty in Japan and Korea. *Japanese Journal of Research on Emotions, 1*(2), 101–123.

Damond, M. E., Breur, N. L., & Pharr, A. E. (1993). The evaluation of setting and a culturally specific HIV/AIDS curriculum: HIV/AIDS knowledge and behavior intent of African American adolescents. *Journal of Black Psychology, 19*(2), 169–189.

Dandash, K. F., Refaat, A. H., & Eyada, M. (2001). Female genital mutilation: A descriptive study. *Journal of Sex and Marital Therapy, 27,* 453–458.

Darwin, C. (1859). *The origin of species.* New York: Modern Library.

Darwin, C. (1872). *The expression of emotion in man and animals.* London: John Murray.

Darwin, C. (1998). *The expression of the emotions in man and animals* (P. Ekman, Ed.) (3rd ed.). New York: Oxford University Press. (Original work published 1872.)

Dasen, P. R. (1975). Concrete operational development in three cultures. *Journal of Cross-Cultural Psychology, 6,* 156–172.

Dasen, P. R., Dembele, B., Ettien, K., Kabran, L., Kamagate, D., Koffi, D. A., & N'Guessean, A. (1985). N'glouele, l'intelligence chez les Baoule [N'glouele: Intelligence among the Ivory Coast Baoule]. *Archives de Psychologie, 53,* 293–324.

Dasgupta, S. D. (1998). Gender roles and cultural continuity in the Asian Indian immigrant community in the U.S. *Sex Roles, 38*(11–12), 953–974.

David, K. H., & Bochner, S. (1967). Teacher ratings of I.Q. and Porteus maze scores of Pitjandjara children. *Perceptual and Motor Skills, 25*(2), 639–640.

Davidson, R. J. (2003). Parsing the subcomponents of emotion and disorders of emotion: Perspectives from affective neuroscience. In R. J. Davidson, K. R. Scherer & H. H. Goldsmith (Eds.), *Handbook of affective sciences* (pp. 8–24). New York: Oxford University Press.

Davis, F. G. (1991). *Who is black? One nation's definition.* University Park: Pennsylvania State University Press.

De Raad, B., & Boddema-Winesemius, M. (1992). Factors in the assortment of human mates: Differential preferences in Germany and the Netherlands. *Personality and Individual Differences, 13,* 103–114.

De Raad, B., Hendriks, A. J., & Hofstee, W. K. (1992, October). Towards a refined structure of personality traits. *European Journal of Personality, 6*(4), 301–319.

De Raad, B., Perugini, M., & Szirmak, Z. (1997). In pursuit of a cross-lingual reference structure of personality traits: Comparisons among five languages. *European Journal of Personality, 11*(3), 167–185.

De Raad, B., Perugini, M., Hrebickova, M., & Szarota, P. (1998, January). Lingua franca of personality: Taxonomies and structures based on the psycholexical approach. *Journal of Cross-Cultural Psychology, 29*(1), 212–232.

de Silva, S., Stiles, D., & Gibbons, J. (1992). Girls' identity formation in the changing social structure of Sri Lanka. *Journal of Genetic Psychology, 153*(2), 211–220.

de Waal, F. B. M. (2002). Apes from Venus: Bonobos and human social evolution. In F. B. M. de Waal (Ed.), *Tree of origin: What primate behavior can tell us about human social evolution* (pp. 39–68). Cambridge, MA: Harvard University Press.

de Waal, F. B. M. (2003). Darwin's legacy and the study of primate visual communication. In P. Ekman, J. Campos, R. J. Davidson & F. B. M. de Waal (Eds.), *Emotions inside out: 130 years after Darwin's the expression of emotion in man and animals* (pp. 7–31). New York: New York Academy of Sciences.

De-Fruyt, F., & Mervielde, I. (1998). The assessment of the Big Five in the Dutch language domain. *Psychologica Belgica, 38*(1), 1–22.

Deci, E. L., & Ryan, R. M. (1985). *Intrinsic motivation and self-determination theory in human behavior.* New York: Plenum.

Deck, L. P. (1968). Buying brains by the inch. *Journal of College and University Personnel Associations, 19,* 33–37.

Dehaene, S., Izard, V., Pica, P., & Spelke, E. (2006). Core knowledge of geometry in an Amazonian indigene group. *Science, 311,* 381–384.

del Pino Perez, A., Meizoso, M. T., & Gonzalez, R. (1999). Validity of the structured interview for the assessment of Type A behavior pattern. *European Journal of Psychological Assessment, 15*(1), 39–48.

DelBello, M. P., Lopez-Larson, M. P., Soutullo, C. A., & Strakowski, S. M. (2001), Effects of race on psychiatric diagnosis of hospitalized adolescents: A retrospective chart review. *Journal of Child and Adolescent Psychopharmacology, 11*(1), 95–103.

Denham, S. A., Renwick, S. M., & Holt, R. W. (1997). Working and playing together: Prediction of preschool social–emotional competence from mother-child interaction. *Child Development, 62*(2), 242–249.

DePaulo, B. M., Stone, J., & Lassiter, G. D. (1985). Deceiving and detecting deceit. In B. R. Schlenker (Ed.), *The self and social life* (pp. 323–370). New York: McGraw-Hill.

Desjarlais, R. R. (1991). Dreams, divination, and Yolmo ways of knowing. *Dreaming: Journal of the Association for the Study of Dreams, 1*(3), 211–224.

Devan, G. S. (2001). Culture and the practice of group psychotherapy in Singapore. *International Journal of Groups Psychotherapy, 51,* 571–577.

Devereux, C. E., Jr., Bronfenbrenner, U., & Suci, G. (1962). Patterns of parent behavior in the United States of America and the Federal Republic of Germany: A cross-national comparison. *International Social Science Journal, 14,* 488–506.

Devine, P. G. (1989). Stereotypes and prejudice: Their automatic and controlled components. *Journal of Personality and Social Psychology, 56,* 5–18.

Devine, P. G., & Malpass, R. S. (1985). Orienting strategies in differential face recognition. *Personality and Social Psychology Bulletin, 11*(1), 33–40.

Devos, T., & Banaji, M. R. (2005). American = White? *Journal of Personality and Social Psychology, 88,* 447–466.

Dhawan, N., Roseman, I. J., Naidu, R. K., Komilla, T., & Rettek, S. I. (1995). Self-concepts across two cultures. *Journal of Cross-Cultural Psychology, 26*(6), 606–621.

Diaz-Loving, R. (1998, January). Contributions of Mexican ethnopsychology to the resolution of the etic-emic dilemma in personality. *Journal of Cross Cultural Psychology, 29*(1), 104–118.

Digman, J. M., & Shmelyov, A. G. (1996, August). The structure of temperament and personality in Russian children. *Journal of Personality and Social Psychology, 71*(2), 341–351.

Dinges, N. G., & Hull, P. (1992). Personality, culture, and international studies. In D. Lieberman (Ed.), *Revealing the world: An interdisciplinary reader for international studies.* Dubuque, IA: Kendall-Hunt.

Dion, K. K. (1986). Stereotyping based on physical attractiveness: Issues and conceptual perspectives. In C. P. Herman, M. P. Zanna, & E. T. Higgins (Eds.), *Ontario symposium on personality and social psychology* (Vol. 3). Hillsdale, NJ: Erlbaum.

Dion, K. K., & Dion, K. L. (1993a). Gender and ethnocultural comparisons in styles of love. *Psychology of Women Quarterly, 17,* 463–473.

Dion, K. K., & Dion, K. L. (1993b). Individualistic and collectivistic perspectives on gender and the cultural context of love and intimacy. *Journal of Social Issues, 49,* 53–69.

Doi, T. (1973). *The anatomy of dependence.* Tokyo: Kodansha.

Domino, G. (1992). Cooperation and competition in Chinese and American children. *Journal of Cross-Cultural Psychology, 23*(4), 456–467.

Dosanjh, J. S., & Ghuman, P. A. S. (1996). The cultural context of child rearing: A study of indigenous and British Punjabis. *Early Child Development and Care, 126,* 39–55.

Dosanjh, J. S., & Ghuman, P. A. S. (1997). Punjabi childrearing in Britain: Development of identity, religion and bilingualism. *Childhood, 4*(3), 285–303.

Douki, S., Moussaoui, D., & Kacha, F. (1987). *Handbook of psychiatry of expert Maghrebin.* Paris: Masson.

Draguns, J. (1997). Abnormal behavior patterns across cultures: Implications for counseling and psychotherapy. *International Journal of Intercultural Relations, 21*(2), 213–248.

DSM-IV-TR workgroup. (2000). *The Diagnostic and Statistical Manual of Mental Disorders,* 4th edition, text revision. Washington, DC: American Psychiatric Association.

Duckitt, J. (1992). Psychology and prejudice: A historical analysis and integrative framework. *American Psychologist, 47,* 1182–1194.

Duckitt, J., Callaghan, J., & Wagner, C. (2005). Group identification and outgroup attitudes in four south African ethnic groups: A multidimensional approach. *Personality and Social Psychology Bulletin, 31,* 633–646.

Dumas, F. (1932). La mimique des aveugles [facial expression of the blind]. *Bulletin de l'Academie de Medecine, 107*.

Dunn, J. (1988). *The beginnings of social understanding*. Cambridge, MA: Harvard University Press.

Durie, M. H. (1997). Maori cultural identity and its implications for mental health services. *International Journal of Mental Health, 26*(3), 23–35.

Dwairy, M., Achoui, M., Abouseire, R., & Farah, A. (2006). Parenting styles, individuation, and mental health of Arab adolescents: A third cross-regional research study. *Journal of Cross-Cultural Psychology, 37*(3), 262–272.

Dyal, J. A. (1984). Cross-cultural research with the locus of control construct. In H. M. Lefcourt (Ed.), *Research with the locus of control construct* (Vol. 3, pp. 209–306). New York: Academic Press.

Eagley, A. (1987). *Sex differences in social behavior: A social role interpretation*. Hillsdale, NJ: Lawrence Erlbaum.

Eagly, A., Ashmore, R. D., Makhijani, M. G., & Longo, L. C. (1991). What is beautiful is good, but . . .: A meta analytic review of research on the physical attractiveness stereotype. *Psychological Bulletin, 110*(1), 109–128.

Earley, P. C. (1989). Social loafing and collectivism: A comparison of the United States and the People's Republic of China. *Administrative Science Quarterly, 34*, 565–581.

Eberhardt, J. L., & Randall, J. L. (1997). The essential notion of race. *Psychological Science, 8*(3), 198–203.

Eberhardt, J. L., Goff, P. A., Pursie, V. J., & Davies, P. G. (2004). Seeing black: Race, crime, and visual processing. *Journal of Personality and Social Psychology, 87*, 876–893.

Ebrahimpour, M., & Johnson, J. L. (1992). Quality, vendor evaluation and organizational performance: A comparison of U.S. and Japanese firms. *Journal of Business Research, 25*, 129–142.

Economic and Social Research Council (2005). Who is a sister and a brother? Biological and social ties. Accessed at http://www. esrcsocietytoday.ac.uk/ESRCInfoCentre/PO/releases/2005/may/index2.aspx.

Edwards, C. P., Knoche, L., Aukrust, V., Kimru, A., & Kim, M. (2006). Parental ethnotheories of child development: Looking beyond independence and individualism in American belief systems. In U. Kim, K.-S., Yang, & K.-K. Hwang (Eds.), *Indigenous and cultural psychology: Understanding people in context* (pp. 141–162). New York: Springer Science and Business Media.

Efron, D. (1941). *Gesture and environment*. Oxford, England: King's Crown Press.

Eibl-Eibesfeldt, I. (1973). The expressive behavior of the deaf-and-blind born. In M. von Cranach & I. Vine (Eds.), *Social communication and movement* (pp. 163–194). London: Academic Press.

Ekman, P. (1972). Universal and cultural differences in facial expression of emotion. In J. R. Cole (Ed.), *Nebraska symposium on motivation, 1971* (pp. 207–283). Lincoln: Nebraska University Press.

Ekman, P. (1972). Universal and cultural differences in facial expression of emotion. In J. R. Cole (Ed.), *Nebraska symposium on motivation, 1971* (pp. 207–283). Lincoln: University of Nebraska Press.

Ekman, P. (1973). *Darwin and facial expression: a century of research in review*. New York: Academic Press.

Ekman, P. (1976). Movements with precise meanings. *Journal of Communication, 26*, 14–26.

Ekman, P. (1992). Are there basic emotions? *Psychological Review, 99*, 550–553.

Ekman, P. (1999). Basic emotions. In T. D. a. T. Power (Ed.), *The handbook of cognition and emotion* (pp. 45–60). Sussex, United Kingdom: John Wiley and Sons.

Ekman, P., & Friesen, W. V. (1971). Constants across culture in the face and emotion. *Journal of Personality and Social Psychology, 17*, 124–129.

Ekman, P., & Friesen, W. V. (1969). The repertoire of nonverbal behavior: Categories, origins, usage, and coding. *Semiotica, 1*, 49–98.

Ekman, P., & Friesen, W. V. (1986). A new pan-cultural facial expression of emotion. *Motivation & Emotion, 10*, 159–168.

Ekman, P., & Heider, K. G. (1988). The universality of a contempt expression: A replication. *Motivation & Emotion, 12*, 303–308.

Ekman, P., & Oster, H. (1979). Facial expressions of emotion. *Annual Review of Psychology, 30*, 527–554.

Ekman, P., Davidson, R. J., & Friesen, W. V. (1990). The Duchenne smile: Emotional expression and brain physiology: Ii. *Journal of Personality & Social Psychology, 58*, 342–353.

Ekman, P., Friesen, W. V., & Ellsworth, P. (1972). *Emotion in the human face*. New York: Garland.

Ekman, P., Friesen, W. V., O'Sullivan, M., Chan, A., Diacoyanni-Tarlatzis, I., Heider, K., et al. (1987). Universals and cultural differences in the judgments of facial expressions of emotion. *Journal of Personality & Social Psychology, 53*, 712–717.

Ekman, P., Friesen, W. V., O'Sullivan, M., & Scherer, K. (1980). Relative importance of face, body, and speech in judgments of personality and affect. *Journal of Personality and Social Psychology, 38*, 270–277.

Ekman, P., Levenson, R. W., & Friesen, W. V. (1983). Autonomic nervous system activity distinguishes among emotions. *Science, 221*, 1208–1210.

Ekman, P., Sorenson, E. R., & Friesen, W. V. (1969). Pancultural elements in facial displays of emotion. *Science, 164*, 86–88.

Ekman, P., Sorenson, E. R., & Friesen, W. V. (1969). Pancultural elements in facial displays of emotion. *Science, 164*, 86–94.

El-Islam, M. F. (1982). Arabic cultural psychiatry. *Transcultural Psychiatric Research Review, 19*, 5–24.

El-Islam, M. F. (1983). Cultural change and intergenerational relationships in Arabian families. *International Journal of Family Psychiatry, 4*, 321–329.

Eley, T. C. (1997). General genes: A new theme in developmental psychopathology. *Current Directions in Psychological Science*, 6(4), 90–95.

Elfenbein, H. A., & Ambady, N. (2002). On the universality and cultural specificity of emotion recognition: A meta-analysis. *Psychological Bulletin, 128,* 205–235.

Elfenbein, H. A., & Ambady, N. (2003a). Cultural similarity's consequences: A distance perspective on cross-cultural differences in emotion recognition. *Journal of Cross-Cultural Psychology, 34,* 92–110.

Elfenbein, H. A., & Ambady, N. (2003b). When familiarity breeds accuracy: Cultural exposure and facial emotion recognition. *Journal of Personality and Social Psychology, 85,* 276–290.

Elfenbein, H. A., Mandal, M. K., Ambady, N., & Harizuka, S. (2002). Cross-cultural patterns in emotion recognition: Highlighting design and analytic techniques. *Emotion, 2,* 75–84.

Elfenbein, H. A., Mandal, M. K., Ambady, N., Harizuka, S., & Kumar, S. (2004). Hemifacial differences in the in-group advantage in emotion recognition. *Cognition & Emotion, 18,* 613–629.

Elkind, D. (1978). Understanding the young adolescent. *Adolescence, 13,* 127–134.

Ellis, A. (1962). *Reason and emotion in psychotherapy.* Secaucus, NJ: Prentice-Hall.

Ellis, B., Kimmel, H., Diaz-Guerrero, R., Canas, J., & Bajo, M. (1994). Love and power in Mexico, Spain, and the United States. *Journal of Cross-Cultural Psychology, 25*(4), 525–540.

Enriquez, V. G. (1992). *From colonial to liberation psychology: The Philippine experience.* Manila: De La Salle University Press.

Erşan, E.E., Doğan, O., Doğan, S., & Sümer, H. (2004). The distribution of symptoms of attention deficit/hyperactivity disorder and oppositional defiant disorder in school age children in Turkey. *European Child & Adolescent Psychiatry, 13*(6), 354–361.

Ervin, S. M. (1964). Language and TAT content in bilinguals. *Journal of Abnormal and Social Psychology, 68,* 500–507.

Eschbach, K., Ostir, G. V., Patel, K. V., Markides, K.S., & Goodwin, J. S. (2004). Neighborhood content and mortality among older Mexican Americans: Is there a barrio advantage? *American Journal of Public Health, 94,* 1807–1812.

Espin, O. M. (1993). Feminist theory: Not for or by white women only. *Counseling Psychologist, 21,* 103–108.

Espin, O. M. (1997). *Latina realities: Essays on healing, migration, and sexuality.* Boulder, CO: Westview.

Everett, F., Proctor, N., & Cartmell, B. (1983) Providing psychological services to American Indian children and families. *Research & Practice, 14,* 588–603.

Exline, R. V., Jones, P., & Maciorowski, K. (1977). *Race, affiliative-conflict theory and mutual visual attention during conversation.* Paper presented at the American Psychological Association Annual Convention, San Francisco.

Eysenck, H. J. (1983). Is there a paradigm in personality research? *Journal of Research in Personality, 17*(4), 369–397.

Eysenck, S. B. G., & Chan, J. (1982). A comparative study of personality in adults and children: Hong Kong vs. England. *Personality and Individual Differences, 3,* 153–160.

Fabrega, H. (1989). Language, culture, and the neurobiology of pain: A theoretical exploration. *Behavioral Neurology, 2*(4), 235–260.

Fagot, B., Leinbach, M.D. & Hagen, R. (1986). Gender labeling and adoption of sex-typed behaviors. *Developmental Psychology, 22,* 440–443.

Faraone, S. V., & Biederman, J. (2004). Attention deficit hyperactivity disorder: A worldwide concern. *Journal of Nervous and Mental Disease, 192*(7), 453–454.

Farmer, T. J. (2002). The experience of major depression: Adolescents' perspectives. *Issues in Mental Health Nursing, Special issue: Child and adolescent mental health, 23*(6), 567–585.

Farver, J. M., Welles-Nystroem, B., Frosch, D. L., Wimbarti, S., & Hoppe-Graff, S. (1997). Toy stories: Aggression in children's narratives in the United States, Sweden, Germany, and Indonesia. *Journal of Cross-Cultural Psychology, 28*(4), 393–420.

Febo San Miguel, V. E., Guarnaccia, P. J., Shrout, P. E., Lewis-Fernandez, R., Canino, G. J., & Ramirez, R. R. (2006). A quantitative analysis of ataque de nervios in Puerto Rico: Further examination of a cultural syndrome. *Hispanic Journal of Behavioral Sciences, 28*(3), 313–330.

Fehr, B. J., & Exline, R. V. (1987). Social visual interactions: A conceptual and literature review. In A. W. Siegman & S. Feldstein (Eds.), *Nonverbal behavior and communication* (Vol. 2nd, pp. 225–326). Hillsdale, NJ: Lawrence Erlbaum.

Fehring, R. J., Cheever, K. H., German, K., & Philpot, C. (1998). Religiosity and sexual activity among older adolescents. *Journal of Religion and Health, 37,* 229–239.

Feingold, A. (1992). Good-looking people are not what we think. *Psychological Bulletin, 111*(2), 304–341.

Feist, J., & Brannon, L. (1988). *Health psychology: An introduction to behavior and health.* Belmont, CA: Wadsworth.

Fejes, F. (1992). "Masculinity as fact: A review of empirical mass communication research on masculinity." In S. Craig (Ed.), *Men, masculinity, and the media,* pp. 9–22. Thousand Oaks, CA: Sage.

Fernandez, A. M., Sierra, J. C., Zubeidat, I., & Vera-Villarroel, P. (2006). Sex differences in response to sexual and emotional infidelity among Spanish and Chilean students. *Journal of Cross-Cultural Psychology, 37,* 359–365.

Ferrante, J. (1992). *Sociology: A global perspective.* Belmont, CA: Wadsworth.

Fischer, R., & Smith, P. B. (2003). Reward allocation and culture: A meta-analysis. *Journal of Cross-Cultural Psychology, 34,* 251–268.

Fishman, J. A. (1960). A systematization of the Whorfian hypothesis. *Behavioral Science, 5,* 323–339.

Fitch, W. T., & Hauser, M. D. (2004). Computational constraints on syntactic processing in a nonhuman primate. *Science, 303,* 377–380.

Fitzgerald, L. F., Drasgow, F., Hulin, C. L., Gelfand, M. J., & Magley, V. J. (1997). Antecedents and consequences of sexual harassment in organizations: A test of an integrated model. *Journal of Applied Psychology, 82,* 578–589.

Fitzgerald, L. F., Gelfand, M. J., & Drasgow, F. (1995). Measuring sexual harassment: Theoretical and psychometric advances. *Basic and Applied Social Psychology, 17,* 425–445.

Flanagan, O. (2000). *Dreaming souls: Sleep, dreams, and the evolution of the conscious mind.* Oxford University Press.

Fletcher, J. M., Todd, J., & Satz, P. (1975). Culture fairness of three intelligence tests and a short form procedure. *Psychological Reports, 37,* (3, Pt 2), 1255–1262.

Forgas, J. P. (1992). On mood and peculiar people: Affect and person typicality in impression formation. *Journal of Personality & Social Psychology, 62*(5), 863–875.

Forgas, J. P. (1994). The role of emotion in social judgments: An introductory review and an affect infusion model (AIM). *European Journal of Social Psychology, 24,* 1–24.

Forgas, J. P., & Bower, H. G. (1987). Mood effects on person perception judgments. *Journal of Personality and Social Psychology, 53*(1), 53–60.

Forgas, J. P., & Fiedler, K. (1996). Us and them: Mood effects on intergroup discrimination. *Journal of Personality and Social Psychology, 70,* 28–40.

Forgas, J. P., & Moylan, J. S. (1991). Affective influences on stereotype judgments. *Cognition and Emotion, 5*(5/6), 379–395.

Forgas, J. P., & O'Driscoll, M. (1984). Cross-cultural and demographic differences in the perception of nations. *Journal of Cross-Cultural Psychology, 15*(2), 199–222.

Forgas, J. P., Furnham, A., & Frey, D. (1989). Cross-national differences in attributions of wealth and economic success. *Journal of Social Psychology, 129,* 643–657.

Forston, R. F., & Larson, C. U. (1968). The dynamics of space: An experimental study in proxemic behavior among Latin Americans and north Americans. *Journal of Communication, 18,* 109–116.

Franz, C. E., & White, K. M. (1985). Individuation and attachment in personality development: Extending Erickson's theory. *Journal of Personality, 53*(2), 224–256.

Freedman, D. G. (1964). Smiling in blind infants and the issue of innate versus acquired. *Journal of Child Psychology and Psychiatry, 5,* 171–184.

Freedman, R. E. K., Carter, M. M., Sbrocco, T., & Gray, J. (2004). Ethnic differences in preferences for female weight and waist-to-hip ratio: A comparison of African-American and White American college and community samples. *Eating Behaviors, 5*(3), 191–198.

Freud, S. (1961). *The interpretation of dreams.* New York: Science Editions. (Original work published 1900.)

Friedman, M., & Rosenman, R. H. (1974). *Type A behavior and your heart.* New York: Knopf.

Friesen, W. V. (1972). *Cultural differences in facial expressions in a social situation: An experimental test of the concept of display rules.* Unpublished doctoral dissertation, University of California, San Francisco.

Friesen, W. V., Ekman, P., & Wallbott, H. (1979). Measuring hand movements. *Journal of Nonverbal Behavior, 4,* 97–112.

Frome, P., & Eccles, J. (1996, March). *Gender-role identity and self-esteem.* Paper presented at the biennial meeting of the Society for Research on Adolescence, Boston.

Fulcher, J. S. (1942). "Voluntary" facial expression in blind and seeing children. *Archives of Psychology, 272,* 5–49.

Fuligni, A., & Stevenson, H. (1995). Time-use and mathematics achievement among American, Chinese, and Japanese high school students. *Child Development, 66,* 830–842.

Furnham, A. (1984). Value systems and anomie in three cultures. *International Journal of Psychology, 19,* 565–579.

Furnham, A., & Alibhai, N. (1983). Cross-cultural differences in the perception of female body shapes. *Psychology Medicine, 13,* 829–837.

Furnham, A., & Singh, A. (1986). Memory for information about sex differences. *Sex Roles, 15,* 479–486.

Furnham, A., Moutafi, J., & Baguma, P. (2002). A cross-cultural study on the role of weight and waist-to-hip ratio on female attractiveness. *Personality and Individual Differences, 32*(4), 729–745.

Gabrenya, W. K., Jr., Wang, Y., & Latané, B. (1985). Social loafing on an optimizing task: Cross-cultural differences among Chinese and Americans. *Journal of Cross-Cultural Psychology, 16,* 223–242.

Galambos, N., Peterson, A., Richards, M., & Gitelson, I. (1985). The Attitudes Towards Women Scale for Adolescents (AWSA): A study of reliability and validity. *Sex Roles, 5/6,* 343–356.

Galati, D., Scherer, K. R., & Ricci-Bitti, P. E. (1997). Voluntary facial expression of emotion: Comparing congenitally blind with normally sighted encoders. *Journal of Personality and Social Psychology, 73,* 1363–1379.

Gallup, G. W., & Bezilla, R. (1992). *The religious life of young Americans.* Princeton, NJ: Gallup Institute.

Garcia-Coll, C. T. (1990). Developmental outcomes of minority infants: A process oriented look at our beginnings. *Child Development, 61,* 270–289.

Garcia-Coll, C. T., Meyer, E. C., & Brillon, L. (1995). Ethnic and minority parenting. In M. H. Bornstein & H. Marc (Eds.), *Handbook of parenting: Vol. 2. Biology and ecology of parenting* (pp. 189–209). Mahwah, NJ: Erlbaum.

Gardner, H. (1983). *Frames of mind.* New York: Basic Books.

Gardner, W. L., Gabriel, S., & Lee, A. Y. (1999). "I" value freedom, but "we" value relationships: Self-construal priming mirrors cultural differences in judgment. *Psychological Science, 10,* 321–326.

Garro, L. C. (1986). Language, memory, and focality: A reexamination. *American Anthropologist, 88*(1), 128–136.

Ge, X., Conger, R., Cadoret, R., Neiderhiser, J., Yates, W., Throughton, E., & Stewart, M. (1996). The developmental interface between nature and nurture: A mutual influence model of child antisocial behavior and parent behaviors. *Developmental Psychology, 32,* 574–589.

Geary, D. C. (1996). International differences in mathematical achievement: Their nature, causes, and consequences. *Current Directions in Psychological Science, 5*(5), 133–137.

Geen, R. G. (1994). Social psychological. In M. Hersen & R. T. Ammerman (Eds.), *Handbook of aggressive and destructive behavior in psychiatric patients* (pp. 51–64). New York: Plenum.

Geen, T. (1992). Facial expressions in socially isolated nonhuman primates: Open and closed programs for expressive behavior. *Journal of Research in Personality, 26,* 273–280.

Geertz, C. (1975). From the natives' point of view: On the nature of anthropological understanding. *American Scientist, 63,* 47–53.

Gelfand, M. J. & Dyer, N. (2000). A cultural perspective on negotiation: Progress, pitfalls, and prospects. *Applied Psychology: An International Review, 49*(1), 62–99.

Gelfand, M. J., Major, V. S., Raver, J. L., Nishii, L. H., & O'Brien, K. (2006). The dynamics of the relational self in negotiations. *Academy of Management Review, 31,* 427–451.

Georgas, J. (1989). Changing family values in Greece: From collectivist to individualist. *Journal of Cross-Cultural Psychology, 20,* 80–91.

Georgas, J. (1991). Intrafamily acculturation of values in Greece. *Journal of Cross-Cultural Psychology, 22,* 445–457.

Georgas, J., Berry, J. W., Van di Vijver, F., Kagitcibasi, C., & Poortinga, Y. H. (2006). *Families across cultures: A 30 nation psychological study.* New York: Cambridge University Press.

Gerber, E. (1975). *The cultural patterning of emotions in Samoa.* Unpublished doctoral dissertation, University of California, San Diego.

Gergen, K. J., Gulerce, A., Lock, A., & Misra, G. (1996). Psychological science in cultural context. *American Psychologist, 51*(5), 496–503.

Gerstner, C. R., & Day, D. V. (1994, Summer). Cross cultural comparison of leadership prototypes. *Leadership Quarterly, 5*(2), 121–134.

Gibbons, J., Bradford, R., & Stiles, D.A. (1989). Madrid adolescents express interest in gender roles and work possibilities. *Journal of Early Adolescence, 9*(1–2), 125–141.

Gibbons, J., Stiles, D. A., & Shkodriani, G. M. (1991). Adolescents' attitudes toward family and gender roles: An international comparison. *Sex Roles, 25*(11–12), 625–643.

Gibbons, J., Stiles, D. A., Schnellman, J. D., & Morales-Hidalgo, I. (1990). Images of work, gender, and social commitment among Guatemalan adolescents. *Journal of Early Adolescence, 10*(1), 89–103.

Gilbert, D. T., & Hixon, J. G. (1991). The trouble of thinking: Activation and application of stereotypic beliefs. *Journal of Personality and Social Psychology, 60*(4), 509–517.

Gilbert, G. M. (1951). Stereotype persistence and change among college students. *Journal of Abnormal and Social Psychology, 46,* 245–254.

Gilovich, T., & Medvec, V. H. (1995). The experience of regret: What, when, and why. *Psychological Review, 102,* 379–395.

Gilovich, T., Medvec, V. H., & Kahneman, D. (1998). Varieties of regret: A debate and partial resolution. *Psychological Review, 105,* 602–605.

Gilovich, T., Wang, R. F., Regan, D., & Nishina, S. (2003). Regrets of action and inaction across cultures. *Journal of Cross-Cultural Psychology, 34,* 61–71.

Gim, R. H., Atkinson, D. R., & Kim, S. J. (1991). Asian-American acculturation, counselor ethnicity and cultural sensitivity, and ratings of counselors. *Journal of Counseling Psychology, 38,* 57–62.

Gladwin, H., & Gladwin, C. (1971). Estimating market conditions and profit expectations of fish sellers at Cape Coast, Ghana. In G. Dalton (Ed.), *Studies in economic anthropology* (Anthropological Studies No. 7, pp. 122–143). Washington, DC: American Anthropological Association.

Gladwin, T. (1970). *East is a big bird: Navigation and logic on Puluwat Atoll.* Cambridge, MA: Harvard University Press.

Gleason, H. A. (1961). *An introduction to descriptive linguistics.* New York: Holt, Rinehart & Winston.

Glick, P., Lameiras, M., Fiske, S. T., Eckes, T., Masser, B., Volpato, C., et al. (2004). Bad but bold: Ambivalent attitudes toward men predict gender inequality in 16 nations. *Journal of Personality and Social Psychology, 86,* 713–728.

Glover, G. (2001). Parenting in Native American families. In N. B. Webb (Ed.), *Culturally diverse parent-child and family relationships: A guide for social workers and other practitioners* (pp. 205–231). New York: Columbia University Press.

Goh, S. E., Ong, S. B., & Subramaniam, M. (1993). Eating disorders in Hong Kong. *British Journal of Psychiatry, 162,* 276–277.

Goldman, A. (1992). Intercultural training of Japanese for U.S.–Japanese interorganizational communication. *International Journal of Intercultural Relations, 16,* 195–215.

Goldman, A. (1994). The centrality of "ningensei" to Japanese negotiating and interpersonal relationships: Implications for U.S.–Japanese communication. *International Journal of Intercultural Relations, 18*(1), 29–54.

Goodenough, F. L. (1932). Expression of emotions in a blind-deaf child. *Journal of Abnormal and Social Psychology, 27,* 328–333.

Goodnow, J. (1988). Parents' ideas, actions and feelings: Models and methods from developmental and social psychology. *Child Development, 59,* 289–320.

Goodwin, R. (1990). Sex differences among partner preferences: Are the sexes really very similar? *Sex Roles, 23,* 501–503.

Goossens, L. (1994). Belgium. In K. Hurrelmann (Ed.), *International handbook of adolescence* (pp. 51–64). Westport, CT: Greenwood Press.

Gordon, P. (2004). Numerical cognition without words: Evidence from Amazonia. *Science Express, 10.1126,* 1–8.

Gordon, R. A. (2001). Eating disorders East and West: A culturebound syndrome unbound. In M. Nasser & M. A. Katzman (Eds.), *Eating disorders and cultures in transition* (pp. 1–16). New York: Brunner-Routledge.

Gorman, J. C. (1998). Parenting attitudes and practices of immigrant Chinese mothers of adolescents. *Family Relations: Interdisciplinary Journal of Applied Family Studies, 47*(1), 73–80.

Gottman, J. M. (1994). *What predicts divorce?* Hillsdale, NJ: Erlbaum.

Gottman, J. M., & Levenson, R. W. (2002). A two-factor model for predicting when a couple will divorce: Exploratory analyses using 14-year longitudinal data. *Family Process, 41,* 83–96.

Graham, J. L. (1983). Brazilian, Japanese, and American Business Negotiations. *Journal of International Business Studies, 14,* 47–61.

Graham, J. L. (1984). *Smart bargaining: Doing business with the Japanese.* Cambridge, MA: Ballinger.

Graham, J. L. (1993). The Japanese negotiation style: Characteristics of a distinct approach. *Negotiation Journal, 9*(2), 123–140.

Graham, J. L., & Andrews, J. D. (1987). A holistic analysis of Japanese and American business negotiations. *Analysis of Business Negotiations, 24*(4), 63–77.

Graham, J. L., Evenko, L. I., & Rajan, M. N. (1992). A empirical comparison of Soviet and American business negotiations. *Journal of International Business Studies, 23,* 387–418.

Graham, J. L., Kim, D. K., Lin, C.-Y., & Robinson, M. (1988). Buyerseller negotiations around the Pacific rim: Differences in fundamental exchange processes. *Journal of Consumer Research, 15*(1), 48–54.

Grant, B. F., Stinson, F. S., Hasin, D. S., Dawson, D. A., Chou, S. P., & Anderson, K. (2004). Immigration and lifetime prevalence of DSM-IV psychiatric disorders among Mexican Americans and Non-Hispanic whites in the United States. *Archives of General Psychiatry, 61,* 1226–1233.

Grant, N. M., Schell, T. L., Elliot, M. N., Berthold, M., & Chun, C.-A. (2005). Mental health of Cambodian refugees 2 decades after resettlement in the United States. *JAMA, 294,* 571–579.

Greenberg, J., Solomon, S., & Pyszczynski, T. (1997). Terror management theory of self-esteem and cultural worldviews: Empirical assessments and conceptual refinements. In M. P. Zanna (Ed.), *Advances in experimental social psychology* (pp. 61–139). San Diego, CA: Academic Press.

Greenberger, E., & Chen, C. (1996). Perceived family relationships and depressed mood in early and late adolescence: A comparison of European and Asian Americans. *Developmental Psychology, 32*(4), 707–716.

Greenfield, P. M. (1997). You can't take it with you: Why ability assessments don't cross cultures. *American Psychologist, 52,* 1115–1124.

Greenfield, P. M., Reich, L. C., & Oliver, R. R. (1966). On culture and equivalence II. In J. S. Bruner, R. R. Oliver, & P. M. Greenfield (Eds.), *Studies in cognitive growth* (pp. 270–318). New York: Wiley.

Greenwald, A. G., & Pratkanis, A. R. (1984). The self. In R. S. Wyer & T. K. Srull (Eds.), *Handbook of social cognition* (Vol. 3, pp. 129–178). Hillsdale, NJ: Erlbaum.

Greenwald, A. G., McGhee, D. E., & Schwartz, J. L. K. (1998). Measuring individual differences in implicit cognition: The implicit association test. *Journal of Personality and Social Psychology, 74,* 1464–1480.

Grisaru, N., Budowski, D., & Witztum, E. (1997). Possession by the "zar" among Ethiopian immigrants to Israel: Psychopathology or culture-bound syndrome? *Psychopathology, 30*(4), 223–233.

Guarnaccia, P. J., & Rogler, L. H. (1999). Research on culturebound syndromes: New directions. *American Journal of Psychiatry, 156*(9), 1322–1327.

Guarnaccia, P. J., Martinez, I., & Acosta, H. (2005). Mental health in the Hispanic immigrant community: an overview. *Journal of Immigrant and Refugee Services, 3,* 21–46.

Gudykunst, W. B. (1993). Toward a theory of effective interpersonal and intergroup communication: An anxiety/uncertainty management (AUM) perspective. In R. L. Wiseman, J. Koester, et al. (Eds.), *International and intercultural communication annual: Vol. 17. Intercultural communication competence* (pp. 33–71). Newbury Park, CA: Sage.

Gudykunst, W. B., & Nishida, T. (1984). Individual and cultural influences on uncertainty reduction. *Communication Monographs, 51,* 23–36.

Gudykunst, W. B., & Nishida, T. (1986b). The influence of cultural variability on perceptions of communication behavior associated with relationship terms. *Human Communication Research, 13,* 147–166.

Gudykunst, W. B., & Shapiro, R. B. (1996). Communication in everyday interpersonal and intergroup encounters. *International Journal of Intercultural Relations, 20*(1), 19–45.

Gudykunst, W. B., & Ting-Toomey, S. (1988). Culture and affective communication. [Special Issue: *Communication and affect.*] *American Behavioral Scientist, 31,* 384–400.

Gudykunst, W. B., Matsumoto, Y., & Ting-Toomey, S. (1996). The influence of cultural individualism-collectivism, self construals, and individual values on communication styles across cultures. *Human Communication Research, 22,* 510–543.

Gudykunst, W. B., Sodetani, L. L., & Sonoda, K. T. (1987). Uncertainty reduction in Japanese-American/Caucasian relationships in Hawaii. *Western Journal of Speech Communication, 51,* 256–278.

Gudykunst, W. B., Yoon, Y., & Nishida, T. (1987). The influence of individualism-collectivism on perceptions of communication in ingroup and outgroup relationships. *Communication Monographs, 54,* 295–306.

Guilford, J. P. (1985). The structure of intellect model. In B. B. Wolman (Ed.), *Handbook of intelligence: Theories, measurements, and applications* (pp. 225–265). New York: Wiley.

Guisinger, S., & Blatt, S. J. (1994). Individuality and relatedness: Evolution of a fundamental dialectic. *American Psychologist, 49,* 104–111.

Gurin, P. (1997). Expert report. Ann Arbor: University of Michigan. http://www.umich.edu/~urel/admissions/legal/expert/gurintoc.html.

Guthrie, G. M., & Bennett, A. B. (1971). Cultural differences in implicit personality theory. *International Journal of Psychology, 6*(4), 305–312.

Hadiyono, J. E. P., & Hahn, M. W. (1985). Personality differences and sex similarities in American and Indonesian college students. *Journal of Social Psychology, 125,* 703–708.

Haghighatgou, H., & Peterson, C. (1995). Coping and depressive symptoms among Iranian students. *Journal of Social Psychology, 135*(2), 175–180.

Haidt, J. (2001). The emotional dog and its rational tail: A social intuitionist approach to moral judgment. *Psychological Review, 108,* 814–834.

Haidt, J., & Keltner, D. (1999). Culture and facial expression: Open-ended methods find more expressions and a gradient of recognition. *Cognition & Emotion, 13,* 225–266.

Hall, E. T. (1963). A system for the notation of proxemic behaviors. *American Anthropologist, 65,* 1003–1026.

Hall, E. T. (1966). *The hidden dimension.* New York: Doubleday.

Hall, E. T. (1973). *The silent language.* New York: Anchor.

Hall, E. T. (1976). *Beyond culture.* New York: Anchor.

Hall, R. H., Jiang, S., Loscocco, K. A., & Allen, J. K. (1993). Ownership patterns and centralization: A China and U.S. comparison. *Sociological Forum, 8*(4), 595–608.

Hamid, P. N. (1994). Self-monitoring, locus of control, and social encounters of Chinese and New Zealand students. *Journal of Cross-Cultural Psychology, 25*(3), 353–368.

Hamilton, L. H., Brooks-Gunn, J., & Warren, M. P. (1985). Sociocultural influences on eating disorders in professional female ballet dancers. *International Journal of Eating Disorders, 4*(4), 465–477.

Hamilton, V. L., Blumenfeld, P. C., Akoh, H., & Miura, K. (1991). Group and gender in Japanese and American elementary classrooms. *Journal of Cross-Cultural Psychology, 22,* 317–346.

Hanna, G. S., House, B., & Salisbury, L. H. (1968). WAIS performance of Alaskan Native university freshmen. *Journal of Genetic Psychology, 112*(1), 57–61.

Hardin, E. E. (2006). Convergent evidence for the multidimensionality of self construal. *Journal of Cross-Cultural Psychology, 37,* 516–521.

Hardin, E. E., Leong, F. T. L., & Bhagwat, A. A. (2004). Factor structure of the self-construal scale revisited: Implications for the multidimensionality of self-construal. *Journal of Cross-Cultural Psychology, 35,* 327–345.

Harkins, S. G. (1987). Social loafing and social facilitation. *Journal of Experimental Social Psychology, 23,* 1–18.

Harkins, S. G., & Petty, R. E. (1982). Effects of task difficulty and task uniqueness on social loafing. *Journal of Personality and Social Psychology, 43,* 1214–1229.

Harkness, S., & Super, C. M. (2006). Themes and variations: Parental ethnotheories in Western culture. In K. Rubin & O. Chung (Eds.), *Parenting beliefs, behaviors, and parent-child relations* (pp. 61–79). New York: Psychology Press.

Harris, A. C. (1996). African Americans and Anglo American gender identities: An empirical study. *Journal of Black Psychology, 22*(2), 182–194.

Harrison, A. O., Stewart, R. B., Myambo, K., & Teveraishe, C. (1995). Perceptions of social networks among adolescents from Zimbabwe and the United States. *Journal of Black Psychology, 21*(4), 382–407.

Harrison, A. O., Wilson, M. N., Pine, C. J., Chan, S. Q., & Buriel, R. (1990). Family ecologies of ethnic minority children. *Child Development, 61,* 347–362.

Hart, I. (1971). Scores of Irish groups on the Cattell Culture Fair Test of Intelligence and the California Psychological Inventory. *Irish Journal of Psychology, 1*(1), 30–25.

Harvey, Y. K. (1979). *Six Korean women: The socialization of shamans.* New York: West.

Haskins, R. (1989). Beyond metaphor: The efficacy of early childhood education. *American Psychologist, 44,* 274–282.

Haslam, N., Bain, P., Douge, L., Lee, M., & Bastian, B. (2005). More human than you: Attributing humanness to self and others. *Journal of Personality and Social Psychology, 89,* 937–950.

Hatfield, E. (1988). Passionate and companionate love. In R. J. Sternberg & M. L. Barnes (Eds.), *The psychology of love* (pp. 191–217). New Haven, CT: Yale University Press.

Hatfield, E., & Rapson, R. L. (1996). *Love and sex: Cross-cultural perspectives.* Boston: Allyn & Bacon.

Hatfield, E., & Sprecher, S. (1995). Men's and women's preferences in marital partners in the United States, Russia, and Japan. *Journal of Cross-Cultural Psychology, 26*(6), 728–750.

Hau, K., & Salili, F. (1991). Structure and semantic differential placement of specific causes: Academic causal attributions by Chinese students in Hong Kong. *International*

Journal of Psychology, 26, 175–193.

Hauser, M. (1993). Right hemisphere dominance for the production of facial expression in monkeys. *Science, 261,* 475–477.

Hays, J. R., & Smith, A. L. (1980). Comparison of WISC-R and Culture Fair Intelligence Test scores for three ethnic groups of juvenile delinquents. *Psychological Reports, 46*(3, Pt. 1), 931–934.

Healey, J. F. (1998). *Race, ethnicity, gender, and class: The sociology of group conflict and change.* Thousand Oaks, CA: Pine Forge.

Heaven, P. C. L., & Rajab, D. (1983). Correlates of self-esteem among a South African minority group. *Journal of Social Psychology, 121*(2), 269–270.

Heaven, P. C. L., Connors, J., & Stones, C. R. (1994). Three or five personality dimensions? An analysis of natural language terms in two cultures. *Personality and Individual Differences, 17*(2), 181–189.

Heelas, P., & Lock, A. (1981). *Indigenous psychologies: An anthropology of the self.* London: Academic Press.

Heider, E. R., & Oliver, D. (1972). The structure of the color space in naming and memory for two languages. *Cognitive Psychology, 3,* 337–354.

Heine, S. J. (2005). Where is the evidence for pancultural self-enhancement? A reply to Sedkides, Gaertner, and Toguchi (2003). *Journal of Personality and Social Psychology, 89,* 531–538.

Heine, S. J., & Lehman, D. R. (1996). Hindsight bias: A cross-cultural analysis. *Japanese Journal of Experimental Social Psychology, 35,* 317–323.

Heine, S. J., & Renshaw, K. (2002). Interjudge agreement, self-enhancement, and liking: Cross-cultural divergences. *Personality and Social Psychology Bulletin, 28,* 578–587.

Heine, S. J., Lehman, D. R., Markus, H. R., & Kitayama, S. (1999). Is there a universal need for positive self-regard? *Psychological Review, 106,* 766–794.

Heine, S. J., Lehman, D. R., Peng, K., & Greenholz, J. (2002). What's wrong with cross-cultural comparisons of subjective likert scales? The reference-group problem. *Journal of Personality and Social Psychology, 82,* 903–918.

Helms, J. E., Jernigan, M., & Mascher, J. (2005). The meaning of race in psychology and how to change it. *American Psychologist, 60,* 27–36.

Henderson, N. D. (1982). Human behavior genetics. *Annual Review of Psychology, 33,* 403–440.

Heppner, P. (2006). The benefits and challenges of becoming cross-culturally competent counseling psychologists: Presidential address. *Counseling Psychologist, 34*(1), 147–172.

Hermans, H. J. M., & Kempen, H. J. G. (1998). Moving cultures: The perilous problems of cultural dichotomies in a globalizing society. *American Psychologist, 53,* 1111–1120.

Herrnstein, R. J., & Murray, C. (1994). *The bell curve: Intelligence and class structure in American life.* New York: Free Press.

Hess, J. A. (1993). Assimilating newcomers into an organization: A cultural perspective. *Journal of Applied Communication Research, 21*(2), 189–210.

Hiatt, L. R. (1978). Classification of the emotions. In L. R. Hiatt (Ed.), *Australian aboriginal concepts* (pp. 182–187). Princeton, NJ: Humanities Press.

Higginbotham, H. N. (1979). Culture and mental health services. In A. J. Marsella, G. DeVos, & F. L. K. Hsu (Eds.), *Perspectives on cross-cultural psychology* (pp. 307–332). New York: Academic Press.

Hippler, A. E. (1974). The North Alaska Eskimos: A culture and personality perspective. *American Ethnologist, 1*(3), 449–469.

Hirschfield, L. A. (1996). *Race in the making: Cognition, culture, and the child's construction of human kinds.* Cambridge, MA: MIT Press.

Ho, D. Y. (1998). Indigenous psychologies: Asian perspectives. *Journal of Cross Cultural Psychology, 29*(1), 88–103.

Ho, M. K. (1984). Social group work with Asian/Pacific-Americans.

Social Work with Groups, 7(3), 49–61.

Hobson, J. A. (1999). The new neuropsychology of sleep: Implications for psychoanalysis. *Neuropsychoanalysis, 1,* 157–183.

Hoch, E. M. (1990). Experiences with psychotherapy training in India. *Psychotherapy and Psychosomatics, 53*(1–4), 14–20.

Hodgetts, R. M., Luthans, F., & Lee, S. M. (1994). New paradigm organizations: From total quality to learning to world-class. *Organizational Dynamics, 22*(3), 5–19.

Hoek, H. W., van Harten, P. N., van Hoeken, D., & Susser, E. (1998). Lack of relation between culture and anorexia nervosa: Results of an incidence study on Curacao. *New England Journal of Medicine, 338*(17), 1231–1232.

Hoffman, W., Gawronski, B., Gschwendner, T., Le, H., & Schmitt, M. (2005). A meta-analysis on the correlation between the implicit association test and explicit self-report measures. *Personality and Social Psychology Bulletin, 31,* 1369–1385.

Hofstede, G. (1980). *Culture's consequences: International differences in work-related values.* Beverly Hills, CA: Sage.

Hofstede, G. (1983). Dimensions of national cultures in fifty countries and three regions. In J. B. Deregowski, S. Dziurawiec, & R. C. Annis (Eds.), *Explications in cross-cultural psychology* (pp. 335–355). Amsterdam: Swets & Zeitlinger.

Hofstede, G. (1984). *Culture's consequences: International differences in work-related values* (abridged ed.). Beverly Hills, CA: Sage.

Hofstede, G. (1996b). Riding the waves of commerce: A test of Trompenaars' "model" of national culture differences. *International Journal of Intercultural Relations, 20*(2), 189–198.

Hofstede, G. (2001). *Culture's consequences: Comparing values, behaviors, institutions, and organizations across nations* (2nd ed.). Thousand Oaks, CA: Sage.

Hofstede, G. H. (2001). *Culture's consequences: Comparing values, behaviors, institutions and organizations across nations* (2nd ed.). Thousand Oaks, CA: Sage.

Hofstede, G. H., & Bond, M. (1984). Hofstede's cultural dimensions: An independent validation using Rokeach's value survey. *Journal of Cross-Cultural Psychology, 15,* 417–433.

Hofstede, G. H., Bond, M., & Luk, C. -L. (1993). Individual perceptions of organizational cultures: A methodological treatise on levels of analysis. *Organization Studies, 14,* 483–503.

Hofstede, G., & Bond, M. (1988). Confucius and economic growth: New trends in culture's consequences. *Organizational Dynamics, 16*(4), 4–21.

Hofstee, W. K. B., Kiers, H. A., De Raad, B., Goldberg, L. R., et al. (1997). A comparison of Big Five structures of personality traits in Dutch, English, and German. *European Journal of Personality, 11*(1), 15–31.

Hollander, E. (1985). Leadership and power. In G. Lindzey & E. Aaronson (Eds.), *The handbook of social psychology* (3rd ed., Vol. 2, pp. 485–537). New York: Random House.

Hollon, S. D., & Beck, A. T. (1994). Cognitive and cognitive behavioral therapies. In A. E. Bergin & S. L. Garfield (Eds.), *Handbook of psychotherapy and behavior change* (4th ed., pp. 428–466). New York: Wiley.

Holmes, L. D., Tallman, G., & Jantz, V. (1978, Fall). Samoan personality. *Journal of Psychological Anthropology, 1*(4), 453–469.

Hong, Y. Y., Morris, M., Chiu, C.-Y., & Benet-Martinez, V.(2000). Multicultural minds: A dynamic constructivist approach to culture and cognition. *American Psychologist, 55,* 709–720.

Hood, R. W., Spilka, B., Hunsberger, B., & Gorsuch, R. (1996). *The psychology of religion* (2nd ed.). New York: Guilford Press.

Hoosain, R. (1986). Language, orthography and cognitive process: Chinese perspectives for the Sapir-Whorf hypothesis. *International Journal of Behavioral Development, 9*(4), 507–525.

Hoosain, R. (1991). *Psycholinguistic implications for linguistic relativity: A case study of Chinese.* Hillsdale, NJ: Erlbaum.

Hopper, K., & Wanderling, J. (2000). Revisiting the developed versus developing country distinction in course and outcome in schizophrenia: Results from ISoS, the WHO collaborative followup project. *Schizophrenia Bulletin, 26*(4), 835–846.

Hornsey, M. J., & Jetten, J. (2004). The individual within the group: Balancing the need to belong with the need to be different. *Personality and Social Psychology Review, 8,* 248–264.

Hothersall, D. (1990). *History of psychology* (2nd ed.). New York: McGraw-Hill.

House, R. J., Hanges, P. J., Javidan, M., Dorfman, P. W., & Gupta, V. (2004). *Culture, leadership, and organizations: The GLOBE study of 62 societies.* Thousand Oaks, CA: Sage.

Howell, J. P., Dorfman P. W., Hibino, S., Lee, J. K., & Tale, U. (1995). *Leadership in Western and Asian countries: Commonalities and differences in effective leadership processes and substitutes across cultures.* Las Cruces: New Mexico State University.

Howell, S. (1981). Rules not words. In P. Heelas & A. Lock (Eds.), *Indigenous psychologies: The anthropology of the self* (pp. 133–143). San Diego: Academic Press.

Howes, C. (1990). Can the age of entry into child care and the quality of child care predict adjustment in kindergarten? *Developmental Psychology, 26,* 292–303.

Howes, C., Whitebrook, M., & Phillips, D. (1992). Teacher characteristics and effective teaching in child care: Findings from the National Child Care Staffing Study. *Child and Youth Care Forum, 21*(6), 399–414.

Hsu, L. (1977). An examination of Cooper's test for monotonic trend. *Educational and Psychological Measurement, 37*(4), 843–845.

Hu, P., & Meng, Z. (1996). *An examination of infant-mother attachment in China.* Poster presented at the meeting of the International Society for the Study of Behavioral Development, Quebec City.

Huang, L. N., & Ying, Y. (1989). Japanese children and adolescents. In J. T. Gibbs & L. N. Huang (Eds.), *Children of color.* San Francisco: Jossey-Bass.

Hudson, W. (1960). Pictorial depth perception in subcultural groups in Africa. *Journal of Social Psychology, 52,* 183–208.

Huff, R. M. (1999). Cross-cultural concepts of health and disease. In R. M. Huff & M. V. Kline (Eds.), *Promoting health in multicultural populations: A handbook for practitioners* (pp. 23–39). Thousand Oaks, CA: Sage.

Hughes, B., & Paterson, K. (1997). The social model of disability and the disappearing body: Towards a sociology of impairment. *Disability and Society, 12*(3), 325–340.

Hui, C. H. (1984). *Individualism-collectivism: Theory, measurement, and its relation to reward allocation.* Unpublished doctoral dissertation, University of Illinois.

Hui, C. H. (1988). Measurement of individualism-collectivism. *Journal of Research in Personality, 22,* 17–36.

Hull, P. V. (1987). *Bilingualism: Two languages, two personalities? Resources in education, educational resources clearinghouse on education.* Ann Arbor: University of Michigan Press.

Hull, P. V. (1990a). *Bilingualism: Two languages, two personalities?* Unpublished doctoral dissertation, University of California, Berkeley.

Hull, P. V. (1990b, August). *Bilingualism and language choice.* Paper presented at the Annual Convention of the American Psychological Association, Boston. Human Synergistics. (1986). *Organizational Culture Inventory.* Isle of Man, UK: Author.

Hundley, G., & Kim, J. (1997). National culture and the factors affecting perceptions of pay fairness in Korea and the United States. *International Journal of Organizational Analysis, 5,* 325–341.

Huntington, R. L., Fronk, C., & Chadwick, B. A. (2001). Family roles of contemporary Palestinian women. *Journal of Comparative Family Studies, 32*(1), 1–19.

Husen, T. (1967). *International study of achievement in mathematics.* New York: Wiley.

Hwang, C. P., & Broberg, A. G. (1992). The historical and social context of child care in Sweden. In M. E. Lamb, K. J. Sternberg, C-P. Hwang, & A. G. Broberg (Eds), *Childcare in context: Cross-cultural perspectives* (pp. 27–53). Hillsdale, NJ: Erlbaum.

Hwu, H. G., & Compton, W. M. (1994). Comparison of major epidemiological surveys using the diagnostic interview schedule. *International Review of Psychiatry, 6,* 309–327.

Hyson, M. C., & Izard, C. E. (1985). Continuities and changes in emotion expressions during brief separation at 13 and 18 months. *Developmental Psychology, 21,* 1165–1170.

Indian Health Service (2006). *Facts on Indian health disparities.* Washington, DC: U.S. Department of Health and Human Services.

Inglehart, R. (1997). *Modernization and postmodernization: Cultural, economic and political change in 43 societies.* Princeton, NJ: Princeton University Press.

Inglehart, R. (1998). *Modernizacion y postmodernizacion. El cambio cultural, economico y polotico en 43 sociedades.* Madrid, Spain: CIS.

International Classification of Diseases—10, (2nd ed.) (2005). Geneva: World Health Organization.

International Displacement Monitoring Centre (2006). *International displacement, global overview of trends and developments in 2005.* Geneva: Norwegian Refugee Council.

Isaac, M., Janca, A., & Orley, J. (1996). Somatization: A culture-bound or universal syndrome? *Journal of Mental Health UK, 5*(3), 219–222.

Iwao, S., & Triandis, C. H. (1993). Validity of auto- and heterostereotypes among Japanese and American students. *Journal of Cross-Cultural Psychology, 24*(4), 428–444.

Iwata, N., & Higuchi, H. R. (2000). Responses of Japanese and American university students to the STAI items that assess the presence or absence of anxiety. *Journal of Personality Assessment, 74,* 48–62.

Izard, C. E. (1971). *The face of emotion.* East Norwalk, CT: Appleton-Century-Crofts.

Izard, C. E. (1971). *The face of emotion.* New York: Appleton-Century-Crofts.

Jackson, J. M., & Williams, K. D. (1985). Social loafing on difficult tasks: Working collectively can improve performance. *Journal of Personality and Social Psychology, 49,* 937–942.

Jackson, L. M., Pratt, M. W., Hunsberger, B., & Pancer, S. (2005). Optimism as a mediator of the relation between perceived parental authoritativeness and adjustment among adolescents: Finding the sunny side of the street. *Social Development, 14*(2), 273–304.

Jaffe, Y., & Yinon, Y. (1983). Collective aggression: The group-individual paradigm in the study of collective antisocial behavior. In H. H. Blumberg, A. P. Hare, V. Kent, & M. F. Davies (Eds.), *Small groups and social interaction* (Vol. 1., pp. 267–175). Chichester, UK: Wiley.

Jahoda, G. (1984). Do we need a concept of culture? *Journal of Cross-Cultural Psychology, 15,* 139–151.

Jalali, B. (1982). Iranian families. In M. McGoldrick, J. Pearce, & J. Giordano (Eds.), *Ethnicity and family therapy* (pp. 288–309). New York: Guilford Press.

Jang, K. L., McCrae, R. R., Angleitner, A., Riemann, R., & Livesley, W. J. (1998). Heritability of facet-level traits in cross-cultural twin sample: Support for a hierarchical model of personality. *Journal of Personality and Social Psychology, 74,* 1556–1565.

Janis, I. L. (1983). *Group think.* Boston: Houghton Mifflin.

Jankowiak, W. R., & Fischer, E. F. (1992). A cross-cultural perspective on romantic love. *Ethology, 32,* 149–155.

Jencks, C., Smith, M., Acland, H., Bane, M. J., Cohen, D., Gintis, H., Heyns, B., & Michaelson, S. (1972). *Inequality: A reassessment of the effect of family and schooling in America.* New York: Harper & Row.

Jensen, A. R. (1968). Social class, race and genetics: Implications for education. *American Educational Research Journal, 5*(1), 1–42.

Jensen, A. R. (1969). How much can we boost IQ and scholastic achievement? *Harvard Educational Review, 39,* 1–123.

Jensen, A. R. (1971). Twin differences and race differences in I.Q.: A reply to Burgess and Jahoda. *Bulletin of the British Psychological Society, 24*(84), 195–198.

Jensen, A. R. (1973). Personality and scholastic achievement in three ethnic groups. *British Journal of Educational Psychology, 43*(20), 115–125.

Jensen, A. R. (1977). Cumulative deficit in IQ of Blacks in the rural South. *Developmental Psychology, 13*(93), 184–191.

Jensen, A. R. (1980). *Bias in mental testing.* New York: Free Press.

Jensen, A. R. (1981). *Straight talk about mental tests.* London: Methuen.

Jensen, A. R. (1983). Effects of inbreeding on mental-ability factors. *Personality and Individual Differences, 4*(1), 71–87.

Jensen, A. R. (1984). The black-white difference on the K-ABC: Implications for future tests. *Journal of Special Education, 18*(3), 377–408.

Jensen, A. R., & Johnson, F. W. (1994). Race and sex differences in head size and I.Q. *Intelligence, 18*(3), 309–333.

Jensen, A. R., & Munro, E. (1979). Reaction time, movement time, and intelligence. *Intelligence, 3*(2), 121–126.

Jensen, A. R., & Reed, T. E. (1990). Simple reaction time as a suppressor variable in the chronometric study of intelligence. *Intelligence, 14*(4), 375–388.

Jensen, A. R., & Whang, P. A. (1993). Reaction times and intelligence: A comparison of Chinese-American and Anglo-American children. *Journal of Biosocial Science, 25*(3), 397–410.

Jensen, L. A. (1997). Different world-views, different morals: America's culture war divide. *Human Development, 40*(6), 325–344.

Ji, L. J., Zhang, Z., & Nisbett, R. (2004). Is it culture or is it language? Examination of language effects in cross-cultural research on categorization. *Journal of Personality and Social Psychology, 87,* 57–65.

Jilek-Aall, L., Jilek, M., Kaaya, J., Mkombachepa, L., & Hillary, K. (1997). Psychosocial study of epilepsy in Africa. *Social Science and Medicine, 45*(5), 783–795.

Joensson, E. G., Cichon, S., Gustavsson, J. P., Greunhage, F., Forslund, K., Mattila-Evenden, M., Rylander, G., Asberg, M., Farde, L., Propping, P., & Noethen, M. (2003). Association between a promoter dopamine D-sub-2 receptor gene variant and the personality trait detachment. *Biological Psychiatry, 53*(7), 577–584.

Johnson, D. L., Johnson, C. A., & Price-Williams, D. (1967). The Draw A Man Test and Raven Progressive Matrices performance of Guatemalan boys and Latino children. *Revista Interamericana de Psicologia, 1*(2), 143–157.

Johnson, T., Kulesa, P., Cho, Y. I., & Shavitt, S. (2004). The relation between culture and response styles: Evidence from 19 countries. *Journal of Cross-Cultural Psychology, 36,* 264–277.

Johnston, L., Hewstone, M., Pendry, L., & Frankish, C. (1994). Cognitive models of stereotype change: IV. Motivational and cognitive influences. *European Journal of Social Psychology, 24*(2), 237–265.

Jones, E. E., & Harris, V. A. (1967). The attribution of attitudes. *Journal of Experimental Social Psychology, 3,* 1–24.

Jones, E. E., & Matsumoto, D. R. (1982). Psychotherapy with the underserved. In L. Snowden (Ed.), *Services to the underserved* (pp. 207–228). Beverly Hills, CA: Sage.

Jones, E. F., Forrest, J. D., Goldman, N., Henshaw, S. K., Lincoln, R., Rosoff, J. I., et al. (1985). Teenage pregnancy in developed countries: Determinants and policy implications. *Family Planning Perspectives, 17,* 53–63.

Joseph, R. A., Markus, H. R., & Tafarodi, R. W. (1992). Gender differences in the source of self-esteem. *Journal of Personality and Social Psychology, 63,* 1017–1028.

Juni, S. (1996). Review of the revised NEO Personality Inventory. In J. C. Conoley & J. C. Impara (Eds.), *12th mental measurements yearbook* (pp. 863–868). Lincoln: University of Nebraska Press.

Kagitcibasi, C. (1996a). The autonomous-relational self: A new synthesis. *European Psychologist, 1,* 180–186.

Kagitcibasi, C. (1996b). *Family and human development across cultures: A view from the other side.* Mahwah, NJ: Erlbaum.

Kakar, S. (1978). *The inner world: A psychoanalytic study of childhood and society in India.* New Delhi: Oxford University Press.

Kamal, Z., & Lowenthal, K. M. (2002). Suicide beliefs and behavior among young Muslims and Indians in the UK. *Mental Health, Religion and Culture, 5*(2), 111–118.

Kane, C. M. (1994). Differences in the manifest dream content of Anglo-American, Mexican-American, and African-American college women. *Journal of Multicultural Counseling and Development, 22,* 203–209.

Karam, E. G., Mneimneh, Z. H., Karam, A. N., Fayyad, J. A., Nasser, S. C., Chatterji, S., Kessler, R. C. (2006). Prevalence and treatment of mental disorders in Lebanon: A national epidemiological survey. *Lancet, 367*(9515), 1000–1006.

Karavasilis, L., Doyle, A. & Markiewicz, D. (2003). Associations between parenting style and attachment to mother in middle childhood and adolescence. *International Journal of Behavioral Development, 27*(2), 153–164.

Karlins, M., Coffman, T. L., & Walters, G. (1969). On the fading of social stereotypes: Studies in three generations of college students. *Journal of Personality and Social Psychology, 13*(1), 1–16.

Kashima, E. S., & Hardie, E. A. (2000). The development and validation of the Relational, Individualism, and Collectivism self-aspects (RIC) Scale. *Asian Journal of Social Psychology, 3,* 19–48.

Kashima, E. S., & Kashima, Y. (1998). Culture and language: The case of cultural dimensions and personal pronoun use. *Journal of Cross-Cultural Psychology, 29,* 461–486.

Kashima, Y., & Triandis, H. C. (1986). The self-serving bias in attributions as a coping strategy: A cross-cultural study. *Journal of Cross-Cultural Psychology, 17,* 83–97.

Kashima, Y., Kokubo, T., Kashima, E. S., Boxall, D., Yamaguchi, S., & Macrae, K. (2004). Culture and self: Are there within-culture differences in self between metropolitan areas and regional cities? *Personality and Social Psychology Bulletin, 30,* 816–823.

Kashima, Y., Yamaguchi, S., Kim, U., & Choi, S. C. (1995). Culture, gender, and self: A perspective from individualism-collectivism research. *Journal of Personality & Social Psychology, 69,* 925–937.

Katigbak, M. S., Church, A. T., Guanzon-Lapena, M. A., Carlota, A. J., & del Pilar, G. H. (2002). Are indigenous personality dimensions culture specific? Philippine inventories and the five-factor model. *Journal of Personality and Social Psychology, 82*(1), 89–101.

Katz, D., & Braly, K. (1933). Racial stereotypes of one hundred college students. *Journal of Abnormal and Social Psychology, 28,* 280–290.

Kay, P., & Kempton, W. (1984). What is the Sapir-Whorf hypothesis? *American Anthropologist, 86,* 65–89.

Kazarian, S. S., & Persad, E. (2001). Cultural issues in suicidal behavior. In S. S. Kazarian & D. R. Evans (Eds.), *Handbook of cultural health psychology* (pp. 267–302). San Diego: Academic Press.

Keats, D. M. (1982). Cultural bases of concepts of intelligence: A Chinese versus Australian comparison. In P. Sukontasarp, N. Yongsiri, P. Intasuwan, N. Jotiban, & C. Suvannathat (Eds.), *Proceedings of the Second Asian Workshop on Child and Adolescent Development* (pp. 67–75). Bangkok: Burapasilpa Press.

Keats, D. M., & Fang, F. X. (1987). Cultural factors in concepts of intelligence. In C. Kagitcibasi et al. (Eds.), *Growth and progress in cross-cultural psychology* (pp. 236–247). Berwyn, PA: Swets North America.

Keitner, G. I., Fodor, J., Ryan, C. E., Miller, I. W., Epstein, N. B., & Bishop, D. S. (1991). A cross-cultural study of major depression and family functioning. *Canadian Journal of Psychiatry, 36*(4), 254–258.

Kelleher, M. J., Chambers, D., Corcoran, P., Williamson, E., & Keeley, H. S. (1998). Religious sanctions and rates of suicide worldwide. *Crisis, 19*, 78–86.

Keller, M., Edelstein, W., Schmid, C., Fang, F.-X., & Fang, G. (1998). Reasoning about responsibilities and obligations in close relationships: A comparison across two cultures. *Developmental Psychology, 34*(4), 731–741.

Kelley, M., & Tseng, H. (1992). Cultural differences in child rearing: A comparison of immigrant Chinese and Caucasian American mothers. *Journal of Cross-Cultural Psychology, 23*(4), 444–455.

Kelly, D. J., Quinn, P. C., Slater, A. M., Lee, K., Gibson, A., Smith, M., et al. (2005). Three-month-olds, but not newborns, prefer own-race faces. *Developmental Science, 8*, F31–F36.

Kelly, J. G. (1990). Changing contexts and the field of community psychology. *American Journal of Community Psychology, 18*(6), 769–792.

Keltner, D. (1995). The signs of appeasement: Evidence for the distinct displays of embarrassment, amusement, and shame. *Journal of Personality and Social Psychology, 68*, 441–454.

Kemmelmeier, M., & Cheng, B. Y.-M. (2004). Language and self-construal priming: A replication and extension in a Hong Kong sample. *Journal of Cross-Cultural Psychology, 35*, 705–712.

Kemmelmeier, M., Jambor, E., & Letner, J. (2006). Individualism and good works: Cultural variation in giving and volunteering across the United States. *Journal of Cross-Cultural Psychology, 37*, 327–344.

Kessler, R. C., Berglund, P., Demler, O., Jin, R., Koretz, D., Merikangas, K. R., Rush, A. J., Walters, E. E., & Wang, P. S. (2003). The epidemiology of major depressive disorder: Results from the National Comorbidity Survey Replication (NCS-R). *JAMA, 289*, 3095–3105.

Keys, J. B., Denton, L. T., & Miller, T. R. (1994). The Japanese management theory jungle revisited. *Journal of Management, 20*(2), 373–402.

Khaleefa, O. H., Erdos, G., & Ashria, I. H. (1996). Creativity in an indigenous Afro-Arab Islamic culture: The case of Sudan. *Journal of Creative Behavior, 30*(4), 268–282.

Kiev, A. (1972). *Transcultural psychiatry*. New York: Free Press.

Kiev, A. (1973). The psychiatric implications of interracial marriage. In I. R. Stuart & L. E. Abt (Eds.), *Interracial marriage: Expectations and realities* (pp. 162–176). New York: Grossman.

Kim, E. Y. (1993). Career choice among second-generation Korean-Americans: Reflections of a cultural model of success. *Anthropology and Education Quarterly, 24*(3), 224–248.

Kim, H. S. (2002). We talk, therefore we think? A cultural analysis of the effect of talking on thinking. *Journal of Personality and Social Psychology, 83*, 828–842.

Kim, U. (2001). Culture, science, and indigenous psychologies: An integrated analysis. In D. Matsumoto (Ed.), *Handbook of culture and psychology* (pp. 51–75). Oxford, UK: Oxford University Press.

Kim, U., & Berry, J. W. (1993). Introduction. In K. Uichol & J. W. Berry (Eds.), *Indigenous psychologies: Research and experience in cultural context* (Cross-cultural research: Indigenous and methodology series, Vol. 17,

pp. 1–29). Newbury Park, CA: Sage.

Kimmel, P. R. (1994). Cultural perspectives on international negotiations. *Journal of Social Issues, 50*(1), 179–196.

King, J. E., & Figueredo, A. J. (1997). The Five-Factor Model plus dominance in chimpanzee personality. *Journal of Research in Personality, 31*(2), 257–271.

King, M., Nazroo, J., Weich, S., McKenzie, K., Bhui, K., Karlsen, S., Stansfeld, S., Tyrer, P., Blanchard, M., Lloyd, K., McManus, S., Sproston, K., & Erens, B. (2005). Psychotic symptoms in the general population of England—a comparison of ethnic groups (The EMPIRIC study). *Social Psychiatry and Psychiatric Epidemiology, 40*(5), 375–381.

Kinzie, J. D., & Sack, W. (2002). The psychiatric disorders among Cambodian adolescents: The effects of severe trauma. In F. J. C. Azima & N. Grizenko (Eds.), *Immigrant and refugee children and their families: Clinical, research, and training issues* (pp. 95–112). Madison, CT: International Universities Press.

Kinzie, J. D., Leung, P. K., & Bui, A. (1988). Group therapy with Southeast Asian refugees. *Community Mental Health Journal, 24*(2), 157–166.

Kinzie, J. D., Leung, P. K., Boehnlein, J., Matsunaga, D., Johnson, R., Manson, S., Shore, J. H., Heinz, J., & Williams, M. (1992). Psychiatric epidemiology of an Indian village: A 19-year replication study. *Journal of Nervous and Mental Disease, 180*, 33–39.

Kirmayer, L. J. (2001). Cultural variations in the clinical presentation of depression and anxiety: Implications for diagnosis and treatment. *Journal of Clinical Psychiatry, 62*(113), 22–28.

Kitayama, S., & Karasawa, M. (1997). Implicit self-esteem in Japan: Name letters and birthday numbers. *Personality and Social Psychology Bulletin, 23*(7), 736–742.

Kitayama, S., & Markus, H. R. (1991). Culture and the self: Implications for cognition, emotion, and motivation. *Psychological Review, 98*, 224–253.

Kitayama, S., & Markus, H. R. (1995). Culture and self: Implications for internationalizing psychology. In N. Rule & J. B. Veroff (Eds.), *The culture and psychology reader* (pp. 366–383). New York: New York University Press.

Kitayama, S., & Markus, H. R. (Eds.). (1994). *Emotions and culture: Empirical studies of mutual influence*. Washington, DC: American Psychological Association.

Kitayama, S., Matsumoto, H., Markus, H. R., & Norasakkunkit, V. (1997). Individual and collective processes in the construction of the self: Self-enhancement in the United States and self-criticism in Japan. *Journal of Personality and Social Psychology, 72*, 1245–1267.

Kleinknecht, R. A., Dinnel, D., Kleinknecht, E. E., Hiruma, N., & Harada, N. (1997). Cultural factors in social anxiety: A comparison of social phobia symptoms and taijin kyofusho. *Journal of Anxiety Disorders, 11*, 157–177.

Kleinman, A. (1978). Culture and depression. *Culture and Medical Psychiatry, 2*, 295–296.

Kleinman, A. (1982). Neurasthenia and depression: A study of somatization and culture in China. *Culture, Medicine and Psychiatry, 6*(2), 117–190.

Kleinman, A. (1988). *Rethinking psychiatry: From cultural category to personal experience*. New York: Free Press.

Kleinman, A. (1995). Do psychiatric disorders differ in different cultures? The methodological questions. In N. R. Goldberger & J. B. Veroff (Eds.), *The culture and psychology* (pp. 631–651). New York: New York University Press.

Kleinman, A. (2004). Culture and depression. *New England Journal of Medicine, 351*, 951–953.

Klingelhofer, E. L. (1967). Performance of Tanzanian secondary school pupils on the Raven Standard Progressive Matrices Test. *Journal of Social Psychology, 72*(2), 205–215.

Kohlberg, L. (1976). Moral stages and moralization: The cognitive-developmental approach. In J.

Lickona (Ed.), *Moral development behavior: Theory, research and social issues* (pp. 31–53). New York: Holt, Rinehart & Winston.

Kohlberg, L. (1984). *The psychology of moral development: The nature and validity of moral stages* (Vol. 2). New York: Harper & Row.

Koltko-Rivera, M. E. (2004). The psychology of worldviews. *Review of General Psychology, 8*, 3–58.

Kontos, S., Howes, C., Shinn, M., & Galinksy, E. (1995). *Quality in family child care and relative care*. New York: Teachers College Press.

Kosic, A., Kruglanski, A. W., Pierro, A., & Mannetti, L. (2004). The social cognition of immigrants' acculturation: Effects of the need for closure and the reference group at entry. *Journal of Personality and Social Psychology, 86*, 796–813.

Kosmitzki, C. (1996). The reaffirmation of cultural identity in cross-cultural encounters. *Personality and Social Psychology Bulletin, 22*, 238–248.

Koss, J. D. (1990). Somatization and somatic complaint syndromes among Hispanics: Overview and ethnopsychological perspectives. *Transcultural Psychiatric Research Review, 27*, 5–29.

Koss-Chioino, J. D. (2000). Traditional and folk approaches among ethnic minorities. In J. F. Aponte & J. Wohl (Eds.), *Psychological intervention and cultural diversity* (2nd ed., pp. 149–166). Boston: Allyn & Bacon.

Kranzler, J. H., & Jensen, A. R. (1989). Inspection time and intelligence: A meta-analysis. *Intelligence, 13*(4), 329–347.

Krappmann, L. (1996). Amicitia, drujba, shin-yu, philia, freundschaft, friendship: On the cultural diversity of a human relationship. In W. M. Bukowski, A. F. Newcomb, & W. W. Hartup (Eds.), *The company they keep: Friendship in childhood and adolescence* (pp. 19–40). Cambridge, UK: Cambridge University Press.

Krause, I. B. (1989). Sinking heart: A Punjabi communication of dis-

tress. *Social Science and Medicine, 29*(4), 563–575.

Krieger, N. (1999). Embodying inequality: A review of concepts, measures, and methods for studying health consequences of discrimination. *International Journal of Health Services, 29*, 295–352.

Kroeber, A. L., & Kluckholn, C. (1952/1963). *Culture: A critical review of concepts and definitions*. Cambridge, MA: Harvard University.

Kruglanski, A. W. (1989). *Lay epistemics and human knowledge*. New York: Plenum Press.

Kudoh, T., & Matsumoto, D. (1985). Cross-cultural examination of the semantic dimensions of body postures. *Journal of Personality & Social Psychology, 48*, 1440–1446.

Kuo, W. H. (1984). Prevalence of depression among Asian Americans. *Journal of Nervous and Mental Disease, 172*(8), 449–457.

Kurasaki, K. S., Sue, S., Chun, C-A., & Gee, K. (2000). Ethnic minority and intervention and treatment research. In J. E. Aponte & J. Wohl (Eds.), *Psychological intervention and cultural diversity* (2nd ed., pp. 167–182). Boston: Allyn & Bacon.

Kurman, J. (2001). Self-enhancement: Is it restricted to individualistic cultures? *Personality and Social Psychology Bulletin, 27*(12), 1705–1716.

Kurman, J., & Ronen-Eilon, C. (2004). Lack of knowledge of a culture's social axioms and adaptation difficulties among immigrants. *Journal of Cross-Cultural Psychology, 35*, 192–208.

Lachlan, R. F., Janik, V. M., & Slater, P. J. B. (2004). The evolution of conformity-enforcing behaviour in cultural communication systems. *Animal Behaviour, 68*, 561–570.

LaFrance, M., & Mayo, C. (1976). Racial differences in gaze behavior during conversations: Two systematic observational studies. *Journal of Personality and Social Psychology, 33*, 547–552.

LaFromboise, T. D., Trimble, J. E., & Mohatt, G. V. (1990). Counseling intervention and American Indian tradition: An integrative approach. *Counseling Psychologist, 18*(4), 159–182.

Lalwani, A. K., Shavitt, S., & Johnson, T. (2006). What is the relation between cultural orientation and socially desirable responding? *Journal of Personality and Social Psychology, 90*, 165–178.

Lamb, M. E., & Sternberg, K. J. (1992). Sociocultural perspectives on nonparental child care. In M. E. Lamb, K. J. Sternberg, C-P. Hwang, & A. G. Broberg (Eds.), *Childcare in context: Cross-cultural perspectives* (pp. 1–23). Hillsdale, NJ: Erlbaum.

Landau, M. S. (1984). The effects of spatial ability and problem presentation format on mathematical problem solving performance of middle school students. *Dissertation Abstracts International, 45*(2-A), 442–443.

Landis, D. &, O'Shea, W. (2000). Cross-cultural aspects of passionate love: An individual differences analysis. *Journal of Cross-Cultural Psychology, 31*(6), 752–777.

Langer, E. J. (1989). Mindfulness. Readings, MA: Addison-Wesley.

Langlois, J. H., Kalakanis, L., Rubenstein, A. J., Larson, A., Hallam, M., & Smoot, M. (2000). Maxims or myths of beauty? A meta-analytic and theoretical review. *Psychological Bulletin, 126*, 390–423.

Langman, P.F. (1997). White culture, Jewish culture and the origins of psychotherapy. *Psychotherapy: Theory, Research, Practice, Training, 34*, 207–218.

Latané, B. (1981). The psychology of social impact. *American Psychologist, 36*, 343–356.

Latané, B., Williams, K., & Harkins, S. (1979). Many hands make light the work: The causes and consequences of social loafing. *Journal of Personality and Social Psychology, 37*, 322–332.

Lau, S. (1989). Sex role orientation and domains of self-esteem. *Sex Roles, 21*(5–6), 415–422.

Leadbeater, B. J., & Way, N. (2001). *Growing up fast: Transitions to early adulthood of inner-city adolescent mothers.* Mahwah, NJ: Erlbaum.

Lee, C. C., Oh, M. Y., & Mountcastle, A. R. (1992). Indigenous models of helping in nonwestern countries: Implication for multicultural counseling. *Journal of Multicultural Counseling and Development, 20*, 3–10.

Lee, F., Hallahan, M., & Herzog, T. (1996). Explaining real life events: How culture and domain shape attributions. *Personality and Social Psychology Bulletin, 22*(7), 732–741.

Lee, H. O., & Boster, F. J. (1992). Collectivism-individualism in perceptions of speech rate: A cross-cultural comparison. *Journal of Cross-Cultural Psychology, 23*, 377–388.

Lee, S. (1995). Reconsidering the status of anorexia nervosa as a culture-bound syndrome. *Social Science and Medicine, 42*, 21–34.

Lee, S. (2001). From diversity to unity: The classification of mental disorders in 21st century China. *Cultural Psychiatry: International Perspectives, 24*(3), 421–431.

Lee, V. K., & Dengerink, H. A. (1992). Locus of control in relation to sex and nationality: A cross-cultural study. *Journal of Cross-Cultural Psychology, 23*(4), 488–497.

Lee, W. M. L., & Mixson, R. J. (1995). Asian and Caucasian client perceptions of the effectiveness of counseling. *Journal of Multicultural Counseling and Development, 23*(1), 48–56.

Lee, Y.-T., Jussin, L. J., & McCauley, C. R. (Eds.). (1995). *Stereotype accuracy: Toward appreciating group differences.* Washington, DC: American Psychological Association.

Lee-Sing, C. M., Leung, Y. K., Wing, H. F., & Chiu, C. N. (1991). Acne as a risk factor for anorexia nervosa in Chinese. *Australian and New Zealand Journal of Psychiatry, 25*(1), 134–137.

Leenaars, A. A., Anawak, J., & Taparti, L. (1998). Suicide among the Canadian Inuit. In R. J. Kosky & H. S. Hadi (Eds.), *Suicide prevention: The global context* (pp. 111–120). New York: Plenum Press.

Leff, J. (1973). Culture and the differentiation of emotional states. *British Journal of Psychiatry, 123*, 299–306.

Leff, J. (1977). International variations in the diagnosis of psychiatric illness. *British Journal of Psychiatry, 131*, 329–338.

Leff, J. (1981). *Psychiatry around the globe: A transcultural view.* New York: Dekker.

Leff, J. (1986). The epidemiology of mental illness. In J. L. Cox (Ed.), *Transcultural psychiatry* (pp. 23–36). London: Croom Helm.

Leong, F. T. L., & Lau, A. S. L. (2001). Barriers to providing effective mental health services to Asian Americans. *Mental Health Services Research, 3*(4), 201–214.

Leong, F. T. L., Wagner, N. S., & Tata, S. P. (1995). Racial and ethnic variations in help-seeking attitudes. In J. G. Ponterotto & J. M. Casas (Eds.), *Handbook of multicultural counseling* (pp. 415–438). Thousand Oaks, CA: Sage.

Lepore, S. J., Revenson, T. A., Weinberger, S. L., Weston, P., Frisina, P. G., Robertson, R., Portillo, M. M., Jones, H., & Cross, W. (2006). Effects of social stressors on cardiovascular reactivity in black and white women. *Annals of Behavioral Medicine, 31*(2), 120–127.

Lerner, B. (1972). *Therapy in the ghetto: Political impotence and personal disintegration.* Baltimore: Johns Hopkins University Press.

Leung, K. (1988). Some determinants of conflict avoidance. *Journal of Cross-Cultural Psychology, 19*, 125–136.

Leung, K. (1989). Cross-cultural differences: Individual-level vs. culture-level analysis. *International Journal of Psychology, 24*, 703–719.

Leung, K. (1996). The role of beliefs in Chinese culture. In M. H. Bond (Ed.), *The handbook of Chinese psychology* (pp. 247–262). Hong Kong: Oxford University Press.

Leung, K., & Bond, H. M. (1989). On the empirical identification of dimensions for cross-cultural comparisons. *Journal of Cross-Cultural Psychology, 20*(2), 133–151.

Leung, K., Bond, M. H., Reimel de Carrasquel, S., Muñoz, C.,

Hernández, M., Murakami, F., et al. (2002). Social axioms: The search for universal dimensions of general beliefs about how the world functions. *Journal of Cross-Cultural Psychology, 33,* 286–302.

Leung, P. W. L., Luk, S. L., Ho, T. P., Mak, T. E., & Bacon-Shone, J. (1996). The diagnosis and prevalence of hyperactivity in Chinese schoolboys. *British Journal of Psychiatry, 168,* 486–496.

Levenson, R. W., & Ekman, P. (2002). Difficulty does not account for emotion-specific heart rate changes in the directed facial action task. *Psychophysiology, 39,* 397–405.

Levenson, R. W., Carstensen, L. L., Friesen, W. V., & Ekman, P. (1991). Emotion, physiology, and expression in old age. *Psychology & Aging, 6,* 28–35.

Levenson, R. W., Ekman, P., & Friesen, W. V. (1990). Voluntary facial action generates emotion-specific autonomic nervous system activity. *Psychophysiology, 27,* 363–384.

Levenson, R. W., Ekman, P., Heider, K., & Friesen, W. (1992). Emotion and autonomic nervous system activity in the Minangkabau of West Sumatra. *Journal of Personality and Social Psychology, 62*(6), 972–988.

Levin, H. M. (1996). Accelerated schools after eight years. In L. Schauble & R. Glaser (Eds.), *Innovations in learning: New environments for education* (pp. 329–352). Mahwah, NJ: Erlbaum.

Levine, J. B. (1991). The role of culture in the representation of conflict in dreams: A comparison of Bedouin, Irish, and Israeli children. *Journal of Cross-Cultural Psychology, 22,* 472–490.

LeVine, R. A. (1977). Child rearing as cultural adaptation. In P. H. Leiderman, S. R. Tulkin, & A. Rosenfeld (Eds.), *Culture and infancy* (pp. 15–27). New York: Academic Press.

LeVine, R. A. (1997). Mother-infant interaction in cross-cultural perspective. In N. L. Segal & G. Weisfeld (Eds.), *Uniting psychology and biology: Integrative perspectives on human development* (pp. 339–354). Washington,

DC: American Psychological Association.

LeVine, R. A., LeVine, S. E., Dixon, S., Richman, A., Leiderman, P. H., & Keefer, C. (1996). *Child care and culture: Lessons from Africa.* Cambridge, UK: Cambridge University Press.

Levine, R. V., & Bartlett, K. (1984). Pace of life, punctuality, and coronary heart disease in six countries. *Journal of Cross-Cultural Psychology, 15,* 233–255.

Levine, R. V., & Norenzayan, A. (1999). The pace of life in 31 countries. *Journal of Cross-Cultural Psychology, 30,* 178–205.

Levine, R. V., Lynch, K., Miyake, K., & Lucia, M. (1989). The type a city: Coronary heart disease and the pace of life. *Journal of Behavioral Medicine, 12,* 509–524.

Levine, R., Sato, S., Hashimoto, T., & Verma, J. (1995). Love and marriage in eleven cultures. *Journal of Cross-Cultural Psychology, 26*(5), 554–571.

Levine, T. R., Bresnahan, M. J., Park, H. S., Lapinski, M. K., Wittenbaum, G. M., Shearman, S. M., et al. (2003). Self-construal scales lack validity. *Human Communication Research, 29,* 210–252.

Levy, G., Lysne, M., & Underwood, L. (1995). Children's and adults' memories for self-schema consistent and inconsistent content. *Journal of Social Psychology, 135*(1), 113–115.

Levy, R. I. (1973). *Tahitians.* Chicago: University of Chicago Press.

Levy, R. I. (1983). Introduction: Self and emotion. *Ethos, 11,* 128–134.

Lewis, G., Croft-Jeffreys, C., & Anthony, D. (1990). Are British psychiatrists racist? *British Journal of Psychiatry, 157,* 410–415.

Lewontin, R. C., Rose, S., & Kamin, L. J. (1984). *Not in our genes: Biology, ideology and human nature.* New York: Pantheon.

Li, H.-z. (2003). Inter- and intra-cultural variations in self-other boundary: A qualitative-quantitative approach. *International Journal of Psychology, 38,* 138–149.

Li-Repac, D. (1980). Cultural influences on clinical perception: A comparison between Caucasian and Chinese-American thera-

pists. *Journal of Cross-Cultural Psychology, 11,* 327–342.

Liebal, K., Pika, S., & Tomasello, M. (2004). Social communication in siamangs (Symphalangus syndactylus): Use of gestures and facial expressions. *Primates, 45,* 41–57.

Liebkind, K. (1996). Acculturation and stress: Vietnamese refugees in Finland. *Journal of Cross-Cultural Psychology, 27*(2), 161–180.

Lightfoot-Klein, H. (1989). *Prisoners of ritual: An odyssey into female genital circumcision in Africa.* New York: Harrington Park Press.

Lijembe, J. (1967). The valley between: A Muluyia's story. In L. Fox (Ed.), *East African Childhood* (pp. 4–7). Nairobi: Oxford University Press.

Lin, E. J.-L., & Church, A. T. (2004). Are indigenous Chinese personality dimensions culture-specific? *Journal of Cross-Cultural Psychology, 35,* 586–605.

Lin, K., Inui, T. S., Kleiman, A. M., & Womack, W. M. (1992). Sociocultural determinants of the help-seeking behavior of patients with mental illness. *Journal of Nervous and Mental Disease, 170,* 78–85.

Lin, M. H., Kwan, V. S. Y., Cheung, A., & Fiske, S. T. (2005). Stereotype content model explains prejudice for an envied outgroup: Scale of anti-Asian American stereotypes. *Personality and Social Psychology Bulletin, 31,* 34–47.

Lin, P., & Schwanenflugel, P.(1995). Cultural familiarity and language factors in the structure of category knowledge. *Journal of Cross-Cultural Psychology, 26*(2), 153–168.

Lindsey, K. P., & Paul, G. L. (1989). Involuntary commitments to public mental institutions: Issues involving the overrepresentation of Blacks and assessment of relevant functioning. *Psychological Bulletin, 106*(2), 171–183.

Linton, R. (1936). *The study of man: An introduction.* New York: Appleton.

Little, D. T., Oettingen, G., Stetsenko, A., & Baltes, B. P. (1995). Children's action-control beliefs about school performance: How do American children compare with

German and Russian children? *Journal of Personality and Social Psychology, 69*(4), 686–700.

Liu, L. G. (1985). Reasoning counterfactually in Chinese: Are there any obstacles? *Cognition, 21*(3), 239–270.

Loewenthal, K. M. (1995). *Mental health and religion*. London: Chapman & Hall.

Lonner, W. J. (1980). The search for psychological universals. In J. W. Berry, Y. H. Poortinga & J. Pandey (Eds.), *Handbook of cross-cultural psychology, vol. 1: Theory and method* (pp. 43–83). Boston: Allyn and Bacon.

Lonner, W. J., & Ibrahim, F. A. (1989). Assessment in cross-cultural counseling. In P. B. Pedersen, J. Dragus, W. Lonner, & J. E. Trimble (Eds.), *Counseling across cultures* (3rd ed., pp. 299–334). Honolulu: University of Hawaii Press.

Lopez, S. R. (1989). Patient variable biases in clinical judgment: Conceptual overview and methodological considerations. *Psychological Bulletin, 106*(2), 184–203.

Lopez, S. R., Hipke, K. N., Polo, A. J., Jenkins, J. H., Karno, M., Vaughn, C., & Snyder, K. S. (2004). Ethnicity, expressed emotion, attributions, and course of schizophrenia: Family warmth matters. *Journal of Abnormal Psychology, 113*, 428–439.

Lott, D. F., & Hart, B. L. (1977, Summer). Aggressive domination of cattle by Fulani herdsmen and its relation to aggression in Fulani culture and personality. *Ethos, 5*(2), 174–186.

Love, K. G., Bishop, R. C., Heinisch, D. A., & Montei, M. S. (1994). Selection across two cultures: Adapting the selection of American assemblers to meet Japanese job performance demands. *Personnel Psychology, 47*, 837–846.

Lucy, J. A. (1992). *Language diversity and thought: A reformation of the linguistic relativity hypothesis*. Cambridge, UK: Cambridge University Press.

Lueptow, L. B., Garovich, L., & Lueptow, M. B. (1995). The persistence of gender stereotypes in the face of changing sex roles:

Evidence contrary to the sociocultural model. *Ethology and Sociobiology, 16*(6), 509–530.

Luria, A. R. (1976). *Cognitive development: Its cultural and social foundations* (M. Lopes & L. Solotaroff, Trans.). Cambridge, MA: Harvard University Press. (Original work published 1974).

Luthar, V. K., & Luthar, H. K. (2002). Using Hofstede's cultural dimensions to explain sexually harassing behaviors in an international context. *International Journal of Human Resource Management, 13*, 268–284.

Lutz, C. (1980). *Emotion words and emotional development on Ifaluk Atoll*. Unpublished doctoral dissertation, Harvard University.

Lutz, C. (1983). Parental goals, ethnopsychology, and the development of emotional meaning. *Ethos, 11*, 246–262.

Luzzo, D. A. (1993). Ethnic differences in college students' perceptions of barriers to careers development. *Journal of Multicultural Counseling and Development, 21*, 227–236.

Lynn, R., Paspalanova, E., Stetinsky, D., & Tzenova, B. (1998). Intelligence in Bulgaria. *Psychological Reports, 82*(3, Pt. 1), 912–914.

Lyons, A., & Kashima, Y. (2001). The reproduction of culture: Communication processes tend to maintain cultural stereotypes. *Social Cognition, 19*(3), 372–394.

Maccoby, E. E., & Jacklin, C. N. (1974). *The psychology of sex differences*. Stanford, CA: Stanford University Press.

Maccoby, E. E., & Martin, J. A. (1983). Socialization in the context of the family: Parent-child interaction. In E. M. Hetherington (Ed.), *Handbook of child psychology: Vol. 4. Socialization, personality, and social development* (4th ed., pp. 1–101). New York: Wiley.

MacDonald, K. (1991). A perspective on Darwinian psychology: The importance of domain-general mechanisms, plasticity, and individual differences. *Ethology and Sociobiology, 12*(6), 449–480.

MacDonald, K. (1998). Evolution, culture, and the five-factor

model. *Journal of Cross-Cultural Psychology, 29*(1), 119–149.

MacLachlan, M. (1997). *Culture and health*. Chichester, UK: Wiley.

Macrae, C. N., Bodenhausen, G. V., & Milne, A. B. (1998). Saying no to unwanted thoughts: Self-focus and the regulation of mental life. *Journal of Personality and Social Psychology, 74*(3), 578–589.

Maddox, K. B. (2005). Perspectives on racial phenotypicality bias. *Personality and Social Psychology Review, 8*, 383–401.

Madon, S., Guyll, M., Aboufadel, K., Montiel, E., Smith, A., Palumbo, P., & Jussim, L. (2001). Ethnic and national stereotypes: The Princeton trilogy revisited and revised. *Personality and Social Psychology Bulletin, 27*(8), 996–1010.

Maher, T. E., & Wong, Y. Y. (1994). The impact of cultural differences on the growing tensions between Japan and the United States. *SAM Advanced Management Journal, 59*, 40–46.

Maio, R. G., & Esses, M. V. (1998). The social consequences of affirmative action: Deleterious effects on perceptions of groups. *Personality and Social Psychology Bulletin, 24*(1), 65–74.

Malik, V., Schulze, M., & Hu, F. (2006). Intake of sugar-sweetened beverages and weight gain: a systematic review. *American Journal of Clinical Nutrition, 84*, 274–288.

Malinowski, B. (1944/1960). A scientific theory of culture and other essays. New York: Oxford University Press.

Malpass, R. S. (1974). Racial bias in eyewitness identification. *Personality and Social Psychology Bulletin, 1*(1), 42–44.

Malpass, R. S. (1993, August). *A discussion of the ICAI*. Symposium presented at the Annual Convention of the American Psychological Association, Toronto.

Malpass, R. S., & Kravitz, J. (1969). Recognition for faces of own and other race. *Journal of Personality and Social Psychology, 13*(4), 330–334.

Manson, S. M., & Shore, J. H. (1981). Psychiatric epidemiological research among American Indian and Alaska Natives: Some methodological issues. *White Cloud Journal, 2,* 48–56.

Manson, S. M., Shore, J. H., & Bloom, J. D. (1985). The depressive experience in American Indian communities: A challenge for psychiatric theory and diagnosis. In A. Kleinman & B. Good (Eds.), *Culture and depression: Studies in the anthropology and cross-cultural psychiatry of affect and disorder* (pp. 331–368). Berkeley: University of California Press.

Manz, C. C. (1992). Self-leading work teams: Moving beyond self-management myths. *Human Relations, 45*(11), 1119–1140.

Maramba, G. G., & Nagayama Hall, G. C. (2002). Meta-analysis of ethnic match as a predictor of dropout, utilization, and level of functioning. *Cultural Diversity and Ethnic Minority Psychology, 8,* 290–297.

Markoff, R. (1977). Intercultural marriage: Problem areas. In W. S. Tsent, J. F. McDermott, Jr., and T. W. Maretzk (Eds.), *Adjustment in intercultural marriage* (pp. 51–61). Honolulu: University of Hawaii Press.

Marks, D. (1997). Models of disability. *Disability and Rehabilitation: An International Multidisciplinary Journal, 19*(3), 85–91.

Markus, H. R. (1977). Self-schemata and processing information about the self. *Journal of Personality and Social Psychology, 35,* 63–78.

Markus, H. R., & Kitayama, S. (1991a). Cultural variation in self-concept. In G. R. Goethals & J. Strauss (Eds.), *Multidisciplinary perspectives on the self* (pp. 18–48). New York: Springer-Verlag.

Markus, H. R., & Kitayama, S. (1991b). Culture and the self: Implications for cognition, emotion, and motivation. *Psychological Review, 98,* 224–253.

Markus, H. R., & Kitayama, S. (1998). The cultural psychology of personality. *Journal of Cross Cultural Psychology, 29*(1), 63–87.

Markus, H. R., Mullally, P. R., & Kitayama, S. (1997). Selfways: Diversity in modes of cultural participation. In U. Neisser & D.

Jopling (Eds.), *The conceptual self in context* (pp. 13–61). New York: Cambridge University Press.

Marmot, M. G., & Syme, S. L. (1976). Acculturation and coronary heart disease in Japanese Americans. *American Journal of Epidemiology, 104,* 225–247.

Marsella, A. J. (1979). Cross-cultural studies of mental disorders. In A. J. Marsella, G. DeVos, & F. L. K. Hsu (Eds.), *Perspectives on cross-cultural psychology* (pp. 233–262). New York: Academic Press.

Marsella, A. J. (1980). Depressive experience and disorder across cultures. In H. C. Triandis & J. Draguns (Eds.), *Handbook of cross-cultural psychology: Vol. 6. Psychopathology* (pp. 237–289). Boston: Allyn & Bacon.

Marsella, A. J. (2000). Culture bound disorders. In A. Kazdin (Ed.) *The encyclopedia of psychology.* Washington, DC: American Psychological Association Press/ Oxford University Press.

Marsella, A. J., Kaplan, A., & Suarez, E. (2002). Cultural considerations for understanding, assessing, and treating depressive experience and disorder. In M. Reinecke & M. Davison (Eds.) *Comparative treatments of depression* (pp. 47–78). New York: Springer.

Marsella, A. J., Sartorius, N., Jablensky, A., & Fenton, F. R. (1985). Cross-cultural studies of depressive disorders. In A. Kleinman & B. Good (Eds.), *Culture and depression* (pp. 299–324). Berkeley: University of California Press.

Marshall, G. N., Schell, T. L., Elliot, M. N., Berthold, S. M., & Chung, C.-A. (2005). Mental health of Cambodian refugees 2 decades after resettlement in the United States. *JAMA, 294,* 571–579.

Mashima, R., Yamagishi, T., & Macy, M. (2004). Trust and cooperation: A comparison of ingroup preference and trust behavior between American and Japanese students (in japanese). *Japanese Journal of Psychology, 75,* 308–315.

Mastor, K. A., Jin, P., & Cooper, M. (2000). Malay culture and personality: A big five perspective. *American Behavioral Scientist, 44,* 95–111.

Masuda, T., & Nisbett, R. (2001). Attending holistically versus analytically: Comparing the context sensitivity of Japanese and Americans. *Journal of Personality and Social Psychology, 81,* 922–934.

Matsumoto, D. (1989). Cultural influences on the perception of emotion. *Journal of Cross-Cultural Psychology, 20,* 92–105.

Matsumoto, D. (1991). Cultural influences on facial expressions of emotion. *Southern Communication Journal, 56,* 128–137.

Matsumoto, D. (1992). More evidence for the universality of a contempt expression. *Motivation & Emotion, 16,* 363–368.

Matsumoto, D. (1993). Ethnic differences in affect intensity, emotion judgments, display rule attitudes, and self reported emotional expression in an American sample. *Motivation and Emotion, 17*(2), 107–123.

Matsumoto, D. (2001). Culture and emotion. In D. Matsumoto (Ed.), *The handbook of culture and psychology* (pp. 171–194). New York: Oxford University Press.

Matsumoto, D. (2002). *The new Japan.* Yarmouth, ME: Intercultural Press.

Matsumoto, D. (2002). Methodological requirements to test a possible ingroup advantage in judging emotions across cultures: Comments on Elfenbein and Ambady and evidence. *Psychological Bulletin, 128,* 236–242.

Matsumoto, D. (2006a). Are cultural differences in emotion regulation mediated by personality traits? *Journal of Cross-Cultural Psychology, 37*(4), 421–437.

Matsumoto, D. (2006b). Culture and cultural worldviews: Do verbal descriptions about culture reflect anything other than verbal descriptions about culture? *Culture and Psychology, 12*(1), 33–62.

Matsumoto, D. (in press). Playing catch with emotions. *CREO.*

Matsumoto, D., & Assar, M. (1992). The effects of language on judgments of universal facial expressions of emotion. *Journal of Nonverbal Behavior, 16,* 85–99.

Matsumoto, D., & Ekman, P. (1989). American-Japanese cultural differences in intensity ratings of facial expressions of emotion. *Motivation and Emotion, 13,* 143–157.

Matsumoto, D., & Ekman, P. (2004). The relationship between expressions, labels, and descriptions of contempt. *Journal of Personality and Social Psychology, 87,* 529–540.

Matsumoto, D., & Fletcher, D. (1996). Cultural influences on disease. *Journal of Gender, Culture, and Health, 1,* 71–82.

Matsumoto, D., & Kudoh, T. (1987). Cultural similarities and differences in the semantic dimensions of body postures. *Journal of Nonverbal Behavior, 11,* 166–179.

Matsumoto, D., & Kudoh, T. (1993). American-Japanese cultural differences in attributions of personality based on smiles. *Journal of Nonverbal Behavior, 17*(4), 231–243.

Matsumoto, D., & LeRoux, J. A. (2003). Measuring the psychological engine of intercultural adjustment: The intercultural adjustment potential scale (icaps). *Journal of Intercultural Communication, 6,* 27–52.

Matsumoto, D., & Willingham, B. (2006). The thrill of victory and the agony of defeat: Spontaneous expressions of medal winners at the 2004 Athens Olympic games. *Journal of Personality and Social Psychology, 91,* 568–581.

Matsumoto, D., & Yoo, S. H. (2006). Toward a new generation of cross-cultural research. *Perspectives on Psychological Science, 1*(3), 234–250.

Matsumoto, D., Consolacion, T., Yamada, H., Suzuki, R., Franklin, B., Paul, S., et al. (2002). American-Japanese cultural differences in judgments of emotional expressions of different intensities. *Cognition & Emotion, 16,* 721–747.

Matsumoto, D., Grissom, R., & Dinnel, D. (2001). Do between-culture differences really mean that people are different? A look at some measures of cultural effect size. *Journal of Cross-Cultural Psychology, 32,* 478–490.

Matsumoto, D., Kasri, F., & Kooken, K. (1999). American-Japanese cultural differences in judgments of expression intensity and subjective experience. *Cognition and Emotion, 13*(2), 201–218.

Matsumoto, D., Keltner, D., O-Sullivan, M., & Frank, M. G. (2006). What's in a face? Facial expressions as signals of discrete emotions. Manuscript submitted for publication.

Matsumoto, D., Kouznetsova, N., Ray, R., Ratzlaff, C., Biehl, M., & Raroque, J. (1999). Psychological culture, physical health, and subjective well being. *Journal of Gender, Culture, and Health, 4*(1), 1–18.

Matsumoto, D., Kudoh, T., & Takeuchi, S. (1996). Changing patterns of individualism and collectivism in the United States and Japan. *Culture and Psychology, 2,* 77–107.

Matsumoto, D., Kudoh, T., Scherer, K., & Wallbott, H. (1988). Antecedents of and reactions to emotions in the United States and Japan. *Journal of Cross-Cultural Psychology, 19*(3), 267–286.

Matsumoto, D., LeRoux, J. A., Bernhard, R., & Gray, H. (2004). Personality and behavioral correlates of intercultural adjustment potential. *International Journal of Intercultural Relations, 28,* 281–309.

Matsumoto, D., LeRoux, J. A., Iwamoto, M., Choi, J. W., Rogers, D., Tatani, H., et al. (2003). The robustness of the intercultural adjustment potential scale (icaps). *International Journal of Intercultural Relations, 27,* 543–562.

Matsumoto, D., LeRoux, J. A., Ratzlaff, C., Tatani, H., Uchida, H., Kim, C., et al. (2001). Development and validation of a measure of intercultural adjustment potential in Japanese sojourners: The intercultural adjustment potential scale (icaps). *International Journal of Intercultural Relations, 25,* 483–510.

Matsumoto, D., Pun, K. K., Nakatani, M., Kadowaki, D., Weissman, M., McCarter, L., Fletcher, D., &

Takeuchi, S. (1995). Cultural differences in attitudes, values and beliefs about osteoporosis in first and second generation Japanese-American women. *Women and Health, 23*(4), 39–56.

Matsumoto, D., Takeuchi, S., Andayani, S., Koutnetsouva, N., & Krupp, D. (1998). The contribution of individualism-collectivism to cross-national differences in display rules. *Asian Journal of Social Psychology, 1,* 147–165.

Matsumoto, D., Weissman, M., Preston, K., Brown, B., & Kupperbusch, C. (1997). Context-specific measurement of individualism–collectivism on the individual level: The IC Interpersonal Assessment Inventory (ICIAI). *Journal of Cross-Cultural Psychology, 28,* 743–767.

Matsumoto, D., Yoo, S. H., & LeRoux, J. A. (in press). Emotion and intercultural communication. In H. Kotthoff & H. Spencer-Oatley (Eds.), *Handbook of applied linguistics (Vol. 7: Intercultural Communication):* Mouton de Gruyter.

Matsumoto, D., Yoo, S. H., Anguas-Wong, A. M., Arriola, M., Ataca, B., Bond, M. H., et al. (2005). *Mapping expressive differences around the world: A thirty country study of cultural display rules.* Manuscript submitted for publication.

Matsumoto, D., Yoo, S. H., Anguas-Wong, A. M., Arriola, M., Ataca, B., Bond, M. H., et al. (2005). Mapping expressive differences around the world: A thirty country study of cultural display rules. *Manuscript submitted for publication.*

Matsuyama, Y., Hama, H., Kawamura, Y., & Mine, H. (1978). Analysis of emotional words. *Japanese Journal of Psychology, 49,* 229–232.

Matsuzawa, T. (2001). *Primate origins of human cognition and behavior.* New York: Springer-Verlag.

Mauro, R., Sato, K., & Tucker, J. (1992). The role of appraisal in human emotions: A cross-cultural study. *Journal of Personality and Social Psychology, 62*(2), 301–317.

Mauss, I. B., Levenson, R. W., McCarter, L., Wilhelm, F. L., &

Gross, J. J. (2005). The tie that binds? Coherence among emotion experience, behavior, and physiology. *Emotion, 5,* 175–190.

McConatha, J. T., Lightner, E., & Deaner, S. L. (1994). Culture, age, and gender as variables in the expression of emotions. *Journal of Social Behavior and Personality, 9*(3), 481–488.

McCracken, L. M., Matthews, A. K., Tang, T. S., & Cuba, S. L. (2001). A comparison of blacks and whites seeking treatment for chronic pain. *Clinical Journal of Pain, 17,* 249–255.

McCrae, R. R. (2001). Trait psychology and culture: Exploring intercultural comparisons. *Journal of Personality, 69*(6), 819–846.

McCrae, R. R., & Costa, P. T. (1997). Personality trait structure as a human universal. *American Psychologist, 52*(5), 509–516.

McCrae, R. R., & Costa, P. T. (1999). A five-factor theory of personality. In L. A. Pervin & O. John (Eds.), *Handbook of personality: Theory and research* (2nd ed., pp. 139–153). New York: Guilford.

McCrae, R. R., Costa, P. T., & Yik, M. S. M. (1996). Universal aspects of Chinese personality structure. In M. H. Bond et al. (Eds.), *The handbook of Chinese psychology* (pp. 189–207). Hong Kong: Oxford University Press.

McCrae, R. R., Costa, P. T., Del-Pilar, G. H., & Rolland, J. P. (1998, January). Cross-cultural assessment of the five-factor model: The revised NEO personality inventory. *Journal of Cross Cultural Psychology, 29*(1), 171–188.

McCrae, R. R., Terracciano, A., Khoury, B., Nansubuga, F., Knezevic, G., Djuric Jocic, D., et al. (2005). Universal features of personality traits from the observer's perspective: Data from 50 cultures. *Journal of Personality and Social Psychology, 88,* 547–561.

McCrae, R. R., Terracciano, A., Leibovich, N. B., Schmidt, V., Shakespeare-Finch, J., Neubauer, A., et al. (2005). Personality profiles of cultures: Aggregate personality traits. *Journal of Personality and Social Psychology, 89,* 407–425.

McCrae, R.R. & Costa, P.T. (2003). *Personality in adulthood: A five-factor theory perspective* (2nd ed.). New York: Guilford Press.

McGoldrick, M., & Preto, N. G. (1984). Ethnic intermarriage: Implications for therapy. *Family Process, 23*(3), 347–364.

McGrew, W. C. (2004). *The cultured chimpanzee: Reflections on cultural primatology.* New York: Cambridge University Press.

McGurk, H., & Jahoda, G. (1975). Pictorial depth perception by children in Scotland and Ghana. *Journal of Cross-Cultural Psychology, 6*(3), 279–296.

McHale, S. M., Crouter, A. C., & Whiteman, S. D. (2003). The family contexts of gender development in childhood and adolescence. *Social Development, 12*(1), 125–148.

McHale, S., Updegraff, K., Helms-Erikson, H., & Crouter, A. (2001). Sibling influences on gender development in middle childhood and early adolescence: A longitudinal study. *Developmental Psychology, 37*(1), 115–125.

McPherson, M., Smith-Lovin, L., & Brashears, M. (2006). Social isolation in America: Changes in core discussion networks over two decades. *American Sociological Review, 71,* 353–375.

Mead, M. (1975). *Growing up in New Guinea.* New York: William Morrow. (Originally published in 1930.)

Mead, M. (1978). *Culture and commitment.* Garden City, NY: Anchor. (Original work published 1928.)

Meglino, B. M., Ravlin, E. C., & Adkins, C. L. (1989). A work values approach to corporate culture: A field test of the value congruence process and its relationship to individual outcomes. *Journal of Applied Psychology, 74*(3), 424–432.

Mehrabi, F., Bayanzadeh, S.-A., Atef-Vahid, M.-K., Bolhari, J., Shahmohammadi, D., & Vaezi, S.-A. (2000). Mental health in Iran. In I. Al-Junūn (Ed.), *Mental illness in the Islamic world* (pp. 139–161). Madison, CT: International Universities Press.

Meissner, C. A., & Brigham, J. C. (2001). Thirty years of investigating the own-race bias in memory for faces: A meta-analytic review. *Psychology, Public Policy, and Law, 7,* 3–35.

Merton, R. (1968). *Social theory and social structures.* New York: Free Press.

Mesquita, B. (2001). Emotions in collectivist and individualist contexts. *Journal of Personality and Social Psychology, 80,* 68–74.

Mesquita, B., & Karasawa, M. (2002). Different emotional lives. *Cognition & Emotion, 16,* 127–141.

Messick, D. M., & Mackie, D. M. (1989). Intergroup relations. *Annual Review of Psychology, 40,* 45–81.

Mezulis, A. H., Abramson, L. Y., Hyde, J. S., & Hankin, B. L. (2004). Is there a universal positivity bias in attributions? A meta-analytic review of individual, developmental, and cultural differences in the self-serving attributional bias. *Psychological Bulletin, 130,* 711–747.

Milgram, S. (1974). *Obedience to authority.* New York: Harper & Row.

Miller, J. G. (1984). Culture and the development of everyday social explanation. *Journal of Personality and Social Psychology, 46,* 961–978.

Miller, J. G., & Bersoff, D. M. (1992). Culture and moral judgment: How are conflicts between justice and interpersonal responsibilities resolved? *Journal of Personality and Social Psychology, 62,* 541–554.

Miller, K. E. (1999). Rethinking a familiar model: Psychotherapy and the mental health of refugees. *Journal of Contemporary Psychotherapy, 29,* 283–306.

Miller, K. E., Worthington, G. J., Muzurovic, J., Tipping, S., & Goldman, A. (2002). Bosnian refugees and the stressors of exile: A narrative study. *American Journal of Orthopsychiatry, 72*(3), 341–354.

Miller, K. M., Kelly, M., & Zhou, X. (2005). Learning mathematics in

China and the United States: Cross-cultural insights into the nature and course of preschool mathematical development. In J. Campbell (Ed.), *Handbook of mathematical cognition* (pp. 163–177). New York: Psychology Press.

Miller, K., & Rasco, L. M. (2004). An ecological framework for addressing the mental health needs of refugee communities. In K. Miller & L. Rasco (Eds.), *The mental health of refugees: Ecological approaches to healing and adaptation* (pp. 1–64). Mahwah, NJ: Lawrence Erlbaum Associates.

Minami, M., & McCabe, A. (1995). Rice balls and bear hunts: Japanese and North American family narrative patterns. *Journal of Child Language, 22*(2), 423–445.

Mintz, J., Mintz, L., & Goldstein, M. (1987). Expressed emotion and relapse in first episodes of schizophrenia. *British Journal of Psychiatry, 151,* 314–320.

Mintz, L. B., & Kashubeck, S. (1999). Body image and disordered eating among Asian American and Caucasian college students: An examination of race and gender differences. *Psychology of Women Quarterly, 23*(4), 781–796.

Miranda, J., & Green, B. L. (1999). The need for mental health services research focusing on poor young women. *Journal of Mental Health Policy and Economics, 2,* 73–89.

Miranda, J., Bernal, G., Lau, A., Kohn, L. Hwang, W.-C., & LaFromboise, T. (2005). State Of The Science On Psychosocial Interventions For Ethnic Minorities. *Annual Review of Clinical Psychology, 1*(1), 113–142.

Miranda, J., Green, B.L., & Krupnick, J. L. (2006). One-year outcomes of a randomized clinical trial treating depression in low-income minority women. *Journal of Consulting and Clinical Psychology, 74*(1), 99–111.

Mirande, M. (1985). *The Chicano experience: An alternative perspective.* Notre Dame, IN: University of Notre Dame Press.

Miron, M. (1975). A study of cross-cultural factorial structure of intelligence. *Psychologia: An International Journal of Psychology in the Orient, 18*(2), 92–94.

Misumi, J. (1985). *The behavioral science of leadership: An inter-disciplinary Japanese research program.* Ann Arbor: University of Michigan Press.

Miura, I.T., Okamoto, Y., Vladovic-Stetic, V., Kim, C., & Han, J. (1999). Language supports for children's understanding of numerical fractions: Cross-national comparisons. *Journal of Experimental Child Psychology, 74*(4), Special issue: The development of mathematical cognition: Numerical processes and concepts, pp. 356–365.

Miyake, K. (1993). Temperament, mother-infant interaction, and early emotional development. *Japanese Journal of Research on Emotions, 1*(1), 48–55.

Miyake, K., Chen, S., & Campos, J. J. (1985). Infant temperament, mother's mode of interaction, and attachment in Japan: An interim report. In I. Bretherton & E. Waters (Eds.), *Growing points of attachment theory.* Monographs of the Society of Research in Child Development, 50(1–2, Serial No. 209).

Miyamoto, Y., Nisbett, R., & Masuda, T. (2006). Culture and the physical environment: Holistic versus analytic perceptual affordances. *Psychological Science, 17,* 113–119.

Moghaddam, F. M., Ditto, B., & Taylor, D. M. (1990). Attitudes and attributions related to psychological symptomatology in Indian immigrant women. *Journal of Cross-Cultural Psychology, 21,* 335–350.

Molinsky, A. L., Krabbenhoft, M. A., Ambady, N., & Choi, Y. S. (2005). Cracking the nonverbal code: Intercultural competence and gesture recognition across cultures. *Journal of Cross-Cultural Psychology, 36,* 380–395.

Monteith, M., Sherman, J., & Devine, P. (1998). Suppression as a stereotype control strategy. *Personality and Social Psychology Review, 1,* 63–82.

Moore, J. T. (1988, March). *Pride against prejudice: The biography of Larry Doby.* New York: Greenwood Press.

Morelli, G. A., Oppenheim, D., Rogoff, B., & Goldsmith, D. (1992). Cultural variations in infant sleeping arrangements: Questions of independence. *Developmental Psychology, 28,* 604–613.

Morris, D., Collett, P., Marsh, P., & O'Shaughnessy, M. (1980). *Gestures: Their origins and distribution.* New York: Scarborough.

Morris, M. H., Avila, R. A., & Allen, J. (1993). Individualism and the modern corporation: Implications for innovation and entrepreneurship. *Journal of Management, 19*(3), 595–612.

Morris, M. W., & Leung, K. (2000). Justice for all? Progress in research on cultural variation in the psychology of distributive and procedural justice. *Applied Psychology: An International Research Journal, 49,* 100–132.

Morris, M. W., & Peng, K. (1994). Culture and cause: American and Chinese attributions for social and physical events. *Journal of Personality and Social Psychology, 67*(6), 949–971.

Mossakowski, K. N. (2003). Coping with perceived discrimination: Does ethnic identity protect mental health? *Journal of Health and Social Behavior, Special issue: Race, Ethnicity and Mental Health 44*(3), 318–331.

Muela, S. H., Ribera, J. M., & Tanner, M. (1998). Fake malaria and hidden parasites: The ambiguity of malaria. *Anthropology and Medicine, 5*(1), 43–61.

Mukai, T., & McCloskey, L. (1996). Eating attitudes among Japanese and American elementary schoolgirls. *Journal of Cross-Cultural Psychology, 27*(4), 424–435.

Mulatu, M. S., & Berry, J. W. (2001). Health care practice in a multicultural context: Western and non-Western assumptions. In S. S. Kazarian & D. R. Evans (Eds.), *Handbook of cultural health psychology* (pp. 45–61). San Diego: Academic Press.

Mule, P., & Barthel, D. (1992). The return to the veil: Individual autonomy and social esteem. *Sociological Forum, 7*(2), 323–333.

Munro, D. (1979). Locus-of-control attribution: Factors among Blacks and Whites in Africa. *Journal of Cross-Cultural Psychology, 10*(2), 157–172.

Munroe, R. H., Shimmin, H. S., & Munroe, R. L. (1984). Gender understanding and sex role preference in four cultures. *Developmental Psychology, 20*(4), 673–682.

Murdock, G. P., Ford, C. S., & Hudson, A. E. (1971). *Outline of cultural materials* (4th ed.). New Haven, CT: Human Relations Area Files.

Murphy, J. M. (1976). Psychiatric labeling in cross-cultural perspective. *Science, 191,* 1019–1028.

Murstein, B., Merighi, J., & Vyse, S. (1991). Love styles in the United States and France: A cross-cultural comparison. *Journal of Social and Clinical Psychology, 10*(1), 37–46.

Myers, D. (1987). *Social psychology* (2nd ed.). New York: McGraw-Hill.

Myers, F. R. (1979). Emotions and the self: A theory of personhood and political order among Pintupi aborigines. *Ethos, 7,* 343–370.

Narayanan, S., & Ganesan, V. (1978). The concept of self among the Irulas of Palamalai. *Journal of Psychological Researches, 22*(2), 127–134.

National Center for Education Statistics (2003). *Highlights from the Trends in International Mathematics and Science Study (TIMSS) 2003.* Washington, DC.: U.S. Department of Education.

National Institutes of Health (2000). *Plain talk about depression.* NIH Publication No. 00-3561. Washington, DC: Government Printing Office.

National Institutes of Health (2006). *Attention Deficit Hyperactivity Disorder.* NIH Publication No. 3572, Washington, DC.

National Institute of Mental Health (2006). *Attention deficit hyperactivity disorder.* NIMH Publication No. 3572.

Nayak, S., Shiflett, S., Eshun, S., & Levine, F. (2000). Culture and gender effects in pain beliefs and the prediction of pain tolerance.

Cross-Cultural Research: The Journal of Comparative Social Science, 34(2), 135–151.

Nazroo, J. Y. (2003). The structuring of ethnic inequalities in health: Economic position, racial discrimination, and racism. *American Journal of Public Health, 93*(2), 277–284.

Neck, C. P., & Manz, C. C. (1994). From groupthink to teamthink: Toward the creation of constructive thought patterns in self-managing work teams. *Human Relations, 47*(8), 929–951.

Nelson, S. H., McCoy, G. F., Stetter, M., & Vanderwagen, W. C. (1992). An overview of mental health services for American Indians and Alaska Natives in the 1990s. *Hospital and Community Psychiatry, 43,* 257–261.

Nemoto, T., Wong, F. Y., Ching, A., Chng, C. L., Bouey, P., Henrickson, M., & Smeber, R. E. (1998). HIV seroprevalence, risk behaviors, and cognitive factors among Asian and Pacific Islander American men who have sex with men: A summary and critique of empirical studies and methodological issues. *AIDS Education and Prevention, 10*(3), 31–47.

Nenty, H. J. (1986). Cross-culture bias analysis of Cattell Culture-Fair Intelligence Test. *Perspectives in Psychological Researches, 9*(1), 1–16.

Nenty, H. J., & Dinero, T. E. (1981). A cross-cultural analysis of the fairness of the Cattell Culture Fair Intelligence Test using the Rasch model. *Applied Psychological Measurement, 5*(3), 355–368.

Newberg, A. B. & Lee, B. Y. (2006). The relationship between religion and health. In P. McNamara (Ed.), *Where god and science meet: How brain and evolutionary studies alter our understanding of religion (Vol. 3): The psychology of religious experience* (pp. 51–81). Westport, CT: Praeger/Greenwood.

Newton, N., & Newton, M. (1972). Childbirth in cross-cultural perspectives. In J. G. Howells (Ed.), *Modern perspectives in psychoobstetrics* (pp. 76–94). New York: Brunner/Mazel.

Ng, H. S., Cooper, M., & Chandler, P. (1998). The Eysenckian personality structure: A "Giant Three" or "Big Five" model in Hong Kong? *Personality and Individual Differences, 25*(6), 1111–1131.

Nguyen, H. H., Messe, L. & Stollack, G. (1999). Toward a more complex understanding of acculturation and adjustment: Cultural involvements and psychosocial functioning in Vietnamese youth. *Journal of Cross-Cultural Psychology, 30*(1), 5–31.

NICHD (2001). Nonmaternal care and family factors in early development: An overview of the NICHD Study of Early Child Care. *Journal of Applied Developmental Psychology, 22*(5), 457–492.

NICHD (2005). Early child care and children's development in the primary grades: Follow-up results from the NICHD study of early child care. *American Educational Research Journal, 42,* 537, 570.

Nichols, R. K., & McAndrew, T. F. (1984). Stereotyping and auto-stereotyping in Spanish, Malaysian, and American college students. *Journal of Social Psychology, 124,* 179–189.

Niedenthal, P., & Beike, D. (1997). Interrelated and isolated self-concepts. *Personality and Social Psychology Review, 1*(2), 106–128.

Nisbett, R. (1993). Violence and U.S. Regional culture. *American Psychologist, 48,* 441–449.

Nisbett, R. E. (2003). *The geography of thought: How Asians and westerners think differently. And why.* New York: The Free Press.

Nisbett, R. E., Peng, K., Choi, I., & Norenzayan, A. (2001). Culture and systems of thought: Holistic versus analytic cognition. *Psychological Review, 108,* 291–310.

Noesjirwan, J. (1977). Contrasting cultural patterns on interpersonal closeness in doctors: Waiting rooms in Sydney and Jakarta. *Journal of Cross-Cultural Psychology, 8,* 357–368.

Noesjirwan, J. (1978). A rule-based analysis of cultural differences in social behavior: Indonesia and Australia. *International Journal of Psychology, 13,* 305–316.

Nomura, N., & Barnlund, D. (1983). Patterns of interpersonal criticism in Japan and United States. *International Journal of Intercultural Relations, 7*(1), 1–18.

Norenzayan, A., & Heine, S. J. (2005). Psychological universals: What are they and how can we know? *Psychological Bulletin, 131,* 763–784.

Norvilitis, J. M., & Fang, P. (2005). Perceptions of ADHD in China and the United States: A preliminary study. *Journal of Attention Disorders, 9*(2), 413–424.

Nydell, M. K. (1998). *Understanding Arabs: A guide for Westerners.* Yarmouth, ME: Intercultural Press.

O'Reilly, C. A. (1989). Corporations, culture, and commitment: Motivation and social control in organizations. *California Management Review, 31,* 9–25.

O'Reilly, C. A., Chatman, J., & Caldwell, D. F. (1991). People and organizational culture: A profile-comparison approach to assessing person-organization fit. *Academy of Management Journal, 34,* 487–516.

O'Sullivan, M., Ekman, P., Friesen, W., & Scherer, K. R. (1985). What you say and how you say it: The contribution of speech content and voice quality to judgments of others. *Journal of Personality & Social Psychology, 48,* 54–62.

O'Toole, A. J., Deffenbacher, K. A., Valentin, D., & Abdi, H. (1994). Structural aspects of face recognition and the other-race effect. *Memory and Cognition, 22*(2), 208–224.

O'Toole, A. J., Peterson, J., & Deffenbacher, K. A. (1996). An "other-race effect" for categorizing faces by sex. *Perception, 25*(6), 669–676.

Oakes, P. J., Haslam, S. A., & Turner, J. C. (1994). *Stereotyping and social reality.* Oxford, UK: Basil Blackwell.

Oesterheld, J. R. (1997). Acceptability of the Conners Parent Rating Scale and Child Behavior Checklist to Dakotan/Lakotan parents.

Journal of the American Academy of Child and Adolescent Psychiatry, 36(1), 55–64.

Ogbu, J. U. (1981). Origins of human competence: A cultural-ecological perspective. *Child Development, 52,* 413–429.

Ogden, C. L., Flegal, K. M., Carroll, M. D., & Johnson, C. L. (2002). Prevalence and trends in overweight among US children and adolescents, 1999–2000. *JAMA, 288,* 1728–1732.

Oh, Y., Koeske, G. F., Sales, E. (2002). Acculturation, stress and depressive symptoms among Korean immigrants in the United States. *Journal of Social Psychology, 142*(4), 511–526.

Okamoto, K. (1993). *Nihonjin no YES wa Naze No Ka? [Why is a Japanese yes a no?].* Tokyo: PHP Research Laboratory.

Okazaki S. (2000). Asian American and White American differences on affective distress symptoms. Do symptom reports differ across reporting methods? *Journal of Cross-Cultural Psychology 31*(5), 603–625.

Okechuku, C. (1994). The relationship of six managerial characteristics to the assessment of managerial effectiveness in Canada, Hong Kong and People's Republic of China. *Journal of Occupational and Organizational Psychology, 67*(1), 79–86.

Okello, E. S., & Ekblad, S. (2006). Lay concepts of depression among the Baganda of Uganda: A pilot study. *Transcultural Psychiatry, 43*(2), 287–313.

Okonkwo, R. (1997). Moral development and culture in Kohlberg's theory: A Nigerian (Igbo) evidence. *IFT Psychologia: An International Journal, 5*(2), 117–128.

Olsson, A., Ebert, J. P., Banaji, M. R., & Phelps, E. A. (2005). The role of social groups in the persistence of learned fear. *Science, 309,* 785–787.

Omi, M., & Winant, H. (1994). *Racial formation in the United States: From the 1960s to the 1990s* (2nd ed.). New York: Routledge.

Opler, M. K., & Singer, J. L. (1959). Ethnic differences in behavior and psychopathology. *Interna-*

tional Journal of Social Psychiatry, 2, 11–23.

Oppedal, B., Roysamb, E. & Sam, D. L. (2004). The effect of acculturation and social support on change in mental health among young immigrants. *International Journal of Behavioral Development, 28*(6), 481–494.

Oquendo, M. A. (1996a). Psychiatric evaluation and psychotherapy in the patient's second language. *Psychiatric Services, 47*(6), 614–618.

Oquendo, M. A. (1996b). Psychiatric evaluation in a second language: Commentary reply. *Psychiatric Services, 47*(9), 1002.

Organista, P. B., Organista, K. C., & Kurasaki, K. (2003). The relationship between acculturation and ethnic minority health. In K. M. Chun & P. B. Organista (Eds.), *Acculturation: Advances in theory, measurement, and applied research* (pp. 139–161). Washington, DC: American Psychological Association.

Organization, W. H. (1997). *World health assembly.* Geneva, Switzerland: World Health Organization.

Orlinsky, D. E., Grawe, K., & Parks, B. K. (1994). Process and outcome in psychotherapy: Noch einmal. In A. E. Bergin & S. L. Garfield, (Eds), *Handbook of psychotherapy and behavior change* (4th ed., pp. 270–376). New York: Wiley.

Orr, E., & Ben-Eliahu, E. (1993). Gender differences in idiosyncratic sex-typed self-images and self-esteem. *Sex Roles, 29*(3–4), 271–296.

Ortega, J. E., Iglesias, J., Fernandez, J., M., & Corraliza, J. A. (1983). La expression facial en los ciegos congenitos [facial expression in the congenitally blind]. *Infancia y Aprendizaje, 21,* 83–96.

Oster, H. (2005). The repertoire of infant facial expressions: An ontogenetic perspective. In J. Nadel & D. Muir (Eds.), *Emotional development* (pp. 261–292). New York: Oxford University Press.

Ostrov, J. M., Crick, N. R., & Staffacher, K. (2006). Relational aggression in sibling and peer relationships during early childhood. *Journal of Applied Developmental Psychology, 27*(3), 241–253.

Oyserman, D. (1993). The lens of personhood: Viewing the self and others in a multicultural society. *Journal of Personality and Social Psychology, 65*, 993–1009.

Oyserman, D., Coon, H. M., & Kemmelmeier, M. (2002). Rethinking individualism and collectivism: Evaluation of theoretical and assumptions and meta-analyses. *Psychological Bulletin, 128*, 3–72.

Oyserman, D., Coon, H. M., & Kemmelmeier, M. (2002). Rethinking individualism and collectivism: Evaluation of theoretical assumptions and meta-analyses. *Psychological Bulletin, 128*, 3–72.

Oyserman, D., Gant, L., & Ager, J. (1995). A socially contextualized model of African American identity: Possible selves and school persistence. *Journal of Personality and Social Psychology, 69*, 1216–1232.

Padilla, A. M., Wagatsuma, Y., & Lindholm, K. J. (1985). Acculturation and personality as predictors of stress in Japanese and Japanese Americans. *Journal of Social Psychology, 125*, 295–305.

Paguio, L. P., Robinson, B. E., Skeen, P., & Deal, J. E. (1987). Relationship between fathers' and mothers' socialization practices and children's locus of control in Brazil, the Philippines, and the United States. *Journal of Genetic Psychology, 148*(3), 202–313.

Paik, J. H. & Mix, K. S. (2003). U.S. and Korean children's comprehension of fraction names: A reexamination of cross-national differences. *Child Development, 74*(1), 144–154.

Pang, O. V. (1991). The relationship of test anxiety and math achievement to parental values in Asian American and European American middle school students. *Journal of Research and Development in Education, 24*(4), 1–10.

Paniagua, F. A. (1998). *Assessing and treating culturally diverse clients: A practical guide.* Newbury Park, CA: Sage.

Paniagua, F. A. (2000). Culture-bound syndromes, cultural variations and psychopathology. In I. Cuellar & F. A. Paniagua (Eds.), *Handbook of multicultural mental health: Assessment and treatment of diverse populations* (pp. 139–169). San Diego: Academic Press.

Papps, F., Walker, M., Trimboli, A., & Trimboli, C. (1995). Parental discipline in Anglo, Greek, Lebanese, and Vietnamese cultures. *Journal of Cross-Cultural Psychology, 26*(1), 49–64.

Pargament, K. I., & Maton, K. I. (2000). Religion in American life. In J. Rappaport & E. Seidman (Eds.), *Handbook of community psychology* (pp. 495–522). New York: Kluwer Academic/Plenum.

Parke, R. (2004). Development in the family. *Annual Review of Psychology, 55*, 365–399.

Parkin, M. (1974). Suicide and culture in Fairbanks: A comparison of three cultural groups in a small city of interior Alaska. *Psychiatry: Journal for the Study of Interpersonal Processes, 37*(1), 60–67.

Parsonson, K. (1987). Intermarriages: Effects on the ethnic identity of the offspring. *Journal of Cross-Cultural Psychology, 18*(3), 363–371.

Pascual, L., Haynes, O. M., Galperin, Z. C., & Bornstein, H. M. (1995). Psychosocial determinants of whether and how much new mothers work: A study in the United States and Argentina. *Journal of Cross-Cultural Psychology, 26*(3), 314–330.

Patzer, G. L. (1985). *The physical attractiveness phenomena.* New York: Plenum Press.

Paulhaus, D. L. (1984). Two-component models of socially desirable responding. *Journal of Personality and Social Psychology, 46*, 598–609.

Paunonen, S. V., & Ashton, M. C. (1998). The structured assessment of personality across cultures. *Journal of Cross-Cultural Psychology, 29*(1), 150–170.

Paunonen, S. V., Jackson, D. N., Trzebinski, J., & Forsterling, F. (1992). Personality structure across cultures: A multi-method evaluation. *Journal of Personality and Social Psychology, 62*(3), 447–456.

Pe-Pua, R. (1989). Pagtatanong-Tanong: A cross-cultural research method. *International Journal of Intercultural Relations, 13*, 147–163.

Pederson, A. K., King, J. E., & Landau, V. I. (2005). Chimpanzee (Pan troglodytes) personality predicts behavior. *Journal of Research in Personality, 39*, 534–549.

Pekerti, A. A., & Thomas, D. C. (2003). Communication in intercultural interaction: An empirical investigation of idiocentric and sociocentric communication styles. *Journal of Cross-Cultural Psychology, 34*, 139–154.

Pelto, P. J., & Pelto, G. H. (1975). Intra-cultural diversity: Some theoretical issues. *American Ethnologist, 2*, 1–18.

Pena, Y., Sidanius, J., & Sawyer, M. (2004). Racial democracy in the Americas: A Latin and U.S. comparison. *Journal of Cross-Cultural Psychology, 35*, 749–762.

Peng, K., & Nisbett, R. (1999). Culture, dialectics, and reasoning about contradiction. *American Psychologist, 54*, 741–754.

Peng, K., Nisbett, R. E., & Wong, Y. C. (1997). Validity problems comparing values across cultures and possible solutions. *Psychological Methods, 2*(4), 329–344.

Pennebaker, J. W., Rime, B., & Blankenship, V. E. (1996). Stereotypes of emotional expressiveness of northerners and southerners: A cross-cultural test of Montesquieu's hypothesis. *Journal of Personality and Social Psychology, 70*(2), 372–380.

Pennisi, E. (2005). How did cooperative behavior evolve? *Science, 309*, 93.

Petersen, D. J., Bilenberg, N., Hoerder, K., & Gillberg, C. (2006). The population prevalence of child psychiatric disorders in Danish 8- to 9-year-old children. *European Child & Adolescent Psychiatry, 15*(2), 71–78.

Peterson, M. (1997). Work, corporate culture, and stress: Implications for worksite health promotion.

American Journal of Health Behavior, 21(4), 243–252.

Peterson, M. F., & Smith, P. B. (1997). Does national culture or ambient temperature explain cross-national differences in role stress? No sweat! *Academy of Management Journal, 40*(4), 930–946.

Petrie, K., Dibble, C., Long-Taylor, M., & Ruthe, G. (1986). A New Zealand information subtest for the WAIS–R. *New Zealand Journal of Psychology, 15*(1), 23–26.

Pfeiffer, W. M. (1982). Culture-bound syndromes. In I. Al-Issa (Ed.), *Culture and psychopathology* (pp. 201–218). Baltimore: University Park Press.

Phillips, D. A., Voran, M., Kisker, E., Howes, C., & Whitebrook, M. (1994). Child care for children in poverty: Opportunity or inequity? *Child Development, 65*(2), 472–492.

Phinney, J. S. (1996). When we talk about American ethnic groups, what do we mean? *American Psychologist, 51*(9), 918–927.

Pierrehumbert, B., Bader, M., Thévoz, S., Kinal, A., & Halfon, O. (2006). Hyperactivity and attention problems in a Swiss sample of school-aged children: Effects of school achievement, child gender, and informants. *Journal of Attention Disorders, 10*, 65–76.

Pike, K. L. (1954). *Language in relation to a unified theory of the structure of human behavior, Pt. 1* (Preliminary ed.). Glendale, CA: Summer Institute of Linguistics.

Piker, S. (1998). Contributions of psychological anthropology. *Journal of Cross-Cultural Psychology, 29*(1), 9–31.

Pines, A. M. (2001). The role of gender and culture in romantic attraction. *European Psychologist, 6*(2), 96–102.

Pinker, S. (1995). *The language instinct: How the mind creates language.* New York: HarperCollins.

Pittam, J., Gallois, C., Iwawaki, S., & Kroonenberg, P. (1995). Australian and Japanese concepts of expressive behavior. *Journal of Cross-Cultural Psychology, 26*(5), 451–473.

Plaks, J. E., Stroessner, S. J., Dweck, C. S., & Sherman, J. W. (2001). Person theories and attention allocation: Preferences for stereotypic versus counterstereotypic information. *Journal of Personality and Social Psychology, 80*(6), 876–893.

Plomin, R. (1990). *Nature and nurture: An introduction to human behavioral genetics.* Pacific Grove, CA: Brooks/Cole.

Pohl, R. F., Bender, M., & Lachmann, G. (2002). Hindsight bias around the world. *Experimental Psychology, 49*, 270–282.

Pollack, R. H., & Silvar, S. D. (1967). Magnitude of the Mueller-Lyer illusion in children as a function of the pigmentation of the fundus oculi. *Psychonomic Science, 8*, 83–84.

Ponce, F. Q., & Atkinson, D. R. (1989). Mexican-American acculturation, counselor ethnicity, counseling style, and perceived counselor credibility. *Journal of Counseling Psychology, 36*, 203–208.

Ponchillia, S. V. (1993). The effect of cultural beliefs on the treatment of native people with diabetes and visual impairment. *Journal of Visual Impairment and Blindness, 87*(9), 333–335.

Ponterotto, J. G., Alexander, C. M., & Hinkston, J. A. (1988). Afro-American preferences for counselor characteristics: A replication and extension. *Journal of Counseling Psychology, 35*(2), 175–182.

Pontius, A. A. (1997). Lack of sex differences among east Ecuadorian school children on geometric figure rotation and face drawings. *Perceptual and Motor Skills, 85*(1), 72–74.

Poortinga, H. Y. (1989). Equivalence of cross-cultural data: An overview of basic issues. *International Journal of Psychology, 24*, 737–756.

Poortinga, H. Y. (1990). *Presidential address IACCP: Towards a conceptualization of culture for psychology.* Unpublished paper, Tilburg University, The Netherlands.

Poortinga, Y. H., Van de Vijver, F. J. R., Joe, R. C., & van de Koppel, J. M. H. (1987). Peeling the onion called culture: A synopsis. In C.

Kagitcibasi et al. (Eds.), *Growth and progress in cross-cultural psychology* (pp. 22–34). Berwyn, PA: Swets North America.

Porter, J. R., & Washington, R. E. (1993). Minority identity and self-esteem. *Annual Review of Sociology, 19*, 139–161.

Porter, R. Y. (2000). Understanding and treating ethnic minority youth. In J. E. Aponte & J. Wohl (Eds.), *Psychological intervention and cultural diversity* (2nd ed., pp. 167–182). Boston: Allyn & Bacon.

Pote, H. L., & Orrell, M. W. (2002). Perceptions of schizophrenia in multi-cultural Britain. *Ethnic Health, 7*(1), 7–20.

Prasadaro, P. S. D. V., & Matam, S. P. (2001). Clinical psychology in India. *Journal of Clinical Psychology in Medical Settings, 8*(1), 31–38.

Pratt, G. (1993). Should I take this job? The organizational culture dimension to career decisions. *Educational Psychology in Practice, 8*(4), 222–224.

Premack, D. (2004). Is language the key to human intelligence? *Science, 303*, 318–320.

Priest, R. (1991). Racism and prejudice as negative impacts on African American clients in therapy. *Journal of Counseling and Development, 70*, 213–215.

Primm, A. B., Lima, B. R., & Rowe, C. L. (1996). Cultural and ethnic sensitivity. In W. R. Breakey (Ed.), *Integrated mental health services: Modern community psychiatry* (pp. 146–159). New York: Oxford University Press.

Prince, R. (1980). Variations in psychotherapeutic procedures. In H. C. Triandis & J. Draguns (Eds.), *Handbook of cross-cultural psychology: Vol. 6. Psychopathology* (pp. 291–349). Boston: Allyn & Bacon.

Prince, R. H. (2000). Transcultural psychiatry: Personal experiences and Canadian perspectives. *Canadian Journal of Psychiatry, 45*, 431–437.

Pugh, J. F. (1991). The semantics of pain in Indian culture and medicine. *Culture, Medicine and Psychiatry, 15*(1), 19–43.

Puloka, M. H. (1997). A common-sense perspective on the Tongan folk healing. *International Journal of Mental Health, 26*(3), 69–93.

Punamaeki, R. L., & Joustie, M. (1998). The role of culture, violence, and personal factors affecting dream content. *Journal of Cross-Cultural Psychology, 29*(2), 320–342.

Punetha, D., Giles, H., & Young, L. (1987). Ethnicity and immigrant values: Religion and language choice. *Journal of Language and Social Psychology, 6,* 229–241.

Pyszczynski, T., Greenberg, J., Solomon, S., Arndt, J., & Schimel, J. (2004). Why do people need self-esteem? A theoretical and empirical review. *Psychological Bulletin, 130,* 435–468.

Quah, S., & Bishop, G. D. (1996). Seeking help for illness: The roles of cultural orientation and illness cognition. *Journal of Health Psychology, 1,* 209–222.

Rabbie, J. M., & Horwitz, M. (1982). Conflicts and aggression among individuals and groups. In H. Hirsch, H. Brandstatter, & H. Kelley (Eds.), *Proceedings of the XXII International Congress of Psychology, Leipzig, DDR: No. 8. Social Psychology.* Amersterdam: Noord-Holland.

Rack, P. (1982). *Race, culture and mental disorder.* London: Tavistock.

Radford, M. H. B., Mann, L., Ohta, Y., & Nakane, Y. (1993). Differences between Australian and Japanese students in decisional self-esteem, decisional stress, and coping styles. *Journal of Cross-Cultural Psychology, 24*(3), 284–297.

Radford, M. H. B., Nakane, Y., Ohta, Y., & Mann, L. (1991). Differences between Australian and Japanese students in reported use of decision processes. *International Journal of Psychology, 26*(1), 35–52.

Rao, V., & Rao, V. (1985). Sex-role attitudes across two cultures: United States and India. *Sex Roles, 13*(11–12), 607–624.

Rattan, M. S., & MacArthur, R. S. (1968). Longitudinal prediction of school achievement for Metis and Eskimo pupils. *Alberta Journal of Educational Research, 14*(1), 37–41.

Redican, W. K. (1982). An evolutionary perspective on human facial displays. In P. Ekman (Ed.), *Emotion in the human face* (pp. 212–280). New York: Cambridge University Press.

Reed, T. E., & Jensen, A. R. (1992). Conduction velocity in a brain nerve pathway of normal adults correlates with intelligence levels. *Intelligence, 16*(3–4), 259–272.

Reed, T. E., & Jensen, A. R. (1993). A somatosensory latency between the thalamus and cortex also correlates with level of intelligence. *Intelligence, 17*(4), 443–450.

Regier, D. A., Farmer, M. E., Rae, D. S., Myers, J. K., Kramer, M., Robins, L. N., George, L. K., Karno, M., & Locke, B. Z. (1993a). One-month prevalence of mental disorders in the United States and sociodemographic characteristics: The Epidemiologic Catchment Area study. *Acta Psychiatrica Scandinavica, 88,* 35–47.

Regier, D. A., Narrow, W. E., Rae, D. S., Manderscheid, R. W., Locke, B. Z., & Goodwin, F. K. (1993b). The de facto US mental and addictive disorders service system: Epidemiologic Catchment Area prospective 1-year prevalence rates of disorders and services. *Archives of General Psychiatry, 50,* 85–94.

Reichers, A. E., & Schneider, B. (1990). Climate and culture: An evolution of constructs. In B. Schneider (Ed.), *Organizational climate and culture* (pp. 5–39). San Francisco: Jossey-Bass.

Remschmidt, H. (2004). Global consensus on ADHD/HKD. *European Child & Adolescent Psychiatry, 14*(3), 127–137.

Reynolds, D. K. (1980). *The quiet therapies.* Honolulu: University of Hawaii Press.

Rhee, E., Uleman, J. S., & Lee, H. K. (1996). Variations in collectivism and individualism by ingroup and culture: Confirmatory factor analyses. *Journal of Personality and Social Psychology, 71,* 1037–1054.

Rhi, B.-Y. (2000). Culture, spirituality, and mental health. *Cultural Psychiatry: International Perspectives, 24*(3), 569–579.

Riemann, R., Angleitner, A., & Strelau, J. (1997). Genetic and environmental influences on personality: A study of twins reared together using the self-and peer-report NEO-FFI scales. *Journal of Personality, 65*(3), 449–475.

Riesman, P. (1977). *Freedom in Fulani social life: An introspective ethnography* (M. Fuller, Trans.). Chicago: University of Chicago Press. (Original work published 1974) Rivers, W. H. R. (1905). Observations on the senses of the Todas. *British Journal of Psychology, 1,* 321–396.

Robbins, J. M., & Krueger, J. I. (2005). Social projection to ingroups and outgroups: A review and meta-analysis. *Personality and Social Psychology Review, 9,* 32–47.

Robbins, M. C., DeWalt, B. R., & Pelto, P. J. (1972). Climate and behavior: A biocultural study. *Journal of Cross-Cultural Psychology, 3*(4), 331–344.

Roberts, B. W., & Helson, R. (1997). Changes in culture, changes in personality: The influence of individualism in a longitudinal study of women. *Journal of Personality and Social Psychology, 72,* 644–651.

Roberts, B. W., Caspi, A., & Moffitt, T. E. (2003). Work experiences and personality development in young adulthood. *Journal of Personality and Social Psychology, 84,* 582–593.

Roberts, B. W., Helson, R., & Klohnen, E. C. (2002). Personality development and growth in women across 30 years: Three perspectives. *Journal of Personality, 70,* 79–102.

Roberts, B. W., Walton, K. E., & Viechtbauer, W. (2006). Patterns of mean-level change in personality traits across the life course: A meta-analysis of longitudinal studies. *Psychological Bulletin, 132,* 1–25.

Robertson, A., & Cochrane, R. (1976). Attempted suicide and cultural change: An empirical investigation. *Human Relations, 29*(9), 863–883.

Robins, L. N., & Regier, D. A. (1991). *Psychiatric disorders in America: The Epidemiologic Catchment Area study*. New York: Free Press.

Rodenhauser, P. (1994). Cultural barriers to mental health care delivery in Alaska. *Journal of Mental Health Administration, 21*, 60–70.

Rodriguez, D., Wigfield, A., & Eccles, J. S. (2003). Changing competence perceptions, changing values: Implications for youth sports. *Journal of Applied Sport Psychology, 15*, 67–81.

Roemer, M. I. (1991). *National health systems of the world*. New York: Oxford University Press.

Rogers, C. R. (1942). *Counseling and psychotherapy*. Boston: Houghton Mifflin.

Rogler, L. H., Malgady, R. G., & Rodriguez, O. (1989). *Hispanics and mental health: A framework for research*. Malabar, FL: Krieger.

Rohde, L. A., Szobot, C., Polanczyk, G., Schmitz, M., & Martins, S.(2005). Attention-deficit/hyperactivity disorder in a diverse culture: Do research and clinical findings support the notion of a cultural construct for the disorder? *Biological Psychiatry, 57*(11), 1436–1441.

Rohner, R. P. (1984). Toward a conception of culture for cross-cultural psychology. *Journal of Cross-Cultural Psychology, 15*, 111–138.

Rokeach, M. (1973). *The nature of human values*. New York: Free Press.

Rolland, J. S. (1993). Mastering family challenges in serious illness and disability. In F. Walsh et al. (Eds.), *Normal family processes* (2nd ed., pp. 444–473). New York: Guilford Press.

Romano, J. L. (1988). Stress management counseling: From crisis to intervention. *Counseling Psychology Quarterly, 1*(2–3), 211–219.

Romero, G. J., & Garza, R. T. (1986). Attributes for the occupational success/failure of ethnic minority and non-minority women. *Sex Roles, 14*, 445–452.

Rosch, E. (1973). On the internal structure of perceptual categories. In T. E. Moore (Ed.), *Cognitive development and the acquisition of language* (pp. 111–144). San Diego: Academic Press.

Rosch, E. (1978). Principles of categorization. In E. Rosch & B. B. Lloyd (Eds.), *Cognition and categorization* (pp. 28–48). Hillsdale, NJ: Erlbaum.

Rose, M. H. (1995). Apprehending deaf culture. *Journal of Applied Communication Research, 23*(2), 156–162.

Roseman, I. J., Dhawan, N., Rettek, S. I., Nadidu, R. K., & Thapa, K. (1995). Cultural differences and cross-cultural similarities in appraisals and emotional responses. *Journal of Cross-Cultural Psychology, 26*, 23–48.

Rosenthal, M.K. (1992). Nonparental child care in Israel: A cultural and historical perspective. In M. E. Lamb, K. J. Sternberg, C-P. Hwang, & A. G. Broberg (Eds). *Childcare in context: Cross-cultural perspectives* (pp. 305–330). Hillsdale, NJ: Erlbaum.

Rosmus, C., Halifax, N. S., Johnston, C., Chan-Yip, A., & Yang, F. (2000). Pain response in Chinese and non-Chinese Canadian infants: Is there a difference? *Social Science and Medicine, 51*(2), 175–184.

Ross, B. M., & Millson, C. (1970). Repeated memory of oral prose in Ghana and New York. *International Journal of Psychology, 5*, 173–181.

Ross, J., & Ferris, K. R. (1981). Interpersonal attraction and organizational outcome: A field experiment. *Administrative Science Quarterly, 26*, 617–632.

Ross, L. (1977). The intuitive psychologist and his shortcomings: Distortions in the attribution process. In L. Berkowitz (Ed.), *Advances in experimental social psychology* (Vol. 10, pp. 174–221). New York: Academic Press.

Rosselló, J., & Bernal, G. (1999). The efficacy of cognitive behavioral and interpersonal treatments for depression in Puerto Rican adolescents. *Journal of Consulting and Clinical Psychology, 67*, 734–745.

Rossiter, J. C. (1994). The effect of a culture-specific education program to promote breastfeeding among Vietnamese women in Sydney. *International Journal of Nursing Studies, 31*(4), 369–379.

Rothbaum, F., Weisz, J., Pott, M. Miyake, K., & Morelli, G. (2000). Attachment and culture: Security in the United States and Japan. *American Psychologist, 55*, 1093–1104.

Rotheram-Borus, M. J., & Petrie, K. J. (1996). Patterns of social expectations among Maori and European children in New Zealand. *Journal of Cross-Cultural Psychology, 27*(5), 576–597.

Rotter, J. B. (1954). *Social learning and clinical psychology*. Englewood Cliffs, NJ: Prentice-Hall.

Rotter, J. B. (1966). Generalized expectancies for internal versus external control of reinforcement. *Psychological Monographs, 80* (Whole No. 609).

Rowe, D.C. (1994). *The limits of family influence: Genes, experience, and behavior*. New York: Guilford Press.

Rozin, P., Lowery, L., Imada, S., & Haidt, J. (1999). The cad triad hypothesis: A mapping between three moral emotions (contempt, anger, disgust) and three moral codes (community, autonomy, divinity). *Journal of Personality and Social Psychology, 75*, 574–585.

Rudmin, F. (2003). Critical history of the acculturation psychology of assimilation, separation, integration, and marginalization. *Review of General Psychology, 7*, 3–37.

Russell, G. L., Fujino, D. C., Sue, S., Cheung, M., & Snowden, L. R. (1996). The effects of the therapist-client ethnic match in the assessment of mental health functioning. *Journal of Cross-Cultural Psychology, 27*(5), 598–615.

Russell, J. A. (1991). Culture and the categorization of emotions. *Psychological Bulletin, 110*, 426–450.

Russell, J. A. (1995). Facial expressions of emotion: What lies beyond minimal universality? *Psychological Bulletin, 118*(3), 379–391.

Ryan, R. M., & Deci, E. L. (2000). Self-determination theory and the facilitation of intrinsic motivation, social development and well-being. *American Psychologist, 55,* 68–78.

Sachdev, P. S. (1990). Whakama: Culturally determined behavior in the New Zealand Maori. *Psychological Medicine, 20*(2), 433–444.

Sakamoto, Y., & Miura, T. (1976, March). An attempt to understand Japanese personality from a family psychiatry point of view. *Australian and New Zealand Journal of Psychiatry, 10*(1-A), 115–117.

Salganik, M. J., Dodds, P. S., & Watts, D. J. (2006). Experimental study of inequality and unpredictability in an artificial cultural market. *311,* 854–856.

Salzman, M. (2001). Cultural trauma and recovery: Perspectives from terror management theory. *Trauma, Violence, and Abuse: A Review Journal, 2,* 172–191.

Sam, D. L. (1994). The psychological adjustment of young immigrants in Norway. *Scandinavian Journal of Psychology, 35,* 240–253.

Sam, D. L. (2000). Psychological adaptation of adolescents with immigrant backgrounds. *Journal of Social Psychology, 140*(1), 5–25.

Sampson, E. E. (1988). The debate on individualism: Indigenous psychologies and their role in personal and societal functioning. *American Psychologist, 43,* 15–22.

Sanchez, A. R., & Atkinson, D. R. (1983). Mexican-American cultural commitment, preference for counselor ethnicity, and willingness to use counseling. *Journal of Counseling Psychology, 30*(2), 215–220.

Sanchez-Burks, J., Lee, F., Choi, I., Nisbett, R., Zhao, S., & Koo, J. (2003). Conversing across cultures: East-West communication styles in work and nonwork contexts. *Journal of Personality and Social Psychology, 85,* 363–372.

Santa, J. L., & Baker, L. (1975). Linguistic influences on visual memory. *Memory and Cognition, 3*(4), 445–450.

Santiago-Rivera, A. L., & Azara, L. (1995). Developing a culturally sensitive treatment modality for bilingual Spanish-speaking clients: Incorporating language and culture in counseling. *Journal of Counseling and Development, 74*(1), 12–17.

Saraswathi, T. (1999). Adult-child continuity in India: Is adolescence a myth or an emerging reality? In T. Saraswathi (Ed.), *Culture, socialization, and human development: Theory, research, and applications in India* (pp. 213–232). Thousand Oaks, CA: Sage.

Sargent, C. (1984). Between death and shame: Dimensions of pain in Bariba culture. *Social Science and Medicine, 19*(12), 1299–1304.

Sato, T. (1998). Agency and communion: The relationship between therapy and culture. *Cultural Diversity and Mental Health, 4,* 278–290.

Satoh, K. (1996). Expression in the Japanese kindergarten curriculum. *Early Child Development and Care, 123,* 193–202.

Saucier, D. A., Miller, C. T., & Douct, N. (2005). Differences in helping whites and blacks: A meta-analysis. *Personality and Social Psychology Review, 9,* 2–16.

Saucier, G., Georgiades, S., Tsaousis, I., & Goldberg, L. R. (2005). The factor structure of Greek personality adjectives. *Journal of Personality and Social Psychology, 88,* 856–875.

Saudino, K. J. (1997). Moving beyond the heritability question: New directions in behavioral genetic studies of personality. *Current Directions in Psychological Science, 6*(4), 86–90.

Scarr, S. (1993). Biological and cultural diversity: The legacy of Darwin for development. *Child Development, 64,* 1333–1353.

Scarr, S., & Weinberg, R.A. (1976). I.Q. test performance of black children adopted by white families. *American Psychologist, 31,* 726–739.

Schachter, F.F., Fuches, M.L., Bijur, P., & Stone, R. K. (1989). Cosleeping and sleep problems in Hispanic-American urban young children. *Pediatrics, 84,* 522–530.

Schaller, M., Conway, L. G., & Tanchuk, T. L. (2002). Selective pressures on the once and future contents of ethnic stereotypes: Effects of the communicability of traits. *Journal of Personality and Social Psychology, 82*(6), 861–877.

Schein, E. H. (1985). *Organizational culture and leadership: A dynamic view.* San Francisco: Jossey-Bass.

Scheper-Hughes, N. (1992). *Death without weeping: The violence of everyday life in Brazil.* Berkeley: University of California Press.

Scherer, K. R. (1997a). Profiles of emotion-antecedent appraisal: Testing theoretical predictions across cultures. *Cognition & Emotion, 11,* 113–150.

Scherer, K. R. (1997b). The role of culture in emotion-antecedent appraisal. *Journal of Personality & Social Psychology, 73,* 902–922.

Scherer, K. R., & Wallbott, H. (1994). Evidence for universality and cultural variation of differential emotion response patterning. *Journal of Personality & Social Psychology, 66,* 310–328.

Schimmack, U. (1996). Cultural influences on the recognition of emotion by facial expressions. *Journal of Cross-Cultural Psychology, 27,* 37–50.

Schliemann, A. D., & Carraher, D. W. (2001). Everyday cognition: Where culture, psychology, and education come together. In D. Matsumoto (Ed.), *Handbook of culture and psychology* (pp. 137–150). New York: Oxford University Press.

Schmidt, S. M., & Yeh, R. (1992). The structure of leader influence: A cross-national comparison. *Journal of Cross-Cultural Psychology, 23*(2), 251–264.

Schmit, M. J., Ryan, A. M., Stierwalt, S. L., & Powell, A. B. (1995). Frame-of-reference effects on personality scale scores and criterion-related validity. *Journal of Applied Psychology, 80*(5), 607–620.

Schmitt, D. P., & Allik, J. (2005). Simultaneous administration of the Rosenberg Self-Esteem Scale in 53 nations: Exploring the universal and culture-specific features of global self-esteem. *Journal of Personality and Social Psychology, 89,* 623–642.

Schmitt, D. P., Alcalay, L., Allensworth, M., Allik, J., Ault, L., Austers, I., et al. (2004). Patterns and universals of adult romantic attachment across 62 cultural regions. *Journal of Cross- Cultural Psychology, 35,* 367–402.

Schneiderman, N. (2004). Psychosocial, behavioral, and biological aspects of chronic diseases. *Current Directions in Psychological Science, 13*(6), 247–251.

Scholz, U., Hutierrez Dona, B., Sud, S., & Schwarzer, R. (2002). Is general self-efficacy a universal construct? *European Journal of Psychological Assessment, 18,* 242–251.

Schwartz, S. H. (1992). Universals in the content and structure of values: Theoretical advances and empirical tests in 20 countries. In M. Zanna (Ed.), *Advances in experimental social psychology* (Vol. 25, pp. 1–65). New York: Academic Press.

Schwartz, S. H. (1994). Are there universal aspects in the structure and contents of human values? *Journal of Social Issues, 50*(4), 19–45.

Schwartz, S. H. (1994). Beyond individualism/collectivism: New cultural dimensions of values. In U. E. Kim, H. C. Triandis, et al. (Eds.), *Individualism and collectivism: Theory, method, and applications.* (Vol. 18, pp. 85–119). Newbury Park, CA: Sage.

Schwartz, S. H. (2004). Mapping and interpreting cultural differences around the world. In H. Vinken, J. Soeters & P. Ester (Eds.), *Comparing cultures, dimensions of culture in a comparative perspective* (pp. 43–73). Leiden, The Netherlands: Brill.

Schwartz, S. H. (in press). Mapping and interpreting cultural differences around the world. In H. Vinken, J. Soeters & P. Ester (Eds.), *Comparing cultures, dimensions of culture in a comparative perspective.* Leiden, The Netherlands: Brill.

Schwartz, S. H., & Bardi, A. (2001). Value hierarchies across cultures: Taking a similarities perspective. *Journal of Cross-Cultural Psychology, 32,* 268–290.

Schwartz, S. H., & Ros, M. (1995). Values in the west: A theoretical and empirical challenge to the individualism-collectivism cultural dimension. *World Psychology, 1,* 91–122.

Scribner, S. (1974). Developmental aspects of categorized recall in a West African society. *Cognitive Psychology, 6*(4), 475–494.

Scribner, S. (1979). Modes of thinking and ways of speaking: Culture and logic reconsidered. In I. O. Freedle (Ed.), *New directions in discourse processing* (pp. 223–243). Norwood, NJ: Ablex.

Sedikides, C., Gaertner, L., & Toguchi, Y. (2003). Pancultural self-enhancement. *Journal of Personality and Social Psychology, 84,* 60–79.

Seelye, H. N., & Brewer, B. M. (1970). Ethnocentrism and acculturation of North Americans in Guatemala. *Journal of Social Psychology, 80,* 147–155.

Segall, M. H. (1979). *Cross-cultural psychology: Human behavior in global perspective.* Pacific Grove, CA: Brooks/Cole.

Segall, M. H. (1984). More than we need to know about culture, but are afraid to ask. *Journal of Cross Cultural Psychology, 15*(2), 153–162.

Segall, M. H., Campbell, D. T., & Hersokovits, J. (1963). Cultural differences in the perception of geometric illusions. *Science, 193,* 769–771.

Segall, M. H., Campbell, D. T., & Hersokovits, J. (1966). *The influence of culture on visual perception.* Indianapolis: Bobbs-Merrill.

Segall, M. H., Dasen, P. R., Berry, J. W., & Poortinga, Y. H. (1990). *Human behavior in global perspective: An introduction to cross-cultural psychology.* New York: Pergamon Press.

Shahim, S. (1992). Correlations for Wechsler Intelligence Scale for Children–Revised and the Weschler Preschool and Primary Scale of Intelligence for Iranian children. *Psychological Reports, 70,* 27–30.

Shakin, M., Shakin, D., & Sternglanz, S. H. (1985). Infant clothing: Sex labeling for strangers. *Sex Roles, Vol. 12*(9–10), 955–964.

Shand, N., & Kosawa, Y. (1985). Culture transmission: Caudill's model and alternative hypotheses. *American Anthropologist, 87*(4), 862–871.

Shane, S., Venkataraman, S., & MacMillan, I. (1995). Cultural differences in innovation championing strategies. *Journal of Management, 21*(5), 931–952.

Shepperd, J., & Wright, R. (1989). Individual contributions to a collective effort: An incentive analysis. *Personality and Social Psychology Bulletin, 15,* 141–149.

Shikanai, K. (1978). Effects of self-esteem on attribution of success and failure. *Japanese Journal of Experimental Social Psychology, 18*(1), 35–46.

Shiller, V. M., Izard, C. E., & Hembree, E. A. (1986). Patterns of emotion expression during separation in the strange-situation procedure. *Developmental Psychology, 22,* 378–382.

Shin, S.-M., Chow, C., Camacho-Gonsalves, T., Levy, R., Allen, I., & Leff, H. (2005). A meta-analytic review of racial-ethnic matching for African American and Caucasian American clients and clinicians. *Journal of Counseling Psychology, 52*(1), 45–56.

Shirakashi, S. (1985). Social loafing of Japanese students. *Hiroshima Forum for Psychology, 10,* 35–40.

Shupe, E. I., Cortina, L. M., Ramos, A., Fitzgerald, L. F., & Salisbury, J. (2002). The incidence and outcomes of sexual harassment among Hispanic and non-Hispanic white women: A comparison across levels of cultural affiliation. *Psychology of Women Quarterly, 26,* 295–308.

Shuter, R. (1976). Proxemics and tactility in Latin America. *Journal of Communication, 26,* 46–52.

Shuter, R. (1977). A field study of nonverbal communication in Germany, Italy, and the United States. *Communication Monographs, 44,* 298–305.

Shweder, R. A. (1979a). Rethinking culture and personality theory: I. A critical examination of two classical postulates. *Ethos, 7*(3), 255–278.

Shweder, R. A. (1979b). Rethinking culture and personality theory: II. A critical examination of two more classical postulates. *Ethos,* 7(4), 279–311.

Shweder, R. A. (1980). Rethinking culture and personality theory: III. From genesis and typology to hermeneutics and dynamics. *Ethos,* 8(1), 60–94.

Shweder, R. A. (1991). *Thinking through cultures: Expeditions in cultural psychology.* Cambridge, MA: Harvard University Press.

Shweder, R. A. (1993). Liberalism as destiny. In B. Puka (Ed.), *Moral development: A compendium* (*Vol. 4*: The great justice debate: Kohlberg criticism, pp. 71–74). New York: Garland.

Shweder, R. A. (1994). Liberalism as destiny. In B. Puka et al. (Eds.), *Moral development: A compendium: Vol. 4. The great justice debate: Kohlberg criticism* (pp. 71–74). New York: Garland.

Shweder, R. A., & Bourne, E. J. (1984). Does the concept of the person vary cross-culturally? In R. A. Shweder & R. A. LeVine (Eds.), *Culture theory: Essays on mind, self, and emotion* (pp. 158–199). Cambridge, UK: Cambridge University Press.

Shweder, R. A., Minow, M., & Markus, H. R. (Eds.). (2002). *Engaging cultural differences: The multicultural challenge in liberal democracies.* New York: Russell Sage Foundation.

Sidanius, J., Henry, P. J., Pratto, F., & Levin, S. (2004). Arab attributions for the attack on America: The case of Lebanese Subelites. *Journal of Cross-Cultural Psychology,* 35, 403–416.

Silk, J. B., Brosnan, S. F., Vonk, J., Henrich, J., Povinello, D. J., Richardson, A. S., et al. (2005). Chimpanzees are indifferent to the welfare of unrelated group members. *Nature,* 437, 1357–1359.

Simich, L., Beiser, M., Stewart, M., & Mwakarimba, E. (2005). Providing social support for immigrants and refugees in Canada: Challenges and directions. *Journal of Immigrant Health,* 7(4), 259–268.

Simmons, C. H., vom Kolke, A., & Shimizu, H. (1986). Attitudes toward romantic love among American, German and Japanese students. *Journal of Social Psychology,* 126, 327–336.

Simonton, D. K. (1996). Presidents' wives and First Ladies: On achieving eminence within a traditional gender role. *Sex Roles 35,* (5–6), 309–336.

Singelis, T. (1994). The measurement of independent and interdependent self-construals. *Personality and Social Psychology Bulletin,* 20, 580–591.

Singelis, T. M. (2000). Some thoughts on the future of cross-cultural social psychology. *Journal of Cross-Cultural Psychology,* 31(1), 76–91.

Singelis, T. M., Triandis, C. H., Bhawuk, S. D., & Gelfand, M. J. (1995). Horizontal and vertical dimensions of individualism and collectivism: A theoretical and measurement refinement. *Cross-Cultural Research,* 29(3), 241–275.

Singelis, T., Bond, M., Sharkey, W. F., & Lai, C. S. Y. (1999). Unpackaging culture's influence on self-esteem and embarassability. *Journal of Cross-Cultural Psychology,* 30, 315–341.

Singh-Manoux, A., Marmot, M. G., & Adler, N. E. (2005). Does subjective social status predict health and change in health status better than objective status? *Psychosomatic Medicine,* 67(6), 855–861.

Sinha, D. (1993). Indigenization of psychology in India and its relevance. In U. Kim & J. W. Berry (Eds.), *Indigenous psychologies: Research and experience in cultural context* (pp. 30–43). Newbury Park, CA: Sage.

Sinha, J. B. P. (1979). The authoritative leadership: A style of effective management. *Indian Journal of Industrial Relations,* 2(3), 381–389.

Slavin, M. O., and Kriegman, D. (1992). *The adaptive design of the human psyche: Psychoanalysis, evolutionary biology, and the therapeutic process.* New York: The Guilford Press.

Slee, R., & Cook, S. (1994). Creating cultures of disability to control young people in Australian schools. *Urban Review,* 26, 15–23.

Sloane, V. M. (1978). *Common folks.* Pepper Passes, KY: Alice Lloyd College.

Small, M. F. (1998). *Our babies, ourselves: How biology and culture shape the way we parent.* New York: Anchor.

Smedley, A., & Smedley, B. D. (2005). Race as biology is fiction, racism as a social problem is real: Anthropological and historical perspectives on the social construction of race. *American Psychologist,* 60, 16–26.

Smith, J. R., Griffith, E. J., Griffith, K. H., & Steger, J. M. (1980). When is a stereotype a stereotype? *Psychological Reports,* 46, 643–651.

Smith, P. B. (1998, October). *Leadership in high power distance cultures: An event management perspective.* Paper presented at the Third Latin-American Reunion of Cross-Cultural Psychology, Toluca, Mexico.

Smith, P. B. (2004). Acquiescent response bias as an aspect of cultural communication style. *Journal of Cross-Cultural Psychology,* 35, 50–61.

Smith, P. B., & Bond, M. H. (1999). *Social psychology: Across cultures* (2nd ed.) Boston: Allyn & Bacon.

Smith, P. B., Dugan, S., & Trompenaars, F. (1996). National culture and the values of organizational employees. *Journal of Cross-Cultural Psychology,* 27(2), 231–264.

Smith, P. B., Dugan, S., & Trompenaars, F. (1997). Locus of control and affectivity by gender and occupational status: A 14-nation study. *Sex Roles,* 36(1–2), 51–77.

Smith, P. B., Dugan, S., Peterson, M. F., & Leung, K. (1998). Individualism–collectivism and the handling of disagreement: A 23-country study. *International Journal of Intercultural Relations,* 22(3), 351–367.

Smith, P. B., Peterson, M. F., & Misumi, J. (1994). Event management and work team effectiveness in Japan, Britain and USA. *Journal of Occupational and Organizational Psychology,* 67, 33–43.

Smith, P. B., Peterson, M. F., & Schwartz, S. H. (2002). Cultural values, sources of guidance, and their relevance to managerial behavior. *Journal of Cross-Cultural Psychology,* 33(2), 188–208.

Smith, P. B., Peterson, M., Misumi, J., & Bond, M. (1992). A cross-cultural test of the Japanese PM leadership theory. *Applied Psychology: An International Review, 41*, 5–19.

Smith, P. B., Wang, Z. M., & Leung, K. (1997). Leadership, decision-making, and cultural context: Event management within Chinese joint ventures. *Leadership Quarterly, 8*(4), 413–431.

Smith, S. M., Stinson, F. S., & Dawson, D. A. (2006). Race/ethnic differences in the prevalence and co-occurrence of substance use disorders and independent mood and anxiety disorders: Results from the National Epidemiologic Survey on Alcohol and Related Conditions. *Psychological Medicine, 36*(7), 987–998.

Snowden L. R. (2001). Barriers to effective mental health services for African Americans. *Mental Health Services Research, 3*, 181–187.

Snowden, L., Masland, M., Ma, Y., & Ciemens, E. (2006). Strategies to improve minority access to public mental health services in California: Description and preliminary evaluation. *Journal of Community Psychology, 34*(2), Special issue: Addressing mental health disparities through culturally competent research and community-based practice, 225–235.

Snowdon, C. T. (2003). Expression of emotion in nonhuman animals. In R. J. Davidson, K. Scherer & H. H. Goldsmith (Eds.), *Handbook of affective sciences* (pp. 457–480). New York: Oxford University Press.

Sodowsky, G. R., & Carey, J. C. (1987). Asian immigrants in America: Factors related to adjustment. *Journal of Multicultural Counseling and Development, 15*, 129–141.

Solis-Camara, P., & Fox, R. A. (1995). Parenting among mothers with young children in Mexico and the United States. *Journal of Social Psychology, 135*(5), 591–599.

Song, M. J., & Ginsburg, H. P. (1987). The development of informal and formal mathematical thinking in Korean and U.S. children. *Child Development, 58*, 1286–1296.

Sorkhabi, N. (2005). Applicability of Baumrind's parent typology to collective cultures: Analysis of cultural explanations of parent socialization effects. *International Journal of Behavioral Development, 29*(6), 552–563.

Spadone, R. A. (1992). Internal-external control and temporal orientation among Southeast Asians and White Americans. *American Journal of Occupational Therapy, 46*(8), 713–718.

Spearman, C. E. (1927). *The abilities of man.* New York: Macmillan.

Spera, C. (2005). A review of the relationship among parenting practices, parenting styles, and adolescent school achievement. *Educational Psychology Review, 17*(2), 125–146.

Spielberger, C. D., & Sydeman, S. J. (1994). State-trait anxiety inventory and state-trait anger expression inventory. In M. E. Maruish (Ed.), *The use of psychological testing for treatment planning and outcome assessment* (pp. 292–321). Hillsdale, NJ: Erlbaum.

Sponsel, L. E. (1998). Yanomami: An arena of conflict and aggression in the Amazon. *Aggressive Behavior, 24*(2), 97–122.

Sprecher, S., & Chandak, R. (1992). Attitudes about arranged marriage and dating among men and women from India. *Journal of Sex Research, 32*, 3–15.

State of the science on psychosocial interventions for ethnic minorities. *Annual Review of Clinical Psychology, 1*(1), 113–142.

Stauffacher, K., & DeHart, G. B. (2006). Crossing social contexts: Relational aggression between siblings and friends during early and middle childhood. *Journal of Applied Developmental Psychology, 27*(3), 228–240.

Steele, C. (1998). How stereotypes shape intellectual identity and performance. *American Psychologist, 52*(6), 613–629.

Steele, C., & Aronson, J. (1995). Stereotype threat and the intellectual test performance of African Americans. *Journal of Personality and Social Psychology, 69*, 797–811.

Steinberg, L., Dornbusch, S. M., & Brown, B. B. (1992). Ethnic differences in adolescent achievement: An ecological perspective. *American Psychologist, 47*, 723–729.

Steinberg, L., Lamborn, S. D., Darling, N., Mounts, N. S., & Dornbusch, S. M. (1994). Over-time changes in adjustment and competence in adolescents from authoritative, authoritarian, indulgent, and neglectful families. *Child Development, 65*, 754–770.

Steinberg, L., Lamborn, S., Dornbusch, S., & Darling, N. (1992). Impact of parenting practices on adolescent achievement: Authoritative parenting, school involvement, and encouragement to succeed. *Child Development, 63*, 1266–1281.

Stephan, W. G., Stephan, C. W., & de Vargas, M. (1996). Emotional expression in Costa Rica and the United States. *Journal of Cross-Cultural Psychology, 27*(2), 147–160.

Steptoe, A., & Wardle, J. (Eds.). (1994). *Psychosocial processes and health: A reader.* Cambridge, UK: Cambridge University Press.

Steptoe, A., Sutcliffe, I., Allen, B., & Coombes, C. (1991). Satisfaction with communication, medical knowledge, and coping styles in patients with metastatic cancer. *Social Science and Medicine, 32*(6), 627–632.

Sternberg, R. J. (1986). *Intelligence applied: Understanding and increasing your intellectual skills.* New York: Harcourt Brace Jovanovich.

Sternberg, R. J. (1988). Triangulating love. In R. J. Sternberg & M. L. Barnes (Eds.), *The psychology of love* (pp. 119–138). New Haven, CT: Yale University Press.

Sternberg, R. J. (2004). Culture and Intelligence. American Psychologist, *59*(5), 325–338.

Sternberg, R. J., Grigorenko, E. L., & Kidd, K. K. (2005). Intelligence, Race, and Genetics. *American Psychologist, 60*(1), 46–59.

Sternberg, R. J., & Lubart, T. I. (1995). *Defying the crowd: Cultivating creativity in a culture of conformity.* New York: Free Press.

Sternberg, R. J., & Lubart, T. I. (1999). The concept of creativity: Prospects and paradigms. In R. J. Sternberg (Ed.), *Handbook of creativity* (pp. 3–15). New York: Cambridge University Press.

Stevenson, H. W., et al. (1985). Cognitive performance and academic achievement of Japanese, Chinese, and American children. *Child Development, 56*(3), 718–734.

Stevenson, H. W., Lee, S., & Stigler, S. Y. (1986). *Beliefs and achievements: A study in Japan, Taiwan, and the United States.* Unpublished manuscript.

Stevenson, H., & Zusho, A. (2002). Adolescence in China and Japan: Adapting to a changing environment. In B. Brown, R. Larson & T. Saraswathi (Eds.), *The world's youth: Adolescence in eight regions of the globe* (pp. 141–170). New York: Cambridge University Press.

Stewart, A. J., & Malley, J. E. (1987). Role combination in women: Mitigating agency and communion. In F. J. Crosby et al. (Eds.), *Spouse, parent, worker: On gender and multiple roles* (pp. 44–62). New Haven, CT: Yale University Press.

Stewart, S. M., Bond, M. H., Zaman, R. M., McBride-Chang, C., Rao, N., Ho, L. M., & Fielding, R. (1999). Functional parenting in Pakistan. *International Journal of Behavioral Development, 23*(3), 747–770.

Stewart, V. (1973). Tests of the "carpentered world" hypothesis by race and environment in American and Zambia. *International Journal of Psychology, 8,* 83–94.

Stigler, J. W., & Baranes, R. (1988). Culture and mathematics learning. In E. Rothkpof (Ed.), *Review of research in education* (Vol. 15, pp. 253–306). Washington, DC: American Educational Research Association.

Stigler, J. W., & Perry, M. (1988). Mathematics learning in Japanese, Chinese, and American classrooms. *New Directions for Child Development, 41,* 27–58.

Stigler, J. W., Lee, S., & Stevenson, H. W. (1986). Digit memory in Chinese and English: Evidence for a temporally limited store. *Cognition, 23,* 1–20.

Stiles, D. A., Gibbons, J. L., & Schnellman, J. (1990). The smiling sunbather and the chivalrous football player: Young adolescents' images of the ideal women and men. *Journal of Early Adolescence, 7,* 411–427.

Stipek, D. J., & Gralinski, J. H. (1991). Gender differences in children's achievement-related beliefs and emotional responses to success and failure in mathematics. *Journal of Educational Psychology, 83*(3), 361–371.

Stone, L. (1990). *Road to divorce: England 1530–1987.* New York: Oxford University Press.

Strathman, A., Gleicher, F., Boninger, D., & Edwards, C. (1994). The consideration of future consequences: Weighing immediate and distant outcomes of behavior. *Journal of Personality and Social Psychology, 66,* 742–752.

Streltzer, J. (1997). Pain. In W. Tseng & J. Streltzer (Eds.), *Culture and psychopathology: A guide to clinical assessment* (pp. 87–100). New York: Brunner/Mazel.

Strodtbeck, F. L. (1964). Considerations of meta-method in cross-cultural studies. *American Anthropologist, 66*(3), 223–229.

Stryker, S. (1986). Identity theory: Developments and extensions. In K. Tardley & T. Honess (Eds.), *Self and identity* (pp. 89–107). New York: Wiley.

Su, L., Yang, Z., Wan, G., Luo, X., & Li, X. (1999). The Child Behavior Checklist used in Chinese children aged 6–11. *Chinese Journal of Clinical Psychology, 7*(2), 70–73.

Suchman, R. G. (1966). Cultural differences in children's color and form perception. *Journal of Social Psychology, 70,* 3–10.

Sue, D. (1998). The interplay of sociocultural factors in the psychological development of Asians in America. In D. R. Atkinson & G. Morten (Eds.), *Counseling American minorities* (5th ed., pp. 205–213). New York: McGraw-Hill.

Sue, D. W. (1994). Asian-American mental health and help-seeking behavior: Comment on Solberg et al. (1994), Tata and Leong (1994), and Lin (1994). *Journal of Counseling Psychology, 41,* 292–295.

Sue, D. W., & Ivey, A. E., & Pedersen, P. B. (1996). A theory of multicultural counseling and therapy. Pacific Grove, CA: Brooks/Cole.

Sue, D. W., & Sue, D. (1999). *Counseling the culturally different: Theory and practice* (3rd ed.). New York: Wiley.

Sue, D., Sue, D. W., & Sue, S. (1990). *Understanding abnormal behavior* (3rd ed.). Boston: Houghton Mifflin.

Sue, D.W., & Sue, D. (2003). *Counseling the culturally diverse* (4th ed.). New York: John Wiley and Sons.

Sue, S. (1977). Community mental health services to minority groups: Some optimism, some pessimism. *American Psychologist, 32,* 616–624.

Sue, S. (1991, August). *Ethnicity and mental health: Research and policy issues.* Invited address presented at the annual meeting of the American Psychological Association, San Francisco.

Sue, S. (1998). In search of cultural competence in psychotherapy and counseling. *American Psychologist, 53,* 440–448.

Sue, S., & Morishima, J. K. (1982). *The mental health of Asian Americans.* San Francisco: Jossey-Bass.

Sue, S., & Zane, N. (1987). The role of culture and cultural techniques in psychotherapy: A reformation. *American Psychologist, 42,* 37–45.

Sue, S., Fujino, D. C., Hu, L. T., Takeuchi, D. T., & Zane, N. W. S. (1991). Community mental health services for ethnic minority groups: A test of the cultural responsiveness hypothesis. *Journal of Counseling Psychology, 59,* 533–540.

Sue, S., Zane, N., & Young, K. (1994). Research on psychotherapy with culturally diverse populations. In A. E. Bergin & S. L. Garfield (Eds.), *Handbook of psychotherapy and behavior change* (4th ed., pp. 428–466). New York: Wiley.

Suggs, D. N., & Miracle, A. W. (Eds.). (1993). *Culture and human sexuality: A reader*. Pacific Grove: Brooks/Cole.

Suhail, K., & Nisa, Z. (2002). Prevalence of eating disorders in Pakistan: Relationship with depression and body shape. *Eating and Weight Disorders, 7*(2), 131–138.

Sun, L., & Stewart, S. (2000). Psychological adjustment to cancer in a collective culture. *International Journal of Psychology, 35*(5), 177–185.

Super, C. M., & Harkness, S. (1986). The developmental niche: A conceptualization at the interface of child and culture. *International Journal of Behavioral Development, 9,* 545–569.

Super, C. M., & Harkness, S. (1994). The developmental niche. In W. Lonner & R. Malpass (Eds.), *Psychology and culture* (pp. 95–99). Boston: Allyn & Bacon.

Super, C. M., & Harkness, S. (2002). Culture structures the environment for development. *Human Development, 45*(4),270–274.

Sussman, L. K., Robins, L. N., & Earls, F. (1987). Treatment seeking for depression by black and white Americans. *Social Science and Medicine, 24,* 187–196.

Swartz, L. (1985). Anorexia nervosa as a culture-bound syndrome. *Social Science and Medicine, 20,* 725–730.

Sy, S., & Schulenberg, J. (2005). Parent beliefs and children's achievement trajectories during the transition to school in Asian American and European American families. *International Journal of Behavioral Development, 29*(6), 505–515.

Szapocznik, J., Scopetta, M. A., & Tillman, W. (1979). What changes, what stays the same and what affects acculturative change? In J. Szapocznik & M. C. Herrera (Eds.), *Cuban Americans: Acculturation, adjustment and the family* (pp. 12–21). Miami: Universal.

Tafarodi, R. W., & Swann, W. B., Jr. (1996). Individualism-collectivism and global self-esteem: Evidence for a cultural trade-off. *Journal of Cross-Cultural Psychology, 27*(6), 651–672.

Tajfel, H. (1982). Social psychology of intergroup relations. *Annual Review of Psychology, 33,* 1–39.

Tajfel, H., & Turner, J. C. (1986). The social identity theory of intergroup behavior. In S. Worchel & W. G. Austin (Eds.), *Psychology of intergroup relationships* (pp. 7–24). Chicago: Nelson-Hall.

Takahashi, K., & Takeuchi, K. (2006). Japan. In J. J. Arnett, R. Ahmed, B. Nsamenang, T. S. Saraswathi, & R. K. Silbereisen (Eds.), *Routledge international encyclopedia of adolescence.* New York: Routledge.

Takahashi, Y. (1997). Culture and suicide: From a Japanese psychiatrist's perspective. *Suicide and Life Threatening Behavior, 27*(1), 137–145.

Takaki, R. (1998). *Strangers from a different shore: A history of Asian Americans* (rev. ed.). Boston: Back Bay Books.

Takano, Y. (1989). Methodological problems in cross-cultural studies of linguist relativity. *Cognition, 31,* 141–162.

Takano, Y., & Noda, A. (1993). A temporary decline of thinking ability during foreign language processing. *Journal of Cross- Cultural Psychology, 24*(4), 445–462.

Takano, Y., & Noda, A. (1995). Interlanguage dissimilarity enhances the decline of thinking ability during foreign language processing. *Language Learning, 45*(40), 657–681.

Takeuchi, D. T., Bui, K.-V. T., & Kim, L. (1993). The referral of minority adolescents to community health centers. *Journal of Health and Social Behavior, 34*(2), 153–164.

Takeuchi, D. T., Higginbotham, N., Marsella, A., Gomes, K., Kwan, L., Ostrowski, B., et al. (1987). Native Hawaiian mental health. In A. B. Robillard & A. J. Marsella (Eds.), *Contemporary issues in mental health research in the Pacific Islands* (pp. 149–176). Honolulu: University of Hawaii Press.

Takeuchi, D. T., Sue, S., & Yeh, M. (1995). Return rates and outcomes from ethnicity-specific mental health programs in Los Angeles. *American Journal of Public Health, 85,* 638–643.

Talamantes, M. A., Lawler, W. R., & Espino, V. (1995). Hispanic American elders: Caregiving norms surrounding dying and the use of hospice services. *Hospice Journal, 10*(2), 35–49.

Tanaka-Matsumi, J. (2001). Abnormal psychology and culture. In D. Matsumoto (Ed.), *The handbook of culture and psychology* (pp. 265–286). New York: Oxford University Press.

Tardif, T., Wellman, H. M., Fung, K., Liu, D., & Fang, F. (2005). Preschoolers' understanding of knowing-that and knowing-how in the United States and Hong Kong. *Developmental Psychology, 41*(3), 562–573.

Tareen, A., Hodes, M., & Rangel, L. (2005). Non-fat-phobic anorexia nervosa in British South Asian adolescents. *International Journal of Eating Disorders, 37*(2), 161–165.

Tata, S. P., & Leong, F. T. (1994). Individualism-collectivism, social-network orientation, and acculturation as predictors of attitudes toward seeking professional psychological help among Chinese Americans. *Journal of Counseling Psychology, 41,* 280–287.

Taylor, C. R., & Stern, B. B. (1997). Asian-Americans: Television advertising and the "model minority" stereotype. *Journal of Advertising, 26*(2), 47–61.

Tedlock, B. (1992). The role of dreams and visionary narratives in Mayan cultural survival. *Ethos, 20*(4), 453–476.

Terracciano, A., Abdel-Khalek, A. M., Adam, N., Adamovova, L., Ahn, C.-K., Ahn, H.-N., et al. (2005). National character does not reflect mean personality trait levels in 49 cultures. *Science, 310,* 96–100.

Terrell, M. D. (1992, August). *Stress, coping, ethnic identity and college adjustment.* Paper presented at the annual meeting of the American Psychological Association, Washington, DC.

Teti, D. (2002). Retrospect and prospect in the psychological study of sibling relationships. In J. McHale & W. Grolnick (Eds.), *Retrospect and prospect in the psychological study of families* (pp. 193–224). Mahwah, NJ: Erlbaum.

Tharp, R. G. (1991). Cultural diversity and treatment of children. *Journal of Consulting and Clinical Psychology, 5*(3), 381–392.

Thomas, A., & Chess, S. (1977). *Temperament and development.* New York: Brunner/Mazel.

Thomas, D. C., & Toyne, B. (1995). Subordinates' responses to cultural adaptation by Japanese expatriate managers. *Journal of Business Research, 32,* 1–10.

Thompson, J. (1941). Development of facial expression of emotion in blind and seeing children. *Archives of Psychology, 37,* 1–47.

Thompson, N., Stradling, S., Murphy, M., & O'Neill, P. (1996). Stress and organizational culture. *British Journal of Social Work, 26*(5), 647–665.

Thurstone, L. L. (1938). *Primary mental abilities.* Chicago: University of Chicago Press.

Timimi, S. (2004). A critique of the international consensus statement on ADHD. *Clinical Child and Family Psychology Review, 7*(1), 59–63.

Ting-Toomey, S. (1991). Intimacy expressions in three cultures: France, Japan, and the United States. *International Journal of Intercultural Relations, 15,* 29–46.

Ting-Toomey, S. (1996). Managing intercultural conflicts effectively. In L. A. Samovar & R. E. Porter (Eds.), *Intercultural communication: A reader* (8th ed., pp. 392–404). Belmont, CA: Wadsworth.

Tobin, J. J., & Friedman, J. (1983). Spirits, shamans, and nightmare death: Survivor stress in a Hmong refugee. *American Journal of Orthopsychiatry, 53,* 434–448.

Tolman, A., & Reedy, R. (1998). Implementation of a culture-specific intervention for a Native American community. *Journal of Clinical Psychology in Medical Settings, 5*(3), 381–392.

Tolson, T. F., & Wilson, M. N. (1990). The impact of two- and three-generational Black family structure on perceived family climate. *Child Development, 61*(2), 416–428.

Tomasello, M. (1999). *The cultural originals of human cognition.* Cambridge, MA: Harvard University Press.

Tomasello, M., Kruger, A. C., & Ratner, H. H. (1993). Cultural learning. *Behavioural and Brain Sciences, 16,* 495–552.

Tomkins, S. S. (1962). *Affect, imagery, and consciousness: Vol. 1. The positive affects.* New York: Springer.

Tomkins, S. S. (1963). *Affect, imagery, and consciousness: Vol. 2. The negative affects.* New York: Springer.

Torrey, E. F. (1972). *The mind game: Witchdoctors and psychiatrists.* New York: Emerson Hall.

Tracy, J. L., & Robins, R. W. (2004). Show your pride: Evidence for a discrete emotion expression. *Psychological Science, 15,* 104–197.

Trafimow, D., Silverman, E. S., Fan, R. M.-T., & Law, J. S. F. (1997). The effects of language and priming on the relative accessibility of the private self and collective self. *Journal of Cross-Cultural Psychology, 28,* 107–123.

Trafimow, D., Triandis, H. C., & Goto, S. G. (1991). Some tests of the distinction between the private self and the collective self. *Journal of Personality and Social Psychology, 60,* 649–655.

Trankina, F. J. (1983). Clinical issues and techniques in working with Hispanic children and their families. In G. J. Powell (Ed.), *The psychological development of minority group children* (pp. 307–329). New York: Brunner/Mazel.

Triandis, H. C. (1972). *The analysis of subjective culture.* New York: Wiley.

Triandis, H. C. (1989). The self and social behavior in differing cultural contexts. *Psychological Review, 96,* 506–520.

Triandis, H. C. (1994). *Culture and social behavior.* New York: McGraw-Hill.

Triandis, H. C. (1995). *New directions in social psychology: Individualism and collectivism.* Boulder, CO: Westview Press.

Triandis, H. C. (1996). The psychologist measurement of cultural syndromes. *American Psychologist, 51*(4), 407–415.

Triandis, H. C., & Lambert, W. W. (1958). A restatement and test of Schlosberg's theory of emotion with two kinds of subjects from Greece. *Journal of Abnormal and Social Psychology, 56,* 321–328.

Triandis, H. C., Bontempo, R., Betancourt, H., Bond, M., Leung, K., Brenes, A., Georgas, J., Hui, C. H., Marin, G., Setiadi, B., Sinha, J. B., Verma, J., Spangenberg, J., Touzard, H., & de Montonollin, G. (1986). The measurement aspects of individualism and collectivism across cultures. *Australian Journal of Psychology, 38,* 257–267.

Triandis, H. C., Bontempo, R., Villareal, M. J., Asai, M., & Lucca, N. (1988). Individualism and collectivism: Cross-cultural perspectives on self-ingroup relationships. *Journal of Personality & Social Psychology, 4,* 323–338.

Triandis, H. C., Bontempo, R., Villareal, M. J., Asai, M., & Lucca, N. (1988). Individualism and collectivism: Cross-cultural perspectives on self-ingroup relationships. *Journal of Personality and Social Psychology, 4,* 323–338.

Triandis, H. C., Leung, K., Villareal, M., & Clack, F. (1985). Allocentric versus idiocentric tendencies: Convergent and discriminate validation. *Journal of Research in Personality, 19,* 395–415.

Triandis, H. C., McCusker, C., & Hui, C. H. (1990). Multimethod probes of individualism and collectivism. *Journal of Personality and Social Psychology, 59,* 1006–1020.

Triandis, H., Marin, G., Lisansky, J., & Betancourt, H. (1984). Simpatia as a cultural script of Hispanics. *Journal of Personality and Social Psychology, 47,* 1363–1375.

Tribe, R., & De Silva, P. (1999). Psychological intervention with displaced widows in Sri Lanka. *International Review of Psychiatry, 11,* 184–190.

Trickett, E. J. (1996). A future for community psychology: the contexts of diversity and the diversity of contexts. *American Journal of Community Psychology, 24,* 209–234.

Trommsdorff, G., & Iwawaki, S. (1989). Students' perceptions of socialization and gender role in Japan and Germany. *International Journal of Behavioral Development*, 12(4), 485–493.

Trompenaars, F. (1993). *Riding the waves of culture*. London: Brealey.

Tronick, E. Z. (1989). Emotions and emotional communication in infants. *American Psychologist*, 44(2), 112–119.

Trull, T. J., & Geary, D. C. (1997). Comparison of the Big-Five factor structure across samples of Chinese and American adults. *Journal of Personality Assessment*, 69(2), 324–341.

Tsai, J. L., & Levenson, R. W. (1997). Cultural influences of emotional responding: Chinese American and European American dating couples during interpersonal conflict. *Journal of Cross-Cultural Psychology*, 28, 600–625.

Tse, D. K., Francis, J., & Walls, J. (1994). Cultural differences in conducting intra- and inter-cultural negotiations: A Sino-Canadian comparison. *Journal of International Business Studies*, 25(3), 537.

Tseng, W. (1977). Family diagnosis and classification. *Annual Progress in Child Psychiatry and Child Development*, 434–454.

Tseng, W., & McDermott, J. F. (1981). *Culture, mind and therapy: An introduction to cultural psychiatry*. New York: Brunner/Mazel.

Tucker, C. J., Updegraff, K. A., McHale, S. M. & Crouter, A. C. (1999). Older siblings as socializers of younger siblings' empathy. *Journal of Early Adolescence*, 19(2), Special issue: Prosocial and moral development in early adolescence, Part II, pp. 176–198.

Tulviste, P. (1978). On the origins of the theoretic syllogistic reasoning in culture and in the child. *Acta et commentationes Universitatis Tortuensis*, 4, 3–22.

Tylor, E. B. (1865). *Researches into the early history of mankind and development of civilisation*. London: John Murray.

U.S. Census Bureau (2000). *Current population reports*. Washington, DC: Government Printing Office.

U.S. Census Bureau. (2002). *Current population reports: Poverty in the United States: 2001*. Washington, DC: Government Printing Office.

U.S. Department of Health and Human Services (1999). *Mental Health: A Report of the Surgeon General—Executive Summary*. Rockville, MD: U.S. Department of Health and Human Services, Substance Abuse and Mental Health Services Administration, Center for Mental Health Services, National Institutes of Health, National Institute of Mental Health.

Uba, L. (1994). *Asian Americans: Personality patterns, identity, and mental health*. New York: Guilford Press.

Uehara, E. S., Takeuchi, D. T., & Smukler, M. (1994). Effects of combining disparate groups in the analysis of ethnic differences: Variations among Asian American mental health service consumers in level of community functioning. *American Journal of Community Psychology*, 22(1), 83–99.

Ueno, A., Ueno, Y., & Tomonaga, M. (2004). Facial responses to four basic tastes in newborn rhesus macaques (Macaca mulatta) and chimpanzees (pan troglodytes). *Behavioural Brain Research*, 154, 261–271.

Uleman, J. S., Rhee, E., Bardoliwalla, N., Semin, G., & Toyama, M. (2000). The relational self: Closeness to ingroups depends on who they are, culture, and the type of closeness. *Asian Journal of Social Psychology*, 3, 1–17.

Urton, G., & Brezine, C. J. (2005). Khipu accounting in ancient Peru. *Science*, 309, 1065–1067.

Uziel-Miller, N. D., Lyons, J. S., Kissiel, C., & Love, S. (1998). Treatment needs and initial outcomes of a residential recovery program for African American women and their children. *American Journal on Addictions*, 7, 43–50.

van de Vijver, F. J. R. (in press). Culture and psychology: A swot analysis of cross-cultural psychology. In Q. Jing, M. R. Rosenzweig, G. d'Ydewalle, H. Zhang, H. C. Chen & K. Zhang (Eds.), *Progress in psychological science* (Vol. 2: Progress in psychological science around the world, Proceedings of the 28th International Congress of Psychology (vol. 2, Social and applied issues)). London: Psychology Press.

Van de Vijver, F. J. R., & Leung, K. (1997a). Methods and data analysis of comparative research. In J. W. Berry, Y. H. Poortinga, & J. Pandey (Eds.), *Handbook of cross-cultural psychology* (2nd ed., Vol. 1, pp. 257–300). Boston: Allyn & Bacon.

Van de Vijver, F. J. R., & Leung, K. (1997b). *Methods and data analysis for cross-cultural research*. Newbury Park, CA: Sage.

Van de Vijver, F. J. R., & Matsumoto, D. (2007). *Cross-cultural research methods in psychology*. New York: Oxford University Press. Manuscript in preparation.

Van de Vliert, E. (2003). Thermoclimate, culture, and poverty as country-level roots of workers' wages. *Journal of International Business Studies*, 34, 40–52.

Van de Vliert, E. (2006). Autocratic leadership around the globe: Do climate and wealth drive leadership culture? *Journal of Cross-Cultural Psychology*, 37, 42–59.

Van de Vliert, E., & Smith, P. B. (2004). Leader reliance on subordinates across nations that differ in development and climate. *The Leadership Quarterly*, 15, 381–403.

Van de Vliert, E., Huang, X., & Levine, R. V. (2004). National wealth and thermal climate as predictors of motives for volunteer work. *Journal of Cross-Cultural Psychology*, 35, 62–73.

Van de Vliert, E., Huang, X., & Parker, P. M. (2004). Do colder and hotter climates make richer societies more but poorer societies less happy and altruistic? *Journal of Environmental Psychology*, 24, 17–30.

Van de Vliert, E., Schwartz, S. H., Huismans, S. E., Hofstede, G. H., & Daan, S. (1999). Temperature, cultural masculinity, and domestic political violence: A cross-national study. *Journal of Cross-Cultural Psychology*, 30, 291–314.

Van den Berghe, P. L. (1981). *The ethnic phenomenon*. New York: Elsevier.

van Herk, H., Poortinga, Y. H., & Verhallen, T. M. M. (2004). Response styles in rating scales: Evidence of methods bias in data from six EU countries. *Journal of Cross-Cultural Psychology, 35,* 346–360.

Van Hoof, J. A. R. A. M. (1972). A comparative approach to the phylogeny of laughing and smiling. In R. A. Hinde (Ed.), *Nonverbal communication* (pp. 209–241). Cambridge, England: Cambridge University Press.

van IJzendoorn, M. H., & Sagi, A. (1999). Cross-cultural patterns of attachment: Universal and contextual dimensions. In J. Cassidy & P. R. Shaver (Eds.), *Handbook of attachment: Theory, research, and clinical applications* (pp. 713–734). New York: Guilford Press.

van Ommeren, M., Sharma, B., Sharma, G. K., Komproe, K., Cardena, E., & de Jong, J. T. V. N. (2002). The relationship between somatic and PTSD symptoms among Bhutanese refugee torture survivors: Examination of comorbidity with anxiety and depression. *Journal of Traumatic Stress, 15*(5), 415–421.

Vandello, J. A., & Cohen, D. (2003). Male honor and female fidelity: Implicit cultural scripts that perpetuate domestic violence. *Journal of Personality and Social Psychology, 84,* 997–1010.

Vega, W. A., Koloy, B., Aguilar-Gaxiola, S., Alderete, E., Catalano, R., & Caraveo-Anduaga, J. (1998). Lifetime prevalence of DSM-III-R psychiatric disorders among urban and rural Mexican Americans in California. *Archives of General Psychiatry, 55,* 771–778.

Verkuyten, M., & Hagendoorn, L. (1998). Prejudice and self-categorization: The variable role of authoritarianism and in-group stereotypes. *Personality and Social Psychology Bulletin, 24*(1), 99–110.

Verkuyten, M., & Pouliasi, K. (2002). Biculturalism among older children: Cultural frame switching, attributions, self-identification, and attitudes. *Journal of Cross-Cultural Psychology, 33,* 596–609.

Vinacke, W. E. (1949). The judgment of facial expressions by three national-racial groups in Hawaii: I. Caucasian faces. *Journal of Personality, 17,* 407–429.

Vinacke, W. E., & Fong, R. W. (1955). The judgment of facial expressions by three national-racial groups in Hawaii: II. Oriental faces. *Journal of Social Psychology, 41,* 184–195.

Vontress, C. E. (1991). Traditional healing in Africa: Implications for cross-cultural counseling. *Counseling and Development, 70,* 242–249.

Vrij, A., & Winkel, F. W. (1991). Cultural patterns in dutch and Surinam nonverbal behavior: An analysis of simulated police/citizen encounters. *Journal of Nonverbal Behavior, 15,* 169–184.

Vrij, A., & Winkel, F. W. (1992). Cross-cultural police-citizen interactions: The influence of race, beliefs, and nonverbal communication on impression formation. *Journal of Applied Social Psychology, 22,* 1546–1559.

Vrij, A., & Winkel, F. W. (1994). Perceptual distortions in cross-cultural interrogations: The impact of skin color, accent, speech style, and spoken fluency on impression formation. *Journal of Cross-Cultural Psychology, 25*(2), 284–295.

Wachs, T., & Bates, J. (2001). Temperament. In G. Bremer & A. Fogel (Eds.), *Blackwell handbook of infant development* (pp. 465–501). Oxford: Blackwell.

Wagner, D. A. (1977). Ontogeny of the Ponzo illusion: Effects of age, schooling and environment. *International Journal of Psychology, 12,* 161–176.

Wagner, D. A. (1980). Culture and memory development. In H. Triandis & A. Heron (Eds.), *Handbook of cross-cultural psychology: Vol. 4. Developmental psychology* (pp. 187–232). Boston: Allyn & Bacon.

Wagner, J. A., III. (1995). Studies of individualism-collectivism: Effects on cooperation in groups. *Academy of Management Journal, 38*(1), 152–172.

Walkey, H. F., & Chung, C. R. (1996). An examination of stereotypes of Chinese and Europeans held by some New Zealand secondary school pupils. *Journal of Cross-Cultural Psychology, 27*(3), 283–292.

Wallace, J. M., & Williams, D. R. (1997). Religion and adolescent health-compromising behavior. In J. Schulenberg, J. L. Maggs, & K. Hurrelmann (Eds.), *Health risks and developmental transitions during adolescence* (pp. 444–468). New York: Cambridge University Press.

Wallbott, H., & Scherer, K. (1988). Emotion and economic development: Data and speculations concerning the relationship between emotional experience and socioeconomic factors. *European Journal of Social Psychology, 18,* 267–273.

Wang, A. V. (1994). Passionate love and social anxiety of American and Italian students. *Psychology: A Journal of Human Behavior, 31,* 9–11.

Ward, C., & Chang, W. C. (1997). "Cultural fit": A new perspective on personality and sojourner adjustment. *International Journal of Intercultural Relations, 21,* 525–533.

Warneken, F., & Tomasello, M. (2006). Altruistic helping in human infants and young chimpanzees. *Science, 311,* 1301–1303.

Wasti, S. A., & Cortina, L. M. (2002). Coping in context: Sociocultural determinants of responses to sexual harassment. *Journal of Personality and Social Psychology, 83,* 394–405.

Wasti, S. A., Bergman, M. E., Glomb, T. M., & Drasgow, F. (2000). Test of the cross-cultural generalizability of a model of sexual harassment. *Journal of Applied Psychology, 85,* 766–778.

Watson, O. M. (1970). *Proxemic behavior: A cross-cultural study.* The Hague, Nederlands: Mouton.

Watson, O. M., & Graves, T. D. (1966). Quantitative research in proxemic behavior. *American Anthropologist, 68,* 971–985.

Watson-Gegeo, K. A. (1992). Thick explanation in the ethnographic study of child socialization: A longitudinal study of the problem of schooling for Kwara'ae

(Solomon Islands) children. In W. A. Corsaro & P. Miller (Eds.), *New directions for child development: Interpretive approaches to children's socialization* (pp. 51–66). San Francisco: Jossey-Bass.

Weatherly, K. A., & Beach, L. R. (1998). Organizational culture and decision making. In L. R. Beach et al. (Eds.), *Image theory: Theoretical and empirical foundations* (pp. 211–225). Mahwah, NJ: Erlbaum.

Weisner, T. S., & Gallimore, R. (1977). My brother's keeper: Child and sibling caretaking. *Current Anthropology, 18*(2), 169–190.

Weiss, A., King, J. E., & Enns, R. M. (2002). Subjective well-being is heritable and genetically correlated with dominance in chimpanzees (Pan troglodytes). *Journal of Personality and Social Psychology, 83*, 1141–1149.

Weiss, A., King, J. E., & Figueredo, A. J. (2000). The heritability of personality factors in chimpanzees (Pan troglodytes). *Behavior Genetics, 30*, 213–221.

Weiss, A., King, J. E., & Perkins, L. (2006). Personality and subjective well-being in orangutans. *Journal of Personality and Social Psychology, 90*, 501–511.

Weiss, S. C. (1980). Porteus Maze performances on nonliterate and literate Campas from Eastern Peru. *Journal of Social Psychology, 112*(2), 303–304.

Weissman, M. M., & Olfson, M. (1995). Depression in women: implications for health care research. *Science, 269*, 799–801.

Weissman, M. M., Bland, R. C., Canino, G. J., Faravelli, C., Greenwald, S., Hwu, H. G., Joyce, P. R., Karam, E. G., Lee, C. K., Lellouch, J., Lepine, J. P., Newman, S. C., Rubin-Stiper, M., Wells, J.E., Wickramaratne, P. J., Wittchen, H., & Yeh, E. K. (1996). Cross-national epidemiology of major depression and bipolar disorder. *Journal of the American Medical Association, 276*, 293–299.

Weisz, J. R., Sigman, M., Weiss, B., & Mosk, J. (1993). Parent reports of behavioral and emotional problems among children in Kenya, Thailand, and the United States. *Child Development, 64*, 98–109.

Weisz, J. R., Suwanlert, S., Chaiyasit, W., Weiss, B., Walter, B. R., & Anderson, W. W. (1988). Thai and American perspectives on over- and under-controlled child behavior problems: Exploring the threshold model among parents, teachers and psychologists. *Journal of Consulting and Clinical Psychology, 56*(4), 601–609.

Weldon, E., & Gargano, G. M. (1988). Cognitive loafing: The effects of accountability and shared responsibility on cognitive effort. *Personality and Social Psychology Bulletin, 14*, 159–171.

Welles-Nystrom, B. (2005). Co-sleeping as a window into Swedish culture: Considerations of gender and health care. *Scandinavian Journal of Caring Sciences, 19*(4), 354–360.

Wessells, M. & Monteiro, C. (2001). Psychosocial interventions and post-war reconstruction in Angola: Interweaving Western and traditional approaches. In D. J. Christie, V. Richards (Eds.), *Peace, conflict, and violence: Peace psychology for the 21st century,* (pp. 262–275). Upper Saddle River, NJ, US: Prentice Hall.

Westaby, J. D. (1995). Presence of others and task performance in Japan and the United States: A laboratory investigation. *International Journal of Psychology, 30*(4), 451–460.

Wheeler, L., & Kim, Y. (1997). What is beautiful is culturally good: The physical attractiveness stereotype has different content in collectivistic cultures. *Personality and Social Psychology Bulletin, 23*(8), 795–800.

White, G. M. (1980). Conceptual universals in interpersonal language. *American Anthropologist, 88*, 759–781.

Whitehorn, J., Ayonrinde, O., & Maingay, S. (2002). Female genital mutilation: Cultural and psychological implications. *Sexual and Relationship Therapy, 17*, 161–173.

Whiten, A., Horner, V., & De Waal, F. B. M. (2005). Conformity to cultural norms of tool use in chimpanzees. *Nature, 437*, 737–740.

Whiting, B. B., & Whiting, J. M. (1975). *Children of six cultures.* Cambridge, MA: Harvard University Press.

Widmer, E. D., Treas, J., & Newcomb, R. (1998). Attitudes toward nonmarital sex in 24 countries. *The Journal of Sex Research, 35*, 349.

Wierzbicka, A. (1994). Semantic universals and primitive thought: The question of the psychic unity of humankind. *Journal of Linguistic Anthropology, 4*(1), 23.

Williams, J. E., & Best, D. L. (1982). *Measuring sex stereotypes: A thirty-nation study.* Beverly Hills, CA: Sage.

Williams, J. E., & Best, D. L. (1990). *Measuring sex stereotypes: A multination study.* Beverly Hills, CA: Sage.

Williams, J. E., & Best, D. L. (1994). Cross-cultural views of women and men. In W. Lonner & R. Malpass (Eds.), *Psychology and culture.* Boston: Allyn & Bacon.

Williams, J. E., Satterwhite, R. C., & Best, D. L. (1999). Pancultural gender stereotypes revisited: The five factor model. *Sex Roles, 40*(7–8), 513–525.

Williams, J. E., Satterwhite, R. C., & Best, D. L. (2000). *Gender stereotypes in 27 countries examined via the five factor model.* Paper presented at the International Association of Cross-Cultural Psychology, Poland.

Willmann, E., Feldt, K., & Amelang, M. (1997). Prototypical behaviour patterns of social intelligence: An intercultural comparison between Chinese and German subjects. *International Journal of Psychology, 32*(5), 329–346.

Wilson, M. N., Kohn, L. P., & Lee, T. S. (2000). Cultural relativistic approach toward ethnic minorities in family therapy. In J. E. Aponte & J. Wohl (Eds.), *Psychological intervention and cultural diversity* (2nd ed., pp. 167–182). Boston: Allyn & Bacon.

Wing, D. M., Crow, S. S., & Thompson, T. (1995). An ethno-nursing study of Muscogee (Creek) Indians and effective health care practices for treating alcohol abuse. *Family and Community Health, 18*(2), 52–64.

Wittenbrink, B., Judd, C. M., & Park, B. (1997). Evidence for racial prejudice at the implicit level and its relationship with questionnaire measures. *Journal of Personality and Social Psychology, 72*, 262–274.

Wlodarek, J. (1994). Poland. In K. Hurrelmann (Ed.), *International handbook of adolescence* (pp. 309–321). Westport, CT: Greenwood Press.

Wober, M. (1974). Toward an understanding of the Kiganda concept of intelligence. In J. W. Berry & P. R. Dasen (Eds.), *Culture and cognition* (pp. 261–280). London: Methuen.

Wohl, J. (1989). Integration of cultural awareness into psychotherapy. *American Journal of Psychotherapy, 43*, 343–355.

Wolf, R. M. (1965). The measurement of environments. In C. W. Harris (Ed.), *Proceedings of the 1964 Invited Conference on Testing Problems*. Princeton, NJ: Educational Testing Service.

Wolff, B. B., & Langley, S. (1968). Cultural factors and the response to pain: A review. *American Anthropologist, 70*(3), 494–501.

Wolpoff, M., & Caspari, R. (1997). *Race and human evolution: A fatal attraction*. New York: Simon & Schuster.

Wong, R. Y.-M., & Hong, Y.-Y. (2005). Dynamic influences of culture on cooperation in the prisoner's dilemma. *Psychological Science, 16*, 429–434.

Wood, P. B., & Chesser, M. (1994). Black stereotyping in a university population. *Sociological Focus, 27*(1), 17–34.

Wood, P. C., Hillman, S. B., & Sawilowsky, S. S. (1995). Comparison of self-esteem scores: American and Indian adolescents. *Psychological Reports, 76*(2), 367–370.

World Health Organization (1948). *Constitution of the World Health Organization*. Geneva: Author.

World Health Organization (2004). The world health report: Changing history, Annex Table 3: Burden of disease in DALYs by

cause, sex, and mortality stratum in WHO regions, estimates for 2002. Geneva.

World Health Organization (2006). Depression. Accessed at http://www.who.int/mental_health/management/depression/definition/en.

World Health Organization. (1973). *Report of the International Pilot Study of Schizophrenia* (Vol. 1). Geneva: Author.

World Health Organization. (1979). *Schizophrenia: An international follow-up study*. New York: Wiley.

World Health Organization. (1981). *Current state of diagnosis and classification in the mental health field*. Geneva: Author.

World Health Organization. (1983). *Depressive disorders in different cultures: Report of the WHO collaborative study of standardized assessment of depressive disorders*. Geneva: Author.

World Health Organization. (1991). *World health statistics quarterly*. Geneva: Author.

Wright, D. B., Boyd, C. E., & Tredoux, C. G. (2001). A field study of own-race bias in South Africa and England. *Psychology, Public Policy, and Law, 7*(1), 119–133.

Wu, C., & Chao, R. (2005). Intergenerational cultural conflicts in norms of parental warmth among Chinese American immigrants. *International Journal of Behavioral Development, 29*(6), 516–523.

Wylie, R. C. (1979). *The self concept: Vol. 2. Theory and research on selected topics*. Lincoln: University of Nebraska Press.

Wynn, K. (1992). Addition and subtraction in human infants. *Nature, 358*, 749–750.

Yamagishi, T. (1986). The provision of a sanctioning system as a public good. *Journal of Personality and Social Psychology, 51*, 110–116.

Yamagishi, T. (1988). The provision of a sanctioning system in the United States and Japan. *Social Psychology Quarterly, 51*, 265–271.

Yamaguchi, S. (2001). Culture and control orientations. In D. Matsumoto (Ed.), *The handbook of culture and psychology*

(pp. 223–243). New York: Oxford University Press.

Yamaguchi, S., Okamoto, K., & Oka, T. (1985). Effects of cofactor's presence: Social loafing and social facilitation. *Japanese Psychological Research, 27*, 215–222.

Yamamoto, J., & Kubota, M. (1983). The Japanese-American family. In G. J. Powell (Ed.), *The psychological development of minority group children* (pp. 307–329). New York: Brunner/Mazel.

Yamamoto, K., Soliman, A., Parsons, J., & Davies, O. L. (1987). Voices in unison: Stressful events in the lives of children in six countries. *Child Psychology and Psychiatry, 28*(6), 855–864.

Yamashita, I., & Koyama, T. (1994). Neurotic spectrum disorders in Japan. In J. E. Mezzich, Y. Honda, & M. O. Kastrup (Eds.), *Psychiatric diagnosis: A world perspective* (pp. 96–101). New York: Springer-Verlag.

Yan, W., & Gaier, L. E. (1994). Causal attributions for college success and failure: An Asian-American comparison. *Journal of Cross-Cultural Psychology, 25*, 146–158.

Yap, P. M. (1974). *Comparative psychiatry: A theoretical framework*. Toronto: University of Toronto Press.

Yates, J. F., Lee, J.-W., & Shinotsuka, H. (1996). Beliefs about overconfidence, including its cross-national variation. *Organizational Behavior and Human Decision Processes, 65*(2), 138–147.

Ybarra, O., & Trafimow, D. (1988). How priming the private self or collective self affects the relative weights of attitudes and subjective norms. *Personality and Social Psychology Bulletin, 24*, 362–370.

Yee, H. A., Fairchild, H. H., Weizmann, F., & Wyatt, E. G. (1993). Addressing psychology's problems with race. *American Psychologist, 48*(11), 1132–1140.

Yeh, C., Hunter, C. D., Madan-Bahel, A., Chiang, L. & Arora, A. K. (2004). Indigenous and interdependent perspectives of healing: Implications for counseling and research. *Journal of Counseling & Development, 82*(4), 410–419.

Yeh, M., Takeuchi, D. T., & Sue, S. (1994). Asian-American children treated in the mental health system: A comparison of parallel and mainstream outpatient service centers. *Journal of Clinical Child Psychology, 23*(1), 5–12.

Ying, Y.-W., & Hu, L.-T. (1994). Public outpatient mental health services: Use and outcome among Asian Americans. *American Journal of Orthopsychiatry, 64*(3), 448–455.

Ying, Y-W., Akutsu, P. D., Zhang, X., & Huang, L. N. (1997). Psychological dysfunction in Southeast Asian refugees as mediated by sense of coherence. *American Journal of Community Psychology, 25*(6), 839–859.

Yip, K. (2005). Chinese concepts of mental health: Cultural implications for social work practice. *International Social Work, Special Issue: China, 48*(4), 391–407.

Yodanis, C. (2005). Divorce culture and marital gender equality: A cross-national study. *Gender and Society, 19,* 644–659.

Young, D. M. (1997). Depression. In W.-S. Tseng & J. Streltzer (Eds.), *Culture and psychopathology: A guide to clinical assessment* (pp. 28–45). New York: Brunner/Mazel.

Zaccaro, S. J. (1984). The role of task attractiveness. *Personality and Social Psychology Bulletin, 10,* 99–106.

Zahn-Waxler, C., Friedman, J. R., Cole, M. P., Mizuta, I., & Hiruma, N. (1996). Japanese and United States preschool children's responses to conflict and distress. *Child Development, 67,* 2462–2477.

Zane, N., Hatanaka, H., Park, S., & Akutsu, P. (1994). Ethnic-specific mental health services: Evaluation of the parallel approach for Asian-American clients. *Journal of Community Psychology, 22*(2), 68–81.

Zhang, L. (2005). Prediction of Chinese life satisfaction: Contribution of collective self-esteem. *International Journal of Psychology, 40,* 189–200.

Zhang, M., Yan, H., & Phillips, M. R. (1994). Community-based psychiatric rehabilitation in Shanghai: Facilities, services, outcome, and culture-specific characteristics. *British Journal of Psychiatry, 165*(24), 70–79.

Zhang, Y., Young, D., & Lee, S. (2002). Chinese Taoist cognitive psychotherapy in the treatment of generalized anxiety disorder in contemporary China. *Transcultural Psychiatry, 39*(1), 115–129.

Zuckerman, M. (1990). Some dubious premises in research and theory on racial differences: Scientific, social, and ethical issues. *American Psychologist, 45*(12), 1297–1303.

Zukow-Goldring, P. (1995). *Sibling interaction across cultures.* New York: Springer-Verlag.

Name Index

Subject Index